"This superb handbook provides us with cutting-edge chapters on European institutions and European integration by today's leading gender politics scholars. Their feminist critical analysis of gender and European politics marks a high point in European studies. It will become a classic text, providing foundational contributions to teaching and research for many years to come."

Yvonne Galligan, *Technological University Dublin, Ireland*

"This handbook is a fantastic intervention into contemporary European studies delving into both the theory and practices of European integration using a gender lens. A one stop shop for all things gender and Europe, the editors have curated an extraordinary collection of contributions. At a time when there is a backlash against insights that centre gender perspectives within Europe and globally, this Handbook demonstrate the need for resistance."

Toni Haastrup, *University of Stirling, UK*

"*The Routledge Handbook of Gender and EU Politics* offers a significant, creative corrective to the his-torically biased nature of most grand narratives addressing the European Union's development. Concentrating on core constructs and institutions, its contributors engage with "mainstream" literature as well as with gender scholarship, pinpointing topics for future research. One can only hope that "malestream" researchers will begin to follow their lead, to ensure a more complete, his- and her-storical picture of what makes the EU "tick" and where it needs to go from here."

Joyce Marie Mushaben, *Georgetown University, USA*

"At a time when gender equality policies are under attack and the European Union is self-destructing, this book is a crucial reminder of the historical importance of European integration to women's rights in the region. This handbook is a must-read for students, researchers, journalists and practitioners. It examines politics in a broad sense, covering most fields of political science with openings towards history, law, political economy and sociology. It offers an up-to-date overview of gender politics and the EU, including timely issues such as austerity, Brexit and populism."

David Paternotte, *Université libre de Bruxelles, Belgium*

The Routledge Handbook of Gender and EU Politics

This handbook maps the expanding field of gender and EU politics, giving an overview of the fundamentals and new directions of the sub-discipline, and serving as a reference book for (gender) scholars and students at different levels interested in the EU.

In investigating the gendered nature of European integration and gender relations in the EU as a political system, this book summarizes and assesses the research on gender and the EU to this point in time, identifies existing research gaps in gender and EU studies and addresses directions for future research. Distinguished contributors from the US, the UK and continental Europe, and from across disciplines from political science, sociology, economics and law, expertly inform about gender approaches and summarize the state of the art in gender and EU studies.

The Routledge Handbook of Gender and EU Politics provides an essential and authoritative source of information for students, scholars and researchers in EU studies/politics, gender studies/politics, political theory, comparative politics, international relations, political and gender sociology, political economy and European law studies.

Gabriele Abels is Jean Monnet Chair of European Integration at the Institute for Political Science, University of Tübingen, Germany.

Andrea Krizsán is Associate Professor at the School of Public Policy, Central European University, Hungary.

Heather MacRae is Associate Professor and former Jean Monnet Chairholder in the Department of Politics at York University, Toronto, Canada.

Anna van der Vleuten is Professor Contesting Europeanization at the Department of Political Science at Radboud University, The Netherlands.

The Routledge Handbook of Gender and EU Politics

*Edited by Gabriele Abels, Andrea Krizsán,
Heather MacRae and Anna van der Vleuten*

LONDON AND NEW YORK

First published 2021
by Routledge
2 Park Square, Milton Park, Abingdon, Oxon OX14 4RN

and by Routledge
52 Vanderbilt Avenue, New York, NY 10017

Routledge is an imprint of the Taylor & Francis Group, an informa business

© 2021 selection and editorial matter, Gabriele Abels, Andrea Krizsán, Heather MacRae and Anna van der Vleuten; individual chapters, the contributors

The right of Gabriele Abels, Andrea Krizsán, Heather MacRae and Anna van der Vleuten to be identified as the authors of the editorial material, and of the authors for their individual chapters, has been asserted in accordance with sections 77 and 78 of the Copyright, Designs and Patents Act 1988.

All rights reserved. No part of this book may be reprinted or reproduced or utilised in any form or by any electronic, mechanical, or other means, now known or hereafter invented, including photocopying and recording, or in any information storage or retrieval system, without permission in writing from the publishers.

Trademark notice: Product or corporate names may be trademarks or registered trademarks, and are used only for identification and explanation without intent to infringe.

British Library Cataloguing-in-Publication Data
A catalogue record for this book is available from the British Library

Library of Congress Cataloging-in-Publication Data
Names: Abels, Gabriele, 1964– editor.
Title: The Routledge handbook of gender and EU politics / edited by Gabriele Abels, Andrea Krizsán, Heather MacRae, and Anna van der Vleuten.
Description: Abingdon, Oxon; New York, NY: Routledge, 2021. |
Series: Routledge international handbooks |
Includes bibliographical references and index.
Identifiers: LCCN 2020043560 (print) | LCCN 2020043561 (ebook) |
ISBN 9781138485259 (hardback) | ISBN 9781351049955 (ebook)
Subjects: LCSH: Women–Political activity–European Union countries. |
Feminism–European Union countries. |
Sex discrimination–European Union countries. | European Union–History.
Classification: LCC HQ1236.5.E85 R68 2021 (print) |
LCC HQ1236.5.E85 (ebook) | DDC 320.082/094–dc23
LC record available at https://lccn.loc.gov/2020043560
LC ebook record available at https://lccn.loc.gov/2020043561

ISBN: 978-1-138-48525-9 (hbk)
ISBN: 978-1-351-04995-5 (ebk)

Typeset in Bembo
by Newgen Publishing UK

Contents

List of figures	*x*
List of tables	*xi*
List of contributors	*xii*
Acknowledgements	*xxii*
List of abbreviations and acronyms	*xxiv*

1 Whose story is it anyway? Studying European integration with
a gender lens   1
Gabriele Abels and Heather MacRae

PART I
Gendering the EU: theoretical perspectives   15

2 The EU as a gender equality regime: a core research concept   17
Angelika von Wahl

3 Europeanization   30
Maxime Forest

4 Social constructivism   43
Emanuela Lombardo and Johanna Kantola

5 Feminist institutionalism   56
Heather MacRae and Elaine Weiner

6 Feminist political economy and its explanatory promise   68
Rosalind Cavaghan and Anna Elomäki

7 The EU, men and masculinities   80
Jeff Hearn, Katarzyna Wojnicka, Iva Šmídová and Keith Pringle

Contents

8   The EU approach to intersectional discrimination in law   93
    Iyiola Solanke

PART II
Gendering the EU polity and structures of governance   105

9   European Parliament   107
    Petra Ahrens and Lise Rolandsen Agustín

10 Gendering the Council system   120
    Gabriele Abels

11 Gender equality and the European Commission   133
    Miriam Hartlapp, Henriette Müller and Ingeborg Tömmel

12 The European External Action Service   146
    Laura Chappell

13 The politics of gender in the field of European agencies   158
    Sophie Jacquot and Andrea Krizsán

14 The Court of Justice of the EU and judicial politics   170
    Jessica Guth and Sanna Elfving

PART III
Gendered politics in the EU   181

15 Enlargement   183
    Cristina Chiva

16 Gender and EU citizenship   195
    Birte Siim and Monika Mokre

17 The privilege of (defining) knowledge: gender differences in political
    knowledge across Europe   208
    Jessica Fortin-Rittberger and Lena Ramstetter

18 Civil society   222
    Sabine Lang

19 Party politics   235
    Petra Ahrens and Lise Rolandsen Agustín

Contents

PART IV
Gender equality and EU policies
251

20 Social and employment policy
253
Susan Milner

21 Economic and monetary union
265
Alexandra Scheele

22 Trade policy
278
Maria García

23 Development policy
290
Petra Debusscher

24 Gender and EU climate policy
302
Gill Allwood

25 Research policy
314
Marcela Linková and Lut Mergaert

26 Security and defence policy
327
Hanna L. Muehlenhoff

27 Migration and asylum policy
339
Ulrike Krause and Helen Schwenken

28 Violence against women and gender-based violence
352
Conny Roggeband

PART V
A gender lens on key issues and debates
365

29 The populist challenge to gender equality
367
Birte Siim and Christina Fiig

30 Economic crisis and the politics of austerity
379
Johanna Kantola and Emanuela Lombardo

31 The gender story of Brexit: from under-representation of women to
marginalisation of equality
392
Roberta Guerrina and Annick Masselot

Index
404

ix

Figures

9.1	Members of the European Parliament, 1952–2019 (%)	109
11.1	Women at the top of the Commission, 1958–2020	135
17.1	Mean number of correct responses on four factual political knowledge questions about the European Union and national parliaments by country and gender, 2009	210
17.2	Mean number of correct responses on four factual political knowledge questions about the European Union and national parliaments by country and gender, 2014	211
17.3	Mean political interest by gender and country, ESS 2018	212
17.4	Average number of "don't know" answers versus substantive answers (whether correct or incorrect) with 99% t-test confidence intervals	215
19.1	Gender composition by European Parliament political group, 1979–2019	242

Tables

19.1	Overview of Europarties and EPGs	238
25.1	Major steps in the evolution of gender equality in RTD, 1993–2020	317

Contributors

Gabriele Abels, Prof. Dr., is Jean Monnet Chair of European Integration at the Institute for Political Science, University of Tübingen, Germany. Her research interests include democratization and parliaments in the EU system, gendering the EU, integration theory, regional governance and the role of regions in the EU. Since 1995, she is co-editor of the journal *Femina Politica*. Her most important publications include *Gendering European Integration Theory: Engaging New Dialogues* (co-edited with Heather MacRae; Barbara Budrich Publishers, 2016) and *Gendering the European Union. New Approaches to Old Democratic Deficits* (co-edited with Joyce M. Mushaben; Palgrave Macmillan, 2012). Her articles have appeared in *European Political Science*, *European Integration online Papers*, *Journal of Common Market Studies*, *Femina Politica*, *Journal of Legislative Studies* and *Zeitschrift für Parlamentsfragen*, *Zeitschrift für Politikwissenschaft*, among others.

Lise Rolandsen Agustín, PhD, is Associate Professor at the Department of Politics and Society, Aalborg University, Denmark. Her research focuses on gender equality, social movements, intersectionality and gender-based violence. She is the author of *Gender Equality, Intersectionality and Diversity in Europe* (Palgrave Macmillan, 2013) and *Sexual Harassment in the Work Place* (with Anette Borchorst, Aalborg University Press, 2017). She has co-edited (with Petra Ahrens) *Gendering the European Parliament: Structures, Policies and Practices* (Rowman & Littlefield, 2019). Her articles have been published in *Journal of Common Market Studies*, *Party Politics*, *Ethnicities* and *Politics*, among others.

Petra Ahrens, Dr., is Senior Researcher in the ERC-funded research project "Gender, party politics and democracy in Europe: A study of European Parliament's party groups" (EUGenDem) at Tampere University, Finland. She works on gender equality policies and politics in the European Union and Germany, gendered power relations and political strategies like gender mainstreaming, and on civil society organizations and participatory democracy. She was founding co-editor of *European Journal of Politics and Gender*. She is the author of *Actors, Institutions, and the Making of EU Gender Equality Programs* (Palgrave Macmillan, 2018) and co-editor, with Lise Rolandsen Agustín, of *Gendering the European Parliament. Structures, Policies, and Practices* (Rowman & Littlefield/ ECPR Press, 2019). Her articles have appeared in *European Politics and Society*, *Journal of Common Market Studies*, *West European Politics* and *Parliamentary Affairs*, among others.

Gill Allwood, PhD, is Professor of Gender Politics at Nottingham Trent University, UK. Her areas of expertise include gender and EU policy, especially development, migration and climate change. She is currently working on gender and European policy. This examines the relation between gender mainstreaming and a range of EU policy areas, including migration, international development and climate change. She is co-author (with Kursheed Wadia) of *Refugee*

Women in Britain and France (Manchester University Press, 2010) and *Gender and Policy in France* (Palgrave Macmillan, 2009). Her articles have appeared in *European Integration online Papers, French Politics, Contemporary Politics, Political Studies Review* and *Women's Studies International Forum,* among others.

Rosalind Cavaghan, Dr., is an independent scholar and public policy consultant located in Edinburgh, UK. Her research interests include the gendering impacts of EU integration and the politics of knowledge, especially in economic policy and research and development policy. Her recent projects include co-editing the 2020 special issue of *Social Politics* entitled "Experts, Idiots and Liars: the gender politics of knowledge in turbulent times", where she has published on intersectionality in gender budgeting. Her book *Making Gender Equality Happen: Knowledge Change and Resistance in EU Gender Mainstreaming* (Routledge, 2017) is based on her PhD thesis, which was awarded the ECPR Gender and Politics Thesis Dissertation Prize in 2013. She has published in *Social Politics, Journal of Common Market Studies Annual Review, Journal of Women Politics and Policy* and *International Feminist Journal of Politics and Critical Policy Studies,* among others.

Laura Chappell, Dr., is Senior Lecturer in European Politics at the University of Surrey. Her research focuses on the Common Security and Defence Policy and the European External Action Service including from a gender perspective, European strategic culture, EU defence capability initiatives and Polish security and defence policy. She has published widely on different aspects of the EU's Common Security and Defence Policy, Polish and German defence policies as well as gender and European security. Her articles have appeared in *Cooperation and Conflict, Journal of European Integration, Journal of Common Market Studies, Contemporary Security Policy,* among others. She is co-author of *The EU, Strategy and Security Policy* (Routledge, 2016), and co-editor of the journal *European Security.*

Cristina Chiva, Dr., is Lecturer in EU Politics at the University of Salford Manchester, UK. Her research interests and published work are in EU gender equality policy and in women's representation in politics in post-communist legislatures and in the European Parliament. Her recent monograph, *Gender, Institutions and Political Representation: Reproducing Male Dominance in Europe's New Democracies* (Palgrave Macmillan, 2017), examines the causal mechanisms that have perpetuated women's under-representation in politics in Bulgaria, the Czech Republic, Hungary, Poland, Romania and Slovakia during the period 1990–2016. Her articles have appeared in *Parliamentary Affairs* and *Perspectives on European Politics and Society,* among others.

Petra Debusscher, Dr., is an independent consultant and associate researcher at the University of Antwerp, Belgium. In her research she focuses on gender equality and diversity policies in the European Union, and in particular on gender mainstreaming in EU development policy, which was the topic of her PhD (2010 Ghent University). She was awarded a postdoctoral fellowship of the Special Research Fund (BOF) and a postdoctoral fellowship of the Research Foundation – Flanders (FWO) on the topic "Successfully Mainstreaming Gender in EU Development Cooperation and the Role of the EU, the Partner Country and Civil Society: A Best and Worst Cases Analysis." She has published and taught extensively on gender mainstreaming, intersectionality and multiple inequalities in EU external and development policy. Her work has appeared in *Development Policy Review, European Journal of Development Research, Journal of Women, Politics & Policy, International Development Planning Review, Political Studies Review* and *Women's Studies International Forum,* among others.

Contributors

Sanna Elfving, Dr., is a Senior Lecturer in Law at the University of Bradford, UK. Her area of expertise is EU Law. She is currently working on gender in asylum cases before the Court of Justice and the right of residence for EU citizens in the UK after Brexit. She has co-authored *Gender and Court of Justice of the European Union* with Jessica Guth (Routledge, 2018)

Anna Elomäki, Dr., is Senior Researcher at the Faculty of Social Sciences at Tampere University, Finland. She works in the ERC project "Gender, party politics and democracy in Europe: a study of European Parliament's party groups." Her research focuses on the intersections of gender, politics and the economy: gendered character and impacts of economic policies and governance, economization of gender equality policies in Finland and in the EU, gender budgeting, the changing conditions of feminist movements, and theoretical questions about gender, neoliberalism and economization. Her work has appeared in *Gender, Work & Organization, European Journal of Women's Studies*, *International Journal of Feminist Politics*, *Journal of Common Market Studies* and *Social Politics*, among others

Christina Fiig, PhD, is Associate Professor of Gender and European Politics at Aarhus University, Denmark. She researches gender and politics. Her research interests and teaching activities include European, Nordic and Danish politics, democracy, the public sphere, media and Nordic enfranchisement. She employs a gender as well as a perspective of intersectionality in her research. Fiig is currently involved in research projects on the populist challenge to gender equality in the European Union, on implementation of gender quotas, on EU's gender equality policies, Nordic enfranchisement and media and gender. Her most recent work appeared in *The Oxford Handbook of Danish Politics* (together with Birte Siim; Oxford University Press, 2020) and the *Encyclopedia of European Union Politics* (2020).

Maxime Forest, PhD, is Senior Lecturer and research associate at Sciences Po Paris (OFCE). His research and teaching interests cover the Europeanization of gender and anti-discrimination policies in a comparative perspective and the politics of gender in the enlarged European Union. He has co-edited (with Emanuela Lombardo) *The Europeanization of Gender Equality Policies: A Discursive-Sociological Approach* (Palgrave MacMillan, 2012) and (with Bronwyn Winter and Réjane Sénac) *Global Perspectives on Same-Sex Marriage: A Neo-Institutional Approach* (Palgrave MacMillan, 2018). His work has appeared in *Comparative European Politics, Perspective on European Politics Societies* and *Revue Internationale de politique compare*, among others.

Jessica Fortin-Rittberger, PhD, is Professor of Comparative Politics at the University of Salzburg, Austria. Her main areas of research interest include political institutions and their measurement with particular focus on electoral rules, women's political representation, political knowledge, as well as the impact of state capacity on democratization. She is co-lead editor of the *European Journal of Politics and Gender*. Her work has appeared in *Comparative Political Studies, European Journal of Political Research, Electoral Studies, European Union Politics, International Journal of Public Opinion Research* and the *Journal of European Public Policy*, among others.

Maria García, Dr., is a Senior Lecturer in the Department of Politics, Languages and International Studies, at the University of Bath, UK. Her research focuses on the politics of trade and economic governance, EU Trade Policy (and Brexit, EU–Latin America/EU–Asia relations/ EU–Australasia relations, and values in trade policy. She leads a GW4 Community focused on examining regional business responses to Brexit in Wales and the South West. Her research on

EU trade policy and the politics of trade agreements has appeared in various journals including *Journal of Common Market Studies* and *Journal of World Trade*. Together with Sangeeta Khorana she is co-editor of *Handbook of EU and International Trade* (Edward Elgar, 2018).

Roberta Guerrina, PhD, is Professor in Politics and Director of the Gender Research Centre at the University of Bristol and currently joint editor of the *Journal Common Market Studies Annual Review*. She is a specialist in the politics of gender, with a particular interest in EU politics and social policy, citizenship and gender equality. She has published in the area of women's human rights, work–life balance, identity politics and the UNSCR 1325. She is author of *Mothering the Union* (Manchester University Press, 2005) and *Europe: History, Ideas and Ideologies* (Arnold, 2002). Her work has appeared in the *Journal of Common Market Studies, International Affairs, Women's Studies International Forum* and *Review of International Studies*, among others.

Jessica Guth, Dr., Reader in Law at Leeds Beckett University. Her areas of expertise include legal education, gender perspectives in EU Law, in particular EU Social Law and Policy, feminist and queer approaches to law and legal study. Her work focuses on the Court of Justice of the EU as a legal and political institution. She has co-authored *Gender and the Court of Justice of the European Union* with Sanna Elfving (Routledge, 2018). Her articles have appeared in the *Journal of Contemporary European Research* and the *Journal of Social Welfare and Family Law*, among others.

Miriam Hartlapp, Prof. Dr., holds the Chair for Comparative Politics: Germany and France at the Otto Suhr Institute of Political Science, Freie Universität Berlin. Her research and teaching focus on European integration and comparative politics, in particular regarding the European Commission, economic and social integration, and questions of power, polarization, and conflict in the EU multilevel system as well as implementation and compliance. She is co-author of *Which Policy for Europe? Power and Conflict Inside the European Commission* (Oxford University Press, 2014) and *Taking the EU to Court: Annulment Proceedings and Multilevel Judicial Conflict* (Palgrave Macmillan, 2019). Her work has been published in *Journal of European Integration, West European Politics, Journal of Common Market Studies* and *Revue française des affaires sociales*, among others.

Jeff Hearn, PhD, is Senior Professor, Gender Studies, Örebro University, Sweden; Professor of Sociology, University of Huddersfield, UK; Professor Emeritus, Hanken School of Economics, Finland; Professor Extraordinarius, University of South Africa; and honorary doctor in Social Sciences, Lund University, Sweden. His work focuses on gender, sexuality, violence, work, organizations, management, social policy, and transnational processes. His many books include: the authored *Men of the World* (Sage, 2015) and *Age at Work* (with Wendy Parkin) (Sage, 2020); and the co-edited *Rethinking Transnational Men* (Routledge, 2013), *Engaging Youth in Activism, Research and Pedagogical Praxis* (Routledge, 2018) and *Unsustainable Institutions of Men* (Routledge, 2019).

Sophie Jacquot, PhD, is Professor of Political Science at the Université Saint-Louis – Bruxelles (IEE, CReSPo). Her research activities are concerned with the transformation of EU public policies and with the effects of Europeanization, especially in the fields of gender equality, social policy and anti-discrimination. She is author of *Transformations in EU Gender Equality. From Emergence to Dismantling* (Palgrave Macmillan, 2015). Her work has been published in *Journal of Common Market Studies, Journal of European Public Policy, West European Politics, Comparative European Politics* and *European Journal of Politics and Gender*, among others.

Contributors

Johanna Kantola, PhD, is Professor of Gender Studies at the Faculty of Social Sciences at the Tampere University, Finland. She directs an ERC Consolidator Grant (2018–2023) funded *Gender, Party Politics and Democracy in Europe: A Study of European Parliament's Party Groups* (EUGenDem) and Director of the Academy of Finland funded project *Gender and Power in Reconfigured Corporatist Finland* (GePoCo). Her books include *Gender and Political Analysis* (with Emanuela Lombardo, Palgrave, 2017) and *Gender and the European Union* (Palgrave, 2010). She has co-edited *The Oxford Handbook on Gender and Politics* (Oxford University Press, 2013) and (with Emanuela Lombardo) *Gender and the Economic Crisis in Europe: Politics, Institutions and Intersectionality* (Palgrave 2017). She is the Editor of Palgrave Macmillan's Gender and Politics Book Series with Sarah Childs.

Ulrike Krause, Prof. Dr., Junior Professor of Forced Migration and Refugees Studies at the Institute for Migration Research and Intercultural Studies (IMIS), Osnabrück University, Germany. Her areas of expertise are the conflict–displacement nexus, gender, (post)colonial approaches and knowledge production. She is author of *Difficult Life in a Refugee Camp. Violence, Gender, and Coping in Uganda* (Cambridge University Press, forthcoming) and co-editor of *Gender, Violence, Refugees* (Berghahn, 2017) and the *German Journal of Forced Migration and Refugee Studies* (Z'Flucht) (Nomos, since 2017). Her articles have appeared in *Development*, *Journal of Refugee Studies* and *Refugee Survey Quarterly*, among others.

Andrea Krizsán, PhD, is Associate Professor at the School of Public Policy and Research Fellow at the Democracy Institute, Central European University (CEU). Her research focuses on policy change in countries of central and eastern Europe in the fields of gender and race equality and gender-based violence, and the role of diverse actors including the EU in promoting gender policy change. She is co-author (with Conny Roggeband) of *The Gender Politics of Domestic Violence. Feminists Engaging the State in Central and Eastern Europe* (Routledge, 2018) and co-editor with Judith Squires and Hege Skjeie of Institutionalizing Intersectionality (Palgrave MacMillan, 2012). Her publications include articles in *Politics and Governance*, *European Journal of Politics and Gender*, *Violence against Women*, *Journal of International and Comparative Social Policy*, *Ethnic and Racial Studies*, *Social Politics* and *Journal for Ethnic and Minority Studies*, among others.

Sabine Lang, PhD, is Professor of European Politics and Director of the Center for West European Studies at the Henry M. Jackson School of International Studies/University of Washington, Seattle. Her research interests include gender and civil society, political representation, and transnational advocacy in the EU. She co-authored (with Petra Ahrens, Katja Schmilewski, and Birgit Sauer) *Gender Equality in Politics – Implementing Party Quotas in Germany and Austria* (Springer, 2020) and is co-editor (with Jill Irvine and Celeste Montoya) of *Gendered Mobilizations. Intersectional Challenges in North American and European Social Movements* (Rowman & Littlefield, 2019). Her articles have appeared in *German Politics*, *European Journal of Women's Studies* and *Publius – The Journal of Federalism*, *Social Politics*, among others.

Marcela Linková, PhD, is the Head of the Centre for Gender and Science at the Institute of Sociology, Czech Academy of Sciences. Her research focuses on gendered organizations, research careers, governance of research and research assessment from a gender perspective as well as research policy analysis from a gender perspective. She is the chair of the ERAC Standing Working Group on Gender in Research and Innovation. She is co-editor of *Gender and Neoliberalism in*

Czech Academia (Sociologické nakladatelství, 2017). Her work has appeared in *European Journal of Women's Studies, Gender and Research* and *Science and Public Policy*, among others.

Emanuela Lombardo, PhD, is Associate Professor at the Department of Political Science and Administration and member of the Institute of Feminist Research of Madrid Complutense University, Spain. Her research concerns gender equality policies in the European context, political analysis, and Europeanization. She currently coordinates the evaluation of research projects on gender in the social sciences at the Spanish Ministry of Research, and co-directs (with Maria Bustelo) the research group Gender and Politics and the research project UNiGUAL. She has recently published with Johanna Kantola *Gender and Political Analysis* (Palgrave Macmillan, 2017) and *Gender and the Economic Crisis in Europe. Politics, Institutions and Intersectionality* (Palgrave Macmillan, 2017). She is co-author (with Petra Meier) of *The Symbolic Representation of Gender: A Discursive Approach* (Ashgate, 2014). Her articles have appeared in *Journal of Common Market Studies, European Journal of Political Research, Policy and Society, Comparative European Politics, Gender, Work and Organization* and *Social Politics*, among others.

Heather MacRae, PhD, is Associate Professor and former Jean Monnet Chairholder in the Department of Politics at York University, Toronto, Canada. She is currently co-editor of the *Journal of Common Market Studies*. Her current research focuses on a variety of aspects of gender policy in the European Union and, specifically, Germany. She is co-editor (with Gabriele Abels) of *Gendering European Integration Theory: Engaging new Dialogues* (Barbara Budrich Publishers, 2016), and (with Elaine Weiner) of *Towards Gendering Institutionalism: Equality in Europe* (Rowman & Littlefield, 2017). Her articles have been published in *Journal of Common Market Studies, West European Politics, European Integration online Papers* and other key journals.

Annick Masselot, PhD, is Professor of Law at the University of Canterbury, New Zealand. Her research interests include gender equality and equal treatment, social and employment law, reconciliation between work and family life, pregnancy and maternity rights in a comparative context. Her current work focuses on the gender impact of Brexit. She is the co-author of *Reconciling Work and Family Life in EU Law and Policy* (Palgrave Macmillan, 2010) and *Caring Responsibility in EU Law and Policy: Who Cares?* (Routledge, 2020), and co-editor of *Importing EU Norms? Conceptual Framework and Empirical Findings* (Springer, 2015). She is co-editor of the *Journal of Common Market Studies*. Her works has appeared in *Social Policy & Society, International Feminist Journal of Politics, European Law Journal, European Law Review* and *International Journal of Comparative Labour Law and Industrial Relations*, among others.

Lut Mergaert, PhD, is Director and Senior Consultant at Yellow Window (Antwerp, Belgium) and has been the project leader and principal investigator of a significant number of policy support studies related to gender, mainly for the European Commission and the European Institute for Gender Equality. Her areas of expertise and research interests include gender in EU research policy, the facilitation of structural change towards gender equality in research organizations, and EU gender equality and gender mainstreaming policies. Her work features in *European Journal of Risk Regulation, European Integration online Papers (EIoP), International Feminist Journal of Politics, Journal of gender-based violence, NORA-Nordic Journal of Feminist and Gender Research, Genus* and *European Journal of Politics and Gender*, among others.

Susan Milner, PhD, is Professor of European Politics and Society in the Department of Politics, Languages and European Studies at the University of Bath, UK. Her areas of expertise include

European social and employment policy, with a focus on policies to support working parents, and to tackle gender pay gaps. She is associate editor of the international journal *Gender, Work & Organization* and was consultant on an EU-funded project on Trade unions and anti-discrimination policies. She is author of *Comparative Employment Relations: France, Germany and Britain* (Palgrave Macmillan, 2015). Her work has appeared in *British Politics, Gender, Work & Organization, Journal of Industrial Relations, Modern and Contemporary France* and *Work, Employment and Society*, among others.

Monika Mokre, Dr., is a political scientist and Senior Researcher at the Institute of Culture Studies and Theatre History of the Austrian Academy of Sciences (ÖAW). She teaches at various universities and is politically active in the field of asylum and migration. Her research interests include asylum and migration, cultural politics, democracy and the public sphere, and gender studies. She is one of the Austrian representatives in the Cost Action "Constitution Making and Deliberative Democracy" and Member of the Executive Committee of ROR-n, Refugee Outreach and Research Network. She is co-editor (with Birte Siim) of *Negotiating Gender and Diversity in an Emergent European Public Sphere* (Palgrave Macmillan, 2013) and (with Jozef Bátora) of *Culture and External Relations: Europe and Beyond* (Routledge, 2011).

Hanna L. Muehlenhoff, Dr., is Assistant Professor in European Studies with a focus on "Europe in the World" at the Department of European Studies, University of Amsterdam (UvA), The Netherlands. Her research interests include EU's human rights promotion, gender and security policies. She is author of *EU Democracy Promotion and Governmentality: Turkey and Beyond* (Routledge, 2019) and has co-edited a special issue on gender in EU external relations for *Political Studies Review* (2020). Her work has been published in *Politics, International Feminist Journal of Politics, Cooperation and Conflict* and *Journal of Balkan and Near Eastern Studies*.

Henriette Müller, Dr., is Visiting Assistant Professor of Leadership Studies at New York University Abu Dhabi. Her research encompasses the comparative study of political leadership and executive politics both at the national and international level with an emphasis on the European Union and the Arab Gulf region. She is author of *Political Leadership and the European Commission Presidency* (Oxford University Press, 2020) and co-editor (with Ingeborg Tömmel) of *Pathways to Power: Women and Leadership in the European Union* (Oxford University Press, 2021). Her research has appeared in journals such as *Politics & Governance, Journal of European Integration* and *West European Politics*.

Keith Pringle, PhD, is Professor Emeritus in Sociology (with a specialism in social work), Uppsala University, Sweden. He has formerly held professorships in sociology, social policy and social work in Sweden, the UK and Denmark. His research interest is the intersections of young age, "race" and gender in the context of comparative welfare analysis, with a special focus on masculinities. He is co-author (with Jeff Hearn) of *European Perspectives on Men and Masculinities: National and Transnational Approaches* (Palgrave Macmillan, 2006) and of *Men and Masculinities in Europe* (Whiting & Birch, 2013). His articles have appeared in *Men and Masculinities, Culture, Society and Masculinities, European Journal of Social Work* and *Critical Social Policy*, among others.

Lena Ramstetter is a PhD candidate in Comparative Politics at the University of Salzburg. Her areas of interest include women's representation in politics, societal polarization, as well as political attitudes from a political psychology perspective, including gendered attitudes on environmental politics. Her work was published in *Environmental Politics*.

Contributors

Conny Roggeband, Dr., is an Associate Professor at the Department of Political Science, University of Amsterdam, The Netherlands. She has written extensively on the politicization of gender-based violence, gender mainstreaming and equality policies, social movements and transnational feminist networking. Her current research focuses on the implications of democratic backsliding for gender equality policies in central and eastern Europe and Latin America. Together with with Andrea Krizsán she has published of *The Gender Politics of Domestic Violence. Feminists Engaging the State in Central and Eastern Europe* (Routledge, 2018) and *Gendering Democratic Backsliding in Central and Eastern Europe. A Comparative Agenda* (Central European University Press, 2019). Her articles have been published in *International Relations, Journal of Civil Society, Politics and Governance, European Journal of Politics and Gender* and *International Migration*, among others.

Alexandra Scheele, PD Dr., is Senior Assistant Professor (Akademische Oberrätin) for Economic Sociology and Sociology of Work, Faculty for Sociology, Bielefeld University, Germany. She is a member of the European Commission's Expert body "Scientific analysis and advice on gender equality in the EU – SAAGE." She is currently co-directing the interdisciplinary and international research group "Global Contestations of Women's and Gender Rights" at the ZiF Bielefeld, Germany. Her areas of expertise include gender inequalities at work and on the labour market, digital economy, and gender policies in the EU. Her work has appeared in *Femina Politica, Global Dialogue, Gender, Work & Organiaztion* and *Journal of Contemporary European Studies*, among others.

Helen Schwenken, Prof. Dr., is Professor for Migration and Society at the Institute for Migration Research and Intercultural Studies (IMIS), Osnabrück University, Germany. Her areas of expertise are gender and migration, labour migration and social movement studies. She is co-editor (with Sabine Ruß-Sattar) of *New Borders and Citizenship Politics* (Palgrave Macmillan, 2014) and (with Helge Schwiertz) of the special issue *Citizenship and Solidarity along Migratory Routes in Europe and the Americas* (Citizenship Studies, 2020). She is editorial board member of the IMISCOE (International Migration, Integration and Social Cohesion in Europe) book series. Her work has appeared in *International Migration, Population, Place & Space, Signs* and *International Feminist Journal of Politics*, among others.

Birte Siim is Professor Emerita in Gender Research, Aalborg University (AAU), Campus Copenhagen, Denmark. Her research interests include gender and politics, citizenship and democracy, populism and nationalism, diversity and migration; she combines citizenship and social movement studies with intersectional analysis. Siim currently works on research projects on "The Populist Challenge to Gender Equality; Populism and Female leadership; Gender and European Citizenship," "The Politics and Practice of Solidarity," and "Gender and Danish Politics." She is co-editor of *Negotiating Gender and Diversity in an Emergent European Public Sphere* (Palgrave Macmillan, 2013), *Diversity and Contestations over Nationalism in Europe and Canada* (Palgrave Macmillan, 2018), and *Citizens Activism and Solidarity Movement in Contemporary Europe: Contending with Populism* (Palgrave Macmillan, 2019). Her articles have been published in *NORA – Nordic Journal of Feminist and Gender Research, Critical Sociology, Ethnicities, Journal of Comparative Social Welfare* and *Politics & Gender* among others.

Iva Šmídová, PhD, is a sociologist and Associate Professor at the Department of Sociology, Faculty of Social Studies, Masaryk University, Brno, Czech Republic. She has worked in the field

xix

of gender studies since the early 1990s, with a particular focus on Critical Studies on Men and Masculinities (CSMM). Her research interests include health, illness and medicine, and death and dying. She is co-author of *Men and Masculinities in Europe* (Whiting & Birch, 2013). Her work has appeared in *Women's Studies International Forum*, among others.

Iyiola Solanke, Prof, Dr. is Chair in EU Law and Social Justice, School of Law, University of Leeds, UK. Her research adopts a socio-legal, historical and comparative focus on EU law, anti-discrimination law, racial integration and intersectional discrimination, and alternative dispute resolution (ADR). Her research interests include black and migrant women in European welfare states and European labour markets, social action and legal reform, synergy and intersectional discrimination, the impact of separate opinions on judicial authority, the Advocate General in the CJEU, and a public health approach to anti-discrimination law. She is author of *Discrimination as Stigma: A Theory of Anti-Discrimination Law* (Hart, 2017), *EU Law* (Pearson, 2015) and *Making Anti-Racial Discrimination Law* (Routledge, 2009). Her articles have been published in *Feminist Legal Studies, European Law Journal, Industrial Law Journal, Columbia Journal of European Law, Modern Law Review* and *West European Politics*, among others. She is founder of the Black Female Professors Forum (blackfemaleprofessorsforum.org), a network of black female professors in the UK.

Ingeborg Tömmel, Dr. habil., is Professor emeritus in International and European Politics and Jean Monnet Chair at the University of Osnabrück, Germany. She is holder of the John F. Diefenbaker Award of the Canadian Council for 2005–2006. Her research focuses on the political system of the EU, European governance and policy-making, policy implementation in the member states, and political leadership in the EU. Recent publications include *Innovative Governance in the European Union* (with Amy Verdun; Lynne Rienner, 2009), *The European Union: What It Is and How It Works* (Palgrave Macmillan, 2014), a special issue on "Political Leadership in the EU" (with Amy Verdun; *Journal of European Integration,* 2017), and *Pathways to Power: Women and Leadership in the European Union* (with Henriette Müller; Oxford University Press, 2021). Her work has appeared in *Journal of European Integration, Journal of Common Market Studies* and *West European Politics*, among others.

Anna van der Vleuten, Dr., is Professor Contesting Europeanization at the Department of Political Science and Public Administration at Radboud University, The Netherlands. Her research and teaching activities focus on the European Union and other regional organizations, theories of international relations, gender and LGBT rights. She is co-coordinator of the multi-disciplinary research group Gender and Power in Politics and Management (GENDER) and she is involved in the multidisciplinary research group Europeanisation of Policy and Law (EUROPAL). Her book *The Price of Gender Equality. Member States and Governance in the European Union* (Ashgate, 2007) reinvestigates the history of EU gender equality policy. Her work has appeared in *Acta Politica, International Relations, Journal of Common Market Studies, Policy & Politics, Political Studies Review* and *West European Politics*, among others.

Angelika von Wahl, Dr., is Professor and Chair of the International Affairs Program at Lafayette College, USA. Her research focuses on gender and social policy in Germany and the European Union. She studies family and labour market policy, gender equality regimes, intersectionality, and the gender policies of the Merkel era. Her current research focuses on the emergence of gender variance in politics and policy. She is currently working on a monograph tracing the emergence of the third gender law in Germany from the local to the global level. Her articles have been published in *Social Politics*, *West European Politics*, *German Politics*, *German Politics and Society*, *Femina Politica* and *Feministische Studien*, and others.

Elaine Weiner, PhD, is Associate Professor in Sociology at McGill University, Canada. Her research interests lie at the intersection of gender, work and Central and East European societies. She is the author of *Market Dreams: Gender, Class, and Capitalism in the Czech Republic* (University of Michigan Press, 2007) and co-editor (with Heather MacRae) of *Towards Gendering Institutionalism: Equality in Europe* (Rowman & Littlefield, 2017). She has published in *European Journal of Women's Studies*, *European Integration Online Papers*, *Social Problems*, *Social Politics* and *Women's Studies International Forum*, among others.

Katarzyna Wojnicka, PhD, is a sociologist and Research Fellow at the Department of Sociology and Work Science and Centre for European Research at the University of Gothenburg, Sweden. She is currently involved in several research projects concerning men and masculinities, migration and social movements in Europe. Before joining the University of Gothenburg she worked as a Postdoctoral Researcher at the University of Leeds, UK and Humboldt University of Berlin as well as Dissens: Institut for Education and Research, Germany, and DeZIM: German Centre for Intergation and Migration Research in Berlin, Germany. Her work has appeared in *NORMA: International Journal for Masculinity Studies*, *International Journal for Crime, Justice and Social Democracy*, *Men and Masculinities* and *Masculinities and Social Change*, among others.

Acknowledgements

Compiling a handbook that is to bring together the state-of-the art in a specific scholarly field of what has been achieved so far and which gaps should be attended to in future research is a demanding task. It requires a large group of highly dedicated people believing in the project and supporting it. We, the editors, had the pleasure to work with many dedicated colleagues, research assistants and publishing managers in the last few years.

The Handbook evolved over a time span of three years, first by bringing together a quartet of editors with diverse backgrounds and expertise in the expanding field of EU studies, but all with a strong commitment to and enthusiasm for gender studies, and with a perseverance necessary for our joint project ahead. First ideas were exchanged in 2017, invitation letters sent out to more than 40 contributors in 2018 and 2019, an intensive workshop held in Tübingen in June 2019, where we discussed chapter outlines style sheet etcs, and intensive rounds of commenting and editing of all chapters followed in 2019 and 2020. Several ideas and aims guided the project: (1) We aimed for a Handbook that represents the state-of-the-art in how gender scholars have explored European integration and the Union today, making the rich research accessible, on the one hand, to non-gender specialists while, on the other hand, also fostering new debates for scholars who are in the field for a long time. (2) We opted for a mainstreaming approach in all chapters, yet to different degree, with regard to how far gender equality has advanced and gender mainstreaming has been implemented and with regard to intersectional concerns. (3) Our third aim was to overcome a geographical bias by including research from and on central and eastern European countries and how this affects a gendered approach to European integration. (4) Finally, besides an often prevalent crisis topos, we wanted to include the most recent developments linked to European elections in 2019, a new Commission coming into power, the release of a new and ambitious Commission Gender Equality Strategy in March 2020. Whether we have achieved these aims is for the reader to decide.

We are very thankful to all contributors for their commitment and diligence throughout several rounds of revisions and editing. Without their work, this Handbook would not have been possible. More than one supersize big thank you goes to our key editorial staff, Anne Cress. She has coordinated the project from the start, sending out numerous emails and reminders to authors and editors alike, setting and monitoring deadlines, circulating papers, and thus keeping the project on track. We also owe a debt of gratitude to our editorial assistants Lena Korn and Joshua Beer, who have checked chapters over and over again to insure coherence and high quality. We are also very grateful to Hailey Murphy for her valuable language-editing support. Finally, we are thankful for the support from Routledge, especially from Andrew Taylor and Sophie Iddamalgoda, who believed in the project and provided continuous support.

Acknowledgements

When we started this "journey," it was not always clear that it would be doable; but it was always worth trying and we are happy and grateful that we made it through the finish line.

We wish all readers "viel Vergnügen und neue Erkenntnisse," "jó szórakozást és sok inspirációt," lots of fun and food for thought, and "Veel genoegen en nieuwe inzichten."

Gabriele Abels, Andrea Krizsán, Heather MacRae and Anna van der Vleuten
Tübingen, Budapest, Toronto and Nijmegen in September 2020

Abbreviations and acronyms

ACP	Africa, Caribbean and Pacific
ACRE	Alliance of European Conservatives and Reformists
AEMN	Alliance of European National Movements
AFCO	Committee on Constitutional Affairs, European Parliament
AfD	Alternative für Deutschland
AGRIFISH	Agriculture and Fisheries Council
AIDCO	EuropeAid Co-operation Office
ALDE	Alliance of Liberals and Democrats for Europe
AP	action programme
APF	Alliance for Peace and Freedom
APPF	Authority for European Political Parties and European Political Foundations
AVFT	Association des victimes de harcèlement moral, psychologique, sexuel, dans le cadre du travail
BME	black and minority ethnic
CAHRV	Coordination Action on Human Rights Violations
CARD	Coordinated Annual Review on Defence
CDU	Christian Democratic Union of Germany
CEAS	Common European Asylum System
CEDAW	Convention on the Elimination of All Forms of Discrimination against Women, United Nations
CEDEFOP	European Center for the Development of Vocational Training
CEE	central and eastern Europe
CETA	Comprehensive Economic and Trade Agreement
CFR	Charter of Fundamental Rights
CFSP	Common Foreign and Security Policy
CJEU	Court of Justice of the European Union
CoE	Council of Europe
CoFoE	Conference on the Future of Europe
COMPET	Competitiveness Council
COREPER	Comité des représentants permanents
CPCC	Civilian Planning and Conduct Capability
CPE	critical political economy

CRC	Combahee River Collective
CROME	Critical Research on Men in Europe
CSDP	Common Security and Defence Policy
CSMM	Critical Studies on Men and Masculinities
CSO	civil society organization
CSPEC	Confederation of Socialist Parties in the European Community
CSR	country-specific recommendation
DEVAW	Declaration on the Elimination of Violence against Women
DF	Dansk Folkeparti, Danish Peoples' Party
DG	Directorate-General
DG CLIMA	Directorate-General for Climate Action
DG DEFIS	Directorate-General for Defence Industry and Space
DG DEVCO	Directorate-General International Cooperation and Development
DG ECFIN	Directorate-General for Economic and Financial Affairs
DG EMPL	Directorate-General Employment, Social Affairs and Equal Opportunities
DG Justice	Directorate-General Justice, Fundamental Rights and Citizenship
DG RELEX	Directorate-General for External Relations
DG RTD	Directorate-General for Research and Innovation
DUP	Democratic Unionist Party
EAEC	European Atomic Energy Community
EASO	European Asylum Support Office
EC	European Communities
ECB	European Central Bank
ECD	European Consensus on Development
ECHR	European Convention on Human Rights and Fundamental Freedoms (Council of Europe)
ECJ	European Court of Justice
ECOFIN	Economic and Financial Affairs Council
ECPM	European Christian Political Movement
ECR	European Conservatives and Reformists
ECSC	European Coal and Steel Community
ECtHR	European Court of Human Rights
ECU	European Currency Unit
EDC	European Defence Community
EDF	European Development Fund
EDP	European Democratic Party
EDP	excessive deficit procedure
EEAS	European External Action Service
EEC	European Economic Community
EES	European Employment Strategy
EFA	European Free Alliance
EFDD	Europe of Freedom and Direct Democracy
EFTA	European Free Trade Association

Abbreviations and acronyms

EGC	European Green Coordination
EGP	European Green Party
EIDHR	European Instrument for Democracy and Human Rights
EIGE	European Institute for Gender Equality
EL	Party of the European Left
ELDR	European Liberal Democrat and Reform Party
ELSA	Ethical, Legal and Social Aspects
EMPL	Committee on Employment and Social Affairs, European Parliament
EMS	European Monetary System
EMU	Economic and Monetary Union
ENF	Europe of Nations and Freedom
ENoMW	European Network of Migrant Women
ENP	European Neighbourhood Policy
ENVI	Environment Council
EP	European Parliament
EPA	Economic Partnership Agreement
EPG	European party groups
EPLO	European Peacebuilding Liaison Office
EPO	European Protection Order
EPP	European People's Party
EPRS	European Parliamentary Research Service
EPSCO	Employment, Social Policy, Health and Consumer Affairs Council
EPSR	European Pillar of Social Rights
ERA	European Research Area
ERG	European Research Group
ERM	Exchange Rate Mechanism
ESC	Economic and Social Committee
ESDP	European Security and Defence Policy
ESF	European Social Fund
ESS	European Security Strategy
ESS	European Social Survey
ETF	European Training Foundation
ETS	Emissions Trading System
ETUC	European Trade Union Confederation
EU	European Union
EUCO	European Council
EUMC	European Monitoring Centre on Racism and Xenophobia
EU OSHA	European Agency for Safety and Health at Work
EUPP	Euro Plus Pact
Euratom	European Atomic Energy Community
EUROFOUND	European Foundation for the Improvement of Living and Working Conditions

EWL	European Women's Lobby
EYCS	Education, Youth, Culture and Sport Council
FAC	Foreign Affairs Council
FEMM	Committee on Women's Rights and Gender Equality, European Parliament
FGM	female genital mutilation
FI	feminist institutionalism
FP	Framework Programme
FPE	feminist political economy/feminist political economist
FRA	European Union Agency for Fundamental Rights
GAC	General Affairs Council
GAD	Gender and Development
GAP	Gender Action Plan
GDP	gross domestic product
GER	gender equality regime
GFP	gender focal person
GIA	gender impact assessment
GM	gender mainstreaming
GSC	General Secretariat of the Council
GSP	Generalised System of Preferences
GUE	European United Left
HR/VP	High Representative for Foreign Affairs and Security Policy/ Vice President
IcSP	Instrument contributing to Stability and Peace
ID	Identity & Democracy Group
ILGA	International Lesbian, Gay, Bisexual, Trans and Intersex Association
ILO	International Labour Organisation
IMF	International Monetary Fund
IPU-PACE	Inter-Parliamentary Union and Parliamentary Assembly of the Council of Europe
ITC	International Trade Centre
JHA	Justice and Home Affairs Council
JRC	Joint Research Centre
LGBT	lesbian, gay, bisexual, transgender
LGBTI	lesbian, gay, bisexual, transgender, intersex
LGBTIQA+	lesbian, gay, bisexual, trans/transgender, intersex, queer/ questioning, and asexual
LI	liberal intergovernmentalism
LIBE	Committee on Civil Liberties, Justice and Home Affairs, European Parliament
MENF	Movement for a Europe of Nations and Freedom
MEP	Member of the European Parliament
MP	Member of Parliament

Abbreviations and acronyms

MPCC	Military Planning and Conduct Capability
MTO	Medium-Term Objective
NATO	North Atlantic Treaty Organization
NFMM	Nordic Association for Research on Men and Masculinities
NGL	Nordic Green Left
NGO	non-governmental organization
NI	new institutionalism
OLP	ordinary legislative procedure
OMC	open method of coordination
OJ	Official Journal of the European Union
OSCE	Organisation for Security and Co-operation in Europe
PES	Party of European Socialists
PESCO	permanent structured cooperation
PHARE	Poland and Hungary Assistance for Economic Reconstruction
PiS	Polish Law and Justice Party
PPEU	European Pirate Party
PPP	public–private partnerships
PTA	preferential trade agreement
PVV	Partij voor de Vrijheid, Dutch Freedom Party
QMV	qualified majority vote
R&D	research and development
RE	Renew Europe
RN	Rassemblement National
RRI	responsible research and innovation
RRP	radical right-wing parties
RRP	radical-right politics
RTD	research and technological development
RWP	right-wing populism
S&D	Progressive Alliance of Socialists and Democrats
SDG	Sustainable Development Goals
SEA	Single European Act
SEDE	Committee on Security and Defence, European Parliament
SGP	Stability and Growth Pact
SIA	sustainability impact assessment
SOTEU	State of the Union address
STOP	Sexual Trafficking of Persons
TCN	third-country national
TEU	Treaty on European Union
TFEU	Treaty on the Functioning of the European Union
TRAN	Committee on Transport and Tourism, European Parliament
TSCG	Treaty on Stability, Coordination and Governance
TSD	trade and sustainable development
TTE	Transport, Telecommunication and Energy Council
TTIP	Transatlantic Trade and Investment Partnership

UDHR	Universal Declaration of Human Rights
UKIP	UK Independence Party
UN	United Nations
UNFCCC	United Nations Framework Convention on Climate Change
UNSC	United Nations Security Council
UNSCR	United Nations Security Council Resolution
V4	Visegrád countries
VAW	violence against women
WasH	Women against sexual harassment
WAVE	Women Against Violence Europe
WEU	Western European Union
WEUCO	Women's European Council
WID	Women in Development policy
WIDE	Women in Development Europe
WPS	Women, Peace and Security
WTO	World Trade Organization

1

Whose story is it anyway?

Studying European integration with a gender lens

Gabriele Abels and Heather MacRae

'The historiography of European integration is dominated by legends of great men … For the Community's supporters they have become saints.'

(Milward 2000, 281)

'There were no women, and for good reason: at the time they were given very little space in the national political life of the six founding states.'

(Denéchère 2016)

The history of Europe, according to Greek mythology, begins with the abduction and rape of a young Phoenician girl, called Europe, by Zeus, a hypermasculine god who had disguised himself as a handsome white bull. Gender issues and a dominance of masculinity hence have been there from the beginning. However, women have been strangely absent in the making of European integration. Scholars in EU studies almost unanimously point to Jean Monnet, Robert Schuman, Konrad Adenauer, Alcide de Gasperi, Paul-Henri Spaak and other 'great men' as the 'founding fathers' of European integration. Certainly, these men played key roles in the early development and the evolution of the European project. Unlike Alan Milward, Yves Denéchère (2016) gives a reason: the male dominance of and corresponding oppression ('little space') of women in politics and political life. But this image of polity formation without women is incredibly misleading. In fact, women were (and continue to be) very much a part of the European project. So, where are they? Why are they excluded from the formal telling of the EU's history? Were there any 'founding mothers'? And if yes, who, and what did they contribute, given the societal restrictions imposed on women?

In gender studies, one common research strategy is to begin by searching for the women and investigating their role in – in this case – political life that has shaped the continent in a remarkable way in previous decades. The focus on European integration as the story of 'great men' is an historicization which presents a myth of European integration as a masculine project, it is Zeus 2.0. It is the EU's 'his-story'. This perspective is reproduced over and over again. An analysis of standard texts on the evolution of European integration (such as Dinan 2006, Griffiths 2014, or Loth 2015) proves that women are hardly, if ever, mentioned as part of the political elite which has shaped European integration, particularly during the first two formative decades. Denéchère (2016) concedes that there were some women, but relegated to the background and with limited impact: 'even if a few women can be identified in the shadows of the founders behind the European project. None of these, however, had a deciding role.' Furthermore, he notes, '[t]his initial absence of women can lead one to believe that they did not share in in the construction of Europe'; but 'what was true of the 1950s and 1960s, was no longer the case from the beginning of the 1980s' (Denéchère 2016). In fact, integration as a purely male project, was not true of the 1950s and 1960s. Rather, one could argue that the contributions of women have been 'written out' of out the history of integration. For example, Marga Klompé, largely forgotten by EU texts was the first woman to join the 78 male members of the ECSC Assembly constituted in 1952. She was appointed rapporteur for the Assembly's opinion on the Messina Declaration, which laid down the foundations for the Treaties of Rome. The inequalities and difficulties with the lack of women's voices did not go unnoticed, even in the 1950s. Madame Ledru, a Belgian expert participating in the elaboration of a European social policy, observed

> that in fact it is rather astonishing that, for a problem which is of such big interest for women, I am here the only woman present. And I am not sure whether this is always a good thing, because I believe that it would be useful that in discussions on equal pay women should be represented with a much more comfortable majority.
>
> *(cited in: Commission 1959, V/4847/59, 203)*

Ledru's role, and the roles of Klompé and other women have been downplayed or rendered invisible in most accounts, contributing to the 'dominant masculinity' of the contemporary EU. We should not overlook these contributions again. Indeed, for the more contemporary period, some women are frequently mentioned as 'shapers' of European integration: for the 1980s this is especially true of British Prime Minister Margaret Thatcher, who is often strongly criticized for her harsh anti-deepening stance; since 2005, German Chancellor Angela Merkel is widely seen as shaping Europe's future (Mushaben 2017, 161–213). Merkel has been depicted as both demon and saviour of Europe *Madame Non* and *Frau Europa* (Madam Europe) in the Euro crisis. However, these women are seen as central to the EU's trajectory largely by virtue of their role as national politicians acting on the EU stage. Very few women are recognized for their roles as European actors.

One telling, although hopefully not representative example, is Desmond Dinan's (2006) account of the origins and evolution of European integration. In the index to this standard textbook the names of 165 men – politicians as well as academic scholars – are mentioned, but only four (!) women: besides Thatcher and Merkel he lists only Miriam Camps, an economist who was involved in the development of the Marshall Plan, and Mariann Fischer-Boel, Commissioner for Agriculture and Rural Development (2004–2009). This grossly imbalanced example illustrates a case of what Jenson (2008) has called 'writing out' women and their contributions – in this case not only out of European history and politics, but also out of academic EU studies. Anna van der Vleuten (2007), in contrast, lists 20 women and 32 men in the index of her feminist account of the history of gender equality in the EU. Quite a different story. There are at least two dangers involved in the masculine representation of history. Not only does it present an inaccurate picture of the process of integration, it does so without critiquing, or even recognizing the ways in which this imbalance continues to shape a masculine bias into the study of European integration.

There are other versions of this narrative, although they are certainly less prevalent. The European history expert Maria Pia Di Nonno has worked on the prehistory and early days of

European integration. In contrast to Dinan's *his*torical account, she has identified at least nine women who deserve the honorary title 'founding mothers'. Di Nonno's list (2019) includes, for example, the French journalist, peace and women's rights activist Louise Weiss (1893–1983), who – using a male (!) pseudonym – founded a newspaper *L'Europe nouvelle* in the inter-war period (see also Denéchère 2016; EPRS_BRI(2019)642289_EN). The newspaper chronicled the political, economic and social life in Europe, and worked towards creating a peaceful and unified Europe, including support for the League of Nations, Franco-German reconciliation, and continental disarmament. Weiss later became a member of the European Parliament (MEP). As the oldest MEP, she gave the inaugural speech of the first-ever directly elected Parliament – and then handed over to the European Parliament's first-ever female president: Simone Veil (see below). Weiss' contribution – as well as Veil's – is acknowledged by the European Parliament which named buildings after these two 'founding mothers'. The European Parliament building in Strasbourg is called the Louise Weiss Building, and the public space in Brussels between the Spinelli Building and the Parlamentarium (i.e. the European Parliament's visitor centre & exhibition), is called the 'Simone Veil Agora'. Denéchère (2016) even concludes: it seems that the 'European Parliament is an institution that has been much more favourable to the engagement of women in the European project' (Denéchère 2016). In contrast to this prominent recognition, in mainstream academic textbooks Weiss is never, and Veil hardly ever mentioned. Indeed, they share this fate of academic and public negligence with numerous other women who have shaped Europe's fate.

These short analyses demonstrate that if we apply a gendered lens to explore the 'her-story' of European integration, we will 'discover' women coming from different walks of life, who have contributed in a variety of different ways, to the making of Europe. We would furthermore illuminate different events, power relations and individuals, and highlight alternate patterns and trajectories of European integration than mainstream accounts tend to acknowledge. As such, a gendered reading can provide a rather different account of the progress in and promoters of the European project. It goes without saying that in this short introduction, we cannot provide this kind of comprehensive gendered re-inspection of the evolution of what is today known as the European Union. This would require – and deserves – in-depth *her*storical studies. But what we can do, is at least draw attention to the existing imbalances and biases and illuminate the importance and urgency of a gendered approach.

For this endeavour, this chapter begins with a discussion of the mainstream understanding of integration, which tends to see the evolution of the European project in the 20th century as a progression of 'fits and starts' along a generally linear path forward, yet always prone to crisis or setback. The general interpretation tends towards an understanding that integration has deepened as a result of crises – and continues to do so in the light of the ongoing 'polycrisis' to which the Covid-19 pandemic and its radical effects further contribute. The second section briefly considers some feminist recounts of European integration. This demonstrates that a different lens can shift our understanding of the EU's progression. When retelling the EU history through a gendered lens, we need to contextualize key events in European integration within the broader social context of a growing and changing women's movement and both individual and collective action. This shows how reconceptualizing the historical narrative can change the overall story. The final part of this chapter gives an overview of how this Handbook is organized. It explains what gendering the EU and EU politics means and entails and which key and cross-cutting questions and perspectives have guided this Handbook. The Handbook adopts an approach, common in gender studies and which represents the move from women's studies to gender studies. This involves not only looking for women and adding them in, but gendering 'the story' of constructing Europe. By this, we mean to investigate, with a gender lens, the ways

Some remarks on mainstream history

By and large, mainstream accounts perpetuate and deepen the masculine hegemonic narrative and offer an incomplete history of the continent and its re-ordering post-1945. Clearly, we cannot recount the full history of European integration over the past 70 years here. Yet, a key finding is that from the very beginning, the process has been strongly affected by crisis. Some would even argue that crisis is constitutive and works as a motor of integration. In this sense, Europe is the crisis (see Fossum and Menéndez 2014) – a crisis that has been accelerating in the last decade, leading to what is today often called a 'poly-crisis', i.e. multiple crises, existing in a parallel and often overlapping manner and shaking up the European project.

The predecessors of what is known today as the European Union, were established in the 1950s and developed directly out of the experiences of World War II. At the time of this writing (summer 2020) the famous Schuman plan, outlining a proposal to create a body with collective authority over aspects of the European economy, celebrates its 70th anniversary. From this plan, proposed on May 9, 1950, the European Coal and Steel Community (ECSC) emerged. The Treaty of Paris, signed in 1951 and enacted in 1952, brought together the six founding member states of France, Germany, Italy and the three Benelux countries (Belgium, the Netherlands and Luxembourg) in a joint economic framework. Following a failed attempt to establish a European Defence Community in 1954, the states took the steps to realize further integration through the European Economic Community (EEC) and the European Atomic Energy Community (EAEC, or frequently, Euratom) in 1957. We have all seen the famous picture of the signing of those two treaties in Rome on March 25, 1957: dozens of black suits worn by (old) white men. What is wrong with this picture? There is not even a single woman. This missing representation of women is emblematic. Even the 'family pictures' of contemporary European summits that bring together the heads of states and governments of the current 27 member states are male-dominated. Yet, this is not the full story, and writing women back in, as we will illustrate below, adds important insights.

Two key concepts that characterize the process of integration since the 1950s are deepening and widening. The first, *deepening*, refers to increasing transfer of competences from national to supranational level, the construction of stronger common institutions, and an 'ever closer Union' – as the Treaty puts it – with remarkable effects on European societies. This incremental transfer of powers and deepening of integration has progressed from economic integration to increasingly social and political forms of integration. The EU became a 'success story' in driving integration forward to previously unknown territory, involving an expanding body of economic, social and environmental regulation, and even the introduction of a common currency several decades later. The second concept, *widening*, refers to an ever-growing Union in terms of membership. Over the course of 70 years, the Union has grown from the initial six founding member states, through successive waves of enlargement to 28 member states. Most recently, due to Brexit (UK withdrawal from the EU), membership has dropped back to 27 as of 2020. In terms of both widening and deepening, 1992 is often held up as a pivotal moment, with the signing of the Maastricht Treaty representing a 'relaunching' of the European project. The Treaty involved the creation of the Common (Internal) Market, the establishment of the Economic and Monetary Union (EMU) with a common currency – the Euro –, and a move towards increased political union with new policy pillars such as Common Foreign and Security Policy and cooperation in Justice and Home Affairs. 1992 marks an important point as states opted to move forward with a concurrent process of deepening integration through the Maastricht 'relaunch' and simultaneously preparing to widen the Union and welcome the post-Communist states to the EU in what was sometimes celebrated as a 'family reunion'.

Neither deepening nor widening have been straightforward processes and they are, in fact, closely interlinked. The process of gradual, yet not linear growth and intensity has been both the product and the source of crisis and contestation. The ambiguity around the ultimate goals and aims of integration, the so-called *finalité politique,* has led to intense debate among both politicians and academics. The nature of the Union itself has changed tremendously through both widening and deepening, with growing heterogeneity and disparities among the member states leaving a mark on politics, law, economics, and even on societies. Gender relations and national gender regimes (see von Wahl in this volume) have not remained untouched by these developments. From a gender perspective, as we will illustrate later, the linearity and continuity of integration as a success story is somewhat more ambivalent.

Actually, these historical accounts are fraught with problems. First, the image of and focus on the 'founding fathers' can be called a 'myth' (Milosevic 2018). They are represented as a 'group of wise leaders [who] had a vision and came up with a plan on how to rise Europe from the ashes of the Second World War', while 'women were not in the spotlight, nor in the narrative about Europe's re-birth' (Milosevic 2018). While certainly a number of politicians were critical for the 'uniting of Europe' (Haas 1958) – those often referred to as 'founding fathers' – social groups and support structures also played an important role in 'getting the job done'. Second, much of the historiography of European integration is, first and foremost, a story of 'big', history-making events and 'high politics', often focussing on treaty ratifications. This tendency to focus on big events – inter-state bargains achieved in night-long, hard negotiations among national leaders – results in a skewed vision of the process as one dominated by men. When we place treaty reforms, and the heads of state and government as well as national diplomats that negotiate these, at the centre of our vision, we prioritize male agency, often at the expense of other actors. Important players in the background, frequently women, are rendered invisible in this account of treaty reform. Certainly, for much of the European Union's history, men have been the de facto leaders, as most of the state leaders have been male. But they are not the only important actors. It is only in recent years that we see more women in executive leadership in the member states – as heads of states and governments and as members of national governments – and in EU institutions. Only recently do we see more women heading key EU institutions such as the Commission, the European Central Bank and the External Action Service. This development certainly requires empirical research (Müller and Tömmel 2021) and conceptualization in terms of what this means for theorizing integration itself (Abels and MacRae 2021b).

But treaty changes and big events do not only change the politico-legal structure of an international or supranational community. These revisions can frequently alter institutions and relationships which affect people's day-to-day lives. This raises a third difficulty with mainstream historical accounts. The policy focus of big events is extremely limited. 'High politics' is often linked to economics, budgetary and monetary policies, defence, or sovereignty-related issues. Current EU ambitions of a 'geopolitical Commission', involves a Union that needs to learn the language of power. This is evident, for example in Commission President Ursula von der Leyen's first State of the Union Address (SOTEU) in which she calls for 'A Union of vitality in a world of fragility' and for increased European sovereignty in order to move in this direction.

This focus on how integration is affected by its linkage to 'core state powers' (Genschel and Jachtenfuchs 2018) marginalizes so-called 'low politics'. Stanley Hoffmann, in the introduction of his intergovernmentalist interpretation of European integration in 1966, drew this distinction between high and low politics, and assumed that integration (i.e. supranationalization) is easier to achieve in low politics than in high. Yet, what is considered high and low politics is far from self-evident. The distinction is open to discussion, especially in times of increasing politicization of EU policies in member states and EU institutions. Indeed, low politics issues, for instance cooperation in health policy and cross-border threats to health (Article 168 TFEU), can become exceptionally salient, as we see in the Covid-19 pandemic that is currently shaking up the Union. These so-called 'low politics' may be directly linked to 'high politics' as in the connection between the Covid-19 crisis and the closing of borders by various member states. Furthermore, a focus on high politics and treaty negotiations ignores that big events can happen in other policy areas and which may affect the life of citizens. For instance, stronger integration among a set of now 16 EU member states in harmonizing jurisdiction over family and divorce law as it pertains to certain bi-national couples (Council Regulation (EC) No 2201/2003) can clearly have repercussions for gender relations. Some national laws are more favourable to one spouse than to the other one in terms of consequential matters of divorce and child custody and shifts in these laws can result in fundamental changes to women's economic status and their rights regarding custody. Additionally, EU accession to the Council of Europe's so-called Istanbul Convention on violence against women is currently strongly contested (see Roggeband in this volume). While one is inclined to assume that all member states should protect women from domestic violence, for some member states, such as Bulgaria or Hungary, this Convention has become an issue of state sovereignty and Europe's undue interference in 'domestic' (in a dual sense) politics (see Krizsán and Roggeband 2018). Thus, what could be 'low politics', can become very politicized 'high politics' – with tremendous effects on the 'life expectancy' of women.

The key point is that the focus on big events, leadership and high politics all contribute to 'writing out' women – and gender relations – of the history of European integration. This leads to the question, that Milosevic (2018) poses: 'Does Europe prefer her sons over daughters?' Moreover, even if we take a big event perspective, we need to be aware of the contributions made by women to these events. For instance, the famous 'Manifesto of Ventotene' (1941) by Altiero Spinelli, Ernesto Rossi und Eugenio Colorni for 'a free and united Europe' is certainly considered to be an important vision for a post-World War II order. But how many people know that this manifesto was spread by female 'letter carriers'? It was Ada Rossi (1899–1993), Rossi's wife and a professor of mathematics, and Ursula Hirschmann (1913–1991), organizer of the first meeting of the European Federalist Movement (1943), who smuggled the manifesto to the mainland and subsequently spread it through the Italian Resistance (Di Nonno 2019, 242). Later on, in 1975, Hirschmann 'planned the inaugural meeting of the group *Women for Europe*, believing that the European project needed a wider participation of women to achieve a true democracy in Europe' (Di Nonno 2019, 243, 255f.). In the 1880s it was Bertha von Suttner, the peace and women's rights activist, who already demanded European integration.

Some might argue that these are details that do not alter the overall story of integration. They may ask, what difference it will make to adopt a 'her-story' standpoint? We are aware that it is problematic to present a his-tory/her-story dichotomy, as this may give the impression that we view women and men as two unique and homogenous social groups where lived experiences are determined by one's identity as either male or female, fully disregarding other identity forms. Here, we use her-story mainly as a marker, a provocation to point out the historical and academic marginalization of gendered experiences in the making of Europe. It seems that the 'founding mothers' were often aware of their gender-based discrimination. Thus, it is maybe no coincidence that they were not only dedicated Europeans but also courageous women's rights activists who wanted a better future for women in a better – i.e. democratic and peaceful – Europe. Many other women have followed their path of shaping the present and future of European integration.

European integration as 'her-story' – some missing bits and pieces

Women have undoubtedly shaped the history of European integration. But they are hardly part of the official historiography. Ana Milosevic concludes, 'What place [do the] EU's Founding Mothers have in European memory? How are these women memorialised? Little and poorly.' Many women have been actively campaigning for (and also against) integration since before its inception. They have been present within the halls of the institutions, as well as in civil society. This section aims to present bits and pieces of what could be called a 'her-story', highlighting the ways in which individual women, and feminist collective action has shaped the integration project. We have to admit that these individual and collective stories have largely been overlooked by EU gender scholars as well. As such, there is still a need for in-depth research and memorialization. Let us start with the (overlooked) 'founding mothers'. Maria Di Nonno forcefully argues:

> While it cannot be denied that European Institutions were born particularly thanks to the good deeds of the Founding Fathers, it is equally true that it would not be fair to downplay the role of women. *The Founding Mothers of Europe were convinced that a real European democracy would have been reached only through a greater involvement and empowerment of all individuals. The economic union was not enough*, it was necessary to act on more fronts – social, cultural and political – in order to bring a change in mentality. Europe was not orphaned by its 'mothers'.
>
> *(Di Nonno 2019, 241, emphasis added)*

The integration story told with a gender lens typically begins with the equal pay Article 119 in the EEC Treaty of 1958 (today Article 157 TFEU) and what has evolved out of this provision since the 1970s, including a rich body of EU gender equality law (see, for many, Jacquot 2015; Kantola 2010; Kantola and Lombardo 2017; Prügl 2006; Rees 1998; see contributions in the policy part of this volume). This article actually represents the birth of social policy in the EU (see Ostner and Lewis 1995). Moreover, it effectively creates a relationship between EU law, the individual and European institutions. In her landmark study, Catherine Hoskyns (1996) retold European integration with a focus on how the political, social and economic sphere are interlinked and how the gender regime developed. Hoskyns draws attention to some individual women who shaped the narrative around equality between women and men. She analyses the struggle over Article 119 EEC and its realization, involving women's strikes, legal court cases and ambitious activists, and above all highlighting the role of Éliane Vogel-Polsky (1926–2015). Without doubt, Vogel-Polsky, a Belgium lawyer and feminist, is a 'founding mother' who has shaped European integration since the 1970s. She was a 'woman of conviction' (Gubin 2008), a dedicated fighter for gender equality in Europe, initiating the ground-breaking '*Defrenne* cases' (see Guth and Elfving in this volume). These cases have illustrated the tremendous amount of sex discrimination still accepted (as natural) in the late 1960s/early 1970s and the negligence of the Commission and member states to implement Article 119 of the EEC Treaty. More than ten years after Hoskyns' groundbreaking book, Anna van der Vleuten's 2007 book breaks down the history of integration from 1955 to 2005 based on four phases of social policy. She traces the roots of gender equality in the EU by analysing why and how the equal pay Article 119 was included in the EEC Treaty's social chapter as early as 1957 – agreed on by an all-male group of diplomats. The key rationale was competition (between member states), not equality (between the sexes)! Van der Vleuten illustrates how the progress in gender equality is influenced by (trans) national mobilization of women's organizations, the perceived economic and ideological costs of equality and unintended consequences of early decisions, which were, actually, driven by the competition norm and not by the gender equality norm. This link of equality to the economic rationale, which is still believed to be at the heart of European integration, has been a mover and shaker of gender equality policies since the 1970s, but it has also imposed strong restrictions on the development of such policies.

Many accounts of the development of gender equality in the EU point to the strong impact of 'critical acts' (Mushaben 1998) as well as 'critical actors' (Childs and Krook 2009) behind them. Vogel-Polsky was certainly a 'critical actor' who was aware of the need for 'critical acts'. Another critical actor was Simone Veil (1927–2017). French lawyer and liberal politician, Holocaust survivor and women's rights advocate Veil became the first female president of the European Parliament in 1979. To elect her as first president following the introduction of direct elections to the European Parliament can be interpreted as a very powerful

> symbol of Franco-German reunification and the best way of turning the page on the world wars forever [...] For a former deportee to become the first President of the new European Parliament seemed to him [the French President Valery Giscard d'Estaing who supported her nomination] to augur well for the future.
>
> *(Veil, quoted in Di Nonno 2019, 245).*

Against the background of the UN 'decade of women', which started in 1976, and with a – in those days – ground-breaking high number of women representatives (16.3% female MEPs), Veil strongly bolstered the move to establish an Ad Hoc Committee on Women's Rights in the Parliament which would be entrusted with a mission to analyse the situation of women in the European Community by means of an own-initiative report. The resulting Maij-Weggen Report 'presented an exhaustive list of points concerning the specific problems and discrimination experienced by women, which were exacerbated by the economic crisis at the time' (www.europarl.europa.eu/workingpapers/femm/105/text_en.htm). The follow-up resolution 'set the parliamentary agenda for years to come', covering issues that remain on the EU's gender equality agenda today (van der Vleuten 2019, 40–41). These events were the keystone of the reputation of the European Parliament 'as a constant promoter for gender equality' (van der Vleuten 2019), which remains today. For her achievements, in 1981, Simone Veil became the first women ever to win the Charles V Prize (2008) awarded by the Fundacion Academia Europea De Yuste and the Charlemagne Prize (1981) awarded by the German city of Aachen. This award is one of the oldest and best-known prizes recognizing contributions to the European integration project. In fact, Veil is one out of only five women of the 62 laureates to ever win this prestigious prize (the other four are, in chronological order: the Norwegian Prime Minister Gro Harlem Brundtland, the Dutch Queen Beatrix, the German Chancellor Angela Merkel and the Lithuanian President Dalia Grybauskaitė).

Other women worked more 'behind the scenes' including, for instance Fausta Deshormes La Valle (1927–2013). She started to work in the Commission in the early 1960s and worked for the EEC information service (later DG Information). Gender equality initiatives had been undertaken in the Commission since the mid-1970s and in response to the court's decisions in the *Defrenne* cases (see Guth and Elfving in this volume). At this time, Deshormes La Valle was managing the Women's Information Service and in 1977 she 'launched the review Women of Europe' in 1977, which 'was an informative sheet, translated in all the languages of the Member States, with the aim to better inform, and consequently to mobilize women' (Di Nonno 2019, 243, 256). Another woman behind the scenes was Jacqueline Nonon, a Commission official who played a key role in the 1960s/1970s in the elaboration of a European gender equality policy by creating a transnational feminist network involving experts such as sociologist Evelyne Sullerot and women activists and trade unionists. In the earliest days of integration, women were relegated to 'office' positions, rendering them all but invisible in academic accounts. Ursula Wenmakers acted as the translator between French-speaking Jean Monnet (then President of the High Authority which later became the Commission) and his German-speaking Vice President, Franz Etzel. According to one account, each man spoke only his native language. 'She was thus the indispensable link between the two most important figures in the High Authority' (Carbonell 2020). Working in the shadows, these women are largely forgotten, or are at best, made anonymous as they are simply referred to as 'an interpreter' in accounts and photo captions. They 'were certainly not at the controls, but they nevertheless took part in the proper functioning of the burgeoning administration' (Carbonell 2020).

A woman was also the inventor of the Erasmus Programme in 1987, widely considered to be one of the success stories of European integration. Sofia Corradi (born 1934), was an Italian professor of pedagogy. While a student, she was awarded a scholarship to study abroad, only to find that her credentials, earned abroad, were not recognized by her home university. She turned this setback into a project, eventually developing the Erasmus programme for university students. For this accomplishment she is called 'Mamma Erasmus' (Di Nonno 2019, 250) and received the Spanish Charles V European Award in 2016.

The first ever female Commissioner, Vasso Papandreou in 1989 saw it as her vocation to convert the Charter for Fundamental Rights into proposals for binding social legislation. It resulted in 47 proposals, which almost all remained blocked in the Council of Ministers by British vetoes. More recently women like Lady Catherine Ashton and Federica Mogherini have shaped the face of the EU's external relations as the first High Representatives of the Union for Foreign Affairs and Security Policy, who had to cope with the challenge of building a new EU body, the European External Action Service (see Chappell in this volume). Importantly, at present and for the first time, the powerful European Commission is headed by a woman, Ursula von der Leyen (see also Hartlapp et al. in this volume). It is too soon to recognize what their impact on the European project will be, or how female leadership styles may shape their respective institutions and roles (see Abels and MacRae 2021b). Other women have worked for Europe from national capitals. For example, Élisabeth Guigou, played a key role in France during François Mitterrand's two terms as president in the 1980s/1990s. Her work was decisive in deciding how to deal with a reunited Germany as part of the process leading to the ground-breaking 1992 Maastricht Treaty (Loth 2015, 310). Clearly, there is much to be researched and brought to the fore in order to bring these and other women into the collective history and recognize their contributions in the European memory.

Despite the clear merits achieved by these women, gender studies must be careful not to step into the trap of simply creating new myths by reproducing the idea that history is made by exceptional individuals – by replacing the 'his-torical hero' with a 'her-storical heroine'. For this reason, we must be cautious when speaking of 'founding mothers'. Nonetheless, the women, those at centre stage and those in the background; those in national capitals and those in Brussels, have made a tremendous contribution to European integration and this needs to be acknowledged. Thus, 'adding the gender perspective to European memory' (Milosevic 2018) is important. These women were not only influential social and political actors in their own right, but acted against a backdrop of strong sex-based discrimination, some of which still lingers today. Alongside academic recognition, there is also a need for public recognition, through for example, the 'Women of Europe Awards'.[1] In 2019 this prize was awarded to Laura Codruța Kövesi, who followed up a career fighting national corruption in her home Romania, to become, in October 2019, the EU's first Chief Public Prosecutor. Taken together, layers of public and academic recognition can begin to entrench a gender-aware narrative to co-exist alongside the mainstream narratives of European history.

Drawing attention to the individual achievements of these women cannot provide us with a detailed history of the integration process. But what these snapshots can do is encourage scholars to broaden their gaze beyond the commonly told stories, to include different, marginalized voices and experiences and show how women were excluded from decision-making processes that strongly have influenced their lives. These stories can also help us to identify research gaps that remain in the mainstream scholarship in EU studies. As memories play an important role in shaping both present and future, individual and collective identities, it is essential to ensure that they are as complete and inclusive as possible.

A focal point for research and for discussing how far we have come could be the starting debate of the 'Conference on the Future of Europe' (CoFoE; for details see EPRS_ATA(2020)651959_EN). This initiative spearheaded by the von der Leyen Commission and the European Parliament, aims to connect European citizens and EU stakeholders in order to increase public involvement and empower individuals in the evolution and potential reforms in the European project. The conference was scheduled to begin in May 2020, and was anticipated to last for two years. Due to the pandemic as well as continued negotiations among the three EU institutions about the mandate and composition of CoFoE, its official start was delayed until most likely, autumn 2020. It is one of the top political priorities on the political guidelines of Commission President von der Leyen. In her words, this conference will give 'a new push for European democracy' (von der Leyen 2019, 19). CoFoE is indeed not the first attempt of this kind. Previous conferences such as the 'Convention on the Future of Europe' in 2002 also aimed at a more inclusive approach to developing an EU Constitution. This convention involved not only national governments as previous Intergovernmental Conferences (IGC) had, but also included a wider set of EU institutions plus parliaments from the member states. What makes the CoFoE potentially different is that will attempt to go a step further in terms of the participation of civil society members. Ideally, it 'should bring together citizens, including a significant role for young people, civil society and European institutions as equal partners' (von der Leyen 2019, 19). What about women? Gender equality is certainly another top priority of von der Leyen political agenda; yet, how much she can fulfil – given strong structural limitations – remains to be seen (Abels and Mushaben 2020). Gender equality in the CoFoE would, first of all, mean parity among the various groups of representatives and participants and, secondly, would involve putting gender equality officially on the agenda as a key challenge for the future of Europe. Yet, the first signs are ambivalent. The good news is that equality between women and men is listed among the 'societal challenges' to be addressed by CoFoE and the EU institutions, which 'should participate on an equal footing' should also ensure gender equality in their delegations. After intense discussion this is now part of the Council position 9102/20 on CoFoE as of June 2020. However, there is no sign of gender mainstreaming of the mandate nor any enforcement mechanisms to ensure gender balanced delegations.

In practice, gender equality could be achieved in relation to the 200–300 citizens who are likely to participate in the various thematic fora ('Agoras'), as selection procedures would allow for gender as a criterion. For the EU institutions themselves, equality of representation does not seem to be much of an issue – despite rhetorical commitments. For the Commission, CoFoE falls within the mandate of one of the female Commissioners, Vice-President for Democracy and Demography, Dubravka Šuica. For the Council of the EU, securing gender equality is a problem given women's strong under-representation in the Council system (see Abels in this volume). But even for the European Parliament, the equality trailblazer among the EU institutions, the signs are not very positive. While there is no list of nominees on the table and not even a final number of how many MEP can participate, the working group set up by the Conference of Presidents of the European Parliament in October 2019 with the mission to prepare the Parliament's work on CoFoE, has only one female member of eight members of this working group (EPRS_BRI(2019)644202_EN). As mentioned, in some respect this conference is seen in comparison to, and as a further development of the 2002 Convention. The Convention had a total of 105 participants – of which only 18 (17%) were women (Lombardo 2005, 422). It is not only key to consider the substantive representation of individuals, but also the ways in which the issues are presented. In the case of the 2002 Convention, gender equality was not addressed in a satisfactory manner, and remained far from what Lombardo would identify as a necessary 'agenda setting' approach (Lombardo 2005; 2007). As scholars (and as feminist activists) we need to analyse and learn from this earlier experience to make an impact on the future of European integration in general and the CoFoE in particular.

Structure and idea of this Handbook

While writing the gendered history/herstory of European integration is an important and ongoing project, we must also continue to apply a gendered lens to the European polity, politics and policies. This Handbook aims to offer an overview of some of the key areas of research, and to initiate a discussion of the state of the field of gender EU studies, and in particular, future research perspective. The Handbook is organized to reflect how gender studies have engaged with European integration since the 1990s and how this field of research has evolved. Today there is a rich body of cross-disciplinary academic research by gender scholars on the EU. The collection in this Handbook reflects the state of the field, with a broad focus on political science and the links to sociology, economics and legal studies. As other handbooks in the field, the general structure follows the three dimensions of polity, politics and policy. Thus, at first glance, the Handbook may appear to be traditional in its organization. However, the perspectives adopted in the different sections and the more than 30 chapters illustrate that gender analysis builds on and, moreover, transcends mainstream approaches by, first, including issues and voices marginalized in the mainstream and, second, by illustrating what is left out and what needs to be included. The editors asked all contributors to illustrate what a gender perspective contributes to the subject of study, and what future research gaps remain. We asked all contributors to put emphasis, first, on the dimension of enlargement in terms of what the effects on gender issues have been and, second, to adopt a gender+ perspective, meaning to include a gender mainstreaming and an intersectional perspective. This implies going beyond the 'add women and stir' approach, to investigate the EU through the lens of gender relations. Furthermore, it means going beyond a focus on women and men only, to include other social categories like race, class, sexual identity etc. A number of contributions show, for instance, how policies are not only gendered, but also racialized. Finally, where appropriate, we asked the contributors to include recent developments related to the change in the EU Commission, the new Gender Equality Strategy (as of March 2020), Brexit, and the Covid-19 pandemic.

The Handbook starts with a theoretical section. The last decade has seen an increasingly intense discussion of how to theorize European integration through a gendered lens and what gender perspective can contribute to the mainstream and/or critical discussion (e.g. Abels and MacRae 2016, 2021a; Kronsell 2012). It becomes obvious that gender perspective can be more easily injected in some integration theories, while other are more 'stubborn'. Some (meta) theories and approaches have shown themselves to be more helpful than others, and these have become widespread in EU gender studies, and accordingly in this Handbook. Europeanization, social constructivism and feminist institutionalism are three of the approaches that dominate the

EU gender studies landscape. Given the dramatic effects of the economic crisis, we also elected to include a chapter on Feminist Political Economy, a more recent approach. A few other theoretical issues are also paramount for EU gender studies and, hence, included in this section. The gender regime approach is key to feminist analysis of European welfare states and discussions on the development of the EU itself. Intersectionality, as outlined above, is a cross-cutting issue that is included in many contributions to this Handbook. Hence, a chapter in the theory section is devoted to introducing the concept and its development in EU law. Finally, even as gender studies shifts its primary object of focus from women to gender relations, a good deal of the research still focuses on the role of women in the EU, and how the EU affects women and femininity. Clearly, the EU also affects men and masculinity. In terms of gender relations this is something that needs further exploration in the future, as the contribution in this Handbook illustrates.

In terms of the historical development in academia, policy studies on the EU came first. One of the first areas of inquiry for gender scholars has been to investigate the effects of EU policies, especially in relation to social and employment policy, on gender relations. This initial focus is rooted in Article 119 of the EEC Treaty as the source of gender equality policy-making in the European Communities (the European Union as of 1993). Ever since the first accounts, the focus has expanded to a number of other policy fields. In the light of gender mainstreaming, all policy areas ought to be gender-aware. There remain a number of contemporary policy fields that still require investigation through a gender lens. Several of the chapters in the Handbook offer some of the first evidence on how these policies are gendered and how they continue to reproduce gendered structures. The policy section investigates nine different policy fields and their development through a gendered lens.

More recently, gender scholars began to scrutinize the role of EU institutions, especially the European Parliament, the Commission and the Court of Justice, on gender issues. Today, it is obvious that the whole range of institutions in the EU polity requires a gender analysis. Thus, the contributions in this Handbook also cover institutions that have, until recently, not been the subject of many studies with a gender lens. This includes, for example, the Council, the EEAS and the numerous EU agencies established since the mid-1970s.

As for the politics dimension, some issues, such as citizenship and enlargement, were quickly incorporated into the research agenda of gender scholars. Recently, and particularly in the light of rising right-winged populism, which goes along with anti-gender and anti-feminist politics, issues such as party politics in the EU and civil society have been addressed with a gender lens. This Handbook addresses these issues, as well as some, such as gender differences in political knowledge, which have been largely overlooked, but which are important to the overall story.

The fifth and final section addresses some key issues and debates that have an impact on gender relations in the EU. The rise of right-wing populist parties and movements in many EU member states, which increasingly affects not only national, but also EU institutions, is one such key issue. Also, the economic crisis and the austerity-driven policy response has affected gender relations in a number of member states, especially in Europe's South and East. This topic has been analysed in recent work that takes on a new importance in light of the unprecedented economic hardship likely to result from the Covid-19 pandemic. The gender effects of Covid-19, the recovery efforts and the remarkable new instrument 'NextGenerationEU' are becoming increasingly apparent (see Klatzer and Rinaldi 2020). Also, national recovery programmes require a gender inspection. Furthermore, at the time of this writing (August 2020), Brexit is not yet fully complete. Formally, the UK has left the Union after almost 50 years of membership, but many details remain unresolved. Brexit will leave a gendered mark on women and gender relations not only in the UK, but also in the Union, even though the UK was often a reluctant participant in the development of gender equality measures. This relationship is analysed in the chapter included in this volume.

It is our aim with this Handbook to offer an overview of the field of Gender and EU Studies, to emphasize the ways in which gender studies has influenced the field of European Integration studies, and continues to do so. Although we could not include all the salient issues and concepts, this Handbook draws attention to trends and patterns and encourages scholars to continue to use a gender lens on the process and institutions of the European Union.

Note

1 This prize was awarded between 1987 to 2003 and then again since 2016 in four different categories – including 'Women in power' for "extraordinary political leadership in Europe" (https://europeanmovement.eu/women-of-europe/). Interestingly, unlike the prestigious and prominent Charlemagne Prize of the City of Aachen, the 'Women of Europe' award is a civic society initiative jointly initiated by the European Movement International and the European Women's Lobby.

A final note on official sources. To avoid an inflation of references with numerous documents, such official sources by the EU institutions and other international organizations are only quoted with their official reference number, e.g. COM(2020) 150 final or Regulation (EC) No 1922/2006. Thus, readers can easily find them.

References

Abels G, MacRae H, eds. (2016): *Gendering European Integration Theory. Engaging New Dialogues*, Opladen: Barbara Budrich.

Abels G, MacRae H (2021a): Gender Approaches, in: Bigo D, Diez T, Fanoulis E, Rosamond B, Stivachtis YA (eds.): *Routledge Handbook of Critical European Studies*, Abingdon, New York: Routledge, 112–124.

Abels G, MacRae H (2021b): Searching for Agency: Gendering Leadership in European Integration Theory, in: Müller H, Tömmel I (eds.): *Pathways to Power. Female Leadership and Women Empowerment in the European Union*, Oxford: Oxford University Press (forthcoming).

Abels G, Mushaben JM (2020): Great expectations – strong limitations. Ursula von der Leyen and the Commission's New Equality Agenda, *Journal of Common Market Studies,* Annual Review, 1–12, doi: 10.1111/jcms.13102.

Childs S, Krook ML (2009): Analysing women's substantive representation. From critical mass to critical actors, *Government and Opposition* **44** (2), 125–145.

Carbonell M (2020): The founding fathers of Europe and the ECSC mother, in: *Digital Encyclopedia of European History* (EHNE), URL: https://ehne.fr/en/article/gender-and-europe/gender-citizenship-europe/founding-fathers-europe-and-ecsc-mother (download: August 20, 2020).

Denéchère Y (2016): The Female Actors of European Construction, in: *Encyclopédie pour une histoire nouvelle de l'Europe* [online], published 18/10/2017, URL: http://ehne.fr/en/node/1110 (download: August 1, 2020).

Dinan, D (2006): *Origins and Evolution of the European Union*, 2nd ed., Oxford: Oxford University Press.

Di Nonno MP (2019): The Founding Mothers of Europe. The Role of Simone Veil and Sofia Corradi in Defence of the European Values, in: Baigorri J, Elvert J (eds.): P*az y valores europeos como posible modelo de integración y progreso en un mundo global / Peace and European values as a potential model for integration and progress in a global world*, Brussels: Peter Lang, 239–258.

Fossum JE, Menéndez AJ, eds. (2014): *The European Union in Crises or the European Union as Crises?*, ARENA Report No 2/14, URL: https://www.sv.uio.no/arena/english/research/publications/arena-reports/2014/report-2-14.pdf (download: August 12, 2020).

Genschel P, Jachtenfuchs M (2018): From market integration to core state powers: The Eurozone crisis, the refugee crisis and integration theory, *Journal of Common Market Studies* **56**, 178–196.

Griffiths RT (2014): The Founding Fathers, in: Jones E, Menon A, Weatherill S (eds.): *The Oxford Handbook of the European Union*, Oxford: Oxford University Press, 181–192.

Gubin E (2008): *Éliane Vogel-Polsky: A Woman of Conviction*, Brussels: Institute for the Equality of Women and Men, URL: https://igvm-iefh.belgium.be/sites/default/files/downloads/13%20-%20Vogel-Polsky_EN.pdf (download: May 15, 2020).

Haas EB (1958): *The Uniting of Europe: Political, Social, and Economical Forces, 1950–1957*, Notre Dame, IN: University of Notre Dame Press.

Hoffmann S (1966): Obstinate or obsolete? The fate of the nation-state and the case of Western Europe, *Daedalus* **95**, 862–914.

Hoskyns C (1996): *Integrating Gender. Women, Law and Politics in the European Union*, London, New York: Verso.

Jacquot S. (2015): *Transformations in EU Gender Equality. From Emergence to Dismantling*, Basingstoke: Palgrave Macmillan.

Jenson J (2008): Writing women out, folding gender in: The European Union 'modernises' social policy, *Social Politics* **15** (2), 131–153.

Kantola J (2010): Feminist Approaches, in: Egan M, Nugent N, Paterson W (eds.): *Research Agendas in EU Studies. Stalking the Elephant*, Basingstoke, New York: Palgrave Macmillan, 305–322.

Kantola J, Lombardo E (2017): EU Gender Equality Policies, in: Heinelt H, Münch S (eds.): *Handbook of European Policies: Interpretive Approaches to the EU*, Aldershot: Edward Elgar, 331–352.

Klatzer E, Rinaldi A (2020). *NextGenerationEU leaves women behind. Gender Impact Assessment on the EC proposal for #nextGenerationEU*, Study commissioned by The Greens/EFA Group in the European Parliament, initiated by Alexandra Geese, MEP, Brussels.

Krizsán A, Roggeband C (2018): *The Gender Politics of Domestic Violence. Feminists Engaging the State in Central and Eastern Europe*, New York: Routledge.

Kronsell A (2012): Gendering Theories of European Integration, in Abels G, Mushaben JM (eds.): *Gendering the European Union*, Basingstoke, New York: Palgrave Macmillan, 23–40.

Lombardo E (2005): Integrating of setting the agenda? Gender mainstreaming in the European constitution-making process, *Social Politics: International Studies in Gender, State & Society* **12** (3), 412–432.

Lombardo E (2007): Gender Equality in the Constitution-Making Process, in Castiglione D, Schönlau J, Longman C, Lombardo E, Pérez-Solórzano Borragán N, Aziz M: *Constitutional Politics in the European Union. The Convention Moment and its Aftermath*, Basingstoke: Palgrave Macmillan, 137–152.

Loth, W (2015): *Building Europe. A History of European Unification*, Berlin: De Gruyter Oldenbourg.

Milosevic A (2018): *Does Europe Prefer Her Sons Over Daughters? Adding the Gender Perspective to European Memory*, URL: https://blogs.lse.ac.uk/gender/2018/04/05/does-europe-prefer-her-sons-over-daughters-adding-the-gender-perspective-to-european-memory/ (download: August 13, 2020).

Milward A (2000): *The European Rescue of the Nation-state*, 2nd ed., London: Routledge.

Müller H, Tömmel I, eds. (2021): *Pathways to Power. Female Leadership and Women Empowerment in the European Union*, Oxford: Oxford University Press (forthcoming).

Mushaben JM (1998): The politics of critical acts. Women, leadership and democratic deficits in the European Union, *The European Studies Journal* **15** (2), 51–91.

Mushaben JM (2017): *Becoming Madam Chancellor. Angela Merkel and the Berlin Republic*, Cambridge: Cambridge University Press.

Ostner I, Lewis J (1995): Gender and European Social Policy, in: Leibfried S, Pierson P. (eds.): *European Social Policy. Between Fragmentation and Integration*, Washington DC: Brookings Institution, 159–193.

Prügl E (2006): Gender and European Union Politics, in: Jørgensen KE, Pollack MA, Rosamond B (eds.): *Handbook of European Union Politics*, London: SAGE, 433–447.

Rees TL (1998): *Mainstreaming Equality in the European Union: Education, Training and Labour Market Policies*, London, New York: Routledge.

van der Vleuten A (2007): *The Price of Gender Equality. Member States and Governance in the European Union*, Abingdon: Ashgate.

van der Vleuten A (2019): The European Parliament as a Constant Promoter for Gender Equality. Another European Myth?, in: Ahrens P, Rolandsen Agustín L (eds.): *Gendering the European Parliament. Structures, Policies and Practices*, London, New York: Rowman & Littlefield, ECPR Press, 35–49.

von der Leyen U (2019): *A Union That Strives for More. My Agenda for Europe: Political Guidelines for the next European Commission 2019–2024. By Candidate for President of the European Commission Ursula von der Leyen*, Brussels: European Commission.

Part I

Gendering the EU

Theoretical perspectives

Theorizing the European integration is an ongoing endeavour. It started in the 1950 when the original three European Communites were established in 1951 and 1957. The challenges for theorizing have always been the famous moving target plus n=1 problems. This means that theoretical interpretations, if they aim to be useful in terms of explanatory power and, potentially, also prognostic power, have to adapt to the dynamic developments in European integration. Today we have a rich toolbox of integration theories and approaches. This toolbox has developed over time and in different stages. A general trend is that, first, 'grand theories' – such as intergovernmentalism and neofunctionalism as well as their offspring – no longer dominate the discussion as they did for several decades. Second, more and more critical voices from different angles and with different foci play a role, which do not only pose the question what the EU is and how it has evolved, but what the EU should and could be like. This normative perspective, prevalent in critical EU studies, is more open to gender studies due to its link to feminism as a normative political project.

Despite the dynamic within theory-development, for decades theorizing in the mainstream was blind to gender implications and gender perspectives in European integration, i.e. investigating the role women have played in the process of European integration or the effects of EU policies on national gender relations. It was not until, first, gender research within EU studies begin to flourish and, second, the socialconstructivist turn in EU studies that the question of integrating gender in integration theory came to the forefront and was raised by gender scholars.

While there is certainly not a single gender theory on European integration, various gender perspectives can contribute to theorizing European integration. Of the collection of gender perspectives, we can only assemble a selection in this volume. Thus, this part leaves many gaps, but includes those perspectives that we consider particularly fruitful and innovative for gendering the EU. This selection includes a re-inspection of neoinstitutionalism, of political economy, socialconstructivism and Europeanization with a gender lens.

For gender scholars, theorizing the EU goes beyond integration theories. Theorizing also includes the conceptualization of the EU as a gender regime, the question how intersectionality plays out in this gender equality and anti-discriminiation regime. These issues go beyond sectoral policy analysis, but address the very nature of the EU in a broader sense including the political, economic and the social dimension of European integration. Such gender-sensitive analysis also implies not only to look at women vs men, but at the construction of different – some of the hegemonic – masculinities and femininities in and by the EU.

2

The EU as a gender equality regime

A core research concept

Angelika von Wahl

This chapter demonstrates the foundational richness and broad application of the gender equality regime as a core concept in research on the European Union (EU). Over the last 25 year, the "gender equality regime" has significantly guided the direction of feminist research agendas representing a foundational and vibrant paradigm. It allows for the systematic analysis of the interaction of central policies, actors, institutions, and discourses, designed to mitigate against women's inequality. Thematically, the majority of research focuses on employment, family, and care work in the EU or its member states. Yet, more broadly this research also covers policies and power relations regarding violence, abortion, migration, race, ethnicity, representation, sexuality etc.

The notion of a EU gender equality regime (GER) emphasizes the importance of supranational-level gender policies but also allows for the consideration of regional or national-level diversity. Less a theory than a heuristic framework, it permits analyzing policies, actors, and institutions across time and place. The level of analysis varies among research studying the nature of the supranational regime itself, the extent of multi-level interaction between nations, regions, and the EU, or the historic legacies and politics of individual nation-states. Influenced by the literature on welfare state regimes, authors analyze regional typologies, transnationalism, and different structural or power relationships among the EU, the member states, market, families and the individual from a feminist perspective.

Despite the relevance of regional or national policy-making, it is generally agreed that "[o]f all the transformations affecting European politics and the position of women, none is more important than the transnational impact of increasing European integration" (Woodward 2015, 851). EU policies have grown over nearly seven decades from a few isolated policies only addressing women's equal pay to a complex web of egalitarian norms, rights, and court rulings, supported by institutions and interconnected opportunity structures also described as "regime." This web has significantly expanded and standardized the aspirations and prospects of European women *and* men.

The gender equality regime's robustness can be viewed as an indicator of the public acceptance of the European project itself. I argue that the policies and institutions making up this regime mirror the overall fate and aspirations of the EU – and that this fate has been under serious strain lately. Since 2009, several large crises – the Euro crisis, the challenges of dealing with the influx

Angelika von Wahl

of refugees, the rise of populist and anti-EU parties, Brexit, and Covid-19 – have exacerbated existing structural and cultural problems. These strains and attendant political reactions have led to cost-cutting, backsliding, downgrading, and even dismantling of certain aspects of the existing gender equality architecture. Simultaneously, activists are pushing back against the spread of neo-nationalism, femonationalism, and masculinist politics (see Hearn et al. and Siim and Fiig in this volume).

A short overview of gender equality in the EU

The Treaty of Rome in 1957 included in Article 119 of the EEC Treaty equal pay for men and women (see Milner in this volume). Lying dormant as part of an international treaty focused on the economic integration of six nations, the promise of equal pay only came alive with the rise of the women's movement in the late 1960s and early 1970s. At this point, equality claims turned into a political and feminist project. In the following years, the member states passed numerous progressive policy innovations with broad legal impact, such as equal treatment and positive action directives in employment. During these heydays of EC/EU optimism and vision, approaches to gender equality grew and branched out considerably. Innovative feminist policies promised equal rights, anti-discrimination, anti-harassment, parental leave, gender mainstreaming and the recognition of difference. Importantly, EU equal employment policies expanded coverage from full-time to part-time workers, from pay to pensions and other forms of remuneration, and included working conditions for the self-employed. With the 1992 Maastricht Treaty, gender equality moved to the center of its – overall rather limited – social policy agenda and became a *raison d'être* of the larger EU value system itself.

The *peak of optimism* and support for the EU and its gender equality initiatives can be situated between the Amsterdam Treaty in 1997 and the following decade, when EU membership grew to 28 states. The treaty declared the advancement of equality between women and men a fundamental EU task and forbid discrimination on the grounds of gender, sex, race, ethnicity, disability, age etc. This is a high point of institutional deepening and diffusion for the EU gender regime. At the same time, member states became ever more economically, politically and culturally diverse and a common denominator of agreed upon woman-friendly and feminist values and goals, if it ever existed, began to fray. Feminism itself also changed and expanded its focus from straightforward equality-oriented policies towards difference feminism and from women to gender. Attention to sexuality and increasingly complex intersectional identities and interests were added (Woodward 2012).

Each wave of new member states brought new equality approaches, but also challenges (see Chiva in this volume): in the 1970s, the United Kingdom, Ireland and Denmark joined; in the 1980s, additional Mediterranean countries; in the early 1990s, the EC expanded north to Scandinavia and east to Austria; and, 15 years after the fall of Communism, the EU accepted countries from central and eastern Europe (henceforth CEE). Each of these accession states brought with them certain regional or national gender arrangements or gender regimes (see EIGE gender equality index: https://eige.europa.eu/gender-equality-index/2019). For example, southern European women in overwhelmingly Catholic, conservative and weakly industrialized states showed low levels of employment and had much to gain from the EU equality directives. On the other hand, women in Sweden, a well-known feminist forerunner, could expect much less from membership. Indeed, Sweden contributed its own policy innovations, thus providing the EU with an egalitarian push: its membership in 1995 led to the introduction of EU work–life balance and reconciliation measures that also included *men*. These measures are most clearly represented in the European diffusion of "father's months" in parental leave policies (Stratigaki 2004).

The accession of CEE states (in 2004, 2007 and 2013) represents the largest and most recent addition of new member states. Authors agree that CEE states have "witnessed the most radical and epochal political and economic transformation of any of the welfare regimes" (Hemerijck 2015, 652). The transformation was at least twofold: politically from state socialism to liberal democracy and economically from a planned economy to a capitalist economy; both deeply affecting society. CEE states under Communism had instituted egalitarian policies in the area of economic and social rights for women, but they lacked democratic legitimacy and an open civil society. Women's movements were allowed only under the tutelage of the state; independent organizations were illegal. Nevertheless, at the time of the demise of Communism, women in CEE states ironically surpassed women in west European states in numerous dimensions, be it labor market participation, equal pay, parental leave or education levels (Fodor 2004; von Wahl 2008). With the implosion of the centrally planned economies in 1989, some of these advances were wiped away and an often-painful adjustment process to Western capitalism began, marked by stronger political rights but weaker social standards, many codified in EU accession rules.

Around 2000, the rise of neoliberalism began to shift EU polices away from an emancipatory egalitarian approach towards a social investment approach (Esping-Andersen et al. 2002; Hemerijck 2015; Jenson 2009). Research argued that the old welfare state model was inert and produced suboptimal life chances due to continued reliance on the male breadwinner model in a phase of deindustrialization combined with demographic decline. In order to be successful in a knowledge-based service economy, women's employment and educational levels, as well as availability of childcare, needed to be improved. Thus, theoretical and political questions of gender equity rose in relevance, pushing work–life balance and reconciliation policies to the forefront.

However, with the start of the global banking and then sovereign debt crisis in 2009, many Euro countries slid into turmoil. That economic crisis and the arrival of over one million refugees from war zones in the Middle East in 2015-2016 produced a political backlash leading to a wave of popular Euroskepticism (Kirchick 2017; Krastev 2017). The Brexit vote seemed to be another nail in the coffin, but seeing how the chaotic Brexit process unfolded, public support for the EU again rose especially among the younger generation, indicating that reports of the EU's demise have been greatly exaggerated. But the Euro crisis and subsequent austerity measures negatively affected social policy and employment, making gender equality concerns look irrelevant or "narrow." Although the roots of this retrenchment were older and based on EU neoliberal preferences, the Euro crisis stalled or even dismantled the realization of further gender equality prospects (Jacquot 2015). Today, gender equality policies, being part and parcel of the larger EU landscape, experience a number of discouraging challenges due to political and economic headwinds. Feminism and gender equality have become targets of budget cuts and the "anti-gender" discourse on the populist right. Most recently, the Covid-19 pandemic has brought the global economy to an unprecedented standstill with additional challenges to gender equality and the integrative power of the EU.

The next section recounts the theoretical origins of the gender regime, and more specifically the gender equality regime approach. Knowing its findings and variations enables scholars to solve empirical puzzles, build theory, and better understand how the broader challenges of European (dis)integration and democracy play out within gendered structures.

Origins of the "gender regime" approach

Theorizing on GERs is a moving target because the EU is constantly changing. The literature on gender more broadly is multi-disciplinary, highly productive, and extensive. The gender regime can be considered one of the most employed frameworks for the analysis of gendered policy and institutions originating in feminist sociology and political science. The sociologist RW Connell (1987, 20) coined the concept "gender regime" and defined it as the "state of play of gender relations in a given institution." Accordingly, it involved a distinct division of labor among the sexes and ideologies about sexual behavior and character, constructing certain ideas of masculinity and femininity. The definition exemplifies the emergence of a constructivist approach to gender hierarchies in feminist sociology. Constructivism sees gender not as a biological given but as socially constructed through interrelated values, institutions, and production systems. For the relationship between gender regimes, Connell used the term "gender order," while other authors use these terms interchangeably (Chappell and Waylen 2013; Clavero and Galligan 2009).

The specific literature on European gender regimes was initially more influenced by sociologist Gøsta Esping-Andersen (1990), who developed the concept of "welfare state regimes," which revolutionized the study of social politics. It redefined the usage of the term "regime" (so far limited to authoritarian states in the field of international relations) to the sociological realm. The reconceptualization of the social welfare state as a broader kind of social and economic "regime" brought the interaction of *domestic* social actors, markets, and states into focus and thus became a subject of comparative politics. Over the next three decades, the GER concept inspired a wealth of feminist responses. To understand the foundation of these debates, it is crucial to grasp the important contributions made by the welfare regime approach.

Esping-Andersen (1990) proposed three ideal regime types, which are not just quantitatively (i.e. more or less welfare payments) but *qualitatively* different from each other. The UK represents the liberal regime type, while Germany stands for the conservative, and Sweden for the social-democratic or Nordic welfare state regime. The latter is identified as most desirable, i.e. most equitable, for the working and middle class. These "regimes" result from different historic legacies in the organization of labor and the state, specifically the extent and ways in which the state intervened in the market. The types are assessed according to three factors: level of de-commodification of workers, stratification of society and specific triadic relations among state, market and family. The degree of "de-commodification" of male workers is vital, meaning the degree to which "individuals or families can uphold a socially acceptable standard of living independently of market participation" (Esping-Andersen 1990, 37).

Feminist scholarship readily engaged with and reacted to this typology. Of special interest were the categorical underpinnings and patriarchal blind spots of the typology around the standard of the male breadwinner model. Feminist research gendered these categories and added new factors to accommodate for women's experiences (Lewis 1992; O'Connor 1993; Orloff 1993). Primary was the critique that women were less looking for the privileges of de-commodification, since many experienced hurdles just entering the labor force, and instead were striving to become "commodified" and gain employment in the first place. From a feminist perspective, de-commodification was also problematic as it conceptualized women as male dependents and not as women on their own autonomous terms. In addition, the areas of family and care work were not sufficiently recognized as forms of labor. In response, feminist counter models theorized putting individuals and care-work at the center instead of the family and (male) employment and called for "de-familiarization." Walby summarizes this changed perspective succinctly: "The theory of gender regimes was developed as an alternative to the reduction of gender to family or culture" (Walby 2020). Scholars developed new kinds of welfare state models, such as the strong, modified, or weak breadwinner model (Lewis 1992) or the male-breadwinner/individual model (Sainsbury 1996). Another alternative conception was a continuum reaching from the male breadwinner to dual earner regimes. As mainstream welfare states foundations – an industrial base and a male breadwinner model – were crumbling across developed nations, Fraser (1994) asked pointedly: What kind of gender model would the welfare state of the future be based on? The universal breadwinner or a caregiver parity model?

An important conceptual advancement occurred in a comparative study of equal employment policies, where the "regime" concept was not applied to traditional transfer payments of welfare states (pensions, unemployment etc.), but specifically to an array of measures such as anti-discrimination and equal pay, affirmative action and quotas, family policies, sexual harassment, and LGBT rights (von Wahl 1999). It was argued that different national arrangements and policies designed to achieve more gender equality in paid and unpaid work could be conceptualized not just as policies but as "gender equality regimes" (*Gleichstellungsregime*). Similarly, research in the next two decades has conceptualized the various kinds of gender equality policies by states or the EU itself as "regimes."

While power resources were seen as the active force in the struggle for a more egalitarian welfare state, feminist scholars saw an important, albeit less organized and incorporated, role for women's movements in their analysis. Research identified the central role of women's and feminist movements, women's policy machinery and the social mobilization of related movements as core drivers of the articulation and application of gender policies (Locher 2012; McBride and Mazur 2010; von Wahl 1999; Zippel 2006). From a social movement perspective, gender regimes can be read as specific kind of political opportunity structure containing hurdles and opportunities for mobilization. While most women's and feminist movements in Europe are local, poorly resourced and small, some groups have formed national as well as transnational networks. Their experts, activists, and allies can have considerable influence in political parties, national governments, as well as in Brussels. Especially so-called femocrats, feminist bureaucrats and administrators bring feminist expertise and ideas into the policy-making processes and institutions. Since 1990, the European Women's Lobby (EWL) represents more than 2,000 women's organizations, while another network, KARAT, represents women's interests from CEE states at the EU since 1997. Other smaller NGO's lobby for migrant women, LGBTI etc. Woodward (2004) has called these dense feminist networks the "velvet triangle."

Conceptualizing the EU as a gender equality regime

Since the beginning of European integration, underlying questions of what place women should occupy, surfaced. This first became evident on issues of women's labor market participation and the inclusion of equal pay in the 1957 EEC founding treaty. Since then, the EU's intervention in questions of gender equality have grown dramatically in scope, breadth, and interconnectedness from equal pay to anti-discrimination, positive action, and work–life reconciliation. In 1996 the EU launched a much broader policy called gender mainstreaming (COM(96) 67final). This idea grew out of international women's conferences in Nairobi (1985) and Beijing (1995) and was intended to integrate a gender perspective into all policy-making. The EU describes mainstreaming as "the (re)organisation, improvement, development and evaluation of policy processes, so that a gender equality perspective is incorporated into all policies at all levels and all stages, by the actors normally involved in policymaking" (https://eige.europa.eu/thesaurus/terms/1185).

In response to this policy expansion, research pondered the place of gender in the EU: **Had the EU itself developed politically and legally to such an extent that it could be described as a sort of gender regime or gender equality regime?** If so, what exactly was the relationship between this new supranational and the various national gender regimes? And what were the effects of the EU regime on member states? As with the larger field of

Europeanization (see Forest in this volume), central fields of theorizing related to political and economic convergence (or continued diversity/fragmentation) and democratic representation. In response to the institutional diversification and political strengthening, scholars began to consider the EU itself as a new kind of GER.

Ostner and Lewis (1995) began this line of inquiry with their study on the "needles eye," ingeniously overlaying the supranational opportunity structure with the national level. They demonstrated that institutional and political "fit" severely limits successful feminist claims at the EU and coined the term "gender policy regimes." Liebert (2003, 480) defined a "gender policy regime" as combining "general social norms about gender relations of a given country, often referred to as 'gender orders,' and the way those gender roles underpin and are in turn affected by general social policy arrangements." Using Ostner and Lewis' approach, she demonstrated that German gender policy was affected by hard and soft EU law, leading to the Europeanization of domestic law.

In 2004, Walby put the term "EU gender regime" on the map. In her broad conceptualization of "varieties of gender regimes," the powers of the EU extend beyond economic considerations and towards a varied and very broad definition of the gender regime as a social system. Walby mixed aspects of Connell's understanding of gender orders as a series of multi-dimensional regimes, domains, and social practices, as well as Esping-Andersen's typology and predicted that as "the EU becomes increasingly important through the deepening of its powers, the increasing number of member states, and increased impact in global governance, this new form of the gender regime grows in importance" (Walby 2004, 24). Similarly, but focusing on employment and related family policy, von Wahl (2005, 2008) proposed that a European GER had emerged. This argument constructed three regional types of equal employment regimes, those more based on anti-discrimination (liberal), social equality (social-democratic) or women's difference (conservative) and came to the conclusion that above and out of these regional differences, a unique equal employment regime was emerging at the EU level.

Others argued that the EU regime represented institutionally a mixed approach (MacRae 2006) or a political "hybrid" (Ferree 2008) out of transnational and global neoliberalism and a "European" social democratic model. In contrast, Kantola viewed the EU as a kind of liberal regime based on a US model of anti-discrimination and focused on the shift from hard to soft law. She similarly found that, "[t]he processes of *Europeanization* raise questions about the member states shifting towards common EU standards" (Kantola 2010, 4, emphasis in original). It should be noted, however, that the differentiation between gender regime and gender equality regime in the literature is not always very clear and the terms are sometimes used synonymously. In the end, the latter concept relates closely to policies, actors, and institutions dealing with questions of fostering equality between the sexes.

Recent research addressed the regime analysis from other angles developing different interpretations of origin and functioning. Neo-Marxists see primarily neoliberal market forces at work, while institutionalists emphasize the power of norms and institutional legacies. The latter put the role of discourses and frames in the center and argue that these are now defined at the EU level (Lombardo et al. 2009; Verloo 2007). Scholars discuss mechanisms of framing the meaning of equality differently as fixing, freezing, bending or stretching (Lombardo et al. 2009). Accordingly, EU institutions have a privileged position in "fixing" the meaning of gender equality. Kronsell (2012, 39) stated that the concept of gender regimes is a "useful concept because it embraced gender as a constructed order, exhibited in institutions and practices that come to the fore in diverse policy domains."

In sum, the literature *shares* the assessment that there is theoretical and empirical utility in conceptualizing the EU as a GER. The research has developed a variety of accounts about its extent, nature and effects. Intensified interaction among member states, the development of new institutions, norms and laws, and the rise of transnational women's groups have led to a process of Europeanization drawing together a extensive and multi-level web of gender-related policies, networks and discourses. By now the concept's applications are widely established not only in reference to national and regional regimes but also to the EU at large (Abels and Mushaben 2012; Jacquot 2017; Kantola 2010; Kronsell 2012; Pascall and Kwak 2005). EU-wide common legal standards have numerous and positive effects on the existing national and regional gender regimes, expanding, for example, parental leave in the liberal regime and equal treatment in the conservative. Top-down Europeanization of nation-level laws and policies has changed national institutions, public expectations and political opportunity structures towards certain common standards, while diversity among state policies still exists. Europeanization research is now moving its focus from policy formulation and outputs to questions of implementation and effect.

The EU gender equality regime since the Great Recession

The Great Recession of 2008–2013 weakened the EU's legitimacy and power. One cause stems from the politics of austerity and the massive cutbacks in social welfare in response to the Euro crisis (see Kantola and Lombardo in this volume). The political – and sometimes populist – backlash against austerity undermined the European project of an "ever closer union" and accelerated the emergence of a new transnational cleavage between winners and losers of integrated markets and globalization (Hooghe and Marks 2018; Kriesi et al. 2008). Although substantial percentages of European citizens have always been "Eurosceptics," these numbers soared as the larger EU project became politicized in new and polarizing ways. The startling idea of member states leaving the union, summed up as "Grexit," "Nexit," or "Brexit," gained much attention and vocal support from nationalists, leading to a successful public referendum in Britain in 2016 to leave the EU (see Guerrina and Masselot in this volume).

Neoliberal policies intended to control the quickly unfurling sovereign debt crisis squeezed countries, communities, and families. In this context, the political space and funding to fight against various forms of gender discrimination, unemployment, and women's poverty shrank. Gender policies were downgraded, the standard example being gender mainstreaming, which has had at best mixed results but is mostly unenforced. In addition, gender equality institutions were downscaled (Klatzer and Schlager 2014). Importantly, the economic crisis added a layer of budget cuts to the public sector and welfare, relying instead on women's traditional care work (Kantola and Lombardo 2017, 4). The financial crisis also led to shifts in national and European gender regimes (Walby 2011, 2015). In institutionalist terms, the crisis represents a "critical juncture" that has the power to undermine and even revert long-term progress already achieved in gender relations (Rubery 2014).

An important problem is backsliding and de-democratization. Backsliding comes in different forms, some as discursive opposition and others as explicit opposition to gender equality principles. Krizsán and Roggeband observed this critical development in four CEE states, manifesting itself to different degrees and in different forms. They state that backsliding "may occur when a policy problem is radically reframed so that the new frame contrasts with gender equality meanings or allows for contrasting interpretations" (Krizsán and Roggeband 2018, 93). Focusing on social mobilization and women's movements, they argue that women's movements hold less weight now as states are more hostile towards them. While backsliding occurs in many member states, in some CEE states repressive techniques against women's groups are quite extreme and

> can range from regulatory tools such as excessive auditing and surveillance to more violent and repressive tools such as police searches, raiding of offices, holding computers or

even arrests of activists. They limit activism both by means of threat but also by demanding unnecessary and mostly unavailable resources for handling excessive auditing.

(Krizsán and Roggeband 2018, 94)

As anti-EU, starkly conservative, nationalist and right-wing populist movements and parties become more vocal and influential, we can expect more backsliding and repressive tactics against women's groups and policies to occur (Krizsán and Roggeband 2018, 91). Interestingly, Krizsán and Roggeband (2018) argue that EU norms are those that backslide the least.

Jacquot (2015, 2017) views the crisis-triggered shift towards neoliberal policy solutions as part of the "dismantling" of the EU gender regime and the EU as undergoing a "deeply trans-formative" change. Not only did budgetary cuts occur during the crisis, but structural changes undermining "the functioning, modes, and means of action, but also the very legitimacy … of equality between men and women as a common value and a fundamental right" (Jacquot 2017, 28). Due to the crises the weight of member states in gender equality policy strengthened (Jacquot 2017, 37), more blockages occurred in the EU Council, and a more cautious approach was taken in the European Commission, the original motor of many equality policies (such as the blockage of quotas on corporate boards, withdrawal of maternity directive proposal). In add-ition, feminists in the European Parliament have less ability to bring reports from the FEMM Committee on Women's Rights and Gender Equality to the plenary due to internal reform processes. While this can be interpreted as "backsliding" or "dismantling," Weiner and MacRae (2017) instead interpret these changes as "politics as usual," because, after all, the EU has always prioritized the market over gender equality and, in crises situations, gender equality stalls or falls by the wayside. But while the general prioritization of the market over equality concerns is a correct assessment, the current backlash against feminist and democratic aspirations seems to have crossed a disconcerting new threshold.

In the broad protests against austerity, gender inequality receded as poverty, class and, particu-larly, issues of race and migration rose to the fore, fueled by the coincidental exodus of over a million refugees from the Middle East to Europe. Social movements and populist parties, already critical of the EU's handling of the economic crisis, emerged on the left in the Mediterranean and on the political right in northern member states, questioning not just austerity, the eco-nomic rationale for the Euro as common currency, and monetary policy, but also giving voice to anti-refugee, anti-migrant and xenophobic sentiments. A division between those who are for and against building a more integrated and pluralistic EU has risen across the continent. Its most dramatic expressions are the rise of right-wing and neo-nationalist parties, the vote for Brexit and the rise of illiberal democracies in Hungary and Poland.

None of this bodes well for the EU as a whole and gender equality specifically. The EU and its prescribed gender equality policies have even become a central focus of mobilization of the political right (Hark and Villa 2015; Köttig et al. 2017). The erosion and regression of established policies has further *intersectional* repercussions for women of color, those from minority religions, women with migration or asylum status, disabilities or marginal sexual identities (see Solanke in this volume). A decade of austerity has sharpened power differentials and inequalities among women in terms of class, race, ethnicity, age and citizenship status in the EU. The Great Recession's ripple effects through the broader GER have negatively affected the resources of transnational women's groups.

Although many CEE states joined the EU with high hopes, several of them have strongly asserted their own national(ist) paths. Authoritarian nationalists are trying to turn the clock back on gender equality and are re-introducing traditional familialism, limiting access to abortion, weakening laws against domestic violence, declaring LGBTI-free zones, ending women's and

The EU as a gender equality regime

gender studies programs at universities and undermining feminist mobilization. In addition, neoliberal ideas continue to roll back or deregulate employment and social rights for the sake of efficiency in member states. The EU market orientation, increasing diversity of gender regimes, introduction of regulatory or outright repressive policies and the organizational weakness of women's and feminist movements have considerably slowed the momentum and imaginative space of the EU's GER. From a political perspective, these mounting hurdles to building a more united feminist vision are disconcerting; from a theoretical perspective, it requires scholars to more accurately theorize forces of repression, de-democratization, disintegration and defiance.

While Europeanization literature has mostly dealt with the many important questions of convergence, the last decade must be seen as a repudiation of integration by parts of the public. It may, however, not so much trigger the return to former national or traditionalist gender regimes, as deeper domestic divides manifesting themselves in unexpected radicalization of neoliberal and populist forces on one side, and, on the other side, a pushback against anti- EU sentiments by the younger generation, the well-educated, urbanites, and current supportive nonvoters, who in theory probably still hold a majority. Currently public opinion seems to be swinging in the opposite direction with the citizens voicing more public support for the EU. At the last Eurobarometer poll in April 2019, 68% of respondents stated that "EU countries overall have benefi ted from being part of the EU – equalling [sic] the highest level recorded since 1983" (EB91).

Achievements, gaps and future directions

The GER literature has generated a wealth of insights, analyses and concepts distinguishable as three waves: (1) *Comparative* accounts belong to the first wave of internationally oriented research. These accounts generated the basic concept and produced critical and feminist counter models to mainstream accounts. These models were theoretically innovative and systematically brought into discussion welfare regimes, state institutions, the women's policy machinery and national cases. Comparative research continues as new research questions are generated.

(2) The second wave of research analyzed the EU as a new kind of *supranational* gender equality regime. The literature on European integration, Europeanization, varieties of gender regime, and the EU GER has analyzed how policies, institutions and actors have together produced a specific EU discourse and approach to achieving gender equality in member states. This discourse is simultaneously ambitious but also limited by the EU's market orientation. In the last two decades, challenges, such as the growing diversity of member states, the Great Recession and anti-democratic tendencies require scholars to shift attention to the EU's Achilles heel: social and economic differences among regions, national resistance to gender equality, and limited powers to implement EU goals.

(3) Transnational and border accounts form a third and more recent perspective are asking, for example, if the EU regime can be viewed as a regional variation of a global model or how transnational migration affects European gender and care regimes (Lutz and Palenga-Möllenbeck 2011; Sainsbury 2006; Siim and Borchorst 2017). Similarly, concerns over dealings with Europe's neighbors, its border regions and the women's and human rights norms of refugees have risen to the forefront or top of concerns (Gerard and Pickering 2014).

New innovative and promising areas of research have emerged, which are of theoretical and normative importance for feminism: Firstly, issues of intersectionality, such as the intersection of hierarchized group identities in the EU and member states (Crenshaw 1990; Davidson-Schmich 2017; Walby et al. 2012). A related and promising endeavor is research investigating the complex intersections of different emerging equality regimes related to race, disability, sexuality etc. that emerged with the Amsterdam Treaty (Krizsán et al. 2014). This research has opened the study of new identities and interest, e.g. through racial, ethnic or religious hybridity, which are producing very complex identities and gender regimes (Ferree 2008; Kantola and Nousiainen 2009). Included are trans and intersex issues, pointing to the emergence of gender variance and the end of a simple gender binary in Europe (Ayoub 2013; de Silva 2018; von Wahl 2019).

Secondly, the disconcerting rise of populism across the continent with its attendant anti-EU sentiments is challenging more than specific EU policies, especially given the centrality of gender issues to the right-wing populist agenda (Sauer 2017). The emergence of a transnational cleavage with a radical right-wing has already shown its power to hollow out, undermine and pervert democratic principles. These developments will challenge and possibly bring about new gender regimes that could be radically re-traditionalizing or even segregating, depending on one's ethnicity, race, sexuality or religion. Systematic analyses of how new theories can explain the shifting political landscape or how the new realities can be theoretically reflected will be crucial.

Conclusion: dismantling, disintegration or defiance

Understanding the GER concept and its analysis of the EU is part of the basic feminist toolkit of European social science research. GERs enable sophisticated analyses of emergence, diffusion and impact of gendered norms, processes and institutions. I have argued here that concepts of the EU GER parallel the development of the EU at large. This is visible along two dimensions. Firstly, market orientation: With the founding of the common market and basic rules for competition, EU law built a foundation to enable women to enter that market on equal terms with men. EU policy was directed to produce equality *for* the market. With the rise of neoliberalism and a number of economic and political headwinds, the more expansive EU vision has shrunk and now only promises equality *despite* the market. Secondly, aspiration: At its founding, the new community inscribed marching orders of an "ever closer union" for itself. With the political fragmentation and dangers of disintegration through repeated and large-scale crises, the EU's ambitions have notably slackened and seem to point more towards "some sort of union," affecting also the ambition and robustness of the EU gender regime.

Over the last four decades, feminist goals of the EU have changed from a one-dimensional focus on encouraging labor market-related equality towards multi-dimensional complexity taking difference, gender, and intersectionality into account. While there is currently less optimism and trust in EU capabilities, feminist mobilization and protest have returned in some states, indicating that there still is a lot of defiance left among activists. Furthermore, the new President of the EU Commission, Ursula von der Leyen, is ambitious on gender issues and comes with a proven domestic track record. Since 2019, she has spearheaded the push for a gender-balanced Commission, appointed a Commissioner on Equality, and released a robust Gender Equality Strategy for 2020–2025 (COM (2020) 152 final). Despite these positive signals, the sense of larger European goals and aspirations has dampened with the series of crises befalling the continent over the last decade. As a result, the future of the EU and the place of gender equality are less predictable, although the EU has a proven track record of "failing forward" and advancing when under duress (Jones et al. 2016).

References

Abels G, Mushaben J M, eds. (2012): *Gendering the European Union: New Approaches to Old Democratic Deficits*, Basingstoke: Palgrave Macmillan.

Ayoub P (2013): Cooperative transnationalism in contemporary Europe. Europeanization and political opportunities for LGBT mobilization in the European Union, *European Political Science Review* **5** (2), 279–310.

Chappell L, Waylen G (2013): Gender and the hidden life of institutions, *Public Administration* **91** (3), 599–615.

Clavero S, Galligan Y (2009): Constituting and reconstituting the gender order in Europe, *Perspectives on European Politics and Society* **10** (1), 101–117.

Connell R W (1987): *Gender and Power*, Cambridge: Polity Press.

Crenshaw K (1990): Mapping the margins. Intersectionality, identity politics, and violence against women of color, *Stanford Law Review* **43** (6), 1241–1299.

Davidson-Schmich L K, ed. (2017): *Gender, Intersections, and Institutions: Intersectional Groups Building Alliances and Gaining Voice in Germany*, Ann Arbor: University of Michigan Press.

de Silva A (2018): *Negotiating the Borders of the Gender Regime Developments and Debates on Trans(sexuality) in the Federal Republic of Germany*, Bielefeld: transcript.

Esping-Andersen G (1990): The three political economies of the welfare state, *International Journal of Sociology* **20** (3), 92–123.

Esping-Andersen G, Gallie D, Hemerijck A, Myles J (2002), *Why We Need a New Welfare State*, Oxford: Oxford University Press.

Ferree M M (2008): Framing Equality: The Politics of Race, Class, Gender in the US, Germany, and the expanding European Union, in: Roth S (ed.): *Gender Politics in the Expanding European Union. Mobilization, Inclusion, Exclusion*, New York: Berghahn.

Fodor E (2004): The state socialist emancipation project. Gender inequality in workplace authority in Hungary and Austria, *Signs: Journal of Women in Culture and Society* **29** (3), 783–813.

Fraser N (1994): After the family wage: gender equality and the welfare state, *Political Theory* **22** (4), 591–618.

Gerard A, Pickering S (2014): Gender, securitization and transit. Refugee women and the journey to the EU, *Journal of Refugee Studies* **27** (3), 338–359.

Hark S, Villa P (2015): *Anti-Genderismus, Sexualität und Geschlecht als Schauplätze aktueller politischer Auseinandersetzungen*, Bielefeld: transcript.

Hemerijck A (2015): European Welfare States in Motion: From Social Protection to Social Investment, in: Magone, J M (ed.) *Handbook of European Politics*, London, New York: Routledge, 640–668.

Hooghe L, Marks G (2018): Cleavage theory meets Europe's crises: Lipset, Rokkan, and the transnational cleavage, *Journal of European Public Policy* **25** (1), 109–135.

Jacquot S (2015): *Transformations in EU Gender Equality. From Emergence to Dismantling*, Basingstoke: Palgrave Macmillan.

Jacquot S (2017): A Policy in Crisis. The Dismantling of the EU Gender Equality Policy, in: Kantola J, Lombardo E (eds.): *Gender and the Economic Crisis in Europe*, Cham: Palgrave Macmillan, 27–48.

Jenson J (2009): Lost in translation: The social investment perspective and gender equality, *Social Politics* **16** (4), 446–483.

Jones E, Kelemen R D, Meunier S (2016): Failing Forward? The Euro Crisis and the Incomplete Nature of European Integration, Comparative Political Studies 49 (7), 1010–1034.

Kantola J (2010): *Gender and the European Union*, Basingstoke: Palgrave Macmillan.

Kantola J, Lombardo E, eds. (2017): *Gender and the Economic Crisis in Europe. Politics, Institutions and Intersectionality*, *Gender and Politics*, Cham: Palgrave Macmillan.

Kantola J, Nousiainen K (2009): Institutionalizing intersectionality in Europe, *International Feminist Journal of Politics* **11** (4), 459–477.

Kirchick J (2017): *The End of Europe. Dictators, Demagogues, and the Coming Dark Age*, New Haven, CT: Yale University Press.

Klatzer E, Schlager C (2014): Feminist Perspectives on Macroeconomics: Reconfiguration of Power Structures and Erosion of Gender Equality Through the New Economic Governance Regime in the European Union, in: Evans M, Hemmings C, Henry M (eds.): *The SAGE Handbook of Feminist Theory*, Thousand Oaks, CA: SAGE, 483–499.

Köttig M, Bitzan R, Petö A, eds. (2017): *Gender and the Far Right in Europe*, Cham: Palgrave Macmillan.

Krastev I (2017): *After Europe*, Philadelphia, PA: University of Pennsylvania Press.

Kriesi H, Grande E, Lachat R, Dolezal M, Bornschier S, and Frey T (2008): *West European Politics in the Age of Globalization,* Cambridge: Cambridge University Press.

Krizsán A, Roggeband C (2018): Towards a conceptual framework for struggles over democracy in backsliding states. Gender equality policy in central eastern Europe, *Politics and Governance* **6** (3), 90–100.

Krizsán A, Skjeie H, Squires J (2014): The changing nature of European equality regimes: Explaining convergence and variation, *Journal of International and Comparative Social Policy* **30** (1), 53–68.

Kronsell A (2012): Gendering Theories of European Integration, in: Abels G, Mushaben J M (eds.): *Gendering the European Union: New Approaches to Old Democratic Deficits*, Basingstoke: Palgrave Macmillan, 23–40.

Lewis J (1992): Gender and the development of welfare regimes, *Journal of European Social Policy* **2** (3), 159–173.

Liebert U (2003): Europeanization and the 'Needles Eye': The transformation of employment policy in Germany, *Review of Policy Research* **20** (3), 479–492.

Locher B (2012): Gendering the EU Policy Process and Constructing the Gender Acquis, in: Abels G, Mushaben J M (eds.) *Gendering the European Union: New Approaches to Old Democratic Deficits*, Basingstoke: Palgrave Macmillan, 63–84.

Lombardo E, Meier P, Verloo M (2009): *The Discursive Politics of Gender Equality. Stretching, Bending and Policy-Making*, Abingdon: Routledge.

Lutz H, Palenga-Möllenbeck E (2011): Care, gender and migration. Towards a theory of transnational domestic work migration in Europe, *Journal of Contemporary European Studies* **19** (3), 349–364.

MacRae H (2006): Rescaling gender relations: The influence of European directives on the German gender regime, *Social Politics* **13** (4), 522–550.

McBride D E, Mazur A (2010): *The Politics of State Feminism: Innovation in Comparative Research*, Philadelphia, PA: Temple University Press.

O'Connor J S (1993): Gender, class and citizenship in the comparative analysis of welfare state regimes: Theoretical and methodological issues, *British Journal of Sociology* **44** (3), 501–518.

Orloff A S (1993): Gender and the social rights of citizenship: The comparative analysis of gender relations and welfare states, *American Sociological Review* **58** (3), 303–328.

Ostner I, Lewis J (1995): Gender and the Evolution of European Social Policies, in: Leibfried S, Pierson P (eds.): *European Social Policy: Between Fragmentation and Integration*, Washington DC: Brookings Institution Press, 159–193.

Pascall G, Kwak A (2005): *Gender Regimes in Transition in Central and Eastern Europe*, Bristol: Policy Press.

Rubery J (2014): From 'Women and Recession' to 'Women and Austerity'. A Framework for Analysis, in: Karamessini M, Rubery J (eds.): *Women and austerity*, London, New York: Routledge, 39–58.

Sainsbury D (1996): *Gender, Equality and Welfare States,* Cambridge: Cambridge University Press.

Sainsbury D (2006): Immigrants' social rights in comparative perspective: Welfare regimes, forms in immigration and immigration policy regimes, *Journal of European Social Policy* **16** (3), 229–244.

Sauer B (2017): Gesellschaftstheoretische Überlegungen zum europäischen Rechtspopulismus. Zum Erklärungspotenzial der Kategorie Geschlecht, *Politische Vierteljahresschrift* **58** (1), 3–22.

Siim B, Borchorst A (2017): Gendering European welfare states and citizenship: revisioning inequalities, in: Kennett P, Lendvai-Bainton N (eds.): *Handbook of European Social Policy*, Aldershot: Edward Elgar, 99–127.

Stratigaki M (2004): The cooptation of gender concepts in EU policies: The case of reconciliation of work and family, *Social Politics* **11** (1), 30–56.

Verloo M (2007): *Multiple Meanings of Gender Equality: A Critical Frame Analysis of Gender Policies in Europe*, Budapest: CEU Press.

von Wahl A (1999): *Gleichstellungsregime: Berufliche Gleichstellung von Frauen in der Bundesrepublik und den USA*, Leverkusen: Leske+Budrich.

von Wahl A (2005): Liberal, conservative, social democratic or … European? The European Union as equal employment regime, *Social Politics* **12** (1): 67–95.

von Wahl A (2008): EU Enlargement and Gender Equality in Employment, in: Roth S (ed.): *Gender Politics in the Expanding European Union. Mobilization, Inclusion, Exclusion,* Oxford, New York: Berghahn Books, 19–36.

von Wahl A (2019): From object to subject: intersex activism and the rise and fall of the gender binary in Germany, *Social Politics: International Studies in Gender, State & Society,* https://doi.org/10.1093/sp/jxz044.

Walby S (2004): The European Union and gender equality: emergent varieties of gender regime, *Social Politics: International Studies in Gender, State & Society* **11** (1), 4–29.

Walby S (2011): *The Future of Feminism,* Cambridge: Polity Press.

Walby S (2015): *Crisis*, Cambridge: Polity Press.

Walby S (2020): Varieties of Gender Regimes, Social Politics: International Studies in Gender, State & Society 27 (3), 414–431.

Walby S, Armstrong J, Strid S (2012): Intersectionality: Multiple inequalities in social theory, *Sociology* **46** (2), 224–240.

Weiner E, MacRae H (2017): Opportunity and Setback? Gender Equality, Crisis, and Change, in: Kantola J, Lombardo E (eds.): *Gender and the Economic Crisis in Europe. Politics, Institutions and Intersectionality,* Cham: Palgrave Macmillan, 73–93.

Woodward A (2004): Building Velvet Triangles: Gender and Informal Governance, in: Christiansen T, Piattoni S (eds.): *Informal Governance in the European Union,* Cheltenham: Edgar Elgar, 76–93.

Woodward A (2012). From Equal Treatment to Gender Mainstreaming and Diversity Management, in: Abels G, Mushaben J M (eds.): *Gendering the European Union: New Approaches to Old Democratic Deficits,* Basingstoke: Palgrave Macmillan, 85–103.

Woodward A (2015): Gender and European Politics, in: Magone, J M (ed.): *Handbook of European Politics,* London, New York: Routledge, 843–856.

Zippel K (2006): *The Politics of Sexual Harassment,* Cambridge: Cambridge University Press.

3

Europeanization

Maxime Forest

The integration process has had an impact on the domestic policies, politics and polities of European Union (EU) member states, on candidate countries and third countries targeted by the European Neighbourhood Policy (ENP). This impact is investigated by "Europeanization" studies. This chapter addresses the interaction of feminist and gender scholarship with the Europeanization literature and its different streams. Europeanization does not rely upon a fully-fledged, empirically tested theory, but rather derives from the analysis of top-down implications of what have long been framed as only bottom-up processes. As member states voluntarily conceded competences to a supranational entity, they got caught in a process of adaptation to EU norms, policy instruments and "ways of doing things" generating a number of scenarios for convergence, divergence or norm contestation, depending on domestic settings, actors and policy domains. Europeanization scholars have attempted to make sense of diverse situations, investigating facilitation and causality mechanisms, different logics underpinning norm adaptation and subsequent policy change, as well as actors' configurations or conflicting discursive uses of the EU.

By changing the lens, Europeanization considerably complicated the picture well beyond the dynamics covered by what had so far constituted the main theories of European integration: Liberal intergovernmentalism, neo-functionalism and, more recently, neo-institutionalism. By shifting the focus to new dimensions such as ideas and discourses, it paved the way for a more substantial contribution to theorizing integration from gender scholarship, well suited to consider power dynamics at play in discursive framing or resources redistribution processes as those unfold by Europeanization (see also Lombardo and Kantola in this volume).

This dialogue has not been straightforward and has involved many scholars from Europeanization and gender and politics studies working in the realm of neo-institutionalism. Significant contributions have been made by countless case and comparative studies on many countries and policy domains, with a specific interest on *soft* Europeanization, particularly through gender mainstreaming. These studies have highlighted the importance of gender regimes (see von Wahl in this volume) in Europeanization outcomes, also capturing Europeanization as a scenario for norm contestation, rather than convergence, especially as the diversity of European polities considerably increased with the accession to EU membership of eight, later 11 post-Socialist states from central and eastern Europe. Although far more limited, theoretical dialogue has also developed with the Europeanization literature, especially as most recent trends in this field are reflected in the literature about gendering Europe.

Those trends derive from the current crises of integration, no longer perceived as a one-way process, geographically diluted and heavily contested. Yet, gendering Europeanization theory in times of "de-Europeanization" (Ágh 2015) is only paradoxical at first sight. Addressing the impact of Europe on the politicization and regulation of gender rights in EU member states and accession countries, offers ways to grasp some of the most revealing dynamics currently at play in Europe. At a time when the common European home is burning, gendering Europeanization studies contributes to revealing the origins of the fire.

To unfold this agenda, we will first disentangle what we understand by Europeanization, introducing the concept and key theoretical issues through which it has been framed in "mainstream" literature. Second, we will explore how gender scholarship has engaged with this literature and addressed "mainstream" questions. Third, based on a brief state-of-the-art we will reflect upon the original contribution from the gender scholarship to the *current* agenda of Europeanization studies. Our core argument is that gender rights have become one of the most divisive and politically loaded issues in the European public space, around which concepts of European identity are built, political alliances shift, and new cleavages emerge. Illustrating these dynamics through examples borrowed from recent EU cases studies, we will outline a potential research agenda to further gendering Europeanization literature.

"When Europe hits home"

As a scholarly concept, Europeanization is intrinsically different from integration theories which have progressively constituted the core – and roughly successive mainstreams – of the discipline, e.g. (liberal) intergovernmentalism, neo-functionalism (and multi-level governance) and the different streams of neo-institutionalism – all primarily attempt to explain why and how integration happens. Instead, Europeanization was forged by the mid-1990s (Ladrech 1994; Mény et al. 1996) to account for the implications of integration for national (and sub-national) polities, hence to make sense of how "Europe hits home" (Börzel and Risse 2002).

Integration theories have focused on processes by which member states were transferring fractions of their sovereignty to an increasingly complex supranational entity, also addressing the emergence of EU policies and of a new transnational administrative and political elite. Liberal intergovernmentalism underlined how member states shape the integration process through pursuing their own interests, whereas neo-functionalism highlighted the largely market- and policy-driven dynamics by which integration happened, such as the spill-over effect as driver for the expansion of EU institutions, capacities and competences. Multi-level governance addressed one of the key aspects of this logics of consequence: the emergence of a multi-layered governance system involving subnational, national and supranational levels and a variety of both hard and soft governmentality instruments. Neo-institutionalism analyzed that institutional arrangements matter and that EU integration is also shaped by institutions through the role of institutional paths (history), discourses and actors, which considerably complicates the picture encapsulated in the traditional "domestic interests vs. bureaucratic expansion" opposition (see MacRae in this volume).

While these theories focus on bottom-up processes (Börzel and Risse 2003, 55), new research objects emerged as result of the EU's geographical and political expansion. Those primarily concern the relation of the EU to its parts – member states and regions with legislative capacity, but also to candidate countries and, ultimately, countries covered by the ENP in so far they are exposed to the influence of EU institutions and European law on their own internal orders. Thus, Europeanization initially emerged by changing the lens on integration: from the "uploading" of policy competency and interests' intermediation from the state to the supra-national level to the "downloading" of EU norms, ways of doing things and how it affects (sub)national *policies* (including policy standards, instruments and narratives), *politics* (including processes of interest aggregation and intermediation) and *polities* (including political and judicial institutions or public administration).

These top-down approaches initially explored the degrees of *convergence* of domestic pol-icies and polities with EU norms. Through case studies carried out on different countries and policy areas, Europeanization scholars explored how the "goodness of fit" (Cowles et al. 2001) between the European and the domestic level determines the degree of adaptational pressure generated by Europeanization on member states. They considered the validity of the idea that "the lower the compatibility (…), the higher the adaptational pressure" (Börzel and Risse 2003, 5). Elaborating on rational choice and sociological institutionalism, such works evidenced two competing, yet not mutually exclusive logics: domestic change as a process of resource redis-tribution, by which domestic actors make use of the windows of opportunities opened by the misfit between national and EU norms, and/or as a process of socialization and learning by which those actors are exposed (notably via norm entrepreneurs or epistemic communities) to new rules, norms, practices or meanings, which they have to incorporate into their own practices or structures.

This discussion has been supported by numerous ever-finer grained studies which have revealed a myriad of configurations for domestic change, evidencing that domestic actors do not fit EU incentives smoothly, and underlining the specificities of the EU accession context. However, many of these studies fail to answer *why* policy change happens. Few works have adopted a broader, normative focus, driven by the strong conditionality of the EU accession process linked to the 1993 Copenhagen Criteria (Hillion 2014; see also Chiva in this volume) and the Eastern Enlargement (Schimmelfennig and Sedelmeier 2005). Falkner and Treib (2008) attempted to draw different regimes − or "worlds" − of *compliance* among member states and candidate countries, based on variables such as domestic policy styles or institutional paths. But the "world of dead letters" they described for those countries, where adaptation to the EU norm often amounts to lip service, incidentally matched with (candidate) countries endowed with more complicated and/or recent paths to market democracy, contradicting the "goodness of fit" approach and raising suspicion of culturalist biases.

The Europeanization literature has become a fast-growing sub-field of European studies, despite (or possibly due to) its lack of a clear focus. Definitions flourished to capture this con-ceptual complexity, some being more authoritative than others, as Radaelli's definition of Europeanization as

> processes of a) construction, b) diffusion and c) institutionalization of formal and informal rules, procedures, policy paradigms, styles, 'ways of doing things' and shared beliefs and norms which are first defined and consolidated in the EU policy process and then incorporated in the logic of domestic (national and subnational) discourse, political structures and public policies.
>
> *(Radaelli 2004, 3)*

However, such an extensive definition did not help clarify whether Europeanization was a new theory (Börzel and Risse 2003) or a mere principle for organizing empirical findings (Radaelli 2004).

Clarification attempts all fell short and disputes have regularly ensued around the degree of concept-stretching and the usefulness of the concept (for example, Radaelli 2000, 2012). Critiques have argued that Europeanization too often involves simply studying convergence/compliance with EU rule. Others show that the concept is often used in a very loose way to address how advanced a polity should be considered vis-à-vis European standards of democracy, or highlight how Europeanization as a concept fails to establish causal mechanisms between EU and domestic variables (Exadaktylos and Radaelli 2012).

A more fundamental critique undermines the status of Europeanization as a fully-fledged theory: arguably, Europeanization draws on other, more established theories for building its own hypotheses and gets operationalized. A large portion of the Europeanization literature has indeed developed at the intersection of different types of new institutionalism (Hall and Taylor 1996): historical, rational choice, sociological and discursive institutionalism (Schmidt 2008, 2010). Elaborating on these three older "new institutionalisms," Schmidt's discursive institutionalism has proven to be the most useful for understanding Europeanization. It attempts to reconcile ideas and institutions by focusing on discourses as mediating factors for explaining why, how and when political actors internalize EU norms by exchanging ideas and (re)framing their strategic interests within the institutional settings in which they act. Schmidt's insights thus help to tackle one of the Europeanization unanswered question: Under which circumstances and in which direction does domestic policy change occur? The over-representation of these four new institutionalist streams in Europeanization literature limited its capacity to evolve towards a new "grand theory" of European integration. As a further evidence of its dubious status, while new institutionalisms all feature along with older theories in the latest edition of Wiener, Börzel and Risse (2019), Europeanization does not; it is only addressed as a mere phase of European integration history.

Despite these limitations, Europeanization studies have contributed to shaping scholarly interest for the largely unexpected ways "Europe hits home", usefully broadening our understanding of European integration as both a bottom-up *and* top-down process. Europeanization as convergence was quickly challenged by eastern enlargement, which dramatically increased the diversity of historical experiences, party systems, welfare states, policy styles or gender regimes, despite its unprecedented conditionality (Caporaso 2008). The real-life experiment of 11 countries – including nine post-socialist states – joining the EU between 2004 and 2013 thus demonstrated that divergence and norm contestation are the rule, rather than the exception.

Europeanization through a gender lens: "going soft" vs. meaning contestation

Gender is a good test case for Europeanization. Gender scholarship has actively contributed to Europeanization's fortune, especially if compared to its earlier, rather limited contribution to theorizing integration (Kronsell 2012). This is certainly due to the attention paid – both from gender and politics and from EU scholars – to the consolidation of gender equality as a pillar of the European Employment Strategy (1994) and as an objective of the Union enshrined in the 1997 Amsterdam Treaty, and the corresponding adoption of gender mainstreaming by EU institutions, policies and (funding) instruments. As the EU was expanding the implementation of gender equality through the broader agenda of non-discrimination held in the new directives adopted from 2000 onwards (see Solanke in this volume), it provided member states and subnational entities with a broad set of incentives for Europeanizing gender. Those included treaty provisions, directives, European Court of Justice's case law (see Guth and Elfving in this volume), and one of EU's most sophisticated soft instrument: gender mainstreaming. For EU integration scholars (Mazey 1998, 2000; Pollack and Hafner-Burton 2000; Shaw 2000), gender equality policies perfectly fitted the spill-over narrative, as EU institutions had found in gender equality their "Trojan horse" for expanding competencies from the market to social policies (Hoskyns 1996). From a neo-institutionalist perspective, mainstreaming gender throughout EU policies and funds offered a number of scenarios for the dual logic of consequence and appropriateness of Europeanization to unfold (Beveridge 2012; Jacquot 2010). Women's interests' intermediation through the European Women's Lobby also received some attention, mainly at EU level (Helfferich and Kolb 2001; see also Lang in this volume).

Initially, few studies discussed national implementation of EU gender equality policies; the first attempts explicitly focusing on the Europeanization of gender and anti-discrimination policies mostly came from the Europeanization literature (Caporaso and Jupille 2001; Geddes and Guiraudon 2004). Liebert (2003) coordinated the first substantial contribution from gender scholarship. In her study, feminist institutionalism was mobilized to map Europeanization patterns in the field of gender equality policies in six member states, identifying three drivers to the Europeanization of gender equality policies: *institutional* (EU legislation, policy and legal sentences); *cognitive* (frames that help mobilizing public opinion and reframing public policy issues); and *interaction* mechanisms (related to developing political representation and building transnational advocacy networks). Liebert's mechanism-based theoretical framework thus attempted to bring together two different strands in Europeanization literature through a gender lens: the top-down strand, focused on convergence, and the horizontal/comparative strand, focused on contestation. With its increased diversity in terms of institutional legacies and gender regimes, eastern enlargement also prompted interest for Europeanizing gender in (new) member states (Krizsán 2009; Roth 2008) as well as for comparisons between the latest enlargement waves in terms of EU gender equality *acquis* transposition (Galligan and Clavero 2012). More recently, the Europeanization of gender interest intermediation also received some attention, for example through the "NGO-ization" of ILGA-Europe, the umbrella of LGBT organizations in Europe (Paternotte 2016).

Gender scholars have engaged with Europeanization literature most directly through *discursive institutionalism*, emphasizing the role of ideas and discourses in shaping political change in order to make sense of Europeanization as *conflict*. Lombardo and Kantola (in this volume) illustrate that discursive politics approaches have flourished (Bacchi 2009; Kantola 2010; Lombardo et al. 2009; Verloo 2007). Rather than approaching discourses as mere rhetorical devices, these scholars have focused on their meaning and contestation, showing that concepts like gender equality have no essential meaning but are rather shaped by political goals. Changes in meaning result from the activities of different policy actors trying to steer the concept's meaning in their intended direction through different strategic framings adapted to specific political and institutional contexts. These approaches, which consider frames not only as intentional strategic interventions to shape discourses but also as *unintentional* (based on deeply entrenched gender norms or stereotypes, for instance), have permeated the analysis of Europeanization of gender equality policies.

Lombardo and Forest (2012) attempted to bring this agenda forward, developing a common analytical framework for studies carried out so far on parallel tracks. Simultaneously, they also sketched a first research agenda for gendering Europeanization studies. Initiated under the EU-funded QUING project, this framework has been pursued since then by scholars located in different parts of the enlarged EU and working on a wide range of issues such as, for example, gender-based violence (Kriszan and Popa 2010), the politics of gender at the subnational level (Alonso 2017), the institutionalization of intersectionality (Kriszan et al. 2012) or the politics of LGBTQ rights (Kuhar 2012).

While 'Europeanization as contention' has largely pervaded the analytical frameworks of gender scholars, the opposite does not apply to the same extent, even as (female) European integration scholars well positioned in the field (Abels and Mushaben 2012; Abels and MacRae 2016) have called for the gendering of Europeanization in theory and practice. This is mainly to be addressed as the result of the most recent trends in Europeanization literature leading to stretching the concept further in empirical and geographical terms.

De-Europeanization? Gendering Europe in troubled times

Times have changed in addressing the Europeanization of domestic policies, politics and polities. The Euro-debt crisis has left profound divisions, evidencing the limits of European solidarity (see Kantola and Lombardo in this volume). These wounds have been revived by the 2015 migratory (Schengen) crisis (see Krause and Schwenken in this volume) and, even more recently, by the initial lack of EU coordination in responding to the Covid-19 pandemic. Brexit has shown that the integration of the continent was not a one-way process but could be reversed at any moment by a majority vote in any of the EU member states – with severe gender consequences (see Guerrina and Masselot in this volume). The legal disputes arising from coordinated attacks on the EU's rule of law demonstrate that eastern enlargement has not fully bridged the East–West divide, and has contributed to a redefinition of political cleavages around different understandings of *Europeanness* throughout Europe.

The multiple crises have monopolized much of the EU agenda for the past decade, leaving little space for expanding social and civil rights or challenging inequalities. From 2009 to 2019, no major policy innovation has thus been pushed forward by the European Commission (see Hartlapp et al. in this volume). The initiatives that have passed have been of mixed success. The 2017 Social Summit, the first in 20 years, led to the adoption of the European Pillar of Social Rights, but this was heavily criticized for its non-legally binding nature and lack of ambition. In 2015, a directive aiming at expanding maternity leave to 18 weeks was withdrawn. Four years later in June 2019, Directive 2019/1158 on work–life balance for parents and carers was adopted, but many of the innovations proposed by the European Commission had been removed due to the opposition from some member states (Chieregato 2020). Whether this directive will constitute a new landmark remains to be seen, especially as welfare states have been put under even greater pressure in the aftermath the Covid-19 crisis.

Similarly, after the 2013 accession of Croatia to the EU, the pace and geographical scope of eastern enlargement have been increasingly contested, relegating the Balkan states to the margins, as shown by the 2019 rebuke in the European Council to open accession negotiations with Albania and North Macedonia (a decision reversed in March 2020). Following armed conflicts with Russia ignited in 2008 and 2014, Georgia and Ukraine remain caught in the nets of the ENP, with very little chance to join the club. Turkey, officially still a candidate country, has demonstrated an ever greater defiance towards the EU, especially in relation to the war in Syria and the control of refugees' paths to Europe. Even inside the club, European scholars have struggled to understand self-proclaimed (Hungary, Poland) and "wannabe" (until recently, Romania and Slovakia) illiberal democracies viewing (top-down) Europeanization as the ultimate evil (see also Siim and Fiig in this volume).

If the "ever closer Union" branded in the EU treaties and the enlargement process have both lost their compass, where does this leave Europeanization? Ironically, the weakness of the concept makes it possible for it to be redefined as a process through which references to EU values, legislation and policies become an asset for political *conflict*. These conflicts may arise when the EU's core principles – the rule of law, freedom of movement, intra-European solidarity or gender equality are being renegotiated, contested and stretched in order to fit reactionary political aims that may be pursued by forces fundamentally opposed to EU integration.

Europeanization "beyond Europe", as conflict or "De-Europeanization"

As a result, the research agenda has largely shifted from top–down approaches, once the trademark of Europeanization, to more bottom-up perspectives. The focus of these perspectives covers a wide range, from assessing different degrees of convergence, to conflicting usages of references to EU norms and policy framework, and from a scenario of greater integration to competing scenarios of *disintegration*. From a Europeanization perspective, this does not mean that the EU no longer affects interest intermediation and national polities, but that its impact can hardly be viewed as generating predictable effects. EU law still prevails, but it is increasingly contested. Domestic agents continue to refer to EU law and policies, but frequently use these to support their views opposing further integration. Policies implemented at the (sub)national level still bear the mark of EU recommendations, methods and funding, but those no longer provide sufficient legitimacy to prevent divergence and conflict. Whereas new efforts are invested in theorizing crises (Wiener 2019, 262), Europeanization scholars focus on different directions.

First, Europeanization expanded towards less politically loaded fields such as climate, energy or research and innovation policies. Although politics also matters in those fields, the pressing and multi-faceted reality of climate change, or the geopolitics of energy and innovation in which the EU member states have a shared understanding of the threats posed by isolationist US and aggressive China and Russia, have led to increasing the pace of EU integration in those areas, with growing convergence as a result.

Second, numerous studies address Europeanization *outside* the EU and candidate countries in countries covered either by the ENP or EU international development policies, where despite the multiple crises in which it has been lately submerged, the Union remains a powerfully attractive supranational entity. As the EU has also become an important actor of international development, its impact both on member states development agencies or NGOs, and in beneficiary countries, has been increasingly assessed in terms of Europeanization (see Debusscher in this volume). Understandably, the geographical expansion of Europeanization beyond the EU or even *beyond Europe* (Schimmelfennig 2012) contributes to further blurring the concept, leaving it frequently disconnected from European integration dynamics.

A third trend consists in focusing on conflicts of norms, rather than norm adaptation. The litmus case brought to 'Europeanization as conflict' is Turkey, where a fully-fledged process of *de-Europeanization* appears to have been reinforced since the failed coup attempt of July 2016 (Gurkan 2019). This process evidences that even in those areas where convergence had been relatively far-reaching, reversal can happen, triggered by the rejection of norms and principles powering the rationale of EU policies. Conflicts around the rule of law, independence of the judiciary or freedom of the press in central European countries also provide case studies to empirically analyze how different usages of the reference to Europe (as a body of values and institutions or a culture under threat) compete, challenging foundational principles such as the supremacy of EU law.

While studying Europeanization only in those areas where convergence prevails, outside Europe or primarily as conflict should lead to posing crucial theoretical questions, it is worth underlying that above outlined streams essentially correspond to empirically oriented research and have not yet materialized in fully articulated theorization efforts.

Reflecting new trends in the Gender and EU scholarship

The gender and EU literature reflects these trends to a different extent. With respect to the first, less politically loaded policy fields, we can observe that whereas an increased number of scholars are tackling the gendered dimension of climate change, there are few works that have addressed this dimension in the field of EU policies. Allwood (2014; in this volume), for instance, underlines the persistent invisibility of gender in EU climate change policy, despite endorsing the role of champion both on advancing gender equality and fighting climate change. Similarly, Linková and Mergaert (in this volume) show that in the area of research and innovation policies the gender agenda has gained momentum for two decades since the EU Commission's first communication on women in science (1999). While there is an extensive literature on the rationale for such a policy, relatively little has been written about the gendered impact from a Europeanization lens. Abels and Mushaben (2012) and Mergaert and Minto (2015) highlighted the gap between the gender agenda brought forward by the EU Commission to the member states and the research sector, and the degree to which it permeates its own policy instruments such as framework programmes and funding schemes. Mergaert and Lombardo (2014) took this agenda forward by analyzing the specific resistances opposed to gendering EU research policies, again primarily at the level of EU Commission services. To date, national (or sub-national) policy settings have been primarily addressed through grey literature (EIGE 2015), evidencing a variegated landscape where, despite the diversity of academic and research environments as well as country-specific resistances, Europeanization keeps generating convergence. Beyond those isolated contributions it is yet arguably the last stream, i.e. "Europeanization as contention" or conflict, that offers more avenues for the gender and Europeanization scholarships to interact.

Gender scholars interested in the impact of EU norms, policies and soft instruments appear to be especially well-equipped to make sense of the unexpected impacts of Europeanization dynamics. Key aspects include the role of soft policy instruments developed in the fields of gender equality and anti-discrimination, in shaping gender advocates' agendas, cognitive learning processes, repertoires of contention and discursive references to the EU. Gender mainstreaming has been supported by the unfolding of EU gender equality strategies, the incorporation of gender equality into structural (such as the Social European Fund) and regional funding schemes, as well as in some specific EU policies such as research and innovation. Beyond providing insight into the multi-layered impact of soft policy instruments, this scholarship also highlights that these processes are far from producing homogeneous effects and do not occur without contention and resistances.

Another crucial contribution is that references to the EU legal and policy order can be mobilized by domestic actors: (1) even in the absence of any EU hard law (or policy) on a specific issue and (2) by both supporters and opponents of convergence with the EU norms. Evidence now abounds that during the latest EU enlargement round, initiated in 2004, gender advocates in parliamentary politics or civil society have discursively framed their claims by referring to EU accession conditionality or 'Europeanization as modernization' even in the absence of EU hard law. This was the case, for example, in passing legislation on gender-based violence, (Kriszan and Popa 2010), or in the battle for same-sex marriage recognition (Forest 2018).

The backlash on gender rights in several central and eastern European member states has further shown that discursive–sociological approaches derived both from neo-institutionalism and feminist institutionalism are well-fitted to grasp the complex "usages" of Europe. In Hungary and Poland, antagonistic references to the EU are thus mobilized both to support gender rights *and* by those defending a concept of Europeanness rooted in traditional Christian family values, which EU norms and institutions are believed to undermine (as in the case of the countries' veto against EU accession to the Istanbul Convention on violence against women; see Roggeband in this volume). In Croatia (2013), Romania and Slovakia (2015), these discursive frames of Europeanization were pitted against each other during debates over the (non)recognition of same-sex marriage and the enshrinement of heterosexual marriage in the constitutions. In Croatia, this debate followed immediately on an earlier referendum in which EU membership had been approved by a wide margin. A similar majority approved the Church-supported bid for constitutionalizing heteronormative marriage. During the campaign conservative voices carefully crafted their message, insisting that the recognition of same-sex marriage went far beyond EU requirements on gender-related issues (Kuhar 2012). Additionally, the implications of the De-Europeanization process in Turkey for gender equality have been extensively covered in Süleymanoğlu-Kürüm and Cin (2020).

Towards a common research agenda: gender, the new cleavage of Europe?

With the surge of right-wing populisms, many with a clear anti-gender agenda, across Europe, as well as the unprecedented challenges to European integration posed by the Covid-19 pandemic, the analytical apparatus developed by the gender and Europeanization literature can make a crucial, but as of yet undefined, contribution to the field. As shown in Liebert (2016, 167), in the aftermath of the Euro-debt crisis, gender approaches to Europeanization provided lessons "on how to make gender equality work despite the double pressure of fiscal consolidation and (…) structural reforms on the one hand, and the present anti-feminist, anti-modern tide of Euroscepticism on the other hand" and thus "help rebuild citizen's trust in the EU." As both debt and trust deficits are deepening, it is again necessary to underline that the gender and EU scholarship does not occupy the position it should in assessing the current stage of EU integration. Its long-standing interest in, and capacity for, addressing 'Europeanization as contention' through diverging discursive and political usages of Europe on domestic and transnational EU polities, as well as its focus on one of the most cross-cutting cleavages in an ever-more divided Europe, makes it especially well-placed for this research.

From the mid-2010s, gender equality has generated unprecedented mobilizations (Kuhar and Paternotte 2018) with multiple demonstrations drawing in millions (Spain) or hundreds of thousands (Poland, Ireland, Switzerland) of participants. Opposition to granting gender rights has also mobilized large crowds in France (millions of participants in the *Manif pour Tous* demonstrations, protesting same-sex marriage legislation) or Poland (tens of thousands to support family values). Referenda called by broad-based unions of conservative forces and backed by the Catholic church to oppose state legislation on same-sex marriage (Slovenia) or support constitutionalizing heterosexual marriage (Croatia, Slovakia and Romania) have also mobilized large numbers, some of them (in Croatia and Slovenia) eventually achieved their goals. This opposition plays a central role in the rhetoric of the most recent wave of far-right populist parties, even in countries that usually rank among the most progressive on gender issues, including Finland, Spain and the Netherlands.

The politicization of gender rights in relation to the defence of nationhood and ethnic homogeneity, traditional values, Christian Europe against the alleged threats of Islamization or secularization is no longer confined to post-socialist Europe, but is increasingly pervading the discourse of anti-establishment political forces in southern, continental and northern Europe. Social media and other non-conventional mobilization strategies for which gender patterns appear to play a great role, facilitate this politicization, and may give masculinist and anti-feminist claims an unprecedented influence on new party programmes. Gender scholarship also highlights that nationalist and ultra-conservative forces engage in strategies of cooptation of the gender rights agenda(s), in the name of European values, articulating women's and LGBTQI's rights as worthy of protection from the alleged rise of non-European populations. This was repeatedly shown during the recent migratory crisis.

Such blatant contradictions are of great relevance to analyzing the current stage of European politics and polities, but they cannot be understood without insights from the gender literature This should not be done only from the perspective of comparative politics, tackling the populist challenge to Europe (see Siim and Fiig in this volume), but also through the gender and Europeanization literature, which brings together institutional, cognitive, behavioral and discursive elements to shed light on how the battle over gender rights has become the new game in town, and drawing out competing usages of Europe in the domestic politics of gender equality (Liebert 2016, 161).

Similarly, the politics of sanction, unfolding between the European Commission and Hungary and Poland for breach of the rule of law, need also be read through a broader context where the politicization of gender rights plays a key role. Even the ENP and EU foreign policies appear to be captured by this cross-cutting cleavage over gender issues. Although primarily aimed at provoking divisions rather than achieving concrete goals, the aggressive political agenda of Russia towards the EU, can hardly be understood without referring to the notion of "gayropa" articulated by Russian foreign policy theorists (Foxall 2019). This vision presents Russia and its allies as the refuge of the hierarchical sexual order, in contrast to a corrupted EU, which is embodied by its policies and institutions that propagate "gender theory" (Moss 2018). This, however, does not mean that the relation of the EU to its margins should be only understood through this clash of norms and discourses. From a post-colonial perspective, Kunz and Maisenbacher (2015) analyze the ambivalence of the EU itself, arguing that colonial practices of Othering and hierarchical Self-Other definitions are also being reproduced through the ENP.

Several questions remain. What are the potential theoretical implications of these political developments? And which way forward? On every single of those topics the gender scholarship can bring valuable insights, including how the EU dis-/empowers itself by de-/legalizing soft policy instruments, as the case of EU gender equality strategies shows. But those contributions have not yet formed a coordinated agenda, nor do they necessarily belong to the realm of European studies. They have remained isolated from each other, carried out from a variety of perspectives including social movement literature and feminist discursive institutionalism. Considering the cross-cutting relevance of the politicization of gender rights in relation to the politics of EU (dis-)integration means that a more coordinated and multi-disciplinary agenda is necessary. This agenda could further contribute to analyzing the impact of Europe on domestic politics and polities, as well as transnational Europeanization paths for gender equality advocates and their opponents. Thus, there must be more intense theoretical interactions between gender scholars and Europeanization scholars.

Another important aspect of a potential common research agenda consists of the growing, although often ambivalent attention that gender scholars pay to intersecting inequalities. This attention has developed to a large extent among those researchers tackling the politics of gender in a European comparative perspective. They have demonstrated that, at the EU level, the shift from gender equality to broader anti-discrimination policies failed to materialize in something other than an uneven focus on multiple discriminations, while the member states and regions were expressing growing interest in tackling intersecting inequalities (Kriszan et al. 2012). Because it contradicts standard policy styles, intersectionality is seldom genuinely institutionalized. When it is mentioned, it is primarily found in soft instruments such as policy programmes or plans. Since the crisis of European integration is partly rooted in its failure to tackle a variety of inequality grounds as they *actually* interact with each other, it remains necessary to further investigate the institutionalization of intersectionality in Europe when gendering Europeanization theory. This endeavour is not only timely, but more urgent than ever as European integration has taken a dangerous path towards democratic delusion and dilution, and desperately requires a socially inclusive and genuinely democratic re-foundation.

References

Abels G, Mushaben J M, eds. (2012): *Gendering the European Union: New Approaches to Old Democratic Deficits*, Basingstoke: Palgrave Macmillan.

Abels G, McRae H, eds. (2016): *Gendering European Integration Theory: Engaging New Dialogues*. Opladen: Barbara Budrich Publishers.

Ágh A (2015): De-Europeanization and de-democratization trends in ECE: from the Potemkin democracy to the elected autocracy in Hungary, *Journal of Comparative Politics* **8** (2), 4–26.

Allwood G (2014): Gender Mainstreaming and EU Climate Change Policy, in: Weiner E, MacRae H (eds.): The Persistent Invisibility of Gender in EU Policy, *European Integration online Papers (EIoP)* **18**(1), 1–20, http://eiop.or.at/eiop/texte/2014-003a.htm.

Alonso A (2017): Who learns what from whom? Implementing gender mainstreaming in multi-level settings, *European Journal of Women's Studies,* **24** (2), 174–188.

Bacchi C (2009): The Issue of Intentionality in Frame Theory: The Need for Reflexive Framing, in: Lombardo E, Meier P, Verloo M (eds.): *The Discursive Politics of Gender Equality. Stretching, Bending and Policymaking*, London: Routledge, 19−35.

Beveridge F (2012): Going Soft? Analysing the Contribution of Soft and Hard Measures in EU Gender Law and Policy in: Lombardo E, Forest M (eds.): *The Europeanization of Gender Equality Policies. A Discursive-Sociological Approach*. Basingstoke: Palgrave Macmillan, 28–48.

Börzel T, Risse T (2002): When Europe Hits Home: Europeanization and Domestic Change *European Integration online Papers (EIoP)* **4**(15), http://eiop.or.at/eiop/texte/2000-015a.htm, 1–24.

Börzel T, Risse T (2003): Conceptualizing the Domestic Impact of Europe' in: Featherstone K, Radaelli C (eds.): *The Politics of Europeanisation,* Oxford, New York: Oxford University Press, 57–80.

Caporaso J (2008): The Three Worlds of Regional Integration Theory in: Graziano P, Vink M P (eds.): *Europeanization. New Research Agendas*, Basingstoke: Palgrave, 23–34.

Caporaso J, Jupille J (2001): The Europeanization of Gender Equality Policy and Domestic Structural Change in: Cowles, M G, Risse T, Caporaso J (eds.): *Transforming Europe. Europeanization and Domestic Change,* Ithaca, NY: Cornell University Press, 21–43.

Chieregato E (2020): A work–life balance for all? Assessing the inclusiveness of the EU Directive 2019/1158, *International Journal of Comparative Labour Law and Industrial Relations*, **36** (1), https://papers.ssrn.com/sol3/papers.cfm?abstract_id=3502888.

Cowles M G, Caporaso J, Risse T, eds. (2001): *Transforming Europe: Europeanization and Domestic Change*, Ithaca, NY: Cornell University Press.

EIGE (2015): *Analytical Paper on the Integration of Gender Equality and Gender Mainstreaming in Research Performing Organizations in the EU28*, European Institute for Gender Equality (EIGE) and DG Research, European Commission.

Exadaktylos T, Radaelli C, eds. (2012): *Research Design in European Studies: Establishing Causality in Europeanization*, Basingstoke: Palgrave Macmillan.

Falkner G, Treib O (2008): Three worlds of compliance or four? The EU15 compared to new member states, *Journal of Common Market Studies* **46** (2), 293–314.

Forest M (2018): Europeanizing vs. Nationalizing the Issue of Same-Sex Marriage in Central Europe: A Comparative Analysis of Framing Processes in Croatia, Hungary, Slovakia and Slovenia, in: Winter B, Forest M, Sénac R (eds.): *Global Perspective on Same-sex Marriage*, Global queer politics series, Basingstoke: Palgrave Macmillan, 127–148.

Foxall A (2019): From Europa to Gayropa: A Critical Geopolitics of the European Union as Seen from Russia, *Geopolitics* **24** (1), 174–193.

Galligan Y, Clavero S (2012): Gendering Enlargement of the EU, in: Abels G, Mushaben J M, (eds.): *Gendering the European Union: New Approaches to Old Democratic Deficits*, Basingstoke: Palgrave Macmillan, 104–125.

Geddes A, Guiraudon V (2004): Britain, France, and EU anti-discrimination policy: the emergence of an EU policy paradigm, *West European Politics* **27** (2), 334–353.

Gurkan S (2019): De-Europeanization through Securitization: Discursive framings of Europe and EU values in Turkey, The European Consortium for Political Research (ECPR), Joint sessions (April 8–12, 2019: Mons, Belgium).

Hall P, Taylor R (1996): Political science and the three new institutionalisms, *Political Studies* **44** (5), 952–973.

Helfferich B, Kolb F (2001): Multilevel Action Coordination in European Contentious Politics: the Core of the European Women's Lobby in: Imig D, Tarrow S (eds.): *Contentious Europeans: Protest and Politics in an Integrating Europe,* Lanham, MD: Rowman & Littlefield, 143–162.

Hillion C (2014): The Copenhagen Criteria and Their Progeny, in: Hillion C (ed.): *EU Enlargement,* Oxford: Hart Publishing, 3–26.

Hoskyns C (1996): *Integrating Gender. Women, Law and Politics in the European Union,* London, New York: Verso.

Jacquot S (2010): The paradox of gender mainstreaming: unanticipated effects of new modes of governance in the gender equality domain, *West European Politics* **33** (1), 118–135.

Kantola J (2010): *Gender and the European Union,* Basingstoke: Palgrave Macmillan.

Krizsán A (2009): From formal adoption to enforcement. Post-accession shifts in EU impact on Hungary in the equality policy field, *European Integration online Papers (EIoP),* Special Issue 2, **13** (22), http://eiop.or.at/eiop/texte/2009-022a.htm.

Krizsán A, Popa R (2010): Europeanization in making policies against domestic violence in central and eastern Europe, *Social Politics* **17** (3), 379–406.

Krizsán A, Skjeie H, Squires J (2012): *Institutionalizing Intersectionality. The Changing Nature of European Equality Regimes,* Basingtoke: Palgrave Macmillan.

Kronsell A (2012): Gendering Theories of European Integration, in: Abels G, Mushaben J M (eds.): *Gendering the European Union: New Approaches to Old Democratic Deficits,* Basingstoke: Palgrave Macmillan, 23–40.

Kuhar R. (2012): Use of the Europeanization Frame in Same-Sex Partnership Across Europe, in: Lombardo E, Forest M (eds.): *The Europeanization of Gender Equality Policies: A Discursive-Sociological Approach,* Basingstoke: Palgrave Macmillan, 168–191.

Kuhar R, Paternotte D (2018): *Campagnes anti-genre en Europe. Des Mobilisations contre l'égalité,* Lyon: Presses universitaires.

Kunz R, Maisenbacher J (2015): Women in the neighbourhood: Reinstating the European Union's civilising mission on the back of gender equality promotion? *European Journal of International relations* **23** (1), 122–144.

Ladrech R (1994): Europeanization of domestic politics and institutions: the case of France, *Journal of Common Market Studies* **32** (1), 69–88.

Liebert U, ed. (2003): *Gendering Europeanization,* Brussels: Peter Lang.

Liebert U (2016): Gendering Europeanisation: Making Equality Work in Theory and Practice in: Abels G, MacRae H (eds.): *Gendering European Integration Theory,* Opladen: Barbara Budrich Publisher, 147–174.

Lombardo E, Meier P, Verloo M, eds. (2009): *The Discursive Politics of Gender Equality. Stretching, Bending and Policymaking,* London: Routledge.

Lombardo E, Forest M, eds. (2012): *The Europeanization of Gender Equality Policies, A Discursive – Sociological Approach,* Basingstoke: Palgrave Macmillan.

Mazey M (1998): The European Union and women's rights: from the Europeanization of national agendas to the nationalization of a European agenda?, *Journal of European Public Policy* **5**(1), 131–152.

Mazey S (2000): Introduction: integrating gender – intellectual and "real world" mainstreaming, *Journal of European Public Policy* **7** (3), 333–345.

Mény Y, Muller P, Quermonne J L (1996): *Adjusting to Europe. The Impact of the European Union on National Institutions and Policies,* London: Routledge.

Mergaert L, Lombardo E (2014): Resistance to implementing gender mainstreaming in EU research policy, in: Weiner E, MacRae H (eds.): The persistent invisibility of gender in EU policy, *European Integration online Papers* (EIoP), Special issue 1, **18** (5), 1–21, http://eiop.or.at/eiop/texte/2014-005a.htm.

Mergaert L, Minto R (2015): Ex ante and ex post evaluations: two sides of the same coin?: The case of gender mainstreaming in EU research policy, *European Journal of Risk Regulation* **6** (1), 47–56.

Moss K (2018): La Russie comme sauveuse de la civilisation européenne. 'Genre' et géopolitique des valeurs traditionnelles in: Kuhar R, Paternotte D (eds.): *Campagnes anti-genre en Europe. Des Mobilisations contre l'égalité,* Lyon: Presses universitaires, 269–290.

Paternotte D (2016): The NGOization of LGBT activism: ILGA-Europe and the Treaty of Amsterdam, *Social Movement Studies* **15** (4), 388–402.

Pollack M A, Hafner-Burton E (2000): Mainstreaming gender in the European Union, *Journal of European Public Policy* **7**, 432–456.

Radaelli C (2000): Whither Europeanisation? Concept Stretching and Substantive Change, *European Integration online Papers* **4** (8), 1–28, http://eiop.or.at/eiop/texte/2000-008a.htm.

Radaelli C (2004): Europeanisation: Solution or Problem? *European Integration online Papers* **8** (16), 1–26, http://eiop.or.at/eiop/texte/2004-016a.htm.

Radaelli C (2012): Europeanization: The Challenge of Establishing Causality, in: Exadaktylos T, Radaelli C (eds.): *Research Design in European Studies: Establishing Causality in Europeanization*, Basingstoke: Palgrave Macmillan, 1–16.

Roth S, ed. (2008): *Gender Politics in the Expanding European Union. Mobilization, Inclusion, Exclusion*, Oxford, New York: Berghahn Books.

Schimmelfennig F, Sedelmeier U, eds. (2005): *The Europeanization of Central and Eastern Europe: the Impact of the European Union on Candidate Countries*, Ithaca, NY: Cornell University Press.

Schimmelfennig F (2012): Europeanization beyond Europe, *Living Reviews in European Governance* **7**(1), http://www.livingreviews.org/lreg-2012-1 (Access date: August 16, 2019).

Schmidt V (2008): Discursive institutionalism: The explanatory power of ideas and discourse, *Annual Review of Political Science* **11**, 303–326.

Schmidt V (2010): Taking ideas and discourse seriously: explaining change through discursive institutionalism as the fourth "new institutionalism", *European Political Science Review* **2** (1), 1–25.

Shaw J (2000): Importing gender: the challenge of feminism and the analysis of the EU legal order, *Journal of European Public Policy* **7** (3), 406–431.

Süleymanoğlu-Kürüm R, Melis C eds. (2020): Feminist Framing of Europeanization. Gender Equality Policies in Turkey and the EU, Basingtoke: Palgrave Macmillan.

Verloo M, ed. (2007): *Multiple Meanings of Gender Equality: A Critical Frame Analysis of Gender Policies in Europe*, Budapest: CPS Books.

Wiener A (2019): Taking Stock of Integration Theory, in: Wiener A, Börzel T, Risse T (eds.): *European Integration Theory*, 3rd ed., Oxford: Oxford University Press, 256–272.

Wiener A, Börzel T, Risse T, eds. (2019): *European Integration Theory*, 3rd ed., Oxford: Oxford University Press.

Woll C, Jacquot S (2010): Using Europe: strategic action in multi-level politics, *Comparative European Politics* **8** (1), 110–126.

4

Social constructivism

Emanuela Lombardo and Johanna Kantola

Social constructivism is well suited to address continuous changes in European integration. As political processes such as the 2008 economic crisis in Europe and Brexit show, theorising a polity in continuous transformation requires analytical approaches capable of grasping this social construction, its structures and agents. Despite such contributions to theorising European integration, core issues are neglected when social constructivism does not integrate gender.

Why is gender a key analytical lens to theorise integration from social constructivist perspectives? What are the contributions of feminist approaches to social constructivism in European Integration theory? In this chapter we argue that feminist social constructivist approaches show that the social construction of the EU and the integration process – with its structures, agents, and discourses – is gendered, that EU socially constructed norms have gender and intersectional effects on people, and that power relations between women and men in the EU are central to understanding inequalities in the process of European integration.

The chapter introduces mainstream approaches to social constructivism in European Integration theory in the following section, identifying what they miss out by not incorporating gender as an analytical lens. It then discusses the contribution of feminist approaches, in particular from gender, intersectional, and deconstructionist perspectives, and how these approaches deepen and expand our theorising about the social construction of EU polity, politics, and policy.

Mainstream approaches to social constructivism in European Integration theory

In this section, we introduce the mainstream approaches to social constructivism in European Integration theory and their role as 'openers' for feminist approaches, but also their limitations. By discussing three main commonalities of social constructivist studies – social construction in continuous change, mutual constitution of agents and structures, and role of meanings, norms, and discourses – we point out what these mainstream approaches miss in their understanding of European integration by neglecting feminist approaches.

Social constructivism and gender approaches are potentially good allies. They both address the EU as a socially constructed reality, the former with an emphasis on the social construction of institutions, processes, and actors, as well as the effects of social 'norms and institutions on individuals, and the latter with a focus on the gendering of such social construction and effects, with particular attention to roles, norms, and power between the people (Galligan 2019; Hoskyns 2004; Kronsell 2012; Locher and Prügl 2009, 2001; Lombardo 2016). While the first gender works make explicit their compatibility with mainstream approaches to social constructivism in understanding the EU (Hoskyns 2004; Kronsell 2005), recognising that constructivism opened the way 'for gender perspectives to enter the mainstream' (Hoskyns 2004, 228), social constructivist studies of European integration do not show the same familiarity with gender analyses of the EU (see Abels and MacRae 2016; Galligan 2019; Hoskyns 2004). By neglecting gender approaches, mainstream social constructivist approaches miss out important analytical insights in their understanding of integration. While the latter are discussed in the next section, this section introduces the features of mainstream approaches.

Social constructivism enters European Integration theory at the end of the 1990s from the discipline of International Relations, which shares sociology's insights about the social construction of reality (Onuf 1989; Rosamond 2000). This 'approach' is employed in different ways depending on the epistemological perspective of researchers, ranging from more reflectivist and discourse-centred approaches, addressing how discourses construct social reality and affect people, to more rationalist, actor-centred approaches, focussing on how actors use ideas to pursue their interests (Kantola and Lombardo 2018; Saurugger 2014; Smith 2001).

Notwithstanding these differences, mainstream approaches to social constructivism share three main ideas: (1) European integration is a social construction that is continuously changing and that results from social interaction; (2) agents and structures are mutually constituted; and (3) ideas, discourses, and meanings are essential elements to understand policy change in Europe (Risse 2019; Rosamond 2013, 2001; Saurugger 2014; Schmidt 2011; Wæver 2004; Wiener et al. 2019).

Considering European integration as a constantly changing social construction means understanding processes of change as the result of social interaction between political actors, through which EU norms are constructed, contested, and diffused within the EU political community (Christiansen et al. 2001; Saurugger 2014). Social constructivists consider integration as a 'socialisation and learning process' in which Europeans become socialised in the EU polity, internalise EU social norms, and this social learning influences the formation of actors' interests and identities (Risse 2004; Rosamond 2001; Saurugger 2014, 152; Schmidt 2011).

The mutual constitution of agents and structures is a key feature of social constructivism. It implies that EU institutions and social norms influence agents' daily practices and social interactions (Chryssochoou et al. 2003; Risse 2004), according to a sociological institutionalist 'logic of appropriateness' that moves actors to conform to rules of appropriate behaviour (March and Olsen 1989). The constitutive effects of EU norms move actors socialised in European contexts to learn 'the rules of appropriate behaviour in the Union', becoming more Europeanised, and constructing their identity as Europeans together with other multiple identity markers (Börzel and Risse 2003; Risse 2004, 164; Saurugger 2014). However, agents can change the structures in which they act and, through processes of social interaction, modify their interests (that constructivists consider 'endogenous'), practices, and identities (Rosamond 2000). This is how the EU has been built and how its institutions and norms have evolved over time (Risse 2004).

Social constructivism attributes a central role to ideas, discourses, and meanings for understanding dynamics of policy change in Europe (Schmidt 2002, 2011). The ways in which discursive approaches are employed differs among European Integration theorists (see Saurugger 2014), including Habermasian's communicative rationality in which actors are open to change their preferences if they are persuaded by the power of good rhetorical arguments (Risse 2004), discourses as expressions of power relations that include some interpretations of an issue while excluding others (Wæver 2004), and actors' use of ideas of the EU to strategically legitimatise and promote specific interests and policy outcomes (Woll and Jacquot 2010). Applying the last two types, Rosamond's (2001) study about globalisation in the EU illustrates the variety of existing discourses about globalisation, the use of such discourses to promote specific interests such as discourses on the lack of alternative to neoliberal politics, and the framing of globalisation as a process that acquires internal meanings within the EU communicative space. Representative of the instrumental discursive approach to European integration, Schmidt's (2002) study illustrates how discourses, through influencing actors' preferences, contributed to promoting different policy change towards economic liberalisation in several EU member states exposed to the same EU market-making norms.

Mainstream social constructivist approaches have advanced theorising integration through their articulation of the EU as a social construction in continuous change, in which structures and agents are mutually constructed in social interaction, and ideas and discourses work as endogenous factors explaining policy change in Europe. However, by neglecting gender theories, they miss out the fact that EU institutions, agents, and discourses are gendered, that EU norms have gender and intersectional effects on people, and that power relations between different genders, between women and men in the EU, are central to understanding inequalities in the process of European integration (Hoskyns 2004; Kantola 2010; Kronsell 2012; Lombardo 2016; van der Vleuten 2012).

Gendering European Integration theory from social constructivist approaches

This section will discuss how feminist approaches contribute to the understanding of European integration from social constructivism theory, and how they widen and deepen our knowledge about the social construction of EU polity, politics, and policy.

Feminist approaches contribute by gendering the analysis of 'the political', that is of the 'distribution, exercise, and consequences of power' (Hay 2002, 3) and its contestations (Kantola and Lombardo 2017a). In particular, this means focusing on how power relations in the EU are gendered since they reproduce gender norms and biases that create gender hierarchies in the EU political arena (Hoskyns 2004; Kronsell 2012). Power is understood in feminist theories not only as power between institutions and governments but also, importantly, in terms of power between the people, a power that has consequences for the equality of different groups of people. At the same time, feminist approaches to integration conceptualise power as a relation of domination but also of transformation of such domination through women's agency (Allen 1999). Finally, feminist approaches show how 'the political' in EU policymaking ought to include the analysis of gender equality policy issues that were formerly considered 'personal', such as violence against women or care, on equal terms with other policy issues (Pateman 1983).

Of the variety of feminist approaches in what follows we consider particularly 'gender', 'deconstruction', and 'intersectionality' approaches, drawing on arguments developed in Kantola and Lombardo (2017a).[1] We suggest that these three feminist approaches offer fruitful insights on the European Integration theory of social constructivism: the first because of its focus on the social construction of gender, the second due to its specific affinity with social constructivist theories, and the third due to its broader concept of gender as intersecting with other inequalities. The three feminist approaches present the following characteristics.

'Gender' approaches treat gender as a social construction and understand gender inequalities as always related to wider societal structures, such as family, labour, or political institutions, and the gender norms and practices they produce. They contribute to theorising focussing on the analysis of the socially constructed unequal roles of women and men in the EU polity, of EU gender equality policies, and of the EU gender regime, with its gendered institutions, norms, and practices (Kronsell 2012; Walby 2009). Through theoretical developments in new institutionalism, feminist institutionalist scholars raise the crucial issue of informal, unwritten, gendered norms and practices creating obstacles to effective gender equality at work, in politics, and in all social spheres (see MacRae and Weiner in this volume; Chappell and Galea 2017; Chappell and Mackay 2017; Haastrup and Kenny 2016; Krook and Mackay 2011; Waylen 2017).

'Deconstructionist' approaches theorise gender as a discourse and a practice that has no fixed meaning but is continuously contested and constructed in political debates that attribute to it a variety of meanings (Bacchi 1999; Ferree 2012; Verloo 2007). They show that a problem such as gender inequality can be represented in EU policymaking in many different ways, with many different solutions, that gender issues can be silenced in political disputes, or that some policy solutions are favoured over others (Bacchi 1999; Lombardo et al. 2009). These discursive constructions have gendered effects on people, constructing norms that contribute to build hegemonies and marginalisation in the EU political community.

'Intersectional' approaches are concerned with inequalities, marginalisation and dominations that the interactions of gender, race/ethnicity, class and other systems of inequality produce (Collins and Chepp 2013; Crenshaw 1989; see Solanke in this volume). These approaches, developed in Black, lesbian and postcolonial feminist theorising and initiated by Crenshaw's (1989) coining of the term 'intersectionality', contribute to integration theory by analysing how the intersection of inequalities of gender, race, class or sexuality have consequences on the life opportunities of people living in the EU ('structural intersectionality'), and how different political, institutional, and social movements' strategies focusing on one inequality have effects on other inequalities ('political intersectionality') (Rolandsen Agustín 2013; Kantola and Nousiainen 2009).

Taken together, feminist approaches of 'gender', 'deconstruction', and 'intersectionality' are particularly apt to contribute to social constructivist theories of integration for the following two main reasons: firstly, they draw on theories of how gender, in intersection with other inequalities, is constructed in the EU through social and institutional practices; secondly, they pay specific attention to gender and intersectional norms, meanings, and power relations that are discursively constructed and contested in the EU political arena.

If the basic premise of constructivism in integration theory is that the EU polity, politics, and policy is a social construct in an ongoing process of change, feminist approaches share such an 'Ontology of becoming' (Locher and Prügl 2001, 114). Jo Shaw (2000) argues that the focus on the ongoing challenges of concepts, institutions, meanings, and social relationships characterising feminist approaches is particularly useful for theorising a constantly changing polity like the EU. In particular, feminist approaches contribute to integration theory through an analysis of the gender and intersectional relations, norms, and discourses as objects of ongoing contestation, construction, and transformation in EU policy debates (Kronsell 2012; Locher and Prügl 2009). For example, gender-blind analyses of crucial transformations in the EU integration process such as Brexit severely limit integration theory's potential for understanding the differentiated effects of this disintegration phenomenon on women and men with different socioeconomic, ethnic or sexual experiences (Guerrina et al. 2018, 254).

Gendering the mutual constitution of agents and structures is the contribution of feminist approaches to the second key premise of social constructivism. Agents and structures, feminist theorist contend, are not abstract nor gender neutral. Agents are embodied subjects, women and men intersected by race, class, sexuality and other inequalities, that interact with EU social and institutional structures that are gendered and thus produce gendered norms and practices (Rolandsen Agustín 2013). Feminist studies show that most powerful political actors in the EU are men – e.g. heads of state and government, commissioners, bankers, top civil servants. Simultaneously, they show that the structures of European economic and political integration tend to devalue women and minorities' experiences and needs, while they value those of men and the majority (Haastrup and Kenny 2016). The result of this genderedness of structures is that policy problems of gender equality and diversity are not top EU priorities, and this has effects on the lives of the different women and men in the EU. For example, the discrimination that women from ethnic minorities experience at work or in their social rights is not a priority in the EU agenda (Rolandsen Agustín 2013), even in times of economic crisis (Emejulu and Bassel 2017).

Feminist social constructivist analyses offer important insights on the gender and intersectional norms, meanings, and power relations that are discursively constructed and contested in the EU. Of the different varieties of social constructivism, feminist studies of EU policymaking have particularly developed a 'reflectivist' approach. This approach takes an interpretative position interested in exposing and reflecting on the role discourses play in the construction of reality and knowledge and its gender and intersectional dimensions, by privileging certain representations of the problem over others, certain gendered constructions of subjects, with differentiated effects on people (Kantola and Lombardo 2018). This interpretative stream draws on theoretical and methodological developments on the discursive politics of gender equality, that addresses the construction and contestation of the multiple meanings that different actors attribute to gender and intersectionality policy issues and gender knowledge produced and challenged in discursive processes (Bacchi 2009, 2017; Cavaghan 2017a; Ferree 2012; Kantola 2006; Krizsán et al. 2007; Lombardo et al. 2009; Verloo 2007).

Such reflectivist approaches are particularly effective for detecting and challenging unintentional gender norms and biases implicitly present in the EU political discourses; they can express sexist, heteronormative, or ethnocentric framings actors are not necessarily aware of as they have internalised these biases in the process of socialisation (Bacchi 2009, 2017; Lombardo et al. 2017; Verloo 2007). Such approaches have analytically contributed to the understanding of gender and intersectional norms and biases both implicitly and explicitly constructed in EU policymaking. They allow us to detect, for example, the EU implicit assumptions about the role of women as primarily carers and men as primarily workers (Lombardo and Meier 2008); they have also developed interpretative methodological innovations such as Bacchi's (1999) 'What's the Problem Represented to be?' approach, Verloo's (2007) Critical Frame Analysis or Cavaghan's (2017a) Gender Knowledge Contestation analysis.

These interpretative approaches contribute to social constructivism in integration theory by showing that the specific ways in which policy problems and solutions about gender equality are framed, or the type of knowledge about gender roles that is implicitly or explicitly put forward, are at the same time silencing alternative representations of a problem and solutions to it, thus limiting possibilities of change. For instance, Cavaghan's (2017a) feminist analysis of the European Commission DG Research's systematic exclusion of considerations about gender inequality in science allows us to understand how the institution supported the continuation of gender-biased practices that limit transformation towards gender equality. Rolandsen Agustín's (2013) frame analysis of EU policy documents on gender violence denounces the risk of stigmatising ethnic minority groups such as migrant Muslim women when EU policies frame the problem of gender violence in cultural ways by considering some types of gender violence as specific to certain ethnic groups rather than treating all manifestations of gender violence as part of the systematic phenomenon of men's domination over women. Such reflectivist discursive approaches can expand the interpretative potential of theorising integration, providing a better understanding of the social construction of the EU and its underpinning gender and intersectional norms.

Overall, feminist approaches from gender, deconstruction, and intersectionality perspectives make one simple but central contribution to social constructivism in integration theory: *power is gendered*. Hence, theorising the social construction of the EU polity, politics and policy will miss out important analytical insights, if gender and intersectionality are not integrated in the theoretical frameworks employed for understanding European integration. Guerrina et al. (2018, 255) clearly state that European Integration theories must adopt gender lenses to ensure that gender is understood not as a variable but rather as 'an intrinsic axis of power'.

Analysing processes of integration (and disintegration) in the EU *polity* will then require the use of concepts such as gender regime, that is a system of gender relations that attributes roles to women and men according to norms, policies, institutions and practices such as the male breadwinner and female caregiver (Walby 2009). Social constructivist studies offer analytical lenses to study how the gender regime and other inequality regimes work in the EU, how it interacts with the gender regimes of the different member states, with what effects on the implementation of EU policies (Kronsell 2012). For example, the EU economic regime in times of crisis has promoted changes in the gender regime (Klatzer and Schlager 2014; Walby 2015) that have promoted gendered and racialised hierarchies in the EU and its integration process (Cavaghan and O'Dwyer 2018), continuing the marginalisation of ethnic minority women's demands (Emejulu and Bassel 2017). The EU gender regime in times of crisis, in interaction with the gender regime of member states, has produced shifts at the national level towards more neoliberal gender regimes that are more exploitative of women's paid work and care (Lombardo 2017; Rubery 2014; Wöhl 2014). In Spain, for example, the EU and Spain's government's austerity politics have promoted a shift of the Spanish gender regime towards more neoliberal public forms, through neoliberal labour reforms, privatisations, labour precariousness, enhanced inequality in the labour market and the quality of employment, and cuts and retrenchment in the welfare state and gender equality policies (Lombardo 2017). However, in some cases shifts towards a more domestic gender regime have been halted by feminist collective struggles that have provided renewed strength for autonomous feminist movements as key players in civil society's response to austerity policies in EU member states, from Finland (Elomäki and Kantola 2017) to the UK, France (Emejulu and Bassel 2017), or Spain (Lombardo 2017).

A feminist study of power contributes to constructivist analyses of EU *politics* through a focus on people. It makes visible those who have power within the EU institutions and processes, and how hegemonic masculinity – or the historical domination of men in institutions and of masculinist practices and norms – are institutionalised in the EU (see Hearn et al. in this volume; Haastrup and Kenny 2016; Kronsell 2012; Locher and Prügl 2009). Feminist studies expose men's overrepresentation in EU political institutions as a problem, not only in itself (Haastrup and Kenny 2016; Hoskyns 2004; Kantola 2010, 50–75; van der Vleuten 2012, 41–62), but also because it favours male-dominated policy practices of support and promotion for EU political positions within opaque 'old boys' networks (Kantola 2010, 50). Further, it constructs a culture of hegemonic masculinity, whiteness, and heterosexuality within the EU that is detrimental to women and minoritised groups (Guerrina et al. 2018; Haastrup and Kenny 2016; Locher and Prügl 2009; Stratigaki 2005). It is thus very relevant to assess 'who is at stake and who has authority to define public policy goals', as Cavaghan and O'Dwyer (2018, 100) do in their analysis of the EU economic governance since the economic crisis.

Brexit is a good example of what effects the marginalisation of women's voices and gender perspectives can have on gender equality and the overall goals and shaping of European integration. Feminist scholars have denounced the marginalisation of gender debates and women's expertise during the Brexit process, including the campaign, referendum, and negotiations (Fagan and Rubery 2018; Guerrina and Masselot 2018; Guerrina et al. 2018; see also Guerrina and Masselot in this volume). The political consequences of this marginalisation are the exclusion of gender equality considerations from fundamental changes that a critical phenomenon such as Brexit will bring about, with gender and other intersecting inequalities being reproduced in all policies (Guerrina and Masselot 2018). For this reason, Guerrina et al. (2018, 253) urge studies of European integration to take gender seriously in theory, because otherwise this lack 'puts the discipline in danger of reproducing power structures that keep traditionally marginal groups, including women, ethnic minorities and migrants, on the periphery of the EU project'. They argue that the construction of knowledge about integration, and the gender biases involved in this construction, contributes to shaping existing social inequalities in the EU, by promoting or counteracting them.

Furthermore, a gender and intersectional analysis of power in EU *policy* contributes to social constructivism in European Integration theory by showing that such policymaking is not gender neutral, but rather constructs norms and meanings that are gendered, racialised, classist, and heteronormative, thus legitimising and prioritising particular framings and groups of people while excluding and marginalising others (Bacchi 2017; Kantola and Lombardo 2018; Lombardo 2016). A good illustration in feminist social constructivist analyses of how power is enacted in EU policymaking is represented by the EU policy response to the crisis (see Kantola and Lombardo in this volume). The discursive construction of neoliberal macroeconomic policy as the main priority on the EU agenda since the 2008 economic crisis, while social and equality policy problems have become secondary exemplifies the profound power inequalities at the heart of European integration (Cavaghan 2017b; Jacquot 2015, 2017; Kantola and Lombardo 2017b). While the marginalisation of reproduction and other relevant women's policy issues is not new in European integration (Hoskyns 2004, 2008), the crisis has heightened gender inequalities in the EU (Jacquot 2017). The lack of gender mainstreaming in EU policy responses to the crisis also shows that gender equality has not been framed as part of the solution to the economic crisis (Bettio et al. 2012; Klatzer and Schlager 2014).

The neoliberal policy solutions to the crisis in terms of austerity politics, e.g. cutting down the public sector, have reproduced traditional gender roles delegating major responsibility of care for women (Karamessini and Rubery 2014). Indeed, gender policies, gender mainstreaming, and gender equality institutions have been downscaled in different EU member states at a time when they would be needed the most to counter the gendered effects of the crisis (Klatzer and Schlager 2014). Feminist approaches have shown consequences of austerity policies in terms of the feminisation of poverty and increases in gender violence. They have differentiated impacts of the crisis in terms of race and ethnicity, disability, and class, such as female refugees in Greece (Athanasiou 2014), young unemployed women and old women pensioners (Karamessini and Rubery 2014), or the construction of new solidarity alliances (Emejulu and Bassel 2017; Kantola and Lombardo 2017b). The discursive construction of the narrative about crisis and recovery in the EU is also relevant for its gender and intersectional impacts. As Cavaghan and O'Dwyer (2018, 103) argue, the message about the EU 'recovery' from the economic crisis that imposes a 'strategic silence' over the people who have been especially negatively affected by the EU economic and austerity policies – women and ethnic minorities – not only 'misrepresents the relationships between the productive and the reproductive economy' but also 'wilfully obscures the deeply entrenched gendered and racialised hierarchies that EU economic policy actively maintains'. A key contribution of feminist approaches to social constructivist integration theories is thus the need to include gender in the theorising of 'the political'. This implies addressing policy issues that were formerly considered 'personal', such as reproduction, in EU policymaking, on equal terms with issues that have been longer been considered 'political' such as economic production, paying due attention to the gender and intersectional dynamics involved in such a comprehensive definition of the political.

Finally, feminist approaches contribute to social constructivist theories of power by addressing power as a relation of struggle and contestation, not only of domination (Allen 1999). By addressing a project such as gender equality, which is a process of continuous struggle by actors that promote change, opposition by actors that defend the unequal status quo, and contestation within the rich variety of feminist movements' positionings around gender equality (Verloo 2018), feminist theories are particularly apt to theorise integration as a process in which changes in power have been the result of feminist alliances and transnational activism. Feminist theories conceive of power also in terms of the collective empowerment of women to oppose male domination and achieve gender equality (Allen 1999). Changes in EU political structures, issues, and processes often resulted from transnational advocacy coalitions, alliances, networks, and 'velvet triangles' of feminist policymakers, activists, and academics (Hoskyns 1996; Rolandsen Agustín 2013; van der Vleuten 2007; Woodward 2004, 76; Zippel 2006). Without the pressure of collective feminist activism and the work of individual feminist actors within EU and member states' institutions, it would not be possible to explain the transposition and implementation of EU gender equality directives (La Barbera and Lombardo 2019; Hoskyns 1996; Kantola 2010; Krizsán and Roggeband 2018; Liebert 2003, 2016; Locher 2012; Lombardo and Forest 2012; van der Vleuten 2007). Not only the power of feminist activism needs to be accounted in social constructivist theories of integration for putting EU gender equality policies into practice, but also, importantly for deepening the quality of democracy in Europe. As articulated in the Special Issue by Verloo and Paternotte (2018), processes of de-democratisation in Europe have profound impacts on gender equality, challenging hard-won advances in equality rights and policies (Alonso and Lombardo 2018; Krizsán and Roggeband 2018). The rise of far-right populism in Europe questions core values of democracy such as equality and respect for minorities through their verbal attacks and policies against gender equality policies, LGBTQI+ rights, sexual and reproductive rights, ethnic minorities, migrant people and refugees' rights (Kantola and Lombardo 2020; Köttig et al. 2017; Norocel 2013). Feminist collective mobilisations have proved key to defend the project of democracy and equality from anti-gender attacks and equality policy backsliding (Krizsán and Roggeband 2018; Kuhar and Paternotte 2017).

In this section, we have introduced different feminist approaches to political analysis and their contribution to integration theory. After arguing about the contribution of feminist approaches in general, we have proposed that the feminist approaches of gender, intersectionality, and deconstruction are particularly apt to contribute to social constructivism in integration theory. We have further suggested that of the different varieties of social constructivism, feminist studies especially contribute to develop a 'reflectivist' approach, which takes a more interpretative position interested in the role language and discourses play in the construction of reality. The specific contribution to social constructivism in integration theory that feminist approaches make has been discussed with reference to the concept of power, understood in gender and intersectional ways, and showing what feminist approaches reveal about EU polity, politics, and policy.

Conclusions

Mainstream approaches to social constructivism have crucially contributed to integration theory by showing that integration is a social construction that is continuously changing, that social interaction is key in promoting such changes, that agents and structures are mutually constituted, and that ideas, discourses, and meanings are essential elements to understand policy change in Europe. Feminist social constructivist approaches have shown that these tenets lack fundamental explanatory capacity by not integrating gender as a key analytical lens. Understanding current challenges such as Brexit or the economic crisis requires the adoption of gender and intersectional approaches that provide a more comprehensive and embodied picture of the ongoing social construction of Europe. Social interactions that move changes are gendered, the mutual constitution of agents and structures is gendered, and so are EU norms, discourses, and meanings.

Feminist studies have developed reflectivist social constructivist approaches that are apt for grasping and challenging gender, heteronormative, or ethnocentric norms and biases that are implicitly present in the EU political discourses. In particular, the feminist approaches of 'gender', 'intersectionality', and 'deconstruction' discussed in this chapter have contributed to the theory of social constructivism in European integration by showing firstly how gender in intersection with other inequalities is constructed in the EU through social and institutional practices and, secondly, how gender and intersectional norms, meanings, and power relations are discursively constructed in the EU. The concepts of polity, politics, and policy in the EU thoroughly change when we apply gender and intersectional lenses, and we are able to theorise what are the differentiated effects of the EU economic crisis, Brexit, or phenomena of de-democratisation on women and men intersecting with inequalities of class, ethnicity, sexuality, age or disability. Feminist approaches show that power in the EU is gendered and that, without analyses of the gendered social construction of agents and structures, we would not be able to understand the continuously changing dynamics of domination and contestation of power that move the integration process.

Whilst feminist social constructivist approaches have brought forward theorising, they show limitations in their capacity to grasp realities such as emotions, affects, and their bodily impacts on women and men, which are important for understanding political processes such as the rising of populisms in Europe or the emotions of anger, empathy, and shame that have emerged during the economic crisis (Kantola and Lombardo 2017a, 2017b). Here is where social constructivist approaches could be complemented with feminist scholarly debates on 'post-deconstruction', that study the role of affects, emotions, and bodily material and their gender and intersectional dimensions (Ahmed 2004; Hemmings 2005; Kantola and Lombardo 2017a; Liljeström and Paasonen 2010; Lykke 2010). By complementing its theorising of European integration as a social construct with post-deconstruction approaches that address the materiality of bodies, emotions, and affects, feminist social constructivism could provide an even broader reach about the causes and consequences of inequality in the process of constructing and contesting the EU.

Note

1   Two approaches developed in the book are not addressed here. The *women approach* asks where women are situated in political structures and processes, helping to analyse the (often marginal) position of women and the (often dominant) position of men in key decision-making places, processes, and institutions. *Post-deconstruction* is a novel approach 'interested in understanding what affects, emotions and bodily material do in gender and politics' (Kantola and Lombardo 2017a, 43). It is widely debated in feminist theory and cultural studies but not employed yet in gender and EU studies or political analysis.

Acknowledgement

Johanna Kantola's research has received funding from the European Research Council (ERC) under the European Union's Horizon 2020 research and innovation program grant number 771676.

References

Abels G, MacRae H, eds. (2016): *Gendering European Integration Theory: Engaging New Dialogues,* Opladen: Barbara Budrich Publisher.

Ahmed S (2004): *The Cultural Politics of Emotion,* Edinburgh: Edinburgh University Press.

Allen A (1999): *The Power of Feminist Theory. Domination, Resistance and Solidarity,* Boulder, CO: Westview Press.

Alonso A, Lombardo E (2018): Gender equality and de-democratization processes: the case of Spain, *Politics and Governance* **6** (3), 78−89.

Athanasiou A (2014): Precarious intensities: gendered bodies in the streets and squares of Greece, *Signs* **40** (1), 1−9.

Bacchi C (1999): *Women, Policy, and Politics: The Construction of Policy Problems,* London: Sage.

Bacchi C (2009): The Issue of Intentionality in Frame Theory: The Need for Reflexive Framing, in: Lombardo E, Meier P, Verloo M (eds.): *The Discursive Politics of Gender Equality. Stretching, Bending and Policymaking,* London: Routledge, 19−35.

Bacchi C (2017): Policies as gendering practices: re-viewing categorical distinctions, *Journal of Women Politics and Policy* **38** (1), 20−41.

La Barbera MC, Lombardo E (2019): The long and winding road. A comparative policy analysis of multi-level judicial implementation of work−life balance in Spain, *Journal of Comparative Policy Analysis: Research and Practice* **21** (1), 9−24.

Bettio F, Corsi M, D'Ippoliti C, Lyberaki A, Lodovici MS, Verashchagina A (2012): *The Impact of the Economic Crisis on the Situation of Women and Men and on Gender Equality Policies,* Brussels: The European Commission.

Börzel TA, Risse T (2003): Conceptualizing the Domestic Impact of Europe, in: Featherstone K, Radaelli CM (eds.): *The Politics of Europeanization,* Oxford: Oxford University Press, 57−80.

Cavaghan R (2017a): Bridging rhetoric and practice: new perspectives on barriers to gendered change, *Journal of Women Politics and Policy* **38** (1), 42−63.

Cavaghan R (2017b): The Gender Politics of EU Economic Policy: Policy Shifts and Contestations Before and After the Crisis, in: Kantola J, Lombardo E (eds.): *Gender and the Economic Crisis in Europe. Politics, Institutions and Intersectionality,* London: Palgrave MacMillan, 49−72.

Cavaghan R, O'Dwyer M (2018): European economic governance in 2017: a recovery for whom? *Journal of Common Market Studies* **56** (1), 96−108.

Chappell L, Galea N (2017): Excavating informal institutional enforcement through 'rapid' ethnography: lessons from the Australian construction industry, in: Waylen G (ed.): *Towards Gendering Institutionalism,* London: Rowman & Littlefield, 104−136.

Chappell L, Mackay F (2017): What's in a Name? Mapping the Terrain of Informal Institutions and Gender, in: Waylen G (ed.): *Towards Gendering Institutionalism,* London: Rowman & Littlefield, 33−69.

Christiansen T, Jørgensen KE, Wiener A (eds.) (2001): *The Social Construction of Europe,* London: Sage.

Chryssochoou DN, Stavridis S, Tsinisizelis MJ, Ifantis K (2003): *Theory and Reform in the EU,* Manchester: Manchester University Press.

Collins PH, Chepp V (2013): Intersectionality, in: Waylen G, Celis K, Kantola J, Weldon L (eds.): *The Oxford Handbook of Gender and Politics,* Oxford: Oxford University Press, 57−87.

Crenshaw K (1989): Demarginalizing the intersection of race and sex: a black feminist critique of antidiscrimination doctrine, feminist theory and antiracist politics, *University of Chicago Legal Forum* **1989** (1), 139−167.

Elomäki A, Kantola J (2017): Austerity Politics and Feminist Resistance in Finland: From Established Women's Organizations to New Feminist Initiatives, in: Kantola J, Lombardo E (eds.): *Gender and the Economic Crisis in Europe. Politics, Institutions and Intersectionality,* Basingstoke: Palgrave Macmillan, 231−256.

Emejulu A, Bassel L (2017): Whose Crisis Counts? Minority Women, Austerity and Activism in France and Britain, in: Kantola J, Lombardo E (eds.): *Gender and the Economic Crisis in Europe. Politics, Institutions and Intersectionality,* Basingstoke: Palgrave Macmillan, 185−208.

Fagan C, Rubery J (2018): Advancing gender equality through European employment policy: the impact of the UK's EU membership and the risks of Brexit, *Social Policy and Society* **17** (2), 297−317.

Ferree MM (2012): *Varities of Feminism. German Gender Politics in Global Perspective,* Stanford, CA: Stanford University Press.

Galligan, Yvonne (2019): European Integration and Gender, in: Wiener A, Börzel T, Risse T (eds.): *European Integration Theory,* Oxford: Oxford University Press, 174−194.

Guerrina R, Masselot A (2018): Walking into the footprint of EU law: unpacking the gendered consequences of Brexit, *Social Policy and Society* **17** (2), 319–330.

Guerrina R, Chappel L, Wright KAM (2018): Transforming CSDP? Feminist triangles and gender regimes, *Journal of Common Market Studies* **56** (5), 1036–1052.

Haastrup T, Kenny M (2016): Gendering Institutionalism: A Feminist Institutionalist Approach to EU Integration Theory, in: Abels G, MacRae H (eds.): *Gendering European Integration Theory*, Berlin: Barbara Budrich, 197–216.

Hay C (2002): *Political Analysis*, Basingstoke: Palgrave Macmillan.

Hemmings C (2005): Invoking affect. Cultural theory and the ontological turn, *Cultural Studies* **19** (5), 548–567.

Hoskyns C (1996): *Integrating Gender: Women, Law and Politics in the European Union*, London: Verso.

Hoskyns C (2004): Gender Perspectives, in: Wiener A, Diez T (eds.): *European Integration Theory*, Oxford: Oxford University Press, 217–236.

Hoskyns C (2008): Governing the EU: Gender and Macroeconomics, in: Rai SM, Waylen G (eds.): *Global Governance. Feminist Perspectives*, Basingstoke: Palgrave Macmillan, 107–128.

Jacquot S (2015): *Transformations in EU Gender Equality*, Basingstoke: Palgrave Macmillan.

Jacquot S (2017): A Policy in Crisis. The Dismantling of the EU Gender Equality Policy, in: Kantola J, Lombardo E (eds.): *Gender and the Crisis in Europe: Politics, Institutions, and Intersectionality*, Basingstoke: Palgrave Macmillan, 27–48.

Kantola J (2006): *Feminists Theorize the State*, Basingstoke: Palgrave Macmillan.

Kantola J (2010): *Gender and the European Union*, Basingstoke: Palgrave Macmillan.

Kantola J, Lombardo E (2017a): *Gender and Political Analysis*, Basingstoke: Palgrave Macmillan.

Kantola J, Lombardo E, eds. (2017b): *Gender and the Economic Crisis in Europe: Politics, Institutions and Intersectionality*, Basingstoke: Palgrave Macmillan.

Kantola J, Lombardo E (2018): EU Gender Equality Policies, in: Heinelt H, Münch S (eds.): *Handbook of European Policies: Interpretive Approaches to the EU*, Cheltenham: Edward Elgar, 331–352.

Kantola J, Lombardo E (2020): Strategies of right populists in opposing gender equality in a polarized European Parliament, *International Political Science Review*, https://doi.org/10.1177/0192512120963953.

Kantola J, Nousiainen K (2009): Institutionalising intersectionality in Europe: introducing the theme, *International Feminist Journal of Politics* **11** (4), 459–477.

Karamessini M, Rubery J, eds. (2014): *Women and Austerity: The Economic Crisis and the Future for Gender Equality*, London: Routledge.

Klatzer E, Schlager C (2014): Feminist Perspectives on Macroeconomics: Reconfiguration of Power Structures and Erosion of Gender Equality Through the New Economic Governance Regime in the European Union, in: Evans M, Hemmings C, Henry M, Madhok S, Waring S (eds.): *Feminist Theory Handbook*, London: Sage, 483–499.

Krizsán A, Roggeband C (2018): *The Gender Politics of Domestic Violence. Feminists Engaging the State in Central and Eastern Europe*, Budapest, New York: CEU Press.

Krizsán A, Bustelo M, Hadjiyani A, Kamutis F (2007): Domestic violence: A Public Matter, in: Verloo M (eds.): *Multiple Meanings of Gender Equality: A Critical Frame Analysis of Gender Policies in Europe*, Budapest, New York: CEU press, 141–187.

Kronsell A (2005): Gender, power and European integration theory, *Journal of European Public Policy* **12** (6), 1022–1040.

Kronsell A (2012): Gendering Theories of European Integration, in: Abels G, Mushaben J (eds.): *Gendering the European Union: New Approaches to Old Democratic Deficits*, Basingstoke: Palgrave Macmillan, 23–40.

Krook M, Mackay F, eds. (2011): *Gender, Politics and Institutions: Towards a Feminist Institutionalism*, Basingstoke: Palgrave Macmillan.

Kuhar R, Paternotte D, eds. (2017): *Anti-Gender Campaigns in Europe: Mobilizing Against Equality*, Lanham, MD: Rowman & Littlefield.

Köttig M, Bitzan R, Pető A, eds. (2017): *Gender and Far Rights Politics in Europe*, Basingstoke: Palgrave Macmillan.

Liebert U, ed. (2003): *Gendering Europeanization*, Brussels: Peter Lang.

Liebert U (2016): Gendering Europeanisation: Making Equality Work in Theory and Practice, in: Abels G, MacRae H (eds.): *Gendering European Integration Theories*, Opladen: Barbara Budrich Publishers, 147–174.

Liljeström M, Paasonen S (2010): Feeling Differences, in: Liljeström M, Paasonen S (eds.): *Working with Affect in Feminist Readings: Disturbing Differences*, London: Routledge, 1–17.

Locher B (2012): Gendering the EU Policy Process and Constructing the Gender Acquis, in: Abels G, Mushaben J (eds.): *Gendering the European Union: New Approaches to Old Democratic Deficits*, Basingstoke: Palgrave Macmillan, 63–84.

Locher B, Prügl E (2001): Feminism and constructivism: worlds apart or sharing the middle ground?, *International Studies Quarterly* **45** (1), 111–129.

Locher B, Prügl E (2009): Gender Perspectives, in: Wiener A, Diez T (eds.): *European Integration Theory*, 2nd ed., Oxford: Oxford University Press, 181–197.

Lombardo E (2016): Social Constructivism, in: Abels G, MacRae H (eds.): *Gendering European Integration Theories*, Opladen: Barbara Budrich Publishers, 123–146.

Lombardo E (2017): Austerity Politics and Feminists Struggles in Spain: Reconfiguring the Gender Regime?, in: Kantola J, Lombardo E (eds.): *Gender and the Economic Crisis in Europe: Politics, Institutions and Intersectionality*, Basingstoke: Palgrave Macmillan, 209–230.

Lombardo E, Forest M, eds. (2012): *The Europeanization of Gender Equality Policies: A Discursive-Sociological Approach*, Basingstoke: Palgrave Macmillan.

Lombardo E, Meier P (2008): Framing gender equality in the European Union political discourse, *Social Politics* **15** (1), 101–129.

Lombardo E, Meier P, Verloo M, eds. (2009): *The Discursive Politics of Gender Equality: Stretching, Bending and Policymaking*, London: Routledge.

Lombardo E, Meier P, Verloo M (2017): Policymaking from a gender+ equality perspective, *Journal of Women, Politics & Policy* **38** (1), 1–19.

Lykke N (2010): *Feminist Studies: A Guide to Intersectional Theory, Methodology and Writing*, New York: Routledge.

March J, and Olsen J (1989): *Rediscovering Institutions. The Organizational Basis of Politics*, New York: The Free Press.

Norocel OC (2013): 'Give us back Sweden!' A feminist reading of the (re)interpretations of the Folkhem Conceptual Metaphor in the Swedish radical right populist discourse, *Nora: Nordic Journal of Feminist and Gender Research* **21** (1), 4–20.

Onuf N (1989): *World of Our Making: Rules and Rule in Social Theory and International Relations*, London: Routledge.

Pateman C (1983): Introduction, *Australian Journal of Political Science* **18** (2), 1–2.

Risse T (2004): Social Constructivism and European Integration, in: Wiener A, Diez T (eds.): *European Integration Theory*, Oxford: Oxford University Press, 159–176.

Risse T (2019): Social Constructivism and European Integration, in: Wiener A, Börzel T, Risse T (eds.): *European Integration Theory*, Oxford: Oxford University Press.

Rolandsen Agustín L (2013): *Gender Equality, Intersectionality and Diversity in Europe*, Basingstoke: Palgrave Macmillan.

Rosamond B (2013): Theorizing the European Union after Integration Theory, in: Cini M, Pérez-Solórzano Borragan (eds.): *European Union Politics*, 5th ed., Oxford: Oxford University Press, 85–102.

Rosamond B (2000): *Theories of European Integration*, Basingstoke: Palgrave Macmillan.

Rosamond B (2001): Discourses of Globalization and European Identities, in: Christiansen T, Jørgensen KE, Wiener A (eds.): *The Social Construction of Europe*, London: Sage, 158–175.

Rubery J (2014): The challenge of austerity for equality: a consideration of eight European countries in the crisis, *Revue de l'OFCE* **133** (2), 15–39.

Saurugger S (2014): *Theoretical Approaches to European Integration*, Basingstoke: Palgrave Macmillan.

Schmidt V (2002): *The Futures of European Capitalism*, Oxford: Oxford University Press.

Schmidt V (2011): Speaking of change: why discourse is key to the dynamics of policy transformation, *Critical Policy Studies* **5** (2), 106–126.

Shaw J (2000): Importing gender: the challenge of feminism and the analysis of the EU legal order, *Journal of European Public Policy* **7** (3), 406–431.

Smith S (2001): Social Constructivisms and European Studies, in: Christiansen T, Jørgensen KE, Wiener A (eds.): *The Social Construction of Europe*, London: Sage, 189–198.

Stratigaki M (2005): Gender mainstreaming vs positive action: an ongoing conflict in EU gender equality policy, *European Journal of Women's Studies* **12** (2), 165–186.

Verloo M, ed. (2007): *Multiple Meanings of Gender Equality: A Critical Frame Analysis of Gender Policies in Europe*, Budapest, New York: CEU Press.

Verloo M, ed. (2018): *Varieties of Opposition to Gender Equality in Europe*, New York: Routledge.

Verloo M, Paternotte D (2018): Feminist project under threat in Europe, *Politics and Governance* **6** (3), 1–5.

Van der Vleuten A (2007): *The Price of Gender Equality: Member States and Governance in the European Union*, Aldershot: Ashgate.

Van der Vleuten A (2012): Gendering the Institutions and Actors of the EU, in: Abels G, Mushaben J (eds.): *Gendering the European Union: New Approaches to Old Democratic Deficits*, Basingstoke: Palgrave Macmillan, 41–62.

Wæver O (2004): Discursive Approaches, in: Wiener A and Diez T (eds.): *European Integration Theory*, Oxford: Oxford University Press, 197–216.

Walby S (2009): *Globalization and Inequalities: Complexity and Contested Modernities*, London: Sage.

Walby S (2015): *Crisis*, Cambridge: Polity Press.

Waylen G, ed. (2017): *Towards Gendering Institutionalism*, London: Rowman & Littlefield.

Wiener A, Börzel T, Risse T, eds. (2019): *European Integration Theory*, Oxford: Oxford University Press.

Woll C, Jacquot S (2010): Using Europe: strategic action in multi-level politics, *Comparative European Politics* **8** (1), 110–126.

Woodward A (2004): Building Velvet Triangles: Gender and Informal Governance, in: Christiansen T, Piattoni S (eds.): *Informal Governance and the European Union*, Cheltenham: Edward Elgar, 76–93.

Wöhl S (2014): The state and gender relations in international political economy: a state-theoretical approach to varieties of capitalism in crisis, *Capital & Class* **38** (1), 83–95.

Zippel K (2006): *The Politics of Sexual Harassment: A Comparative Study of the United States, the European Union, and Germany*, Cambridge: Cambridge University Press.

5

Feminist institutionalism

Heather MacRae and Elaine Weiner

"[A]lmost any Europeanist with a minimal level of self-respect flags herself [sic!] as an 'institutionalist' at the moment" Aspinwall and Schneider (2000, 3) claim. One can only assume that the authors believed that by adopting the female pronoun to describe "Europeanists," they were being inclusive and gender-aware. In fact, gender awareness, institutionalist approaches and EU studies have seldom crossed. While many (predominantly male) researchers apply new institutionalist approaches to European Union (EU) studies, until very recently, few do so with a gender lens. However, through the "feminist institutionalist" project of the past two decades, nuanced variations of new institutionalist approaches have emerged to offer gendered insights into the study of European institutions.

This chapter considers the contributions of feminist institutionalism (FI) to the study of gender and the EU. We outline first, the premises and central concepts of both new institutionalism (NI) and of FI to highlight how feminist scholars have borrowed and built upon concepts they found insufficient to elucidate the gendered nature of the EU and its policies. In the second section, we look to specific examples of FI research to highlight some key contributions and to show the depth of analysis generated through FI. Finally, we consider some of the potential directions in which FI could evolve, and the ways in which this could further a collective research agenda in EU studies.

From new institutionalism to feminist institutionalism

FI is "decidedly pluralistic" (Haastrup and Kenny 2016) with scholars drawing on diverse tools from NI and gender studies to offer a gendered reading of the interactions and constitution of institutions. While the majority of FI scholars draw on tools developed by historical institutionalism, tools and methods prevalent in other NI strands, i.e. sociological institutionalism and discursive institutionalisms, and from the broader field of gender studies are also quite prevalent (see Erikson 2019; Gains and Lowndes 2014; Haastrup and Kenny 2016). To understand the interplay between FI and NI in European studies, it is helpful to briefly review the ways in which NI approaches have shaped the past 35 years of research and why these are insufficient to provide a gendered reading of EU integration and institutions.

NI is an umbrella term encompassing a variety of schools and strands (Aspinwall and Schneider 2000). Although we can see an increasing convergence of these strands in contemporary scholarship, most analysts continue to reference four main strands: rational choice, historical, sociological and discursive institutionalism. All of these have found extensive application in EU studies, and each brings specific strengths and underlying methodological and epistemological assumptions to its analysis. In general, new institutional theorists maintain that institutions are central to the organization of political and social relations and that this organization matters to social and political outcomes. They understand institutions broadly, as "the rules of the game." These "rules" may be formal or informal and include norms, values and principles that shape an organization, structure interactions and set standards of logical, appropriate and inappropriate behavior (March and Olsen 1989). In general, NI scholars are all concerned with understanding how and why institutions change (or not); and they seek to understand changes and continuity through an analysis of institutions and their reactions to endogenous and exogenous pressures.

The application of these strands has been varied. For example, rational choice institutionalists have tended to look for patterns of rational behavior in the institutions and the EU as a whole (Pollack 2003). In contrast, historical institutionalism tends to look for changes in an institution over time (Pierson 2004), leading to the development of concepts such as "path dependency" and "feedback loops" as means of explaining the general stability of institutions. Sociological institutionalism considers the cultural and contextual meaning of rules, and the impact of values and beliefs on actors and institutions. It investigates, for example, why national policy differences continue despite EU directives or guidelines. Each strand of the approach brings slightly different observations to EU studies. While some critics see this methodological pluralism as a lack of conceptual clarity, for others it merely means that there are more "tools" in our analytical toolbox, which can only enrich our analyses. As Vivian Schmidt (1999, 3) has commented, "Europeanists should use whichever of the three institutionalisms (among other methods) is appropriate to elucidating the problem at hand. And to gain a full sense of reality, they could try to combine all three." The difficulty for feminist scholars is that none of the new institutionalist schools is "appropriate to elucidating the problem at hand" – the gendered nature of EU institutions and European integration.

Feminist institutionalism as a response to new institutionalism

Although there is some disagreement as to whether FI ought to be considered an independent branch or a means of bringing gender into the mainstream NI approaches, FI scholars generally acknowledge a significant degree of conceptual overlap with mainstream NI (Lowndes and Roberts 2013; Weiner and MacRae 2017). Like NI, FI scholars also understand institutions as essential to unpacking political and social phenomena; recognize both formal and informal aspects of institutions; show an interest in institutional creation, stability and change; and interrogate the relationship between structures and agents and the distribution of power within institutions (Erikson 2019; Mackay et al. 2010; Minto and Mergaert 2018; Weiner and MacRae 2017). The fundamental difference, however, is that FI scholars begin from the premise that it is not only institutions that matter but their *gendered nature*: "constructions of masculinity and femininity are intertwined in the daily culture or 'logic' of political institutions" (Haastrup and Kenny 2016, 201). Within a single organization such as the EU, institutions can be differently gendered, or reflect gendered relationships and cultures differently. For example, while the European Parliament might reflect one understanding of gender relations and may act within a set of gendered rules that is appropriate to that body, individual parliamentary groups or the European Commission might follow a different set of gendered rules and will work within the confines of a different understanding of masculinity and femininity. FI allows for investigating gender "as both institutional – that is, playing out within institutions – and also institutionalised – that is, incorporated into the very structure of institutions" (Weiner and MacRae 2014, 3). There is furthermore, an understanding that identifying the gendered power structures is essential to bringing about change. As Annica Kronsell (2016a, 104) notes, if "masculine power is embedded in European integration and not carefully examined, it is simply reproduced." There is thus an implicit and explicit political project embedded within FI.

There are four aspects of institutions FI can address more thoroughly than NI approaches. These are interconnected and, taken together, result in a nuanced and systematic account of the institutional landscape. First, FI draws attention to the ways in which institutions are inherently *gendered*. More recently, FI scholars have expanded this definition to include "complex gender equality" (Ahrens and van der Vleuten 2020), which recognizes the interplay of multiple forms of structurally embedded inequalities including class, race, ethnicity and religion. Second, FI acknowledges *informal rules* and norms and uses these to demonstrate how institutions produce gendered outcomes and other inequalities. Third, FI interrogates gendered *power* relations and problematizes the location of power within institutions. Fourth, feminist institutionalism is well equipped to recognize both *change* and continuity as elements of institutions and leaves space for analysts to explore "potential, as well as actual change" (MacRae and Weiner 2017, 211). It has embraced a more recent historical institutionalist conceptualization of change as gradual and incremental, which consequently sees the institutions are far less path dependent and constant than many NI scholars assume. In its analysis of power and of change, FI considers the roles of specific individuals and groups within a given institutional context. As such, FI seeks a balance between NI approaches, which are often too focused on structures, and the broader feminist literature which is typically more interested in agency than structure (Thomson 2018). FI brings these strengths into dialogue with some of the concepts developed by NI to generate a nuanced approach that overcomes many of the weaknesses of NI. Before we turn our attention to how FI can augment research in EU studies, we first briefly address some of the concepts central to both FI and NI.

Central concepts

One of the widely-borrowed concepts comes from historical institutionalism (HI) and has been central to both mainstream and FI approaches to the EU. HI often describes institutions as "path dependent" (Pierson 1996), or essentially stable. Simply put, "path dependency" suggests that early institutional choices and policy decisions tend to "lock in," or commit institutions to a particular trajectory or path, constraining future options. "Feedback dynamics," or reinforcing behaviors, can further entrench the status quo, making path-breaking change even more unlikely. If an institution does deviate from its general path, it is often considered to be the result of a "critical juncture." These are relatively short moments in time when two or more choices about institutional organization may be available and which may lead to fundamental change and a break from the former path.

Path dependency has become central to FI scholars seeking to explain how and why gendered norms are so deeply embedded into institutions. Kronsell (2016a), for example, has drawn on path dependency and a FI approach to demonstrate the dominance of "military masculinities" throughout the EU's security and defense regime, even though gender mainstreaming efforts ought to have brought a gendered outlook into this policy sphere. However, if one takes path dependency to the logical conclusion, the result is structural determinism such that individuals and groups are fundamentally unable to alter the institutions. This would render the gender project impossible. Emphasizing continuity as the norm, path dependency assumes fundamental change is the result of large-scale, rapid upheaval. As a result, NI was initially quite blind to the potential of small, incremental changes (Streek and Thelen 2005). As Mackay, Kenny and Chappell (2010, 579) note: "This has meant that the global and regional political trend of incorporation of women in formal institutions that arguably has left no political or state institution untouched, has passed 'under the radar' of NI scholars." The proliferation of gender quotas in the institutions, gender mainstreaming initiatives, the introduction of gender budgeting and even the development of new formal institutions such as the European Institute for Gender Equality (EIGE) (see Jacquot and Krizsán in this volume) have been almost completely overlooked by mainstream EU scholars from within the NI traditions. When NI fails to see these changes, it also fails to recognize the role of gender dynamics in the overall institutional configuration and processes.

More recent NI scholarship has recognized its own bias towards continuity over change. In an effort to be more aware of gradual change, scholars have introduced concepts such as "policy drift," "layering," "conversion" and "displacement." These are particularly helpful in EU gender analyses where we frequently see a partial or incomplete policy shift in gendered assumptions, but not a full-scale replacement. "Layering," for example, involves "the introduction of new rules on top of or alongside existing ones" (Mahoney and Thelen 2010, 15) and can be especially helpful in unpacking the nuances of gender regimes. As different and sometimes contradictory rules exist within a single policy space, different institutional "logics" may coexist (MacRae 2006). The "logic of appropriateness," a concept borrowed from sociological institutionalism asserts that actors interpret their environment in order to understand which actions are most "appropriate" given the institutional constraints (March and Olsen 1989). The logic can thus reinforce existing patterns of behavior, even as formal rules shift. FI scholars have used this concept to highlight the informal rules of the game and the ways in which gendered norms, for example around women's position in committees, or the role of the European Parliament's FEMM committee in relation to other parliamentary committees, can work to produce and reproduce gendered assumptions (Ahrens 2016; Erikson 2019).

FI scholars have also developed their own terminology to describe how institutions are gendered. One of the most used typologies has been the four orders of rules. These orders consider "four sets of variables: rules about gender; rules that have gendered effects (but are not specifically about gender); the gendered actors who work with rules; and gendered policy outcomes" (Gains and Lowndes 2014, 527). This offers FI scholars a starting point to investigate the ways in which these different institutional dimensions are related. For example:

> Studying gendered outcomes might involve examining policy reforms that were designed to introduce new rules to promote gender equality. Such rules might encourage more diverse representation in political organizations by drawing in more women actors. These actors might in turn challenge rules with gendered effects, such as the timing of meetings or dominant styles of political leadership.
>
> *(Gains and Lowndes 2014, 530)*

This focus on the interplay between institutions, actors, formal and informal rules is at the center of much of the FI research in EU studies. In the following section, we draw on specific examples to elaborate on the contributions FI makes to EU studies.

Feminist institutionalism in EU studies

By the mid-1990s, NI approaches were fairly common in EU studies and, by the early 2000s, they arguably had taken on a dominant position in the field. Nonetheless, the feminist variant did not make substantial headway in the field until more than a decade later. Certainly, as this Handbook highlights, there has been a wide array of feminist literature that has investigated women and political institutions in Europe, if to a lesser degree the EU. It is worth noting that there are several studies from much earlier, which are very much in the spirit of FI, but where the author(s) do not specifically identify themselves as FI scholars. For example, Alison Woodward's important study on the institutional pathways of gendered policy-making analyzed the interaction between three different types of actors in formal and informal European governance. Looking specifically at EU employment policies, Woodward (2004) argues that "femocrats," civil society and epistemic communities can work together in a "velvet triangle" to support the incorporation of a gender perspective into European pol-icies. Her research focuses specifically on the informal interactions and personal connections that are at play in the formulation of employment policies. Although she does not identify herself as a feminist institutionalist, this study is very much in line with FI methodology and epistemology. Woodward has a clear focus on informal institutions and agents and seeks to understand the origins of institutional change.

Going back even further, we could suggest that Catherine Hoskyns' (1996) seminal work also contained elements of FI. In an era when feminist theorizing of the EU was all but non-existent, Hoskyns openly rejected the mainstream theories of the time, and turned to "emerging theories" to describe the process of gendering European institutions and policies. She brought these newer theories, some of which were influenced by NI thought (e.g. Wolfgang Streek), into dialogue with insights from feminist and gender studies and focused on elements that today would be considered central to FI. She writes:

> I found these emerging perspectives more helpful than the earlier ones in situating the women's policy and helping to explain its particular shape and effects ... [the] narrow focus of the neo-functionalist/neo-realist debate had the effect of sideling other agendas and masking the way in which a certain type of politics was growing up around the European structures. The failure to pay attention to informal politics and keep democratic values to the fore had the effect, by default at least, of endorsing such developments.
>
> *(Hoskyns 1996, 21)*

Again, we see a focus on structures and the ways in which agents are empowered and constrained by these structures. Hoskyns looks to formal and informal interactions, values and norms, as well as the historical trajectory of policy through time. What is still missing from both Woodward and Hoskyns approaches, however is a theory of gendered power. Although they both hint at the fact that power is not always concentrated in the formal institutions, and both recognize the role of gender within institutions, they do not really interrogate the "gendered character and the gendering effects" of the institutions themselves (Mackay 2011, 181). Thus, although they – and other "pre-FI" feminist approaches – drew attention to the ways in which women and feminists were active in the EU institutions, and how women have navigated the formal and informal institutional configuration of the EU to bring about gendered change, they did not consciously interrogate the power relations embedded in the institutions. This element of theorizing power is one of the main outcomes of feminist analysis of European integration.

One of the earliest collections of FI theorizing about the EU is Weiner and MacRae's (2014) *EIoP* special issue. After 2014, we notice a fairly rapid proliferation of FI approaches as gender and EU scholars consciously adopt the FI terminology and nomenclature. The following section looks at a few of these key contributions to demonstrate the strengths of FI as: (1) its ability to see gender in all institutional configurations and policy areas; (2) its attention to agents in the development of gradual and incremental change and resistance to change; (3) the role of formal and informal institutions and especially their interaction; and (4) its openness to concepts from other compatible approaches. When we take these all together, we recognize that, within EU studies, FI contributions are working towards a comprehensive understanding of gendered institutional power.

Seeing gender when others are blind

It is a commonly accepted adage within gender studies that institutions are not neutral, but contain within them gendered power relations. Consequently, we know that no policy or policy area is truly gender neutral; nonetheless, we must seek to develop gender-aware or gender-friendly outcomes in all policy fields. Many earlier studies of gender in the EU tended to focus on "women's policy," or on policy areas which clearly have differential impacts on men and women, such as employment and social policy. Recently, FI has opened the scope for research to include the gendered nature of all policy areas including the exceptionally male domain of security and defense policies (CSDP).

Drawing attention to the gendered nature of these supposedly "gender-neutral" policy areas contributes not only to FI scholarship, but also to the mainstream. Guerrina, Chappell and Wright (2018) "identify key institutional actors operating in the context of CSDP" by adapting Woodward's "velvet triangle." They argue that CSDP has typically had "special status," which has contributed to a limited implementation of gender mainstreaming principles. Using path dependency and policy layering they show that gender silences persist in the CSDP partly because of the prevalence of gendered norms, and partly because of systems of power that continue to undermine efforts at mainstreaming. Hence, obstacles to gender mainstreaming may constrain the EU's ability to work as an effective gender actor in external policy and, as such, may constrain its overall position as a norm setter in the international community. Clearly, this observation is relevant not only for gender analyses, but also for mainstream scholars of foreign and defense policy.

Kronsell (2016b) also looks to CSDP to draw attention to a hegemonic masculinity which permeates the EU. What is unique about her investigation is that she hones in on the various images of masculinity and femininity that are simultaneously at work in the EU military institutions. She finds that everyday acts, norms, values, routines and behaviors are reproduced in the institutions, perpetuating a notion of "protector masculinity" and "female vulnerability" (see Hearn et al. in this volume). This shapes the EU's interactions with other communities on the global stage. In contrast to mainstream scholars who frequently seek to understand the EU's military power as a benign power or a civilian power (see Muehlenhoff in this volume), this characterization of the EU military as a masculine power, reproducing specific gendered beliefs can shift our lens away from the typical questions of how the EU exercises power over other regions. By beginning from the perspective of the "hegemonic masculinity" inherent in CSDP, one might instead see the EU's interventions as "tainted by desires for masculine power and domination and a gender path dependence that casts masculinities and femininities into historically established gender war roles" (Kronsell 2016b, 329). The ways in which gender plays out in the institutions has implications for the broader interactions of the EU as a whole.

Gender permeates all aspects of institutions, not only at a personal or social level, but within the daily culture or "logic" of political institutions. NI scholars recognize the importance of institutionalized power relations and inequalities within institutions. Aspinwall and Schneider (2000, 3) clearly see that power is at play in the construction and maintenance of institutions when they note that "[i]nstitutions contain the bias individual agents have built into their society over time, which in turn leads to important distributional consequences." And yet, even as they consider institutions to be inherently biased, NI scholars fail to recognize and articulate gender as an overarching and structural bias. FI scholars have shown that the EU institutions, which have been constructed and occupied almost exclusively by individual *male* agents, are infused with a masculine bias. Thus, it is important to study what happens when *female* agents, such as Ursula von der Leyen (first female Commission President) or Christine Lagarde (first female President of the European Central Bank) increasingly take up key positions in the institutions.

Agents of change and resistance

Actors are clearly not gender neutral, but occupy female or male (or non-binary) bodies and are socialized such that their behaviors will fall somewhere along a masculine/feminine spectrum. It matters if masculine or feminine bodies construct the institutions and it matters if positions within the institutions are occupied by masculine or feminine bodies. Although the EU's institutions were designed largely by men, women are not, nor have they ever been, absent from the institutional configurations of the European project (see Milner in this volume). A historical analysis of the EU's institutions and gender policy can show how gendered power came to be embedded in the institutions. Debusscher and van der Vleuten (2017) offer an FI reading of the history of EU gender policy. Their analysis revolves around four critical junctures and determines that policy can, but does not always, move forward at these junctures. Gender-friendly change, even when the opportunity is presented, is highly dependent on the agency of key actors.

Whereas NI tended, at least initially, to focus on large, exogenous pressures as the originator of change, FI looks to subtler, more incremental and endogenous factors. The role of individual actors, as they respond to these changes in their environment is key (Ansorg and Haastrup 2018). Ironically, given the importance of actors as agents of institutional change, there are surprisingly few studies on the EU drawing explicitly on FI and focusing specifically on women's agency. FI scholars generally pay only implicit attention to agents as they take note of the ways in which individuals and groups work within institutions and often factor this into a comprehensive analysis of both structures and agents (Abels and MacRae, *forthcoming*).

Recently, some FI scholars have turned their attention to actors and their ability to prevent change, rather than feminist actors' ability to influence change (Erikson 2019; Mergaert and Lombardo 2014). They show that actors can work within the institutionalized "logic of appropriateness" to affirm or reinforce a particular norm or gendered value, thus hindering change. This opens a new avenue for analysis in the ways that daily practice (a form of informal norm) can override official and formal policy. Building on research on resistance, Erikson (2019) focuses her attention on actors' perceptions of the institutional contexts within which they operate. This goes beyond a simple understanding of agency and the ability to act within the confines of the institutions, to also investigate the meaning that actors place on the formal and informal norms that structure the environment within which they operate. This serves to dig deeper into the "hidden life" (Waylen 2017) of institutions and goes beyond simple interconnections, to consider why agents and individuals act in particular ways. Adopting a constructivist FI approach Erikson (2019, 279–280) argues that

> it is not sufficient to analyze how the institutional context in itself conditions actors' behavior in a gendered way; it is also necessary to address how actors perceive the context and how such perceptions are gendered, when we seek to understand their choice of actions.

Her focus on meaning generates a deeper understanding of the interests, actors, cultures and values that are shaping European policy and can, in the future, help to bring about more gender-equitable policy.

Formal and informal rules and values

Even as some scholars are pushing the boundaries of FI approaches, others continue to use FI in those fields where it has proven itself to be exceptionally perceptive. Much of the earliest FI research looked at women's representation, quotas and recruitment of women. FI has also been very effective in showing how women's representation in particular political bodies can make a difference to the overall institutional environment and consequently to policy outputs. Minto and Mergaert (2018) are very explicit in their analysis of the interaction between formal and informal norms within the European Commission (see Hartlapp et al. in this volume). They see gender mainstreaming as an example of institutional layering which can help us to see why this instrument has been, at best, only partially successful in bringing about gender change in the EU. Like Guerrina et al. (2018), Minto and Mergaert (2018, 214) find that "informal institutions serve to undermine gendered institutional change." In other words, transformative change, such as was initially envisioned from gender mainstreaming, cannot succeed, if it is not accompanied by a fundamental restructuring of the formal and informal institutions in a more gender-aware manner.

Applying FI to formal committees and organizations remains one of the key strengths and likely forms the most common application of FI to regions outside the EU, although it remains under-developed in EU studies. Petra Ahrens (2016) uses FI to develop a detailed study of how actors within the European Parliament's FEMM committee are not only constrained by rules, but are also empowered to use them in a strategic and progressive way to bring about feminist change (see Ahrens and Rolandsen Agustín (European Parliament) in this volume). Her study gets to the heart of questions of power relations between committees, demonstrating that while FEMM may possess the same formal powers as other parliamentary committees, actors can use informal rules to promote the committee and enhance its actual position. "FEMM committee has developed the capacity to exploit the rules and routines of the EU's institutional setting thereby challenging their gendered impact" (Ahrens 2016, 786). To do this, the committee used the gendered logic of appropriateness within the European Parliament to its own advantage, thus creating strategic advantages where they were not immediately visible (Ahrens 2016, 790). This empowerment of actors and reorganization of gendered power within the institutions is only visible through a gendered lens. With this lens, we are able to more fully grasp the dynamics of change in the EU.

Conceptual openness

One important take away from this chapter is that FI approaches are incredibly flexible and open to conceptual stretching or bending. While we present this here as a strength of FI, this observation does not much differ from some of the initial and strong critiques that NI faced in the 1990s. Critics initially attacked NI as being too pluralistic and lacking conceptual clarity. For some, NI's definition of an institution was so broad that anything could be considered an institution; others charged that there was so much conceptual variation within NI that it could not possibly be considered a single approach (for an overall critique, see Lowndes 1996). Over the past decade, NI approaches have begun to converge around some central concepts. Although FI remains almost as diverse as NI, with some scholars borrowing from discursive approaches, others from sociological or historical and others drawing on all of these, we see a methodological convergence taking place within FI. Indeed, there is already convergence around the overarching political project of highlighting gender power within political and social institutions, with an aim to changing these.

Particularly in the field of EU studies, the methodological plurality of FI can be viewed as a real asset. The lack of theoretical constraints has meant that scholars have frequently brought FI into dialogue with other compatible approaches and, in so doing, have extended its scope beyond what was initially intended (see Lombardo and Kantola in this volume). This can be especially useful since the *sui generis* nature of the EU has led to the proliferation of specialized approaches, many of which could be combined with insights from feminist institutionalism. Ahrens and van der Vleuten (2020), for instance, offer one example of how FI can be "modified" to offer insight into questions that are quite specific to the EU. They investigate the European Commission's "White Paper on the Future of Europe" through an FI lens to highlight the invisibility of gender in the Commission's plans. This foray into the future requires them to adapt FI in a number of ways, but the flexibility of FI allows this without compromising the approaches internal integrity. They acknowledge that they "stretch feminist institutionalism by focusing on *potential* gendered outcomes" (Ahrens and van der Vleuten 2020, 294), and that this look into the future means there are no concrete formal or informal rules to examine. They overcome this by assuming a degree of path dependency and by using tools of gender assessment to aid in their predictions. They "expected that rules that are not specifically about gender equality may have gendered effects because they interact with institutions governing the economy, finance, welfare, security and violence" (Ahrens and van der Vleuten 2020, 294). Thus, drawing on FI tools they extrapolate to understand possible outcomes and make predictions based on those potentialities. This allows FI to move from the explanatory to a more predictive tool, which may be of value in identifying locations of gendered power before they become firmly entrenched.

FI's "stretchiness" has also made it possible for gender scholars to continue using the approach even as many have become more aware of the need for nuance within feminist and gender studies. FI considers an institution to be gendered in that it has different consequences for women's lives and men's lives and it may prioritize the experiences and interests of men or women (Ahrens and van der Vleuten 2020; Gains and Lowndes 2014; von Wahl in this volume). Although it is not generally openly critiqued, this position may be viewed as fostering a binary understanding of gender equality. This binary is often implied through FI's terminology, although as Ahrens and van der Vleuten (2020, 294) elaborate, "rather than conceptualizing women and men as two homogenous groups we acknowledge that EU governance can exacerbate or tackle inequalities selectively at the intersections of gender, class, race/ethnicity and sexual orientation." They use the term "complex gender equality" to acknowledge the intersection of gender and other forms of inequality. This is not unusual for gender scholars who are increasingly aware of multiple positionalities and intersectional inequalities. Kantola and Rolandsen Agustín (2019, 771) summarize what has become a common viewpoint: "Gender is also always intersectional: it is cut through with race and ethnicity, sexuality, age, and class to name but few of the relevant inequality categories in today's Europe." The conceptual openness that allows for this shift from "women" to "gender" to "intersectionality" is a real strength of FI and one around which we may see increased conceptual convergence (see von Wahl in this volume).

Moving forward

Despite the prevalence of theorists who are quick to acknowledge the need for an intersectional approach in EU studies, this is one area that remains somewhat undertheorized. However, the methodological flexibility of FI leaves plenty of room for the incorporation of a more intersectional approach. It is our contention that moving forward, in the field of EU studies, FI needs to take a more conscious and meaningful approach to intersectionality in order to unpack the power hierarchies evident not only within and among institutions, but also within and among differently positioned women, men and individuals. Weiner and MacRae (2017, 213) stressed that FI needs to consider "how disparate modes of manhood/masculinity and womanhood/femininity matter for the rules of the game." While there has been some exceptional intersectional FI scholarship in recent years, there is still more to do for FI to really bring intersectionality into the field.

According to Kronsell (2016a, 105) it is still commonplace within feminist EU studies for "gender" to be used to refer to "women" only, and for policies to be "evaluated for their effects on women, while gender as a power relation is at best implicit." To highlight the relational aspect of gender, Kronsell looks to understand masculinities and femininities in relation to one another. While this approach overcomes the "gender as women perspective," it only begins to bring ethnicity and other forms of inequality into the analysis as it considers how and where different forms of masculinity or femininity may take hold within the EU military. Magnusdottir (2016) stresses that power relations built on ethnicity have been largely overlooked in institutionalist theorizing of the EU and Europe, and looks to FI to fill this void.

There are, however, already some exceptional feminist institutional analyses that are clearly intersectional. Yet, only very few apply this framework to EU studies. Guth and Elfving (this volume) draw on insights from the CJEU and its ruling to show the importance of a truly intersectional approach. The CJEU's tendency to consider different forms of discrimination as separate issues, may "privilege the interests of advantaged subgroups, specifically white women and ethnic minority men." We must thus go beyond gender in order to fully understand the power relations within and among institutions.

Several analyses, particularly in the area of EU CSDP reviewed above, have highlighted that EU policies have differential impact on differently positioned women, and that social, political and economic contexts are important in understanding the gendered hierarchies within the institutions. In this way, intersectional approaches can offer an important starting point into the larger investigation of the layers of power and hierarchy evident in the institutional framework. By bringing in the experiences and perspectives of differently positioned women and problematizing the role of race, ethnicity, class and religion in the shaping of European norms and values, FI can expose additional power hierarchies in EU institutions. This is an important observation, not only for feminists, but in terms of the democratic nature of the European project. Through an FI lens, we can highlight silences and exclusions, which are important not only for gender equality, but for transnational democracy more broadly.

Where does this take us?

This discussion has shown the incredible diversity of EU scholarship that is currently in progress under the rubric of FI. Its primary strength is to reminds us that gender matters and institutions matter. As such, FI challenges us to look for connections between structures and agents; formal and informal; discourse and text; meaning and action. It is not possible for a single analysis to investigate all of these interactions. However, in feminist EU studies, we are slowly piecing together observations about the institutions, the position of gender therein and the forces of change that work to create and hinder a more equitable society. As these pieces come together, FI is beginning to bring together the components of a very detailed theory of power. Power is gendered; it is structural and it is institutionalized.

One of the greatest challenges and research objectives in the coming years will be to bring this theory of power and other strengths of FI into a meaningful dialogue with NI approaches and with other dominant approaches to European integration (see Abels and MacRae 2016). In a recent contribution to a well-regarded textbook, Mark Pollack (2019) outlines the role of institutionalist theories to European integration. He limits his discussion to only historical and rational choice institutionalisms and, in 20+ pages, does not make a single mention of gender or feminist contributions to these approaches. Instead, the editors of the textbook have chosen to address all feminist approaches collectively and separately in a single chapter. While this at least recognizes gender approaches as relevant and the editors include them in their synthesizing chapters, this theoretical isolationism is nevertheless reflective of the continued marginalization of gender and equity issues within the EU policy fields.

At present, FI approaches are still marginalized by the mainstream, and even within gender studies. It is the role of FI scholars to draw attention to the inherent gender biases within the institutions, and to strive for institutional change. Perhaps, when institutional change is more prevalent, we will also observe a more meaningful incorporation of feminist and intersectional tools into the new institutionalist toolbox.

References

Abels G, MacRae H (forthcoming): Searching for Agency: Gendering Leadership in European Integration Theory, in: Müller H, Tömmel I (eds.): *Pathways to Power – Female Leadership and Women Empowerment in the European Union*, Oxford: Oxford University Press.

Abels G, MacRae H, eds. (2016): *Gendering European Integration Theory: Engaging New Dialogues*. Opladen: Barbara Budrich.

Ahrens P (2016): The committee on women's rights and gender equality in the European Parliament: taking advantage of institutional power play, *Parliamentary Affairs* **69** (4), 778–793.

Ahrens P, van der Vleuten A (2020): Fish fingers and measles? Assessing complex gender equality in the scenarios for the future of Europe, *Journal of Common Market Studies* **58** (2), 292–308.

Ansorg N, Haastrup T (2018): Gender and the EU's support for security sector reform in fragile contexts, *Journal of Common Market Studies* **56** (5), 1127–1143.

Aspinwall MD, Schneider G (2000): Same menu, separate tables: the institutionalist turn in political science and the study of European integration, *European Journal of Political Research* **38** (1), 1–36.

Debusscher P, van der Vleuten A (2017): Equality Policies in the EU Through a Feminist Historical Institutionalist Lens, in: MacRae H, Weiner E (eds.): *Towards Gendering Institutionalism. Equality in Europe*, London: Rowman and Littlefield, 3–24.

Erikson J (2019): Institutions, gendered perceptions, and frames of meaning. explaining strategic choices of women MPs in Swedish prostitution policy, *Journal of Women, Politics & Policy* **40** (2), 263–285.

Gains F, Lowndes V (2014): How is institutional formation gendered, and does it make a difference? A new conceptual framework and a case study of policy and crime commissioners in England and Wales, *Politics and Gender* **10**, 524–548.

Guerrina R, Chappell L, Wright KAM (2018): Transforming CSDP? Feminist triangles and gender regimes, *Journal of Common Market Studies* **56** (5), 1036–1052.

Haastrup T, Kenny M (2016): Gendering Institutionalism: A Feminist Institutionalist Approach to EU Integration Theory, in: Abels G, MacRae H (eds.): *Gendering European Integration Theory: Engaging New Dialogues*. Opladen, Toronto: Barbara Budrich Publishers, 197–216.

Hoskyns C (1996): *Integrating Gender. Women, Law and Politics in the European Union*, London: Verso.

Kantola J, Rolandsen Agustín L (2019): Gendering the representative work of the European Parliament. A political analysis of women MEP's perceptions of gender equality in party groups, *Journal of Common Market Studies* **57** (4), 768–786.

Kronsell A (2016a): The power of EU masculinities. a feminist contribution to European integration theory, *Journal of Common Market Studies* **54** (1), 104–120.

Kronsell A (2016b): Sexed bodies and military masculinities. Gender path dependence in EU's common security and defense policy, *Men and Masculinities* **19** (3), 311–336.

Lowndes V (1996): Varieties of new institutionalism: a critical appraisal, *Public Administration* **74** (2), 181–197.

Lowndes V, Roberts M (2013): *Why Institutions Matter. The New Institutionalism in Political Science*, Basingstoke: Palgrave Macmillan.

Mackay F (2011): Conclusion: Towards a Feminist Institutionalism, in: Krook ML, Mackay F (eds.): *Gender, Politics and Institutions. Towards a Feminist Institutionalism*, Houndsmill: Palgrave, 181–197.

Mackay F, Kenny M, Chappell L (2010): New institutionalism through a gender lens: towards a feminist institutionalism?, *International Political Science Review* **31** (5), 573–588.

MacRae H (2006): Rescaling gender relations: the influence of European directives on the German gender regime, *Social Politics: International Studies in Gender State & Society* **13** (4), 522–550.

MacRae H, Weiner E (2017): Conclusion: Common Ground and New Terrain, in: MacRae H, Weiner E, (eds.): *Towards Gendering Institutionalism. Equality in Europe*, Lanham, MD: Rowman & Littlefield, 207–214.

Magnusdottir GL (2016): Immigrant representation in the Swedish Parliament: towards homogeneity or united diversity? *Social Change Review* **14** (2), 97–120.

Mahoney J, Thelen K (2010): A Theory of Gradual Institutional Change, in: Mahoney J, Thelen K (eds.): *Explaining Institutional Change. Ambiguity, Agency and Power*, Cambridge: Cambridge University Press, 1–37.

March, JG Olsen, JP (1989): *Rediscovering Institutions*, New York: Free Press.

Mergaert L, Lombardo E (2014): Resistance to Implementing Gender Mainstreaming in EU Research Policy, in: Weiner E, MacRae H (eds.): The persistent invisibility of gender in EU policy, *European Integration online Papers (EIoP)* 18 (5), 1–21, URL: http://eiop.or.at/eiop/texte/2014-005a.htm.

Minto R, Mergaert L (2018): Gender mainstreaming and evaluation in the EU. Comparative perspectives from feminist institutionalism, *International Feminist Journal of Politics* **20** (2), 204–220.

Pierson P (1996): The path to European integration: a historical institutionalist analysis, *Comparative Political Studies* **29** (2), 123–163.

Pierson P (2004): *Politics in Time History, Institutions, and Social Analysis*, Princeton, NJ: Princeton University Press.

Pollack MA (2003): *The Engines of European Integration. Delegation, Agency, and Agenda Setting in the EU*, Oxford, New York: Oxford University Press.

Pollack MA (2019): Institutionalism and European Integration, in: Wiener A, Börzel TA, Risse T (eds.): *European Integration Theory*, 3rd ed., Oxford, New York: Oxford University Press, 108–127.

Schmidt V (1999): ECSA review forum. approaches to the study of European politics, *ECSA Review*, Spring (XII: 2), 2–3.

Streek W, Thelen K (2005): Introduction: Institutional Change in Advanced Political Economies, in: Streek W, Thelen K (eds.): *Beyond Continuity: Institutional Change in Advanced Political Economies*, Oxford: Oxford University Press, 1–39.

Thomson J (2018): Resisting gendered change: feminist institutionalism and critical actors, *International Political Science Review* **39** (2), 178–191.

Waylen G (2017): *Gender and Informal Institutions*, London: Rowman & Littlefield.

Weiner E, MacRae H (2014): The Persistent Invisibility of Gender in EU Policy: Introduction, in: Weiner E, MacRae H (eds.): The persistent invisibility of gender in EU policy, *European Integration online Papers (EIoP)*, Special issue 1, **18** (3), 1–20, URL: http://eiop.or.at/eiop/texte/2014-003a.htm.

Weiner E, MacRae H (2017): Introduction, in: MacRae H, Weiner E (eds.): *Towards Gendering Institutionalism. Equality in Europe*, Lanham, MD: Rowman & Littlefield, xv–xxxi.

Woodward A (2004): Building Velvet Triangles: Gender and Informal Governance, in: Christiansen T, Piattoni S (eds.): *Informal Governance in the European Union*, Cheltenham: Edward Elgar, 76–93.

6

Feminist political economy and its explanatory promise

Rosalind Cavaghan and Anna Elomäki

Feminist EU studies have recently witnessed an expansion in attempts to theorise European integration (see Abels and MacRae 2016, 2020), accompanied by efforts to analyse the profound institutional and political shifts brought about since the financial and Eurozone crises (Kantola and Lombardo 2017). Surprisingly, insights from feminist political economy (FPE) (e.g. Bakker 1994; Elias and Roberts 2018; Young et al. 2011) have not yet been extensively incorporated into feminist EU studies. This chapter lays out some of the core concepts and analytical foci in FPE literature that have the potential to deepen our understanding of the gendered character and impacts of EU integration.

The approaches of critical political economy (CPE) that pay attention to the mutual constitution of the 'political' and the 'economic' – as well as societal power relations in the processes of European integration – have been increasingly applied to studying the EU since the early 1990s. The global financial crisis of 2007–2008 and the ensuing Eurozone crisis have spurred these activities. Critical political economists have shown how European integration and the EU's socioeconomic governance have become increasingly neoliberal since the mid-1980s (Gill 1998; van Apeldoorn 2002). They have further pointed out how the EU's crisis response and its new post-crisis economic governance structures have enhanced neoliberal capitalism, created class-based and other inequalities, reshaped the democratic sphere in the EU, prioritised particular economic ideas and reshaped the relationships between different policy areas (Bruff 2014; Crespy and Menz 2015; Ryner 2015). The multidisciplinary and wide-ranging field of FPE – with influences from Marxist/Socialist feminism, gender and development scholarship, Black feminist scholarship and feminist economics, among others – adds to CPE approaches by paying specific attention to how power, gender and the productive and reproductive economies intertwine (Elias and Roberts 2018). While most FPE literature has focused on global political economy and development, there has been an increasing interest in the application of FPE to the EU.

We argue that FPE concepts and approaches can be used to analyse the EU in various policy areas, ranging from the internal market to agriculture, trade, defence, gender equality policy, development and climate change (see policy section in this volume). To date, however, macro-economic policies and economic governance are the policy areas in which these ideas have been applied most (e.g., Bruff and Woehl 2016; Cavaghan and O'Dwyer 2018; Klatzer and Schlager 2019; O'Dwyer 2017; Young 2018). In this chapter, we show the analytical potential of FPE in these fields, which have also been the focus for most CPE scholars. As we argue, the EU's macro-economic policies, such as fiscal and monetary policies, as well as the governance mechanisms through which they are implemented, are pivotal for the future of gender equality in the EU because they actively maintain gendered and racialised hierarchies in the economy in the EU (Cavaghan and O'Dwyer 2018; Klatzer and Schlager 2014). Focusing on these fields, we illustrate the strengths and potential of FPE in theorising the EU's wider development.

CPE approaches to EU integration

CPE has been applied to multiple policy areas, including the internal market, the Economic and Monetary Union (EMU; see Scheele in this volume), trade policies (see García in this volume), the euro crisis and its management (see Kantola and Lombardo in this volume), and the EU's socioeconomic governance. CPE approaches are characterised by a focus on the interrelations in the economic and political spheres. They often draw on historical materialist and neo-Gramscian approaches and take capitalism and class as their central concepts. These theoretical and methodological starting points set CPE apart from 'traditional' perspectives on European integration. CPE sees the integration processes and EU governance as being intrinsically linked to the dynamics of global capitalism and the wider restructuring of the global political economy. CPE scholars have also conceptualised integration as a hegemonic project of dominant transnational and national social forces and stressed the unequal effects of these processes for different social classes and groups as well as the societal conflicts (Cafruny and Ryner 2012).

CPE scholars have highlighted how the European integration process has become increasingly neoliberalised since the mid-1980s. They have typically emphasised how this trajectory reflects shifts in the global political economy and identified the social and political forces and concrete actors that have supported the hegemony of the neoliberal project at the expense of social democratic alternatives (van Apeldoorn 2002). CPE scholars have further argued that the EMU and its constitutional and other legally binding enforcement mechanisms have reinforced the neoliberal discipline, strengthening financial capitalism in the EU and separating economic policies from political accountability (Gill 1998). The successes of the neoliberal project have led to an asymmetry between policies promoting market efficiencies and those promoting social protection and equality, whereby the former are increasingly regulated at the EU level and the latter left to the member states (Scharpf 2002).

Since the financial and Eurozone crises, CPE approaches have been used both to explain the causes of these crises and to understand their political and social effects. In the following, we focus on some key contributions connected to the EU's response to the financial and Eurozone crises: (1) the rationale and distributional effects of the austerity-focused policy response; (2) the political and democratic impacts of new economic governance structures implementing austerity; and (3) the consequent shifts in the relationship between the EU's economic and social goals.

The EU responded to the financial crisis by encouraging 'austerity' – large-scale cuts in public spending – nominally to reduce sovereign debt (Blyth 2013). This approach assumed that cutting public spending would reduce national debt and promote private sector confidence and investment, thereby ultimately restoring growth. However, critics have pointed out that the evidence supporting this approach is, at best, contextual and nuanced rather than unequivocal (Clarke and Newman 2012). Austerity's distributional impacts have also been well documented. Austerity re-allocates the costs of the financial crisis away from the private financial institutions that caused it and towards the public – particularly its poorest sectors – while mobilising a moral narrative that states overspent and that everyone needs to 'tighten their belts' (Blyth 2013; Clarke and Newman 2012).

CPE approaches have also examined the measures put in place to coordinate member states' implementations of austerity, drawing attention to the constitutionalisation of austerity and the de-democratisation and de-politicisation of economic policy in the EU (Bruff 2014). The successively adopted new sets of rules – the 'Six Pack', the 'Two Pack' and the 'Fiscal Compact' – strengthened and complemented the debt and deficit rules of the 'Stability and Growth Pact' – adopted in 1997 – to ensure the stability of the EMU. They introduced, among other things, new sanctions, a requirement to include a balanced budget rule in national legislation and the annual process of economic surveillance and coordination called the European Semester (Bruff 2014; Oberndorfer 2015; see Scheele in this volume for more details). The reconfiguration of policy rules has shifted power from national and EU-level democratic bodies to executive branches and non-transparent, technocratic financial bureaucracy. It has also made austerity a permanent policy by constraining member states' policy choices. CPE scholars have referred to this shift as 'authoritarian neoliberalism' (Bruff 2014) or 'authoritarian constitutionalism' (Oberndorfer 2015). These concepts draw attention to the way in which the post-crisis reforms of EU economic governance restrict the possibilities for future generations to overturn the permanent austerity and the undemocratic policy-making processes that maintain and marginalise dissenting social groups and oppositional politics. From the CPE perspective, new EU economic governance rules help to institutionalise and maintain the neoliberal political–economic order and defend it from efforts to push for greater democratisation (Bruff 2014).

CPE has also made visible how the EU's strengthened economic governance has shifted towards a technocratic expert regime that relies on a specific form of economic knowledge and ideas. These include, for instance, ideas about constitution-like rules as the basis of market-society characteristic of ordoliberalism, a German variant of neoliberalism (Ryner 2015), heterodox economic assumptions accepting and tacitly promoting the supremacy of the market (Bruff and Tansel 2019) and economic ideas promoting austerity (Helgadóttir 2016). The economic knowledge that disseminates these ideas masks their deeply political ideological commitments with a veneer of technocratic inevitability.

Finally, CPE scholars have argued that the post-crisis shifts in the EU's socio-economic governance have further subjugated the EU's social goals and policies to the objectives of budget discipline and macro-economic balance (Crespy and Menz 2015), which are supported by the ever-stronger rules and surveillance and sanction mechanisms (de la Porte and Heins 2015). Although some commentators describe a gradual 'socialisation' of some economic governance processes (Zeitlin and Vanhercke 2018), social policies must still conform to the EU's market-making logic (see Milner in this volume). In CPE literature, the economy/social relationship has thus been mainly discussed in terms of policies, governance mechanisms and actors, rather than in terms of knowledge and epistemologies.

CPE approaches have, therefore, highlighted how EU monetary and economic integration has reshaped the contours of the political arena, restricting opportunities to contest economic policy at the member-state level and enhancing the power of EU institutions. They have also helped us to understand the ideational underpinning of the EU's economic policies and governance and highlighted the imbalance between economic and social integration. While these approaches have emphasised the category of class, they have tended to neglect concerns about gender and race. As we will show below, by neglecting these analytical angles, CPE approaches miss important dynamics that legitimise EU economic governance, core aspects of its ideological basis and some of the most important structural factors mediating distributional impacts.

Feminist political economy – conceptualising the economy and identifying gendered impacts

In contrast to CPE, FPE is characterised by a significant degree of intellectual and methodological eclecticism. What unites FPE, however, is its focus on 'how gender is performed, enacted, embodied, constructed, institutionalised and reconstituted in the global economy and how these processes work through other many and varied structures of oppression … and are in turn actively resisted' (Elias and Roberts 2018, 5). Broadly speaking, FPE literature points out the central role of gender (inequalities) in the maintenance of capitalist economies and the state (Elias and Roberts 2018; Woehl 2014). Where CPE focuses on the co-construction of the political and the economic, FPE goes further. It points out that the functioning of the economy and much of economic policy depend on the maintenance and reproduction of particular relations between the state and households, which are held in place by the gendered socialisation of human bodies (Griffin 2010, 87). The delegation of care work to households, in which mainly women perform this labour –unpaid – is one of the most important of these relations (Elias and Roberts 2018, 5). Similarly, the low wages paid for work as nursing, childcare and elder care, or in domestic work such as cleaning, rest on an undervaluation of care and reproductive work and the people typically regarded as suitable for it (Elias and Roberts 2018). These female-dominated jobs and public care services are often seen as a cost, rather than an investment (Elson 2017). Feminists argue in contrast that this situation constitutes a reproductive tax extracted from women to subsidise the productive economy (Rai et al. 2014). The current Covid-19 pandemic illustrates the productive economy's reliance on this reproductive subsidy particularly well. Under-funded health and elder care systems unable to cope with the pandemic have led to a near total economic shut down in an effort to suppress transmission so that health care systems will not be overwhelmed. As a result, responsibility for care work and education has been moved back into the home where workers struggle to perform their normal paid work while also having newly intensified caring duties. Early studies have indicated that these shifts are exacerbating gendered and racialised inequalities (Amnesty International 2020; EIGE 2020).

Multiple, more detailed theoretical perspectives and empirical studies flow from these core premises of FPE. FPE's insistence on the centrality of gender to the functioning of capitalism is one of the key differences distinguishing it from CPE. It also places FPE at odds with many of the central assumptions in dominant approaches to economics. Core among these entrenched assumptions is a tendency – particularly within neo-classical economic paradigms – to argue that economic policy is 'gender neutral' (Bakker 1994). This perspective is, in turn, premised on several disciplinary concepts and commitments that discourage consideration of the interactions between different 'levels' and sectors of the economy.

First among these is the presumed division between the 'productive' sector – that is, paid labour – and the (social) reproductive sector in which (predominantly unpaid) care work is performed. FPE points out that the productive economy is *dependent* on the care sector, which creates functioning humans who can work (Çağlar 2009, 166). This dependency is, however, consistently ignored in most economic modelling and economic policy. Instead, dominant approaches simply assume an unlimited supply of care (Rai et al. 2014).

Two other disciplinary assumptions have been problematised by FPE scholars: divisions between the macro-, meso- and micro-economy and the concept of 'homo economicus' or the rational economic man. Neo-classical disciplinary assumptions of the kind often used to underpin austerity policies are premised on the assumption that the individual behaviour of a self-interested 'rational economic man' is the driving causal force in the economy at all levels – micro, meso and macro. Within this paradigm, macro-economic analysis is nothing more than the study of the aggregate effects of individual activities (Bakker 1994, 8; Çağlar 2009, 163). This differs from heterodox approaches, which accept that macro levels of the economy may have their own dynamics that are more complicated than the aggregate effects of individuals' actions (Çağlar 2009, 163). These concepts are an important target of feminist critique because they underpin economic policy-makers' common arguments that social impacts are not a macro-economic concern. Within the neo-classical mind-set, macro-economic policy and analysis is *by definition* not concerned with individuals, but rather with aggregate measures that can be modelled, such as output levels, rates of growth and budget surplus/deficit (Bakker 1994, 8). Under these logics, the social impacts of economic policies (like austerity) and the gender inequalities they entrench are decoupled from the policies causing them.

FPE scholars have challenged these assumptions by thoroughly demonstrating the social impacts of macro-economic policies (Gill and Roberts 2011). However, the presumed separation between the economic and the social, which seems absurd from a feminist perspective, remains influential in mainstream economic thinking and practice. As a result, FPE perspectives argue that these ideas and disciplinary assumptions maintain a 'strategic silence' (Bakker 1994; Young et al. 2011), which serves both to constitute and to obscure unequal economic relations between men and women (Bakker 1994). They also underpin increasing tensions between the capitalist economy and social reproduction, discussed below.

In addition to these kinds of critiques of economic disciplinary assumptions, FPE approaches have shown how both gender and race can structure many economic transactions so that women and men (and other people whose identities may not conform to binary gender classifications) participate in markets on unequal terms (Bakker 1994, 5; Gill and Roberts 2011). These dynamics are relevant both within and among countries. FPE scholars show how states often exploit women's subordination, marketing their under-paid labour as a competitive advantage to attract international manufacturing (Dedeoğlu 2013). In this way, global production chains that bring affordable goods to the Global North, such as food, clothing and technology, are often rendered possible by continued gendered exploitation (Dedeoğlu 2013).

State and corporate claims of non-responsibility for social reproduction have also resulted in it, too, becoming a globalised commodity, with stark gendered and racialised impacts. As states continue to retrench public services, a small proportion of highly educated women can buy in labour to perform care work, which the state supports and subsidises less and less. Usually, this labour takes the form of either female migration or ethnicised labour– a practice that gender-selective and racist national border regimes often facilitate (Sauer and Woehl 2011). The migration 'care chains' (Hochschild 2000) established by these policies also mean that gender regimes are no longer 'fenced in' by the nation state, instead stretching between countries sending and receiving migrants (Hochschild 2000; Sauer and Woehl 2011). This has clear effects on classed and racialised hierarchies among women.

In order to contest these gender-biased and gender-blind understandings entrenched in mainstream economic policy, FPE scholars have devised concepts and measures that capture the gendered inputs into the economy and the gendered outcomes of policy. These include the application of human rights perspectives to macro-economic policy (Balakrishnan et al. 2010), gender budgeting (see below), 'social infrastructure (Elson 2017), and attempts to theorise 'depletion' (Rai et al. 2014). These concepts and approaches attempt to account for the input of social reproductive labour, the impacts of investing in it and the impacts of cutting state support for it. They provide analyses that span different levels of the economy and expose the interrelations between the productive and reproductive economy and the economic and social spheres.

Finally, FPE has also pointed out global patterns in the production and mobilisation of economic knowledge. These critiques have identified the types of knowledge commonly held in esteem in economic policy-making. Peterson (2012, 9) highlights the grip of 'positivism, modernism and masculinisation' in economic policy-making. She describes positivism in terms of 'rationalist approaches' characterised by dichotomised thinking and stable definitions of homogenous and discrete phenomena that enable calculation and prediction as well as control over ambiguity, contestation and critical reflection. She describes modernism as privileging of Western-centric knowledge-production, governed by individualism and instrumental rationality and with a tendency to devalue the voices of 'others'. Finally, masculinism is the tendency to base economic theory on essentialised notions of a generic atomistic and self-interested man (for a discussion of masculinities see Hearn et al. in this volume). These kinds of approaches drive mainstream economic analysts to pursue 'objective' measures of the impacts of, for instance, the crisis rather than analyses that concede the complex social and cultural realities leading to it (Griffin 2013).

The dominance of positivism, modernism and masculinism in economic policy-making also underpins a tendency to confer onto white male perspectives the mantle of 'expertise' while rejecting competing perspectives from peripheral or marginalised voices. Basing economic theory explicitly on (Western, white) *men* also glosses over relationships between differently located people, thus normalising inequalities. FPE approaches, in contrast, emphasise multidisciplinary approaches, which include analyses of inter alia gendered practices and processes in institutions, such as the World Bank or multinational corporations; sites of analyses, such as the household; and methods such as ethnography – foci traditionally overlooked by 'malestream' political economy scholars (Elias and Roberts 2018).

Finally, FPE concepts have been applied to show how the dominance of these epistemological tendencies in economic policy-making shape the possibilities for feminist interventions in economic policy. A key example of this is the widespread tendency to support gender equality policies with arguments and empirical knowledge about efficiency, business benefits and positive effects on employment rates, economic growth and competitiveness. FPE analyses argue that promoting gender equality measures on this basis ignores the historical and structural causes of gender inequality, legitimises neoliberal economic policies and corporate capitalism, reproduces gendered understandings of the economy and reduces gender equality commitments to an investment strategy (Elomäki 2015, 2020). Such promotion also restricts the justifications feminists can use in support of gender equality measures to arguments premised on efficiency, while drawing feminists into the frustrations of working within restrictive 'technicalised' policy development and implementation processes (Ferguson 2015).

Feminist political economy in EU studies

As stated at the outset, FPE approaches have, surprisingly, not yet been extensively or systematically applied to the study of European integration. The policy area in which FPE approaches – or their influence – can be most readily seen in feminist EU studies is the EU's economic governance. Feminist researchers have applied some of the concepts from FPE to illustrate that the economic goals and macro-economic policies pursued are gender-biased and that the EU ignores women and marginalised groups as citizens and as economic actors (Bruff and Woehl 2016; Cavaghan and O'Dwyer 2018; Klatzer and Schlager 2014, 2019; Young 2018). In particular, the reconfigurations of the EU's economic governance after the economic and euro crises have been used to justify cuts to gender equality policies and public services (Kantola and Lombardo 2017; see also Kantola and Lombardo in this volume) and have reshaped gendered subjectivities in conflicting ways. In the wake of austerity-driven cuts to public services, women find themselves lumbered with more care work, performing traditionally conceived feminised roles, while also experiencing more pressure to behave in competitive and risky ways traditionally conceived as masculine (Bruff and Woehl 2016). FPE concepts have been particularly useful in drawing attention to how the EU's fiscal rules and austerity policies set limits on the potential scope of the welfare state, thus driving a crisis in social reproduction as households and individuals are forced to absorb more and more reproductive work and risk (Klatzer and Schlager 2014; Woehl 2017; Young 2002, 2018). These redistributions of work and risk have affected migrant and Black and minority ethnic women the most acutely, deepening existing intersectional inequalities between women (Bassel and Emejulu 2017).

While CPE scholars have described authoritarian neoliberalism and authoritarian constitutionalism, FPE scholars have examined how EU economic governance constitutionalises masculine norms (Bruff and Woehl 2016, 93). EU-level and national fiscal bureaucracy, such as the European Commission's Directorate-General for Economic and Financial Affairs (DG ECFIN), the European Central Bank (ECB), the 'Eurogroup' and national ministries of finance – who have gained in power and influence – are more male-dominated than the European Parliament and national parliaments that have been sidelined, or those parts of the European Commission that have traditionally led EU gender equality policy (Cavaghan 2017a; O'Dwyer 2019). Analysis has shown that the male domination of these economic institutions corresponds to masculine norms, informal institutional rules and the practices within them (Klatzer and Schlager 2019, 51–53). Feminists have found these institutions very difficult to access, encountering stiff resistance to gender mainstreaming efforts and spurious and under-conceptualised critiques of the relevance of gender equality in macro-economic policy (Cavaghan 2017a, 61; Hoskyns 2008, 12).

Feminist scholars have also drawn explicit attention to the gendered forms of expertise and gendered epistemologies underpinning EU economic governance (Cavaghan and O'Dwyer 2018; O'Dwyer 2019). This adds to the mainstream political arguments that have pointed out the dominance and consequences of the ordoliberal ideas within the EU's economic governance (e.g. Helgadóttir 2016; Ryner 2015). Building even further on CPE analysis, feminist approaches have also shown that the EU's efforts to legitimate its economic policy through a discourse of neutrality or expertise also excludes feminist concerns – which do not fit easily within the veneer of objectivity – from economic governance discourses (O'Dwyer 2019, 169). FPE analyses have thus highlighted whose interests are included as 'economic concerns' in EU economic policy-making and whose are not.

This has been linked to the well-documented 'downgrading' of the EU's gender equality policy and a closing of policy opportunities for feminist activists (Jacquot 2015). Feminist actors targeting the EU now confront policy processes that are dominated by economic actors and concerns in which social goals have been subsumed by macro-economic ones (Cavaghan 2017b, 210). In this context, EU gender equality policy has increasingly become framed in a discourse of (individualised) 'rights' and economic benefits, which fits well with neoliberal tendencies to eschew engagement with structural inequalities (Elomäki 2015; Jacquot 2015).

This summary shows the promise of FPE perspectives to highlight the important role of economic policy and ideology in the EU's gender regime. FPE analyses span different levels and sectors of the economy, elaborating links, for example, between economic ideology promoted at the EU level and the gendered subjectivities promoted to citizens in member states. These analyses also show the interrelationships between evolving EU economic governance processes and the declining levels of democratic control. They illustrate how power has shifted away from institutions and parts of the European Commission that are traditionally more open to gender equality claims and towards institutions, such as DG ECFIN, in which entrenched economic disciplinary assumptions place limits on the acceptability and intelligibility of gender equality claims. Understanding the jargonistic vocabularies and methods of these parts of the Commission is much easier when we draw on FPE. Hence, FPE provides promising frameworks with which to theorise links between the EU level, member states and individuals, thus highlighting very important phenomena that are currently shaping gender equality outcomes.

Moving forward – key issues

In this final section, we explore the possibilities of – and barriers to – a feminist transformation of the EU's gendered macro-economic policies and economic governance processes informed by FPE theoretical thinking. We also discuss EU policy fields in which FPE approaches could be applied in greater depth.

Gender budgeting – and to a lesser extent, gender mainstreaming – have been seen as a way to implement the critical insights of feminist economics and FPE in practice (O'Hagan 2018). Gender budgeting is a feminist strategy for bringing an intersectional gender lens to macro-economic policies and budgets and pushing these in a more gender-equal direction. Its radical potential lies in the way it challenges entrenched gender-biased understandings of the economy that underpin macro-economic policies (O'Hagan 2018). However, in EU policy-making, the promise of gender budgeting has not been actualised. Efforts to integrate a gender perspective into macro-economic policies and economic governance as part of the EU's commitment to gender mainstreaming have been disappointing – and often met with hostility (Hoskyns 2008; O'Dwyer 2017; Villa and Smith 2014). The few examples of gender budgeting or gender mainstreaming that can be found in EU macro-economic policies do not challenge the gender biases entrenched in EU macro-economic policies and economic epistemologies. Instead, only gender equality commitments that support existing macro-economic priorities of growth, jobs and competitiveness have been adopted (Hoskyns 2008; O'Dwyer 2017). Even these rather meagre gender equality commitments can be undermined, however, when they are passed to member states for implementation, and budgetary discipline remains the ultimate priority (Cavaghan and Elomäki 2020). The apparent legitimacy of the gendered economic model, which is blind to the importance of reproductive labour, and the economic policies that sustain inequalities therefore remain largely intact in the EU.

FPE helps us to understand these disappointing outcomes. It throws our attention onto how the institutional barriers to gender budgeting and gender mainstreaming that have been identified by gender and EU scholars are intertwined with economic ideological and epistemological barriers. The disciplinary divisions between the macro- and micro-economies explain why the EU's macro-economic policies have been resistant to gender equality claims while gender perspectives have been integrated into the EU's employment policies – an area traditionally understood as micro-economic policy (Cavaghan 2017a; Hoskyns 2008). Moreover, the hierarchy and associated boundary between the economic and the social – the productive and the reproductive economy – serves to exclude certain concerns, such as the unpaid economy and the crisis of social reproduction (enhanced by the economic crisis) from the EU's core economic agendas. These barriers are also connected to power and privilege. Reconfiguring the distribution of social reproduction would erode the 'tax' currently being extracted from women that subsidises the productive economy. It is therefore not a surprise that policy-makers resist tackling these injustices, which have benefited capitalist accumulation and supported gendered and racialised power relations.

FPE approaches therefore have a double role to play in the feminist transformation of the EU's macro-economic policies and economic governance. On the one hand, FPE insights can inform the efforts to challenge these policies. On the other hand, a broader application of FPE-informed research is needed to examine the full array of EU policies and the ways in which integration reconfigures power and relationships that extend from individual subjectivities within households up to the highest levels of EU policy-making.

Many areas of EU policy that have not been thoroughly researched by feminists are ripe for the application of FPE approaches. Young (2018), for example, points out that FPE has not engaged sufficiently with the impact of EU monetary policy, such as quantitative easing. Similarly, trade has not been extensively explored using the full range of FPE concepts. A handful of existing analyses have highlighted gender equality issues related to EU trade policy (see García in this volume). True (2009), for example, has shown that EU trade policy – thoroughly imbued with neoliberal assumptions – shapes the inclusion of any gender equality clauses into the familiar 'business case' mould. Garcia and Masselot (2015; see also García in this volume) have shown that even these conceptually weak rhetorical commitments are not adequately implemented. FPE perspectives on trade also hold the potential to theorise the effects of EU disintegration when we try to work out, for instance, how the UK's exit from the EU and the new trading relationships it might build could affect gender equality in the UK, the EU and third countries (see Guerrina and Masselot in this volume).

It is also surprising that, despite acknowledgements of the impacts that austerity has had on social reproduction – and migrant women in particular – and the fairly large body of research on EU migration (see Krause and Schwenken in this volume), feminist EU studies have not turned to FPE to join these findings together and to theorise the role of the care chains in migration within and into the EU. Such an analysis would provide an excellent opportunity to examine the racialised and classed relationships – not just between men and women, but also between women – that state and corporate non-responsibility for social reproduction – supported by a myriad of EU policies – embeds as a part of the EU's broader gender regime. Nor have the relationships between EU economic ideologies and climate policy and the environment been extensively explored (see Allwood in this volume), yet FPE has provided many analyses of these phenomena in other international arenas (Elias and Roberts 2018).

FPE's analytical vocabularies thus have considerable potential to elucidate the links between multiple levels of the EU polity and the ways in which gendered economic goals and concepts structure activities throughout them. This focus on the economic – conceived in a feminist political sense – sets FPE approaches apart from competing feminist approaches to the analysis of European integration. FPE perspectives push us to understand the links between EU economic ideologies – and the processes putting them into action – and the lived experiences of businesses, households and individuals. They show us how integration has shaped the gendered contours of the political arena and highlight the importance of gendered epistemologies and hierarchies between policy areas, thus providing analytical tools that can be applied to many policy areas. The application of FPE perspectives in feminist EU studies thus has the potential to deepen and widen feminist theorisation of the EU as a whole, providing fresh perspectives that could help to show the full complexities of the role of gender (inequalities) in the maintenance of the European project. FPE concepts should also play a crucial role in studying the gendered and racialised effects of the multiple crises caused by the Covid-19 pandemic and the gendered and racialised effects of the containment and recovery measures (see Klatzer and Rinaldi 2020).

References

Abels G, MacRae H, eds. (2016): *Gendering European Integration Theory*, Opladen, Toronto: Barbara Budrich Publisher.

Abels G, MacRae H (2020): Gender Approaches, in: Didier B, Diez T, Fanoulis E, Rosamond B (eds.): *Routledge Handbook on Critical European Union Studies*, Abingdon, New York: Routledge, 112–124.

Amnesty International (2020): *Policing the Pandemic: Human Rights Violations in the Enforcement of Covid-19 Measures in Europe*. London: Amnesty International, URL: https://www.amnesty.org/en/documents/eur01/2511/2020/en/.

Bakker I (1994): Engendering Macro-Economic Policy Reform in the Era of Global Restructuring and Adjustment, in: Bakker I (ed.): *The Strategic Silence. Gender and Economic Policy*, London: Zed Books, 1–26.

Balakrishnan R, Elson D, Patel R (2010): Rethinking macro economic strategies from a human rights perspective, *Development* **53** (1), 27–36.

Bassel L, Emejulu A (2017): *Minority Women and Austerity. Survival and Resistance in France and Britain*, Bristol: Policy Press.

Blyth, M (2013): *Austerity: The History of a Dangerous Idea*, Oxford: Oxford University Press.

Bruff I (2014): The rise of authoritarian neoliberalism, *Rethinking Marxism* **26** (1), 113–129.

Bruff I, Tansel CB (2019): Authoritarian neoliberalism. Trajectories of knowledge production and praxis, *Globalizations* **16** (3), 233–244.

Bruff I, Woehl S (2016): Constitutionalizing Austerity, Disciplining the Household. Masculine Norms of Competitiveness and the Crisis of Social Reproduction in the Eurozone, in: Hozic A, True J (eds.): *Scandalous Economics. The Spectre of Gender and Global Financial Crisis*, Oxford: Oxford University Press, 92–108.

Cafruny A, Ryner M (2012): The Global Financial Crisis and the European Union. The Irrelevance of Integration Theory and the Pertinence of Critical Political Economy, in: Nousios P, Overbeek H, Tsolakis A (eds.): *Globalisation and European Integration. Critical Approaches to Regional Order and International Relations*, Abingdon Oxon: Routledge, 32–50.

Çağlar G (2009): *Engendering der Makrooekonomie und Handelspolitik. Potenziale transnationaler Wissensnetzwerke*, Wiesbaden: VS Verlag.

Cavaghan R (2017a): The Gender Politics of EU Economic Policy. Policy shifts and Contestations Before and After the Crisis, in Kantola J, Lombardo E (eds.): *Gender and the Economic Crisis in Europe. Politics, Institutions and Intersectionality*, Cham: Palgrave Macmillan, 49–71.

Cavaghan R (2017b): *Making Gender Equality Happen. Knowledge, Change and Resistance in EU Gender Mainstreaming*, London: Routledge.

Cavaghan R, O'Dwyer M (2018): European economic governance in 2017: Whose recovery is it anyway?, *Journal of Common Market Studies Annual Review* **56,** 96–108.

Cavaghan R, Elomäki A (2020): Gendered Epistemologies in the EU's New Economic Governance, paper presented at the 27th International Conference of Europeanists, June 22–24, Reykjavik: University of Iceland.

Clarke J, Newman J (2012): The alchemy of austerity, *Critical Social Policy*, **32** (3), 299–319.

Crespy A, Menz G (2015): Commission entrepreneurship and the debasing of social Europe before and after the eurocrisis, *Journal of Common Market Studies* **53** (4), 753–768.

Dedeoğlu S (2013): Patriarchy reconsolidated. Women's Work in Three Global Commodity Chains of Turkey's Garment Industry, in: Dunaway AW (ed.): *Gendered Commodity Chains. Seeing Women's Work and Households in Global Production,* Stanford, CA: Stanford University Press, 105–118.

de la Porte C, Heins E (2015): A new era of European integration? Governance of labour market and social policy since the sovereign debt crisis, *Comparative European Politics* **13** (1), 8–28.

Elomäki A (2015): The economic case for gender equality in the European Union. Selling gender equality to decision-makers and neoliberalism to women's organizations, *European Journal of Women's Studies* **22** (3), 288–302.

Elomäki A (2020): Economization of expert knowledge about gender equality in the European Union, *Social Politics: International Studies in Gender, State & Society*, https://doi.org/10.1093/sp/jxaa005.

Elias J, Roberts A, eds. (2018): *Handbook on the International Political Economy of Gender.* Aldershot: Edward Elgar.

Elson D (2017) Towards a Gender-Aware Macroeconomic Framework, in: Bargawi H, Cozzi G, Himmelweit S (eds.): *Economics and Austerity in Europe. Gendered Impacts and Sustainable Alternatives*, London: Routledge, 15–26.

European Institute for Gender Equality (EIGE) (2020): *Covid 19 and Gender Equality*, URL: https://eige.europa.eu/topics/health/covid-19-and-gender-equality.

Ferguson L (2015): This is our gender person, *International Feminist Journal of Politics* **17** (3), 1–18.

García M, Masselot A (2015): EU–Asia free trade agreements as tools for social norm/legislation transfer, *Asia Europe Journal* **13** (3), 241–252.

Gill S (1998): European governance and new constitutionalism: Economic and Monetary Union and alternatives to disciplinary Neoliberalism in Europe, *New Political Economy* **3** (1), 5–26.

Gill S, Roberts A (2011): Macroeconomic Governance, Gendered Inequality, and Global Crises, in: Young B, Bakker I, Elson D (eds.): *Questioning Financial Governance from a Feminist Perspective,* Abingdon: Routledge 155–172.

Griffin P (2010): Gender, governance and the global political economy, *Australian Journal of International Affairs* **64** (1), 86–104.

Griffin, P (2013): Gendering global finance. crisis, masculinity, and responsibility, *Men and Masculinities* **16** (1), 9–34.

Helgadóttir O (2016): The Bocconi boys go to Brussels. Italian economic ideas, professional networks and European austerity, *Journal of European Public Policy* **23** (3), 392–409.

Hochschild A (2000): Global Care Chains and Emotional Surplus Value, in: Giddens T, Hutton W (eds.): *On the Edge. Globalization and the New Millennium,* London: Sage. 130–146.

Hoskyns C (2008): Governing the EU: Gender and Macroeconomics, in: Rai SM, Waylen G (eds.): *Global Governance: Feminist Perspectives,* Basingstoke: Palgrave Macmillan, 107–128.

Jacquot S (2015): *Transformations in EU Gender Equality. From Emergence to Dismantling,* Basingstoke: Palgrave Macmillan.

Kantola J, Lombardo E (2017): Gender and the Politics of the Economic Crisis in Europe, in: Kantola J and Lombardo E (eds.): *Gender and the Economic Crisis in Europe. Politics, Institutions and Intersectionality,* London: Palgrave Macmillan, 1–21.

Klatzer E, Rinaldi, A (2020): Next Generation EU leaves women behind: Gender Impact Assessment on the EC proposal for a #nextGenerationEU. Study commissioned by The Greens/EFA Group in the European Parliament, initiated by Alexandra Geese, MEP, ULR: https://alexandrageese.eu/wp-content/uploads/2020/06/Gender-Impact-Assessment-NextGenEU_Klatzer_Rinaldi.pdf (download: July 8, 2020).

Klatzer E, Schlager S (2014): Feminist Perspectives on Macroeconomics. Reconfiguration of Gendered Power Structures and Erosion of Gender Equality Through the New Economic Governance Regime of the European Union, in: Evan CM, Hammings MH, Henry M et al. (eds.): *The Sage Handbook of Feminist Theory,* Thousand Oaks, CA: Sage, 483–499.

Klatzer E, Schlager C (2019): Losing Grounds. Masculine-Authoritarian Reconfigurations of Power Structures in the European Union, in: Wöhl S, Springler E, Pachel M, Zeilinger B (eds.): *The State of the European Union. Fault Lines in European Integration,* Wiesbaden: Springer VS, 45–75.

Oberndorfer L (2015): From new constitutionalism to authoritarian constitutionalism. New Economic Governance and the state of European democracy, in: Jäger, J, Springler E (eds.): *Asymmetric Crisis in Europe and Possible Futures. Critical Political Economy and Post-Keynesian Perspectives,* London: Routledge, 186–207.

O'Dwyer M (2017): The *Role of Gender in European Economic Governance,* PhD Thesis, University College Dublin.

O'Dwyer M (2019): Expertise in European Economic Governance: a feminist analysis, *Journal of Contemporary European Research* **15** (2), 162–178.

O'Hagan A (2018): Conceptual and Institutional Origins of Gender Budgeting, in: O'Hagan A, Klatzer E (eds.): *Gender Budgeting in Europe Developments and Challenges,* Cham: Palgrave Macmillan, 19–42.

Peterson VS (2012): Rethinking theory. inequalities, informalization and feminist quandaries, *International Feminist Journal of Politics* **14** (1), 5–35.

Rai SM, Hoskyns C, Thomas D (2014): Depletion, *International Feminist Journal of Politics* **16** (1), 86–105.

Ryner M (2015): Europe's ordoliberal iron cage. Critical political economy, the euro area crisis and its management, *Journal of European Public Policy* **22** (2), 275–294.

Scharpf F (2002): The European social model, *Journal of Common Market Studies* **40** (4), 645–670.

Sauer B, Woehl S (2011): Feminist perspectives on the internationalization of the state, *Antipode* **43** (1), 108–128.

True J (2009): Trading-off Gender Equality for Global Europe. The European Union and Free Trade Agreements, in: E. Lombardo, P. Meier, M. Verloo (eds.): *The Discursive Politics of Gender Equality: Stretching, bending and policymaking,* London: Routledge, 122–142.

van Apeldoorn B (2002): *Transnational Capitalism and the Struggle over European Integration,* London: Routledge.

Villa P, Smith M (2014): Policy in the Time of Crisis. Employment policy and gender equality in Europe, in: Karamessini, M and Rubery J (eds.): *Women and Austerity. The Ecomomic Crisis and the Future for Gender Equality,* London: Routledge, 273–294.

Woehl S (2014): The state and gender relations in international political economy. A state-theoretical approach to varieties of capitalism in crisis, *Capital & Class* **38** (1), 87–99.

Woehl S (2017): The Gender Dynamics of Financialization and Austerity in the European Union. The Irish Case, in: Kantola J, Lombardo E (eds.): *Gender and the Economic Crisis in Europe: Politics, Institutions and Intersectionality,* London: Palgrave Macmillan, 139–161.

Young, B (2018): Financialization, Unconventional Monetary Policy and Gender Inequality, in: Elias J, Roberts A (eds.): *Handbook on the International Political Economy of Gender,* Aldershot: Edward Elgar, 241–251.

Young B, Bakker I, Elson D (2011). *Questioning Financial Governance from a Feminist Perspective,* Abingdon: Routledge.

Zeitlin J, Vanhercke B (2018): Socializing the European semester. EU social and economic policy co-ordination in crisis and beyond, *Journal of European Public Policy* **25** (2), 149–174.

7

The EU, men and masculinities

Jeff Hearn, Katarzyna Wojnicka, Iva Šmídová and Keith Pringle

Critical approaches on men and masculinities are relevant whether we are talking about EU politics as an amalgam of national and local politics, institutionally or geographically, or the international or transnational politics in or of the EU itself and its various constituent institutions and bodies. They are relevant in the analysis of political institutions, social movements and political actors, both individual and collective, as well as the very question of what counts as politics in the first place, seen as pervasive and not only formal politics in the public domain. Thus, politics is not just mainstream politics in the public domain; rather politics pervades gender ordering of and across societies.

Men and masculinities are just as gendered as women and femininities, individually and collectively: whether we are talking about party politicians, policy-makers, professionals, activists, supporters, clients, citizens, migrants or refugees, amongst many other political actors and groupings. This may seem obvious (to some), but is still frequently forgotten or obscured, in both mainstream and critical analyses. It is so much the case that political institutions and organisations – whether local, national, transnational or European – are often described in either gender-neutral or implicitly masculinised terms, into which women move or which affect women, albeit in differential ways. The centre, the One (as opposed to the presumed Other[s]), typically and easily remains undeconstructed. Likewise, the EU and its institutions and processes may appear, to many, as gender-neutral or implicitly masculinised.

Three basic points are important: (1) studies on men and masculinity are not new, sometimes explicitly, more often implicitly; (2) studying men and masculinity is in itself no guarantee of criticality; and (3) the 'Man/Men Question' has figured long and strong in feminism and related gender theory and practice. There has been an expansion for over 50 years of focused, explicitly critical research, sometimes referred to as Critical Studies on Men and Masculinities (CSMM) (Hearn and Howson 2019; Kimmel et al. 2005). CSMM refers to critical, explicitly gendered studies of men and masculinities that engage with feminist critiques, as well as some men's positive responses to feminism, along with critiques from LGBTIQA+, poststructural and post-colonial positions, among other critical perspectives.

Approaches range across disciplines, methodologies, ontologies and epistemologies – psychological, institutional, societal, ethnographic, discursive, and so on. Significantly, there has generally been a greater development within sociology. The relative neglect in political science is gradually being addressed, especially in respect of international relations, nationalism, populism, and war and peace (e.g. Bjarnegård 2013; Enloe 2013; Hooper 2001). Certain themes have been stressed, notably around work and family, sometimes in contradiction with what may be assumed dominant definitions and priorities of men, rather more than, say, political organising. Research has often been local, bodily, immediate, interpersonal in focus, as in the 'ethnographic moment' (Connell 2000). Increasingly there is a turn to the 'big picture' of globalisations (Connell 1993, 1998), world-centred approaches (Connell 2014), transnational patriarchies, and transnational change (Hearn 2015; Hearn et al. 2013a, 2013b; Ruspini et al. 2011).

The explicitly gendered 'naming men as men' (Collinson and Hearn 1994; Hanmer 1990) has been made within this critical context, not to essentialise or reify men, but to see men and masculinities as an object of critique and critical interrogation. This insight applies whether we are talking of men as explicit public or implicit political actors, and whether as individuals, collectively or institutionally. Importantly, CSMM is certainly not the preserve or property of men, as in some ambiguous or even anti-feminist versions of 'Men's Studies' (as if most academic work is not already), but comprises studies by women, men and further genders. CSMM can be characterised as:

- *a critical explicit focus* on men and masculinities, rather than an implicit or incidental focus on men and masculinities;
- informed by *feminist, gay, queer, trans and other critical gender scholarship*;
- *gendered, socially constructed, (re)produced,* not just 'naturally this way';
- *variable and changing* across time (history), space (culture), within societies, and across the life course and biographies;
- emphasising men's differential relations to *gendered power*;
- spanning the *material and the discursive* in analysis;
- (re)produced in the *intersections of gender and further social divisions* (see Connell et al. 2005, 3) – or to put this another way, men are not only men.

CSMM comprise *historical, cultural, relational, materialist, deconstructive, anti-essentialist* studies, seen throughout within gender relations (Hearn and Pringle 2006). The most cited approach is what can be called 'masculinities theory' (e.g. Carrigan et al. 1985; Connell 1995), in which different masculinities are framed in relation to gender hegemony, patriarchy and patriarchal relations. The concept of hegemonic masculinity – a central pillar – has been defined most notably as 'the configuration of gender practice which embodies the currently accepted answer to the problem of legitimacy of patriarchy, which guarantees (or is taken to guarantee) the dominant position of men and the subordination of women' (Connell 1995, 77). Related concepts, e.g. complicit masculinity, have been interrogated far less.

Numerous applications and interpretations of hegemonic masculinity exist, in theoretical, empirical and policy studies (Bridges and Pascoe 2014; Connell and Messerschmidt 2005; Hearn et al. 2012; Messerschmidt 2012). The concepts of masculinity and hegemonic masculinity have also been critiqued for: lack of clarity in meaning; challenges from comparative, postcolonial, transnational and queer approaches; and usefulness of 'hegemonic masculinity' as a heuristic rather than a precise concept (Hearn 1996). A number of reframings have followed, such as the move to 'the hegemony of men [that] seeks to address the double complexity that men are both a *social category formed by the gender system* and *dominant collective and individual agents of social practices*' (Hearn 2004, 59). Overall, CSMM involves critical gendering of men, 'naming men as men', and simultaneously problematizing and deconstructing both masculinities and the social category of men.

Jeff Hearn et al.

Research in and on the EU

This section summarises and assesses previous research studies, policy developments and activist interventions on men, masculinities and the EU. In so doing, we relate such research and policy to the broad persistence of intersectional gender inequalities and domination across the EU.

The EU political and policy context

Paramount is the lack of a gender perspective in much mainstream research on the formation of the EC/EU, its workings and many studies thereof. A lack of gender perspective typically means an implicit perspective of certain (kinds of) men, and an assumed 'male-as-norm' (Kronsell 2012), whether in politics and/or political analysis. The whole concept of EU integration was very much masculine and men-orientated from the beginning, following the post-war situation, the ECSC, and the Common Market. The Founding *Fathers* entrenched the lack of women's involvement in institutional and political development within the so-called 'Reign of old men' (Wallström 2008), reflecting men's overwhelming domination of political parties and mainstream public politics in the early post-World War II period. Indeed, women were largely excluded as politicians from the integration project until the 1970s and the first direct elections to the European Parliament in 1979 (see Ahrens and Rolandsen Agustín (European Parliament) in this volume). Until then, women were implicitly included via Article 119 of the EEC Treaty on equal pay for equal work (van der Vleuten 2007), but they rarely took part in the decision-making processes as individuals. Thus, one might even talk of the concept of a 'Maleuropean Union' and point to critical analysis of the concept of the 'masculinity/femininity of EU', and various supposedly gender-neutral, but meaning 'men-oriented' EU politics, initiatives and agencies.

According to researchers working on the nexus of gender and EU integration, until recently masculine norms that are still predominant in this particular approach have remained unquestioned (e.g. Abels and MacRae 2016a; Kronsell 2005, 2016). Despite adding a 'gender perspective' to EU policies and research thereon, certain policies and political designs, often seen as 'neutral', in fact reinforce 'traditional' male norms (e.g. Prügl 2011). Such a 'gender perspective' has usually focused on gender equality and women and, until now, mainly on workplace issues (Hubert 2012; see Milner in this volume). In fact, the 'gender turn' initiated in the 1970s was initially limited to equality and the (paid) workplace, and in its initial form lasted until the early 1980s. In research terms, feminist and critical gender analyses of European integration did not become well established until into the 1990s (Abels and MacRae 2016b, 20–26; Hoskyns 1996), and even since then in-depth gendered analyses of men and masculinities in the integration project have not been widely developed in most countries.

The first phase of, and approach to, 'gender equality' policy saw women as participants in the labour market; its main goal was to enable female workers equal position in the market (Kantola 2010). This position was based on male norms; a 'sameness approach' was promoted as equality seen through the lens of equal opportunities. This lasted until the 1980s when it was replaced with 'positive action' aimed at switching 'from equality of access to creating conditions more likely to result in equality of outcome' (Rees 1998, 34). Positive action enabled recognition of the different social positioning of men and women and was primarily aimed at improving the situation of women in the workplace. In 1997 (Amsterdam Treaty) this approach was superseded by gender mainstreaming as the primary policy tool for achieving gender equality. Thus, gender equality was defined as beyond women-targeted policies, with the incorporation of a gender perspective into all EU policies and activities recommended at every stage: from design, through implementation and monitoring, to evaluation.

Increasingly, questions of gender identity and sexuality have also been brought into sharper policy focus. For example, the Treaty of Amsterdam introduced a broader anti-discrimination provision (Article 13), involving appropriate action to combat discrimination based on sex, racial or ethnic origin, religion or belief, disability, age or sexual orientation. This was and is clearly important for LGBTIQA+ persons (see Solanke in this volume). The Employment Equality Directive 2000 bans direct or indirect discrimination based on religion, belief, disability, age or sexual orientation, and seeks to implement the principle of equal treatment in employment and training irrespective of religion or belief, sexual orientation and age (Council Directive 2000/ 78/EC).

Having said that, the significant and more recent growth of both gender (equality) policies in practice and gendered studies of the EC/EU have been largely in terms of adding women's perspectives, that is responding to women's demands for greater equality and including women in gendered analysis more explicitly. This does not necessarily entail gendering men and masculinities in a critical and thoroughgoing way; indeed, many otherwise excellent EU documents and reports, and related academic and research texts on gender equality, power, processes and policy fail to begin to do that. What is needed is to make explicit the position and actions of different groupings of men and different masculinities in the structuring and operation of the very institutions of the EU and in the phenomenon of the EU itself; in short, gender is clearly not a synonym for women (Bieling and Diez 2016). For example, some studies have addressed men and masculinities within the European Commission (e.g. Woodward 1996), and in the construction of the EU and 'Europe' (Novikova et al. 2005).

Historically the EU and its member states have often separated the issue of trafficking women and children from prostitution and pornography; moreover, policy debate around trafficking has often been dealt with in the broader context of policies on inward migration. This association, even confusion, in policy terms, along with the allied topic of racism, demonstrates how power relations associated with dominant forms of masculinity enter into processes that construct the idea of 'Europe'. Racism is widespread throughout Europe, even if its precise configurations vary across cultural contexts. Yet, issues around dominant forms of masculinity and men's practices are remarkably absent in academic and policy debates on racism in Europe. Often central to racism in Europe and how EU member states treat migrants are such questions as what is 'Europe', who is 'European', and who is 'more European' – who is 'other'? These questions are often partly about 'whose masculinity' is 'purer' or 'superior'. Yet both member states and the European Commission itself have largely avoided confronting those highly gendered issues in their policies to combat racism and address migration. Power relations associated with dominant forms of masculinity in the processes of 'Europe creation' – including both the pre-2004 and newer member states – have often been disguised and ignored.

Meanwhile, Western European nations, especially the Nordic countries, may often have been over-privileged as comparative 'benchmarks' when different European societies are being assessed for their alleged degree of 'European-ness', in terms of how far they have achieved gender equality. Such assessments often utilise international comparisons adopting conventional economic, political, educational, and wellbeing measures (e.g. World Economic Forum 2017). By contrast, it is instructive to realize that even in the Nordic countries some major forms of men's domination still stubbornly persist, e.g. business, violence to women, sexual violence to children, the military, academia and religion (Hearn and Pringle 2006; Hearn et al. 2018; Pringle 2011, 2016).

Looking towards the future, Walby (2018) notes that the EU is currently engaged in a major process of shifting its subsidiarity boundaries in response to severe global economic and geo-political challenges: moving the levels of competence and implementation toward the EU level and away from member states. The potential gender implications, positive and negative, are immense: 'Whether this change is to the detriment of gender equality depends on the extent to which the EU gender-equality project is mainstreamed into the new or reformed institutions that will be created or developed' (Walby 2018, 320).

Research developments

A wide variety of critical research on many different aspects of men and masculinities in most parts of the EU exists. Initially, most studies were developed in Germany, the Nordic region, and the UK; topics included family, care, work, sexuality and violence. In the last case, this involved focusing on perpetrators, as well as the structural roots of violent practices in the dominant gender order, and its symbolic grounding in the patriarchal system of masculine domination. Critical approaches to sexism and the relation of men and masculinities to violence were pre-dominant in the German and Nordic contexts, with further focus on education and also men's role in gender (im)balance in the private and public spheres, involved fatherhood being among the central issues. The question *Can Men Do It?* – move towards gender equality – was aptly elaborated in a book by the Norwegian sociologist, Øystein Gullvåg Holter (2003). In a number of countries, there have been various popular and research texts on nurturing or involved father-hood, such as the German case (Richter and Schäfer 2007), published in several languages. In addition, a number of online portals exist that provide networking and research information. The theme of men and care, the gendered understanding of care and of men's involvement in care, is at the core of the research and policy agenda (Hanlon 2012).

Specific institutes or divisions of existing institutions have been founded (e.g. Dissens in Berlin in 1989, the Men's Counselling Centre [now Association for Men and Gender Issues Styria] in Graz in 2001) critically researching issues on men and masculinities (see Hearn and Howson 2019). Academic courses have been incorporated into university social sciences curricula. Critical attention has been paid to structural positionings of men – as an analyt-ical category, as well as social actors – in broader relations of power, reproduction and dis-mantling of institutions sustaining the status quo. Focused journals have been launched, notably *NORMA: The International Journal for Masculinity Studies*, originating in the Nordic region, and *MCS – Masculinities & Social Change* in Spain.

Attention to geopolitical divisions and borders and emergent attempts at dismantling or re-institutionalising them form another established agenda. Examples include those addressing the post-Socialist experience (Novikova and Kambourov 2003; Wojnicka and Ciaputa 2011), and work on intimate and global citizenships (Oleksy 2008, 2009). There are now also extensive studies in Portugal focussing on the postcolonial and recently trans-masculinities (Aboim 2010, 2016), and in some parts of central and eastern Europe (CEE), notably Slovenia (Hrženjak 2016).

Thematic issues of a number of journals mark the network of involved scholars in the Czech Republic and Poland among other research publications (Šmídová et al. 2015; Wojnicka and Kluczyńska 2015), as well as publications analysing issues such as men's migration in the European and global contexts (Charsley and Wray 2015; Wojnicka and Pustuka 2017). There is also growing interest in the Balkans and the Baltics. Following the aforementioned post-Socialist focus (Novikova and Kambourov 2003), there are networks of scholars in Estonia (Kadri Aavik in the Gender Studies Research Group in Tallinn) and Latvia (Irina Novikova at the Gender Centre in Riga).

The CSMM community has built international networks by cooperation on cross-border projects. Conferences have been organised by very active, as well as well established, institutionalised research centres, such as GEXcel in Sweden that has organised several intense international workshops and conferences and published papers from them. Several international conferences grounded in critical approaches to studying men and masculinities have been organised by the Nordic Association for Research on Men and Masculinities (NFMM) for those from the region and beyond (Oslo 2012, Reykjavik 2014, Göteborg 2016, Örebro 2017). Moreover, critical perspectives on men and masculinities have recently become an integral part of more general sociological conferences: e.g. at European Sociological Association Congresses (e.g. Geneva 2011, Manchester 2019) and also at national venues (e.g. during Polish Sociological Association congresses 2016 and 2019).

European Commission-funded interventions

Several research projects addressing men, masculinities and gender relations in EU member states have been funded by the European Commission. These provide a mass of information and analysis on men, masculinities and intersectional gender relations. The first such projects were the 1995 Arianne policy-orientated project on boy pupils in schools, and the Fourth Framework Programme-funded (FP) European Profeminist Men's Network (1997–1999), which was primarily a resource-gathering project with a clear political positioning. These projects can be understood in relation to various contemporary academic and policy developments in the 1980s and 1990s within some European countries, especially those in northern Europe. For example, relatively early examples include the formation of the Finnish Council for Equality Subcommittee on Men's Issues from 1988, and the Nordic Council of Ministers Men and Gender Equality programme 1995–2000.

A key development was the formation of the (initially) ten-country EU-funded European Research Network on Men in Europe, which in turn led to the creation of the collective – Critical Research on Men in Europe (CROME; www.cromenet.org). The Network formally operated from 2000, though planning began much earlier. The Network was initially funded as part of the FP5 project 'The Social Problem and Societal Problematisation of Men and Masculinities 2000–2003'. This was an important step forward in bringing together women and men, feminist and profeminist researchers and policy-makers in Europe. The Network comprised researchers with backgrounds in a range of academic disciplines and from a number of European countries – initially Estonia, Finland, Germany, Ireland, Italy, Latvia, Norway, Poland, the Russian Federation and the UK; from 2003 Bulgaria, Czech Republic, Denmark and Sweden became affiliated member countries. Data in the form of academic research, statistical sources, policy/law, and media representations that focused on men's relations to work and family, violence, health, and social exclusions, were assembled and critically examined (Hearn and Pringle 2006; Pringle et al. 2013). This work pointed to:

- great variations in the state of men and masculinities across Europe;
- differences in how the social problem of men came onto public political, policy and media agendas in different countries and regions;
- the challenges of unified English language conceptualisations (not least the difficulty of using the term 'masculinities'); and
- the identification of gaps for both research and policy.

Special note should be made of the adoption of the priority themes of 'Men and Equality' by the EU Swedish Presidency in 2001, and the EU Finnish Presidency, with accompanying conferences in Örebro and Helsinki (Varanka et al. 2006) respectively. Some other relevant projects have a more specific focus. For example, an important initiative that was not specifically on men and masculinities, but was heavily imbued with those concerns was the EU Fifth Framework project 'Work Changes Gender' (2002–2004; Puchert et al. 2005). This examined how relations to work, paid and unpaid, constitute a major factor in the construction of gender (including men and masculinities), together with the implications for changing men and masculinities. Detailed studies were conducted in Austria, Bulgaria, Germany, Norway, Spain and Israel, at the national, corporate and individual worker levels. It was found that a culture of work, based on 'traditional' models of masculinity, along with tax policies and paternal leave regulations, still promotes the breadwinner mode.

A related concern is men's place in the gender structuring and policy politics of care, as taken up critically in the EU 'FOCUS – Fostering Caring Masculinities project (see Hrženjak et al. 2006) that ran in 2006–2007 in five countries. This broad approach has subsequently been taken up in policy work, such as the 'Fostering Caring Masculinities' national programme of MenCare Switzerland 2014–2027.

Another key area bringing research and policy together has been the issue of violence and anti-violence (see Roggeband in this volume). The FP6 Coordination Action on Human Rights Violations (CAHRV) provided and synthesised a mass of information and research, mainly on men's violence to women and children (Hagemann-White et al. 2008). It also continued some of the previous work of the CROME network. The Council of the EU's Positive Recommendations on men and gender equality, published in 2006, also highlighted the problem of men's violence, noting that 'the vast majority of gender-based acts of violence are perpetrated by men' and urging

> Member States and the Commission to combine punitive measures against the perpetrators with preventive measures targeted especially at young men and boys and to set up specific programmes for victims as well as for offenders, in particular in the case of domestic violence.

Meanwhile, though separate from the EU, a wide variety of further formal international policy and legal work, such as that of the UN, CEDAW, the Council of Europe's Istanbul Convention on preventing and combating violence against *women* and domestic violence has provided general frames for changing men, and specifically stopping men's violence.

One of the most extensive research projects, entitled 'The Role of Men in Gender Equality', was conducted between 2011 and 2013 by the consortium of European scholars representing several research institutes and universities (Bergmann et al. 2014; Scambor and Seidler 2013; Scambor et al. 2014, 2015, 2013; Wojnicka 2015). The project connected more than a hundred European researchers and policy-makers, supported by an international advisory board. It gave a special attention to questions of education, work, care and family, violence, health and political representation in the EU and EFTA countries. A key finding was that traditional concepts of work slowly disappear and men's share of care work as well as a gender equal balance become visible in some parts of Europe. Caring masculinities emerged as a central path forward, and one that is increasingly taken up in practice, together with women's increasing education and professional role, and rising expectations of gender balanced task divisions. This focus means engaging with the large variations in the extent of men's unpaid care work, as well as with the dangers of a possible return to and re-emphasis on the heteronormative 'rights of fathers'. Instead

The EU, men and masculinities

of widening the definition of masculinity and gender roles, a fathers' rights approach focuses on promoting patriarchal understanding of family, where the power is solely male prerogative (Bergmann et al. 2014; Wojnicka 2016). In order to take a broad strategic approach to the politics of care, and not conflating it with fatherhood politics, the research consortium adopted the advocacy of 'caring masculinities' as a policy aim, which could be applied not only in families and households, but also in men's care and caring in workplaces, politics, and so on.

Following analysis of the men's and boys' situation with regard to education, positioning in the workplace and labour market, involvement in care work mostly in family contexts as well as men's health issues, gender-based violence and institutionalised and non-institutionalised politics, based on secondary quantitative data analysis, national reports, qualitative interviews, and other research methods, important policy-related recommendation were developed. Those recommendations were presented in terms of how men and boys can contribute to greater gender equality. This network of researchers has continued under the auspices of a planned COST (European Cooperation in Science & Technology) project, as yet unfunded. (The authors of this chapter have been involved in almost all of these projects above.)

Finally, men and masculinities issues have become an integral part of the gender equality research framework implemented by European Institute for Gender Equality (EIGE), based in Vilnius (see Jacquot and Krizsán in this volume). In 2011, EIGE presented the outcomes of its study on European profeminist social activism undertaken by men in 27 countries. The goal of the study 'was to map relevant stakeholders in all EU Member States whose activity could be considered as contributing to a more effective involvement of men in the promotion of gender equality' (Ruxton and van der Gaag 2012). Since then EIGE has supported several profeminist initiatives mainly through cooperation with the European network, MenEngage Europe.

Gaps and intersections

This section paints in broad brush strokes some key gaps and intersections in research and policy. We build on analyses provided by the CROME network and subsequent EU projects, particularly relations between home and work, social exclusion, violence, and health. Interestingly, these analyses suggest that key lacunae in both research and policy tend to occur where there are intersections between these four themes, with clear intersectional relationships between social problems that some men create and those that some men experience (Hearn and Pringle 2006; Hearn et al. 2018).

Regarding intersections between social exclusion and work, we observe an incremental dichotomy within many European (and other) societies governed by neoliberal principles along the dimensions of increased unemployment of some men in tandem with the stubborn retention of political economic power by other men. Thus, the social marginalisation of the former is primarily the responsibility of the latter. New forms of social exclusion have developed, with shifts from industrial to more post-industrialised society. Long-established oppressive power relations between men colliding with new social labour constellations have left major gaps for research and policy. The intersectional relations between the dynamics of social exclusion in the form of racism and some dominant forms of masculinity have been under-researched and often ignored in policy initiatives.

Likewise, there is the need to recognise that men's sexual violence to children is a major global (including European) gendered problem, and a profound form of social exclusion of the violated in itself, to be treated as such in research and policy (Hearn et al. 2013; Pringle 2016). The linkage between men as parents and carers, and men as violent partners or violent fathers/parents, has also often been seriously neglected in research and policy. In most of Europe,

87

Jeff Hearn et al.

fatherhood and men's violence are treated as separate policy issues. In research and policy, splits between 'problems which some men experience' and 'problems which some men create' need to be bridged.

An integrated policy approach to joined-up policy areas is needed: there is no contradiction between positively promoting the role of men as carers, and emphasising the prime requirement of protecting children from (what are typically constructed as other) men's violence. This applies to policy machineries and political processes at both national and supranational, such as EU, levels. What is striking is how rarely such an integrated dual approach is adopted. There are profound tensions in integrating policies encouraging positive fathering while protecting families from violent fathers. In parallel, (with some exceptions) childhood studies have tended to neglect the dimension of men's violence, while research on men's violence has tended to underplay men's violence to children compared with men's violence to women and men's violence to each other (Pringle 2016).

Turning to the intersections of health, violence, work and social exclusion, we find further issues where both sufficient research and policy attention has been lacking. There is a considerable body of research conducted across many countries illustrating correlations between poor health, including men's health, and social disadvantage associated with class, ethnicity and other social divisions. However, we note that a study of 51 countries suggested a significant association between levels of patriarchy (as indicated by female homicide rates) and men's higher mortality and morbidity (Stanistreet et al. 2005). Following such findings, we need to unpick a range of potential factors, for instance:

- the tendency of some men not to seek medical help early enough, partly perhaps because of a masculinist desire to 'cope' or not face reality, to be 'tough';
- the suggestion that some men may demonstrate greater reluctance to make emotional contact with others to deal with emotions, and this may relate to social isolation and mental wellbeing, including suicide;
- men's, especially young men's, higher mortality and morbidity rates potentially being partly associated with a range of 'dominant and dominating' men's practices, such as accidents and risk-taking behaviours in traffic, crime (including victimisation), sexuality (including non-condom use and multiple sexual partners), gambling, self-created stress at work in trying to 'get ahead', and drinking/drug-taking/other self-destructive behaviours.

Framing a range of men's profound health difficulties within this more power-oriented perspective is insufficiently developed in European research and policy.

Finally, in terms of our intersecting themes, social exclusion/inclusion can be seen as an important element entering into the dynamics of all the other themes – not only as usually seen as immediate social welfare matters for white, host, supposedly autochthonous populations, but also the rise of far-right groups and racist refugee politics.

Conclusion: future directions

This overview raises key issues for future directions. First, the development of critical research and informed policy is very uneven and also changeable across different regions of Europe (Hearn and Howson 2019). These concerns are far from mainstream agendas in much of Europe, especially so in CEE countries, as with Gender Studies and feminist theories more generally. This is even if a certain level of institutionalisation of issues relating to men and masculinities in gender equality policy has taken place, in the EU, the European Commission, and in some countries within that region. In Poland, the political climate is a crucial obstacle in increasing critical research on men and masculinities. The country seems to follow Hungary's steps as Gender Studies are subjected to a high level of (right-wing, conservative) critique, with fewer and fewer resources allocated to gender-focused research, including those on men and masculinities. Growing populism and conservative political agendas do not favour incorporation of these themes into state policies or other forms of institutionalisation (see Siim and Fiig in this volume). There remains an urgent need to support scholarly initiatives on men and masculinities, especially with processes of re-masculinisation, in CEE societies, where democracy is still fragile or obscured, but also elsewhere in Europe. Thus, institutionalisation and sustainability of bodies ensuring the agenda of targeting gender inequality with focus on men and masculinities is of critical importance in such geopolitically turbulent times. Examples are ready at hand. An expert working group on Men and Gender Equality was founded in 2012, affiliated to the Czech Government Office and its Advisory Board on Gender Equality, or another Czech initiative, the Genderman (2017–2018), is a prize awarded to a man defending gender equality and combating sexism in the public domain. However, the latter initiative solely depends on non-governmental funding, and the sustainability of the former on political will.

Secondly, and relatedly, current social and political events across Europe provide much topical and fruitful material for critical analysis and reflection on men and masculinities: men in power, polarisation of public debates regarding gender issues, and assessment of 'crises' of men and masculinities. The place of men and masculinities is increasingly clear in EU politics, party politics and policy-making. The political elite in V4 (Visegrad) countries, but also across the EU, provide a rich source of data for critical reflection, as are moves towards the political right and far-right. Far-right groups, dominated by men in their leadership and voting patterns (Spierings and Zaslove 2015), are gaining greater popularity, including attacking (male) immigrants and refugees coming from other parts of the world (see Siim and Fiig in this volume). The urgency for stepping up such research and policy attention is clear not only in the run up to and aftermath of the Brexit referendum (Dustin et al. 2019), but also in other profound crisis manifestations across Europe associated with the intersections of nationalism, (opposition to) migration, and economic inequality and exclusion. Such trends connect to the resurrection of authoritarian, racist, Islamophobic and homophobic masculinities, as well as creating new marginalised masculinities. These matters need to be problematised in the light of a crisis of liberal democracy and attacks on the value of gender equality. Such turbulent times can also lead to unexpected alliances for critical scholars with critical media and NGOs and other activists. Global, international support networks play an invaluable role in this context. In this respect, the work of the German–UK-based network, 'Political Masculinities', which has organised conferences, a summer school and publications on these themes, is especially relevant.

Thirdly, further specific studies are needed on men and masculinities within the machinery of the EU and the European Commission, and in the very construction of the EU and 'Europe', including how 'lesser others' outside, and sometimes within, are constructed, both through both formal and informal practices.

Finally, there is a need for much more critical engagement with men and masculinities, especially dominant and dominating forms, as they apply across a whole range of further social and political fields. These include ageing, migration, environment, consumption, travel and transport, gender identity, religion, big business, finance, militarism, and impacts of such new technologies such as information and communication technologies, artificial intelligence, robotics and biotechnologies.

References

Abels G, MacRae H, eds. (2016a): *Gendering European Integration Theory: Engaging New Dialogues*, Opladen: Barbara Budrich.

Abels G, MacRae H (2016b): Why and How to Gender European Integration Theory: Introduction, in Abels G, MacRae H (eds.): *Gendering European Integration Theory: Engaging New Dialogues*, Opladen: Barbara Budrich, 9–37.

Aboim S (2010): *Plural Masculinities*, Aldershot: Ashgate.

Aboim S (2016): Trans-masculinities, embodiments and the materiality of gender: Bridging the gap, *NORMA. The International Journal for Masculinity Studies* **11** (4), 225–236.

Bergmann N, Scambor E, Wojnicka K (2014): Framing involvement of men in gender equality in Europe. Between institutionalized and non-institutionalized politics, *Masculinities and Social Change* **3** (1), 61–82.

Bieling, HJ, Diez, T (2016): Linking Gender Perspectives to Integration Theory: The Need for Dialogue, in: Abels G, MacRae H (eds.): *Gendering European Integration Theory: Engaging New Dialogues*, Opladen: Barbara Budrich, 279–292.

Bjarnegård E (2013): *Gender, Informal Institutions and Political Recruitment: Explaining Male Dominance in Parliamentary Representation*, Basingstoke: Palgrave Macmillan.

Bridges T, Pascoe CJ (2014): Hybrid masculinities: new directions in the sociology of men and masculinities, *Sociology Compass* **8** (3), 246–258.

Carrigan T, Connell R, Lee J (1985): Towards a new sociology of masculinity, *Theory and Society* **14** (5), 551–604.

Charsley K, Wray H (2015): Introduction: The invisible (migrant) man, *Men and Masculinities* **18** (4), 403–423.

Collinson DL, Hearn J (1994): Naming men as men: implications for work, organizations and management, *Gender, Work and Organization* **1** (1), 2–22.

Connell R (1993): The big picture: masculinities in recent world history, *Theory and Society* **22** (5), 597–623.

Connell R (1995): *Masculinities*, Cambridge: Polity.

Connell R (1998): Masculinities and globalization, *Men and Masculinities* **1** (1), 3–23.

Connell R (2000): *The Men and the Boys*, Cambridge: Polity.

Connell R (2014): Margin becoming centre: for a world-centred rethinking of masculinities, *NORMA: The International Journal for Masculinity Studies* **9** (4), 217–231.

Connell R, Hearn J, Kimmel M (2005): Introduction, in: Kimmel M, Hearn J, Connell R (eds.): *Handbook of Studies on Men and Masculinities*, Thousand Oaks, CA: SAGE, 1–12.

Connell R, Messerschmidt JW (2005): Hegemonic masculinity: rethinking the concept, *Gender & Society* **19** (6), 829–859.

Dustin M, Ferreira N, Millns S, eds. (2019): *Gender and Queer Perspectives on Brexit*, Basingstoke: Palgrave Macmillan.

Enloe C (2013): *Seriously! Investigating Crashes and Crises as if Women Mattered*, Berkeley, CA: University of California Press.

Hagemann-White C, Gloor D, Hanmer J, Hearn J, Humphreys C, Kelly L, Logar R, Martinez M, May-Chahal C, Novikova I, Pringle K, Puchert R, Schröttle M (2008): *Gendering Human Rights Violations: The Case of Interpersonal Violence*, Brussels: European Commission.

Hanlon N (2012): *Masculinities, Care and Equality: Identity and Nurture in Men's Lives*, Basingstoke: Palgrave.

Hanmer J (1990): Men, Power and the Exploitation of Women, in: Hearn J, Morgan D (eds.): *Men, Masculinities and Social Theory*, London: Unwin Hyman/Routledge, 21–42.

Hearn J (1996): 'Is Masculinity Dead?' A Critical Account of the Concepts of Masculinity and Masculinities, in: Mac an Ghaill M (ed.): *Understanding Masculinities: Social Relations and Cultural Arenas*, Milton Keynes: Open University Press, 202–217.

Hearn J (2004): From hegemonic masculinity to the hegemony of men, *Feminist Theory* **5** (1), 49–72.

Hearn J (2015): *Men of the World*, London: Sage.

Hearn J, Howson R (2019): The Institutionalization of (Critical) Studies on Men and Masculinities: Geopolitical Perspectives, in: Gottzén L, Mellström U, Shefer T (eds.): *The International Handbook of Masculinity Studies*, London: Routledge.

Hearn J, Blagojević M, Harrison K (eds.) (2013a): *Rethinking Transnational Men: Beyond, Between and Within Nations*, New York: Routledge.

The EU, men and masculinities

Hearn J, Nordberg M, Andersson K, Balkmar D, Gottzén L, Klinth R, Pringle K, Sandberg, L (2012): Hegemonic masculinity and beyond. 40 years of research in Sweden, *Men and Masculinities* **15** (1), 31–55.

Hearn J, Pringle K, with members of Critical Research on Men in Europe (2006): *European Perspectives on Men and Masculinities: National and Transnational Approaches*, Basingstoke: Palgrave Macmillan.

Hearn J, Pringle K, Balkmar D (2018): Men, Masculinities and Social Policy, in: Shaver S (ed.): *Handbook of Gender and Social Policy*, Oxford: Edward Elgar, 55–73.

Hearn J, Novikova I, Pringle K, Šmídová I, Bjerén G, Jyrkinen M, Iovanni L, Arranz F, Ferguson, H, Kolga V, Müller U, Oleksy EH, Balkmar D, Helfferich C, Lenz I, Wojtaszek M, Pičukāne E, Rosa V, with an Appendix by Connell R (2013b): *Studying Men's Violences in Europe: Towards a Research Framework*, Örebro: Örebro University CFS Report Series 25.

Holter ØG (2003): *Can Men Do It? Men and Gender Equality – The Nordic Experience*, Copenhagen: Nordic Council of Ministers.

Hooper C (2001): *Manly States: Masculinities, International Relations and Gender Politics*, New York: Columbia University Press.

Hoskyns, C (1996): *Integrating Women, Law and Politics in the European Union*, London: Verso.

Hrženjak M (2016): *Transformations of Fatherhood: Men between Parenthood and Work*, Ljubljana: Piece Institute.

Hrženjak M, Humer Ž, Kuhar R (2006): *Fostering Caring Masculinities: Slovenian National Report*, Ljubljana: Peace Institute, Institute for Contemporary Social and Political Studies.

Hubert A (2012): Gendering Employment Policy. From Equal Pay to Work–Life Balance, in Abels G, Mushaben JM (eds.): *Gendering the European Union: New Approaches to Old Democratic Deficits*, Basingstoke: Palgrave Macmillan, 146–168.

Kantola J (2010): *Gender and the European Union*, Basingstoke: Palgrave Macmillan.

Kimmel M, Hearn J, Connell R, eds. (2005): *Handbook of Studies on Men and Masculinities*, Thousand Oaks, CA: Sage.

Kronsell A (2005): Gender, power and European integration theory, *Journal of European Public Policy* **12** (6), 1022–1040.

Kronsell A (2012): Gendering Theories of European Integration, in: Abels G, Mushaben JM (eds.) *Gendering the European Union: New Approaches to Old Democratic Deficits*, Basingstoke: Palgrave Macmillan, 23–40.

Kronsell A (2016): The power of EU masculinities: a feminist contribution to European integration theory, *Journal of Common Market Studies* **54** (1), 104–120.

Messerschmidt JW (2012): Engendering gendered knowledge. Assessing the academic appropriation of hegemonic masculinity, *Men and Masculinities* **15** (1), 56–76.

Novikova I, Kambourov D (eds.) (2003): *Men in the Global World: Integrating Post-socialist Perspectives*, Helsinki: Aleksanteri Institute.

Novikova I, Pringle K, Hearn J, Müller U, Oleksy E et al. (2005): Men, 'Europe' and Post-socialism, in: Kimmel M, Hearn J, Connell R (eds.): *Handbook of Studies on Men and Masculinities*, Thousand Oaks, CA: Sage, 141–162.

Oleksy E, ed. (2008): *Tożsamość i obywatelstwo w społeczeństwie wielokulturowym*, Warsaw: Wydawnictwo Naukowe PWN.

Oleksy E, ed. (2009): *Intimate Citizenships Gender, Sexualities, Politics*, London: Taylor & Francis.

Pringle K (2011): Comparative Studies of Well-Being in Terms of Gender, Ethnicity and the Concept of Bodily Citizenship: Turning Esping-Andersen on His Head?, in: Oleksy E, Hearn J, Golańska D (eds.): *The Limits of Gendered Citizenship: Contexts and Complexities*, London: Routledge, 137–156.

Pringle K (2016): Doing (Oppressive) Gender via Men's Relations with Children, in: Häyrén A, Henriksson HW (eds.): *Critical Perspectives on Masculinities and Relationalities: In Relation to What?*, New York: Springer, 23–34.

Pringle K, Hearn J, Ferguson H, Kambourov D, Kolga V, Lattu E, Müller U, Nordberg M, Novikova I, Oleksy E, Rydzewska J, Šmídová I, Tallberg T, Niemi H (2013): *Men and Masculinities in Europe*, 2nd revised ed., London: Whiting & Birch.

Prügl E (2011): *Transforming Masculine Rule. Agriculture and Rural Development in the European Union*, Ann Arbor: The University of Michigan Press.

Puchert R, Gärtner M, Höyng S, eds. (2005): *Work Changes Gender. Men and Equality in the Transition of Labour Forms*, Leverkusen: Barbara Budrich Publishers.

Rees T (1998): *Mainstreaming Equality in the European Union. Education, Training and Labour Market Policies*, London: Routledge.

Richter R, Schäfer E (2007): *Das Papa-Handbuch. Alles, was Sie wissen müssen zu Schwangerschaft, Geburt und dem ersten Jahr zu dritt*, 3rd ed., München: Gräfe und Unzer.

Ruspini E, Hearn J, Pease B, Pringle K, eds. (2011): *Men and Masculinities around the World: Transforming Men's Practices*, New York: Palgrave Macmillan.

Ruxton S, van der Gaag N (2012): *The Involvement of Men in Gender Equality Initiatives in the European Union*, Luxembourg: Office of the European Union.

Scambor E, Bergmann, N, Wojnicka K, Belghiti-Mahut S, Hearn J, Holter ØG, Gärtner M, Hrženjak M, Scambor C, White A (2014): Men and gender equality – European insights, *Men and Masculinities* **17** (5), 552–577.

Scambor E, Hrženjak M, Bergmann N, Holter ØG (2015): Men's share of care for children and professional care, *Studia Humanistyczne AGH* **14** (2), 53–71.

Scambor E and Seidler V (2013): Boys in education in Europe: theoretical reflections and the case of early school leaving, *THYMOS: Journal of Boyhood Studies* **7** (1), 3–20.

Scambor E, Wojnicka K, Bergmann N, eds. (2013): *Study on the Role of Men in Gender Equality*, Brussels: European Commission.

Šmídová I, Vodochodský I, Hearn J, eds. (2015): *Challenging Men and Masculinities: The Czech Context and Beyond, Gender, rovné příležitotosti, výzkum* [*Gender, Equal Opportunities, Research*] **16** (1).

Spierings N, Zaslove A (2015): Gendering the vote for populist radical-right parties, *Patterns of Prejudice* **49** (1–2), 135–162.

Stanistreet, D, Bambra C, Scott-Samuel A (2005): Is patriarchy the source of men's higher mortality? *Journal of Epidemiological Community Health* **59** (10), 873–876.

van der Vleuten A (2007): *The Price of Gender Equality: Member States and Governance in the European Union*, London: Routledge.

Varanka J, Närhinen A, Siukola R, eds. (2006): Men and Gender Equality: Towards Progressive Policies, *Reports of the Ministry of Social Affairs and Health* **75**, Helsinki: Ministry of Social Affairs.

Walby, S (2018): Gender in the crisis and remaking of Europe: re-gendering subsidiarity, *European Journal of Gender and Politics* **1** (3), 307–324.

Wallström M (2008): Wallström vill inte bli minister, *Sydsvenska Dagbladet*, February 8.

Wojnicka, K (2016): Masculist groups in Poland: aides of mainstream antifeminism, *International Journal for Crime, Justice and Social Democracy* **5** (2), 36–49.

Wojnicka K (2015): Men, masculinities and physical violence in contemporary Europe, *Studia Humanistyczne AGH* **14** (2), 15–31.

Wojnicka K, Ciaputa E (2011): *Karuzela z mężczyznami: Problematyka męskości w polskich badaniach społecznych*, Kraków: Impuls.

Wojnicka K, Kluczyńska U (2015): Men and masculinities research in the European dimension. Guest editors' introduction, *Studia Humanistyczne AGH* **14** (2), 7–14.

Wojnicka K, Pustułka P (2017): Migrant men in the nexus of space and (dis)empowerment, *NORMA: The International Journal for Masculinity Studies* **12** (2), 89–95.

Woodward AE (1996): Masculinities and European Bureaucracies, in: Collinson DL, Hearn J (eds.): *Men as Managers, Managers as Men: Critical Perspectives on Men, Masculinities and Management*, London: Sage, 167–185.

World Economic Forum (2017): *The Global Gender Gap Report 2017*, Geneva, 2017, URL: www3. weforum.org/docs/WEF_GGGR_2017.pdf (download: December 10, 2018).

8

The EU approach to intersectional discrimination in law

Iyiola Solanke

The principle of non-discrimination has been part of the DNA of European integration since the 1957 Treaty of Rome creating the European Economic Community (EEC). This treaty contained just two relevant provisions: Article 12 of the EEC Treaty (now Article 18 TFEU) on nationality and Article 119 of the EEC Treaty (now Article 157 TFEU) on equal pay between women and men. Both were introduced as mechanisms to support the creation of the common (now single) market: non-discrimination on the grounds of nationality is the fundamental principle underpinning the four freedoms – free movement of goods, persons, services and capital – while non-discrimination on the grounds of gender was intended to prevent any national economic advantage based on the exploitation of women. As such, it was more a market measure than a tool to promote equality between the sexes (van der Vleuten 2007). A first directive giving substance to this provision was created in 1976 – Council Directive 76/207/EEC on access to employment, vocational training and promotion, and working conditions. It required decades of case law and significant activism to give substance to the prevention of gender discrimination in EU law (Solanke 2009a; see also Guth and Elfving in this volume).

It took a further 40 years of political advocacy for the EU to recognise discrimination on other grounds (Solanke 2009a; Givens and Evans 2014). A broad prohibition of discrimination was first introduced into EU law with the 1997 Amsterdam Treaty. In adopting Article 19 TFEU, the member states agreed to 'take appropriate action to combat discrimination based on sex, racial or ethnic origin, religion or belief, disability, age or sexual orientation' (Article 19(1) TFEU).

Further powers were given to the European Parliament and the Council, using the Ordinary Legislative Procedure, to

> adopt the basic principles of Union incentive measures, excluding any harmonisation of the laws and regulations of the Member States, to support action taken by the Member States in order to contribute to the achievement of the objectives referred to in paragraph 1.
>
> *(Article 19(2) TFEU)*

This article was subsequently activated to create two new directives: the 'Race Directive' 2000/43/EC of 2000 obliged member states to create a prohibition of racial discrimination in national law where none previously existed (Solanke 2009a). A second Employment Equality Framework

Directive (2000/78/EC) of 2003 focuses only on labour market equality in relation to all grounds set out in Art. 19 TFEU. While the first prohibits direct and indirect discrimination, and harassment in a range of spheres including social welfare, goods and services, education and employment, the latter prohibits discrimination on grounds of religion, belief, disability, age and sexual orientation in relation to employment and occupation only. Both explicitly call for recognition of 'multiple discrimination' (Hannett 2003) as a facet of gender: preambular paragraphs (Article 3(2)) state that, in implementing the principle of equal treatment, the Community should aim to eliminate inequalities and to promote equality between men and women, especially since women are often the victims of multiple discrimination.

The term 'intersectionality' regularly used in sociology and political science relates more to multiple discrimination than intersectional discrimination. Multiple discrimination has been adopted as an umbrella term encompassing different types of pluralist approaches in anti-discrimination law, such as 'additive', 'cumulative' and 'intersectional'. However, as I explain below, additive and cumulative discrimination significantly differ from intersectional discrimination (Crenshaw 1989) as they lack the synergy at the core of intersectional discrimination (Solanke 2011). As the EU approach focuses on multiple discrimination, it has yet to properly address intersectional discrimination and recognise black women in its law and policy-making.

My chapter will proceed as follows. First, I sketch the evolution of intersectional discrimination, multiple discrimination and intersectionality from enslaved African women to critical race feminism (see also Cooper 2016). I then discuss intersectional and multiple discrimination in Europe, looking at EU institutions and case law before the Court of Justice of the European Union (CJEU) in Luxembourg and the European Court of Human Rights (ECtHR) in Strasbourg. Though the EU is not yet a signatory to the European Convention on Human Rights (ECHR), the ECHR remains inherently connected to EU law, through the EU Charter on Fundamental Rights. However, the courts in Strasbourg and Luxembourg take different approaches to intersectional and multiple discrimination, thus affecting European regulation in a wider sense.

The final section will explore the future of intersectional discrimination in the EU and how improvement is possible. I suggest that in order to effectively tackle intersectional discrimination three things are necessary: first, the biological categories of anti-discrimination law must be replaced with an alternative logic that emphasises social meaning; secondly, it must be brought out from the shadow of gender and of multiple discrimination and finally the concept of race must be recognised and used. In the absence of these three things, black women – the paradigm group of intersectional discrimination – will remain at the margins of EU law and policy.

Intersectional discrimination, multiple discrimination and intersectionality

Anti-discrimination law and policy is 'zero-sum' – it is premised upon the idea that discrimination will relate to a single characteristic – race *or* gender *or* disability *or* age. This law has been designed to prevent discrimination based upon individual biological and immutable traits such as skin colour or sex. Each characteristic traditionally operated as a 'silo' – separate to and distinct from other characteristics. This structural design is linked to its evolution through social equality campaigns, such as the civil rights movement in the USA or the suffragettes in Britain, that also focused on single characteristics (Solanke 2009b) – as succinctly put in a book title, all the women were white and all the blacks men (Akasha et al. 1982).

Only a few examples exist where Black women (here used to refer to women of African, Asian or Caribbean descent) per se were the focus of campaigns for legal reform (Davis 1983). One notable example from the USA is the Combahee River Collective (CRC) which established

Intersectional discrimination in law

a Black feminist movement to challenge multiple oppressions. Black feminism was both the starting point 'to combat the manifold and simultaneous oppressions that all women of color face' and the position from which to free all women because '[i]f Black women were free, it would mean that everyone else would have to be free since our freedom would necessitate the destruction of all the systems of oppression' (cf. Eisenstein 1979, 362–372). It called for a complete reform of social, political and economic organisation.

The concept of intersectional discrimination adopted a similarly synergistic approach, focusing specifically on the 'physical and material representation of the intersection of race and gender' (Caldwell 1991, 372). Synergy emphasises co-determination and interdependence, whereby the component elements work together to create something new. Just as oxygen and hydrogen produce water not 'oxydrogen', or tin and copper together make bronze, not 'tinper', the synergy in intersectional discrimination creates a new subject – Black women (Solanke 2011). Set within critical race feminism (Wing 1997), this intersectional approach insists that anti-discrimination law recognise that inequality occurs in a synergistic manner rather than in neat categories that can be separated from each other. As originally conceived, it entwined race and gender in 'historical, social and political context' (Aylward 1999, 3) to highlight the experience of discrimination by Black women workers in the wake (Sharpe 2016) of white patriarchal employment practices.

The CRC and intersectional discrimination both draw upon the intellectual legacy pioneered by enslaved women activists (Davis 1983), rooted in the society, politics and law of the slave plantation economy. These women[1] examined the plantation through their own eyes to develop a philosophy of structural inequality (Solanke 2013, 450–452). They articulated how the synergy between their sexual and racial identity made their life and political struggles unique: white women could campaign for their emancipation whereas 'the Black woman, doubly enslaved, could but suffer and struggle and be silent' (Cooper 1988, 202). Intersectional discrimination took its purpose from this legacy – to highlight the synergies in anti-discrimination law and 'disrupt' the dominant narratives so as to expose structures of power and discrimination experienced by groups at the cusps of the 'silos'.

The radical potential in law of intersectional discrimination can be seen in *Degraffenreid* (*DeGraffenreid v General Motors Assembly Division*, St. Louis, 413 F.Supp. 142, 143 (E.D.Mo. 1976)), where a group of black women workers at General Motors in St. Louis questioned employment and equality law practices. Due to the lingering impact of slavery, African American women workers were the last to be hired in jobs beyond domestic service. Despite the importance of their earnings to their household income, they were seen by the employer as the least important workers. When an economic downturn occurred, the combination of the seniority system and discrimination meant that African American women were always the first to lose their jobs. Five women fired by General Motors in St. Louis claimed this was intersectional discrimination. In 1977, 22% of the city's working population were African American women, yet prior to 1970, GM – one of the largest employers in the city – employed only one black woman as a janitor. GM admitted in court that until May 1970, all women at its St. Louis plant were excluded from any assembly line work that required shifts longer than nine hours but the company did employ some white women in the cushion room producing automobile seats and upholstery.

Five women who were employed for around six months charged GM with sex and race discrimination. Emma DeGraffenreid applied for employment with GM in 1968 and in 1973; she was hired in June 1973 but, due to recession, was fired in January 1974. Brenda Hines applied for employment twice in 1971 and 1973; eventually hired in June 1973, she went on sick leave in September and was eventually made redundant in January 1974. Alberta Chapman applied for employment with GM in 1971, was hired in 1973 and, by January 1974, was made redundant. Brenda Hollis and Patricia Bell both applied for employment in November 1970 and were hired by December 1970. However, Hollis was made redundant by December 1971; Bell was laid off in May 1972, re-hired in May 1973 and laid off again in January 1974. In total, GM hired just six black female workers in 1970, 11 in 1971, none in 1972, and 137 in 1973. By the end of 1973, GM had 155 black women workers out of a total workforce of 8,500. Yet by January 1974, all of GM's black women workers had been made redundant: only the black female janitor remained.

They claimed that were it not for GM's past discriminatory policies, they would have been hired in the mid-1960s. They also claimed that the seniority system and union-sanctioned 'last hired first fired' termination rule discriminated against them because it perpetuated the effect of GM's past race and sex discrimination. They asserted that, as black women, they experienced discrimination as a 'synergistic' combination of two degraded statuses: 'the disabilities of blacks and the disabilities which inhere in their status as women' and that this synergy left them in a condition 'more terrible than the sum of their two constituent parts' (Scales-Trent 1989, 9).

These brave women therefore challenged not only entrenched labour market structures but also the structure of anti-discrimination law and policy; they argued that in their existence as black women racism and sexism converged. There was no 'either/or' proposition giving them a choice over which one would haunt their lives and which one they would be free of. They had to manage both (Jones and Shorter-Gooden 2003). They therefore asked the courts to recognise them as Black women per se, as an 'integrated, undifferentiated, complete whole' (Austin 1989, 540), who lived in society as 'twice-stigmatised ... twice kin to the despised majority of all the human life that there is' (Jordan 1981, 143).

They lost. The district court did not see synergy but looked at each characteristic individually, adopting a 'sex-plus' (as established in *Phillips v Martin Marietta Corp* 400 US 542 (1971)), or *multiple* discrimination, analysis, dealing with the claim as gender plus racial discrimination. It saw intersectional discrimination as a 'super-remedy' for black women and rejected the idea, reasoning that to find race and sex discrimination would create a new sub-category within Title VII of the Civil Rights Act of 1964 (42 USC § 2000e-2(a)). Furthermore, this would open a 'Pandora's box', unleashing 'new classes of protected minorities, governed only by the mathematical principles of permutation and combination' (*DeGraffenreid*). It thus applied the zero-sum logic: the sex claim was dismissed; the race claim was consolidated with a complaint brought by African American men against GM (*Moseley v General Motors,* 497 F.Supp. 583 (E. D. Mo. 1980)) and was also unsuccessful.

Without synergy, intersectional discrimination lost its radical potential. It was made to fit into existing political perceptions and legal paradigms by reduction to 'sex-plus', or multiple discrimination. The *Degraffenreid* case illustrates that multiple discrimination does not disrupt prevailing frameworks of discrimination law but, rather, re-defines intersectional discrimination so that it can be accommodated into them. As a consequence of this conflation of intersectional discrimination into multiple discrimination, some feminists wondered if it were not a bankrupt concept by 2007 (Grabham et al. 2009).

This de-radicalisation also re-marginalised the black women workers at the centre of the concept: synergy facilitates the shift of perspective centralising marginalised voices and without it these voices are re-marginalised allowing the white male norm to return to the centre of anti-discrimination law. Overall, in the absence of synergy, the idea of intersectional discrimination loses its systemic critique and is reduced to the first stage of identity politics in which 'scholars chronicle the harms visited on subordinated groups' (Harris 1996, 217). In its place emerges the prospect of potentially unlimited 'combination' of characteristics (Ferree 2009; Lenz 2007; McCall 2005; Urbanek 2009) – as feared by the court in *DeGraffenreid*.

I argue that this is the approach taken in the EU: intersectional discrimination has been reduced to multiple discrimination – in relation to anti-discrimination. The EU has multiplied its vision (what it sees) but without shifting its perspective (the way it sees).

Intersectional and multiple discrimination in Europe

As we see in the Race and Equal (Employment) Treatment Directives, multiple discrimination has been entrenched in EU law (Burri and Schiek 2006; European Commission 2007; FRA 2013; Schiek and Lawson 2011; Sheppard 2011). According to Knapp (2005) this approach to intersectional discrimination was the secret of its success: stripped of its 'baggage' of slave history, it was able to move rapidly into different parts of the academy. Furthermore, over the past 30 years this deradicalised version of intersectional discrimination has become popularised as 'intersectionality' and developed into a general methodological concept, applied across fields to studies at the 'nexus' (Bauer 2014; Gardner 2005; Taylor et al. 2010; Wilson 2013; Zemore et al. 2011).

In addition, the general idea of intersectionality has eclipsed the more specific legal idea of intersectional discrimination and, with it, the critical race feminism centring of black women. It is sometimes hard to see that intersectionality is rooted in critical race theory – it has been de-racialised as well as de-radicalised to become a 'historically disembodied cipher which serves to erase home-grown anti-racist feminist struggles and theoretical debates which go back to the 1980s and 1990s' (Erel et al. 2010, 57). Power asymmetries in politics and education have allowed the tail to wag the dog: intersectional discrimination has been 'hollowed out' and replaced by superficial 'tokenized' attitudes (May 2014, 100) wherein any combination of characteristics will do (Bilge 2010; Hancock 2007; Stasiulis 1999). It is this de-radicalised and de-racialised version of intersectional discrimination that exists in the EU.

The problem in the EU is twofold: it is not just that intersectional discrimination has been replaced by multiple discrimination but, as discussed below, there is no uniform approach to multiple discrimination in the EU or in the member states.

There are different levels of awareness of multiple discrimination in the main EU institutions. While the European Parliament and the European Commission recognise intersectionality (as described above) in EU law, the EU Fundamental Rights Agency (FRA) seems to no longer do so. Its Handbook (FRA 2011) on non-discrimination law mentions neither 'multiple discrimination' nor 'intersectionality', although it has recently published a report on multiple discrimination in healthcare (FRA 2013). The European Institute for Gender Equality (EIGE; see Jacquot and Krizsán in this volume) failed to specifically mention multiple discrimination in its new vision for a gender-equal Europe, but chose an image that included Black women to accompany the statement on its webpage.

This is also evident in the national legal systems. While some countries (e.g. Bulgaria, Croatia, Germany) have incorporated multiple discrimination into law, others (e.g France, Ireland, the Netherlands) have chosen not to do so (Solanke 2013). Most discrimination cases in the member states concern employment, yet few cover race, which can be attributed to the rejection of race[2] as a meaningful social and political category in many EU member states (Barskanmaz 2011; Solanke 2009a).

Multiple discrimination is also visible in legal systems at the European level. The ECtHR in Strasbourg, which oversees the ECHR, provides one separate framework for protection from discrimination in Europe. Created by the Council of Europe in 1950, Article 14 of the ECHR prohibits discrimination but only applies with regard to the 'enjoyment of the rights and freedoms … without discrimination on any ground such as sex, race, colour, language, religion,

Iyiola Solanke

political or other opinion, national or social origin, association with a national minority, property, birth or other status' (see also Harris 2014; O'Neill 2013; O'Connell 2009; Wintemute 2004).

The ECHR system exists alongside the EU system for protection of human rights, as set out in the EU Charter of Fundamental Rights (CFR). The CJEU has ultimate oversight over the CFR, but must interpret rights in the CFR that also exist in the ECHR in line with interpretation by the ECtHR. Article 52(3) CFR says that:

> In so far as this Charter contains rights which correspond to the rights guaranteed by the Convention for the Protection of Human Rights and Fundamental Freedoms, the meaning and scope of those rights shall be the same as those laid down by the said Convention.

However, this provision does not prevent EU law providing more extensive protection.

These two European courts also take different approaches to intersectional discrimination. It has been explicitly mentioned by the ECtHR while in the CJEU there is silence, although it has dealt with two cases that can arguably be described as such: *Achbita* (C-157/15) and *Bougnaoui* (C-188/15) (a further example is C-443/15 *Parris*). Both cases concerned Muslim women who chose to wear the headscarf at work.

Achbita worked at G4S, a Belgium private company where she was employed to provide reception services for organisations in the public and private sector. Achbita informed her line managers that she intended to wear a hijab at work – she was told this was contrary to G4S's informal position of workplace neutrality. The G4S works council subsequently introduced an official ban of employees 'wearing any visible signs of their political, philosophical or religious beliefs and/or from engaging in any observance of such beliefs' at work'. Soon thereafter Achbita was dismissed for wearing her hijab at work. Her legal action for discrimination against G4S failed before the local and appeal court, which held that as the G4S prohibition covered both religious and philosophical beliefs, it complied with Directive 2000/78/EC on equal treatment in employment and occupation. A question was then referred to the CJEU on the interpretation of the Directive's Article 2(2)(a): Should this be interpreted as meaning that the prohibition on a female Muslim wearing a hijab at work does not constitute direct discrimination where the employer's rule prohibits all employees from wearing outward signs of political, philosophical and religious beliefs at the workplace?

The CJEU likewise concluded that because the rule was applied to all workers in the same way, there was no direct discrimination (paras 27–28). It found the rule indirectly discriminatory but justifiable: '27. […] the desire to display, in relations with both public and private sector customers, a policy of political, philosophical or religious neutrality must be considered legitimate' (*Achbita* (C-157/15)). Yet, for business rules of neutrality as set out in Article 16 CFR to be legitimate, they must apply only to those workers '28. … required to come into contact with the employer's customers' (*Achbita* (C-157/15)). The G4S rule could be deemed 'strictly necessary for the purpose of achieving the aim pursued' if it covered only those G4S workers interacting with customers and appropriate to its aim of ensuring neutrality in the workplace as long as it was 'genuinely pursued in a consistent and systematic manner.'

Achbita therefore won an important principle; the CJEU suggested that if such an appearance rule applied to workers who did not come into contact with customers, it would not be legitimate, as it would be unnecessary to achieve the stated goal of neutrality. However, she lost her case: the national court was instructed to ascertain whether, instead of dismissing her, G4S could have offered her an alternative post without visual contact with customers.

It is a disappointing judgement: as in *Degraffenreid* the CJEU overlooks the intersectional discrimination and effectively sanctions the banning of the hijab in public life, enabling

Intersectional discrimination in law

discrimination against Muslim women. The suggestion that women wearing the hijab should be hidden from the sight of customers does little to promote equality in the 21st century. Instead it harkens back to the rampant discrimination common in 1960s Britain, where Black workers would only be given non-client facing roles and could not progress into any other position.

In the second case, Ms Bougnaoui (C-188/15) also wore a hijab to her job in IT. Sent to work on location for a particular client, she was dismissed when she refused to comply with the client request to not wear her hijab when working at their premises. The client argued its own clients had complained about this. When Bougnaoui was dismissed without her severance pay, she brought an action for discrimination on grounds of religion contrary to Directive 2006/78/EC. After losing at the Labour Tribunal of Paris and the Court of Appeal in Paris, the case landed before the French Cour de Cassation, who referred a question to the CJEU under Article 267 TFEU. Given that Bougnaoui's employer sought to defend its action as a genuine occupation qualification, the Cour de Cassation asked whether Article 4(1) of Directive 2000/78/EC covered this (para. 19). Fortunately for Ms Bougnaoui, the CJEU answered in the negative – such a preference could not constitute a genuine and determining occupational requirement:

> 40 ... the concept of a "genuine and determining occupational requirement", within the meaning of that provision, refers to a requirement that is objectively dictated by the nature of the occupational activities concerned or of the context in which they are carried out. It cannot, however, cover subjective considerations, such as the willingness of the employer to take account of the particular wishes of the customer.
>
> (Bougnaoui (C-188/15))

However, in coming to this decision the CJEU did not consider the intersectional aspects nor examine whether there had been discrimination: its reasoning focused on the definition of a 'genuine and determining occupational requirement'. In addition, while it negated the idea that the wishes of a customer to not receive services of an employer provided by a worker wearing the hijab cannot be considered a genuine and determining occupational requirement within the meaning of that provision, it did not state that this wish was per se direct discrimination. A key opportunity was therefore missed to address two issues in the one case.

The CJEU also rarely addresses multiple discrimination in its case law, although the EU Race and Equal Treatment Directives include multiple discrimination. One recent example is *Odar* (C 152-11), where the CJEU found disability discrimination but no age discrimination in relation to German national rules on the calculation of an occupational social security scheme.

The ECtHR takes a different approach to intersectional discrimination: it was explicitly mentioned in *BS v Spain* (no 47159/08; ECtHR) (see also Yoshida 2013), which concerned racial profiling and racial harassment by police of a black women working as a prostitute in Spain. The ECtHR referred to the research on intersectional discrimination and decided that, in light of evidence that the police had allegedly called BS a 'black whore' (para. 61), the absence of an investigation into racism indicated a failure by the domestic courts to 'take account of the applicant's particular vulnerability inherent in her position as an African woman working as a prostitute' (47159/08, paras 56–62). Failure to acknowledge the verbal abuse of the police led to a breach of Article 3 ECHR in conjunction with Article 14; the Spanish authorities had violated the Convention through failure to ascertain whether or not a discriminatory attitude might have played a role in the events (para. 63). While a very limited statement, it suggests that the idea of intersectional discrimination has a procedural impact in European human rights law: just as the US Federal Court of Appeals had done in *Jeffries*,[3] an intersectional approach was adopted to highlight a procedural failure.

Iyiola Solanke

The future of intersectional discrimination in the EU

What is needed to improve the EU approach to intersectional discrimination? I argue that three things are crucial: first, the zero-sum biological categories of anti-discrimination law must be replaced with an alternative logic that emphasises social meaning; secondly, intersectional discrimination must be brought out from the shadow of gender and multiple discrimination; and, finally, the idea of race as a socially salient category must be recognised. In the absence of these three things, intersectional discrimination in the EU will remain as multiple discrimination, and black women – the paradigm[4] group of intersectional discrimination – will remain at the margins of EU anti-discrimination law and policy.

From immutability to stigma

Historically, in the EU as elsewhere, anti-discrimination law has been designed to prevent discrimination because of individual biological traits such as skin colour or sex that are seen as immutable – unchosen, permanent and unchanging. This focus on specific characteristics creates a political–legal framework of grounds assessed in isolation from each other. Jurisprudence and anti-discrimination (legal) scholarship has followed this pattern set by legislation, with intellectual concepts and expertise being developed according to each distinct protected characteristic – race, sex, age, disability etc. Accommodation of an idea that merges two characteristics, such as 'black women', in this rigid framework premised upon immutability is challenging. What is needed therefore is anti-discrimination law that uses an alternative logic – that of stigma.

A stigma is a mark or 'stain' that tarnishes the whole identity. It is used to set an individual apart from others and discredit them so that they are seen as less worthy and excluded from everyday interaction. Those who are stigmatised have no control over the powerful meaning given by society to their attributes or characteristics and cannot escape stigmatisation.

Scholarship on stigma has moved from the behavioural approach of Erving Goffman (1990) to a critical approach. Critical studies identify stigma as a concept with multiple components (Link and Phelan 2001) that is multi-level (Pescosolido et al. 2008) and structurally embedded (Hannem and Bruckert 2012). It is a far more complex concept than the 'face to face'. With its focus on social relationships, critical stigma – as opposed to behavioural stigma – draws attention to the individual, context and power; it links psychological processes with social conditions, creating a continuum of five factors – labelling, stereotyping, exclusion, status loss and discrimination. Stigma arises when they converge (Link and Phelan 2001, 1).

From this perspective, discrimination is a direct consequence of stigmatisation, understood as an expression of socio-cultural power rather than a simple manifestation of individual behaviour.

Stigma is not new to legal systems (Solanke 2017) but rarely used. It has been mentioned in cases before the ECHR (Yoshida 2013) and the CJEU (*Chez Razpredelenie Bulgaria*, C 83/14). Clearly not all stigma leads to discrimination but by thinking about discrimination as stigma, we disrupt existing categories so that we are no longer thinking about identity per se, but about the social meaning arbitrarily attached to certain attributes, statuses and conditions in a way that strips away the right to equal regard. It may be that there is just one attribute, status or condition that stigmatises or it may be that there are many that intersect. Synergy is thus inherent in the anti-stigma principle (Solanke 2017, 133–159).

The shadow of gender and multiple discrimination

Despite acknowledging its existence, the EU – like member states – has struggled to address intersectional discrimination. Legal recognition currently focuses on 'multiple discrimination' (additive and cumulative) rather than intersectional discrimination. Multiple discrimination anchors intersectional discrimination within zero-sum categorical thinking rather than 'disrupting' categories. Additive and cumulative discrimination lack the 'synergy' (Scales-Trent 1989, 24; Solanke 2011, 336) that is central to intersectional discrimination: it must be recognised as distinct from multiple discrimination.

The problem is less the absence of a gender lens but rather the extent to which gender eclipses race. Gender overwhelms intersectional discrimination: whereas in its paradigm legal formulation intersectional discrimination speaks to the unique social, political and economic experiences of black women, in the European sociological interpretation intersectional discrimination focuses solely on women. This recognition proceeds from gender alone, adopting the zero-sum approach. This seems unnecessary, especially as the wording of Article 19 TEU does not prioritise gender. The impulse of intersectional discrimination is also against any prioritisation – it calls instead for a pursuit of social justice that is both local and universal, for disruption in a non-dichotomous way, resistance of dominant rationalities and discovery of 'nondominant resisting rationalities' (Hoagland 2010, 140). This should be the goal of the EU approach to intersectional discrimination.

Perhaps more than anything else, a successful EU approach depends upon recognition of race as a salient social category and the study of race in Europe. The deracialisation of intersectional discrimination in EU policy and law re-marginalises the black women workers originally at the centre of the concept. Thus, in many countries in Europe, black women and their specific experiences are invisible in law, policy and politics (Solanke 2009a). Where race is not recognised as a meaningful socio-political category (Roig and Barskanmaz 2013; Ruble 2014), black women remain 'at the margins' (Crenshaw 1989). Ironically absence of a public discussion of race in Europe supports the refusal to collect data disaggregated by race, creating the conditions for perpetuation of racism and ultimately prevents an effective European approach to intersectional discrimination.

Conclusion

Intersectional discrimination remains an important concept. Although the labour market is now a precarious space for the majority of workers, evidence shows that, as work disappears, this is felt more by black workers (Johnston and Lordan 2014). Data also shows that during any economic downturn, such as that caused by Covid-19, black women– predominantly employed in service and entertainment sectors – experience disproportionately high unemployment rates (ENAR 2019; FRA 2018). A remedy for intersectional discrimination thus remains necessary across Europe where there are migrant and non-migrant, skilled or unskilled, documented and undocumented, black women whose labour market experience differs from both black men and white women.

The EU approach to intersectional discrimination is mediated through the lens of gender, which was indeed its starting point for the legal prohibition of discrimination. It was only in 1997 that additional grounds, including race, became prohibited. This is not per se problematic: gender is as integral to the original idea of intersectional discrimination as race and the synergy between the two is fundamental to it. What is problematic is that gender continues to overshadow race in Europe. This has caused a conversion of intersectional discrimination into 'sex-plus' or multiple discrimination. This is again evident in the new Gender Equality Strategy of the European Commission, which is a current example of how the EU has multiplied its vision (what it sees) without changing the way it sees. The new strategy aims to mainstream intersectionality but in defining this as 'the *combination* [author's emphasis] of gender with other personal characteristics or identities' (COM(2020) 152 final, 2) anchors intersectionality in multiple discrimination. The ambition is to be applauded but the aim to collate comparable data to tackle gender-based violence (COM(2020) 152 final, 5) will be difficult given that – as mentioned above – member states do not collect data disaggregated by race and/or ethnicity. This shows that while the *idea* of intersectional discrimination has stimulated widespread interest across Europe, discussion and policy innovation has really been on multiple discrimination.

The success in tackling intersectional discrimination in the EU depends upon understanding synergy, especially between race and gender. Understanding synergy can be difficult given the zero-sum structural design of anti-discrimination. However, this can be addressed by replacing the principle of immutable biological categories with the anti-stigma principle that is per se synergistic. Using the anti-stigma principle, categories can be created that move away from the single dimension model. The greater the distance from this model, the better the understanding of synergy will be. When intersectional discrimination is released from single dimension thinking as well as the shadow of both gender and multiple discrimination, the more effective the EU approach to intersectional discrimination will be.

Notes

1 Frances EW Harper created the first African American heroine, Iola Leroy, in her novel *Iola Leroy or Shadows Uplifted* (1892); Ida B Wells was the daughter of slaves, she was orphaned as a teenager and founded a newspaper in Memphis. An anti-lynching campaigner, she was also a founder of the first Black Women's Suffrage Club (Davis 1983, 111) and friend of Susan B Anthony; Mary Church Terrell, daughter of a slave, was the third black woman college graduate in the USA, university professor, first President of the National Association of Colored Women's Clubs' created in 1896, and first black woman appointed to the Board of Education of the District of Columbia (Davis 1983, 134–135).
2 Ethnicity is used instead although this arguably belies the specific 'set of political and moral rights and obligations that are argued to arise from a certain history' (Harris 1996, 212).
3 Dafro Jefferies, a Black woman, applied for a vacancy at her organization for a Field Representative. This position had previously been staffed by a white female and a black male. An Appeal Court insisted that her claim of intersectional discrimination be properly examined. *Jefferies v Harris Cty. Community Action Association* 615 F. 2nd 1025 (5th Cir. 1980).
4 This does not of course mean that the concept cannot apply to those who are not black women.

References

Austin R (1989): Sapphire bound, *Wisconsin Law Review* **3**, 539–578.
Akasha G, Bell-Scott P, Smith B (1982): *All the Women are White, All the Blacks Are Men, But Some of Us Are Brave*, New York: Feminist Press.
Aylward CA (1999): *An Intersectional Approach to Discrimination. Addressing Multiple Grounds in Human Rights Claims*, Discussion Paper, Ontario Human Rights Commission.
Barskanmaz C (2011): Rasse – Unwort des Antidiskriminierungsrechts? [Race – taboo of anti-discrimination law?], *Kritische Justiz* **3**, 382–389.
Bauer GR (2014): Incorporating intersectionality theory into population health research methodology. Challenges and the potential to advance health equity, *Social Science & Medicine* **110**, 10–17.
Bilge S (2010): Recent feminist outlooks on intersectionality, *Diogenes* **57** (1), 58–72.
Burri S, Schiek D (2006): Multiple Discrimination in EU Law. Opportunities for Legal Responses to Intersectional Gender Discrimination? Brussels: European Commission.

Caldwell P (1991): A hair piece: perspectives on the intersection of race and gender, *Duke Law Journal*, 365–396.

Cooper AJ (1988): *A Voice from the South. By a Woman from the South*, Oxford, New York: Oxford University Press.

Cooper B (2016): Intersectionality in: Disch L, Hawkesworth, M (eds.): *The Oxford Handbook of Feminist Theory*, Oxford, New York: Oxford University Press.

Crenshaw K (1989): Demarginalising the intersection of race and sex. A black feminist critique of antidiscrimination doctrine, feminist theory and antiracial politics, *University of Chicago Legal Forum* no. 1, 139–167.

Davis AY (1983): *Women, Race and Class*, London: Vintage Books.

Eisenstein ZR, eds. (1979): *Capitalist Patriarchy and the Case for Social Feminism*, New York: Monthly Review Press.

European Network against Racism (ENAR) (2019): Racism and Discrimination in Employment in Europe. ENAR Shadow Report 2013–2017, Brussels: ENAR.

Erel U, Haritaworn J, Rodríguez EG, Klesse C (2010): On the Depoliticisation of Intersectionality Talk. Conceptualising Multiple Oppressions in Critical Sexuality Studies, in: Taylor Y, Hines S, Casey ME (eds.): *Theorizing Intersectionality and Sexuality*, London: Palgrave Macmillan, 56–77.

European Commission (2007): *Tackling Multiple Discrimination Practices, Policies and Laws*, Luxembourg: Office for Official Publications of the European Communities.

European Union Agency for Fundamental Rights (FRA) (2011): *Handbook on European Non-Discrimination Law*, Luxembourg: Publications Office of the European Union.

European Union Agency for Fundamental Rights (FRA) (2013): *Inequalities and Multiple Discrimination in Access to and Quality of Healthcare*, Luxembourg: Publications Office of the European Union.

European Union Agency for Fundamental Rights (FRA) (2018): *Being Black in the EU. Second European Union Minorities and Discrimination Survey*, Luxembourg: Publications Office of the European Union.

Ferree MM (2009): Inequality, Intersectionality and the Politics of Discourse: Framing Feminist Alliances', in: Lombardo E, Meier P, Verloo M (eds): *The Discursive Politics of Gender Equality. Stretching, Bending and Policy Making*, Abingdon: Routledge, 84–101.

Gardner M (2005): *Linkage Activism: Ecology, Social Justice and Education for Social Change*, Abingdon: Routledge.

Givens TE, Evans R (2014): *Legislating Equality. The Politics of Antidiscrimination Policy in Europe*, Oxford: Oxford University Press.

Grabham E, Cooper D, Krishnadas J, Herman D (2009): Intersectionality and Beyond. Law Power and the Politics of Location, Abingdon: Routledge.

Goffman E (1990): *Stigma. Notes on A Spoiled Identity* (1st ed. 1963), London: Penguin.

Hancock AM (2007): When multiplication doesn't equal quick addition. Examining intersectionality as a research paradigm, *Perspective on Politics* **5** (1), 63–79.

Hannem S, Bruckert C, eds. (2012): *Stigma Revisited. Re-Examining the Mark*, Ottawa: University of Ottawa Press.

Hannett C (2003): Equality at the intersections. The legislative and judicial failure to tackle multiple discrimination, *Oxford Journal of Legal Studies* **23** (1) 65–86.

Harper FEW (1892): *Iola Leroy or Shadows Uplifted*, Mineola, NY: Dover Publications.

Harris AP (1996): The unbearable lightness of identity, *Berkeley Women's Law Journal* **11**, 207–221.

Harris D (2014): *O'Boyle, and Warbrick Law of the European Convention on Human Rights*, Oxford: Oxford University Press.

Hoagland SL (2010): Resisting Rationality, in: Tuana N, Morgen S (eds.): *Engendering Rationalities*, Albany, NY: SUNY Press, 125–150.

Johnston DW, Lordan G (2014): When Work Disappears. Racial Prejudice and Recession Labour Market Penalties, *CEP Discussion Paper* Nr. 1257, URL: http://cep.lse.ac.uk/pubs/download/dp1257.pdf (download: April 14, 2020).

Jones C, Shorter-Gooden K (2003): *Shifting. The Double Lives of Black Women in America*, New York: Harper Collins.

Jordan J (1981): *Civil Wars*, New York: Simon and Schuster.

Knapp GA (2005): Race, Class, Gender. Reclaiming Baggage in Fast Travelling Theories, *European Journal of Women's Studies* **12** (3), 249–265.

Lenz I (2007): Power People, Working People, Shadow People … Gender, Migration, Class and Practices of (In)Equality, in: Lenz I, Ullrich C, Fersch B (eds.): *Gender Orders Unbound? Globalisation, Restructuring and Reciprocity*, Opladen: Barbara Budrich, 99–119.

Link BG, Phelan JC (2001): Conceptualizing stigma, *Annual Review of Sociology* **27**, 363–385.
May VM (2014): Speaking into the void. Intersectionality critiques and epistemic backlash *Hypatia* **29** (1), 94–112.
McCall L (2005): The complexity of intersectionality, *Signs* **30** (3), 1771–1800.
Neill AO (2013): *EU Law for UK Lawyers*, Oxford: Hart Publishing.
O'Connell R (2009): Cinderella comes to the Ball. Art 14 and the right to non-discrimination in the ECHR, *Legal Studies* **20**, 211–231.
Pescosolido BA, Martin J, Lang A, Olafsdottir S (2008): Rethinking theoretical approaches to stigma. A Framework Integrating Normative Influences on Stigma (FINIS), *Social Science & Medicine* **67**, 431–440.
Roig E, Barskanmaz C (2013): La République gegen Rasse. URL: http://verfassungsblog.de/la-republique-against-race/ (download: April 13, 2020).
Ruble K (2014): Sweden Plans to Thwart Racism by Eliminating the Mention of Race from Its Laws, URL: https://news.vice.com/article/sweden-plans-to-thwart-racism-by-eliminating-the-mention-of-race-from-its-laws (download: April 13, 2020).
Scales-Trent J (1989): Black women in the constitution. Finding our place and asserting our rights, *Harvard Civil Rights-Civil Liberties Law Review* **24**, 9–44.
Schiek D, Lawson A (2011): *European Union Non-Discrimination Law and Intersectionality,* Farnham: Ashgate.
Sharpe C (2016): *In the Wake. On Blackness and Being,* Durham, NC: Duke University Press.
Sheppard C (2011), Multiple Discrimination in the World of Work, *ILO Working Paper No 66,* Geneva: ILO.
Solanke I (2009a): *The Evolution of Anti-Racial Discrimination Law,* Abingdon: Routledge.
Solanke I (2009b): Putting race and gender together. A new approach to intersectionality, *Modern Law Review* **72** (5), 723–749.
Solanke I (2011): Infusing the silos in the Equality Act 2010 with synergy, *Industrial Law Journal* **40**, 336–358.
Solanke I (2013): A Method for Intersectional Discrimination in EU Labour Law, in: Bogg A, Costello C, Davies (eds.): *Research Handbook on EU Labour Law,* Cheltenham: Edward Elgar, 445–473.
Solanke I (2017): *Discrimination as Stigma. A Theory of Anti-Discrimination Law,* Oxford: Hart Publishing.
Stasiulis D (1999): Feminist Intersectional Theorizing, in: Li SP (ed.): *Race and Ethnic Relations in Canada,* Oxford: Oxford University Press, 347–397.
Taylor Y, Hines S, Casey ME, eds. (2010): Theorizing Intersectionality and Sexuality, New York: Palgrave Macmillan.
Urbanek D (2009): Towards a processual intersectional policy analysis, URL: www.iwm.at/projects/quing/www.quing.eu/files/WHY/urbanek.pdf (download: April 14, 2020).
van der Vleuten A (2007): *The Price of Gender Equality: Member States and Governance in the European Union,* Abingdon: Ashgate.
Wilson AR (2013): *Situating Intersectionality. Politics, Policy and Power (The Politics of Intersectionality),* London: Palgrave Macmillan.
Wing AK (1997): *Critical Race Feminism. A Reader,* New York: New York University Press.
Wintemute, R (2004): 'Within the ambit'. How big is the 'gap' in Article 14 European Convention on Human Rights, *European Human Rights Law Review* **12** (4), 366–382.
Yoshida K (2013): Towards intersectionality in the European Court of Human Rights. The case of B.S. v Spain, *Feminist Legal Studies* **21**, 195–204.
Zemore SE, Karriker-Jaffe KJ, Keithly S, Mulia N (2011): Racial prejudice and unfair treatment. Interactive effects with poverty and foreign nativity on problem drinking', *J Stud Alcohol Drugs* **72** (3), 361–370.

Part II

Gendering the EU polity and structures of governance

Institutions and structures of governance have traditionally been at the centre of the study of European integration. Since the early days of neo-functionalist and intergovernmental analyses, mainstream scholars have investigated the powers of the various institutions and the ways in which these institutions interact with one another and the member states. Until the mid 1990s, both the gender of the individuals in those institutions, as well as the gendered practices of the institutions themselves went largely uninvestigated. However, as equality between women and men emerged as an important policy area for the EU, scholars began to dig more deeply into the gender aspects of the institutions themselves. Gender analyses have since highlighted that the dominance of men within the EU and EU studies has contributed to a hegemonic masculinity that permeates both the EU and its academic field of study. Considering these institutions and their powers through a gendered lens opens new avenues of inquiry and draws attention to different forms of power within and between the institutions.

Compared with some other aspects of gender and the EU that are addressed in this Handbook, the EU institutions have garnered a fair amount of attention from gender scholars over the years. Beginning with Catherine Hoskyns' 1996 work *Integrating Gender: Women Law and Politics in the European Union*, feminists have turned their attention to the EU institutions to show how they contribute to, and hinder, the development of women's rights. At least three themes are readily identifiable. First, many feminist scholars have looked at questions of gender and participation and representation in the individual institutions. This leads them to ask questions about where women are in the institutions, and what sort of power, women (and members of other marginalized groups) are able to exercise. From these observations, scholars have since begun to consider how diversity of representation may influence policy outcomes. In other words, they are interested in understanding how policy outcomes might change through the increased participation and inclusion of marginalized individuals. In the past decades, this strand of research has included a significant amount of research around gender mainstreaming, gender budgeting, positive action and gendered policy outcomes. Finally, in recent years gender scholars have increasingly turned their attention to the ways in which the institutions, rules, norms and processes of the EU are themselves embedded with an inherent masculinity.

The chapters in this part all focus on one or more of these themes. Chapters consider the three legislative institutions as well as the courts. Additionally, several authors pay attention to supporting institutions including agencies and the External Action Service. By considering the interaction between women and the structures, these chapters shed light on the institutional barriers to equality, as well as the ways in which these advocates use the structures to advance a gender-friendly agenda. It becomes apparent that, overall, the European institutions have generally been active advocates for gender equality, although the level of commitment varies among institutions and over time. Some bodies, like the Parliament were early adopters of institutionalized gender equality machinery, while other institutions such as the Council may be viewed as less gender-friendly. However, the chapters importantly also show where the EU institutions fall short of their formal commitment to gender equality.

Not surprisingly, there are still a number of avenues of inquiry that remain underexplored, both in this Handbook and in the broader field of gender and EU studies. In particular, scholars must continue to broaden their application of a gendered lens to the myriad of institutions in the European Union. Bodies such as Comité des représentants permanents (COREPER), expert networks, informal decision-making bodies and smaller, but extremely important bodies, such as the governing Council of the European Central Bank must be subjected to a gender analysis in order to gain a fuller understanding of the gender structures at play in the EU. Furthermore, the relationship between institutions, for example in the trilogue process, could be analyzed through a gendered lens to highlight systemic inequalities resulting from informal rules and norms. Finally, gender scholars need to continue to address intersectional inequalities and the role of intersectional politics in the institutions. While some scholars have started to look at intersectionality in the institutions, this research is mainly confined to the European Parliament. In coming years this needs to be broadened to include all of the European institutions.

The chapters in this part are a strong indication of how much headway gender analyses have made in field of EU studies. We hope that these discussions will continue to spark debate and spur on research across other bodies and institutions.

9

European Parliament

Petra Ahrens[1] and Lise Rolandsen Agustín

The first direct elections to the European Parliament were held in 1979. However, its predecessor, the Common Assembly of the European Coal and Steel Community, dates back to 1951. This body was part of the European Economic Community and the European Atomic Energy Community and had nationally appointed, rather than elected, members. The first meeting of the current institution took place in 1958, when it was called the European Parliamentary Assembly; the name was changed to European Parliament in 1962. Since 1979, members of the European Parliament (MEPs) have been elected through nationally organized elections every five years, based on the 1976 European Electoral Act. The elections are governed by common European rules as well as specific national provisions (EPRS Briefing (2019) 642250). According to the former, European Union (EU) citizens are entitled to vote and run for European elections in their member state of residency even if they are not nationals of that country. For example, a German living in Spain can vote and run for office in Spain. Elections are based on proportional representation and member states decide whether to use an open or closed list system or single transferable vote system. Similarly, national provisions differ in terms of election days, thresholds, voting age, number of constituencies, and compulsory voting.

Competences have increased over time and the European Parliament is seen as a second, equally important channel for creating legitimacy within the EU. Arguably, increasing the power of the only directly elected EU institution has helped to diminish the infamous democratic deficit of the EU (see Moravcsik 2002). The changing powers and composition of the European Parliament has meant that the parliamentarization of EU politics has gained more scholarly attention over time (see Crum and Fossum 2013; Ripoll Servent 2018). With the introduction of the co-decision procedure in 1992 the European Parliament's powers have gradually evolved. In the Amsterdam Treaty, co-decision was expanded to an increased number of policy areas; in 2009, the Lisbon Treaty renamed the process, the ordinary legislative procedure (OLP), implying the new norm of including Parliament as co-legislator in most policy decisions. The European Parliament also shares budgetary authority to decide and approve the annual budget with the Council of the EU (see Abels in this volume).

The European Parliament is also involved in vetting and approving the European Commission (see Hartlapp et al. in this volume). Additionally, Article 17 of the Treaty on the Functioning of

107

the EU (TFEU) specifies that the European Parliament and the Council "are jointly responsible for the smooth running of the process leading to the election of the President of the European Commission"; it specifically notes that the process shall take "account of the elections to the European Parliament". In practice, the Parliament votes to approve the Commission President and subsequently the entire College of Commissioners, as a collective body. It has objected individual Commission candidates several times. In 2004, for example, the conservative Rocco Buttiglione (EPP) was rejected due to his comments on the traditional role of women in households and homosexuality as a sin (Corbett et al. 2016, 344). After the 2019 elections, it rejected three candidates: French liberal Sylvie Goulard (Renew Europe), who responded too vaguely to the scrutinizing committee's questions on its ethical concerns about her conduct as former MEP and the broad nature of the Internal Market portfolio that she was foreseen for; the Romanian social democrat Rovana Plumb (S&D) and the Hungarian conservative László Trócsányi (EPP) were rejected before their parliamentary hearings due to potential conflict of interests assessed on the basis of their declarations of financial interests.

Over time, the European Parliament has developed new practices to further enact, sustain and extend its own powers. Beginning in 2014, it encouraged its political groups to nominate candidates for the position of Commission President, also known as the *Spitzenkandidatur* process. This contributed to actual campaigns for the Commission presidency as part of the European election campaign and included televised debates among pan-European candidates. However, there is no formal obligation for the European Council to accept this process, and the 2019 nomination of German conservative Ursula von der Leyen as Commission President, despite not being a *Spitzenkandidatin*, is an example of the power struggle among EU institutions.

This chapter considers the gendered nature of the European Parliament as an institution by accounting for recent gender research and relating this to mainstream EU literature. The first section addresses four key elements of parliamentary politics in the EU: candidates and MEPs, political groups, committees, and structures and policies. The second section focuses on research gaps and directions for future research on three selected areas: intersectionality; the role of the Parliament in relation to the other EU institutions; and national/transnational dynamics.

Gendering the European Parliament

Research on the European Parliament is rich and diverse (e.g. Corbett et al 2016; Ripoll Servent 2018), but gender aspects have been largely disregarded in mainstream literature. Research specifically on gender and the European Parliament has focused on the ways in which the institutions and its main components (elections, political groups, committees) are gendered and, moreover, how policies adopt, or fail to adopt, a gender perspective. The former relates mainly to descriptive and substantive representation (that is, how many women are represented and where their interests are represented), as well as to the gendered practices of politics. The latter concerns agenda-setting and policy-making processes as well as the structures hindering or facilitating gender awareness and implementation. The European Institute for Gender Equality (EIGE 2020; see Jacquot and Krizsán in this volume) builds upon this systematization in its "Gender-sensitive Parliaments Tool". The European Parliament is currently ranked number three in this tool (scoring 75.8 out of 100) compared to member states' national parliaments. In the following we address these various dimensions by presenting and discussing research on candidates and MEPs, political groups, committees, as well as structures and policies.

Candidates and MEPs

European elections have been often characterized as "second-order elections", implying they are less important than national elections (Ripoll Servent 2018). This is reflected in the argument that the electoral campaigns are not about European politics as such, but rather, a matter of voters evaluating national parties and punishing or rewarding these national parties for political decisions in the domestic sphere (Hix and Lord 1997). Indeed, electoral turnout has followed a downward development over the years, from 62% in the first direct elections in 1979 to an all-time low of 43% in 2014 (European Parliament 2019, 34). The 2019 elections showed a slight increase across member states, with an overall turnout of 51% and national differences ranging from a low of 28% in Slovakia to a high of 88% in Belgium (European Parliament 2019, 36). According to Kostelka, Blais and Gidengil (2019, 446–448), the gender gap in national elections has closed over time, but remains for supranational (and sub-national) elections. In 2019, the average turnout was still higher among men (52%) than women (49%), but the gap had narrowed considerably in all countries. Moreover, while more men voted in 15 countries, in 13 countries more women voted (European Parliament 2019, 38; Fortin-Rittberger and Ramstetter in this volume). A key reason is an "unequal psychological engagement in politics" that is amplified for "elections of lower importance" such as European elections (Kostelka et al. 2019, 452–456). Whether the recent changes mean that European elections are becoming more salient or whether women are becoming more politically engaged requires further research.

The number of MEPs has gradually increased to 751 due to the enlargement of the EU; this is the maximum number set in the treaties. However, due to the UK withdrawal the number

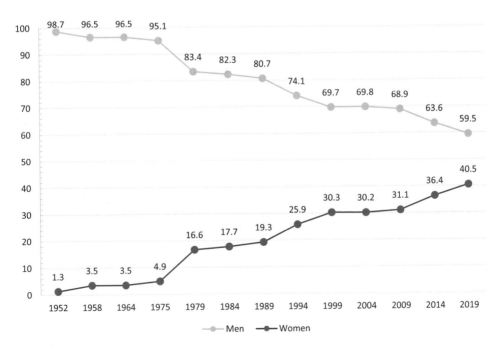

Figure 9.1 Members of the European Parliament, 1952–2019 (%)

Source: Graph and calculation by authors. Data from European Parliament 2018b, 5 and https://election-results.eu/mep-gender-balance/2019–2024/.

of MEPs has decreased by 46 seats so that the Parliament, as it stands right now (March 2020), is composed of 705 MEPs. The seats are distributed among the member states on the basis of the size of the population and the principle of degressive proportionality; accordingly, larger member states (Germany: 96) have proportionally fewer seats than smaller member states (Malta, Cyprus: 6). The gender gap among the elected MEPs has decreased over the years (see Figure 9.1); whereas only 15% women MEPs were elected in 1979, the results of the 2019 European elections showed the highest descriptive representation of women in the history of the institution, with 40.6% women candidates gaining a seat (39.5% after Brexit; European Parliament 2020). Often, "the European Parliament is heralded as one of the most gender-equal elected bodies in the world" (Fortin-Rittberger and Rittberger 2014, 1).

A study commissioned by the European Parliament shows that the remaining gender gap is largely due to underrepresentation of women candidates. National parties act as gatekeepers and the composition of electoral lists are to blame, rather than voter preferences (EPRS_BRI(2019)635548). Analysing the 2014 European elections, Aldrich (2018, 2) argues that party strategy and electoral rules matter to the gendered composition of electoral lists but "these effects are mediated by party organization … The nomination of women in parties utilizing centralized selection is much less likely to be affected by electoral conditions" and vice versa. This means that "party-level contextual factors" need to be considered when discussing the conditions leading to a more gender-balanced representation on electoral lists (Aldrich 2018, 2). A study conducted by the European Parliament itself also highlights the lack of encouragement by Europarties towards their national member parties to support measures enhancing women's representation on party lists (EPRS_BRI(2019)635548, 7). The Parliament itself has adopted several resolutions welcoming quota initiatives at national level; however, recent attempts to include gender quotas in reforming the European Electoral Act have been rejected by the Council (EPRS_BRI(2019)635548, 9), even though we have witnessed a "gender quota revolution" (Lépinard and Rubio-Marín 2018) at national level. Party and legislative quotas are on the rise in member states and such quota then also pertain to European elections (see EPRS Briefing (2019) 642250).

Currently, descriptive representation of women in the European Parliament is significantly above the national parliamentary average of 30%. Thus, one of the key questions addressed in the literature tries to understand this difference. Following the 2019 EU elections, women MEPs made up 40.5% of the representatives (Abels 2020). Sweden had sent the most women MEPs (55%), followed by Finland with 54% and several member states reached 50% gender representation (Austria, France, Latvia, Luxembourg, Malta, the Netherlands and Slovenia). At the bottom, we find Cyprus, with no women among the state's six representatives. Slovakia (15%), Romania (22%) and Greece (24%) also fared poorly (European Parliament 2019a). National variations make the European Parliament especially appropriate to look for explanations of the descriptive representation gap between the European and member states' parliaments. Two basic models, which distinguish between the supply-side, focusing on the candidates and their motivations and characteristics, and the demand-side, including recruitment patterns, electoral rules, party dynamics, etc., explain the gap (Krook 2010; Norris and Lovenduski 1995). Supply-side explanations suggest that women are more motivated to run for European elections (compared to the national level), whereas demand-side explanations look at electoral rules and the parties' role in recruiting women candidates for European elections. Fortin-Rittberger and Rittberger (2014) argue that electoral rules are not causally related to descriptive representation in the case of the European Parliament, refuting the claim that proportional electoral systems can explain the gender gap. Also drawing on a demand-side explanation, Chiva (2014) argues that the electoral system or the left–right divide of the political parties, offer at best, limited explanations of the variations in women's representation in the new member states. Instead, she finds that the party's position on European integration is a key explanatory factor for gendered recruitment strategies. Accordingly, "political parties with a positive stance towards European integration are more likely to take the norms of equality they perceive as dominant in the European Union into consideration when selecting their candidates" (Chiva 2014, 461). Forest (2015) compares trends in the old and the new member states and finds that in central and eastern Europe, women candidates represent an intellectual political elite with stronger political capital and longer educational background than women candidates in the old member states.

Chiva (2019) further argues that, because the "rules of the game" differ between the national and European context, substantive representation of women is also different. Gender equality is an established norm in the EU treaties and policy-making, creating an environment more conducive to the participation of women MEPs. Moreover, she finds that there is "little evidence to suggest that the [European Parliament] has become more conservative after the Eastern enlargement" (Chiva 2019, 197); rather women MEPs from the central and eastern European member states seem to have been socialized into the gender equality norms of the EU institutions, and the European Parliament in particular. Further research is required to trace the origins of socialization pressures and whether they also operate for other groups of MEPs, for instance newly incoming MEPs from old member states.

Another hypothesis considers European elections as "second-order" and thus less important than national elections, because they are not about power politics in terms of forming a government. This suggests that women have easier access to this arena since the level of competition is lower (Vallance and Davies 1986). Hence, as the powers of the EU have gradually grown, we would expect the representation gap between national and European levels to decrease (Fortin-Rittberger and Rittberger 2014). Similarly, the representation of women should decrease as the Parliament's powers increase. This has not happened. Instead women's representation has grown along with the expansion of European Parliament powers. Consequently, Abels (2019, 19) suggests that the relationship between feminization and parliamentarization of the European Parliament is "highly complex".

Political groups

Candidates typically run for election as representatives of their national parties. As elected MEPs, they represent their national party and their electoral constituency and, at the same time, they organize as part of transnational political groups (see Ahrens and Rolandsen Agustín (European Parliament) in this volume). A political group is composed of at least 23 MEPs representing a minimum of seven member states. After elections each political group elects a chair or several co-chairs as well as a bureau and a secretariat. In the 2019–2024 legislature (post-Brexit) there are seven political groups representing a classical left–right spectrum of political affiliation and ideology: the European People's Party (EPP; 187 MEPs), the Progressive Alliance of Socialists and Democrats (S&D; 147 MEPs), Renew Europe (98 MEPs), Identity and Democracy (ID; 76 MEPs), Greens/European Free Alliance (Greens/EFA; 67 MEPs), European Conservatives and Reformists (ECR; 61 MEPs), and the European United Left/Nordic Green Left (GUE/NGL; 39 MEPs). MEPs choosing not to belong to a political group are defined as "non-attached members" (29 MEPs).

The gender composition of these political groups varies between 32% in the ECR to almost 53% in the Greens/EFA group. Historically, the Greens/EFA have had the highest representation of women, with the exception of the 2014–2019 legislature (Kantola and Rolandsen Agustín 2019).

Renew Europe (formerly Alliance of Liberals and Democrats for Europe) shows the steepest development from 8% in 1979 to 47% in 2019. The two largest groups, EPP and S&D, have followed similar development paths, with S&D typically having approximately 10% more female representation than the EPP. In the period from 1979 to 2019, women's representation increased from 8% to 34% for the EPP and 21% to 43% for S&D. Women's representation even grew in the Eurosceptic right-wing groups, starting at 13% in 2009 and currently at 32% (ECR group) and from 31% in 2014 to 40% in 2019 in ID (formerly ENF) (see Figure 19.1 in this volume). The development over time shows that all groups have contributed to the general increase in women's descriptive representation in the European Parliament. However, with very few exceptions, centre-left and leftist groups deliver higher percentages of female representation than centre-right and right-wing groups. Greens/EFA have consistently been at the top, except for the 2014 elections when the group was surpassed in women's representation by GUE/NGL and S&D.

This increase does not translate into leadership positions such as chairs and co-chairs in the same way. In the 2019–2024 legislature, only 30% of political group chairs are women. Yet, all political groups in the current legislature have an equal share of women and men among committee chairs, except for S&D (60% women) and Greens/EFA (100%, one woman) as well as GUE/NGL (100%, one man). Political groups usually assign leadership positions (including rapporteurships) to national delegation leaders or long-term MEPs, who are predominantly men, thus once more reproducing gender imbalances.

Substantive representative of women in the political groups can be understood by considering their positioning in different policy fields (see Ahrens and Rolandsen Agustín (Party politics) in this volume). Political groups follow the classic left/right divide with left-leaning groups demonstrating more gender equality and gender-sensitivity in their policies, and typically also showing a high degree of women's descriptive representation (Kantola and Rolandsen Agustín 2016; 2019). The right-leaning groups have weaker gender-awareness and gender equality policies. This is reflected in their voting patterns on gender equality proposals. However, gender equality issues can be highly controversial and the specific position of a political group is highly dependent on the context of the policy issue at hand. For example, policies such as sexual and reproductive health and rights can highlight large internal differences within the individual groups (Kantola and Rolandsen Agustín 2019). Mainstream literature argues that political groups are increasingly coherent with party discipline strictly enforced. Yet, Bowler and McElroy (2015) showed that divisive policy issues between political groups lower intra-group cohesion. Similarly, gendered analyses found that the politicized nature of gender equality results in lower intra-group cohesion in the 2009–2014 and 2014–2019 legislature (Warasin et al. 2019). Yet, the lower cohesion rates (compared to all policy areas on average) vary strongly between the political groups: they are lower for EPP, ALDE, EFDD, ENF and ECR and higher for S&D, Greens/EFA and GUE/NGL. This allows the latter to build a strong alliance in the Committee on Women's Rights and Gender Equality (FEMM) (Warasin at al. 2019, 148–149).

Furthermore, gender research emphasizes the role of internal rules and networks within parties as a means of enhancing women's representation and supporting gender equality policies. For instance, in the European Parliament, the Greens/EFA, have rules in place to ensure a gender balance in appointments and elections. Several other groups have adopted various measures to support women candidates (EPRS_BRI(2019)635548). The EPP has the "W group" (for "Women"), which is an informal network pushing for more women in European Parliament leadership positions and coordinating efforts to put gender equality on the political group agenda (Kantola and Rolandsen Agustín 2019). Whether or not such measures improve substantive representation requires more research.

Committees

The largest portion of day-to-day work is carried out in committees consisting of between 25 and 73 MEPs, with groups represented proportional to their position in the Parliament. Currently, there are 20 standing committees divided into specific policy areas, plus two sub-committees. Each committee has a chair, a bureau and a secretariat, and MEPs acting as rapporteurs. In the committees, policy reports are drafted, debated, amended and voted upon before they reach the plenary where they are adopted or rejected. The committees are characterized by a rather traditional gendered division of labour with high representation of women in the FEMM committee and the committees on Employment and Social Affairs (EMPL), and Civil Liberties, Justice and Home Affairs (LIBE), and low representation in Constitutional Affairs (AFCO), Security and Defense (SEDE), and Transport and Tourism (TRAN) (Abels 2020; European Parliament 2014).

Gender research has mainly focused on FEMM as the European Parliament's gender equality machinery, along with the High Level Group on Gender Equality and Diversity, the Gender Mainstreaming Network, and the Group of Equality and Diversity Coordinators as well as the Equality and Diversity Unit in the European Parliament administration. The FEMM committee, fully established in 1984, institutionalized earlier ad hoc committees initiated as early as 1979. It differs from most other parliamentary committees, because its membership is voluntary and "neutral" (i.e. MEPs can still be full member of another committee), and its output is predominantly non-legislative (Ahrens 2016). Renman and Conroy (2014) argue that European Parliament committees headed by women are weak in power terms; FEMM, in particular, is powerless and hardly involved in legislative procedures. Moreover, "men are significantly less likely to be on the FEMM Committee than women, and once on the committee are less likely to take an active role in the work of the committee" (Nugent 2019, 138). In contrast, Ahrens (2016) has found that FEMM has made creative use of its power and institutional possibilities to the fullest, ensuring "institutional persistence", "thematic inclusion" and "networked integration". It has drafted own-initiative reports "in order to promote public debate on questions of gender equality in a range of areas" (Jacquot 2017, 38). Nonetheless, in 1998 and again in 2000, as gender mainstreaming initiatives led to the (presumed) inclusion of gender perspectives in other European Parliament committees, there was discussion as to whether FEMM ought to be abolished (Ahrens 2016; Lombardo and Verloo 2009).

The FEMM Committee is often characterized as a consensus-seeking, feminist-activist arena where important agenda-setting for EU gender equality policy takes place (Ahrens 2018a; Jacquot 2015; Rolandsen Agustín 2012). In recent legislatures, FEMM has also attracted MEPs of the right-wing groups, who denounce EU gender equality policy and the work of FEMM as "gender ideology" (Korolczuk and Graff 2018). Anti-gender attacks occur in FEMM and in plenary (Kemper 2014), even though MEPs from populist and radical right parties rarely engage as (shadow) rapporteur in any parliamentary committee or in inter-institutional "trilogues"[2] (McDonnell and Werner 2019; Ripoll and Panning 2019; including FEMM, see Ahrens 2018b). Thus, contestation over gender equality thrives both within and between political groups.

Additional formal and informal structures

Abels (2019) underlines that the European Parliament has not followed the expected dynamic of "power in, gender out", in other words, women's representation has increased as the European Parliament has gained institutional power. The share of women in parliamentary leadership positions has also steadily increased over time. At the top leadership level, the President of the Parliament along with the chairs of the political groups set the agenda and timetable of the

European Parliament; they agree on the committee setup. The first President of the elected European Parliament was Simone Veil (1979–1982); since then, however, only one of the following 16 presidents was a woman, namely Nicole Fontaine (1999–2002). In the 2019–2024 legislature, women provide 55% of the committee chairs (12 out of 22), and 57% of the vice-presidents (eight out of 14); this is a significant increase from the previous legislature (36% and 21%, respectively). Apart from data on descriptive representation, at present, no research investigates how gender equality inside the European Parliament is influenced by various political–administrative functions.

Mushaben (2019, 80), however, finds that the potential "critical mass" of more than 30% women within the European Parliament is undermined by "gender-blind institutional reforms". Here, she refers specifically to the new power balances emerging from the rise of intergovernmentalism and the increased use of trilogues to fast-track legislation, at the expense of transparency. Mushaben argues that women have increased their representation in the European Parliament, but have not experienced a similar rise in their influence. Hence, women have gained descriptive but not substantive representation.

So-called intergroups, i.e. informal groups with MEPs and external (informal) members from civil society organizations, are also important as they focus on specific political topics not directly covered by committees (Landorff 2019). One of the longest standing informal groups is the Lesbian, Gay, Bisexual & Transgender Rights – LGBT Intergroup, established in 1997, which has had an important role in mobilizing for LGBT rights, particularly during the enlargement to central and eastern Europe (Kristoffersson et al. 2016, 50–52). Other intergroups, such as the Intergroups on Anti-Racism & Diversity, on Disability, or on Ageing and Intergenerational Solidarity, also draw attention to intersectional equality.

A wide variety of other administrative groups are important to the smooth operation of the European Parliament. This includes, for example, the European Parliamentary Research Service (EPRS) and the secretariats supporting parliamentary committees. The EPRS, for instance, publishes fact sheets and reports on gender equality, often commissioned by FEMM. Yet, all of these structures are under-researched, particularly from a gender perspective.

European Parliament policies and gender equality

Gender research has also focused on specific policy areas, addressing the parliamentary policy processes as part of the bigger picture of EU integration. Policy areas such as employment, economy and gender-based violence have been analysed extensively (see Cengiz 2019; Jacquot 2017; Montoya 2013). These studies highlight that the EU is not a unitary actor; we must analyse and evaluate differences between and also within institutions, from a gender perspective. The European Parliament, or more specifically the FEMM Committee, typically acts as the main gender actor in policy-making and seeks to add a gender perspective on otherwise "ungendered" issues. FEMM, for instance, played an important agenda-setting role on the issue of domestic violence, leading the European Parliament to become a frontrunner on the policy issue in the 1980s, well ahead of many member states (Montoya and Rolandsen Agustín 2013). Through strategic framing the Parliament was able to maximize its policy-making influence. This illustrates the ways in which the institution has used its powers to the fullest. Accepting a de-gendered framing of violence against women as a public health problem, the European Parliament maximized its influence and took advantage of the fact that the issue fell under the co-decision procedure, giving the European Parliament more power than it may have otherwise had (Rolandsen Agustín 2013; see Roggeband in this volume). A similar strategic move secured the 1992 maternity leave directive. However, the European Parliament was unable to bring a revised version of the directive in 2015 (Kluger Dionigi 2017; Milner in this volume).

Another example of FEMM's agenda-setting and institutionalization power is the effort to adopt and implement gender mainstreaming in the European Parliament itself. To this end, FEMM engineered a system of monitoring and evaluation, which made "it almost impossible for the EP to forget about the new [gender mainstreaming] rules" and served to enhance its power (Ahrens 2019, 100). With respect to the economic and financial crisis, FEMM was agenda-setter again, emphasizing the gendered consequences of austerity policies (see Kantola and Lombardo in this volume). The Committee was also an important reflection of the contestation among political groups around the issue of solidarity. Attempts to influence policies and policy-making in the Commission and the Council were unsuccessful, and the overall EU policy remained quite gendered (Cavaghan 2017; Guerrina 2017; Jacquot 2017; Kantola and Rolandsen Agustin 2016). The European Parliament is characterized as an "institutional advocate of gender budgeting", but has been similarly unsuccessful in bringing about actual policy change, partly due to the "fragmented nature of the Parliament as an institution comprising of various committees and groups with varying priorities and interests" (Cengiz 2019, 104) and "its limited veto powers within the budgetary process vis-a-vis the national governments and the overarching neoliberal efficiency and competitiveness discourse dominating EU policies and politics" (Cengiz 2019, 119). The European Parliament's role in promoting gender equality in foreign affairs and development policy is even less pronounced; gender aspects are appended, treated in a narrow way, and typically addressed in separate institutional units instead of as a cross-cutting issue (Allwood 2013; Debusscher in this volume).

Without doubt, the European Parliament has played a prominent role in setting the agenda and advancing specific gender equality policies at the supranational level. It has been decisive in expanding the policy scope of the EU from gender equality related exclusively to the labour market to other areas including education, gender-based violence and migration (van der Vleuten 2019). Concurrently, the European Parliament has contributed to the re-interpretation of the EU's policy competences in the field of gender equality by articulating a supranational argument for the development of new policies and the expansion into new policy fields. Thus, in many regards the Parliament has driven gender equality policy and its Europeanization forward. In the process, the institution has also been active in branding itself as the key "equality promoter" of the EU (Ahrens 2019). In addition, a significant amount of gender knowledge is produced by the European Parliament through studies and reports. Despite this active role, recent research has questioned the notion of the Parliament as a consistently progressive gender equality actor. Van der Vleuten (2019) argues that the European Parliament's history and its development illustrates that women's substantive representation and support for gender equality policies has not increased in parallel with descriptive representation. Nonetheless, the norm entrepreneurship of "committed individuals" has been important and it has strengthened women's substantive representation, with the FEMM Committee working as "a node of a transnational 'velvet' network of engaged individuals, experts and femocrats, national MPs and non-governmental organizations", which was especially influential in the 1980s and 1990s (van der Vleuten 2019, 47). Finally, the European Parliament has made efforts to enhance EU legitimacy by emphasizing social policies, including gender equality policies. However, van der Vleuten (2019) finds that the legitimacy argument has become less powerful given the economic costs of gender equality policies along with the ideological contestation of gender ideology from the right-wing.

Moving forward: research gaps and directions for future research

Even though gender research into the European Parliament is growing, there are still numerous gaps that deserve more attention. In the following, we highlight three points for future research: intersectionality, institutional interrelations and national/transnational dynamics.

There is a lack of research around the composition of the Parliament and its political groups from an intersectional perspective, e.g. including ethnic background, disability, sexual orientation. An intersectional approach could similarly offer insight into European Parliament policies and debates. Some light has been shed on how intersectionality was addressed in, for instance, internal struggles about whether to establish a specific gender equality agency, EIGE, or an integrated equality body (Lombardo and Verloo 2009; on EIGE see Jacquot and Krizsán in this volume) and to gender-based violence policies (Lombardo and Rolandsen Agustín 2011) as reflection of #MeToo in the European Parliament. Yet, overall research on its structures, policies and practices from an intersectional perspective is rare.

The relationships among the European Parliament and other EU institutions, stakeholders and civil society have also received considerably less attention than its internal dimensions and elements. There is a need to explore the Parliament's role in the broader context of today's EU gender equality policy-making, not least because the new provisions of the 2009 Lisbon Treaty, which provide the European Parliament with more power, are still changing existing practices and rules. Feminist institutionalism suggests that institutions and their formal and informal rules are gendered (see MacRae and Weiner in this volume); thus, the implementation of new treaties may create opportunities to reshape power balances into more gender-equal practices and rules. Moreover, previous (personal) networks of gender equality actors between the different institutions and civil society have been shaken up with gender equality currently institutionalized in different places (van der Vleuten 2019). How this institutionalization shapes and affects the work of parliamentary committees, political groups and individual MEPs requires attention from a gender perspective.

Finally, differences between various national and EU-level politics are largely neglected from a gender perspective. Scholars need to consider the ways in which different levels of governance relate to each other and become institutionalized at the EU level through the parliamentary arena. Research on how national parliaments are "Europeanized" and involved in EU politics, is still an emerging topic (Abels 2019; Crum and Fossum 2013; Hefftler et al. 2015; Högenauer et al. 2016), and its impact on supranational gender equality policies has not yet been addressed. Research into this area could include agenda-setting; gendered discourses (for example in parliamentary debates); party practices for selection and nomination of European Parliament candidates; as well as the translation of populism and radical politics from the national to the European sphere. Likewise, interparliamentary cooperation between the European Parliament and its national counterparts receives some attention in mainstream research (Brack and Deruelle 2016), but has not yet been addressed through a gendered lens. There is evidence of this interparliamentary cooperation. For example, the FEMM committee is actively organizing inter-parliamentary committee meetings with sectoral committees from national parliaments. Addressing the nature, dynamics and development of democracy in relation to the European Parliament from a gender perspective is crucial, not least given that the Parliament is highlighted as the most democratic institution of the EU and, as such, the democratic legitimacy of the EU itself largely depends on it.

Notes

1 Petra Ahrens' work received funding from the European Research Council (ERC) under grant agreement No 771676 of the European Union's Horizon 2020 research and innovation programme.
2 Trilogues are informal meetings in the EU legislative process between European Parliament, Council and Commission representatives to speed up decision-making and to avoid time-consuming "third-reading" conciliation processes.

References

Abels G (2019): The Powers of the European Parliament. Implications for Gender Equality Policy, in: Ahrens P, Rolandsen Agustín L (eds.), *Gendering the European Parliament: Structures, Policies, and Practices*, London: Rowman & Littlefield International, 19–34.

Abels G (2020): Gendering the 2019–2024 European Parliament, in: Kaeding M, Müller M, Schmälter J (eds.), *Die Europawahl 2019: Ringen um die Zukunft Europas*, Wiesbaden: Springer VS, 407–421.

Ahrens P (2016): The Committee on Women's Rights and gender equality in the European Parliament. Taking advantage of institutional power play, *Parliamentary Affairs* **69** (4), 778–793.

Ahrens P (2018a): *Actors, Institutions, and the Making of EU Gender Equality Programs*, London: Palgrave Macmillan.

Ahrens P (2018b): Anti-feministische Politiker*innen im Frauenrechtsausschuss des Europäischen Parlaments – Wendepunkt oder Resilienz in der EU Gleichstellungspolitik?, *Feministische Studien* **36** (2), 403–416.

Ahrens P (2019): Working Against the Tide? Institutionalizing Gender Mainstreaming in the European Parliament, in: Ahrens P, Rolandsen Agustín L (eds.): *Gendering the European Parliament: Structures, Policies, and Practices*, London: Rowman & Littlefield International, 85–101.

Aldrich A (2018): Party organization and gender in European elections, *Party Politics*, 1–14. https://doi.org/10.1177/1354068818806630.

Allwood G (2013): Gender mainstreaming and policy coherence for development: Unintended gender consequences and EU policy, *Women's Studies International Forum* **39**, 42–52.

Bowler S, McElroy G (2015): Political group cohesion and "hurrah" voting in the European Parliament, *Journal of European Public Policy* **22** (9), 1355–1365.

Brack N, Deruelle T (2016): Towards a More Politicized Interparliamentary Cooperation? The EP's Political Groups and the European Parliamentary Week, in: Lupo N, Fasone C (eds.): *Interparliamentary Cooperation in the Composite* European Constitution, Oxford: Hart Publishing, 131–146.

Cavaghan R (2017): The Gender Politics of EU Economic Policy. Policy Shifts and Contestations Before and After the Crisis, in: Kantola J, Lombardo E (eds.): *Gender and the Economic Crisis in Europe. Politics, Institutions and Intersectionality*, London: Palgrave Macmillan, 49–71.

Cengiz F (2019): Gendering the EU Budget. Can European Parliament Play the Role of a Gender Budgeting Advocate?, in: Ahrens P, Rolandsen Agustín L (eds.): *Gendering the European Parliament: Structures, Policies, and Practices*, London: Rowman & Littlefield International, 103–120.

Chiva C (2014): Gender, European integration and candidate recruitment. The European Parliament elections in the new EU member states, *Parliamentary Affairs* **67** (2), 458–494.

Chiva C (2019): Overcoming Male Dominance? The Representation of Women in the European Parliament Delegations of the Post-Communist EU Member States, in: Ahrens P, Rolandsen Agustín L (eds.): *Gendering the European Parliament: Structures, Policies, and Practices*, London: Rowman & Littlefield International, 177–197.

Corbett R, Jacobs F, Neville D (2016): *The European Parliament*, 9th ed., London: John Harper.

Crum B, Fossum JE, eds. (2013): *Practices of Inter-Parliamentary Coordination in International Politics. The European Union and Beyond*, Colchester: ECPR Press.

European Parliament (2014): *Women in the European Parliament. Political posts*, URL: www.europarl.europa.eu/RegData/publications/2014/0001/P7_PUB(2014)0001_EN.pdf (download: February 6, 2020).

EIGE (2020): Gender-sensitive Parliaments, URL: https://eige.europa.eu/gender-mainstreaming/toolkits/gender-sensitive-parliaments (download: March 24, 2020).

European Parliament (2019a): 2019 European election results: MEPs' gender balance by country: 2019, URL: https://europarl.europa.eu/election-results-2019/en/mep-gender-balance/2019–2024/ (download: March 24, 2020).

European Parliament (2019b): *Review of European and National Election Results. Update September 2019*, URL: https://op.europa.eu/en/publication-detail/-/publication/1f2a7ac7-d8f7-11e9-9c4e-01aa75ed71a1 (download: February 6, 2020).

European Parliament (2020): At a Glance: Women in Parliaments, Infographic February 2020, URL: https://www.europarl.europa.eu/RegData/etudes/ATAG/2020/646189/EPRS_ATA(2020)646189_EN.pdf (download: April 6, 2020).

Forest M (2015): Did newcomers (finally) make a difference? Framing gender equality in the EU-28, Paper presented at the *13th Congress of the French Political Science Association*, June 22–24.

Fortin-Rittberger J, Rittberger B (2014): Do electoral rules matter? Explaining national differences in women's representation in the European Parliament, *European Union Politics* **15** (4), 496–520.

Guerrina R (2017): Gendering European Economic Narratives: Assessing the Costs of the Crisis to Gender Equality, in: Kantola J, Lombardo E (eds.): *Gender and the Economic Crisis in Europe. Politics, Institutions and Intersectionality*, London: Palgrave Macmillan, 95–116.

Hefftler C, Neuhold C, Rozenberg O, Smith J, eds. (2015): *The Palgrave Handbook of National Parliaments and the European Union*, Basingstoke: Palgrave Macmillan.

Hix S, Lord C (1997): *Political Parties in the European Union,* London: Macmillan.

Högenauer A-L, Neuhold C, Christiansen T (2016): *Parliamentary Administrations in the European Union,* Basingstoke: Palgrave Macmillan.

Jacquot S (2015): *Transformations in EU Gender Equality. From Emergence to Dismantling,* London: Palgrave Macmillan.

Jacquot S (2017): A Policy in Crisis. The Dismantling of the EU Gender Equality Policy, in: Kantola J, Lombardo E (eds.): *Gender and the Economic Crisis in Europe. Politics, Institutions and Intersectionality,* Basingstoke: Palgrave Macmillan, 27–48.

Kantola J, Rolandsen Agustín L (2016): Gendering transnational party politics: the case of European Union, *Party Politics* **22** (5): 641–51.

Kantola J, Rolandsen Agustín L (2019): Gendering the representative work of the European Parliament. A political analysis of women MEP's perceptions of gender equality in party groups, *Journal of Common Market Studies* **57** (4): 768–786.

Kemper A (2014): *Keimzelle der Nation, Teil 2. Wie sich in Europa Parteien und Bewegungen für konservative Familienwerte, gegen Toleranz und Vielfalt und gegen eine progressive Geschlechterpolitik radikalisieren.* Berlin: Friedrich-Ebert-Stiftung.

Kluger Dionigi M (2017): *Lobbying in the European Parliament. The Battle for Influence*, Cham: Palgrave Macmillan.

Korolczuk E, Graff A (2018): Gender as 'Ebola from Brussels': the anti-colonial frame and the rise of illiberal populism, *Signs: Journal of Women in Culture and Society* **43** (4): 797–821.

Kostelka F, Blais A, Gidengil E (2019): Has the gender gap in voter turnout really disappeared?, *West European Politics* **42** (3): 437–63.

Kristoffersson M, van Roozendahl B, Poghosyan L (2016): European Integration and LGBTI Activism: Partners in Realising Change?, in: Slootmakers K, Touquet H, Vermeersch P (eds.): *The EU Enlargement and Gay Politics. The Impact of Eastern Enlargement on Rights, Activism and Prejudice,* Basingstoke: Palgrave Macmillan, 45–67.

Krook, M-L (2010): Why are fewer women than men elected? Gender and the dynamics of candidate selection, *Political Studies Review* **8**: 155–168.

Landorff L (2019): *Inside European Politics. Informality, Information and Intergroups.* Basingstoke: Palgrave Macmillan.

Lépinard E, Rubio-Marín R, eds. (2018): *Transforming Gender Citizenship. The Irresistible Rise of Gender Quotas in Europe,* Cambridge: Cambridge University Press.

Lombardo E, Verloo M (2009): Institutionalizing intersectionality in the European Union? Policy Developments and contestations, *International Feminist Journal of Politics* **11** (4), 478–495.

Lombardo E, Rolandsen Agustín L (2011): Framing gender intersections in the European Union. What implications for the quality of intersectionality in policies?, *Social Politics* **19** (4): 482–512.

McDonnell D, Werner A (2019): *International Populism. The Radical Right in the European Parliament,* London: Hurst.

Montoya C (2013): *From Global to Grassroots. The European Union, Transnational Advocacy, and Combating Violence against Women,* Oxford, New York: Oxford University Press.

Montoya C, Rolandsen Agustín L (2013): The othering of domestic violence: the EU and cultural framings of violence against women, *Social Politics* **20** (4), 534–557.

Moravcsik A (2002): In defence of the "democratic deficit": reassessing the legitimacy of the European Union, *Journal of Common Market Studies* **40** (4), 603–634.

Mushaben J (2019): Undermining Critical Mass. The Impact of Trilogues and Treaty Reforms on Gender-Sensitive Decision-Making in the European Parliament, in: Ahrens P, Rolandsen Agustín L (eds.): *Gendering the European Parliament: Structures, Policies, and Practices,* London: Rowman & Littlefield International, 69–83.

Norris P, Lovenduski L (1995): *Political Recruitment: Gender, Race and Class in the British Parliament,* Cambridge: Cambridge University Press.

Nugent M (2019): "Feminist to Its Fingertips"? Gendered Divisions of Labour and the Committee on Women's Rights and Gender Equality, in: Ahrens P, Rolandsen Agustín L (eds.): *Gendering the European Parliament: Structures, Policies, and Practices,* London: Rowman & Littlefield International, 123–140.

Renman V, Conroy C (2014): Advances in EU gender equality: missing the mark?, *European Policy Institutes Network* **41**, 1–12.

Ripoll Servent A (2018): *The European Parliament,* Basingstoke: Palgrave Macmillan.

Ripoll Servent A, Panning L (2019): Eurosceptics in trilogue settings. Interest formation and contestation in the European Parliament, *West European Politics* **42** (4),755–775.

Rolandsen Agustín L (2012): (Re)defining women's interests? Political struggles over women's collective representation in the context of the European Parliament, *European Journal of Women's Studies* **19** (1), 23–40.

Rolandsen Agustín L (2013): *Gender Equality, Intersectionality and Diversity in Europe*, New York: Palgrave Macmillan.

Vallance E, Davies E (1986): *Women of Europe: Women MEPs and Equality Policy*, Cambridge: Cambridge University Press.

van der Vleuten A (2019): The European Parliament as a Constant Promoter of Gender Equality. Another European Myth?, in: Ahrens P, Rolandsen Agustín L (eds.): *Gendering the European Parliament: Structures, Policies, and Practices,* London: Rowman and Littlefield International, 35–49.

Warasin M, Rolandsen Agustín L, Kantola J, Coughlan C (2019): Politicisation of Gender Equality in the European Parliament. Cohesion and Inter-Group Coalitions in Plenary and Committees, in: Ahrens P, Rolandsen Agustín L (eds.): *Gendering the European Parliament: Structures, Policies, and Practices,* London: Rowman and Littlefield International, 141–158.

Woodward A, Hubert A (2007): Reconfiguring state feminism in the European Union Changes from 1995–2006, Paper presented at the *EUSA Tenth Biennial International Conference*, May 17–19, Montreal.

10

Gendering the Council system

Gabriele Abels*

As 'masters of the treaties' the EU member states are represented by the Council, a body 'of utmost importance in the institutional system of the EU' (Naurin and Wallace 2008, 2). The Council is more than a *single* institution, however, involving a complex, opaque *system* of negotiation and decision-making. We first need to differentiate between the European Council and the Council of the EU; consisting of multiple councils, the latter relies on preparatory bodies and various committees in its essential operations. Its key purpose is to secure a balance between the intergovernmental mode of decision-making and the supranational community method. Regardless of one's theoretical perspective, the Council(s) comprise the intergovernmental component of EU decision-making processes, accounting for 'a substantial body of literature' (Naurin 2018, 1526).

Infused with an aura of secrecy and high diplomacy, the inner workings of the Council are nonetheless difficult to research. Scholars are 'generally hampered by the scarcity of information …, with hard data sorely lacking, and soft data scattered and fragmentary' (Naurin and Wallace 2008, 2). Although recent studies have 'reached a new phase of sophistication', 'there are still many dark corners waiting to be revealed' (Naurin and Wallace 2008, 1–2). This chapter shines a gender spotlight to re-inspect what we already know about the Councils and to determine what is still lurking in its 'dark corners.' It revisits core aspects of the Council system, such as

> 'the stability and content of political cleavages, the roles played by formal rules and informal norms, by political ideologies and bureaucratic procedures, and by national and European identities, the impacts of opaqueness or transparency on the way politics is played out, and the forms of power exercised in the complex games which governments play in Brussels.'
>
> *(Naurin and Wallace 2008, 3)*

To investigate their hidden and explicit gendered implications, I begin by deconstructing the complex Council system, including its gender composition and the Councils' significance in the EU system. I then discuss research findings to date, viewed through a gender lens, concluding with our knowledge gaps and future research needs.

---

* I am most grateful to Joyce M. Mushaben and to Alexander Schilin for their valuable comments on an earlier version.

The Council system

We begin with the 'Council system', i.e. how it works and its role in EU politics. The *Council of the EU* (hereafter: the Council) was incorporated into the founding treaties as the Council of Ministers, as an intergovernmental body representing the member states governments. Its legal position changed along the way from the 1952 Paris Treaty to the 2009 Lisbon Treaty. The powers conferred on the Council under Article 16 of the Treaty on European Union (TEU) were re-specified in Articles 237 to 243 of the Treaty on the Functioning of the European Union (TFEU). As the main decision-making body, it exercises legislative and executive functions. Council culture draws on subsidiarity, that is the right to defend national competences against undue supranational interference. For a long time, the Council was the only body possessing legislative and budgetary authority. It approves international agreements, actively engages in Eurozone governance, coordinates member state economic policies and can also adopt non-legislative acts, which are actually the majority of decisions. It is the final decision-maker regarding foreign affairs and security policy. The Council formally appoints the members of various EU auxiliary bodies, like the Court of Auditors, European Economic and Social Committee and the Committee of the Regions.

The original Council had only six members of 'ministerial' rank, one from each of the founding countries. Through subsequent enlargements it grew into a 28-member body (27 after Brexit), which altered its internal dynamics and necessitated procedural reforms. Although legally speaking, the Council functions as a *single* entity, it conducts its operations through ten different sectoral councils, meeting with different frequency. Devoid of a formal hierarchy, any configuration can adopt any legislative act. The General Affairs Council (GAC), made up of European affairs ministers, plays a coordinating role, and is responsible for institutional, administrative and 'horizontal' matters. Also possessing a special remit, the Foreign Affairs Council (FAC) is the most active in terms of meetings and can convene defence ministers (addressing common security and defence policy), development ministers (development cooperation) or trade ministers (deliberating commercial or trade policies). FAC is the only council chaired by the High Representative of the Union for Foreign Affairs and Security Policy (see Muehlenhoff in this volume). The Council for Economic and Financial Affairs (ECOFIN, the 'Eurogroup') has gained in significance since the 2008 financial crisis. Further configurations included agriculture and fisheries (AGRIFISH); competitiveness (COMPET); education, youth, culture and sport (EYCS); employment, social policy, heath and consumer affairs (EPSCO); environment (ENVI); justice and home affairs (JHA) and, finally, transport, telecommunication and energy (TTE). No explicit gender equality council exists.

The Council presidency rotates among member states every six months (January to June, July to December), based on a fixed scheme. National governments use this position to enhance their representation at EU level and to raise awareness about EU affairs among their own citizens. Each presidency proposes an agenda reflecting national priorities as well as common challenges. The Lisbon Treaty introduced the 'trio presidency' (triumvirate) consisting of the previous, acting and subsequent presidency, to ensure consistency in the policy process.

When acting as legislator (Article 16 (8) TEU), the Council's meetings are public; all other sessions occur behind closed doors. Its procedural rules have changed over time: initially requiring unanimity, decision-making became more difficult with ever more member states. The 1986 Single European Act (SEA) introduced qualified majority voting (QMV). Modified over time, the member states possess 'weighted votes' broadly reflecting population size (more people, more votes). QMV usually suffices for most types of decision. A fixed threshold of 74% of the weighted votes ensures a power balance between big and small states, preventing structural dominance on the part of any one group. The Lisbon Treaty simplified the voting system, rendering it more transparent and democratic by requiring a 'double majority' for Commission proposals or those of the High Representative. QMV now requires that 55% (presently 15 of 27 national governments) approve a decision and that the yes votes represent at least 65% of the EU population. Abstentions count as 'nays.'

Proposals originating in other institutions call for a 'reinforced QMV', with at least 72% of the member states in favour, likewise representing 65% of the EU population. While QMV applies to most decisions, particularly sensitive matters still require unanimity. This includes issues such as EU membership, citizenship, EU finances or taxation, but also 'certain provisions' impinging on justice and home affairs, e.g., family law or the 'harmonization' of national social security and social protection legislation (www.consilium.europa.eu/en/council-eu/voting-system/unanimity/). The latter are particularly relevant for gender equality.

Not to be confused with the Council of Europe or 'Council of Ministers', the role of the *European Council* (in short EUCO) is 'both ambiguous and hybrid in nature' (Wessels 2016, 5). Initiated in the 1960s, it has undergone an incremental evolution: it moved 'from fireside chats' to key decision-maker status (www.consilium.europa.eu/en/history/?filters=2031). Established at the 1974 Paris summit, EUCO organizes frequent biannual and quarterly meetings (since 1996). While the SEA formalized its meetings, the 1992 Maastricht Treaty accorded it a formal role, and the Lisbon Treaty transformed it into a full-blown EU institution (Article 13 TEU). The heads of state and government assemble along with the EUCO President and the President of the European Commission. Its purpose is to 'provide the Union with the necessary impetus for its development and define the general political directions and priorities thereof' (Article 15 TEU). Lower levels pass complex, controversial and sensitive issues up to EUCO, which often produces package deals emerging from long, day-and-night negotiations. It now serves as a constitutional actor, deciding on treaty negotiations convening intergovernmental conferences. In addition, its 'strengthened role' today compared to the status quo before the Lisbon Treaty is 'mainly due to developments during the multiple crises'; EUCO 'carries out various roles …, some being Treaty-based and others the result of practice and of the political and economic situation over time' (European Parliament 2019a, 52). Without doubt, it has become a chief crisis-manager over the last decade, involving regular summits and numerous 'extraordinary, informal and special meetings' (Wessels 2016, 4). It has ordained new 'constitutional' instruments, such as the Euro Group (only for euro-area members). While this group's first meetings were informal and ad hoc, it was formalized through the Fiscal Compact agreement of 2012, now meeting every six months. EUCO actively engaged with the 'Schengen crisis' (see Krause and Schwenken in this volume), the 'Brexit crisis' (see Guerrina and Masselot in this volume) and now the health crisis.

The EUCO president is elected for a 2.5-year term (renewable once); thus far all have been male: Herman van Rompuy, 2009–2014; Donald Tusk, 2014–2019; Charles Michel, since 2019. The President convenes and chairs Council meetings, acting as mediator as well as a leader in negotiations, especially when decisions require unanimity. For some decisions, i.e. appointments for presidency, nomination of candidate for Commission president, it can utilize QMV.

Both Councils are assisted by the *General Secretariat of the Council* (GSC, part of the EU civil service), whose Secretary-General is appointed by the Council of the EU. The GSC ensures that the Councils 'operate smoothly', lending them the necessary assistance 'so they [the Councils] can perform the missions conferred on them by the treaties to further the development of the Union' (GSC n.d.). COREPER (Comité des représentants permanents) is a significant component of the Councils' preparatory system, encompassing national ambassadors to the EU and supplying an important link between the national and EU levels. These senior-ranking diplomats usually abstain from partisan politics; strongly grounded in European affairs, they serve long tenures, assisted by civil servants from different ministries delegated to each country's permanent representation in Brussels. COREPER is actually divided in two groups: COREPER I (deputies) and COREPER II (ambassadors). Work is divided according to policy portfolios (EPSCO falls under COREPER I). Ambassadors use weekly meetings to prepare Council decision-making (117 times in 2018; European Parliament 2019b); they also coordinate activities related to joint legislation with the European Parliament. As a 'veritable decision-making factory', COREPER is a place where many EU decisions are effectively made (Lewis 2017, 344). Its vote is indicative of final Council decisions.

Finally, the Council system also relies on a hundred specialized *working parties,* bringing together delegates from national ministries. The member state holding the rotating Council Presidency chairs the meetings. Attempts are made to prepare decisions and reach an agreement among national governments at the working parties level. In 2018 the 138 working parties met more than 4,300 times (European Parliament 2019b). If agreement is not possible, problems are 'uploaded' to the next higher level. Agreed upon items are formally adopted by the Council of the EU as 'A items.' The ministers themselves only debate and vote on 'B Items', when no agreement has been secured at lower levels or when a member state requests discussion. The Council is officially responsible for all decisions, no matter at which level and in which configuration they were taken. Council working parties and COREPER rely on the same decision-making rules used in ministerial meetings. Voting rarely occurs in the preparatory bodies or COREPER; consensus and deliberative culture usually prevail (Puetter 2007, 2014).

The Councils cultivate strong *relations with other EU institutions.* EUCO nominates and elects candidates for select leadership posts: e.g. the European Central Bank and European Commission presidents, and the High Representative of the Union for Foreign Affairs and Security Policy. The latter participates in EUCO meetings. The first two High Representatives were women, Catherine Ashton (2009–2014) and Federica Mogherini (2014–2019), followed by Josep Borrell as of 2019. In other cases, e.g. international trade policy, the Council extends a mandate to the Commission, which represents the Union and negotiates treaties on its behalf. Both the Council and its preparatory bodies actively engage with the Commission; their working parties are interlinked via 'comitology', that is committees consisting of national and Commission delegates that prepare and implement EU legal acts. The Council now shares most legislative competencies with the European Parliament. Most legislation is adopted under the Ordinary Legislative Procedure (OLP) combined with 'trilogues' i.e. inter-institutional negotiations between Council, European Parliament and Commission.

Gendering mainstream research on the Council system

The main topics dominating Council research, along with its 'dark corners' merit re-inspection employing a gender lens. EU studies conducted by gender scholars have posed new questions ignored by 'mainstream' researchers. One crucial issue pertains to *agency* and the ways in which a dearth of women in the Council system undermines gender-democratic representation in terms of styles, power and policies.

Fiona Hayes-Renshaw and Helen Wallace (2006) published the first comprehensive account of the Council in 1997. By then intergovernmentalism had become the 'baseline theory' (Moravcsik and Schimmelfennig 2019, 64; Naurin 2018) for Council research. Its origins owe to high politics, i.e. constitutional issues. Work on ground-breaking policies and budgetary issues in the 1960s inspired Hoffmann's classic conceptualization in 1966; Moravcsik's (1998) focus on the 1992 Maastricht Treaty gave rise to liberal intergovernmentalism (LI), while post-Maastricht developments, especially the Euro crisis or currently the Covid-19 pandemic, saw a shift to new intergovernmentalism (Bickerton et al. 2015; Puetter 2014). LI 'is by far the most frequently used theoretical source' (Naurin 2018, 1527) – and also the most criticized. It is applied not only to the 'grand bargains' of intergovernmental conferences and treaty negotiations but also to everyday low politics. LI proponents claim that state preferences, resulting from international or domestic politics, are decisive for understanding member state behaviour at the EU level. Agreements among national governments result from interstate bargaining, essentially rendering EU institutions 'agents' of their national 'principals.'

From a gender perspective, intergovernmentalism ranks as a 'dinosaur' among European integration theories (van der Vleuten 2016). Even if it appears in different shades, the 'focus on national governments is too limited', although van der Vleuten (2016, 94) argues that it 'could be strengthened further by including feminist agency.' This requires knowledge about *where and how women are actually represented* in the Council system. The Council system is still overwhelmingly male, despite the fact that it is subject to a high degree of personnel turnover, among all configurations (including EPSCO), which affects its role in the legislative process (Perez and Scherpereel 2017; Scherpereel and Perez 2015). Given the large number of member states with average national electoral cycles of four to five years, roughly six to seven national elections per year can potentially redefine the party and gender composition of national governments – and thus bodies comprising the Council system. A rising number of women in the Councils is attributed to women's growing representation in national parliaments. Currently 21 EU member states utilize gender quotas (11 with compulsory legislative quotas), which we would expect to influence the number of female ministers; this is true of their increasing presence in Council of the EU. During the third quarter of 2019, women, on average, held 30% of the senior positions in EU-28 national governments.[1] The Scandinavian countries are the frontrunners reaching (almost) gender parity; yet, others in western and southern Europe have also seen increases (see below). Eight member states qualify as laggards with fewer than 20% female ministers. A growing number of female ministers no longer correlates strongly with left-wing parties – the traditional pattern until 2000; liberal parties are also promoting women in office (Stockemer and Sundström 2018, 668). Eventually, we see governments where female ministers are in fact the majority such as in the current Spanish Social Democratic government under Prime Minister Pedro Sanchez (50% women), or in the French government under President Emmanuel Macron (53%). Both leaders made parity part of their progressive agenda. Conservative-dominated governments under German Chancellor Merkel also raised the number of female ministers; 44% of her cabinet post (including her own) are held by women. In the new conservative–green government in Austria (March 2020) women hold 53% of ministerial post, including a female minister for EU affairs who is a GAC member. Often changes in government bring in more female ministers (Stockemer and Sundström 2018), reflecting greater electoral volatility, growing fragmentation in party systems and difficulties in coalition-building. More women in power at the national level brings more women ministers into the Council. While women were usually assigned to 'gendered' portfolios in the past, more are now being assigned to formerly 'male' portfolios, mirrored in the sectoral councils (for assignment patterns see Annesley et al. 2019). In 2019, five of 28 EU defence ministers are currently women (Denmark, France, Germany, Netherlands and Spain), though only two (from Bulgaria and Sweden) hold seats in the FAC. Among the different Council configuration women's representation ranges between 21% (ECOFIN) and 38% (EYCS) and varies strongly among member states (European Parliament 2019b, 6).

Gender imbalance is much more prevalent in the EUCO. While 'women have made important strides in attaining executive office in Europe', as presidents and prime ministers, the 'durable glass ceiling' persists (Jalalzai 2014, 591). Currently (December 2020), EUCO has three female

Gendering the Council system

members: the prime ministers of Denmark and Finland as well as the German Chancellor (www.consilium.europa.eu/en/european-council/members/). Germany offers something of an exceptional case: Holding office since 2005, Angela Merkel is the longest serving head of a European government and certainly an influential leader (Mushaben 2017). Other Council bodies remain male-dominated. The General Secretariat employs almost 3,000 people as officials or as temporary staff delegated by the member states (September 2019); although 59% of the GSC staff is female, women occupy only one-third of the senior and middle management positions (www.consilium.europa.eu/en/general-secretariat/staff-budget/). They are overrepresented among assistants, secretaries and in the translation service.

The national diplomatic corps in Brussel was all-male for a long time until in 1995 the first woman was appointed to COREPER I (Hayes-Renshaw and Wallace 2006, 74–75). In fact, it is still very male today with about 20% of women among the member state ambassadors. It is difficult to obtain reliable membership information for numerous Council committees and working parties, due to constant change. These bodies, along with national representatives' networks, engage in highly political, not just technical work (e.g. the Advisory Committee on Equal Opportunities), necessitating further research (Ahrens 2018, 56).

While descriptive gender representation matters, a key dimension of gender studies, one cannot assume a direct impact on substantive representation, i.e. how gender equality concerns are incorporated into actual policies. The lack of a formal gender equality council per se is problematic. Yet, informal meetings are frequently organized. Despite changes in the gender and party composition of Council bodies, Council negotiations evince a high degree of policy continuity. Differences among national gender regimes can affect the internal dynamics and legislative decision-making in the Council system, e.g., in shaping a Polish or Swedish presidency.

Representing national preferences, the Council responds not only to economic interests, but also to social practices and normative beliefs. National gender regimes, norms and traditions (see von Wahl in this volume) make a difference, influencing governments' position and strategies regarding equality policies. Gender ideologies shape national welfare state models, with consequences for implementation back home. The 2019 Gender Equality Index, developed by the European Institute for Gender Equality (EIGE; see Jacquot and Krizsán in this volume), gives Sweden a score of 83.2, compared to Greece and Hungary with a score of 51 (https://eige.europa.eu/gender-equality-index/2019).

Another focus of mainstream research, the internal working of the Councils, ignores its impact on the making of gender equality policy. Power imbalances between large and small, old and new, west and east, north and south contribute to a complex system of relative power sharing (Thomson 2010), which affects coalition-building, consensus-formation, voting behaviour, the speed of decision-making speed and the role of veto-players. The Council remains a highly complex 'consensus machine', relying on formal as well as informal rules (see MacRae and Weiner in this volume). Although QMV is legally prescribed, consensual decision-making still dominates. From a rationalist perspective, national governments do not want to find themselves in a (defeatable) minority position; they prefer compromises that keep them part of the majority.

Constructivist interpretations emphasize the 'culture of consensus' developed and internalized by national institutions. Actual voting was sooner the exception than the rule exception (Hayes-Renshaw et al. 2006; Warntjen 2010) – and remains so today. A rising number of right-wing populist governments, however, triggers more ideological conflicts over gender equality beyond an economic framing of equality. The EU accession to the Council of Europe's 'Convention on preventing and combating violence against women and domestic violence' (Istanbul Convention), for example, is still blocked (December 2020) by several member states, which resist gender concepts countering their traditional views on the family.

The Council's preparatory bodies have been covered in mainstream research, albeit without a gender lens. National representatives at different levels, such as COREPER (Lewis 2017), committees and working parties (Beyers and Dierickx 1998) – and the Council itself – regularly adhere to social norms and follow a logic of appropriateness. COREPER, for instance, constitutes a 'dense normative environment' (Lewis 2017, 347), in which 'thick trust', fostered by long tenure, leads to the development of a 'club' following its own rules. Many scholars emphasize the strong effect of 'EU socialization' among these, despite differences in the conditions for cooperative negotiations (Lewis 2010).

> 'Rather than constituting faithful voices of domestic political equilibria, Brussels negotiators may be vulnerable to the influence of socialization, persuasion and informal norms inherent to the negotiation "environment", possibly deriding (sic) them from the path determined in the domestic political game.'
>
> *(Naurin 2018, 1530)*

How might this play out with regard to gender equality policies? Given the Council's key legislative tasks, relations to the European Parliament are especially important. Both seek leverage over the balance of power between them, yet, 'day-to-day decision-making is ... characterized by a high level of consensus ... also between the institutions' (Mühlböck and Rittberger 2015, 3). The European Parliament is considered a 'champion' of gender equality; studies attest that, in contrast to the European Parliament, the Council continues to offer a difficult environment for adopting gender equality policies at the EU level as well as for effective implementation at the national level. National filters, referred to as the 'needle's eye' (Ostner and Lewis 1995) or 'policy hinterland' (Mazey 1998) have a restrictive effect; this implies that exogenous, domestic preferences dominate EU politics (a key LI argument). In the 1980s and 1990s, however, the Council did adopt ten directives advancing gender equality, which had a tremendous effect in 'Europeanizing' national policies (see chapters by von Wahl, Forest and Millner in this volume).

Northern enlargement in 1995 was a game changer, thanks to progressive, social-democratic gender regimes in Sweden and Finland. This led to the 'revolutionary' inclusion of gender mainstreaming in the 1996 Amsterdam Treaty (Lomazzi and Crespi 2019). One needs 'to look at issue-specific actor constellations in order to explain agenda-setting and the adoption of or resistance to gender equality policies'; these, in turn, are 'shaped by the institutional setting (intergovernmental or supranational decision-making structures) and the underlying power relations' which are also gendered (van der Vleuten 2016, 94). Member state preferences not only derive from domestic politics; the EU context has its own impact, coupled with Council party politics (Hagemann and Hoyland 2008; Tallberg and Johansson 2008). Political parties' responsiveness to gender equality vary, although centre-left parties tend to be more sensitive than centre-right or right-wing populist parties (see Ahrens and Rolandsen Agustín (Party politics) in this volume).

Gender research focuses primarily, though not exclusively on social policy, a domain in which the Council shares legislative competencies with the European Parliament. Council positions depend on multiple factors, including national gender regimes. Strong, neoliberal trends shaping EU politics often invoke strong resistance against gender equality and anti-discrimination directives, which allegedly generate costly public expenditures and bureaucratic burdens for the economy. In 2008 the Commission proposed a directive aimed at extending protection against discrimination by applying 'equal treatment' outside the labour market; it failed to secure consensus in the Council. The global financial crisis intensified resistance against social policy; economic issues were prioritized, and gender equality was dismissed as too expensive (Ahrens 2018, 59). Gender equality, anti-discrimination and even violence against women are often framed in terms of improving women's labour market integration, rather than as human rights violations. Although this framing is often criticized (Walby and Olive 2014; Young 2000), it has allowed for the adoption of hard law, despite strong resistance.[2]

The Council is not limited to hard legislation; it also adopts non-legislative resolutions, conclusions and decisions on gender equality, including the medium-term action programmes on equal opportunities for women and men in the 1990s, and its 2001 decision on the framework strategy on gender equality strategy (Ahrens 2018, 51, 57). As part of the Europe 2020 Strategy, the Council adopted a European Pact for Gender Equality (2011–2020) in March 2011, to encourage action at national level (Lomazzi and Crespi 2019, 41). EPSCO is the Council configuration most concerned with gender equality, although the latter entails more than social policy. Gender mainstreaming mandates that gender concerns should be addressed across *all* policy domains, yet certain policy sectors are immune to gender concerns, as empirical studies demonstrate (see policy chapters in this volume).

Missing are studies assessing which member states oppose gender equality policies, their reasons for doing so, and the conditions that might change their preferences. Researchers have neglected legislative patterns in the EPSCO (or other Council formations), investigating whether gender parity has an impact. Does the gender of officials influence their interests and, if so, how might gender imbalance influence 'the way in which negotiations are conducted as well as their outcomes' (van derVleuten 2016, 87). Early research on gender differences in international negotiations has uncovered surprising results regarding the impact of gender stereotyping. Studying EU diplomats, Naurin et al. (2019) determined unconscious gender interactions can produce 'chivalry patterns', rendering male negotiators more inclined to yield to demands of female counterparts. Gender mainstreaming also requires us to investigate other Council formations and bodies in the Council system regarding gendered patterns of deliberation and negotiation. Now that a majority of EU policies fall under the OLP, trilogue interactions between the Council and the European Parliament, mediated by the Commission also harbour gender consequences, as Mushaben (2019) argues.

Another key issue is *leadership* in an increasingly heterogeneous Union. Hoffmann's classical account of intergovernmentalism highlighted a need to analyze the quality of leadership early on. Although histories of European integration frequently reference key leaders like 'the founding fathers', this approach is less common in political science. Exceptions include 'grand decisions' by Jacques Delors (over the internal market) or Helmut Kohl (monetary union). Ongoing crises have raised new leadership questions, e.g. regarding Chancellor Merkel's performance during the Euro-crisis (Mushaben 2017, 161–211; Schoeller 2018). Van der Vleuten (2016, 94) suggest that a leadership focus 'would open up the possibility of examining the role of gender when more women are in power at the highest levels', for example, in the Council of Ministers and European Council. Positional leadership is one dimension, while the behavioural approach poses the questions: Does gender matter (Müller and Tömmel forthcoming, Sykes 2014, Tömmel 2013)? How has Merkel's leadership style shaped her policy decisions (Mushaben 2017)? Does her performance differ from that of Scandinavian and east European heads of state or government?

Council *presidencies* also provide fertile ground for gendering leadership research, given presidential bargaining power and their broker-role among member states (Tallberg 2010; Tömmel 2017). Who places gender equality makes on the Council agenda, how and why? Pioneering Scandinavians have used the presidency for fostering gender equality. Assuming the presidency for the first time in 1999, Finland encouraged debate on member state implementation of gender mainstreaming in national employment programmes, and prepared to monitor outcomes regarding the progress report of Beijing World Conference on Women (Beijing+5). During its second rotation (2006), Finland focussed on family policy, work–family reconciliation and equality. The third Finnish presidency (2019) focused heavily on labour market issues, emphasizing the need for a gender equality strategy that combined mainstreaming, specific actions and gender budgeting. Finland drafted a related Council conclusion adopted by the EPSCO Council in December 2019. Sweden focussed during its first presidency in 2001 on labour market integration, in 2009 on better protection against gender-based discrimination. The 2012 Danish presidency highlighted women's underrepresentation on company boards, gender equality in education, violence against women, and commissioned a report on gender and climate change (see Allwood in this volume).

Others have also stressed gender equality, such as Ireland (2013), Lithuania (2013), Italy (2014), Luxembourg (2015), Malta (2017), Austria (2018), Romania (2019) and Germany (2020; see Abels 2020). Labour market discrimination and violence against women are common themes. The Belgian presidency in 2001 was the first to put gender budgeting on the agenda; a theme taken up by the 2019 Finnish presidency. In 2018, the Austrian presidency convened informal meetings of gender equality ministers (under EPSCO auspices) as an ad hoc substitute for the lack of a permanent Gender Equality Council. These presidencies' agenda-setting and framing processes merit further study.

Future perspectives

Despite a growing body of research on the Council system, few scholars have applied a gender lens. Experts have analyzed the Council's legislator role with regard to gender equality and anti-discrimination policies, but not the 'gendering' of the Council system per se. Three dimensions offer particularly fertile ground for future research: a focus on women's agency, treatments of the diverse and subtle dimensions of power; and the democratic quality of EU governance.

For starters, researchers need to broaden their *epistemological and theoretical perspectives on the Council,* beyond intergovernmentalism and its critique. EU gender scholars have never been fond of intergovernmentalism, characterized as a 'dinosaur' still roaming the landscape of European integration theory. Given its state-centric and rationalist axioms, intergovernmentalism essentially 'reproduces existing gender relations' (Kronsell 2005, 1025), though it can be a helpful heuristic tool, if domestic social relations serve as a 'starting point' (Galligan 2019, 183). Gender scholars need to scrutinize its 'baseline' as to who and what is included/excluded. This calls for exploring women's agency, gendered power structures and domestic preference formation. Governments do respond to public opinion with their Council voting behaviour when the issues are especially salient (Hagemann et al. 2017), but what creates saliency? Eurobarometer data attest to strong support for gender equality among national publics; the question is, how this might be reflected in Council negotiations.

Just as understanding EU complexity requires multiple theoretical approaches, there can be no single gender integration theory (Abels and MacRae 2016). Scholars need to utilize a broad range of theories, including neo-institutionalism, social constructivism and other critical approaches (Stivachtis et al. 2020), which pinpoint factors shaping government preferences on gender policies. Considering the Commission and the European Parliament as equality advocates, pushing strong '"constitutional" advocacy of gender equality' (Galligan 2019, 177), questioning the 'logic of appropriateness' and existing socialization effects: these approaches could work in favour of gender equality. However, norm-based advocacy is 'conditional', as Galligan (2019, 177) argues: policy domains bearing directly on gender equality (e.g. family law, social protection) 'are subject to the unanimous decision-making rule in the Council – a higher bar than is required in other policy areas.'

128

The rise of right-wing populism in many member states challenges gender policies and gender mainstreaming, in line with post-functionalism (Hooghe and Marks 2009) and growing politicization (Kriesi 2016), because it espouses traditional gender ideologies and identities (see Siim and Fiig in this volume). These changes influence EU negotiations, as shown by the debate over EU accession to the Istanbul Convention. This legally binding instrument to combat violence against women has been blocked by Bulgaria, Czech Republic, Hungary, Latvia and Lithuania, whose governments defend the family as a 'protected sphere', rather than as a potential realm of domestic violence, and who oppose the concept of gender as such.

Furthermore, while there is a growing knowledge base regarding the Councils' *internal operations*, researchers need to consider the potential impact of gender representation on negotiations, including existing imbalances and stereotyping effects. Preliminary evidence (Naurin et al. 2019) suggests a need to extend our investigations to other 'dark corners.' The role of the Council Presidency also requires further scrutiny.

In addition, there is a further need to study women and gender in relation to *executive leadership*. Gender parity with respect to top EU positions first became a central topic of discussion following the 2019 European Parliament elections (de La Baume and Bayer 2019). Indeed, the EU recently elected its first female Commission President, Ursula von der Leyen; Council members also chose the first female President of the European Central Bank, Christine Lagarde. Both pledged to place equality high on their agenda; as a first step, von der Leyen has deliberately set out to ensure gender parity in constituting the new Commission itself (see Hartlapp et al. in this volume). These Commissioners, in turn will have to work closely with the two Councils, invoking research on their potential impact on EU governance.

Finally, the *relations* among the Councils, Council Presidencies and/or select national governments as well as with the European Parliament, and widely ignored external stakeholders, need to be researched. Many EU gender studies are policy-driven and, thus, investigate the complex EU policy process, while others emphasize civil society involvement and the role of women's and LGBT movements. Efforts by civil society organizations to lobby the Councils have not been thoroughly examined nor has lobbying by member states, with regard to the changing Council Presidencies, for example (Panke 2012). The recently established Women's European Council (WEUCO) functions as an informal European summit convened before European Council's meetings 'to commit women leaders and civil society towards a renewed vision of European Union' (http://europeanwomenalliance.eu/weuco/). WEUCO brings together European Parliament delegates, Commissioners and individuals representing the rotating Council Presidency, to generate 'concrete proposals and undertake actions to change European public policies through a gender perspective' (http://europeanwomenalliance.eu/weuco/). This initiative could also prove worthy of researching, given its effort to tackle the democratic deficit and increase the responsiveness of the Councils by linking EU institutions and civil society. It would allow us to widen the policy scope beyond rather narrowly defined equality policies to gender mainstreaming at large.

Gender scholars agree that political institutions are never gender-neutral; this would also apply to the Councils and the Council system. Studies along these lines would count as a step in lifting the curtain of ignorance with regard to EU operations not easily accessible to informed publics. Efforts to unveiling the gendered nature of the Council are still in their infancy, but they should be recognized as an urgent task in relation to our respective research agendas.

Notes

1   See https://eige.europa.eu/gender-statistics/dgs/browse/wmidm/wmidm_pol/wmidm_pol_gov. For more detailed data on development over time see EIGE's Gender Statistics Database on women and

men in decision-making: https://eige.europa.eu/gender-statistics/dgs; https://eige.europa.eu/gender-equality-index/2019/domain/power

2 After years of legislative inaction, and intense negotiation, the Council approved the directive on work-life balance for parents and care-givers (2019/1158/EU) in May 2019. Member states must implement it by 2022, to narrow the gender employment gap.

References

Abels G (2020): Making progress, fighting rollback: Germany's EU Council Presidency must secure gender equality achievements and reach new milestones, #BerlinPerspectives No. 7, Berlin: Institut für Europäische Politik (IEP), URL: http://iep-berlin.de/wp-content/uploads/%202020/12/Berlin-Perspectives-Volume-7.pdf.

Abels G, MacRae H, eds. (2016): *Gendering European Integration Theory: Engaging new Dialogues,* Opladen: Barbara Budrich Publishers.

Ahrens P (2018): The birth, life, and death of policy instruments. 35 years of EU gender equality policy programmes, *West European Politics* **42** (1), 45–66.

Annesley C, Beckwith K, Franceschet S (2019): Cabinets, Ministers, & Gender, Oxford: Oxford University Press.

Beyers J, Dierickx G (1998): The working groups of the Council of the European Union. Supranational or intergovernmental negotiations?, *Journal of Common Market Studies* **36** (3), 289–317.

Bickerton CJ, Hodson D, Puetter U (2015): The new intergovernmentalism. European integration in the post-Maastricht Era, *Journal of Common Market Studies* **53** (4), 703–722.

Council, General Secretariat (GSC), n.d.: GSC mission statement, URL: www.consilium.europa.eu/media/29311/gsc-mission-statement.pdf (download: September 21, 2019).

de La Baume M, Bayer L (2019): 'The 14 women who could take over the EU', Politico, May 15, 2019, URL: www.politico.eu/article/the-14-women-who-could-take-over-the-eu-top-jobs/ (download: October 10, 2019).

European Parliament (2019a): The European Council under the Lisbon Treaty: How has the institution evolved since 2009? EPRS Study, PE 642.806, December 2019, Brussels, URL: www.europarl.europa.eu/RegData/etudes/STUD/2019/642806/EPRS_STU%282019%29642806_EN.pdf (download: December 12, 2019).

European Parliament (2019b): Council of the European Union: Facts and Figures, EPRS Briefing, BRI (2019) 646113, December 2019, Brussels, URL: www.europarl.europa.eu/RegData/etudes/BRIE/2019/646113/EPRS_BRI(2019)646113_EN.pdf (download: December 12, 2019).

Galligan Y (2019): European Integration and Gender, in: Wiener A, Börzel TA, Risse T (eds.): *European Integration Theory,* 3rd ed., Oxford: Oxford University Press, 174–194.

Hagemann S, Hoyland B (2008): Parties in the Council?, *Journal of European Public Policy* **15** (8), 1205–1221.

Hagemann S, Hobolt SB, Wratil C (2017): Government responsiveness in the European Union: evidence from Council voting, *Comparative Political Studies* **50** (6), 850–876.

Hayes-Renshaw F, Wallace H (2006): *The Council of Ministers,* 2nd ed., Basingstoke: Macmillan.

Hayes-Renshaw F, van Aken W, Wallace H (2006): When and why the EU Council of Ministers votes explicitly, *Journal of Common Market Studies* **44** (1), 161–194.

Hoffmann S (1966): Obstinate or obsolete? The fate of the nation-state and the case of western Europe, *Daedalus* **95** (1), 862–915.

Hooghe L, Marks G (2009): A Postfunctionalist theory of European integration: from permissive consensus to constraining dissensus, *British Journal of Political Science* **39** (1), 1–23.

Jalalzai F (2014): Gender, presidencies, and prime ministerships in Europe: Are women gaining ground?, *International Political Science Review* **35** (5), 577–594.

Kriesi H (2016): The politicization of European integration, *Journal of Common Market Studies* **54** (1), Annual Review, 32–47.

Kronsell A (2005): Gender, Power and European Integration Theory, *Journal of European Public Policy* **12** (6), 1022–1040.

Lewis J (2010): How institutional environments facilitate co-operative negotiation styles in EU decision-making, *Journal of European Public Policy* **17** (5), 648–664.

Lewis J (2017): COREPER: National Interests and the Logic of Appropriateness, in: Hodson D, Peterson J (eds.): *The Institutions of the European Union,* 4th ed., Oxford: Oxford University Press, 334–356.

Lomazzi V, Crespi I (2019): *Gender Mainstreaming and Gender Equality in Europe,* Bristol: Policy Press.

Mazey S (1998): The European Union and women's rights: from the Europeanization of national agendas to the nationalization of European agenda, *Journal of European Public Policy* **5** (1), 131–152.

Moravcsik A (1998): *The Choice for Europe: Social Purpose and State Power from Messina to Maastricht,* Ithaca, NY: Cornell University Press.

Moravcsik A, Schimmelfenning F (2019): Liberal Intergovernmentalism, in: Wiener A, Börzel TA, Risse T (eds.): *European Integration Theory,* 3rd ed., Oxford: Oxford University Press, 64–84.

Mühlböck M, Rittberger B (2015): The Council, the European Parliament, and the paradox of inter-institutional cooperation, *European Integration online Papers (EIoP)* **19** (4), URL: http://eiop.or.at/eiop/texte/2015-004a.htm (download: December 12, 2019).

Mushaben, JM (2017): *Becoming Madam Chancellor. Angela Merkel and the Berlin Republic,* Cambridge: Cambridge University Press.

Mushaben, JM (2019): Undermining Critical Mass. The Impact of Trilogues and Treaty Reforms on Gender-Sensitive Decision-Making in the European Parliament, in: Ahrens P, Rolandsen Agustín L (eds.): *Gendering the European Parliament: Structures, Policies and Practices,* Lanham, MD: Rowman & Littlefield, 69–83.

Müller H, Tömmel I (forthcoming): Women and Leadership in the European Union. Introduction, in: Müller H, Tömmel I (eds.): *Women and Leadership in the European Union,* Oxford: Oxford University Press.

Naurin D (2018): Liberal intergovernmentalism in the Councils of the EU: a baseline theory?, *Journal of Common Market Studies* **56** (7), 1526–1543.

Naurin D, Wallace H, eds. (2008): *Unveiling the Council of the EU: Games Governments play in Brussels,* Basingstoke: Palgrave.

Naurin A, Naurin E, Alexander A (2019): Gender stereotyping and chivalry in international negotiations: a survey experiment in the Council of the European Union, *International Organization* **73** (2), 469–488.

Ostner I, Lewis J (1995): Gender and European Social Policies, in: Leibfried S, Pierson P (eds.): *European Social Policy. Between Fragmentation and Integration,* Washington DC: The Brookings Institution, 153–193.

Panke D (2012): Lobbying institutional key players: how states seek to influence the European Commission, the Council Presidency and the European Parliament, *Journal of Common Market Studies* **50** (1), 129–150.

Perez LK, Scherpereel JA (2017): Vertical intra-institutional effects of ministerial turnover in the Council of the European Union, *Journal of European Public Policy* **24** (8), 1154–1171.

Puetter U (2007): Providing venues for contestation: the role of expert committees and informal dialogue among ministers in European Economic Policy Coordination, *Comparative European Politics* **5** (1), 18–35.

Puetter U (2014): *The European Council and the Council. New intergovernmentalism and institutional change,* Oxford: Oxford University Press.

Scherpereel JA, Perez LK (2015): Turnover in the Council of the European Union: what it is and why it matters, *Journal of Common Market Studies* **53** (3), 658–673.

Schoeller MG (2018): The rise and fall of Merkozy: Franco-German bilateralism as a negotiation strategy in Eurozone crisis management, *Journal of Common Market Studies* **56** (5), 1019–1035.

Stivachtis Y, Bigo D, Diez T, Fanoulis E, Rosamond B, eds. (2020): *Routledge Handbook of Critical European Studies,* London: Routledge.

Stockemer D, Sundström A (2018): Women in cabinets: the role of party ideology and government turn-over, *Party Politics* **24** (6), 663–673.

Sykes PL (2014): Does Gender Matter?, in: Rhodes RAW, t'Hart P (eds.): *The Oxford Handbook of Political Leadership,* Oxford: Oxford University Press, 690–704.

Tallberg J (2010): The power of the chair: formal leadership in international cooperation, *International Studies Quarterly* **54** (1), 241–265.

Tallberg J, Johansson KM (2008): Party politics in the European Council, *Journal of European Public Policy* **15** (8), 1222–1242.

Thomson R (2010): The Relative Power of Member States in the Council: Large and Small, Old and New, in: Naurin D, Wallace H (eds.): *Unveiling the Council of the European Union. Games Governments Play in Brussels,* Basingstoke: Palgrave Macmillan, 238–260.

Tömmel I (2013): The presidents of the European Commission: transactional or transforming leaders?, *Journal of Common Market Studies* **51** (4), 789–805.

Tömmel I (2017): The standing president of the European Council: intergovernmental or supranational leadership?, *Journal of European Integration* **39** (2), 175–189.

van der Vleuten A (2016): Intergovernmentalism: Gendering a Dinosaur?, in: Abels G, MacRae H (eds.): *Gendering European Integration Theory: Engaging new Dialogues,* Opladen: Barbara Budrich Publishers, 77–97.

Walby S, Olive P (2014): *Estimating the costs of gender-based violence in the European Union,* Report, Luxembourg: EIGE.

Warntjen A (2010): Between bargaining and deliberation: decision-making in the Council of the European Union, *Journal of European Public Policy* **17** (5), 665–679.

Wessels W (2016): *The European Council,* Basingstoke: Palgrave Macmillan.

Young B (2000): Disciplinary neoliberalism in the European Union and gender politics, *New Political Economy* **5** (1), 77–98.

11

Gender equality and the European Commission

Miriam Hartlapp, Henriette Müller and Ingeborg Tömmel

The European Commission (Commission) is one of the core institutions of the EU political system. It is headed by a president and 26 Commissioners (one for each member state) and structured into a number of services employing around 32,000 officials. The Commission interacts with other EU institutions and governments and administrations of the member states in decision-making and policy implementation. It holds a quasi-monopoly on the proposal of legislation and acts as a powerful agenda-setter. Furthermore, the Commission is endowed with monitoring and enforcement powers to ensure the implementation of commonly agreed mandates. These roles render the Commission a central actor in shaping the course and substance of European integration.

Within this broad spectrum of functions and responsibilities, the Commission has played a role in setting up, expanding and, more recently, limited updating of gender equality policies, both at European and member state levels and within its own ranks (Ahrens 2019; Jacquot 2015). Its activities in these realms have often been impelled by advocacy and pressure from internal as well as external actors – notably the European Parliament, women's lobbies, and the women's movement more broadly. This has resulted in the establishment of basic principles of gender equality at the European level, in the heightened awareness and development of policy tools for counteracting sex discrimination across the Union, and in transforming the Commission from a male-dominated into a more gender-balanced institution.

There is a rich literature of studies and critical commentary on the Commission's actions in the realm of gender equality, with focal points typically encompassing legislative initiatives, policy developments, implementation strategies, and the impact of legislation. By contrast, research on women's participation and representation in the Commission and the agency of its leading female Commissioners, managers, and civil servants has been very scarce.

Against this background, this chapter pursues four aims. First, it analyzes the development and current state of gender equality in the Commission. It explores how the increase in women's participation and representation has altered the Commission's organizational structure. Second, the chapter focuses on the Commission's record in fostering gender equality through governance modes and policy tools. It shows the Commission's commitment, but also the manifold constraints it faces to proactive policy-making and implementation. Third, the chapter provides an overview of the policies and regulations that the Commission has adopted to improve gender equality within its own ranks. It highlights the Commission's successes and setbacks in gradually transforming its own institutional structure. Fourth, the chapter examines the question of agency in the enhancement of gender equality policies both within the Commission and across the EU. Here, we explore the Commission's gender strategy in the context of interinstitutional dynamics and constraints, as well as pressures from civil society actors.

We conclude that the Commission, when pressured by other actors and institutions, has shown a strong commitment to gender equality. However, when pressures are weak or member state resistance strong, the Commission's engagement has been reduced to the expression of noble policy objectives.

The state of gender equality in the European Commission

With its dual role as agenda-setter and guardian of the treaties, the Commission has political and administrative roles. The Commissioners and the President constitute the political apex. They give political guidance to their portfolios and take all decisions on Commission affairs collectively. The administrative level consists of the Directorates-General (DGs), also called the services, which bear responsibility for the individual portfolios. Each DG is headed by a Director-General.

To date, a total of 63 women have held top-level positions of Directors-General and Commissioners in the Commission. Beginning with just two women working at the upper echelons of the Commission in the late 1980s, the number has increased to 24 in the von der Leyen Commission (December 2019). The share of women working in the administrative staff has increased as well. This increase in women's participation and representation has altered the organizational makeup of the Commission in its College and the DGs over time and across sectors.[1] For the analysis, we differentiate by term in office (not individual) and for each legislature separately, since Commissioners may be appointed for more than one term, either on the same portfolio or on different ones. This is quite typical for Directors-General, too. We also distinguish between the different leadership positions the individuals occupy in the Commission, i.e. Commissioners (political level) versus Directors-General (administrative level). The characteristics of women in these positions are likely to differ, not least because they enter the Commission via different career paths.

Figure 11.1 shows that in the first 35 years of integration no women achieved top-level positions, but since the Delors II Commission (1989–1993) more and more women have ascended to those ranks.

Looking at women in political positions, we see that they first entered the Commission as members of the Delors II College. In 1989, Vasso Papandreou from Greece became Commissioner for Employment and Social Affairs, and Christiane Scrivener from France became Commissioner for Tax Policy. There were five female Commissioners under Santer and Prodi, eight and ten under Barroso I and Barroso II respectively, nine under Juncker, and 12 under von der Leyen. Research assumes that women may exert more influence to put issues on the political agenda or to shape discourse and decision-making dynamics once they reach a critical mass of roughly 30% (Childs and Krook 2008). This threshold was first reached under Prodi (35%) and Barroso II (37%), as well as under Juncker (32%). Since then, female empowerment at the political top of the Commission gained traction again and reached near-parity under von der Leyen (44%).

We can link these developments to changes in the appointment process of Commissioners, who are proposed by their national governments and approved by the European Parliament. Over time, the power of national governments in this process has been constrained, rendering it more

The European Commission

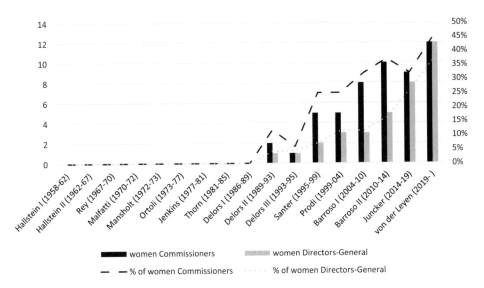

Figure 11.1 Women at the top of the Commission, 1958–2020
Source: authors' analysis, women's terms with N = 87, 52 women Commissioners and 35 women Directors-General including double entries of persons serving in more than one Commission (as per June 2020).

difficult to appoint men only. First, votes on the Commission President and the new College of Commissioners moved from unanimity to majority decisions in the European Council and the Council. Second, in 1995 the Parliament empowered itself to scrutinize individual candidates in hearings (Wonka 2007, 169–189). Third, largely as a consequence of those hearings, the selection process has become much more publicly visible. This has allowed the Commission President and the European Parliament to be more demanding of member states to put forward candidates that meet their criteria, facilitating the quest for more female candidates.

Commission President Prodi is reported to have been the first incumbent who, "understanding at least the rhetoric of balanced participation … explicitly encouraged member states to put forward women's names for consideration to the College of Commissioners" (MacRae 2012, 310). Public debate about gender balance in the top EU jobs has further increased with the *Spitzenkandidaten* process, first employed in the European elections of 2014.

Women's representation has also been on the rise in the Commission's top administrative positions. However, here the trend set in later and, until recently, remained much less robust. Shortly after the appointment of the first female Commissioners, Colette Flesch from Luxembourg followed as the first female Director-General. Heading the DG for Communication on the administrative side, she remained the only female Director-General under Delors III; the number of female DG heads subsequently grew, more or less steadily, to three (Prodi), five (Barroso II), eight (Juncker) and now 12 (von der Leyen).

Historically, national networks and national quotas had been crucial to the appointment of individuals to the Commission's administrative top positions. Officials were sometimes "parachuted" into the services by their national governments without having worked in the EU before. For much of the integration process this seems to have benefited men more than women. Following the alleged mismanagement and resignation of the Santer Commission in 1999, the career system in the Commission underwent important changes. Administrative careers in the body are now much more merit-based (Bauer 2008), and there are many more women in top-level positions. The share of female Directors-General has increased from a little less than 3% under Delors II to 40% today. In particular, the Barroso and Juncker Commissions continuously advanced the share of female administrative leaders.

The Commission's administrative base has also become more gender balanced, although internal differences persist. Schmidt (2005, 197) shows that between 1984 and 2000 female staff increases were most pronounced at the D level (qualified workers) and LA level (heads of linguistic units, interpreters, and translators). The composition of the C grade (secretaries), comprising around 80% of the Commission's female staff, hardly changed. The B level (principal assistants) remained stable as well (between 38% and 40% women). In contrast, female representation at the A level grew from almost 10% in 1984 to about 21% in 2000 (Schmidt 2005, 198). Between 2008 and 2014, female representation continued to grow, from 21% to 28% in senior management, from 20% to 31% in middle management, and from 40% to 44% in non-management positions (Connelly and Kassim 2017, 19). Overall, despite the increased access to management positions, women comprise a much greater share of work as secretaries, translators, and interpreters than men. Women's relative gains in management positions have largely been at the lower ranks and they still tend to only slowly work their way up through the Commission hierarchy.[2]

Regarding sectoral distribution, the majority of portfolios have been headed by women at the political and/or administrative level for at least some amount of time. Exceptions are the DGs for Economic and Financial Affairs, and for Enlargement. Counting each Commission term in which a female Commissioner or a female Director-General presided over a DG, the number of women has been highest in the areas of Education (seven terms), Health and Safety and Justice (six terms each) as well as in the European External Action Service (five terms) – indeed, Justice and the External Action Service have now been led by women on both the political and administrative sides for three or more successive terms. The three DGs of Communication, and Budget (five terms each) also stand out as relatively "female" portfolios.

Concentration of women leaders in conventionally "female" portfolios such as social welfare and education is typical at the national level, too (Goddard 2018). Yet, in contrast to the national level, women in the Commission seem to be more likely to work in budget, foreign affairs, competition, and justice. For these traditionally "male" portfolios, women's empowerment seems to have been driven by political decisions, while on the administrative side, female Directors-General were more often nominated for "female" portfolios. This points to the differences in the career paths of Commissioners and Directors-General. While a powerful member state may be eager to push high-ranking politicians into important portfolios – including women if this increases its chances of securing desired posts – Directors-General typically are recruited to the Commission at earlier stages of their career and work their way up through the administration. On this path, they are likely to end up in portfolios that are perceived as dealing with "women's issues," perhaps due to self-selection as well as internal promotion logics.

In sum, while the data indicate the growth of female empowerment in the Commission, the rise of women into leadership positions has been slow. At the political level, it started earlier; in top administrative positions, a "critical mass" of women has been reached only recently. Today, the Commission is approaching parity, with 44% (political) and 36% (administration) women in the top posts. These numbers may well increase further under President Ursula von der Leyen, who, upon assumption of her office, strongly urged member states to nominate female Commissioners. While the Commission's agency has been constrained by member states' political interests, other actors and institutions, in particular the European Parliament, have pushed and pulled for female empowerment, as we will see below.

Gendering EU policies

Despite its mainly male top-level composition, the Commission embarked early on policy initiatives aimed at fostering gender equality in the European Community/Union. Starting in the mid-1970s, the Commission's activities in promoting gender equality evolved in three phases: the first focused exclusively on policy-making in the workplace, with the initiation of European legislation to ensure equal pay for men and women; the second widened the perspective to the societal position of women, in which gender-mainstreaming constituted the main policy approach to foster gender equality across a broad set of policy areas; and the third took all forms of discrimination into account, while gender inequalities were addressed mainly through the updating of prior commitments and heightened attention to implementation deficits (for a similar distinction of phases, see also Jacquot 2015 and Solanke in this volume).

Phase one: fostering equal pay for men and women

In the mid-1970s, in the context of the increased commitment by the then European Community (EC) to complement economic integration with social policy, the issue of equal pay for men and women reached the legislative agenda (Mazey 1988). Referring to a provision in the EEC Treaty of 1957 that stipulated equal pay for men and women for equal work (Article 119; now Article 157 TFEU), the Commission proposed a series of directives to enforce various aspects of the general rule. Over the course of two decades, this resulted in the adoption of six directives at European level.

The Equal Pay Directive (75/117/EEC) mainly regulated equal pay for men and women for work of equal value. The Equal Treatment Directive (76/207/EEC) mandated that men and women be treated equally "with respect to access to employment, training and promotion, and working conditions" (Kantola 2010, 34). Furthermore, it "ruled out all forms of direct and indirect discrimination on grounds of sex, particularly to reference of marital or family status" (Ostner 2000, 28). The Social Security Directive (79/7/EEC) covered all aspects of social security payments, "providing protection against the risks of sickness, invalidity, accidents at work, occupational diseases and unemployment" (Mazey 1988, 69). The Occupational Pensions Schemes Directive (86/378/EEC) applied these principles to pension schemes, while the Equal Treatment Directive for the Self-Employed (86/613/EEC) expanded the rules to other social security schemes (Ostner 2000, 28). Finally, the Pregnant Workers Directive (92/85/EEC) ensured protections for expectant mothers as well as workers who had recently given birth (Falkner et al. 2005, 73–77). Beginning in 1982, the Commission also initiated a series of multi-annual action programs, aimed at fostering additional legislative acts and complementing them with measures of positive action (Hoskyns 2000; Mazey 1998; Reinalda 1992). Other proposals for directives launched by the Commission during those years (concerning part-time work, atypical work, and parental leave) were rejected by the Council (Mazey 1988, 76–77). Nevertheless, the six directives as well as the action programs were important steps in the establishment of a gender policy at the European level, especially since at the time these regulations and measures by far transcended those of most member states.

According to many scholars, however, the directives focused too narrowly on the workplace and ignored women's overall position in society. Furthermore, they changed the situation of working women by law, but not in substance (MacRae 2010). As Mazey (1988, 63) states: "In short, the socio-structural causes of sex discrimination lie beyond the reach of existing Equality Directives."

Phase two: broadening the perspective through gender mainstreaming

In the mid-1990s, the Commission introduced the gender mainstreaming approach as a means to raise attention to sex discrimination across the whole policy spectrum at both the European and member state levels, marking the beginning of the second phase. This change in direction – or even "paradigm shift" (Ostner 2000, 34) – was induced by the Commission's concern about labor shortages. Accordingly, the Commission aimed to improve women's access to the labor market by removing some of the manifold barriers, such as the lack of childcare facilities (Jenson 2008).

In 1996, the Commission officially launched gender mainstreaming, defining its foundation as "the systematic consideration of the differences between the conditions, situations and needs of women and men in all Community policies and actions" (COM(1996)67final, 5). It identified six areas for future action; among these, employment and the labor market figured most prominently (COM(1996)67 final, 6–10). Furthermore, it envisaged mobilizing political and financial support through the Structural Funds (COM(1996)67 final, 15–20). The Action Program 4, also launched in 1996, used mainstreaming as its "main organizing principle" (Hoskyns 2000, 53). The Amsterdam Treaty (adopted in 1997) further underpinned the Union's commitment to a gendered policy by promoting "throughout the Community … equality between men and women" (Article 2 TEC, now Article 8 TFEU) and listing a broad set of policy areas where this principle had to be applied (Article 3(2) TEC, now Article 8 TFEU).

The gender mainstreaming approach rested on so-called new modes of governance, that is, steering instruments not reliant on legislation. It encompassed a broad set of nonbinding measures such as raising awareness, providing information, stimulating the commitment and cooperation of the actors actually involved into policy-making, coordinating their performance, and monitoring policy progress (Ahrens 2019; Jacquot 2010; Mazey 2002; Woodward 2012, 96).

During this phase, the Commission also continued to launch legislative initiatives, although success was limited by fierce opposition from national governments. Directives on part-time work, atypical work, and parental leave were subsequently adopted via the European Social Dialogue. This procedure, introduced with the Treaty of Maastricht, allows the social partners – employers' and workers' representatives – to negotiate legislative texts, while the Council only formally adopts the results of those negotiations (Falkner et al. 2005, 142–144, 161–164). Furthermore, the Commission succeeded in pushing through a general framework directive for equal treatment in employment and occupation (2000/78/EC) and for equal treatment of men and women regarding the access to and supply of goods and services (2004/113/EC).

The rich literature on the second phase mainly focuses on the gender mainstreaming approach. Scholars have criticized the voluntary approach (Abels and Mushaben 2012), the lack of appropriate incentives (Hafner-Burton and Pollack 2009), and the huge differences in implementation between various policy areas and sectors of intervention as well as member states (e.g. Mergaert and Lombardo 2014). Overall, the second phase was characterized by an anti-discrimination policy going beyond the focus on the employment relationship that had characterized the first phase. New initiatives, however, mostly took the form of soft measures, resulting in a dilution of the Commission's innovative policy approach and protracted implementation.

Phase three: focusing on wider aspects of discrimination and updating earlier gender equality policies

From 2005 onwards, the Commission once more changed direction by no longer focusing exclusively on gender inequality, but increasingly on broader and more differentiated grounds of discrimination. Starting with race, it soon expanded its anti-discrimination policies to a broad spectrum of "other disadvantaged groups and minorities" groups.

In terms of concrete gender measures, the Commission replaced the action programs, first by a Roadmap for Equality (2006–2010), followed by a Strategy for Equality between Women and Men (2010–2015), and finally by a Strategic Engagement for Gender Equality (2016–2019) (Ahrens 2019, 58–61; SWD(2015)278 final; Woodward 2012, 100). In 2010, it also adopted a charter for women's rights (COM(2010)78 final). The most recent Strategic Engagement issued by the Juncker Commission is not an official Communication, but only a staff working document, which "might mean the end of gender equality programmes as a policy instrument" (Ahrens 2019, 61). Much like in the second phase, the most prominent objective of all these documents remained increasing female participation in the labor market. Additional objectives included equal pay for work of equal value, equality in decision-making, ending gender-based violence, and promoting gender equality beyond the EU (SWD(2015)278 final). The Commission's commitment also became apparent in a number of other steps. The Commission updated and revised existing directives, such as ones addressing the equal treatment of men and women in matters of employment and occupation (2006/54/EC), self-employment (2010/41/EC), and work-life balance for parents and carers (2019/1158/EC). More ambitious legal initiatives advanced by the Commission with potentially higher implementation costs (e.g. the Anti-Discrimination Framework Directive) were, however, blocked by member states. In short, while the Commission updated the policy objectives of earlier phases, it proposed few if any successful new initiatives.

Unsurprisingly, the Commission formulated the corresponding policy tools in vague terms, that is predominantly in the form of intentions and purposes. The Strategic Engagement for Gender Equality, for instance, mentioned as concrete measures: "continuing to support"; "continue to collect and disseminate further data"; "consider measures"; "provide guidance to the Member States"; and "reach the target" (SWD(2015)278 final, 20–33). In sum, the Commission's recent engagement with gender policy has consisted in coaxing others through weak instruments and vague formulations; in other words, it continues to rely on soft modes of governance.

Feminist scholarly assessments of this phase of the Commission's gender equality policy are extremely critical. Woodward (2012, 100) argued that "the anti-discrimination framework seems like a step backward for gender." Jacquot (2015, 181) saw the Commission's equality policy as in a state of "progressive dismantling," and Ahrens (2019, 62) concluded that the Commission intentionally avoided giving legal status to its latest policies, the better to "retain the power to design policy instruments that suit its interests." This perspective, however, might be biased by a focus on gender equality narrowly defined. Others, looking from a broader policy-making perspective and highlighting anti-discrimination directives as scarce examples of hard law-making in the area of EU social policy, argue that the Commission was able to advance the policy field against opposing interests at least in some cases (Hartlapp 2017).

The third phase of the Commission's gender equality policy is thus characterized by its repositioning within the context of a broader conception of discrimination. In an era of "new intergovernmentalism" (e.g. Bickerton et al. 2015) and extremely heterogeneous member state interests, Commission policy-making on gender issues has been relegated to a prodding role with uncertain impact. It remains to be seen whether and to what extent the new Gender Equality Strategy 2020–2024, initiated by the von der Leyen Commission in March 2020, will be able to change this trend.

Gendering the European Commission

By the end of the 1980s, the Commission had also started to work at improving the gender balance within its own ranks. For this purpose, it defined a set of measures, laid down first in

Miriam Hartlapp et al.

positive action programs (APs) and, later, in so-called strategies – not to be confused with the APs and strategies directed toward member states. The APs and strategies comprise mainly soft measures and recommendations rather than hard legislation and enforcement. They thus correspond to the new governance approach underlying the Commission's gender equality policy of the second and third phases as described above, and clearly mirror the respective policy shifts. The initiatives presented here contributed to a slow improvement of the gender balance in the Commission's services, as well as their working culture (Schmidt 2005, 48; also see MacRae 2012, 303).

The First Positive Action Programme (1988–1990) and the Second Positive Action Programme (1992–1996) targeted female personnel only (though in the second AP as part of an integrated human resources policy, MEMO/04/46), and aimed at expanding women's career opportunities through vocational training and recruitment, as well as raising awareness of the importance of equal opportunities among officials and staff. As of 1995, the Second Positive Action Programme also set annual targets for the gender composition of the Commission's staff, especially with regard to A-grade posts (SEC(2004)447/5, 4). It also established the Equal Opportunities Unit to evaluate and monitor the progress and implementation of the gender equality measures (Schmidt 2005, 47). As previously mentioned, both APs met with limited success, at least in regard to the Commission's top leadership positions (see also MEMO/04/46).

The Third Action Programme for Equal Opportunities for Women and Men (1997–2000, extended until 2001 and de facto until 2003 (SEC(2004)447/5, 4) went hand in hand with the introduction of the gender mainstreaming approach; consequently, the Commission applied this approach to its own administration (SEC(2004)447/5, 6). This meant moving beyond "positive action," as the Commission's measures no longer exclusively targeted the underrepresented sex, but envisaged more holistic strategies for creating equal opportunities within the institution. The Commission now published annual reports on the progress of gender mainstreaming in each DG (Schmidt 2005, 191), and DG Administration applied stricter oversight of the recruitment of new officials, ensuring, for instance, that female applicants did not face all-male juries (Schmidt 2005, 193). Beginning in 2000, DG Employment and Social Affairs (DG EMPL) included gender mainstreaming in its training courses for directors and heads of units as well as new officials and staff (Schmidt 2005, 201f.). An evaluation of the Third Action Programme by Commission officials and staff, however, revealed mixed results (SEC(2004)447/5). The AP's measures were seen as weak and patchy and the consensus view was that "there has been a serious lack … in developing information on, awareness of and sensitization to gender equality matters. Inconsistency of implementation and lack of priority are also underlined" (SEC(2004)447/5, 5).

The Fourth Positive Action Programme for Equal Opportunities for Women and Men at the European Commission (2004–08), introduced as part of the Prodi-Kinnock reforms (1999–2005), stipulated that the onus of proof concerning any form of discrimination no longer lay with the accuser but in all cases with the institution (European Commission 2005, 10). The Commission introduced the publication of an annual "gender equality scoreboard" to improve transparency and consistency across the DGs concerning equal opportunity achievements (SEC(2004)447/5, 12), and established a Senior Women's Network "to encourage women in senior management positions to meet and discuss issues of mutual interest on a regular but informal basis" (SEC(2004)447/5, 10). Soft and indirect measures thus continued to characterize the Commission's promotion of gender equality.

With the launch of a new Equal Opportunities Strategy (2010–2014), the Commission slowly shifted the focus from equal gender representation to creating a more inclusive and diverse organization (IP/10/1742, 1). Nevertheless, it aimed to further increase the number of women in senior and middle management positions and the recruitment of women administrators. In this regard, targets were set for each DG individually (DG Human Resources, IP/10/1742, 1). To reduce structural barriers to women in management (Ban 2013, 186) and to improve the overall work–life balance, greater emphasis was placed on flexible working methods, such as flextime, telework, and part-time work (IP/10/1742, 1). A target of 25% female representation in senior management posts was set for 2014 (SEC(2010)1554/3, 5). Overall, the strategy only continued already established measures, though with greater visibility and regular reporting of each DG's achievements (SEC(2010) 1554/3, 8).

Finally, in 2017, the Commission adopted the strategy for A better workplace for all: from equal opportunities towards diversity and inclusion. The aim was to ensure compliance with nondiscrimination of all types – not just on the basis of sex and gender. The Commission explicitly incorporated the perspective of stakeholders ranging from women to staff with disabilities, LGBTI (lesbian, gay, bisexual, transgender, and intersex) staff, and older staff into its new approach (C(2017)5300 final, 5). In line with this commitment, the Commission also adopted its first Diversity and Inclusion Charter on July 19, 2017, which set guiding principles for the institution's human resources policies. A target of at least 40% female representation in middle and senior management by 2019 was set, which was indeed achieved by the Juncker Commission (IP/19/6139). DG Human Resources was charged with preparing talented staff for management and leadership courses, monitoring progress in diversity and inclusion, drafting the Commission's diversity and gender equality reports, and galvanizing the exchange of best practices across the different portfolios. The DGs, in turn, were encouraged to set up management programs for female staff (C(2017) 5300 final, 14–15, 21).

In the heyday of gender mainstreaming the Commission thus enthusiastically committed itself to the advancement of equal gender representation within its own ranks, though mainly with soft and indirect measures. Since the mid-2000s, the focus has widened to encompass broader issues of diversity and inclusion. Though some advocates of gender equality perceive this as diluting previous goals, we have recently seen a steep increase in the number of female Directors-General (see Figure 11.1), at last reaching that self-imposed 40% target. With more gender-balanced cohorts advancing up the hierarchy, the Commission is finally turning its goal of greater gender balance into reality.

The Commission's agency: between pressure and constraints

The Commission's gender equality policy did not evolve as a self-evident process; on the contrary, during each phase it was actively driven by committed actors – mostly women – within the Commission (so-called femocrats) and advocacy groups from without. The feminist literature has paid much attention to the interaction and networks of like-minded gender advocates in the bureaucracy and civil society (Woodward 2004). In addition, pressure from the European Parliament and, more recently, a "critical mass" of female Commissioners in the College has played an important role.

During the 1970s, such a coalition pushed gender equality in the workplace onto the legislative agenda (phase one) (Kantola 2010, 31–33; Reinalda 1992, 84–88; Schmidt 2005, 41). Advocacy by a small but proactive non-governmental group (Women for Europe) and cause lawyers such as Éliane Vogel-Polsky, who launched the three famous *Defrenne* cases (see Guth and Elfving in this volume) in front of the Court of Justice of the European Union (C-80/70, C-43/75 and C-149/77), enabled committed women inside DG EMPL – such as the French official Jacqueline Nonon – to draft and advance new legislation. The women's movement of those years, as well as the accession of three new member states to the Community in 1973 (United Kingdom, Ireland, and Denmark) each with its own advanced equal opportunity laws,[3] further facilitated the Commission's agency – not least since Ireland provided the new Commissioner for DG EMPL (Reinalda 1992, 84).

After the second direct European elections in 1984, the European Parliament established a Committee on Women's Rights and Equal Opportunities (renamed the Committee on Women's Rights and Gender Equality (FEMM) in 2004). This committee, as well as the Parliament as a whole, served as a strong voice for gender equality policy, often successfully pressuring the Commission to act in a responsive manner (Ahrens 2016; Mazey 1988, 77–78). For example, in 1995, when the European Parliament had first obtained the power to give or deny consent to the incoming Commission, it announced it would accept the Commission only if it comprised at least 25% female members as previously suggested by the FEMM committee (PE 205.666/final, January 27, 1994). This resulted in a sharp increase in the number of female Commissioners (Figure 11.1). The following year, the Santer Commission – pressured by the Parliament – then created the Group of Commissioners on Equal Opportunities. This group officially launched the gender mainstreaming concept (phase two). At the staff level, the group was supported by an Inter-Service Group on Gender Equality (founded in 1996) and the Group of Gender Mainstreaming Officials composed of heads of units and directors (Schmidt 2005, 206). A European Women's Lobby, established in 1990 in Brussels, acted as a committed external voice on behalf of anti-discrimination policies.

During the presidency of Prodi, the Commissioner for Employment and Social Affairs, Anna Diamantopoulou, pushed for the adoption of additional gender equality directives, against resistance from within the Commission and the member states. When she left the Commission in 2004, her Director-General, Odile Quintin, continued to skillfully advance the agenda (Hartlapp et al. 2014, 71–77). A number of legislative initiatives were subsequently adopted that consolidated existing principles, codified case law advances, and clarified their application.

The Commission's interest in continuing to advance gender policy-making, even against increasing member state opposition in the Council, led it to forge new alliances, in particular with NGOs already involved in the fight against other forms of discrimination (phase three) (Hartlapp 2017). In 2010, under Barroso's second presidency, the gender equality issue became the responsibility of DG Justice, Fundamental Rights, and Citizenship and consequently embedded within broader human rights and anti-discrimination policies. Viviane Reding, the responsible Commissioner, successfully launched "A Women's Charter" (COM(2010)78 final) and pushed other gender equality proposals, such as a directive on gender balance on company boards (COM(2012)0614 final). Though it was forcefully supported by the European Parliament, this latter proposal could not gain the necessary support in the Council. Since then, the Parliament has pushed the Council to continue the debate on legislative action (most recently, in the Employment, Social Policy, Health and Consumer Affairs Council, June 13–14, 2019). Nevertheless, DG EMPL continued to advance gender equality both inside the Commission (jointly with DG Administration), and externally toward member states. In the subsequent Juncker Commission (2014–2019), Věra Jourová acted as Commissioner for Justice, Consumers and Gender Equality. During this period, as previously detailed, the Commission's agency in the field of gender equality was limited, focusing mainly on updating earlier policy objectives. In 2019, Commission President von der Leyen for the first time nominated a Commissioner for Equality, Helena Dalli.

Overall, the Commission's engagement in the promotion of gender equality has evolved largely in reaction to the pressure of external actors, most notably various advocacy coalitions and networks, the European Parliament, and the women's movement more broadly. Within the

Commission, deeply committed women in leadership positions – Commissioners, Directors-General, and other high-level civil servants – took up the ball and pushed forward the gender equality agenda. Throughout the three phases described above, however, especially during the last decade, the Commission faced strong resistance from the member states, inhibiting substantial advances in equal treatment.

Conclusion

This chapter has provided a comprehensive overview of the development and current state of women's representation within the Commission as well as the organization's record in promoting gender equality policies throughout the Union and implementing them within its own ranks. It has also provided an overview of the main actors who have influenced the Commission's agency in this domain. On the basis of this analysis, we can draw the following conclusions.

The Commission has evolved from an initially male-dominated institution to one whose top leadership is now around 40% female, both at the political and administrative levels. Beginning in the mid-1970s, it has established gender equality policies for the member states. These policies developed out of a limited legal approach involving a broad, but soft governance concept, leading more recently to a set of revisions of earlier commitments and weak voluntary measures. Since 1988, the Commission has also actively promoted growth in the share of female leaders and staff across the different ranks of its administration through a variety of policies, measures, and tools, though again mainly voluntary in nature.

Assessing the Commission strategies for establishing and implementing gender equality policies both intra- and inter-institutionally, we see a strong commitment early on, triggered by the women's movement of the 1970s and an effective advocacy coalition at the European level. This resulted in the enshrinement of certain basic principles of gender equality in the form of directives and treaty articles. In the 1990s, this legally based approach expanded through the application of the concept of gender mainstreaming to all EU policy areas as well as, institutionally, to the Commission itself. The broad policy objectives have been pursued through soft modes of governance, making their implementation contingent on the commitment of the actors involved. Since the mid-2000s, the Commission has focused less on specific gender equality policies in favor of a more sweeping approach, covering a variety of discrimination grounds.

The Commission's strategies and particularly its periodic revisions of its gender policy reflect fundamental developments in European integration and society at large. When the issue of sex discrimination was highly politicized, as in the 1970s, the Commission reacted with a progressive and authoritative policy approach, clearly transcending the policies of the member states at the time. When such pressures were weaker, the Commission reacted to perceived problems in the market – that is, shortages in the labor supply – with a more diffuse and less assertive approach, characterized by soft modes of governance. This turn was also a reaction to externally imposed constraints, as national governments increasingly sought to curb legislative initiatives at European level. Given the significant increase in female representation within the Commission's leadership, now at more than 40%, it will be interesting to observe if there is a corresponding improvement in gender equality policies.

Future research would benefit from more systematic study of the link between women's representation in positions of power and authority and their substantive representation of political interests in a number of policy areas. The field is ripe for innovative research that targets female empowerment in "male" portfolios and considers whether and under what conditions women leaders might make a difference in fostering gender equality. Research on this issue will

Miriam Hartlapp et al.

be of particular consequence in the years to come as, with Ursula von der Leyen's election to the presidency, for the first time a woman has accessed the highest leadership position in the European Commission.

Notes

1   Data is taken from the PEU data base on the Commission (Hartlapp 2019). The database covers information about individuals (e.g. names, sex/gender, nationality or DG affiliation) as well as organizational features of the Commission and can be accessed at www.polsoz.fu-berlin.de/polwiss/forschung/international/de-fr/Forschung/PEU-Database1/index.html.
2   Data can be accessed at https://eige.europa.eu/genderstatistics/dgs/indicator/wmidm_adm_eur__wmid_euadmin_eurins/line (download: March 1, 2019).
3   Oral history interview with Jacqueline Nonon, recorded October 25, 2010, accessed via the EUI Archives, reference Code INT226.

References

Abels G, Mushaben J M (2012): Introduction: Studying the EU from a Gender Perspective, in: Abels G, Mushaben J M (eds.): *Gendering the European Union. New Approaches to Old Democratic Deficits*, Basingstoke, Palgrave Macmillan, 1–22.

Ahrens P (2016): The Committee on Women's Rights and Gender Equality in the European Parliament: taking advantage of institutional power play, *Parliamentary Affairs* **69** (4), 778–793.

Ahrens P (2019): The birth, life, and death of policy instruments: 35 years of EU gender equality policy programmes, *West European Politics* **42** (1), 45–66.

Ban C (2013): *Management and Culture in an Enlarged European Commission. From Diversity to Unity?* Basingstoke: Palgrave Macmillan.

Bauer M W (2008): Diffuse anxieties, deprived entrepreneurs. Commission reform and middle management, *Journal of European Public Policy* **15** (5), 691–707.

Bickerton C J, Hodson D, Puetter U (2015): The new intergovernmentalism: European integration in the post-Maastricht era, *Journal of Common Market Studies* **53** (4), 703–722.

Childs S, Krook M L (2008): Critical mass theory and women's political representation, *Political Studies* **56** (3), 725–736.

Connelly S, Kassim H (2017): Beyond the Numbers: Gender and Careers in the European Commission, paper prepared for presentation at the EUSA Fifteenth Biennial Conference, Miami, Florida.

European Commission (2005): Staff Regulations of the Officials of the European Communities, Brussels, URL: https://ec.europa.eu/eurostat/cache/metadata/Annexes/prc_colc_nat_esms_an2.pdf (download: May 20, 2019).

Falkner G, Treib O, Hartlapp M, Leiber S (2005): *Complying with Europe. EU Minimum Harmonisation and Soft Law in the Member States*, Cambridge: Cambridge University Press.

Goddard D (2018): Entering the men's domain? Gender and portfolio allocation in European governments, *European Journal of Political Research* **48** (8), 631–655.

Hafner-Burton E M, Pollack M A (2009): Mainstreaming gender in the European Union: getting the incentives right, *Comparative European Politics* **7** (1), 114–138.

Hartlapp M (2017): How time empowers agency. Combining the EU Commission's political powers and its administration's advantage of acting from a long-term perspective, *Journal of European Integration* **39** (3), 303–317.

Hartlapp M (2019): Position Formation in the EU Commission, Version 1.0.0, WZB Berlin Social Science Center, dataset.

Hartlapp M, Metz J, Rauh C (2014): *Which Policy for Europe? Power and Conflict inside the European Commission*, Oxford: Oxford University Press.

Hoskyns C (2000): A Study of Four Action Programmes on Equal Opportunities, in: Rossilli M (ed.): *Gender Policies in the European Union*, New York: Peter Lang, 43–59.

Jacquot S (2010): The paradox of gender mainstreaming: unanticipated effects of new modes of governance in the gender equality domain, *West European Politics* **33** (1), 118–135.

Jacquot S (2015): *Transformations in EU Gender Equality. From Emergence to Dismantling*, Basingstoke: Palgrave Macmillan.

Jenson J (2008): Writing women out, folding gender in: The European Union "modernises" social policy, *Social Politics* **15** (2), 131–153.

Kantola J (2010): *Gender and the European Union*, Basingstoke: Palgrave Macmillan.

MacRae H (2010): The EU as a Gender Equal Polity: Myths and Realities, *Journal of Common Market Studies* **48** (1), 155–174.

MacRae H (2012): Double-Speak: the European Union and gender parity, *West European Politics* **35** (2), 301–318.

Mazey S (1988): European Community action on behalf of women: the limits of legislation, *Journal of Common Market Studies* **27** (1), 63–84.

Mazey S (1998): The European Union and women's rights: from the Europeanization of national agendas to the nationalization of a European agenda? *Journal of European Public Policy* **5** (1), 131–152.

Mazey S (2002): Gender mainstreaming strategies in the EU: delivering on an agenda?, *Feminist Legal Studies* **10** (3–4), 227–240.

Mergaert L, Lombardo E (2014): Resistance to Implementing Gender Mainstreaming in EU Research Policy, in: Weiner E, MacRae H (eds.): *The persistent invisibility of gender in EU policy, European Integration online Papers (EIoP)* **18**, Special Issue 1, 1–21, URL: http://eiop.or.at/eiop/pdf/2014-005.pdf.

Ostner I (2000): From Equal Pay to Equal Employability. Four Decades of European Gender Policies, in: Rossilli M (ed.): *Gender Policies in the European Union*, New York: Peter Lang, 25–42.

Reinalda B (1992): Totstandkoming, ontwikkeling en doorwerking van het EG-beleid inzake gelijke behandeling van vrouwen en mannen, in: Tömmel I (ed.): *Europese gemeenschap en nationale staat: Integratie en diversificatie door overheidsbeleid*, Amsterdam: Thesis, 82–104.

Schmidt V (2005): *Gender Mainstreaming – An Innovation in Europe? The Institutionalisation of Gender Mainstreaming in the European Commission*, Opladen: Barbara Budrich Publishers.

Wonka A (2007): Technocratic and independent? The appointment of European Commissioners and its policy implications, *Journal of European Public Policy* **14** (2), 169–189.

Woodward A E (2004): Building Velvet Triangles: Gender and Informal Governance, in: Christiansen T, Piattoni S (eds.): *Informal Governance in the European Union*, Cheltenham: Edward Elgar, 76–93.

Woodward A E (2012): From Equal Treatment to Gender Mainstreaming and Diversity Management, in: Abels G, Mushaben J (eds.): *Gendering the European Union. New Approaches to Old Democratic Deficits*, Basingstoke: Palgrave Macmillan, 85–103.

12

The European External Action Service

Laura Chappell

One of the primary innovations within the Lisbon Treaty was the creation of the European External Action Service (EEAS). The idea was to provide the EU with its own diplomatic service, ensuring coherence and efficiency in its external relations, an area that has seen rapid expansion since the creation of the Common Security and Defence Policy (CSDP) in 1999. Not only is the EEAS there to ensure the EU speaks with a common voice in developing and implementing foreign, security and defence policies, but also to reflect the EU's key values globally. Gender equality, considered a foundational EU norm (MacRae 2010), has been integrated into a variety of communitised policies. The question is whether the EEAS has been able to mainstream gender both internally in its own structures and externally in the external relations policies it creates, promotes and implements.

The creation of the EEAS represented a window of opportunity to fully incorporate a gender perspective into the EU's external activities. However, the structure of the EEAS has made this particularly challenging. First, the EEAS was created from the European Commission's Directorate-General for External Relations (DG RELEX), DG E in the Council as well as seconded officials from the member states. As a result, there was at least initially, a lack of a general *esprit de corps* (Davis Cross 2011; Vanhoonacker and Pomorska 2013). Second, the EEAS is partly dependent on diverse gender norms coming from the EU member states. Thus, the EEAS does not have control over its entire staff base when it comes to implementing a common culture or *esprit de corps* (see below) or mainstreaming gender with implications for gender equality policies, in the context of foreign, security and defence policies. This is particularly evident in how gender mainstreaming is viewed: is it seen purely as a tick box exercise or as a substantive and integrated part of the EEAS's activities (see Muehlenhoff in this volume)?

Considering the serious implications of a lack of gender mainstreaming both within the EEAS and the policies it promotes and implements, it is surprising that little academic work has been conducted from a gender perspective (although see Deiana and McDonagh 2018 Guerrina et al. 2018; Guerrina and Wright 2016; Haastrup 2018; Kronsell 2015, 2016; Novotnà 2015, 2016; Muehlenhoff 2017). The small body of work on gender and the EEAS has focused on the challenges in mainstreaming gender in the EEAS in respect to mediation and CSDP structures. Hence the literature identifies a lack of feminist constellations (Guerrina et al. 2018; Haastrup 2018), underscores the 'dominance of male bodies' (Kronsell 2016, 111) within CSDP

146

institutions and highlights the 'reproduction of gender hierarchies of the masculinized CSDP onto the feminized mediation institution' (Haastrup 2018, 232), in addition to emphasising the lack of women in various parts of the service. Nonetheless, the recently created position of the Principal Advisor on Gender and on the Implementation of UNSCR 1325 initiated in the summer 2015 and currently held by Mara Marinaki, along with her albeit small office of the gender advisor, represents an advancement in how and where gender is placed on the agenda. This in turn has raised the visibility of gender mainstreaming within the EEAS. Importantly it has facilitated the utilisation of such tools as the informal task force on women, peace and security and increased attention in respect to gender equality within EEAS staffing.

This chapter focuses on where gender can be found within EEAS structures and whether this provides a foundation for gender mainstreaming within foreign, security and defence policies (see Muehlenhoff in this volume). It is important to consider gender not only in the societies the EEAS engages with, but also that the EEAS acts as a positive example through a gender awareness in its in-house gender norms, personnel practices, training and resources. Hence, for the EU to be a normative gender actor it must embody and practice this value (see Chappell and Guerrina 2020). This chapter will underscore the challenges for the EEAS in entrenching gender into its core. This allows us to consider a variety of gaps in the research, including structural and normative impediments to mainstreaming gender, training, resource allocation, perceptions of gender and gender mainstreaming within the EEAS and the member states, and intersectionality, which in turn links to the overall agenda of diversity. These, in turn, set an overarching research agenda, which shall be elaborated upon in the final section.

Creating the EEAS: a gendered agenda?

The Treaty of Lisbon gives little detail on the structure and workings of the EEAS. Instead the service was briefly mentioned in the context of the new post of High Representative for Foreign Affairs and Security Policy (HR):

> The High Representative shall be assisted by a European External Action Service. … The organisation and functioning of the European External Action Service shall be established by a decision of the Council. The Council shall act on a proposal from the High Representative after consulting the European Parliament and after obtaining the consent of the Commission.
>
> *(Article 27(3) TEU)*

Hence, it was the task of the first HR, Catherine Ashton, to 'create' the EEAS. Thus, it took just over a year from the entering into force of the treaty in December 2009, to the formal launch of the EEAS on 1 January 2011. The EEAS's key tasks were outlined rather broadly in the Council Framework decision of 26 July 2010: supporting the HR to fulfil her duties in respect of CFSP and CSDP and in particular, 'to contribute by his/her proposals to the development of that policy … and to ensure the consistency of the Union's external action' (2010/427/EU, 32). Additionally, EU delegations to third countries and international organisations were transferred to the EEAS from the Commission.

The EEAS's personnel came from three distinctive backgrounds located in the Commission, the Council and the member states. While the former two can be considered career EU officials who remain in the EEAS, the latter are seconded from the member states. This has implications for both gender equality and gender mainstreaming. In respect to whom these officials are, gender balance was raised as an issue early in the drafting process. The first mention of this occurred in the 2009 Swedish Presidency report on the EEAS which outlined that recruitment should aim 'towards gender balance' (Council of the European Union 2009, 7; European Parliament 2013, 12). However, geographical balance was of greater concern to the member states and gender was not consistently part of discussions until the draft Council Decision on the EEAS in March 2010 (European Parliament 2013, 14). Rather than this element coming from the HR, it appears that it was the Green Party in the European Parliament that placed gender onto the agenda and ensured that it became a consistent central focus, along with geographical balance (European Parliament 2013; Guerrina et al. 2018, 1044).

Nonetheless, the European Parliament had little role to play following the set-up of the EEAS. Thus its gender advocacy role has not acted as a subsequent motor for gender equality as clearly highlighted by the organigram of the EEAS, and the gender distribution of member states' personnel in such directorates as the EU Military Staff and the Civilian Planning and Conduct Capability (CPCC) (see Chappell and Guerrina 2020). While the idea of gender balance was there at the foundation of the EEAS, the focus was on *adding* women into the EEAS's structures to ensure *adequate* representation. Hence the culture of the EEAS or how gender would be mainstreamed in the organisation or its policies was not part of discussions. Considering the neoliberal gender regime coming from the EU's employment agenda (see Milner in this volume) and militarised masculinity originating from the military component, which was to be part of the EEAS's competences (Chappell and Guerrina 2020; Kronsell 2016), the question remained how prominent a role gender was going to play in the EEAS itself.

Understanding the EEAS as an institutional actor: internal dynamics and institutional connections

The original focus of the EEAS concerned its construction and the development of its core business. There are three general areas of investigation: first, how the EEAS fits into the EU's overarching institutional arena; second, the internal development of the EEAS pertaining to its staffing, training and culture; third, the EEAS's tasks. In what follows we will consider these three areas in turn and link them to the nascent literature on gender and the EEAS, allowing us to identity the gaps in the current literature.

The EEAS and the Commission: partners or competitors?

The EEAS was created in a contested institutional space. Indeed, the Commission successfully managed to retain competences in foreign affairs including enlargement, the European Neighbourhood Policy, and aid highlighting issues of coherence for the EU's CFSP and broader foreign policy role. This grab for competencies set up the Commission and the EEAS as potential competitors, highlighting the idea of a 'turf war' between the two institutions (Furness 2013; Riddervold and Trondal 2017, 40). As Duke (2014, 25) highlights, the EEAS has yet to find its institutional place' and has a confusing view of its role and mission. Hence there is a gap between expectations of the EEAS and 'its ability to deliver', which Duke (2014, 43) attributes to budgets, resources and the member states and other EU institutions lack of willingness to 'give the EEAS the necessary room to develop and grow'.

A more positive view of the institutional landscape has been taken by Bátora (2013), Riddervold and Trondal (2017) and, to a lesser extent, by Shepherd (2016). Bátora states that the EEAS could become an 'innovative kind of diplomatic agency' (Bátora 2013, 610), framing it as an 'interstitial organisation' (Bátora 2013, 599), which brings together conflicting principles, practices and expectations. Thus, the EEAS's origins – combining different policy areas and personnel – could become its strength. More recently, Riddervold and Trondal (2017, 34) consider how the EEAS 'may settle and become "normalised" into families of existing organisations'. They find that the EEAS officials act independently of the member states and that the EEAS is coordinated with the Commission, indicating 'administrative integration', which is an evolution from the earlier competitive atmosphere, contributing to a potential communitisation of CFSP (Riddervold and Trondal 2017, 40, 44). Meanwhile Shepherd highlights that the EEAS has 'the potential to enhance inter-institutional coordination and better connect CSDP with internal security' (Shepherd 2016, 96). Hence, the mainstream literature underlines the evolution of the EEAS from a competitor to a partner for the Commission. However, Shepherd (2016) also introduces the idea of stove-piping, in which tasks get 'stuck' in a particular part of the EU. This is important because the question is whether and how gender has been integrated into the EEAS.

Internal developments in the EEAS

The subsequent potential partnership between the EEAS and the Commission underscores questions relating to whether this is a partnership of equals and how gender norms have been integrated into the EEAS. The EEAS's place in the EU's institutional architecture should be taken as context for its organisation and functioning. Here the focus is on the function of the EU delegations, the background of officials, training and the idea of an *esprit de corps* (Davis Cross 2011; Henökl 2015; Juncos and Pomorska 2016 2014; Vanhoonacker and Pomorska 2013). First, the EU delegations were moved from the Commission into the EEAS and thus the focus is not on their creation but rather on their legitimacy (Maurer and Morgenstern-Pomorski 2018). Although they were largely viewed positively, they still had to 'gain legitimacy', which was done through 'adding value on the ground', although the level of success depended on 'experience of the diplomats' and 'the input of the EU ambassador' (Maurer and Morgenstern-Pomorski 2018, 311, 313). Legitimacy building proved more difficult in international organisational settings where the question remains who speaks for Europe. This raises questions concerning who these officials were, and how success was defined. On what values was success premised and how does gender fit into 'success'?

Regarding the internal creation, Missiroli (2010, 442) states that 'the strategic rationale and ultimate ambition behind the establishment of the EEAS was (and still is) the creation of a common culture and practice among EU officials and diplomats'. In line with this, Davis Cross (2011, 453) highlights that 'EEAS diplomats will naturally identify with one another, and an *esprit de corps* should be virtually automatic'. However, she also stresses that the institutional backgrounds of EEAS staff may be challenging as these may encompass 'organizational and cultural clashes' (Davis Cross 2011, 454). This latter point is taken up by Vanhoonacker and Pomorska (2013, 1316) who emphasise the 'credibility challenge' due to 'divergences in knowledge and expertise' and the fact that they are from 'different epistemic communities' (Vanhoonacker and Pomorska 2013, 1323–1324). Likewise, Henökl (2015, 679) emphasises competing institutional (intergovernmental vs. supranational) logics within the EEAS influencing officials' decision-making. In summary, developing an '*esprit de corps*', with shared beliefs, values, aims and goals, is challenging (Juncos and Pomorska 2014, 302). Despite these challenges, Henökl and Trondal (2015, 1441) confirm that EEAS officials do identify with their primary institution rather than the one they have come from. Juncos and Pomorska (2013, 1338–1340) concur, highlighting support for both the EEAS and the idea of a unified foreign policy.

Training within the EEAS could also be used to build a shared culture or an *esprit de corps* and its absence from the EEAS review was a 'lost opportunity' (Duke 2014, 42; see also Davis Cross 2011; Smith 2013, 1311). Duke (2012, 106–107) notes that that while socialisation is important, nonetheless, knowledge and skills development should be the primary focus of any training. However, Duke (2012, 114) also notes that training could potentially become 'a primary tool for the strategic development of not only the EEAS, but the external action of the European Union itself'. Hence the development of an *esprit de corps*, while not impossible, is difficult to achieve in light of the progress in developing a common perspective concerning the running and tasks of the EEAS and the training imparted. Connecting this to gender, one area of exploration is the extent to which gender is intertwined with officials' identification with the EU and its foreign policy. This interconnects with an *esprit de corps* because, if one is to develop, it will have to integrate a gender dimension.

The question here relates to the impact such a system has had on the promotion of gender within the EEAS. Here Duke (2014, 41) underscores the personal commitment of Catherine Ashton and her role in selecting senior appointments along with Helga Schmidt's role in the professional development of women in the EEAS. Allwood (2019, 7), also points to Ashton's and her successor Federica Mogherini's commitment to 'bring about institutional cultural change'. However, barriers still remain at particular grades. Indeed, one focal point of the literature on the EEAS and gender relates to where are the women in the institution. This includes their seniority, and where within the EEAS they are located. It is important to note that while gender does not equate to women, as Haastrup (2018, 220) argues in the context of institutionalised mediation, 'the treatment of women and their situation within the EU's security institution is essential to understanding how gender works'. Women remain underrepresented at all levels with the exception of traditional women dominated positions such as assistants/secretaries (Novotnà 2015, 426). This is despite Ashton's supposed commitment as highlighted above by Duke (2014). However, the EEAS does not have responsibility for the entirety of its staff base, and more women are being recruited from the EU institutions than from the EU member states (Novotna 2015). Hence some of the responsibility for gender imbalances lies at the door of the member states.

The representation of women has improved under the second HR, Federica Mogherini, although the balance between men and women in senior positions is a long way from reaching parity. The EEAS organigram indicates that the numbers of women in senior positions fluctuates between 19% and 23% depending on the year (Chappell and Guerrina 2020; Davis 2019; European External Action Service 2017; Haastrup 2018; Novotnà 2016, 3). For EU Special Representatives or Special Envoys, just four women have been appointed to these posts out 'of 54 such posts since 1996, and two of these are currently in post' (Davis 2019, 6–7).

It is notable that, within the EEAS and the EU delegations, there are fewer women heading up ambassadorial posts in the EU's strategic partners. In EU delegations to international organisations, e.g. the UN, 'women were in charge of around 60% of these multilateral EU delegations'. Novotnà (2015, 433) suggests that these are seen as 'soft power positions, which in the eyes of some are better filled by women'. Connecting this to Maurer and Morgenstern-Pomorski's (2018) argument above, women leaders can be found where there is difficultly in building legitimacy as opposed to those scenarios where the EU's role is less likely to be questioned. This underscores the idea of women being promoted in situations of political crisis or where the organisation's role is under question.

One might furthermore expect that areas of the EEAS dealing with defence would be less gender equal than those dealing with the civilian side of CSDP. However, this is manifestly not the case (see Chappell and Guerrina 2020). It is thus important to go beyond the numbers and ask why there is a dominance of male bodies. Kronsell (2015) argues that the absence of women reflects traditional understandings of gender and what is security. She further suggests that there is a 'gendered path dependency that naturalizes the association between men, masculinity and military matters' (Kronsell 2016, 110) and includes the construction of men as

The European External Action Service

'protectors, defenders and security actors' of the 'EU homeland femininity' (Kronsell 2016, 111–114). However, the EU's military masculinity is 'civil-minded' with a focus on training rather than warfighting (Kronsell 2016, 114). Hence the way in which the EU's gender regime is constructed leads to a reproduction of gendered inequalities and integrates the civilian element of CSDP with military masculinity. Similarly, Haastrup (2018, 232) finds that because CSDP has been the focus of gender inclusivity, the gendered hierarchies within this policy area have been reproduced in the mediation structures, which has had 'unintended consequences' in the area of mediation. She also highlights the 'narrow view of women's roles', which is built on 'essentialist understandings of what women's roles in conflict … can be' (Haastrup 2018, 228). This reification of traditional gender roles in turn impacts on how seriously gender issues are taken within the EEAS.

Meanwhile, Guerrina et al. (2018) and Guerrina and Wright (2016) underscore a lack of feminist constellations that bring together gender champions, civil society organisations and epistemic communities. Hence 'adding' women to the EEAS does not in itself lead to gender equality. Indeed, Muehlenhoff (2017, 155) underscores that 'simply adding gender equality to existing policies does not necessarily transform them unless a broad understanding of the structural causes of marginalization is included'. To ensure that a gendered agenda is successfully followed within policy-making, a feminist constellation is required. As Guerrina and Wright summarise:

> The EEAS's failure to establish itself as a champion for WPS, the absence of femocrats within the EEAS, the inability of civil society and epistemic communities to find a way to lobby the institution and promote an alternative narrative about security have all contributed to perpetuating the silence of gender in external affairs.
>
> *(Guerrina and Wright 2016, 305)*

Nonetheless Haastrup (2018, 227) points out that there are individual gender focal points who do push the agenda in respect to 'resources for gender inclusive activities' and gender mainstreaming. However, overall there is a lack of gender equality norms in the EEAS, which impacts on its ability to pursue gender sensitive policies and mainstream gender in its workings across the institution in a systematic way.

This issue is taken up by McDonagh and Deiana (2017, 3) who highlight that 'both EEAS/CSDP officials and contributing states also need to address masculine culture, complicity and male privilege' and that the idea of the EU as 'progressive' in comparison to the countries and societies they are engaging in 'evokes colonial undertones'. This emphasises the question of intersectionality within the inequalities perpetuated by the EEAS, an issue that has been overlooked in current research. This brings us back to the issue of hegemonic masculinity (see Hearn et al. in this volume) in the EEAS and the member states. Overall, the EEAS is part of the problem and fails to lead by example.

Consequently, the most important innovation regarding gender equality and mainstreaming has been the creation in 2015 of the position of Principal Advisor on Gender and on the Implementation of UNSCR 1325, an initiative of Sweden and Finland. In a statement on UNSCR 1325 shortly after being the first person to take up the post, Mara Marinaki (2015) states: 'I will work to enhance the visibility and effective prioritisation of gender and WPS in the EU's external action and to assist the work of the UN, in close consultation with all UN services and agencies'. While the feminist literature considers this a positive step, criticism remains. First, this is not a Special Representative post and thus it does not follow UN identified best practice. Second, the Gender Advisor does not report directly to the HR (see Guerrina et al. 2018;

151

Guerrina and Wright 2016). Finally, the office set up to support the Gender Advisor is small with just two officials, an administrator and a secretary (Chappell and Guerrina 2020; Guerrina et al. 2018; Guerrina and Wright 2016). Nonetheless this is still a recognised improvement and ensures that there is an office that priorities gender equality and mainstreaming and acts as a focal point. There are other officials within the EEAS who also have gender as part of their portfolio such as a gender and human rights advisor in the crisis management and planning directorate (CMPD)[1], a focal point on women's participation in peace processes in the Mediation Support Team, and the Advisor for Equal Opportunities and Careers, created in 2018 and is a role directly attached to the Secretary General (Chappell and Guerrina 2020; Davis 2019; Deiana and McDonagh 2018). However, for gender equality to take hold necessitates the mainstreaming of gender throughout the EEAS, which involves all officials considering the gendered impact of their work, not just those very few officials with gender in their brief. Thus, it is important to 'avoid responsibility for gender equality being assigned to a junior, often, temporary, member of staff' (Allwood 2019, 6).

This has led to several positive steps including more prioritisation of the informal task force on WPS. This has been identified as 'an opening for critical voices seeking to increase the reach of gender mainstreaming' and which has 'a nuanced understanding of the power of gender norms' (Guerrina and Wright 2016, 310). The UN is also an important means of 'providing technical expertise and advice' on UNSCR 1325 (i.e. the Security Council resolution on women and peace and security adopted in October 2000) and gender mainstreaming, and the EEAS acts as 'a willing recipient of new impetus from outside due to a lack of experience and resources', suggesting that the relationship between the UN and the EEAS regarding UNSCR 1325 is 'unique' (Joachim et al. 2017, 113–114). However, as Deiana and McDonagh (2018, 43) highlight, there is still an issue with how gender mainstreaming is understood by officials, which then travels into CSDP operations and missions only in respect to how it serves operational requirements (see Muehlenhoff in this volume). They also point to officials' understanding of gender as a 'women's issue', that 'working with women was enough' and that training on gender mainstreaming was not essential (Deiana and McDonagh 2018, 44; see also Haastrup 2018).

Considering the importance of training in underpinning an *esprit de corps*, the (mis) understanding of gender with a focus on women rather than on men and thus masculinities is problematic. Indeed, gender equality is considered something that needs to be done outside of Europe rather than inside the EEAS, as highlighted by Deaina and McDonagh (2018,46), who state: 'Interviewees … tend to associate questions of gender equality with spaces other than Europe … and crucially with spaces such as Afghanistan. By contrast they tend to present themselves as liberal, progressive and "not discriminators".' This is despite evidence to the contrary, in which a 'pick and mix' approach is applied to gender mainstreaming such that it is supported only if 'framed through an operational language, rather than in terms of gender equality' (Deaina and McDonagh 2018, 47). The universal applicability of WPS, both within and outside of the EU, has been underlined in the Council Conclusions 15086/18 on this particular area in 2018 along with the EU's strategic approach to WPS of the same year (see Muehlenhoff in this volume).

The EEAS as a foreign policy actor

The final area concerns the policies the EEAS pursues and how far the institution can be an autonomous actor (Furness 2013). HR Ashton, in particular, thought of the EU as a 'civilizing force' reflecting the EU's normative approach and placed emphasis on the EU neighbourhood including developing strategic partnerships (Vanhoonacker and Pomorska 2013, 1326). Again,

The European External Action Service

this connects with McDonagh and Deiana's (2017, 3) point above about 'colonial undertones', which points to a 'white saviour' narrative and underscores cultural bias.

Meanwhile Bátora (2013, 606) outlines a range of tasks given to the EEAS under external action including not just diplomacy but also 'political engagement, development assistance and civil and military crisis management', which have met with mixed success. Indeed, CSDP was sidelined under HR Ashton for example. Hence considering the importance of the civilian dimension to the EEAS role, this might imply that gender mainstreaming becomes easier than might otherwise be the case with a more defence-led agenda due its existence in communitised EU policies, while also being mindful of Shepherd's (2016) idea of stove-piping.

Looking at the principal–agent relationship between the EU member states, the Commission and the EEAS, Furness (2013) underscores the lack of EEAS autonomy in areas such as CSDP and diplomacy where it is a facilitator rather than an independent actor. Wessel and Van Vooren (2013) concur in so far as diplomatic and consular protection are concerned. They identify a tension between the EU's ambitions and international law as well as a schism between the EU and member states in areas that are intergovernmental and thus are seen to be under the latter's prerogative. Smith (2013, 1308) points to divisions between development cooperation and security policy agendas as well as between humanitarian assistance and emergency/disaster response agendas leading to a clash between the EEAS and the Commission. Furness and Gänzle (2017, 483–484) also highlight tensions regarding issues of competences between these two organisations and underscore that EEAS officials consider the institution to focus on foreign affairs and defence rather than development. They subsequently highlight the persistence of 'pillar thinking', although this was abolished in the Lisbon treaty (Furness and Gänzle 2017, 484). This is despite the fact that the HR Federica Mogherini located her office in Berlaymont, i.e. the Commission's headquarters, rather than in the EEAS building across the street at Place Schuman, following a request from Commission President Juncker (Furness and Gänzle 2017, 482; Henökl 2015, 679–680). Of key concern is the EU's lack of strategy which impinges on the EEAS's ability to set priorities 'because they will not have a strong sense of the organization's interests beyond maximizing its own bureaucratic responsibilities' (Furness 2013, 124; see also Furness and Gänzle 2017, 481). However, the question is where gender appears in any such strategy, particularly in respect to the 2016 EU Global Strategy (see Muehlenhoff in this volume).

Linking this to a normative gender dimension, raises questions concerning the EEAS's ability to promote EU norms in the context of EU member states' conflicting opinions on the role of the EEAS that circumscribes its action. Moreover, the EEAS and certain EU member states are still equating gender with women and the rationale for including women relates to the effectiveness in implementing tasks rather than seeing gender equality as a fundamental norm to be implemented because it is right to do so (Bratosin D'Almeida et al. 2017; Guerrina and Wright 2016, 307). Hence, men are the 'norm' and naturally associated with the EEAS and its tasks, while women are 'other'. Bratosin D'Almeida, Haffner and Hörst (2017, 317) underscore that when women take up positions, particularly in conflict environments or in male-dominated areas such as the police, their competence to do the job can be questioned by their male colleagues and that 'women from civilian backgrounds faced even greater prejudice'. It is here that the visibility of the Gender Advisor in visiting missions and operations is particularly important in advancing work on gender (Bratosin D'Almeida et al. 2017, 320). Additionally, as the personnel come from the member states, challenging gendered structures of power requires the EEAS and member states to work together, something which is rather difficult considering the difference in gender norms between the member states. Finally, Allwood (2019, 12, 14) points to the absence of gender when development (see Debusscher in this volume) intersects with other external policy areas such as migration and climate change, where the 'discourse of crisis' is attached. This

153

indicates that other agendas take over, and thus gender gets lost, as it is not prioritised, rather than getting stuck in one part of the EU's institutional structure, as stove-piping would suggest.

Researching gender and the EEAS: a call to action

Considering the debates outlined, the focus of this section is to highlight a range of different areas where a gender lens could be applied to create new understandings of the EEAS as an institution, to underscore how structures of power can be challenged and changed thus connecting to the emancipatory project of feminist research. This chapter has demonstrated that there is a developing literature that explores gender within the EEAS, an area that the mainstream literature fails to engage with in any meaningful way. However, significant research gaps remain when exploring the EEAS's lack of success in closing the gender gaps despite its seeming commitment to do so. This raises several areas for further research. The first is how the EEAS and the individual member states define gender, gender equality and gender mainstreaming. For some member states, gender simply equates to women and girls, leading to a particular understanding of gender equality and mainstreaming (for gender regimes see von Wahl in this volume). Considering that one third of officials come from the member states it is imperative that a closer examination is provided on this issue.

Second, research on human resources is required, particularly on what work the EEAS is doing to improve internal gender equality. The Secretary General created two task forces on equal opportunities and careers resulting in one report each with recommendations in 2017. Subsequently an implementation roadmap was put together. These policies need fully assessing along with recent structural changes to the EEAS as underlined in the recent organigram released in 2019. Bacchi's (1999) 'what is the problem represented to be' approach acts as a relevant starting point. This leads to particular solutions depending on how this is framed. Is it women whom are responsible for their own empowerment as per neoliberal rationality (see Muehlenhoff 2017)? Why is there a focus on gender equality? Is it because this is a key EU norm or, because of reasons related to the EEAS's functionality, i.e. that more diverse teams make better teams? Indeed, there is little explicit research on intersectionality in the context of the EEAS. The only characteristic taken into account in hiring processes is gender and this may have led to a focus on gender without the necessary thought being given to LGBTQI+, race, religion, age or class for example and how these structural power inequalities interact with gender (see Solanke in this volume). Hence it is not just about 'adding' people from diverse backgrounds to create a better functioning EEAS, but to consider what are the barriers to preventing people from these backgrounds to consider the EEAS as a place to work. How is the EEAS constructed as a workplace and what training is being done to facilitate equality and diversity? Although there is some understanding that family-friendly policies are needed, the 'problem' appears to be placed on women not applying, particularly from the member states, rather than looking at the gendered structures and tasks in the EEAS which may perpetuate inequality and gender stereotyping.

Third, the civilian areas of the EEAS need to be further explored institutionally, particularly regarding gender regimes. This is important considering that the human rights, global and multilateral issues directorate, which includes civilian areas such as development, migration and human security, has not been a central feature of feminist research (although see Allwood (2019) regarding development policy; see Debusscher in this volume). Additionally, considering that human rights and gender are often subsumed together in the security and defence areas of the EEAS, it is critical to understand how gender is integrated in this directorate. Is this different to the military and, if so, how? Moreover, what roles are women and men expected to play and how gendered are these? As has been highlighted in the military domain, increasing the number of women in military operations is seen to be 'good' not because it is a norm but because it makes these operations more effective (see Guerrina and Wright 2016; Muehlenhoff 2017). This leads to a neoliberal understanding of gender equality in which gender needs to be useful in order to be engaged with. Hence women are not the 'norm' in the masculinised institution of the EEAS and the activities it performs. They are thus reduced to a resource to be fitted into the EEAS as a security institution rather than the EEAS being transformed into a gender-sensitive body which puts gender equality at the forefront of its developing *esprit de corps*.

Conclusion

In summary, the puzzle at the centre of this chapter is how the EU can, on the one hand, purport to have gender equality as part of its DNA (European External Action Service 2015), while, on the other hand, have significant difficulties in promoting and achieving gender equality within the EEAS. Building on feminist institutionalist (see MacRae and Weiner in this volume) and gender regime literature, feminist scholarship has started to interrogate the hegemonic masculinities inherent in the EEAS. While the mainstream literature has underscored the idea of building an *esprit de corps* and highlighting issues of coherence within the EU's foreign and security policy architecture, there is no consideration regarding how gender norms would enter such an *esprit de corps* or how they would travel from the Commission to the EEAS.

Starting with Enloe's (1990) 'where are the women' this chapter highlighted the lack of women within the EEAS's senior leadership team, proliferation of male bodies in the militarised components of the EEAS and how militarised masculinity has travelled to the civilian dimension (Haastrup 2018; Kronsell 2016). Work by Guerrina et al. (2018) and Guerrina and Wright (2016) has also underscored the lack of feminist constellations as a block to gender equality. Clearly the implementation of gender equality throughout the EEAS in Brussels and in the EU delegations would lead to a more gender-sensitive approach in EU officials' engagements in the field and a deeper understanding of the gender agenda rather than it being seen as an 'add on' to existing more important security activities. The application of feminist lenses to the EEAS as an institution, how it is structured, the location of gender and its relative importance is essential to a policy area which has traditionally been seen to be 'gender neutral'.

Note

1. The EEAS has been re-structured and the CMPD no longer exists. Instead security and defence activities are located inter alia within the following departments: Integrated Approach for Security and Peace, and Security and Defence Policy.

References

Allwood, G (2019): Gender equality in European Union development policy in times of crisis, *Political Studies Review*, Special Issue, 1–17, URL: https://doi.org/10.1177/1478929919863224.

Bacchi C (1999): *Women, Policy and Politics: The Construction of Policy Problems*, London: Sage.

Bátora J (2013): The 'Mitrailleuse effect'. The EEAS as an interstitial organization and the dynamics of innovation in diplomacy, *Journal of Common Market Studies* **51** (4), 598–613.

Bratosin D'Almeida I, Haffner R, Hörst C (2017): Women in the CSDP: strengthening the EU's effectiveness as an international player, *European View* **16** (2), 313–324.

Chappell, L and Guerrina R (2020): Understanding the gender regime in the European External Action Service, *Cooperation and Conflict*, 1–20, URL: https://doi.org/10.1177/0010836719895296.

Council of the European Union (2009): *Presidency report to the European Council on the European External Action Service*, 14930/09, Brussels: Council of the European Union.

Davis, L (2019): Civil Society Dialogue Network Background Paper EU Support to Women Mediators: Moving Beyond Stereotypes, EPLO Working Paper, URL: http://eplo.org/wp-content/uploads/2019/05/EPLO_CSDN_Background-Paper_EU-Support-to-Women-Mediators.pdf (download: 4 April 2020).

Davis Cross M (2011): Building a European diplomacy. Recruitment and training to the EEAS, *European Foreign Affairs Review* **16** (4), 447–464.

Deiana M, McDonagh K (2018): 'It is important, but …': Translating the Women Peace and Security (WPS) agenda into the planning of EU peacekeeping missions, *Peacebuilding* **6** (1), 34–48.

Duke S (2012): Diplomatic training and the challenges facing the EEAS, *The Hague Journal of Diplomacy* **7** (1), 95–114.

Duke S (2014): Reflections on the EEAS Review, *European Foreign Affairs Review* **19** (1), 23–44.

Enloe C (1990): *Bananas, Beaches and Bases,* Berkeley, Los Angeles: University of California Press.

European External Action Service (2015): 'Statement by First Vice-President Timmermans, High-Representative/Vice-President Mogherini and Commissioners Mimica, Avramopoulos, Thyssen, Stylianides and Jourová on the Occasion of International Women's Day', 8 March 2015, URL: http://europa.eu/rapid/press-release_STATEMENT-15-4573_en.htm (download 20 August 2019).

European External Action Service (EEAS) (2017), *Organisation Chart*. 1 June

European Parliament (2013): *Achieving Geographical and Gender Balance in the European External Action Service*, EXPO/B/AFET/2012/02, URL: www.europarl.europa.eu/RegData/etudes/etudes/join/2013/457106/EXPO-JOIN_ET(2013)457106_EN.pdf (download 20 August 2019).

Furness M (2013): Who Controls the European External Action Service? Agent Autonomy in EU External Policy, *European Foreign Affairs Review* **18** (1), 103–126.

Furness M, Gänzle S (2017): The security–development nexus in European Union foreign relations after Lisbon: policy coherence at last?, *Development Policy Review* **35** (4), 475–492.

Guerrina R, Chappell L, Wright KAM (2018): Transforming CSDP? Feminist triangles and gender regimes, *Journal of Common Market Studies* **56** (5), 1036–1052.

Guerrina R, Wright KAM (2016): Gendering normative power Europe: Lessons of the women, peace and security agenda, *International Affairs* **92** (2), 293–312.

Haastrup T (2018): Creating Cinderella? The unintended consequences of the women peace and security agenda for EU's mediation architecture, *International Negotiation* **23** (2), 218–237.

Henökl TE (2015): How do EU foreign policy-makers decide? Institutional orientations within the European External Action Service, *West European Politics* **38** (3), 679–708.

Henökl TE, Trondal J (2015): Unveiling the anatomy of autonomy. Dissecting actor-level independence in the European External Action Service, *Journal of European Public Policy* **22** (10), 1426–1447.

Joachim, J, Schneiker, A and Jenichen, A (2017): External networks and institutional idiosyncrasies. The Common Security and Defence Policy and UNSCR 1325 on women, peace and security, *Cambridge Review of Internaitonal Affairs*, **30** (1), 105–124.

Juncos AE, Pomorska K (2013): 'In the face of adversity'. Explaining the attitudes of EEAS officials vis-à-vis the new service, *Journal of European Public Policy* **20** (9), 1332–1349.

Juncos AE, Pomorska K (2014): Manufacturing esprit de corps: the case of the European External Action Service, *Journal of Common Market Studies* **52** (2), 302–319.

Kronsell A (2015): Sexed bodies and military masculinities. Gender path dependence in EU's Common Security and Defense Policy, *Men and Masculinities* **19** (3), 1–26.

Kronsell A (2016): The power of EU masculinities. A feminist contribution to European integration theory, *Journal of Common Market Studies* **54** (1), 104–120.

Marinaki M (2015): 15th anniversary and Global Review of UNSCR 1325, 13 November 2015, URL: https://eeas.europa.eu/headquarters/headquarters-homepage/5846/node/5846_ro (download 20 August 2019).

McDonagh K, Deiana M (2017): Add Women and Hope? Assessing the Gender Impact of the EU Common Security and Defence Policy (CSDP) Missions, Policy Report, Dublin: Dublin City University.

Novotnà T (2015): Women in the EEAS and EU Delegations: Another Post-Westphalia Change?, in: Spence D, Batora J (eds.): *The European External Action Service European Diplomacy Post-Westphalia*, Basingstoke: Palgrave Macmillan, 392–402.

Novotnà T (2016): Not a leap but a step in the right direction. Mogherini's structural and personnel reform of the EU's diplomatic service, *Europeum Monitor*, March.

MacRae H (2010): The EU as a gender equal polity: myths and realities, *Journal of Common Market Studies* **48** (1), 155–174.

Maurer H, Morgenstern-Pomorski JH (2018): The quest for throughput legitimacy. The EEAS, EU delegations and the contest structures of European diplomacy, *Global Affairs* **4** (2–3), 305–316.

Missiroli A (2010): *The EU 'Foreign Service': Under Construction*, RSCAS Policy Papers 2010/04, Florence: European University Institute.

Muehlenhoff H (2017):Victims, soldiers, peacemakers and caretakers: the neoliberal constitution of women in the EU's security policy, *International Feminist Journal of Politics* **19** (2), 153–167.

Riddervold M, Trondal J (2017): Integrating nascent organisations. On the settlement of the European External Action Service, *Journal of European Integration* **39** (1), 33–47.

Shepherd AJK (2016): CSDP and the Internal–External Security Nexus, in: Chappell L, Mawdsley J, Petrov P (eds.): *The EU, Strategy and Security Policy. Regional and strategic challenges*, Abingdon: Routledge, 87–103.

Smith ME (2013): The European External Action Service and the security–development nexus. Organizing for effectiveness of incoherence, *Journal of European Public Policy* **20** (9), 1299–1315.

Vanhoonacker S, Pomorska K (2013): The European External Action Service and agenda-setting in European foreign policy, *Journal of European Public Policy* **20** (9), 1316–1331.

Wessel R, Van Vooren B (2013): The EEAS's diplomatic dreams and the reality of European and international law, *Journal of European Public Policy* **20** (9), 1350–1367.

13

The politics of gender in the field of European agencies

Sophie Jacquot and Andrea Krizsán

Agencies are important instruments of European governance. The European Union (EU) itself differentiates between four main types of agencies: agencies under Common Security and Defense Policy, EURATOM agencies and bodies, executive agencies (set up for a limited period by the European Commission to help manage EU programs), and decentralized agencies. This chapter focuses on this last type, i.e. agencies set up for an indefinite period and aimed at supporting the EU institutions in the elaboration and implementation of EU policies. These are defined as "EU level public authorities with a legal personality and a certain degree of organizational and financial autonomy that are created by acts of secondary legislation in order to perform clearly specific tasks" (Kelemen and Tarrant 2011, 929). Based on these characteristics they are classified as independent structures. However, some authors consider them as "semi-autonomous", given that they receive funding directly from the EU budget and are subject to supervision of the Commission – and indirectly of the European Parliament (EP) through budget control (Andoura and Timmerman 2008). Agencies' existence is justified either by the need to perform tasks of technical nature or to manage an issue within the framework of European competences. With transfer of competences to the EU, by 2014 there were over 30 independent EU agencies active in highly specialized sectors, including gender equality. Academic literature devotes increasing attention to EU agencies (Trivino and Jordana 2016). In general, it is important to remember that agencies are an integral part of the administrative network of the EU, which marks an important difference from non-governmental organizations such as the European Women's Lobby (EWL), or expert groups such as the European Equality Law Network, which are not part of the EU's administrative constellation.

While agencies are frequently investigated in their own right with designated theoretical lenses, the gender and politics literature has also paid attention to their powers, especially with regard to women's policy and gender equality agencies. Widely advocated for within the UN Women's World Conference processes, women's policy agencies are recognized as fundamental policy instruments. These are instruments of state feminism and can be "state-based structures at all levels and across all formal government arenas assigned to promote the rights, status, and condition of women or strike down gender-based hierarchies" (McBride and Mazur 2010, 655). The 1995 Beijing Platform for Action provided a blueprint for the creation of institutional mechanisms enabling the advancement of women as "the central policy-coordinating unit inside government. Its main task is to support government-wide mainstreaming of a gender-equality perspective in all policy areas" (United Nations 1995). As such, gender equality agencies are instruments for women's voices, for knowledge production and coordination in the gender equality project.

We look at how gender equality is articulated in the arena of agencies coming from gender and politics and EU governance literatures. We aim to understand if, and how, the importance given to independent agencies as gender equality advancement mechanisms by gender advocates is effective within the EU regulatory system, and to what degree. Gender equality agencies are relevant from a variety of perspectives. First, gender equality policy is a specialized field in the EU, which has its own specific agency: the European Institute for Gender Equality (EIGE). The politics leading to EIGE's creation and the role and efficiency of EIGE in the framework of EU gender policy is one of the issues we discuss. Second, the field of anti-discrimination and the EU Agency for Fundamental Rights (FRA), created to address broader questions of inequality, is another policy area of relevance for gender. FRA has gender equality among the rights it has to cover, and some of its activities are crucially contributing to this purpose. Third, gender mainstreaming (GM) is the principle guiding the EU approach to gender equality. As such, gender should become a horizontal principle integrated in the work of all EU agencies. Whether this is the case, to what extent, and through what mechanism is also an important yet under-researched issue. Finally, gender equality bodies (agencies) are one of the "hard law" based components of gender equality, thus, being an integral part of Europeanization in the field.

In the chapter, we first look at theoretical debates around agencies in mainstream literature. We then turn to each of the four perspectives outlined above to understand how EU agencies are relevant for gender. We conclude with some remarks on the potential impact of recent political changes, including the economic crisis and attacks on gender equality, and with identifying gaps in research and literature in the field for future consideration.

Agencies as a (new) form of governance in the EU

Two main ideas stood at the basis of creating European-level independent agencies: first, the need for independent expert knowledge to support implementation and monitoring of various European policies, and, second, discussions around centralization vs. power delegation in a changing context of legitimacy in the EU.

Although a first wave led to the creation of Community-level agencies in the 1970s, the number grew significantly during the 1990s in the wake of the single market program (Majone 1996). This is referred to as the second wave of "agencification" (Andoura and Timmerman 2008). The basic concern behind the development of the EU's regulatory capacity at this time was the necessity to reconcile free movement of goods with protection imperatives (in fields such as environmental or consumer protection, food safety, public health, workers' health and safety, etc.). This led the Commission – with a mandate from the Council – to set up autonomous structures in which expertise could be developed and shared.

In parallel, agencies came as responses to power-sharing dilemmas within the EU. Institutional complexity, that is to say the multiplicity of sites of power, decision and execution, is one of the long-time trademarks of European governance. From the outset, member states conceived a polycentric institutional system that would avoid any concentration of power. Since the beginning of the 1990s, the EU has confronted a two-pronged legitimacy crisis: on the one hand, citizens are in increasing defiance of the European building process; on the other hand, member states are expressing ever-greater distrust, or even resistance, towards the power-delegation mechanisms. It is this double-faced phenomenon that has prompted the development of what has been called "new governance" as a solution to the EU's legitimacy crisis, and the onset of a third wave of agency creation, which accounts for more than 60% of the total of EU independent agencies (Tömmel and Verdun 2009). Independent agencies were indeed one of the instruments of the new European governance that could contribute to developing the EU's modus operandi by introducing a model of "governance by delegation" (Boussaguet et al. 2011). In this context, the idea behind the creation of independent agencies was the delegation of a number of prerogatives both from the European Commission and from the member state level to autonomous European-level administrative structures. This third wave, around the start of the new millennium, was embedded in this governance turn in the context of debates on legitimacy and transparency in policies and in the European system, along with demands for the Commission to systematically ground its proposals based on scientific data. New forms of EU regulation are based on the principle of a supposedly neutral technical and scientific expertise, aimed at informing political decision – what Majone called "the primacy of information over persuasion" (Majone 1997, 263). The recent multiplication of agencies reflects both the centrality of expertise and technocratic policy work, and the demands on delegation of power in the context of the legitimacy crisis.

Recent analyses of EU agencies (32 of them) show that, despite the intention for agencies to bring decentralization and improved control by member states over a variety of policy issues, in practice the activities of most agencies are under the control of the European Commission as a "parent" rather than a "partner" (Egeberg et al. 2014). Agencies tend to serve as facilitators of EU policy implementation through enforcement mechanisms, various regulatory activities or through production and dissemination of knowledge and expertise and networking with national policy agents. Some literature places different forms of agencies according to their functions on a spectrum with quasi-regulatory enforcement agencies as the strongest at one end of the scale, and information-providing agencies as the weakest at the other end of the spectrum (Trivino and Jordana 2016).

EIGE was created in 2006 (inaugurated in 2010), to "contribute to and strengthen the promotion of gender equality, including in all EU policies and the resulting national policies" (https://eige.europa.eu/about). FRA was inaugurated in 2007, to collect and analyze data on fundamental rights listed in the Charter for Fundamental Rights (including gender equality). With their introduction the EU has now made gender equality a policy domain addressed by EU agencies. The creation of these two agencies has been part of the trend towards "governance by delegation", but is also very much in line with the demand for information and expertise especially in the context of GM. Compared to other EU agencies – in terms of independence and distribution of power between member states and the European Commission – Egeberg et al. (2014) classify both EIGE and FRA as agencies subordinated under their "parent" DG (Justice) more than accountable to member states. Looking at their function, both EIGE and FRA classify as information and networking service providers to the Commission (Trivino and Jordana 2016). That is, both are on the less independent and more limited mandate end of the spectrum of EU agencies and clearly not endowed with a regulatory mandate.

The European Institute for Gender Equality

The creation process of EIGE

Gender equality was first made part of EU administration structures in 1976 when the first specific unit on equal treatment at work for women and men was created in DG V (Employment and Social Affairs), alongside with the Women's Information Service in DG X (Information).

A permanent EP Committee on Women's Rights and Gender Equality (FEMM) was also made part of EU structures in 1984 (see Ahrens and Rolandsen Agustín (European Parliament) in this volume). These structures were further complemented with a series of committees, high-level groups and expert groups dealing with gender equality (Jacquot 2015). The idea of supplementing this institutional regime with an independent structure aimed at coordinating and diffusing information and knowledge on the subject within the EU system was first evoked in the mid-1990s.

This idea of an independent agency responsible for providing expertise on gender equality and supporting policy-making was supported by Sweden, which organized a first joint seminar with EU partners on this question as early as 1999 (Hubert and Stratigaki 2011, 179). The rationale for its creation consisted of three aspects: systematic knowledge production, legitimacy and participation, and the need to keep gender equality policy clearly identifiable (European Parliament 2004; EWL 2005). A resolution and an EP report followed in 2004 and the Commission officially proposed the EIGE creation in 2005. The new EIGE was finally established by a regulation of the EP and the Council in 2006 (Regulation (EC) No 1922/2006). The operational and functional budget was agreed in 2007, yet, because of recruitment problems, EIGE became fully operational only in 2010. The objectives adopted were more scientific and technocratic than political, compared to the originally targeted ones. The focus was more on knowledge management than production, and also the formal participation of women's organization was limited (Hubert and Stratigaki 2011, 170).

The institutional and political compromises found during the long negotiation period had a direct impact on the functioning of the new structure. Firstly, EIGE has been installed in Vilnius, away from the other EU institutions, complicating its initial relationship with other sectoral actors. Secondly, its budget was very small compared to other agencies – it has only one third of the budget allocated to FRA at its disposal; yet, the administrative burden imposed on it was equivalent to other, much larger agencies. Hence, a large part of the budget had to be allocated for handling administrative burdens, at the expense of content. Third, the composition of the internal governance bodies has awarded a large part of the decisional power to representatives of member states and a small part to civil society organizations.[1] These aspects have strongly hindered EIGE's ability of finding a place in the "velvet triangle" (Woodward 2004), or policy community, of the EU gender equality policy. Many DG Justice officials, EP members, members from the EWL and from the EIGE forum of experts used to express skepticism and dissatisfaction with the functioning of EIGE in its first years of existence (Jacquot 2014, 312, 313f). Weaknesses were visible not only in how EIGE performed on the participation objective but also in its performance regarding the knowledge-production objective, given its limited in-house expertise and the need to subcontract most tasks under conditions of stringent European Commission administrative rules. However, recent accounts underline its progressive professionalization. The same findings could be applied with regard to its relations with the main members of the EU gender equality policy community. After a rocky start, exchanges have progressively developed, even if distance remains and confirms that EIGE has more the status of a dependent "parent" than of an autonomous "partner" (Egeberg et al. 2014).

As mentioned before, a recent comparative assessment of activities of EU agencies (Trivino and Jordana 2016) classifies EIGE as mainly an information provider and networking service entrusted with both limited mandate and autonomy. EIGE's objectives are stated in its founding regulation:

> to contribute to and strengthen the promotion of gender equality, including gender mainstreaming in all Community policies and the resulting national policies, and the fight against discrimination based on sex, and to raise EU citizens' awareness of gender equality by

providing technical assistance to the Community institutions, in particular the Commission, and the authorities of the Member States.

(EC Regulation 1922/2006, Article 2)

To our knowledge, no systematic research on EIGE activities exists. Based on a non-systematic search of their website, the main areas of activity are the preparation of the gender equality index, provision of technical knowledge on violence against women, and some selected areas for GM such as gender in research and academia. The website also operates as a hub for information, data, policies, and expertise on gender equality, broken down by policy fields. However, in the absence of a more thorough assessment, it is unclear how systematic these sets of data are and to what extent they serve as a source of knowledge for GM.

One of its most widely referenced outputs is likely the gender equality index (https://eige. europa.eu/gender-equality-index), which aims to compare countries' degree of gender equality achieved. The index is an interesting example of an instrument produced by gender expertise, which has had some success (both in the media and in terms of use in comparative scholarly works) as a quantitative measurement that offers simplified results and a stylized vision of reality. This index can operate in a "naming and shaming" perspective in line with the new governance and new public management ethos. Beginning in 2019, it will be updated on an annual basis.

Finally, it should be mentioned that EIGE has also became visible in public debates and news lately in connection to organizational anomalies including repeated cases of sexual harassment and budgetary problems around procurement and contracting. These have recently weighted on the relationship between the agency and its partners (Hervey 2018). However, in the absence of systematic research into EIGE's activities it is difficult to discuss the significance and consequences of these problems on the influence of the organization within the EU as well as on how it is perceived in the EU galaxy of agencies.

EIGE and the question of the de-politicization of gender expertise

The creation of EIGE is part of a general trend towards de-politicization linked to a managerial dynamic that affects all organizations responsible for gender equality, as well as a certain number of feminist organizations. As such, the agency is characteristic of the transformation of "feminist activism" and knowledge into "gender expertise" (Cavaghan 2017; Prügl 2013), or of the emergence of "market feminism" (Kantola and Squires 2012) in a general context of "knowledge democracy" at the EU level (Gornitzka and Krick 2018). Indeed, in a situation of high regulatory complexity, of complex and interconnected public problems, EU policy-makers are increasingly expected to draw on specialized and technical information in order to elaborate and formulate "evidence-based" proposals. The "expertization" of contemporary EU governance, or increased reliance of policy-making on knowledge is seen as a way to add procedural legitimacy to policy solutions. However, some voices have raised concerns that this general trend towards a more, or even completely, exclusive technocratic approach to gender equality policy-making will result in gender expertise being hollowed out and emptied of feminist and political perspectives for bureaucratic purposes (Paterson 2010; Verloo 2005; Warat 2018).

Even though it was initially conceived as a tool aimed at producing and distributing gender expertise along with liaising with a variety of gender equality actors, in practice EIGE produces technical knowledge rather than alternatives or a political vision (Hubert and Stratigaki 2011). This focus on evidence-based policy-making contributes to downplay both political mobilization and polarization of public opinion on gender issues, which then appear as less salient. Simultaneously, this makes EIGE more similar to other agencies leading to a dilemma, which concerns many EU independent agencies, but which is particularly acute for gender equality and perfectly illustrated by EIGE's situation. On the one hand, a necessity to produce technical knowledge in order to gain legitimacy for intervening in the policy process exists. Ferguson (2018) claims that in most institutional settings, such as the EU, it is constantly necessary to defend the "validity" of specialist gender expertise. On the other hand, this emphasis on technical expertise contributes to a more general trend towards de-politicization, but also dismantling and marginalization of EU gender equality policy (Jacquot 2015).

Gender vs. diversity? Anti-discrimination and the question of the unification of equality agencies

With the Amsterdam Treaty (1999) and the Charter for Fundamental Rights (2000) coming into force, the EU has not only extended its scope of action on gender equality, but has also introduced the prohibition of discrimination on grounds beyond gender: race and ethnicity, disability, age, sexual orientation, and religion (see Solanke in this volume). Two new directives introduced in the early 2000s have signalled an important shift in EU equality policy from a single focus on gender (up until 2000), to a multiple focus in which a total of six inequality grounds are now protected (Kantola and Nousiainen 2009). This dynamics has now been institutionalized with the von der Leyen Commission and the appointment of a "Commissioner for Equality", with an understanding of "equality" both as gender equality and anti-discrimination, whose portfolio covers "inclusion and equality in all of its senses, irrespective of sex, racial or ethnic origin, age, disability, sexual orientation or religious belief" (https://ec.europa.eu/commission/commissioners/2019–2024/dalli_en). In the same line, the new EU Gender Equality Strategy 2020–2025 highlights the importance of intersectionality as a cross-cutting principle alongside GM.

This shift has had various implications. The extension of the number of protected inequality grounds and, most specifically, the heightened protection against race discrimination, was important progress. The extension of the list can also be analyzed as a move towards levelling protection for all inequality grounds and a way towards better integration of intersectionality (Lombardo and Verloo 2009). Concurrently, gender scholars have noted a number of concerns. The privileged protection gender has previously received was now challenged: rather than celebrating wider overall protection, competition for resources was feared in which the special status of gender was difficult to justify, especially in the context of striving for more efficiency (Cullen 2014). The other worry was about more limited protection of "new" grounds, potentially seen by decision-makers as an alternative to the comprehensive protection gender equality strived for. The newly introduced anti-discrimination approach was largely individualist, with its actions relying heavily on the initiatives of the victims (Kantola 2014; Krizsán 2012). Meanwhile EU-level protection for gender equality was based on the complementarity of three approaches, which in addition to anti-discrimination and equal treatment also included positive action and mainstreaming (Booth and Bennet 2002), implying a much more proactive approach from the executive.

This shift from a single gender focus to one on multiple inequalities not only meant an extension of the *acquis communautaire*. It has also impacted EU-level thinking about the field of equality policy, its location within the EU regulatory framework, and, consequently, EU agencies addressing the field. As the idea of an EU gender equality agency was developing, the anti-discrimination agenda was also strengthened, and questions about the legitimacy of a separate gender equality field were raised and had to be defended. Amidst preparatory work for EIGE, the EU proceeded to also create FRA, in charge of the protection of rights under the Charter of Fundamental Rights. FRA was created as the successor to the European Monitoring Centre on Racism and Xenophobia (EUMC) in Vienna. Throughout this political process and in much of the gender equality literature on EIGE, FRA was perceived as a competitor, a challenge to the legitimacy of the specific gender equality agency (European Parliament 2004; Hubert and Stratigaki 2011; Lombardo and Verloo 2009). Ultimately, the dual structure of EIGE and FRA was maintained with both agencies receiving roughly similar competencies: both working mainly as information providers, and, to some extent, as networkers, but with little to no independent regulatory functions (Trivino and Jordana 2016). No comprehensive research compares them in their competences and activities. However, based on a limited analysis, differences seem evident: FRA has roughly three times EIGE's budget, and a staff that is two times EIGE's staff, besides the geographical marginalization of EIGE (based in Vilnius compared to FRA in Vienna).

The parallel creation of EIGE and FRA has helped to raise questions concerning the maintaining of specific mechanisms and institutional structures aimed at gender equality, and the transversal integration of gender in the broader perspective of anti-discrimination. Yet, what is FRA's role in promoting gender equality? FRA works on the promotion of *all* rights under the Charter – including gender equality. In its early years, worry existed that given FRA's predecessor (EUMC) FRA will be likely to follow the path and make race and ethnicity the core issue for its activities (Lombardo and Verloo 2009). In practice, in the first years of its activities, FRA's output mainly focused on anti-discrimination issues more widely (with few exceptions dealing with procedural questions such as data protection and access to justice). Moreover, FRA conducted one of the most prominent pieces of EU-level gender research in the last decades, the European comparative gender-based violence survey (FRA 2014), and published several related reports. Another important output is the EU-wide survey of LGBT hate crime and discrimination and related reports (FRA 2013). The relevance of its work to gender equality is evident. There is no research available on the rationale for FRA taking up gender topics, whether based on cooperative or rather competitive relations with EIGE.

Mainstreaming gender within EU agencies?

While gender equality became the specific focus of EU agencies only with EIGE and FRA, gender equality and its different aspects are included under activities of various other EU agencies. Even though GM was only introduced as an EU-level principle in 1996 (COM(1996)0067), gender issues were covered already by agencies established in the early waves.

The two agencies created in the first wave both had high relevance to gender equality in the traditional EU policy area for gender equality, i.e. employment. Established in the 1970s, the European Center for the Development of Vocational Training (CEDEFOP) had within its scope policies on vocational training for women, while the European Foundation for the Improvement of Living and Working Conditions (EUROFOUND) dealt with reconciliation of work and care issues. The European Training Foundation (ETF) and the European Agency for Safety and Health at Work (EU OSHA), also of relevance, were established in the second wave. Current websites of all of these agencies devote specific attention to gender equality. However, it is important to underline that no systematic analysis of the gender aspects of these or other agencies is available, which is clearly a major research gap. A brief analysis of all agencies' websites and publications presents rather inconsistent results. While some agencies mention the fact that they include a gender perspective into their work (such as the European Asylum Support Office), and some other include gender as a specific issue of concern (like the European Monitoring Centre for Drugs and Drug Addiction), most of them produce sex-disaggregated statistics but do not take gender into account beyond that. A systematic analysis of how gender is integrated in activities of agencies other than EIGE or FRA would be central to understanding the spread of GM to a large number of EU policy fields.

EIGE is part of different agency networks both at the level of its parent domain (Justice and Home Affairs Agencies) and, more widely, of the network of European agencies. Both of these networks allow EIGE to work towards mainstreaming gender to the activities of other European agencies by introducing gender topics in network meetings or upon presiding these networks. Overall, however, it is important to note that GM has not delivered its promises when it comes to infusing a gender equality perspective in the work of most of the EU agencies. A recent FEMM opinion issues regrets and voices criticisms concerning the lack of implementation of GM in the Commission's budget in general and the absence of a gender perspective in the agencies' work in particular (2018/2166(DEC)).

Europeanization and the transformation of governance through agencies at the national level

Gender equality agencies are also part of the EU gender equality *acquis communautaire*. The *acquis* prescribed the requirement of establishing "equality bodies" for race and ethnicity in its 2000 Race Directive (Council Directive 2000/43/EC). A similar requirement was set for gender in 2002, reasserted in the 2006 Recast Directive (Directive 2006/54/EC). This Directive requires member states to designate a body "for the promotion, analysis, monitoring and support of equal treatment of all persons without discrimination on grounds of sex" (Directive 2006/54/ EC, Article 20). The creation of such bodies for better enforcement of EU norms became a key requirement especially for the new, central and eastern European member states where there was a tendency to harmonize laws with EU equality norms, but do little about their enforcement (Falkner et al. 2008), but also set new requirements for many old member states by explicitly requiring that these bodies provide "independent assistance to victims of discrimination in pursuing their complaints about [sex] discrimination" (Directive 2006/54/EC, Article 20).

Equality bodies are discussed widely in the literature on EU enlargement (Avdeyeva 2015; Bego 2015; Krizsán 2009; see also Chiva in this volume) as easy standards to capture the level of Europeanization. They were feasible indicators not only to measure continued compliance with gender equality norms after accession (Sedelmeier 2009), but also to show eloquently the gendered impact on countries of the economic crisis and de-democratization (Krizsán and Roggeband 2018). Research showed remarkable budget cuts, reframing and even dismantling of gender equality agencies in recent years (Bettio 2012; Kantola and Lombardo 2017) also indicative of the limited importance the EU has devoted to gender dimensions in crisis management (Krizsán and Zentai 2017).

Another strand of literature discusses gender equality agencies in the context of the diversity debate detailed above, where gender equality agencies may have to compete for resources with other inequality grounds. Gender equality agencies in most EU member states, including many central and eastern European new member states (Krizsán 2012), were created much earlier than their introduction was demanded by EU hard law, with the purpose of giving voice to the gender perspective in policy-making. The novelty of the new EU norms was their focus on addressing complaints. In this, the norms defined for race and gender looked similar in that they required now the creation of enforcement agencies for anti-discrimination norms. Nousiainen (2008) has analyzed how the EU favored the development of human rights-based equality bodies at the expense of ombudsman type of equality bodies – the former enjoying more independence, but less political influence and conceiving their work in a less proactive manner. The institutional shifts across Europe were widely discussed (Krizsán et al. 2012; Verloo and Walby 2012). Research showed that despite fears about the disappearance of gender equality agencies by integration within agencies covering all inequality grounds under one institutional umbrella, in most cases Europeanization induced changes ended up adding a new layer of equality institutions. Besides the agencies addressing gender equality already in place, new anti-discrimination enforcement agencies were introduced in many member states, which indeed addressed gender together with several other inequality grounds (Krizsán 2012; Krizsán et al. 2012).

EU agencies and gender in the context of the crisis and illiberalism

The early years of EIGE are characterized by two processes, both detrimental to progress in gender equality: (1) the economic crises are seen to have hit particularly hard on gender equality agencies at national level (Bettio et al. 2012; Kantola and Lombardo 2017; Krizsán and Zentai 2017; see also Kantola and Lombardo in this volume), but also gender equality policy at EU level (Jacquot 2017); (2) the increasing attacks on the legitimacy of the gender equality project, particularly from the far right (Kuhar and Patternote 2017; Verloo and Patternote 2018).

The creation of EIGE was already a contested issue in 2009, at the beginning of the crisis. So, it could be said that it has not suddenly changed the game, but it has intensified a process of dismantling already underway for some time (Jacquot 2015). Backsliding on several aspects of gender equality policies across member states (Kantola and Lombardo 2017) indicate a combination of the failure of GM, in this case in gendering interventions into the crisis (Karamessini and Rubery 2014; Walby 2015), and even the instrumentalization of the economic crisis to dismantle some of the gender *acquis*.

Moreover, attacks on gender equality are a prevalent phenomenon in many European countries (see Siim and Fiig in this volume). They are mainly concentrated on sexuality, family policy, and reproductive rights issues. Yet, especially in countries where populist parties with an anti-gender agenda enter national governments, they also undermine implementation of all gender policies including the functioning of relevant agencies and how they frame their objectives (Krizsán and Roggeband 2018). While these discourses clearly engage with the role of Europe in spreading "gender ideology" (Korolczuk and Graff 2018), their presence in the EU arena is not yet documented very thoroughly. It is unclear if there have been any direct attacks against EIGE or FRA. Yet, importantly, these trends potentially affect EIGE's work and the extent to which FRA's agenda includes gender equality issues or not.

Conclusion and directions for future research

This chapter has taken stock of academic knowledge on gender and EU independent regulatory agencies. We see important research gaps. Except for EIGE and FRA, gender scholarship has been largely silent on the interaction between the system of governance by EU agencies and gender. Considering that this delegation of governance to independent institutions is on the rise in a period of intense legitimacy crisis, analyzing this phenomenon from a gender perspective appears all the more important. Moreover, existing research on EIGE and FRA focuses on the political process of creation (quite similarly with other agencies; see Trivino and Jordana 2016), while limited attention is paid to the analysis of their activities. Further attention should be devoted to their efficiency, conception(s) of gender used, relationship with other agencies (at European level), and with gender equality agencies operating at national level. Also relations developed (if at all) with women's movement actors (at both European and national levels), or independence from the European Commission and member states and their scope of influence are important. As illustrated, independent agencies are not blind spots in EU gender research.

However, the panorama presented here demonstrates that there is still a lot of ground to cover and that agencies are crucial pieces to understand the dynamics of gender politics at EU level.

Indeed, agencies are sometimes considered as satellites within the EU political and institutional system and cosmology. This chapter aims to show that they can be meaningful points of observation concerning the dynamics of gender politics at EU level. Looking at agencies actually shows a number of features of the EU gender equality policy on the eve of the third decade of the 21st century. From a policy design point of view, it underlines the weaknesses of GM as a policy instrument. It also underlines the difficulty in combining positive actions and specific structures for women with a GM commitment. It finally underlines the ambiguities of the institutionalization of intersectionality and diversity at EU level. From an institutional point of view, the functioning of EIGE exemplifies the transformation of the balance of powers within the EU gender equality policy. Indeed, the creation of EIGE means for the Commission an important externalization of its expertise, which has historically been one of its main sources of leverage and influence in order to develop gender equality policy (Mazey 1995). It remains to be seen how this transfer will impact upon the larger governance of the policy sector. More fundamentally, the limited strength and marginality of the agency exemplifies the decreasing importance of both gender expertise and gender equality as a policy field in the EU. Finally, the emergence and evolution of EIGE and FRA illustrate the difficulties of the EU gender equality "velvet triangle" as a support base for policy-making and, ultimately, an attempt to de-politicize gender equality. We see a weak role of civil society actors, and their limited voice in shaping the activities of the agencies, alongside the changing strategies of gender advocates, who have to rely on a less normative and more technical expertise, while not necessarily increasing their chance of being heard in the policy process. Whether a stance of de-politicization remains possible in the current context of attacks on gender equality remains to be seen.

More generally, our analysis shows the fragile and vulnerable nature of gender equality policy and institutions in a period of – both economic and political – crisis. Even though, the creation of EIGE has constituted a way to "normalize" the EU gender equality policy and to apply to this domain the standards of "new" and "good" governance, legitimacy remains an ongoing challenge for gender equality at EU level.

Note

1   EIGE's management board, i.e. its main decision-making body, is made up of a representative of the Commission and 18 representatives of member states, rotating every three years. The Expert Forum (consultative body) is made up of one qualified person (generally from one of the national equality body) appointed by each member state, two persons appointed by the EP and three persons appointed by the Commission (one NGO representative, one union representative and one employer representative).

References

Andoura S, Timmerman P (2008): Governance of the EU: The Reform Debate on European Agencies Reignited, Working Paper 19, European Policy Institutes Network, URL: www.ceps.eu/wp-content/uploads/2009/08/1736.pdf (download: June 6, 2019).

Avdeyeva O (2015): *Defending Women's Rights in Europe Gender Equality and EU Enlargement*, Albany, NY: SUNY Press.

Bego I (2015): *Gender Equality Policy in the European Union,* Basingstoke: Palgrave Macmillan.

Bettio F (2012): Women, men and the financial crisis: seven lessons from Europe, *European Gender Equality Law Review* **2**, 4–13.

Bettio F, Corsi M, D'Ippoliti C, Lyberaki A, Samek Lodovici M, Verashchagina A (2012): *The Impact of the Economic Crisis on the Situation of Women and Men on Gender Equality Policies*, Brussels: European Commission.

Booth C, Bennett C (2002): Gender mainstreaming in the European Union: toward a new conception and practice of Equal Opportunities?, *The European Journal of Women's Studies* 9 (4), 430–446.

Boussaguet L, Dehousse R, Jacquot S (2011): The "Governance Turn" Revisited, in: Dehousse R (ed.): *The Community Method*, Basingstoke: Palgrave Macmillan, 186–198.

Cavaghan R, (2017): *Making Gender Equality Happen. Knowledge, Change and Resistance in EU Gender Mainstreaming*, London: Routledge.

Cullen P (2014): Feminist NGOs and the European Union: contracting opportunities and strategic responses, *Social Movement Studies* 14 (4), 410–426.

Egeberg M, Trondal J, Vestlund NM (2014): Situating EU Agencies in the Political-Administrative Space, *ARENA Working Papers* 6. URL: www.sv.uio.no/arena/english/research/publications/arena-working-papers/2014/wp6-14.pdf (download: June 5, 2019).

European Parliament (2004): *Role of a Future European Gender Institute*, Study for the European Parliament's Committee on Women's Rights and Gender Equality, IPOL/C/IV/2003/16/03.

European Women's Lobby (EWL) (2005): *Position paper of the EWL on the setting up of a European Gender Institute*, Brussels, 30 May, URL: www.womenlobby.org/IMG/pdf/EWL_position_paper_European_gender_institute_EN.pdf (download: June 5, 2019).

Falkner G, Treib O, Holtzleithner E, eds. (2008): *Compliance in the Enlarged European Union. Living Rights or Dead Letters?*, Aldershot: Ashgate.

Ferguson L (2018): Feminist Political Economy Perspectives on Gender Expertise, in: Elias J, Roberts A (eds.): *Handbook on the International Political Economy of Gender*, Cheltenham: Edward Elgar Publishing, 298–310.

Fundamental Rights Agency (FRA) (2013): *EU LGBT Survey – European Union Lesbian, Gay, Bisexual and Transgender Survey – Results at a Glance*, Luxembourg: Publications Office of the European Union.

Fundamental Rights Agency (FRA) (2014): *Violence Against Women: An EU-Wide Survey*, Luxembourg: Publications Office of the EU.

Gornitzka A, Krick E (2018): The Expertisation of Stakeholder Involvement in EU Policymaking, in: Gora M, Holst C, Warat M (eds.): *Expertisation and Democracy in Europe*, London: Routledge, 51–70.

Hervey G (2018): Sexual harassment plagues EU body meant to fight it, *Politico*, April 12, 2018, URL: www.politico.eu/article/sexual-harassment-eu-gender-equality-agency/ (download: June 6, 2019).

Hubert A, Stratigaki M (2011): The European Institute for Gender Equality: a window of opportunity for gender equality policies?, *European Journal of Women's Studies* 18, 169–181.

Jacquot S (2015): *Transformations in EU Gender Equality. From Emergence to Dismantling*, Basingstoke: Palgrave Macmillan.

Jacquot S (2014): *L'égalité au nom du marché?*, Brussels: P.I.E. Peter Lang.

Jacquot S (2017): A Policy in Crisis. The Dismantling of the EU Gender Equality Policy, in: Kantola J, Lombardo E (eds.): *Gender and the Economic Crisis in Europe. Politics, Institutions and Intersectionality*, Basingstoke: Palgrave Macmillan, 27–48.

Kelemen RD, Tarrant AD (2011): The political foundations of the Eurocracy, *West European Politics* 34 (5), 922–947.

Kantola J (2014): The paradoxical gendered consequences of the EU policy on multiple discrimination: The Nordic case, *European Integration online Papers (EIoP)* 18 (7), 1–19, URL: http://eiop.or.at/eiop/texte/2014-007a.htm (download: June 5, 2019).

Kantola J, Lombardo E (2017): *Gender and the Economic Crisis in Europe. Politics, Institutions and Intersectionality*, Basingstoke: Palgrave Macmillan.

Kantola J, Nousiainen K (2009): Institutionalising intersectionality in Europe: legal and political analyzes, *International Feminist Journal of Politics* 11 (4), 459–477.

Kantola J, Squires J (2012): From state feminism to market feminism, *International Political Science Review* 33, 382–400.

Karamessini M, Rubery J, eds. (2014): *Women and Austerity. The Economic Crisis and the Future for Gender Equality*, London: Routledge.

Korolczuk E, Graff A (2018): Gender as "ebola from Brussels": the anti-colonial frame and the rise of illiberal populism, *Signs: Journal of Women in Culture and Society* 43 (4), 797–821.

Krizsán A (2009): From Formal Adoption to Enforcement. Post-Accession Shifts in EU Impact on Hungary in the Equality Policy Field, in: Schimmelfennig F, Trauner F (eds): Post-accession compliance in the

EU's new member states, *European Integration online Papers* **13** (22), URL: http://eiop.or.at/eiop/texte/2009-022a.htm (download: June 5, 2019).

Krizsán A (2012): Equality architectures in central and eastern European countries. A framework for analyzing political intersectionality in Europe, *Social Politics* **19** (4), 539–571.

Krizsán A, Roggeband C (2018): Towards a conceptual framework for struggles over democracy in backsliding states. Gender equality policy in central eastern Europe, *Politics and Governance* **6** (3), 90–100.

Krizsán A, Skjeie H, Squires J, eds. (2012): *Institutionalizing Intersectionality: The Changing Nature of European Equality Regimes*, Basingstoke: Palgrave Macmillan.

Krizsán A, Zentai V (2017): Policy paper summarizing findings on backsliding in equality policies and inclusion measures addressing gender, disability and ethnicity-based inequalities, *Transcrisis* (Deliverable 6.2), URL: www.transcrisis.eu/wp-content/uploads/2017/05/D6.2-Backsliding-in-area-of-constitutional-safeguards-and-independent-institutions-corruption-control-and-general-equality-and-minorities-1.pdf (download: June 6, 2019).

Kuhar R, Paternotte D, eds. (2017): *Anti-Gender Campaigns in Europe. Mobilizing against Equality*, London: Rowman & Littlefield.

Lombardo E, Verloo M (2009): Institutionalizing intersectionality in the European Union?, *International Feminist Journal of Politics* **11** (4), 478–495.

McBride D, Mazur A (2010): *The Politics of State Feminism. Innovation in Comparative Research*, Philadelphia, PA: Temple University Press.

Majone G (1996): *Regulating Europe*, London: Routledge.

Majone G (1997): The new European agencies: regulation by information, *Journal of European Public Policy* **4** (2), 262–275.

Mazey S (1995): The development of EU equality policies: bureaucratic expansion on behalf of women?, *Public Administration* **73** (4), 591–610.

Nousiainen K (2008): Unification (or not) of equality bodies and legislation, *European Gender Equality Law Review* **2**, 24–33.

Paterson S (2010): What's the problem with gender-based analysis?, *Canadian Public Administration* **53** (3), 395–416.

Prügl E (2013): Gender Expertise as Feminist Strategy, in: Caglar G, Prügl E, Zwingel S (eds.): *Feminist Strategies in International Governance*, London: Routledge, 57–73.

Sedelmeier U (2009): Post-Accession Compliance with EU Gender Equality Legislation in Post-Communist New Member States, in: Schimmelfennig F, Trauner F (eds.): Post-accession compliance in the EU's new member states, *European Integration online Papers* **13** (23), URL: http://eiop.or.at/eiop/texte/2009-023a.htm (download: June 5, 2019).

Tömmel I, Verdun A, eds. (2009): *Innovative Governance in the European Union. The Politics of Multilevel Policymaking*, Boulder, CO and London: Lynne Rienner.

Trivino J C, Jordana J (2016): *EU Agencies: A Literature Review*. The Transcrisis Project. URL: www.transcrisis.eu/wp-content/uploads/2016/05/EU-Agencies-A-Literature-Review.pdf (download: June 5, 2019).

United Nations (1995): *Beijing Declaration and Platform for Action*, URL: www.un.org/womenwatch/daw/beijing/pdf/BDPfA%20E.pdf (download: June 5, 2019).

Verloo M (2005): Displacement and empowerment: reflections on the concept and practice of the Council of Europe approach to gender mainstreaming and gender equality, *Social Politics* **12** (3), 344–365.

Verloo M, Patternote D, eds. (2018): The feminist project under threat in Europe. Special Issue, *Politics and Governance* **6** (3).

Verloo M, Walby S (2012): Introduction. The implications for theory and practice of comparing the treatment of intersectionality in the equality architecture in Europe, *Social Politics* **19** (4), 433–445.

Walby S (2015): *Crisis*, Cambridge: Polity Press.

Warat M (2018): Uneasy Relation: Gender Expertise and Gender Equality Policy in Poland, in: Gora M, Holst C, Warat M (eds.): *Expertisation and Democracy in Europe*, London: Routledge, 146–170.

Woodward A (2004): Building Velvet Triangles: Gender and Informal Governance, in: Christiansen T, Piattoni S (eds.): *Informal Governance and the European Union*, Cheltenham: Edward Elgar, 76–93.

14

The Court of Justice of the EU and judicial politics

Jessica Guth and Sanna Elfving

This chapter deals with the Court of Justice of the European Union (CJEU) as both a political and legal institution. The CJEU has often been described as political because of its prominent role in developing EU law as well as promoting further integration within the EU through its judgments. These judgments constitute a major source of EU law and apply in all member states. In terms of equality law, the judgments concerning equal pay, pensions, retirement ages and the protection afforded to workers due to pregnancy and maternity have been very influential, and many of these cases have also developed the EU legal order and strengthened its influence in member states (see Guth 2016). This first section briefly outlines the court's composition, power and position. Section two focuses on existing work on gendering the CJEU, outlining key themes and key gaps. Research on the CJEU can be divided into two main categories: first, gendering the court itself and how it works and, second, the case law i.e. the outcomes of that work. These approaches highlight how applying a gender lens can help us better understand the power dynamics and relationships at play in the institutional structure. The final section of this chapter focuses on the way forward and, particularly, the relationship between the CJEU and the European Court of Human Rights (ECtHR) as an area for future research. In spite of the CJEU's and the ECtHR's very distinct jurisdictions, their decisions in areas of law where fundamental human rights play a role are mutually reinforcing, and therefore the relationship between these courts could be important for the future of substantive gender equality.

The CJEU is made up of two individual courts. In the post-Brexit Court of Justice (ECJ) there are 27 judges plus 11 Advocates General, and on the General Court there are two judges from each member state (54). Out of the current total 92 judicial-level appointments, only 22 are women (seven in the ECJ[1] and 15 on the General Court) and, historically, very few women have been appointed, leaving the CJEU dominated by men. The CJEU's main role is to enforce EU law in a consistent and uniform way and thus accountable act as an arbitrator between individuals, organisations, and the political institutions holding the EU's executive and legislative power, namely the European Parliament, the Commission and the Council (see Ahrens and Rolandsen Agustín (European Parliament), Hartlapp et al. and Abels in this volume). Its decisions arguably drive the legal integration of Europe, necessitating 'cooperation among Member States in economic, political, and social domains' (Peritz 2018, 427). The CJEU deals principally with three types of legal procedures, each promoting legal integration to varying degrees. The so-called infringement proceedings are used by the Commission to bring a non-compliant member state in line in case of a breach of EU law. Further, private and public institutions, at both the national and EU level, may seek annulment of acts of the EU institutions due to lack of competence or breach of procedural rules directly before the CJEU. Lastly, and perhaps most importantly, citizens and businesses may challenge any national rules that are inconsistent with EU law. They do this in their national courts, which, in the course of their proceedings, may seek preliminary rulings on specific legal questions from the CJEU.

Scholarship on judicial politics lies at the intersection of law, social and political science. It theorises and empirically studies the relationships and balance of power between judiciary, the legislature and the executive (Dunoff and Pollack 2017, 233). Literature on the judicialisation of politics tends to focus on the changes to the status of law, the values influencing judicial decision-making, and revision of the balance of power between different government agencies (Hersant and Vigour 2017, 292). The judicial politics methodology often combines 'a qualitative research grounded at least partly in observation and interview … with the study of documents, videos, or quantitative data (systematic case analyses)' (Hersant and Vigour 2017, 294). The traditionally understood form of judicial politics generates statistical analysis of case law which is subsequently used to measure judicial behaviour (Chalmers and Chaves 2012). This can be done by theorising judges as rational actors who seek to maximise their influence on policy making by realising their policy preferences (Rachlinski et al. 2017). Much of the existing literature focuses on the US federal courts, whereas less has been written about the CJEU judges and the institution (Dunoff and Pollack 2017, 233). According to scholars, the dynamics of EU judicial politics are inseparable from the analysis of the litigated legal norms, identity of the litigants, and the judgment of the CJEU itself, and hence only a few EU legal norms are susceptible to the traditionally understood form of judicial politics (Chalmers and Chaves 2012, 25). We focus on cases brought to the CJEU using the preliminary reference procedure. However, obtaining the empirical evidence to substantiate the extent of political influences in the context of the CJEU, where deliberations are secret and no dissenting opinions are published, is challenging (Dyevre 2010, 303). Additionally, most existing studies take the US federal courts as their starting point, with far fewer studies placing the EU at the centre. In those that do, early work tended to conceptualise the CJEU as an institution doing the bidding of the most powerful member states (see Guth 2016 for a summary of the literature). However, this perspective oversimplifies matters and underestimates the power of judicial independence. Reflecting the growing influence of economic thinking on political and social science, political scientists have increasingly stressed the role of institutional factors as the main determinants of judicial decision-making (Dyevre 2010; Epstein and Knight 2000). Even legal scholars are not oblivious to the fact that the political climate has some bearing on the judges (Adams and Bomhoff 2012; De Londras and Dzehtsiarou 2015; Dzehtsiarou 2018, 90; O'Brien 2017a).

The CJEU is not specifically gender aware even though the case law demonstrates some small victories in the course of its development (Guth and Elfving 2018, 2). Petra Ahrens (2018, 46) concludes that even though the CJEU has been instrumental at times in advancing gender equality, it has been excluded from gender equality policy-making under the Europe 2020 Strategy (COM (2010)2020). Additionally, one could argue that the CJEU has occasionally been viewed as working against the equality agenda (Guth and Elfving 2018). However, since law is not gender neutral, there is very little the CJEU can do to address gender or intersectional inequalities, if national or European legislation is drafted in discriminatory terms, or the legal questions arriving at the court have had gender filtered out of them. Even the most liberal judiciary can only act within the limits of its powers and the confines of the legislation granting those powers.

Gendering the CJEU

There is currently very little work that examines the CJEU as a political and legal institution from a gendered perspective (Guth 2016). Most key publications in this area centre on a consideration of equality law. For instance, Karen Alter and Jeannette Vargas (2000) considered the highly successful litigation strategies of the UK Equal Opportunities Commission, which utilised EU law to drive legal changes in the 1980s. Jo Shaw (2001) has been more critical of the idea that the CJEU is gender aware by pointing out that many of its decisions, which are fundamental in terms of equality law, were self-serving, and that the court has 'cloaked itself in something akin to a feminist cloak almost always only where some gain can be obtained in terms of reinforcing its own legitimacy within the system' (Shaw 2001, 142). Chalmers and Chaves (2012, 37) have arrived at a similar conclusion, that the court's interest in its judgments is principally self-serving, namely 'to secure authority for itself and its work'. Some of the earliest work in this area reminds us that law does not exist in isolation, and that judicial decisions are often the product of political struggles and activism (Cichowski 2007; Hoskyns 1996). Indeed, the role of civil society, legal mobilisation, and strategies that help drive policy areas forward are equally important (Cichowski 2007; Hoskyns 1996; McIntosh Sundstrom et al. 2019). This aspect of how the CJEU functions is often ignored in both political science and legal scholarship. Catherine Hoskyns' 1996 work is fascinating also because it shows how the CJEU approaches diverse types of cases differently. According to her, the CJEU is more gender aware and bold in relation to employment cases, but much more conservative in relation to social security, for example. She therefore reminds us that gendering the CJEU as an institution is not enough; we also need to take into account the context and subject matter of the decisions. Gendering the court means gendering the institution itself, the way it works, and the outcome of that work, namely the judicial decisions.

Gendering the CJEU as an institution and the way it works has not been done frequently. Sophie Turenne (2015, 2017) has explored some of the issues in her work looking at judicial systems from a comparative perspective and, in particular, the extent to which judiciaries can, and should, reflect the societies they serve. Angela Zhang (2016) has considered appointment to the CJEU and judicial independence of the EU judges in some detail and, although her work lacks gendered analysis, it is useful in posing some gendered questions. It highlights that the appointment process has many political hallmarks with all the gendered assumptions and biases that might come with that. Her findings support earlier gendered analysis by Kenney (2002), who likened appointments to the CJEU to diplomatic appointments, which, depending on the context, may reward or punish the nominees. These arguments have been expanded in the authors' own work, which suggests that the CJEU's current composition means that the court overall, and the chambers in particular, remain male dominated to the detriment of diversity of experience (Guth and Elfving 2018, 43–44; Kenney 2013; Malleson 2003).

The existing body of work on the CJEU highlights several key gaps in the literature. Some of these gaps apply generally to the study of the court (although they may exacerbate gendered considerations) and some are gender specific. One of the gaps arises from a lack of access to the CJEU and its judges, which makes understanding of individual motivations of the judges difficult. In the CJEU context the lack of dissenting opinions exacerbates its impenetrability. As a result, there is an absence of a systematic analysis of how the judges' backgrounds impact on their decision-making at this level. Other gaps include the application of a gendered lens to policy areas where gender is less obvious consideration, and the failure to consider multiple forms of discrimination. We deal with these in turn.

In order to fully understand the CJEU and how it operates, we need to understand its personnel. This includes not only the judges and Advocates-General but also others working in the court. Access is, of course, always difficult, but while a detailed analysis of case law in specific areas can tell us something, it cannot provide an understanding of individual judges' decision-making, influence, or the dynamics of judging at the CJEU (Guth and Elfving 2018). We do not have dissenting opinions, information about how decisions were reached, or the extent of any disagreement. We can certainly gain some information about Advocates-General and their opinions; yet, by and large, we need detailed empirical work with the judges and the staff at the CJEU to understand how the personalities, background, training and dynamics shape the institution and its decisions. We know from work on national judiciaries, particularly in the US, that it matters who our judges are (Boyd 2016; Boyd et al. 2010; Collins et al 2010; Glynn and Sen 2015; Rackley 2013; Sotomayor 2002). This work needs to now be applied and tested in the European context. While research in the US has shown that most judges think that, on average, they are more skilful at avoiding the influence of race and gender bias than their colleague (Negowetti 2015; Rachlinski et al. 2017), a gendered analysis shows that judges are not as good at this as they think. According to Sotomayor (2002, 92), 'personal experiences affect what facts judges choose to see'. It is this personal experience that researchers now need to begin to capture in a systematic way.

To fully understand how the CJEU should take gender into account, we need a systematic review of the existing work in order to ask questions that can form the basis of a research agenda that takes us further towards a judicial politics and that is not only gender aware but gender active. We need a more comprehensive understanding of the importance of non-governmental organisations, lobbying and interest groups, as well as advocates, in the process of furthering cases in supranational courts. We need a more holistic understanding of how gender plays out in national systems, particularly in cases that raise EU law related questions. We need a better understanding of legal mobilisation, access to justice, and about how processes and procedures work to exclude or include gender as an issue for the court to consider. We need to understand the interplay between the European Convention on Human Rights and the fundamental rights provided in the framework of the EU as well as the relationships between courts at all levels, including between the CJEU and the ECtHR.

Additionally, EU member states have ratified the Istanbul Convention on Violence against Women from May 11, 2011 (CETS No. 210), which requires Parties to the Convention to ensure the practical realisation of the principle of equality between women and men by abolishing discriminatory laws and practices; adopting legislative measures preventing and condemning all forms of discrimination against women, and enshrining the principle of equality of men and women in national constitutions or other appropriate legislation (Article 4(2)). As is evident from this provision, the Convention is not limited to preventing domestic violence since it 'places detailed legally binding obligations on states parties as regards the measures that they must adopt in relation to violence against women' (McQuigg 2017, 6).

By studying the outcomes of the judicial work, i.e. the case law, we can gain insights into how particular issues are dealt with. Almost all of this work from a gender perspective has focused on gender equality law, and even the authors' own work has not gone much beyond areas of law with obvious gender implications (Guth 2016; Guth and Elfving 2018). In addition, little scholarship is systematically and explicitly focused on the CJEU, but rather considers case law as part of a wider framework, or as an aside. This work is incredibly valuable in understanding gender implications in various policy areas and highlight different approaches in different areas (Hoskyns 1996).[2] However, there is no systematic gender analysis across all policy areas, which could tell us something about how the court deals with gender per se. The lack of this systematic research is not that surprising as it would be a huge undertaking to examine the CJEU's decisions in areas as diverse as trade, EU citizenship, and competition law, or decisions dealing with acts of annulment, for example. However, to fully understand the impact of gender we need to understand how the CJEU operates specifically in areas in which gender is not an obvious factor. A starting point might be to review existing work in various policy areas to draw parallels and identify differences that can then be further researched. Such research might then begin to highlight the extent to which gender is integrated into judicial decision-making and politics and whether the CJEU is genuinely gender aware.

What we can see from the current research is that a gendered analysis of the CJEU reveals that law is not gender neutral, and that the processes through which cases arrive at the court means that gendered considerations are potentially blocked at the various stages: the facts provided to the court, the legal question asked and the arguments made will already have been filtered based on the experience and background of the advocates and the national judiciary. This therefore highlights the importance of legal mobilisation, gender aware advocacy, gender awareness in the national courts, and the CJEU's willingness to hear the gendered voices in danger of being drowned out by formalistic procedures and dominant legal discourse. These aspects have so far not been subjected to thorough and rigorous analysis by researchers.

While gender has been under-researched, questions of multiple forms of discrimination have garnered even less attention. Although the CJEU has dealt with racial discrimination and xenophobia in a small number of cases (European Commission 2018, 24), it is yet to look at discrimination caused by multiple factors, e.g. gender and race or gender and religion. This is unsurprising given that neither EU law nor most national legislation explicitly prohibits multiple discrimination.

Further, 'adding inequalities' together does not provide any advantage in litigation and might, in fact, make it more difficult to prove discrimination in the first place. The lack of intersectional approach has been argued to divert attention from the dynamics of advantage privileging dominant groups because it may foster a sense of hierarchy among marginalised groups (McCall 2005). However, treating multiple inequalities as separate issues tends to privilege the interests of advantaged subgroups, specifically white women and ethnic minority men (Holmsten et al. 2010; Krook and Nugent 2016). The impact of multiple forms of discrimination needs exploration in relation to the people who make up the CJEU, and we need to consider that judges' views are influenced by political and ideological considerations as well as their background and position in society (Kairys 1998). Griffith (1997, 7) makes this point in relation to the English judiciary, noting specifically that many judges of the highest courts belong to a narrow social background. Therefore, female judges in the English courts are perhaps likely to have more in common with their male peers than with, for instance, women belonging to ethnic or sexual minorities. If, however, female and minority judges' experiences and viewpoints are different from those of their white male colleagues, they may present 'political, legal, moral, and popular interests' of underrepresented individuals and groups (Sen 2017, 375, 379). This needs to be explored in relation to the judicial decisions made in the same way that we suggest above in relation to gender only.

Where do we go from here: future directions

In this section we suggest three key directions for gendered research: first, detailed empirical work with CJEU staff at all levels; second, more systematic work considering the impact of gender across the range of the CJEU's work, including consideration of intersectional issues; and, finally, research that fully considers the relationship between the CJEU and the ECtHR, particularly in relation to gender and intersectionality. Our first two suggestions have already been explored in the previous sections. Suffice it to say that empirical work with staff could focus on life history interviews, which capture their background, education, training and perceptions of their work, as well as on specific questions about how the CJEU works, and the influence of characteristics and politics. This could be supplemented with work analysing decisions, taking into account the composition of chambers, the Advocate-General assigned to the case, and, where available, other staff working on the case. Analysis of areas of work can be done by careful reading of the case law and interrogating each case, applying a gender lens. This allows the researcher to ask different questions about what and who was included or excluded; where was the focus; what was deemed important and why; could other questions have been asked, and what would that mean for the outcome of a case (for further suggestions on this type of methodology, see Guth and Elfving 2018).

Our third suggestion is worth considering in a little more detail. Although all individual EU member states, as signatories to the European Convention, are subject to the jurisdiction of the ECtHR, the EU itself is not formally bound by the Convention (Spaventa 2015, 35–36). This would only be the case if the EU itself ratified and then acceded to the Convention, primarily to allow individuals to appeal the decisions of the CJEU to the ECtHR. Such appeals would have been possible only in very specific circumstances and after the individuals have exhausted all other judicial avenues (Craig 2013; Dzehtsiarou et al. 2014). However, in its *Opinion 2/13* (ECLI:EU:C:2014:2454), the CJEU stated that external scrutiny of EU law by an outside body would run counter to the primacy, unity and effectiveness of EU law as guaranteed by the EU Treaty. It is therefore unlikely that decisions of EU institutions will be subjected to ECtHR jurisdiction in the foreseeable future. The situation is the same for the Istanbul Convention. Although the Commission's Gender Equality Strategy 2020–2025 (COM(2020) 152 final) makes the EU's accession to the Convention a priority, from the legal point of view this will not be able to occur before the CJEU has resolved the EU institutions' disagreement over which treaty articles can be used as a legal basis for the accession (*Opinion 1/19*) – the outcome of which is likely to either speed up or block the accession. The disagreement relates to a number of factors, including the lack of explicit EU competence to legislate in fields that have traditionally been exclusive member state competence (e.g. criminal law and family law) as well as views that member states cannot be forced to provide in their national law the legal recognition for same-sex couples or the necessity for transgender women to benefit from the protection provided in the 1951 Convention on the Status of Refugees (Prechal 2019). There are views, however, that regardless of whether the EU becomes a party to this Convention, the Istanbul Convention contains overlapping requirements with EU law and the EU could legislate within existing competence in order to achieve the aims of the Convention. Additionally, the Istanbul Convention is likely to have an impact on the decisions of the CJEU through the substantial body of the ECtHR case law on domestic violence that the CJEU is likely to consult (McQuigg 2017, 4; Nousiainen 2017).

The lack of scrutiny over the EU institutions by the ECtHR does not mean that its work is irrelevant. Although legal academics disagree over the level of co-operation between the CJEU and the ECtHR, both courts make frequent referrals to one another's jurisdiction (for criticism of the CJEU's lack of referrals to the ECtHR and the ECtHR case law, see de Búrca 2013). An obvious example of such area is equality case law (see Radacic 2008; Suk 2017). Additionally, the ECtHR's decisions have been argued to constitute the benchmark for the CJEU when interpreting provisions of EU law relating to family life and family reunification (Lambert 2014, 211). Indeed, the CJEU has indicated its readiness to follow the ECtHR's jurisprudence on Article 8 ECHR (right to private life) in such cases (e.g. *Parliament v Council* (C-540/03); *Ruiz Zambrano* (C-34/09)). This is in spite of the fact that the two courts' approaches often differ considerably because they operate in different legislative frameworks (Lambert 2014, 214). There is also evidence of the two courts' efforts to find a workable framework to address the protection of fundamental rights in Europe in the area of European arrest warrants (von Danwitz 2019).

Further evidence that the CJEU's decisions often follow guidance from the judgments of the ECtHR can be found in the area of asylum law. Gendered readings of decisions concerning applications for asylum highlight how men and women experience the asylum process differently, and how ignoring gender can leave women vulnerable to exploitation and abuse. However, both courts have shown themselves to be, at best, gender blind in this area. The interplay between the two courts is most visible in the CJEU's decision in *NS* (C-411/10; C-439/10) and the ECtHR's decision in *MSS v Belgium and Greece* (Application No. 30696/09). Both courts concluded that there were substantial grounds for believing that there were systemic flaws in the national asylum procedures and reception conditions. This resulted in the amendment of Article 3(2) of Regulation (EU) No. 604/2013 (Dublin Regulation) to include a prohibition to return of an asylum-seeker to the member state that s/he had first entered as this could result in 'a risk of inhuman or degrading treatment' within the meaning of Article 4 of the Charter of Fundamental Rights of the EU (2010/C 83/02) (prohibition of torture and inhuman or degrading treatment or punishment). There are several other ECtHR decisions concerning reception conditions in a number of EU member states (for further discussion of the relevant case law, see Garlick 2015a, 2015b). In 2017, the CJEU extended the scope of Article 4 to encompass possible deterioration of psychological wellbeing of a Syrian asylum applicant who had recently given birth (C-578/16 PPU). The court recognised that the impact of a transfer from one member state to another within the framework of the Dublin Regulation could have potential negative psychological consequences for the new mother who suffered from post-natal depression with violent and suicidal predispositions. Although there was a strong presumption that the medical treatment offered to asylum-seekers in all member states would be adequate, due to her serious mental or physical illness her transfer could not proceed, if there was any possibility of a permanent deterioration of her health as this would constitute 'a real and proven risk of inhuman or degrading treatment' (C-578/16 PPU, §§ 70/96). The court did not, however, definitely rule out the possibility of her transfer at a later stage, making an explicit reference to the ECtHR decisions where poor mental health was not a barrier to expulsion of non-EU citizens. In *Dragan v Germany* (Application No. 33743/03, § 927) the ECtHR found that authorities were not prevented from proceeding with the deportation of a stateless woman to her native Romania despite explicit suicide threats, provided that specific steps were taken to prevent such threats from being actualised. While Case 578/16 might look like a good gender-aware decision, the judgment focuses on mental health generally and does not draw out the particulars of, for example, post-natal depression. The CJEU had the potential to go further and be explicit about women's rights but chose not to, leaving women in similar situations vulnerable to transfer and deportation when their health is poor.

Although increased collaboration between the two courts is positive, intersectional reading of case law provides further evidence that we need a better understanding of how the courts deal with interaction between gender, race and other categories of difference. The need to consider intersectional issues in order to offer better strategies to try and achieve substantive equality is evident in both the ECtHR decision in *Şahin v Turkey* (Application No. 44774/98) and the CJEU's decisions in *Bougnaoui* (C-188/15) and *Achbita* (C-157/15). These decisions fail to recognise that a seemingly neutral criterion or practice, which requires all employees to hide visible symbols of their faith (e.g. headscarves), is likely to have a more significant impact on specific minorities (e.g. Muslim women). More gender-aware jurisprudence from either court could have a significant impact on the other as their relationship evolves. Therefore, research, which

The Court of Justice

clearly demonstrates how recognising gender and its intersection with other characteristics shape the way in which the court deals with and decides such cases, could help both courts strive for better decision making.

In order to fully understand how the influences between these courts play out and what they mean for gender, we need to include not only gendered, but intersectional aspects, in a systematic analysis of the case law. This also means that the same detailed empirical work we suggest for the CJEU should be done for the ECtHR. Unlike the CJEU, the ECtHR has the ability to issue dissenting opinions. Therefore, it could be easier to investigate the impact of gender and multiple inequalities within the ECtHR. However, although dissenting opinions are allowed on the ECtHR, they are rare (Dyevre 2010). Therefore, empirical testing of whether more female or minority judges will have a significant impact on the decision-making processes or the outcome of cases in either court may be challenging (Volcansek 2000, 7). According to Voeten (2007), it is possible to gain a more accurate representation of the ideological positions of individual judges only if dissenting opinions are common. He analysed the votes of 97 judges on 709 cases between 1960 and 2006, concluding that there was both a liberal and a conservative wing in the ECtHR. He further found statistically significant support for the view that judges from member states, which are more favourably disposed toward European integration or have joined the EU more recently, were likely to rule in favour of the individual applicant than the state. A similar detailed analysis focusing on the impact of gender would provide valuable insights. The structural issues at play in relation to the ECtHR would offer further rich sites for analysis. For example, the data on the gender breakdown of cases, including those concerning gender equality, brought before the ECtHR demonstrates that women remain underrepresented among the litigants (Council of Europe 2015), and further research is needed to fully understand the barriers faced by women in particular.

A gendered analysis of areas of overlap between the CJEU and ECtHR must therefore fully understand both courts, their make-up, ways of working, and the different legal and political contexts in which they operate as well as how the jurisprudence of one might influence the other.

Conclusion

This chapter introduced some of the key ideas and concepts around judicial politics from both political science and legal perspectives as they can be applied to the CJEU. It has shown that while there is some progress in terms of understanding the impact gender has, there is a lot of work yet to be done to achieve gender parity within the court. In addition, we need to systematically map and understand how gender shapes the CJEU, its work, its relationship with other courts and, of course, gender equality across the European Union.

Notes

1 Eleanor Sharptson, the UK's Advocate General, whose term will expire at the end of October 2021 was replaced by a new male Advocate General from Greece, sworn in more than a year before the end of her term.

2 See e.g. work on the following policy areas: citizenship (O'Brien 2017a, 2017b, 2017c); migration and mobility (Allwood 2015); climate change (Allwood 2014); external relations (Guerrina and David 2013); Brexit (Guerrina et al. 2018; Guerrina and Masselot 2018); caring responsibilities (di Torella and Masselot 2010, 2016; Guerrina 2005); security policy (Guerrina and Wright 2016; Haastrup 2018), and economic policy (Cavaghan 2017; Kantola and Lombardo 2017) to name just a few. See also part 3 in this volume.

References

Adams M, Bomhoff J, eds. (2012): *Practice and Theory in Comparative Law*, Cambridge: Cambridge University Press.

Ahrens P (2018): *Actors, Institutions, and the Making of EU Gender Equality Programs*, Basingstoke: Palgrave Macmillan.

Allwood G (2014): Gender Mainstreaming and EU Climate Change Policy, in: Weiner E, MacRae H (eds.): The Persistent Invisibility of Gender in EU Policy, *European Integration online Papers* **1** (18), 1–26, URL: http://eiop.or.at/eiop/texte/2014-006a.htm.

Allwood G (2015): Horizontal policy coordination and gender mainstreaming: the case of the European Union's global approach to migration and mobility, *Women's Studies International Forum* **48**, 9–17.

Alter KJ, Vargas J (2000): Explaining variation in the use of European litigation strategies. European Community law and British gender equality policy, *Comparative Political Studies* **33** (4), 452–482.

Boyd CL (2016): Representation on the courts? The effects of trial judges' sex and race, *Political Research Quarterly* **69** (4), 788–799.

Boyd CL, Epstein L, Martin AD (2010): Untangling the causal effects of sex on judging, *American Journal of Political Science* **54** (2), 389–411.

Cavaghan R (2017): The Gender Politics of EU Economic Policy: Policy Shifts and Contestations Before and After the Crisis, in: Kantola J, Lombardo E (eds.): *Gender and the Economic Crisis in Europe: Politics, Institutions and Intersectionality*, Cham: Palgrave MacMillan, 49–71.

Chalmers D, Chaves M (2012): The reference points of EU judicial politics, *Journal of European Public Policy* **19** (1), 25–42.

Cichowski R (2007): *The European Court and Civil Society*, Cambridge: Cambridge University Press.

Collins PM Jr, Manning KL, Carp RA (2010): Gender, critical mass, and judicial decision making, *Law and Policy* **32** (2), 260–281.

Council of Europe (2015): *Equality and non-discrimination in the access to justice*, Report of the Committee on Equality and Non Discrimination, Doc 13740, 18th Sitting, April 24, 2015.

Craig P (2013): EU accession to the ECHR: competence, procedure and substance, *Fordham International Law Journal* **36** (5), 1114–1150.

de Búrca G (2013): After the EU Charter of Fundamental Rights: The Court of Justice as a human rights adjudicator?, *Maastricht Journal of European and Comparative Law* **20** (2), 168–184.

De Londras F, Dzehtsiarou K (2015): Managing judicial innovation in the European Court of Human Rights, *Human Rights Law Review* **15** (3), 523–547.

di Torella E, Masselot A (2010): *Reconciling Work and Family Life in EU Law and Policy*, Basingstoke: Palgrave Macmillian.

di Torella E, Masselot A (2016): *Caring Responsibilities in European Law and Policy: Who Cares?* London: Routledge.

Dunoff JL, Pollack MA (2017): The judicial trilemma, *American Journal of International Law* **111** (2), 225–276.

Dyevre A (2010): Unifying the field of comparative judicial politics. Towards a general theory of judicial behaviour, *European Political Science Review* **2** (2), 297–327.

Dzehtsiarou K (2018): What is law for the European Court of Human Rights?, *Georgetown Journal of International Law* **49** (1), 89–134.

Dzehtsiarou K, Konstadinides T, Lock T, O'Meara N, eds. (2014): *Human Rights Law in Europe. The Influence, Overlaps and Contradictions of the EU and the ECHR*, London: Routledge.

Epstein L, Knight J (2000): Toward a strategic revolution in judicial politics: a look back, a look ahead, *Political Research Quarterly* **53** (3), 625–661.

European Commission (2018): *European Equality Law Review*, Luxembourg: European Union 2018.

Garlick M (2015a): International protection in court: The asylum jurisprudence of the Court of Justice of the EU and UNHCR, *Refugee Survey Quarterly* **34** (1), 107–130.

Garlick M (2015b): Protecting rights and courting controversy: leading jurisprudence of the European Courts on the EU Dublin Regulation, *Journal of Immigration, Asylum and Nationality Law* **29** (2), 192–210.

Glynn AN, Sen M (2015): Identifying judicial empathy: does having daughters cause judges to rule for women's issues?, *American Journal of Political Science* **59** (1), 37–54.

Griffith JAG (1997): *Politics of the Judiciary*, 5th ed., London: Fontana Press.

Guerrina R (2005): *Mothering the Union: Gender Politics in the EU*, Manchester: Manchester University Press.

Guerrina R, David M (2013): Gender and European external relations: dominant discourses and unintended consequences of gender mainstreaming, *Women's Studies International Forum* **39**, 53–62.

Guerrina R, Exadaktylos T, Guerra S (2018): Gender, ownership and engagement during the European Union referendum: gendered frames and the reproduction of binaries, *European Journal of Politics and Gender* **1** (2), 387–404.

Guerrina R, Masselot AM (2018): *Walking into the footprint of EU Law. Unpacking the gendered consequences of Brexit, Social Policy and Society* **17** (2), 319–330.

Guerrina R, Wright KAM (2016): Gendering normative power Europe: lessons of the women, peace and security agenda, *International Affairs* **92** (2), 293–312.

Guth J (2016): Law as the Object and Agent of Integration. Gendering the Court of Justice of the European Union, Its Decisions and Their Impact, in: Abels G, MacRae H (eds.): *Gendering European Integration Theory*, Opladen: Barbara Budrich Verlag, 175–195.

Guth J, Elfving S (2018): *Gender and the Court of Justice of the European Union*, London: Routledge.

Haastrup T (2018): Creating Cinderella? The unintended consequences of the women peace and security agenda for EU's mediation architecture, *International Negotiation* **23** (2), 218–237.

Hersant J, Vigour C (2017): Judicial politics on the ground, *Law and Social Inquiry* **42** (2), 292–297.

Holmsten SS, Moser RG, Slosar MC (2010): Do ethnic parties exclude women? *Comparative Political Studies* **43** (10), 1179–1201.

Hoskyns C (1996): *Integrating Gender: Women, Law and Politics in the European Union*, London: Verso.

Kairys D (1998): *The Politics of Law: A Progressive Critique*, 3rd ed., New York: Basic Books.

Kantola J, Lombardo E, eds. (2017): *Gender and the Economic Crisis in Europe: Politics, Institutions and Intersectionality*, Cham: Palgrave MacMillan.

Kenney SJ (2002): Breaking the silence: gender mainstreaming and the composition of the European Court of Justice, *Feminist Legal Studies* **10** (3–4), 257–270.

Kenney SJ (2013): *Gender and Justice: Why Women in the Judiciary Really Matter*, London: Routledge.

Krook ML, Nugent MK (2016): Intersectional institutions: representing women and ethnic minorities in the British Labour Party, *Party Politics* **22** (5), 620–630.

Lambert H (2014): Family unity in migration law. The evolution of a more unified approach in Europe, in: Chetail V, Bauloz C (eds.): *Research Handbook on International Law and Migration*, Cheltemham: Edward Elgar, 194–215.

Malleson K (2003): Justifying gender equality on the bench. Why difference won't do, *Feminist Legal Studies* **11** (1), 1–24.

McCall L (2005): The complexity of intersectionality, *Signs* **30** (3), 1771–1800.

McIntosh Sundstrom L, Sperling V, Sayoglu M (2019): *Courting Gender Justice: Russia, Turkey and the European Court of Human Rights*, Oxford: Oxford University Press.

McQuigg RJA (2017): *The Istanbul Convention, Domestic Violence and Human Rights*, New York: Routledge.

Negowetti NE (2015): Implicit bias and the Legal profession's 'diversity crisis': a call for self-reflection, *Nevada Law Journal* **15**, 930–958.

Nousiainen K (2017): *Legal implications of EU accession to the Istanbul Convention. Current Reflections on EU Gender Equality Law*, URL: www.era-comm.eu/oldoku/SNLLaw/15_Istanbul_Convention/117DV31_Nousiainen_EN.pdf (download: November 10, 2019).

O'Brien C (2017a): The ECJ sacrifices EU citizenship in vain: Commission v. United Kingdom, *Common Market Law Review* **54** (1), 209–243.

O'Brien C (2017b): *Unity in Adversity: EU Citizenship, Social Justice and the Cautionary Tale of the UK*, Oxford: Hart.

O'Brien C (2017c): Union Citizenship and Disability: Restricted Access to Equality Rights and the Attitudinal Model of Disability, in Kochenov D (ed.): *EU Citizenship and Federalism: The Role of Rights*, Cambridge: Cambridge University Press, 509–539.

Peritz L (2018): Obstructing integration: domestic politics and the European Court of Justice, *European Union Politics* **19** (3), 427–457.

Prechal S (2019): The European Union's Accession to the Istanbul Convention in: Lenaerts K, Bonichot JC, Kanninen K, Naômé C, Pohjankoski P (eds.): *An Ever-Changing Union? Perspectives on the Future of EU Law in Honour of Alan Rosas*, London: Hart Publishing, 279–292.

Rachlinski JJ, Wistrich AJ, Guthrie C (2017): Judicial politics and decisionmaking: a new approach, *Vanderbilt Law Review* **70** (6), 2051–2103.

Rackley E (2013): *Women, Judging and the Judiciary: From Difference to Diversity*, London: Routledge.

Radacic I (2008): Gender equality jurisprudence of the European Court of Human Rights, The *European Journal of International Law* **19** (4), 841–857.

Sen M (2017): Diversity, qualifications, and ideology: how female and minority judges have changed, or not changed, over time, *Wisconsin Law Review* **2**, 367–399.

Shaw J (2001): Gender and the European Court of Justice, in: de Búrca G, Weiler, JHH (eds.): *The European Court of Justice*, Oxford: Oxford University Press, 87–142.

Sotomayor S (2002): A Latina judge's voice, *Berkeley La Raza Law Journal* **13** (1), 87–93.

Spaventa E (2015): A very fearful court? The protection of fundamental rights in the European Union after Opinion 2/13, *Maastricht Journal of European and Comparative Law* **22** (1), 35–56.

Suk JC (2017): Equality after Brexit: evaluating British contributions to EU antidiscrimination law, *Fordham International Law Journal* **40** (5), 1535–1552.

Turenne S, ed. (2015): *Fair Reflection of Society in Judicial Systems: A Comparative Study*, Heidelberg: Springer.

Turenne S (2017): Institutional constraints and collegiality at the Court of Justice of the European Union: a sense of belonging?, *Maastricht Journal of European and Comparative Law* **24** (4), 565–581.

Voeten E (2007): The politics of international judicial appointments. Evidence from the European Court of Human Rights, *International Organization* **61** (4), 669–701.

Volcansek, M.L. (2000): *Constitutional Politics in Italy*, Basingstoke: Palgrave Macmillan Press

von Danwitz L (2019): *In Rights We Trust*, URL: https://verfassungsblog.de/in-rights-we-trust/ (download: August 22, 2019).

Zhang AH (2016): The faceless court, *University of Pennsylvania Journal of International Law* **38** (1), 71–135.

Part III

Gendered politics in the EU

Adding to the gender analysis of formal political institutions and policies in the EU, this section turns to consider the gendered aspects of EU politics. Politics is gendered through its actors, and the ways they are constituted, the capacities they have and the access they are allowed. Gendering also takes place through discourses used, the ways in which they include or exclude and silence topics relevant for gender equality. This section looks at how research on EU politics engages with gender aspects, and how gender research contributes to complement gaps in the mainstream EU politics research.

Democratic deficit is widely discussed in the EU institutional framework. It has gendered aspects: it impacts women and other politically excluded groups more than others. Giving voice and political representation to women and mainstreaming a gender perspective requires a scrutiny that goes beyond formal institutions and looks into the gendered aspects of European constituency formation, the inclusivity of political processes and, more specifically, political actors beyond formal political institutions. While politics is part of other sections in this volume, this section zooms into some specific aspects not covered in previous sections.

First, how the political community is defined has deeply rooted gendered aspects. The section first looks at the politics of constituency formation: namely citizenship and the politics of EU enlargement.

Literature on EU citizenship including recent attempts to critically analyze it through an interdisciplinary lens (such as the BEUCitizen project) remains remarkably silent on gendered inclusions and exclusions implicit in the concept of EU citizenship. Gender research that is directly engaging with EU citizenship is also relatively limited. This research mainly contributes by bringing an intersectional analysis in which mechanisms of exclusion and inclusion are scrutinized through gender, ethnicity/religion/nationality and class lenses. Such analysis promises to extend perspectives of research on citizenship, particularly in the current context of legitimacy crisis for EU citizenship.

Along with research on citizenship, another approach to understand EU constituency formation and the politics of gendered inclusion and exclusion that accompany it is analysis of EU enlargement. Mainstream enlargement research discusses gender equality policy as one of many other policy fields where harmonization of norms takes place in one way or another. The gender equality acquis is one of the policy fields where de jure progress was remarkable and remained largely stable even beyond the period of accession and into the period of populist attacks on gender equality. Gender research contributes to this field with demonstrating the complexity of the benefits and drawbacks of the enlargement process, particularly as it was instituted in the case of the enlargement wave towards central and eastern Europe. Gender research provides a better understanding of the dual nature of enlargement: of its benefits for a wider more inclusive Europe, but also the limited power and efficiency of the EU to move from de jure norm consistency to de facto. By bringing a constructivist lens as well as a focus on implementation and policy outcomes, not just outputs, gender research on EU enlargement not only highlights the limitations of the enlargement policy in terms of efficient EU integration but also provides tools to understand the weakness of the EU in the face of recent attempts to curtail gender equality in the context of the economic crisis or the context of populist governments.

Politics is gendered not only through how membership is defined in the political community but also through the capacity of its constituents to speak in the debates, be included and recognized members of political debate. Political knowledge is a key element in this process. While mainstream research on political knowledge treats knowledge as genderless, gender research contributes by showing the relevance of a gender lens within this field asking the questions what women know, and how, and how this may lead to exclusionary processes. This emerges as particularly relevant and in need of further research in the EU context where the distance of politics from citizens is much larger, and politics also tends to be much more technocratic and less accessible to ordinary citizens.

Political parties and civil society are the main entry points for gender equality and women into EU politics. A gender analysis of how they operate in EU politics highlights important mechanisms of exclusion but also shows the ways in which these actors can facilitate a more inclusive European arena. These two arenas are venues for a more inclusive European politics, but may be venues for channeling a backlash against inclusion into the EU arena. Mainstream research in both fields includes gender aspects in limited ways only. The scope of contributing for gender research is rather extensive.

While analysis of voting patterns or membership of women in parties are better covered by party politics research, gender analysis of EU parties as organizations, and as discursive actors, related in various ways to national level political agendas are fields of research that emerge only lately and provide opportunities for gender research to intervene and complement mainstream research agendas.

Mainstream civil society research is relatively detached from analysis of women's rights and gender equality related EU-level civil society. Given the diversity of gender equality actors, the tradition of feminist struggle as well as the demonstrated propensity of women to activism and civil society engagement, research using a gender lens can widely contribute to understanding EU civil society dynamics. A gap can be identified here in gender research as well: few studies, mainly of a sectoral nature, do a gender analysis of EU civil society dynamics, and few attempt to address gender equality related civil society comprehensively in its diversity particularly in the context of a financial and legitimacy crisis across the EU. Further research could contribute to this field.

Overall the section has identified important gaps in mainstream EU politics research, critical contributions made by gender research but, foremost, it has detected various arenas where gender research can contribute to understanding dynamics, inclusions and exclusions in EU politics in the future.

15

Enlargement

Cristina Chiva

The European Union's policy on enlargement has evolved significantly over time. In the 1957 Treaty of Rome, membership conditionality consisted in the requirement that applicant states be 'European' – a statement that initially referred to geographical positioning but was gradually expanded to encompass adherence to the European Union's values, including non-discrimination and equality between men and women. For the period between 1957 and 1993, membership conditionality was minimal, with virtually no formal criteria for membership except geographical positioning in Europe, and no significant attempts to monitor candidate countries' progress towards accession. By the early 1990s, the prospect of EU expansion to post-communist Europe had exposed the risks that such a minimalist approach to enlargement conditionality held for the EU, especially when confronted with enlarging to ten post-communist countries at the same time. The prospect of the eastern enlargement thus forced the EU to formulate and implement a new accession policy, one designed to deal with the complex issues arising from bringing the former communist countries into the fold. The policy was originally developed for the post-communist countries that joined in 2004 (the Czech Republic, Estonia, Hungary, Latvia, Lithuania, Poland, Slovakia, Slovenia) and 2007 (Bulgaria and Romania). It was also applied to Croatia during the accession negotiations leading to membership in 2013. Most importantly, the template for enlargement policy originally developed in the 1990s and 2000s remains in place for the current candidates for EU membership: Albania, North Macedonia, Montenegro, Serbia and Turkey.

This chapter argues that the EU's eastwards expansion in particular marked a watershed moment in the development of the EU's enlargement policy, and that this had momentous consequences for gender equality policy in the new member states. Specifically, the EU deliberately used its leverage vis-à-vis central and eastern European countries (CEECs) to monitor progress towards gender equality during the accession process. Thus, gender equality formed an intrinsic part of EU accession conditionality, prompting institutional and legislative change in the candidate countries both before and after accession. These changes were unprecedented by comparison to previous enlargement rounds, where the general requirement that applicant states adopt the EU's *acquis* (including the *acquis* on gender equality) after accession was deemed sufficient. In contrast, CEECs were required to transpose the *acquis communautaire* (in short: acquis; i.e. the body of EU law consisting of treaties, legislation, legal acts and decisions

183

of the Court of Justice of the EU) before accession, and to abide by political conditionality concerning human rights, respect for minorities, non-discrimination and equality between men and women.

The overarching argument of this chapter is twofold. First, I argue that the EU's distinctive membership conditionality towards post-communist candidates made it possible for commentators, feminist activists and scholars to analyse the precise impact of accession on applicant states in ways that were not available for previous enlargement rounds. In particular, since previous applicants (such as the UK in 1973, Spain in 1986 or Sweden in 1995) were free to adopt the EU *acquis* at leisure after accession, the extent to which they complied with the European Communities (EC)/EU gender equality *acquis* would normally become apparent only after these countries had already joined the EC/EU. Furthermore, although the problem of democratic conditionality did arise previously within the context of the Spanish, Portuguese and Greek accessions, the EC at the time had not yet developed mechanisms of Europeanisation such as benchmarking and monitoring that could be used to keep an eye on progress towards gender equality. In sum, the precise relationship between gender and EU enlargement is the result of a historical process whereby the EU gradually incorporated gender into its accession process – both as part of the requirement prior to accession, and as part of the democracy criterion for membership.

Secondly, I argue that, perhaps as a consequence of overwhelming interest in the eastern enlargement round, the literature on gender and enlargement is overwhelmingly focused on the process whereby prospective member states 'download' EU policy templates into domestic settings. In contrast, the impact of enlargement on the EU's commitment to gender equality as a whole has yet to be studied in depth.

This chapter is structured in four main sections. First, I provide an overview of the development of EU membership conditionality, the ways in which eastern enlargement differed from previous rounds, and the ways in which gender equality was incorporated into membership conditionality towards CEECs. Secondly, I trace the evolution of the enlargement literature, focusing primarily on the CEEC enlargement. Thirdly, I examine the existing literature, identifying the core terms of engagement of feminist scholarship with the process of EU accession, particularly in post-communist Europe. Fourth, I identify directions for future research, focusing on existing research gaps.

Although conceptually and empirically distinct, the EU's policy on enlargement and the broader process of Europeanisation (see Forest in this volume) in candidate countries respectively were closely interlinked in practice. The EU's deliberate use of membership conditionality vis-à-vis CEECs resulted in a 'top-down' Europeanisation of gender equality in the post-communist applicant states. The primary analytical focus of this chapter is on enlargement policy, with reference being made to processes of Europeanisation only in so far as this is strictly necessary for conceptualising the effects of enlargement.

The evolution of the EU's membership conditionality

The evolution of the literature on gender and EU enlargement is inextricably linked with the historical development of EU's membership conditionality. Thus, in order to understand how the EU's policy has developed and to evaluate its relationship to gender equality, it is useful to begin by contrasting the initial formulation of membership conditionality in the 1957 Treaty of Rome with the equivalent provisions in the 2009 Lisbon Treaty.

For the first three decades, EC policy on enlargement was succinctly stated in Article 237 of the EC Treaty, which outlined two key elements: (1) a membership criterion, i.e. only countries on the European continent were eligible for membership; (2) the core procedural features according to which applications were to be reviewed by the Commission, whose recommendation, in turn, would be taken into account by the Council when making a decision about enlargement under unanimity. In addition, enlargement was to result in a separate agreement between the parties – in other words, the legal instrument known as the Treaties of Accession for new entrants. Gender equality was incorporated indirectly by means of the expectation that new member states would eventually transpose and implement the EC's *acquis*, including the equal pay provisions of Article 119 of the Treaty on the European Economic Community (EEC) and the subsequent secondary legislation on gender equality, as developed from the 1970s onwards (see von Wahl as well as Milner in this volume).

The original provisions on enlargement still form part of Article 49 of the Treaty on European Union (TEU) but have been clarified and expanded in a number of ways.

> Any European State which respects the values referred to in Article 2 and is committed to promoting them may apply to become a member of the Union. The European Parliament and national Parliaments shall be notified of this application. The applicant State shall address its application to the Council, which shall act unanimously after consulting the Commission and after receiving the consent of the European Parliament, which shall act by a majority of its component members. The conditions of eligibility agreed upon by the European Council shall be taken into account.

Reference to Article 2 of the TEU marked an important shift away from viewing membership in purely geographic terms, towards an understanding of the EU as a 'community of values'. This shift was written into the 1997 Amsterdam Treaty, the first to refer to adherence to democratic values, including equality between men and women. In its current form, Article 2 TEU states that the EU is 'founded on the values of respect for human dignity, freedom, democracy, equality, the rule of law and respect for human rights, including the rights of persons belonging to minorities' and it explicitly refers to 'pluralism, non-discrimination, tolerance, justice, solidarity and equality between women and men prevail' as values shared by the member states. Article 49 TEU also refers to a number of institutional innovations adopted since 1957, such as a stronger role for the European Parliament in the enlargement process and the role of European Council, assembling the heads of states and governments since 1974, in setting the conditions for membership. Most importantly, the 'community of values' includes, at least at declaratory level, a strong commitment to non-discrimination and equality between men and women. Candidate countries seeking to join are thus explicitly required to abide by EU values, including gender equality.

Changes in relevant treaty provisions were paralleled by a slowly evolving EU policy on enlargement. The question of how to deal with neighbouring countries that were not fully-fledged democracies or that were even outright autocratic regimes first arose in relation to Spain's request for an association agreement in the early 1960s. This prompted some thinking on the EC side about democracy as a condition for membership. Thus, the Birkelbach Report adopted by the European Parliamentary Assembly in 1962 stated unambiguously that 'the guaranteed existence of a democratic form of state, in the sense of a free political order, is a condition for membership' (cited in Janse 2018, 66). However, since Spain had become a democracy by the time it eventually joined in 1986, the issue of 'a democratic form of state' did not actually form part of the agenda during Spain's accession process. Instead, the impetus for explicit political conditionality came a few decades later. The EU was concerned about post-communist countries' democratic and economic institutions being too fragile to sustain the pressures of EU accession. In 1993, EU member states addressed the issue of enlargement conditionality by formulating a set of four criteria for membership, collectively known as 'the Copenhagen criteria' (Council Conclusions, SN 180/1/93 REV 1), which were to shape enlargement policy for the foreseeable future.

Succinctly formulated and consistently implemented ever since their initial adoption, the accession criteria are: (1) 'stability of institutions guaranteeing democracy, the rule of law, human rights and respect for and protection of minorities' (political criterion); (2) 'a functioning market economy and the capacity to cope with competition and market forces' (economic criterion); (3) the administrative and institutional capacity to effectively implement the *acquis* and the ability to take on the obligations of membership (administrative criterion); and (4) 'the Union's capacity to absorb new members, while maintaining the momentum of European integration'. Accordingly, even if a candidate country is ready for membership, the EU may well decide against enlargement. Within this context, progress on gender equality was formally assessed as part of two distinct criteria: political conditionality (that is, the extent to which women were included on an equal basis with men in the new post-communist democracies); and the administrative criterion (progress towards transposing the EU's long-standing *acquis* on gender equality).

Over time, the prospect of enlarging eastwards prompted the EU to flesh out the fairly vague conditions into a fully-fledged policy template. In fact, although it was certainly not for the first time that the EU had made membership available to new democracies on the continent, the eastern enlargement was unprecedented in several respects. First, given that previous enlargement negotiations had been conducted with at most four candidates at the same time, the sheer complexity of negotiating accession with ten candidate countries presented a momentous challenge for EU institutions and member states alike. Secondly, while preparation for membership occurred during the negotiating period in previous rounds, EU institutions, member states and applicant states undertook an enormous amount of preparatory work *prior* to starting accession negotiations with the CEECs (Grabbe 2006, 26). Thirdly, power asymmetries gave the EU significant leverage in shaping the process of democratic consolidation in CEE. As Vachudova (2005) argues, while in the early 1990s the EU exercised a 'passive leverage' over post-communist Europe by virtue of the prospect of future membership, by the late 1990s it had moved on to 'active leverage' by monitoring candidate countries' progress in meeting the Copenhagen conditions and gate-keeping access to membership accordingly. As shown below, this process of 'Europeanisation through conditionality' (Grabbe 2006) had a significant impact on gender equality policy in the applicant countries. Finally, although the European Parliament and member states were closely involved, the European Commission was the most forceful advocate of enlarging eastwards among EU institutions; thus DG Enlargement remained the principal gatekeeper for the Commission's (and, by extension, the EU's) decision-making throughout the accession process.

Membership criteria were ranked in order of importance, with political conditionality having priority over economic conditionality, which, in turn, took precedence over administrative conditionality (Smith 2003). Thus, for example, when Slovakia in 1997 was deemed by the Commission not to meet political conditionality due to Vladimir Mečiar's less than impeccable track record concerning the treatment of ethnic minorities, the Commission recommended that accession negotiations not be opened with Slovakia (Smith 2003, Vachudova 2005). Slovakia then made a systematic effort to overcome this hurdle, eventually catching up with the 'frontrunners'. Concerning economic conditionality, both Bulgaria and Romania had difficulties in meeting the criteria, even after negotiations started in 2000. Finally, the administrative criterion was subject to a maximalist interpretation by the Commission, with candidate countries required to transpose the 80,000-page *acquis* prior to accession – a principle Grabbe (2006) described as 'the *acquis*, the whole *acquis* and nothing but the *acquis*'.

The Commission's influential opinions (*avis*) and regular reports on preparation for membership also make it clear just that the EU's position on progress on equality between men and women evolved over time. In general terms, political conditionality covered those areas of gender equality that did not form part of the *acquis*. In the 1997 opinion known as *Agenda 2000*, the Commission's pronouncements on gender equality were rather vague, noting variously that, in Bulgaria and Romania, 'laws in favour of women are not always applied in practice and the situation of women appears to have deteriorated'. By 2000, more specific issues begin to be highlighted in the Commission's regular reports, such as trafficking in women and the need for candidate countries to ratify the UN Optional Protocol to the Convention on the Elimination of All Forms of Discrimination against Women (CEDAW), which entered into force in 2000. This strategy continued well beyond the 2004/2007 enlargement round, with the Commission gradually expanding the scope of monitoring to a variety of equality-related areas. Within this context, new EU legislation continued to be adopted throughout the accession process. For example, Council Directive 2000/43/EC against discrimination on grounds of race and ethnic origin (the Racial Equality Directive) and Council Directive 2000/78/EC against discrimination at work on grounds of religion or belief, disability, age or sexual orientation (the Framework Directive) were adopted two years into the negotiations process, significantly expanding the scope of equality policy under the *acquis*.

The Commission's activism on political conditionality had a significant impact on ethnic minority women, especially Roma women, in the post-communist region. This 'intersectionality effect' emerged only gradually, dating back to the Commission's decision to highlight the plight of the Roma populations in its regular reports. For example, the early reports for Hungary, Bulgaria and Romania highlight the issue of ethnic minority rights for Roma, and related issues of Russophone populations in the Baltic states (Sasse 2008). Although the situation of Roma women is not explicitly mentioned in the earlier reports, over time intersectionality became a particular concern for the Commission. The 2019 report on Serbia, for instance, highlights Roma women's disadvantaged position, especially in terms of education and employment. Within this context, it is difficult to over-state the sheer magnitude of the impact of accession on raising awareness of the Roma issue across CEE. The Commission's regular reports essentially placed the Roma issue on the domestic political agenda of candidate countries, gradually incorporating intersectionality, and the need for national governments to attend to the situation of Roma women.

As far as compliance with the administrative criterion is concerned, the Commission noted, from early on, that candidate countries needed to make the necessary adjustments in order to align domestic legislation with the EU *acquis* on parental leave, non-discrimination or equal pay. Over time, new requirements arose, such as the strengthening of institutional capacity through the establishment of equality bodies throughout the region (see Jacquot and Krizsán in this volume). Within this context, the EU's impact on candidate countries can best be described as mixed. On the one hand, since adoption of the *acquis* was the least significant part of membership conditionality, non-compliance by candidate countries was unlikely to trigger the withdrawal of the membership offer by the EU. This is particularly the case within the area of gender equality, where the requirement to transpose the *acquis,* while formally compulsory, was in practice loosely monitored and enforced. For example, Poland and the Czech Republic had actually not adopted the 'gender *acquis*' in its entirety by the time of accession in 2004: eventually, it took several additional years to transpose the relevant legislation. On the other hand, even if frequently patchy, the *acquis* was utterly transformative in CEE, where gender equality legislation had made very little progress beyond broad constitutional safeguards after the fall of communism.

Cristina Chiva

There were several key mechanisms through which the EU deliberately used membership conditionality to trigger change in CEE. According to Grabbe (2006, 75–89), the EU had five distinct Europeanisation mechanisms in place: (1) the provision of legal and institutional templates; (2) aid and technical assistance; (3) benchmarking and monitoring; (4) advice and twinning; and (5) gate-keeping (access to negotiations and further stages of the accession process). Each of these mechanisms was explicitly used in the policy area of gender equality during accession.

The provision of legal and institutional templates promoted adaptation of candidate countries to the EU's legal and institutional norms. The regular reports of the Commission frequently commend, or, alternatively, criticise countries for establishing (or failing to establish, as the case may be) equality bodies of the type specified in the gender equality directives.

The PHARE programme was the core of the EU's pre-accession aid and technical assistance. Originally an acronym for 'Poland and Hungary Assistance for Economic Reconstruction', PHARE, with approximately 1.5 billion euros a year, was made available to the ten candidate countries in the early 2000s (Grabbe 2006, 80). The programme funded a number of initiatives designed to strengthen institutional capacity, including in the area of gender equality. This was often combined with twinning, where civil servants from the member states shared best practice with civil servants from candidate countries. For instance, a 2001 PHARE-funded twinning programme between Spain and Romania resulted in the establishment of the National Agency for Equal Opportunities.

The benchmarking and monitoring mechanism and the gate-keeping mechanism were closely intertwined, as the Commission would typically evaluate progress toward membership via monitoring, and then condition access to further stages of the process on candidate countries' meeting benchmarks and criteria relevant for that particular policy field. The success of the Commission's approach was distinctly double-edged. While, for example, accession was successful in bringing issues affecting the Roma population in general and Roma women in particular to the attention of national policy-makers across the region, the applicant states' incentive to comply was mild at best, because non-compliance was unlikely to cause the EU to withdraw the membership offer. In sum, the EU's deliberate use of its membership conditionality, and the mostly consistent application of the various instruments at the EU's disposal, had a significant impact on the content and scope of gender equality legislation and institutions in the candidate countries, but this impact was also mitigated by the fact that applicant states knew that non-compliance in this policy area would be unlikely to trigger a denial of membership by the EU.

The broader literature on EU enlargement

The study of gender and enlargement has been shaped by two wider debates. First, scholarship on enlargement draws attention to the distinction between integration ('deepening') and enlargement ('widening'), arguing that the two processes require different theoretical approaches. Schimmelfennig and Sedelmeier (2002, 503) argue that the distinction between 'deepening' and 'widening' corresponds to that between vertical and horizontal institutionalisation, where 'institutionalisation' refers to 'the process by which the actions and interactions of social actors come to be normatively patterned'. Thus, enlargement is a process whereby the norms of an international organisation spread to outside actors interested in joining (or even further afield, to neighboring countries not (yet) intent on membership) (Schimmelfennig and Sedelmeier 2002, 503). From this perspective, enlargement brings about the diffusion of EU gender equality norms to prospective members and associated countries.

Second, scholars such as Börzel and Risse distinguish between a 'bottom-up' and a 'top-down' perspective on Europeanisation – that is, 'the dynamics and the outcome of the European institution-building process' versus 'the impact of European integration and Europeanisation on domestic political and social processes of the member states and beyond' (Börzel and Risse 2000, 1). Thus, candidate countries largely 'download' gender equality norms from the EU level, with various degree of success regarding long-term implementation. Within this context, the EU's deliberate use of its gender equality norms as part of accession conditionality can have discernible download effects on the adoption of respective policies in the candidate countries.

Two main strands of the broader literature on enlargement are relevant from the perspective of gender: first, scholarship on compliance with EU law before and after accession; secondly, scholarship on the impact of EU accession on ethnic minority groups in the CEECs. The first, i.e. compliance with the social policy *acquis*, attracted intense scholarly interest in the early 2000s, with rich theoretical perspectives seeking to explain how and (if applicable) why current and prospective member states transpose and enforce EU legislation in areas such as employment or gender equality. Thus, Falkner and Treib (2008) as well as Falkner et al. (2008) distinguish between four 'worlds of compliance'. The four CEECs covered in their study (Slovenia, Slovakia, Hungary, Czech Republic) joined Italy and Ireland in the 'world of dead letters' category, where countries tend to comply with EU law in terms of transposition but less so when it comes to monitoring and enforcement. This finding is largely congruent to the theoretical presuppositions of the external incentives model of Europeanisation in the CEECs (Schimmelfennig and Sedelmeier 2002, 2005, 2020). According to the model, the EU 'drives Europeanisation through sanctions and rewards that alter the cost-benefit calculations of governments in candidate countries' (Schimmelfennig and Sedelmeier 2020, 815). Furthermore, non-compliance with social policy at the transposition stage was unlikely to lead to the EU denying membership; hence, the effects of Europeanisation in this respect were limited to the transposition stage. Unsurprisingly, some post-communist national governments wanted to be seen as having transposed the *acquis* correctly, in the safe knowledge that enforcement problems were to be dealt with after accession their overarching goal having been achieved.

A second strand of scholarship on EU enlargement does not engage directly with feminist research, but has direct relevance for the study of gender equality in the EU. This scholarship is primarily concerned with the impact of EU accession on ethnic minority rights in the CEECs (Sasse 2008; Schwellnus 2005). For example, Sasse found that 'rational cost-benefit calculations about accession may inform legal changes in candidate countries, but this does not necessarily mean that legal changes are underpinned by successful socialization into European norms' (2008, 856) – a conclusion that lends support to the external incentives model. However, within the literature on ethnic minority rights and enlargement, there is virtually no examination of the impact of EU accession on groups other than ethnic minorities, even if the comprehensive nature of the EU's *acquis* on non-discrimination suggests that there are potential linkages to be examined.

Overall, scholarship on enlargement tends to share at least three assumptions: (1) a shared focus on Europeanisation as the 'download' of EU policies to the domestic level; (2) treating Europeanisation as equivalent to convergence with EU norms in particular policy fields; and (3) the absence of an intersectional approach in studies on the impact of EU accession on different social groups. First, existing literature on EU enlargement generally focuses on the 'download' of EU policies by the candidate states, with the overwhelming majority of studies focusing primarily on eastern enlargements of the past and on lessons these enlargements hold for future expansions of the EU. Before the eastern enlargement, there was no deliberate strategy on the EC/EU side to achieve 'horizontal institutionalisation' by bringing applicant states into the fold prior to accession. In contrast, during CEEC enlargement the EU sought to achieve compliance with its norms *prior* to accession. In this respect, Europeanisation in enlargement prior to 2004 consisted of two steps: the 'upload' of policy preferences to the EU level, and then, if/once adopted, the 'download' of EU policies through transposition and implementation. In the case of post-communist Europe, there is an additional stage *at the time of joining*, where applicant countries were required to adopt EU norms prior to accession. Strictly speaking, enlargement refers only to this latter additional step, while the other two steps are characteristic of European integration.

Second, as Forest and Lombardo (2012, 2–3) note, the literature largely assumes that the idea of Europeanisation refers to 'convergence with the EU norm', thereby glossing over just how differentiated policy responses to the EU's pressure have actually been. Focusing specifically on gender equality policy, they argue for a combination of sociological institutionalism, which emphasises processes of socialisation and persuasion as mechanisms of EU impact, with discursive institutionalism, which helps us understand 'how EU norms are internalized and which endogenous reasons [processes of social learning and framing, or usages of the EU] shape domestic policy change' (Forest and Lombardo 2012, 6). They also suggest it is necessary to look at 'soft measures' outside the scope of 'hard' EU conditionality – in this case, policies that, although not part of the EU's *acquis,* were nevertheless influential in shaping policy-making in the candidate countries. Within the broader framework of a discursive–sociological perspective Krizsán and Popa (2012) show that during EU accession, policy-makers and civil society activists in CEE used accession and 'Europe' strategically to legitimise action in favour of adopting policies against domestic violence throughout the region.

Third, scholarship on enlargement tends to discuss equality between men and women separately from other fields such as ethnic minority rights or LGBT rights (of which more below). An intersectional approach, however, remains largely absent, with ethnic minority rights and gender equality forming separate subjects of scholarly inquiry. This partially reflects the evolution of the EU's 'equality *acquis*', and the fact that it has historically addressed gender and ethnic minority issues in isolation from each other. However, the European Commission's emphasis on the status of Roma women in its regular reports (as noted above, especially in relation to the current candidate countries such as Serbia), suggests that an intersectional analysis to enlargement is empirically feasible, as well as desirable.

As this brief overview illustrates, the shared emphasis is largely on the 'download' of gender equality and other policies from the EU to the domestic level during the accession period. This shared emphasis takes various forms, such as a focus on compliance (Falkner et al. 2008), on mechanisms of Europeanisation (especially the external incentives model, Schimmelfennig and Sedelmeier 2002, 2005, 2020), or analyses of the impact of EU enlargement on various social groups, such as ethnic minorities.

Scholarship on the impact of EU enlargement on gender equality

Feminist analyses of the impact of enlargement on gender equality policies in CEE can be broadly divided into four strands: (1) comparative studies of the impact of EU accession on gender equality policy in the post-communist region; (2) scholarship on the relationship between EU enlargement and women's activism in CEE, (3) literature examining the impact of enlargement on LGBT groups; and (4) scholarship on intersectionality in post-communist Europe. Despite their differences in emphasis and approach, many feminist studies demonstrate that enlargement was a missed opportunity for gender mainstreaming throughout the region (Bretherton 2001). EU accession has resulted, with very few exceptions such as possibly structural funds (Krizsán 2009), in gender equality being incorporated in a variety of gender-related fields, but not mainstreamed in policy areas that are not directly gender-related. This constitutes the flip side of what is otherwise a story of successful adoption of gender equality policies throughout post-communist Europe, as shown below.

Feminist comparative studies draw on a broad range of literature in order to provide a comprehensive picture of the ways in which the pressures of EU conditionality and EU membership interact with gender equality policies in the region. Avdeyeva (2015) investigates compliance in Poland, the Czech Republic and Lithuania. She finds that post-communist states kept the institutions and policies adopted due to pre-accession conditionality in place after accession. This is explained through a combination of factors, such as the role of political parties, the existence of supportive social actors, and the presence of women in national cabinets. Bego analyses the cases of Bulgaria, the Czech Republic, Latvia and Poland, drawing on the state feminism conceptual framework to argue that the EU 'initially created a broad incentive structure for candidate states to adopt gender equality policy, but its adoption and implementation success are mediated by domestic facilitating factors' (Bego 2015, 138). She finds that the role of women's policy agencies may be 'necessary for institutionalizing the relationship with civil society and eliminating the potential future negative effects of lack of political will or Euroscepticism' (Bego 2015, 139). Smaller comparative studies, such as Chiva (2009) and Velluti (2014) reach similar conclusions, highlighting the complexity of factors driving Europeanisation in the post-communist member states.

Scholarship on the impact of EU enlargement and women's activism in CEE has also yielded quite a few excellent insights into how EU accession altered the opportunity structures for women's movements across the post-communist region. Regulska and Grabowska (2008) argue that, in Poland, enlargement has led to a stronger collective agency for women's movements and has enhanced their ability to engage politically. Haskova and Krizkova (2008) find that Czech women's groups transformed rapidly during the accession process, especially in terms of better access to funding and greater opportunities for influencing government. Kakucs and Peto (2008) trace the huge discrepancy between de jure and de facto implementation of gender equality policies in Hungary to the relative absence of civil society mobilisation combined with lack of government support for gender mainstreaming. Krizsán and Popa (2012) examine the impact of EU accession in the area of domestic violence policy, where there was no 'hard' conditionality to be met by candidate countries, but women's movements were successful in pressing for change. They argue that, in contrast to the external incentives model, Europeanisation can and does occur even in the absence of direct EU influence, through mechanisms of social learning and norm contestation in domestic political settings.

Scholars have also recently begun to study the impact of EU enlargement on LGBT politics in the post-communist region (Ayoub 2015; Ayoub and Paternotte 2014; O'Dwyer 2010, 2012; Slootmaeckers et al. 2016). Contributors to Sloootmaeckers et al. (2016) shed light on the interplay between enlargement and LGBT activism in post-communist Europe. Ayoub (2015) argues that the diffusion of LGBT norms to post-communist Europe can be at least partially explained by the fact that new-adopter states are 'more dependent on international resources for making new issues visible and are more inclined to see policy adoption as a means to gain external legitimacy and improve reputation', and that the transnational embeddedness of LGBT groups in CEE explains differentiation in their success. Overall, the emphasis in the literature on LGBT rights is on documenting the impact of EU enlargement in equality policy in this area, and explaining the factors determining policy adoption in the new EU member states and candidate countries.

A fourth and final strand of scholarship concerns intersectionality and EU enlargement. This is perhaps the area in which there is the greatest scope for additional work. Koldinska (2009) argues that coercive sterilisation of Roma women in the Czech Republic was a case of intersectional discrimination and needs to be addressed from the perspective of intersectional equality, a process where civil society actors prove to be indispensable. Krizsán and Zentai (2012) argue that, although post-communist Europe has witnessed a shift from the total absence of formal equality policies towards an increasing recognition of equality concerns, intersectionality is incorporated in a limited way into the equality regimes of the region.

Hence, there have been significant advances in scholarship in terms of understanding and conceptualising the impact of EU enlargement policy vis-à-vis the post-communist member states. These advances notwithstanding, there remains significant scope for further research.

Directions for future research

Scholarship on gender and EU enlargement could fruitfully develop further issues in future research, such as the following: (1) an integrated approach towards enlargement and Europeanisation that brings together analyses of the EU-15 and the new member states; (2) an exploration of the sources and nature of opposition to gender equality across Europe within the context of EU membership; (3) an examination of the role of informal norms in the process of EU enlargement, especially within the area of gender equality.

Since membership conditionality was minimal in the enlargement rounds prior to 2004, it is difficult to draw precise comparisons between the established and the new member states. It appears that potentially the most promising avenue of research is to compare the member states *after* accession through the theoretical framework of Europeanisation. Specifically, are there any differences between new and old democracies in terms of how they 'upload' their preferences to the EU level in the field of gender equality? Are the CEECs likely to resist the notion of gender equality to a greater extent than the older member states in a Union that is increasingly vulnerable to the forces of populism and democratic backsliding (see Siim and Fiig in this volume)? These questions are still unanswered, not least because the post-communist countries' input into EU policy-making still has to be studied in depth.

Recently, opposition to gender equality has been increasing in Europe; some of the post-communist member states, as well as some established democracies, have been at the forefront of these developments (Verloo 2018). We need to understand the precise terms of such opposition from a broader comparative perspective, which includes both the EU-15 and the post-communist member states. For instance, as van der Vleuten (2007, 179) argues, resistance to the adoption of gender equality policies in the 'old' member states was often framed in economic terms – 'when women become costly, states become contrary'. There is some evidence suggesting that this may well be true for CEE as well, in the context of the economic crisis. However, there is also evidence that, in the CEECs, resistance to the adoption of EU gender equality legislation may be supported by a different set of considerations that do not fit an economic cost–benefit frame. For instance, when President Vaclav Klaus vetoed the equal opportunities bill adopted by the Czech legislature in 2008, he argued that the Act addressed 'a natural phenomenon' – inequality. The issue of whether the notion of gender equality plays out differently in political debates in CEE thus needs to be examined in greater detail.

Finally, many studies have focused on the *formal* process of accession, including how conditionality became a part of accession, and the degree to which candidate countries met formal membership requirements. Given the growing literature on the role of *informal* institutions in national and international politics (see, for example, Waylen 2017), it is important to reflect on how informal norms shape the process of EU enlargement, especially in the western Balkans, where accession is still unfolding.

References

Avdeyeva OA (2015): *Defending Women's Rights in Europe: Gender Equality and EU Enlargement*, Albany: State University of New York.

Ayoub P (2015): Contested norms in new-adopter states. International determinants of LGBT rights legislation, *European Journal of International Relations* **21** (2), 293–322.

Ayoub P, Paternotte D, eds. (2014): *LGBT Activism and the Making of Europe: A Rainbow Europe?*, Basingstoke: Palgrave Macmillan.

Bego I (2015): *Gender Equality Policy in the European Union. A Fast Track to Parity for the New Member States*, Basingstoke: Palgrave Macmillan.

Börzel T, Risse T (2000). When Europe hits home. Europeanization and domestic change, *European Integration Online Papers* **4** (15), http://eiop.or.at/eiop/texte/2000-015a.htm.

Bretherton C (2001): Gender mainstreaming and EU enlargement: swimming against the tide?, *Journal of European Public Policy* **8** (1), 60–81.

Chiva C (2009): The limits of Europeanisation. EU accession and gender equality in Bulgaria and Romania, *Perspectives on European Politics and Society* **10** (2), 195–209.

Falkner G, Treib O (2008): Three worlds of compliance or four? The EU-15 compared to new member states, *Journal of Common Market Studies* **46** (2), 293–313.

Falkner G, Treib O, Holzleithner E (2008): *Compliance in the Enlarged European Union: Living Rights or Dead Letters?*, Aldershot: Ashgate.

Forest M, Lombardo E (2012): The Europeanisation of Gender Equality Policies: A Discursive–Sociological Approach, in: Lombardo E, Forest M (eds.): *The Europeanisation of Gender Equality Policies: A Discursive-Sociological Approach*, Basingstoke: Palgrave Macmillan, 1–27.

Grabbe H (2006): *The EU's Transformative Power. Europeanisation through Conditionality in Central and Eastern Europe*, Basingstoke: Palgrave Macmillan.

Haskova H, Krizkova A (2008): The Impact of EU Accession on the Promotion of Women and Gender Equality in the Czech Republic, in: Roth S (ed.): *Gender Politics in the Expanding European Union: Mobilisation, Inclusion, Exclusion,* Oxford: Berghahn Books, 155–173.

Janse R (2018): The evolution of the political criteria for accession to the European Community, 1957–1973, *European Law Journal* **24** (1), 57–76.

Kakucs N, Peto A (2008): The Impact of EU Accession on Gender Equality in Hungary, in: Roth S (ed.): *Gender Politics in the Expanding European Union: Mobilisation, Inclusion, Exclusion*, Oxford: Berghahn Books, 174–192.

Koldinska K (2009): Institutionalizing intersectionality: a new path to equality for new member states of the EU?, *International Feminist Journal of Politics* **11** (4), 547–563.

Krizsán A (2009): From formal adoption to enforcement. Post-accession shifts in EU impact on Hungary in the equality policy field, *European Integration Online Papers* **13** (2), http://eiop.or.at/eiop/texte/2009-022a.htm.

Krizsán A, Popa R (2012): Meanings and Uses of Europe in Making Policies Against Domestic Violence in Central and Eastern Europe, in: Lombardo E, Forest M (eds.): *The Europeanisation of Gender Equality Policies: A Discursive-Sociological Approach*, Basingstoke: Palgrave Macmillan, 49–74.

Krizsán A, Zentai V (2012). Institutionalizing Intersectionality in Central and Eastern Europe: Hungary, Poland, Romania, and Slovenia, in: Krizsán A Skjeie H, Squires J (eds.): *Institutionalising Intersectionality: The Changing Natures of European Equality Regimes*, Basingstoke: Palgrave Macmillan, 179–208.

O'Dwyer C (2010): From conditionality to persuasion? Europeanization and the rights of sexual minorities in post-accession Poland, *Journal of European Integration* **32** (3), 229–47.

O'Dwyer C (2012): Does the EU help or hinder gay-rights movements in post-communist Europe? The case of Poland, *East European Politics* **28** (4), 332–352.

Regulska J, Gabrowska M (2008): Will it Make a Difference? EU Enlargement and Women's Public Discourse in Poland, in: Roth S (ed.) *Gender Politics in the Expanding European Union: Mobilisation, Inclusion, Exclusion*, Oxford: Berghahn Books, 137–154.

Sasse G (2008): The politics of EU conditionality. The norm of minority protection during and beyond EU accession, *Journal of European Public Policy* **15** (6), 842–860.

Schimmelfennig F, Sedelmeier U (2002): Theorizing EU enlargement. Research focus, hypotheses, and the state of research, *Journal of European Public Policy* **9** (4), 500–528.

Schimmelfennig F, Sedelmeier U, eds. (2005): *The Europeanisation of Central and Eastern Europe*, Ithaca, NY: Cornell University Press.

Schimmelfennig F, Sedelmeier U (2020): The Europeanisation of Eastern Europe. The external incentives model revisited, *Journal of European Public Policy* **27** (6), 814–833.

Schwellnus G (2005): The Adoption of Non-Discrimination and Minority Protection Rules in Romania, Hungary and Poland, in: Schimmelfennig F, Sedelmeier U (eds.): *The Europeanisation of Central and Eastern Europe*, Ithaca, NY: Cornell University Press, 29–50.

Slootmaeckers K, Touquet H, Vermeersch P, eds. (2016): *The EU Enlargement and Gay Politics. The Impact of Eastern Enlargement on Rights, Activism and Prejudice*, Basingstoke: Palgrave Macmillan.

Smith KE (2003): The Evolution and Application of EU Membership Conditionality, in: Cremona M (ed.): *The Enlargement of the European Union*, Oxford: Oxford University Press, 105–140.

Vachudova MA (2005): *Undivided Europe: Democracy, Leverage and Integration after Communism*, Oxford: Oxford University Press.

van der Vleuten A (2007): *The Price of Gender Equality. Member States and Governance in the European Union*, Aldershot: Ashgate.

Verloo M, ed. (2018): *Varieties of Opposition to Gender Equality in Europe*, London: Routledge.

Velluti S (2014): Gender regimes and gender equality measures in central eastern European countries post-accession: the case of Hungary and Poland, *Journal of International and Comparative Social Policy* **30** (1), 79–91.

Waylen G, ed (2017): *Gender and Informal Institutions*, London: Rowman & Littlefield.

16

Gender and EU citizenship

Birte Siim and Monika Mokre

The effects of EU citizenship arrangements are gendered. While EU citizenship establishes equal rights, the underlying concept has a flipside that mirrors national citizenship: it promises inclusion to all EU citizens at the expense of excluding outsiders. European citizenship distinguishes between three groups: national citizens, EU citizens, and third country nationals (TCNs). The gendered effects of European citizenship mirror those of national citizenship, privileging mobile male wageworkers at the expense of women who are mothers and caretakers, and mobile over stay-at-home citizens, and denying migrant women access to social rights as third country workers.

This chapter first presents the classic concept of citizenship and feminist approaches to reframing that concept. Secondly, it gives an overview of the gendered effects of EU citizenship and identifies key gender equality problems connected with the institutionalization of gender equality in the EU and the practice of equal rights. It employs an intersectional approach to the gendered effects of EU citizenship focusing on the synergies between gender and diversity and gender and migration. The third section examines recent political developments in the EU, the European Parliament, and EU member states that have placed abortion, gender equality, and women's rights on the political agenda and discusses feminist strategies to preserve these rights. The conclusion sums up the main points and reflects on the challenges for future gender research on EU citizenship. It proposes that one fruitful strategy is the further development of the multi-layered and intersectional approach to EU citizenship.

The construction of citizenship

The concept of citizenship

Various concepts of citizenship date back to ancient times, but the development of modern citizenship is a child of the French Revolution. Active political citizenship as a status that was, in principle, universally applicable became closely related to the concept of the nation state with its clear-cut demarcation between nation states and their respective citizens (Brubaker 1994, 78). This concept of citizenship has to be understood against the economic background

Birte Siim and Monika Mokre

of the rise of capitalism, which made the centralized administration of large territories and cohesive populations (the imagined national community, see Anderson 1996) useful, if not necessary:

> The net effect of these [...] processes was to create a "people", who were entitled to be treated as equals before the law and possessed equal rights to buy and sell goods, services and labour; whose interests were overseen by a sovereign political authority emanating from their corporate unity; and who shared a national identity that shaped their allegiance to each other and to their state. All three elements became important for democratic citizenship.

> *(Bellamy et al. 2006, 4)*

In the beginning, slaves, people without property, and women were legally excluded from citizenship rights (Brubaker 1994, 71) – as far as women are concerned, this was reflected in the three core slogans of the French Revolution: liberty, equality, and *brother*hood. Although these legal exclusions were gradually removed (enfranchisement of women being an important indicator), they have continued to govern the practice of citizenship:

> [E]ven when citizenship is formally extended to ever-broader groups of subjects, widespread enjoyment or practice of citizenship is not thereby guaranteed. Rather, there is often a gap between possession of citizenship status and the enjoyment and performance of citizenship in substantive terms.

> *(Bosniak 2005, 195)*

As far as the situation of women is concerned, the fact that political rights and protections have mostly been restricted to the public sphere presents a crucial problem since women's lives have, to a substantial degree, been concentrated in the private sphere. "The integrative effect of citizenship rights applied to male citizens while for women, family relationships and marriage were supposed to form the most important social relations" (Appelt 1999, 89; translation by the authors). This illustrates the possible conflict between the principles of equality and difference spelled out by Mary Wollstonecraft (1759–1797). In her famous work *A Vindication of the Rights of Woman* (1792), Wollstonecraft pointed to the way in which women's participation in the public sphere as equal citizens reproduces inequality if one denies their difference and fails to take women's experiences as women into account. Feminist approaches to gendered citizenship have conceptualized this "Wollstonecraft dilemma", claiming that Marshall's classic model leads to the marginalization of women as second-class citizens. They conclude that the public/private divide has led to the inclusion of men in the public sphere as independent citizens/workers/voters and the exclusion of women relegated to the private sphere as dependent wives/mothers (Lister 2003; Pateman 1988; Siim 2000).

Scholars have analyzed the interaction between the public and private arenas and proposed various strategies for women's empowerment and increased participation in politics that could be pursued from above, by political institutions, or from below, by civil society activism (Siim 2000). In this vein, Carol Pateman (1988) proposed a differentiated model of citizenship designed to include women both as women and as equal citizens. Ruth Lister (2003) assumes that a creative tension exists between a universalistic "ethic of justice", on the one hand, and a particularistic "ethic of care" which may give equal status to women and men in their diversity, on the other hand. She suggests that a model of "differentiated universalism" (Lister 2003, 90) could resolve this tension.

Political rights and human rights

The conjunction of nationality and citizenship leads to the exclusion of the citizens of other nation states from fundamental rights (both by definition and by law). The aim of the United Nations' Universal Declaration of Human Rights (UDHR), proclaimed in 1948, was to resolve this contradiction between the universalist claim to citizenship and its realization in particular contexts (Mackert and Müller 2000, 12). On the one hand, Article 15 of the UDHR postulates the right of every person to citizenship, i.e. to be a citizen of some country, and prohibits its arbitrary withdrawal. On the other hand, the declaration also defines rights owed to an individual independently of their citizenship. Yet, these stipulations alone are incapable of fully remedying the "rightlessness" of non-citizens. As Hannah Arendt maintained in the 1950s, rights not related to citizenship can never compensate for the lack of citizenship rights. According to Arendt (1951, 297), rights depend on one's belonging to a polity. Consequently, human beings must have the right to be part of a polity in order to enjoy the only truly decisive human right: the right to have rights (Arendt 1951, 177).

Arendt's considerations, which drew on her experiences with statelessness and mass migration during World War II, are of considerable importance to contemporary migration societies, including those in the EU. Here, we can observe an erosion of the homogenizing effect of citizenship as recourse is increasingly being taken to qualities that supposedly precede political affiliation, such as cultural characteristics:

> The problem with the logics of exclusion and enclosure is that they assume that such identities as 'woman' and 'immigrant' preceded citizenship and were excluded from it. Becoming political involves questioning such essential categories as 'woman' or 'immigrant' as given and assumes that they were produced in the process of constituting citizenship and that they are internally, not externally, related to it.
>
> *(Isin 2002, 4)*

Differences – notably of nationality, gender, and class – thus affect the granting and withholding of legally established citizenship rights, and Arendt's radical conclusion that the exclusion from political rights amounts to an exclusion from humanity must apply to the situation of every human being who is not, or not fully, recognized as a bearer of political rights. This brings us back to the partial inclusion of women in the concept of citizenship. As long as the lives of many women largely take place outside the political sphere, the universality of political rights remains an unfulfilled promise.

Key issues and debates for EU citizenship

The experience of war, totalitarianism, and the annihilation of millions of people made Hannah Arendt a strong supporter of European integration. She expressed her support for the contention of "the Dutch underground" that "a good peace is not conceivable unless the States surrender parts of their economic and political sovereignty to a higher European authority" (Arendt 1994, 113).

Even as the war ended, Arendt was in no doubt that a sustainable post-war settlement presupposed the political integration of Europe. As early as the 1950s, Arendt had already grasped the eminently political character of the project of European integration. The concept and issue of European citizenship forms one of the core elements of the political dimension of European integration. Officially implemented only by the 1993 Treaty of Maastricht, European citizenship was arguably anticipated by the process of European integration from the outset. It already featured in a rudimentary form in the 1952 Treaty establishing the European Coal and Steel Community (ECSC) in the guise not of an individual right but of a (limited) option for the free movement of coal and steel workers (Maas 2005). The Treaty on the European Economic Community (EEC) of 1957 then granted citizens the general right to move freely in order to work or search for work in another member state and prohibited the discrimination of citizens of other member states with regard to employment (Article 7 EEC Treaty). Motivated principally not by political but by economic considerations, these provisions addressed the citizens of the European member states as employees and employers rather than political actors, creating a form of "market citizenship" (Bell 2007, 329; see Milner in this volume).

It is worth mentioning, however, that individual citizens were able to lodge complaints with the Court of Justice of the European Union (CJEU; previously called European Court of Justice, ECJ) from the time of its foundation in 1952. In this way, the individual rights of citizens of the then still called European Community (EC) member states were directly recognized. The CJEU's judgments from the 1960s onwards re-enforced these rights and laid crucial foundations for the subsequent official definition of European citizenship (see Guth and Elfving in this volume). Most importantly, the CJEU sanctioned EC citizens' right of free movement between member states. It also maintained, however, that this right applied only to EC citizens not to TCNs residing in the member states, thus illustrating a crucial feature of European citizenship, namely that it presupposes citizenship in one of the member states (Valchars 2017, 138–149).

The EU did not begin to roll out individual political citizenship rights until 1979, when it introduced direct elections to the European Parliament (see Ahrens and Rolandsen Agustín (European Parliament) in this volume). Further steps in this direction discussed in the 1970s were: the unconditional right to take up residence in another member state (without the condition of gainful employment) and the right of EC citizens to participate in local or even general elections in the member state in which they reside, regardless of their nationality. The possible introduction of a common European passport and abolition of border controls within the EC was already debated at this time.

None of these proposals were realized until much later, mostly in a reduced form. The right of residency for people without employment in member states other than that whose citizen they are was implemented in 1989 only for students, pensioners, and people with sufficient financial means of their own and adequate insurance. Moreover, it was limited to five years and could be withheld for reasons of public safety and thus substantially fell short of the unconditional right of EC citizens to reside in any member state (Valchars 2017, 75). European passports – or, more precisely, national passports in a unitary, European format – were introduced in 1985, the same year as the first Schengen Agreement stipulated the abolition of border controls between its signatory states until 1990 (Valchars 2017, 77–84).

The Treaty of Maastricht (1993) eventually implemented the right of EU citizens to participate in local and European elections in the member state in which they reside, irrespective of their nationality. Although the right to vote in general, national or regional, elections was still limited to the nationals of the respective member states, this officially established the status of EU citizenship. In addition, the rights to freedom of movement, to consular protection, to apply to the European Ombudsman and to submit petitions to the European Parliament were extended (these last two rights in fact apply to every person residing in the EU) (Valchars 2017, 87). The Treaty also included a general ban on the discrimination of citizens of other member states (Article 6 TEU). The Treaty of Lisbon (2009), while not adding any new rights, enshrined the European Charter of Fundamental Rights in EU primary law.

The restriction of European citizenship to those who already hold the citizenship of one of the member states has been contested for decades. The issue was raised once again in the run up to the adoption of the Treaty of Amsterdam (1997), when civil society organizations proposed a redefinition of European citizenship to stipulate that "every person holding the nationality of a Member State and every person residing within the territory of the European Union [shall be a citizen of the Union]" (Wiener 2001, 85). Yet to date, the implementation of such aspirations has gone no further than the Maastricht Treaty's introduction of visa-free travel for TCNs within the EU for a maximum period of three months.

Due to the direct derivation of EU citizenship from national citizenship, the ability of TCNs to obtain EU citizenship is dependent on the conditions for naturalization in the respective member state. These conditions usually include proof of gainful employment and sufficient financial means. In addition, naturalization ordinarily depends on a certain period of continuous residence in a particular member state. Thus, mobile TCNs are less likely to obtain European citizenship than their "static" counterparts. This arguably contradicts the fundamental aspiration underpinning European integration: the creation of a common economic and political space.

EU citizenship has a dual character: it embodies the promise of a future world in which the links between citizenship and the nation state are much weaker, while simultaneously it has also created new boundaries. EU citizenship has transformed the bipolar system of national citizenship into a three-layered system of privileges and exclusions encompassing national citizenship, EU citizenship, and third country citizenship. In practice, this system is complemented by further distinctions. For example, citizens of new member states have temporarily been excluded from certain rights associated with the freedom of movement. Conversely, certain rights guaranteed by the EU apply only to "mobile" citizens, i.e. citizens who live (or have lived) in the EU but outside their country of origin (Bruzelius et al. 2017; Valchars 2017, 157).

Gendering EU citizenship

In this section, we will illustrate what a gendering of EU citizenship would imply with regard to several dimensions and groups.

Citizenship rights

As EU citizenship presupposes national citizenship in a member state, the legal status of EU citizens can be complex. It hinges on EU law that directly protects key citizenship rights (above all the right to free movement), on EU regulations enshrined in national legislation, and on purely national laws (Bakker and van der Kolk 2016). The member states take a "link approach" or engage in a "marketization" of citizenship, hence they may adopt conditions on entry and residency that systematically disadvantage specific groups of citizens (Bakker and van der Kolk 2018). They may link access to rights to gainful employment in the country of residency, excluding persons who care for family members, people in low-paid jobs, job seekers etc. In practice, this approach to citizenship creates a gender bias (Pennings et al. 2016). Economically inactive citizens of other states are required to demonstrate some degree of existing integration, frequently linked to a specific family status. While EU law allows EU citizens to bring their family members to another EU member state, only spouses and dependent children or relatives automatically qualify as family. The extent to which other forms of partnership fulfil the conditions for residency depends on national legislation (de Waele and Solis Santos 2016). In addition, the fact that the legal status of spouses hinges on their relationship to a gainfully employed partner leads to a high level of personal dependence (Anderson et al. 2016a).

Limited, as it originally was, to employed people, EU citizens' most important right, i.e. the freedom of movement, excluded the majority of women since the male breadwinner model was still dominant in most member states at the time. While freedom of movement was extended to non-employed people in 1989, they still need to demonstrate an ability to support themselves, which continues to exclude more women than men. The same holds true for restrictions that render the freedom of movement of citizens from new member states conditional on their income and wealth.

Freedom of movement is not only the most important right conveyed directly by the EU to its citizens; it is also a precondition for the enjoyment of other specific rights. This is a general problem inherent in EU citizenship since only 3% of EU citizens make use of their right to move to another EU country. It also creates a gender bias, since women are frequently less mobile than men are due to family and care obligations (Appelt 1999; Mokre and Siim 2018).

Like national concepts of citizenship, in principle EU citizenship encompasses social rights. However, since these rights mostly depend on national legislation they are never as far-reaching as those for national citizens. Migrating EU citizens are not entitled to social assistance payments within the first three months of their stay in another member state, although they can export a previously acquired entitlement to unemployment benefits to their new country of residency. As long as the standard of living in the member states was roughly similar, this was a good way of fostering social equality. However, following the accession of much poorer central and eastern European countries since 2004, it is no longer possible to live, say, on Romanian unemployment benefits in Germany (Seeleib-Kaiser 2017; on enlargement see Chiva in this volume). Given the gender pay gap in all EU countries, these inequalities tend to affect women in particular.

Citizen participation

Theories of democracy distinguish between two concepts of citizenship: the liberal concept focusing on legal rights, and the republican concept focusing on political identity and participation (Dell'Olio 2005; Kymlicka and Norman 1995; Leydet 2011; Marshall 1965). Scholars frequently point out that EU citizens are less interested in voting on the EU level than they are in national elections. Possibly, because the associated legal rights are too weak and citizens lack knowledge about EU issues, EU citizens generally show limited interest in active political participation in the EU's affairs (Bakker and van der Kolk 2018). For the majority of citizens, their national citizenship rights are much more important than their rights as EU citizens. Hence, they do not develop a strong European identity. The democratic legitimacy of the European Parliament has remained precarious, since citizens' political identities and sense of belonging continue to be tied mainly to local/regional and national communities rather than transnational politics. Thus, voter turnout in European Parliament elections is low (on average 20–25 percentage points lower than in national elections), and lower social classes in particular tend not to vote, which may distort election results to favour the interests of more affluent citizens.

Though gender does not affect the franchise as such, one may assume that this poses a problem for the representation of the interests of economically deprived women (Eberl and Seubert 2016). In addition, feminist scholars have identified a twofold democratic deficit with regard to women's participation, an institutional deficit involving women's underrepresentation across European institutions and decision-making; and a deeper gender democratic deficit reflecting the lack of gender sensitivity in EU policy-making (Mushaben and Abels 2012, 228–247).

The European Parliament, as the only directly elected EU institution, nevertheless offers a positive example of women's growing influence. The number of female members (MEPs) has

Gender and EU citizenship

increased dramatically from 5% in 1979 to an historical 39% elected in 2019 (Abels 2020; Fella et al. 2019). It is remarkable that this increase in women's political representation has gone hand in hand with an expansion of the European Parliament's powers. A recent analysis emphasizes the multiple relations between gender and power in the European Parliament (Ahrens and Rolandsen Agustín 2019) and the extent to which the quantitative increase in female representation, in conjunction with the Parliament's expanded powers, might genuinely strengthen the cause of women's rights and gender equality. Yet relevant studies also acknowledge the recent challenges posed by the opposition of right-wing nationalists, conservatives, and Eurosceptics to gender equality (Abels 2020; Meier et al. 2019; see also Ahrens and Rolandsen Agustín (Party politics) in this volume).

Third country nationals

The political impact of EU citizenship is debatable. It can be credited with the creation of the infamous "fortress Europe", on the one hand, that has strengthened the exclusionary side of citizenship (Lister 2003, 47), and a post-national model of citizenship based on a de-territorialized notion of individual rights, on the other (Soysal 1994). EU legislation prohibits the discrimination of EU citizens but, by privileging EU citizens, actually stipulates the discrimination of TCNs. Since the terrorist attacks of 9/11, strict security regulations and measures such as border patrols, language tests, and the tightening of age restrictions on dependents allowed to join their relatives in the EU, have been introduced. Consequently, it has become increasingly difficult for TCNs to enter the EU and obtain legal residency, and for immigrants to obtain EU citizenship and enjoy civil equality (Karyotis 2007).

Restrictions on immigration (see Krause and Schwenken in this volume) have led to gender-specific problems for residents who are not EU citizens. In many countries, men are still the main breadwinners, which makes women dependent wives, denied the right to employment. Female migrants (and refugees) entering the EU to join relatives are largely invisible and experience specific problems, for example as workers with dependent children or as dependent wives. Lack of education and employment often force women into traditional caretaking roles. The fact that naturalization in most member states is dependent upon a regular income or sufficient means to sustain oneself frequently impedes access to EU citizenship. Joyce Mushaben's (2012) analysis of EU initiatives promoting, and barriers to, gender-sensitive migration policies points to a critical synergy between gender- and migration-related processes of integration. She shows that policies defining who may or may not enter any given territory or acquire citizenship are one of the last bastions of national sovereignty, hence the many barriers to the integration of migrants and their offspring (Mushaben 2012, 225).

Just as social rights are increasingly linked to (previous) salaried work for national citizens, TCNs must usually prove their financial independence in order to acquire and maintain a residency permit. Thus, even when TCNs are entitled to social benefits (for example, after some time of employment) they may endanger their further residency by claiming them (Shutes 2016). This also holds true for naturalization, which in most EU countries calls for continuous gainful employment and sufficient financial resources as a precondition of citizenship. To the extent that women are more likely than men to be engaged in care work or have part-time, low-paid, precarious jobs with limited social rights, these prerequisites are particularly likely to exclude them (Anderson et al. 2016b; Shutes 2016).

However, given the EU's general anti-discrimination provisions introduced with Article 13 of the 1997 Amsterdam Treaty (see Solanke in this volume), EU policies also affect TCNs in positive ways, and the shift in focus from gender to diversity in the EU's equality policies has further

201

Birte Siim and Monika Mokre

expanded the scope of these provisions. Intersectional politics address the intersections of gender and other forms of inequality, such as class, sexuality, race/ethnicity, nationality, and religion, and of national and transnational dimensions (Krizsán et al. 2012; Siim and Mokre 2013). From an intersectional perspective, the Amsterdam Treaty represents a milestone because it extended individual freedoms and protection against discrimination from gender to a range of distinctions in terms of race, religion, nationality, age, disability, and sexual orientation. The EU's turning its attention to the implementation of equality legislation and its establishment of new types of equality institutions addressing gender, race, and ethnicity marked a significant step forward (Krizsán et al. 2012, 20). Even so, the treaty maintained the distinction between EU citizens and TCNs and it did not designate unequal treatment on the grounds of this distinction a form of illegal discrimination (see Article 3(2) of the Race Equality Directive 2000/43/EC; Bell 2007, 10).

Recent developments

The delineation of the private and public realms, of women's and human rights, has recently become a matter of extensive political deliberation again in Europe. Debates on gender are increasingly focusing on reproductive rights and abortion, on the discrimination of LGBTQIA (lesbian, gay, bisexual, transsexual, queer, intersex, asexual) people, and on minority/migration rights.

The recent economic and financial crisis has stimulated the growth of Eurosceptic nationalist parties (see Siim and Fiig in this volume). A comparative study of the radical right-wing parties (RRP) represented in the European Parliament has shown that opposition to gender equality and emphasis on family values are often instrumentalized to serve nationalist, racist, and populist aims (see Krizsán and Siim 2018, 54–57). The study points to similarities and differences in the ways in which gender and family issues are framed by Euroscepticism, by domestic gender, welfare, and migration regimes, and in a range of political opportunity structures. It concludes that, against the backdrop of the opposition, or lack of commitment, to gender equality of various religious, cultural, and ethnic subgroups, the examined RRP take varying positions on the issue of gender equality, depending on their respective reference groups. In addition, they instrumentalize family values to legitimize other core objectives of RRP ideology, such as the implementation of exclusive, chauvinist welfare systems premised on nationalist and ethnicized hierarchies that disadvantage Roma, migrants, and the citizens of other EU member states.

The recent economic crisis has also exacerbated tensions inherent in EU citizenship (see Kantola and Lombardo in this volume) and stimulated political debates between nationalist/nativist Eurosceptics and pro-European parties regarding EU interventions in social policy. A recent study by the European Parliament's Committee on Women's Rights and Gender Equality (FEMM) documents the extent to which controversies concerning, and resistance to, EU interventions have escalated in the EP, especially when women or migrants and ethnic or religious minorities are concerned (see Nissen and Rolandsen Agustín 2018).

Future research should focus on the ways in which EU citizenship impacts nationalist approaches to issues of gender and the extent to which public perceptions of EU citizenship have helped strengthen nationalist agendas. Do citizens assume that their counterparts from other member states living among them enjoy their rights at the expense of the national population or attribute the erosion of social rights to the neoliberal bias of European integration?

Moving forward: key issues and debates

Globalization and Europeanization present theoretical and normative challenges for gender and citizenship research, albeit in different ways (Delanty 2000; Siim 2013). EU citizenship can be defined as a supplementary, third form of citizenship derived from national citizenship, a form of nested citizenship based upon residency. European integration has thus created new tensions between the national and transnational dimensions of EU citizenship and new distinctions between insiders and outsiders. Scholars have proposed that citizenship should be redefined to focus not on nationality but on residency, thus giving mobile citizens and TCNs the right to enter and to acquire fully enfranchised EU citizenship rights (Bauböck 2006).

Scholars have argued that European citizenship, despite its present limitations, has opened up new institutional possibilities for democratic citizenship for some groups (students, pensioners, and people capable of sustaining themselves financially) that are indeed premised on residency rather than birth (Delanty 2000). According to Faist and Kivisto (2007), EU citizenship has facilitated a trend towards dual citizenship, given that citizens of one member state are not required to renounce their original citizenship upon naturalization in another. This can be interpreted as a pluralization of citizens' ties across the borders of sovereign states. This strand of scholarship focuses primarily on human rights and rarely addresses issues of gender equality and women's rights.

Europeanization has also precipitated normative debates about the need to develop a differentiated, variegated concept of citizenship within the EU. Engin Isin is among the scholars who emphasize contemporary changes in citizenship legislation and the ways in which various citizenship rights are increasingly "blurring the boundaries between human and civil, political and social rights and the articulation of rights by (and to) cities, regions and across states" (Isin 2009, 367). They have proposed new concepts suited to tackle contemporary global and European political transformations and support the development of a post-national, pluri-national, or even international, situated and transformative form of EU citizenship (Balibar 1988; Benhabib 2002; Isin 2017; Kochenov 2016; Shaw 2016; Valchars 2017).

Globalization and Europeanization have also inspired feminist scholarship exploring post-national conceptions of citizenship, from the local to the global level, from a gender perspective (Liebert 2003; Siim 2013). For example, Nira Yuval-Davis's (2011) influential approach rethinks the nation/nation state and transnational citizenship from a gender perspective that proposes a multi-layered model of citizenship and transnational identities and understands contemporary citizenship as resulting from the negotiation of competing political projects of belonging to a range of political communities (Yuval-Davis 2011, 68–71). This approach identifies contested questions related to boundaries, such as "who has the right to have rights?" and "who cares for whom?", emphasizing that people's citizenship is linked in intersectional ways to a multi-layered polity consisting of sub-, cross-, and supra-state political communities (Yuval-Davis 2011, 201–203).

Gender studies are concerned with the EU's democratic deficit (Abels and Mushaben 2012), the remaking of citizenship in multicultural Europe (Halsaa et al. 2012) and, most recently, with the gendering of the European Parliament (Ahrens and Rolandsen Agustín 2019). One important area is studies of women's citizenship rights and the lived citizenship of various groups of women, exploring how women across the EU exercise their rights or negotiate their lack of rights, and express their sense of belonging to a range of local, national, and transnational arenas. Another area is a focus on relevant practices and affiliations on how the remaking of national and EU citizenship works across different social groups, gender, ethnicity/race, religion, and nationality. Furthermore, it is worth analyzing how citizens link EU citizenship to gender issues. Do citizens perceive of the principle of gender equality as something imposed by the EU against traditional national values, or see less progressive EU gender legislation as a threat to national gender equality norms? The nexus between gender questions and the exclusion of non-national populations is likewise of academic interest. Do citizens consider EU citizens' freedom of movement a threat to national conceptions of gender relations, or, conversely, assume that the exclusionary character of EU citizenship offers a defense against non-European notions of gender? Can one develop a form of EU citizenship that reduces the attraction of nationalist ideologies and increases gender equality?

Conclusion

EU citizenship has helped weaken the close link between citizenship and the nation state and demonstrated the need to strengthen transnational civil, social, and political rights premised not on nationality but on residency. Still, in this chapter we have identified three main forms of exclusion inherent in EU citizenship: first, the dominant market citizen concept mainly restricted to male breadwinners; second, the positive discrimination of mobile EU citizens in contrast to "static" family members; and, third, the exclusion of TCNs from social rights. As Derrida (2000, 11–12) maintains: even if we replace the term "brotherhood" by a gender-neutral word such as "solidarity", the original exclusion of women remains effective – women are incorporated not as sisters but as a special case of brothers.

Gender research has compared the impact of Europeanization (see Forest in this volume) on policies across European member states, and scholars have proposed intersectional and multi-layered analytical approaches to the nexus between gender and other social categories across Europe, focusing on local, regional, national, and transnational communities. Migration itself, and the recent governance crisis that has arisen as Europe grapples with large numbers of refugees and the issue of asylum, have once again placed citizenship and human rights centre stage. It points to the political need for common European solutions in dealing with asylum seekers and refugees and protecting the human rights of all citizens, TCNs, immigrants, and minorities living within the EU. Against this backdrop, it is a major problem that homeland security concerns, re-enforced by increasing nationalism and right-wing populism, continue to trump human rights and undermine the cause of equality.

The implications of EU citizenship for gender relations and the rights of women are ambiguous. On the one hand, freedom of movement within a supranational territory forms an advantage for human beings of every sex and gender, equality between women and men has been part of European integration from the outset, and the introduction of more encompassing anti-discrimination politics has further re-enforced this tendency. On the other hand, the concept of EU citizenship has mostly reproduced the male bias of national and differentiated forms of citizenship leading to further forms of discrimination. Perhaps most importantly, the increasingly rigid control and exclusion of TCNs endangers human rights and, again, affects women in particular ways. This confirms Hannah Arendt's contention, which she articulated 70 years ago, that human rights have little impact on the real-life situation of migrants and refugees unless they are accompanied by political rights.

Even so, gender scholars generally agree that EU citizenship has played an important role in strengthening gender equality and women's and LGBTQIA rights in the member states. Arguably, one of the most important achievement lies in the fact that it has weakened – though not broken – the direct and seemingly inevitable link between citizenship and the nation state. This has inspired researchers to think in more concrete terms about supranational and transnational citizenship. Feminist researchers have prominently contributed to this research, especially by conceptualizing citizenship in a broader way that is not limited to a legal status but conceptualizes citizenship as an integral dimension of people's everyday lives. In this sense, citizenship is understood as resulting from the negotiation of competing political projects of belonging to a range of communities at the local, national, and transnational level. Within a globalized world of immigration and emigration societies, the importance of the EU as a supra-national polity, however flawed and problematic, can hardly be overstated.

In sum, EU citizenship has helped weaken the close link between citizenship and the nation state and research has demonstrated the need to strengthen transnational civil, social, and political rights premised not on nationality but on residency. Feminist scholarship proposes that we need more intersectional studies of how the remaking of national and EU citizenship influences different social groups, gender, ethnicity/race, religion, and nationality.

References

Abels G (2020): Gendering the 2019–2024 European Parliament, in: Kaeding M, Müller M, Schmälter J (eds.): *Die Europawahl 2019: Ringen um die Zukunft Europas,* Wiesbaden: Springer VS, 407–421.

Abels G, Mushaben JM eds., 2012: *Gendering the European Union,* Basingstoke: Palgrave Macmillan.

Ahrens P, Rolandsen Agustín L, eds. (2019): *Gendering the European Parliament. Introducing Structures, Policies and Practices,* London: Rowman & Littlefield.

Anderson B (1996): *Die Erfindung der Nation. Zur Karriere eines folgenreichen Konzepts,* Frankfurt am Main, New York: Campus.

Anderson B, Lepianka D, Baričević V, Murphy K, Gal J, Alfasi-Hanley M, Keidar E, Shutes I, Walker S, Ramos Martín NE (2016a): *Citizenship and Work. Case Studies of Differential Inclusion/Exclusion,* Oxford: bEUcitizen, URL: https://zenodo.org/record/61788#.X6FgslAxnZs (download: May 6, 2020).

Anderson B, Shutes I, Walker S (2016b): *European Policy Brief. Mobility and Citizenship in Europe. From the Worker-Citizen to Inclusive European Union Citizenship. Policy scenarios and recommendations from bEUcitizen. A research project on the barriers to realise and exercise citizenship rights by European Union citizens,* Oxford: bEUcitizen, URL: www.uu.nl/en/research/beucitizen-european-citizenship-research/publications (download: May 6, 2020).

Appelt E (1999): *Geschlecht – Staatsbürgerschaft – Nation. Politische Konstruktionen des Geschlechterverhältnisses in Europa,* Frankfurt am Main, New York: Campus.

Arendt H (1951): *The Origins of Totalitarianism,* New York: Harcourt Brace.

Arendt H (1994): Approaches to the "German Problem", in: Arendt, H: *Essays in Understanding, 1930–1954. Formation, Exile, and Totalitarianism,* New York: Harcourt Brace, 106–120.

Bakker W, van der Kolk M (2016): *Towards Impact Assessment indicators for EU citizenship,* Utrecht: bEUcitizen, URL: www.uu.nl/en/files/towards-impact-assessment-indicators-for-eu-citizenship-d11-2pdf (download: May 6, 2020).

Bakker W, van der Kolk M (2018): *Scenarios for EU Citizenship in 2030. Repertoires for Action in Thinkable Futures,* Utrecht: bEUcitizen, URL: www.uu.nl/en/files/scenarios-for-eu-citizenship-in-2030-repertoires-for-action-in-thinkable-fiturespdf (download: May 6, 2020).

Balibar É (1988): Propositions on citizenship, *Ethics* **98** (4), 723–730.

Bauböck R (2006): *Who are the citizens of Europe?,* URL: www.eurozine.com/who-are-the-citizens-of-europe/ (download: May 6, 2020).

Bell M (2007): Civic citizenship and migrant integration, *European Public Law* **13** (2), 311–333.

Bellamy R, Castiglione D, Shaw J (2006): Introduction. From National to Transnational Citizenship, in: Bellamy R, Castiglione D, Shaw J (eds.): *Making European Citizens. Civic Inclusion in a Transnational Context,* Basingstoke: Palgrave Macmillan, 1–28.

Benhabib S (2002): *The Claims of Culture. Equality and Diversity,* Princeton, NJ: Princeton University Press.

Bosniak L (2005): Citizenship, in: Tushnet M, Cane P (eds.): *The Oxford Handbook of Legal Studies,* Oxford, New York: Oxford University Press, 183–201.

Brubaker R (1994): *Staats-Bürger. Deutschland und Frankreich im historischen Vergleich,* Hamburg: Junius.

Bruzelius C, Reinprecht C, Seeleib-Kaiser M, (2017): Stratified social rights limiting EU citizenship, *Journal of Common Market Studies* 55 (6), 1239–1253.

de Waele H, Solis Santos T (2016): *Cross-Task Analysis,* Antwerpen: bEUcitizen, URL: www.uu.nl/sites/default/files/cross-task-analysis-d7-7.pdf (download May 6, 2020).

Delanty G (2000): *Citizenship in a Global Age. Society, culture, politics,* Buckingham: Open University Press.

Dell'Olio F (2005): *The Europeanization of Citizenship: Between the Ideology of Nationality, Immigration and European Identity,* Aldershot: Ashgate.

Derrida J (2000): *Politik der Freundschaft*, Frankfurt am Main: Suhrkamp.

Eberl O, Seubert S (2016): *European Policy Brief. European Political Citizenship 2030: Postdemocracy with Populist Activism or an Integrated Political and Social Citizenship? Policy scenarios and recommendations from bEUcitizen, a research project on the barriers to realise and exercise citizenship rights by European Union citizens*, Frankfurt am Main: bEUcitizens, URL: http://publikationen.ub.uni-frankfurt.de/frontdoor/index/index/year/2017/docId/43904 (download: May 6, 2020).

Faist T, Kivisto P, eds. (2007): *Dual Citizenship in Global Perspective. From Unitary to Multiple Citizenship*, Basingstoke: Palgrave Macmillan.

Fella S, Uberoi E, Cracknell R (2019): *European Parliament Elections 2019. Results and analysis*, House of Commons Library Briefing Paper 8600 (June 26), London: House of Commons, URL: http://researchbriefings.files.parliament.uk/documents/CBP-8600/CBP-8600.pdf (download: May 6, 2020).

Halsaa B, Roseneil S, Sümer S, eds. (2012): *Remaking Citizenship in Multicultural Europe. Women's Movement, Gender and Diversity*, Basingstoke: Palgrave Macmillan.

Isin EF (2009): Citizenship in the flux. The figure of the activist citizen, *Subjectivity* **29**, 367–388.

Isin EF (2002): *Being Political. Genealogies of Citizenship*, Minneapolis: University of Minnesota Press.

Isin EF (2017): Enacting International Citizenship, in: Basaran T, Bigo D, Guittet EP, Walker RBJ (eds.): *International Political Sociology: Transversal Lines*, London: Routledge.

Karyotis G (2007): European migration policy in the aftermath of September 11. The security–migration nexus, *Innovation: The European Journal of Social Science Research* **20** (1), 1–17.

Kochenov D (2016): EU Citizenship and Withdrawals from the Union: How Inevitable Is the Radical Downgrading of Rights?, *LSE 'Europe in Question' Discussion Paper Series, LEQS Paper* **111**, London: LSE European Institute.

Krizsán A, Siim B (2018): Gender Equality and Family in European Populist Radical Right Agendas. European Parliamentary Debates, in: Knijn T, Naldini M (eds.): *Gender and Generational Division in EU Citizenship*, Cheltenham: Edward Elgar, 39–59.

Krizsán A, Skjeie H, Squires J, eds. (2012): *Institutionalizing Intersectionality. The Changing Nature of European Equality Regimes*, Houndmills: Palgrave Macmillan.

Kymlicka W, Norman W (1995): Return of the Citizen. A Survey of Recent Work on Citizenship Theory, in: Beiner R (ed.): *Theorizing Citizenship*, Albany: State University of New York Press, 283–322.

Leydet D (2011): Citizenship, *Stanford Encyclopedia of Philosophy*, URL: http://plato.stanford.edu/entries/citizenship (download: May 6, 2020).

Liebert U, ed. (2003): *Gendering Europeanisation*, Brussels: Peter Lang.

Lister R (2003): *Citizenship. Feminist Perspectives*, Basingstoke: Palgrave Macmillan.

Maas W (2005): The genesis of European rights, *Journal of Common Market Studies* **43** (5), 1009–1025.

Mackert J, Müller HP (2000): Der soziologische Gehalt moderner Staatsbürgerschaft. Probleme und Perspektiven eines umkämpften Konzepts, in: Mackert J, Müller HP (eds.): *Citizenship. Soziologie der Staatsbürgerschaft*, Wiesbaden: Westdeutscher Verlag, 9–42.

Marshall TH (1965): *Class, Citizenship, and Social Development*. Essays, New York: Anchor Books.

Meier P, Ahrens P, Rolandsen Agustín L (2019): ★Gender★Power★? On the Multiple Relations Between Gender and Power in the European Parliament, in: Ahrens P, Rolandsen Agustín L (eds.): *Gendering the European Parliament. Introducing Structures, Policies and Practices*, London: Rowman & Littlefield, 199–212.

Mokre M, Siim B (2018): Negotiating Equality and Diversity. Transnational Challenges to European Citizenship, in: Fossum JE, Kastoryano R, Siim B (eds.): *Diversity and Contestation over Nationalism in Europe and Canada*, London: Palgrave Macmillan, 187–209.

Mushaben JM (2012): Women on the Move: EU, Migration and Citizenship Policy, in: Abels G, Mushaben JM (eds.): *Gendering the European Union*, Basingstoke: Palgrave Macmillan, 208–277.

Mushaben JM, Abels G (2012): Conclusion: Rethinking the Double Democratic Deficit in the EU, in Abels G, Mushaben JM (eds.): *Gendering the European Union. New Approaches to Old Democratic Deficits*, Basingstoke: Palgrave Macmillan, 228–247.

Nissen A, Rolandsen Agustín L (2018): Rights for Women, Migrants and Minorities. Consensus and Silences in the European Parliament, in: Knijn T, Naldini M (eds.): *Gender and Generational Division in EU Citizenship*, Cheltenham: Edward Elgar, 21–38.

Pateman C (1988): *The Sexual Contract*, Cambridge: Polity.

Pennings F et al. (2016): *EU Citizenship and Social Rights, a Comparative Report*, Utrecht: bEUcitizen, URL: http://dspace.library.uu.nl/handle/1874/346314 (download: May 6, 2020).

Seeleib-Kaiser M (2017): *European Policy Brief. Limited Social Rights and the Case for a European Minimum Income Scheme*, Oxford: bEUcitizen, URL: www.uu.nl/sites/default/files/limited-social-rights-and-the-case-for-a-european-minimum-income-scheme.pdf (download: May 6, 2020).

Shaw J (2016): Citizenship, migration and free movement in Britain, *German Law Journal* **17** (1), 99–104.

Shutes I (2016): Work-related conditionality and the access to social benefits of national citizens, EU and non-EU citizens, *Journal of Social Policy* **45** (4), 691–707.

Siim B (2000): *Gender and Citizenship. Politics and Agency in France, Britain and Denmark*, Cambridge: Cambridge University Press.

Siim B (2013): Citizenship, in: Waylen G, Celis K, Kantola J, Weldon SL (eds.): *The Oxford Handbook of Gender and Politics*, Oxford, New York: Oxford University Press, 756–780.

Siim B, Mokre M, eds. (2013): *Negotiating Gender and Diversity in an Emergent European Public Sphere*, Basingstoke: Palgrave Macmillan.

Soysal YN (1994): *Limits of Citizenship. Migrants and Postnational Membership in Europe*, Chicago, IL: University of Chicago Press.

Valchars G (2017): *"… destined to be the fundamental status." Anspruch und Ausgestaltung der europäischen Citizenship-Architektur*, PhD Thesis, University of Vienna.

Wiener A (2001): Zur Verfassungspolitik jenseits des Staates. Die Vermittlung von Bedeutung am Beispiel der Unionsbürgerschaft, *Zeitschrift für Internationale Beziehungen* **8** (1), 73–104.

Yuval-Davis N (2011): *The Politics of Belonging: Intersectional Contestations*, London: SAGE.

17

The privilege of (defining) knowledge

Gender differences in political knowledge across Europe

Jessica Fortin-Rittberger and Lena Ramstetter

Democratic theory holds that citizens must be sufficiently knowledgeable about public matters to meaningfully participate in politics. In simple terms, political knowledge is to know "what government is and does" (Barber 1969, 38) in order to make "reasoned decisions" (Lupia and McCubbins 1998). Political knowledge is key for the functioning of democracy as both a foundation and facilitator of many features of good citizenship: it increases political tolerance, efficacy, and interest in politics (Delli Carpini and Keeter 1996), fosters different forms of political participation, from casting a ballot to being involved with a political party (Verba et al. 1997; Zaller 1993), empowers people to vote for those who are consistent with their own ideology (Singh and Roy 2014) and, most important, enables them to hold office-holders accountable (de Vries and Giger 2014). Thus, "a broadly and equitably informed citizenry helps assure a democracy that is both responsive and responsible" (Delli Carpini and Keeter 1996, 1). Yet, across the globe, citizens seem to be poorly informed about political institutions, processes, and policies. Europe has not escaped this trend: the relatively scarce research in this field (Braun and Tausendpfund 2019; Maier and Bathelt 2013; Niedermayer and Sinnott 1995) suggests that citizens' overall level of knowledge about European institutions is soberingly low.

To make matters worse, knowledge is unequally distributed. Men seem to know more than women, whites more than members of ethnic minorities, the rich more than the poor. Why is this problematic? Because knowledge differences translate into inequalities in other resources citizens have at their disposal. Not knowing which of the candidates running for office matches my preferences makes it unlikely that I will choose the right one. Not understanding the complexities of the political world makes it unlikely that I will build a coherent world view around it, and perhaps even make me susceptible to misinformation. In the end, not knowing makes it unlikely my voice is heard. This imbalance carries grave implications for the functioning of representative democracy: while those who know might be fairly represented in politics, those who do not are effectively silenced. In a Europe facing a legitimacy crisis, these pockets of systematically less informed citizens pose a particular challenge that has yet to be addressed.

The privilege of (defining) knowledge

In this chapter, we shed light on the most puzzling of these patterns: gender gaps in political knowledge. The overwhelming majority of studies looking at differences across genders document a sizable and consistent gap between the performance of men and women on traditional items measuring political knowledge, suggesting that women know less about politics than men do (Burns et al. 2001; Delli Carpini and Keeter 1996; Fortin-Rittberger 2016; Fraile 2014a; Fraile and Gomez 2017; Mondak and Anderson 2004; Pereira et al. 2015; Sanbonmatsu 2003).

The existence of such gendered knowledge differences stands largely undisputed. However, recent research shows that the content and format of political knowledge questions employed in surveys could shake some of the foundations on which this conclusion rests. If we ask who defines what is worth knowing, what is political and what is not, what is true and what is false, the gendered nature of traditional understandings of political knowledge comes to light. Research suggests that women might not know less, but know differently (Stolle and Gidengil 2010). The EU's multilevel setting raises further questions regarding the alleged consensus on knowledge gaps: does knowledge about supranational politics and the complex institutional set-up follow the same lines as knowledge about (inter-)national political matters? Might the gender gap widen as European politics is even more distant from people's daily lives? Or does the EU, a vanguard in terms of women's representation, shape knowledge in a different way? If we want to address the causes and consequences of gendered knowledge, answering these questions will be one of the major challenges awaiting researchers in this field.

This chapter discusses the state of the art by outlining the key debates surrounding the gender gap in political knowledge. We proceed as follows. A first section traces the antecedents of political sophistication and points out potential sources of gendered differences in knowledge. In this regard, socialization effects reign supreme since they affect socio-economic resources at all stages of life. The second section moves to questions about measurement and asks whether existing research has measured what it had intended to measure. We explore the scope and breadth of what is commonly referred to as political knowledge, revealing that the way this knowledge is defined and assessed has profound effects on the size and shape of gender gaps. The third section points to limitations in existing research and to questions that remain to be answered. In the concluding section we reflect upon the different approaches to measure political knowledge and encourage further research to engage with the meaning of different facets of political sophistication for "good citizenship."

Gender gaps in political knowledge: tracing the roots

Existing literature paints a dim picture of political knowledge in our societies: not only do citizens know little about political institutions, processes, and policies (Converse 1964; Delli Carpini and Keeter 1996), but what they know is unevenly distributed. One of these lines along which knowledge is split is gender. Across countries and over time, a ubiquitous gender gap in political knowledge has been abundantly documented in advanced industrial democracies, such as the United States (Delli Carpini and Keeter 1996; Dolan 2011; Lizotte and Sidman 2009), Canada (Gidengil et al. 2008), and Europe (Fraile 2014a; Frazer and Macdonald 2003).

Figure 17.1 confirms the presence of this gap among the EU-27 countries in 2009 (also documented in Fraile 2014a and Kostelka et al. 2019). Women are less likely to provide correct answers to political knowledge questions than men in all surveyed countries. In the four questions fielded in the European Election Study, which tap into basic knowledge (such as membership in the EU, the number of member countries, and how institutions are staffed), women provided fewer correct answers. What is more, this gender gap is present and statistically significant for the four survey items in all 27 countries. Looking at the same countries five

209

Jessica Fortin-Rittberger and Lena Ramstetter

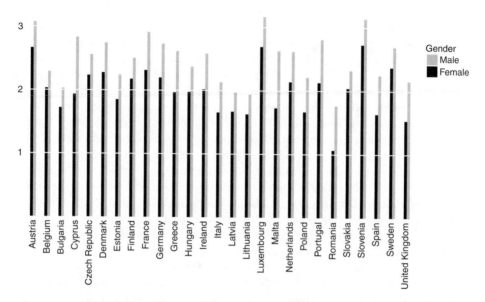

Figure 17.1 Mean number of correct responses on four factual political knowledge questions about the European Union and national parliaments by country and gender, 2009

Source: European Parliament Election Study 2009. Four questions about knowledge of the EU and national parliaments. 27,069 respondents in 27 EU countries. A series of t-tests (not shown) confirm that all differences are statistically significant. Don't know and refused answers were coded as incorrect answers.

years later in 2014 (see Figure 17.2), we observe the same imbalance. Such concordant findings are not only rare, they are also baffling considering that EU countries are some of the most egalitarian in terms of educational achievements and values. While contributors argue that the overall level of knowledge about the EU has been rising post EU-crisis (Hobolt and de Vries 2016), lingering differences across genders have not subsided. Such a systematic imbalance has the potential to be consequential for the EU: knowledge about its functioning affects how satisfied citizens are with the way democracy works (Karp et al. 2003), conditions their voting behavior on European issues (Tillman 2012), and shapes their degree of trust in EU institutions (Armingeon and Ceka 2014).

Also puzzling is the gender gap's persistence over time. Women have redefined their place in society more vigorously than ever before in the course of a few decades. In the political, economic, or private sphere, women reached an unprecedented level of influence. Today, women in the EU are more likely than men to complete tertiary education (Eurostat 2018), the level of descriptive representation in national lower houses increased from 11.7% on average in 1999 to 24.3% in 2019 (Inter-Parliamentary Union 2019), and the labor force participation rate of women is approaching that of men in OECD countries (OECD 2018). Despite these considerable advances in gender equality in all realms of society, gender differences in political knowledge remain widespread and show no sign of diminishing (Delli Carpini and Keeter 1996; Fortin-Rittberger 2020; Jennings 1996).

The privilege of (defining) knowledge

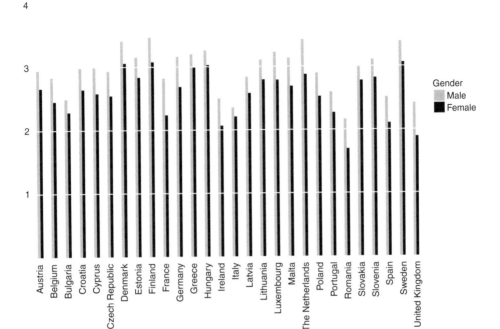

Figure 17.2 Mean number of correct responses on four factual political knowledge questions about the European Union and national parliaments by country and gender, 2014

Source: European Parliament Election Study 2014. Four questions about knowledge of the EU and national parliaments. 30,064 respondents in 28 EU countries. A series of t-tests (not shown) confirm that all differences are statistically significant. Don't know and refused answers were coded as incorrect answers.

What explains this stunningly universal and persistent gender gap? Why are women seemingly less knowledgeable than men when it comes to politics? Research has followed two different pathways to address this question. One branch looks into *substantive* factors accounting for gender differences in political sophistication. The other turns the question upside down, suggesting that women do not know less, but that they know differently. Defining political knowledge in a narrow, fact-focused manner and using *measurement approaches* favoring men, studies either fail to adequately capture women's knowledge or systematically inflate that of men.

To understand why differences exist, we have to take a step back and ask, what, in the first place, is needed to acquire and make use of information about politics? Research highlights three prerequisites: it takes the *motivation* to learn about politics, the *opportunity* to gather the necessary information, and the *ability* to process it. All three of these prerequisites are affected by *socialization*. Men and women have been and remain molded into different social roles. Gendered expectations self-evidently shape thinking and acting at all stages and in all spheres of life, including the acquisition of political knowledge (Bennett and Bennett 1989). Early on, children develop gendered perceptions of politics. Taking full effect in late adolescence, socialization leads boys to outperform girls in both political awareness and factual knowledge questions (van Pereira et al. 2015; Simon 2017; van Deth 2017). Even more alarming, by the age of 18, female students are considerably less attentive to political news and feel a lower degree of internal efficacy than their male classmates (Wolak and McDevitt 2011). It is here, in the formative years, when *motivation* is experiencing a gender twist. In most cases, this twist remains permanent or even intensifies (Ferrín et al. 2019; Fraile and Sánchez-Vítores 2020).

Among adults, women are more inclined to perceive politics as distant and hardly amenable to influence. Contributors have noted the presence of a gender gap in efficacy, i.e. the belief that they can have an impact on politics (Verba et al. 1997). In parallel, women also exhibit lower degrees of political interest (Fraile and Gomez 2017), which is the strongest predictor of political knowledge (Burns et al. 2001). Figure 17.3 visualizes this gender gap in political interest in European countries. This lower interest in politics, in turn, affects the attention one pays to media covering political news. Exploring media consumption in Europe, Benesch (2012) noted that women consumed fewer news programs about current affairs and politics, a difference so large it remained visible even after controlling for known sociodemographic factors. Being less exposed to political news, again, feeds the negative spiral as it reduces knowledge of that domain, resulting in a further decrease of political efficacy and interest (Fraile and Gomez 2017).

Gender roles affect political knowledge also in more intricate ways. Gendered *socioeconomic resources* are the elephant in the room (Burns et al. 2001). Though disparities are slowly decreasing, women continue to earn lower incomes than men (Harkness 2018), are still underrepresented in leadership positions (O'Brien 2015), and more likely to take the responsibilities of child-raising (Gidengil et al. 2008). These structural factors systematically decrease women's *opportunity* to get informed about politics: gendered patterns of employment, associated timely constraints, and material deficiencies complicate and discourage involvement with politics (Frazer and

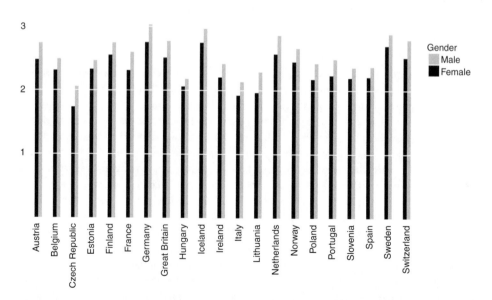

Figure 17.3 Mean political interest by gender and country, ESS 2018
Source: European Social Survey 2018. 39,391 respondents in 21 European countries. Political interest measured via responses to the question "How interested would you say you are in politics – are you…" with answer option ranging from not interested at all (1) to very interested (4). A series of t-tests (not shown) confirms that all differences are statistically significant.

Macdonald 2003; Quaranta and Dotti Sani 2018). Who, in the end, would blame a double-day working mother at the edge of poverty not to be informed about the latest statements from the prime minister or the decisions taken by yet another European Council crisis summit?

Education is one of the strongest individual-level predictors of political knowledge (Burns et al. 2001; Delli Carpini and Keeter 1996) and constitutes another aspect of socioeconomic resources, which bears on socialization effects. Education is crucial for political knowledge to develop, it fosters norms of civic duty and political engagement, thus raising the *motivation* to engage with politics. It promotes the cognitive capacities and hence the *ability* to deal with the complexity of politics. It also provides a unique *opportunity* to get informed about the foundations of political processes and institutions. While inequalities in access to education might explain gender gaps in political knowledge in the past, access to education has become gender-equal in Europe (Eurostat 2019). In fact, with few exceptions, women are actually more likely to complete tertiary education across Europe than men. This closing of the educational gender gap in Western societies (Inglehart and Norris 2003) is a ground for hope. Yet, women were – and in the majority of countries worldwide still are – put at a disadvantage when it comes to educational attainment (United Nations Girls' Education Initiative 2018).

Recent research also suggests that learning methods and environments might be gendered (Simon 2017; Wolak and McDevitt 2011). Hence, even if men and women enjoy the same education, women reap smaller returns, scoring lower on political knowledge tests (Dow 2009) and expressing less confidence (i.e. perceived ability) to understand politics (Gidengil et al. 2008). In short, education seemingly favors "male" habits of acquiring knowledge.

Not only individual-level factors involve gender differences but so do *contexts.* In most countries, women remain less visible in the public sphere in general and in politics in particular. Lacking female role models who fill leadership positions and political offices, women are more likely to believe that politics is a men's game. This depresses their *motivation* to engage with politics and they may consequently turn their backs on it. In turn, we would expect that increases in gender equality reduce the gender gap in political knowledge. Evidence in this regard is inconclusive. The effect of gender equality on knowledge gaps is at best partial (Fraile and Gomez 2017; Quaranta and Dotti Sani 2018) and temporary (McAllister 2019). In European countries, the increasing presence of women in the political sphere has not closed gender knowledge gaps (Fortin-Rittberger 2016). In spite of a consistently higher proportion of women in the European Parliament than in national parliaments, research either found no significant differences in the size of gender gaps in political knowledge about the EU versus national politics (Fraile 2014a) or an even larger gap at the EU level (Kostelka et al. 2019).

No matter how many female politicians are in charge of societal decisions, women remain less knowledgeable about politics than men. According to Dassonneville and McAllister (2018) there is a silver lining to this unsettling finding: it is not the degree of women's representation in the year the respective survey was conducted that affects gender differences in political knowledge, it is the degree of women's representation that prevailed during the years of political socialization that matters. Women coming of age in a society where women have a say in political matters are more likely to become cognitively involved in politics and, consequently, know more about it. Hence, the increasing level of women's representation throughout Europe (Inter-Parliamentary Union 2019) is a dawn of hope. As European Parliament mandates steadily become more gender-equal with each successive election since 1979 (see Ahrens and Rolandsen Agustín in this volume), gender differences in political knowledge might fade over generations.

Incentives to engage with politics can be implicit, as in this case, and their effects on political knowledge slow-moving. Certain circumstances, however, impart explicit impulses for parties to encourage women to participate in politics. Kittilson and Schwindt-Bayer (2012) hypothesize that proportional electoral rules (PR) increase the interest of political parties to mobilize women who, in turn, become more knowledgeable about politics. This implies good grades for Europe, where proportional electoral systems dominate. On the downside, recent research indicates that although PR might boost women's interest, any institutional effect is likely cancelled out by the second order character of European Parliament elections. As voting in such elections is even more contingent on political interest and knowledge, Kostelka et al. (2019) found that women's turnout was systematically lower than men's in European elections, whereas no such gap exists in national elections (Norris 2002).

Whether women engage with the political sphere might also depend on the *institutionalization of the party system*. Fraile and Gomez (2017) hypothesize that stable party systems increase women's *opportunities* to enter elective office and bring women's issues on the agenda, boosting their interest in politics. Both factors, in turn, raise levels of political knowledge among women. This finding is particularly troublesome, as we currently experience a destabilization of party systems across Europe (Dalton and Flanagan 2017).

Female unknowing – or knowing differently?

Research reviewed heretofore suggests that the antecedents of political knowledge are gendered. We assumed that women know less about politics than men as a consequence. Recent studies, however, come to a different conclusion: women do not know less, they just know differently. What seems to be a gap in size at first sight might turn out to be a difference relating to ways knowledge is measured at second glance. Survey mode, interviewer effects, and question content give undue privilege to male ways of knowing, creating a spurious knowledge gap.

With regard to *survey mode,* two factors are at play. First, the mere presence of the "don't know" category has considerable effects on respondent behavior. For one, men are hypothesized to display a higher propensity to guess than women, who are more likely to select "don't know" when they are unsure. Given that "don't know" is often treated as an incorrect response in analyses, this propensity to guess gives rise to artificial differences in levels of political knowledge (Atkeson and Rapoport 2003; Ferrín et al. 2018; Fortin-Rittberger 2020; Frazer and Macdonald 2003; Lizotte and Sidman 2009; Mondak and Anderson 2004; Mondak and Canache 2004). Figure 17.4 illustrates this gender gap in substantive responses.

Second, the format of the answers proposed to respondents – *closed or open-ended* – has differential impacts across genders. A closed format with few responses is generally less demanding to respond to and therefore elicits more correct responses (Mondak and Anderson 2004). Yet women score higher when confronted with multiple-choice questions rather than with "true/false" or open-ended format questions (Fortin-Rittberger 2016). One of the culprits of these differences lies again in men's higher propensity to guess, which is highest when answer sets are smaller (Luskin and Bullock 2011; Rodriguez 2005).

Closely linked to the mode is the survey *setting*. Research indicates that *stereotype threat* increases gender gaps in political knowledge (Ihme and Tausendpfund 2018; McGlone et al. 2006). Concerned to confirm negative expectations, women who are exposed to explicit (i.e. overt reference to the stereotype) or implicit cues (e.g. the interviewer's gender) that make the alleged gender gap in political knowledge salient, perform lower in tests. Men, in contrast, experience the opposite: stereotype lift. The awareness that an outgroup is negatively stereotyped, raises the ingroup members' performance. Hence, men knowing that women are less likely to score high on political knowledge tests will perform better than they would otherwise (Ihme and Tausendpfund 2018).

The privilege of (defining) knowledge

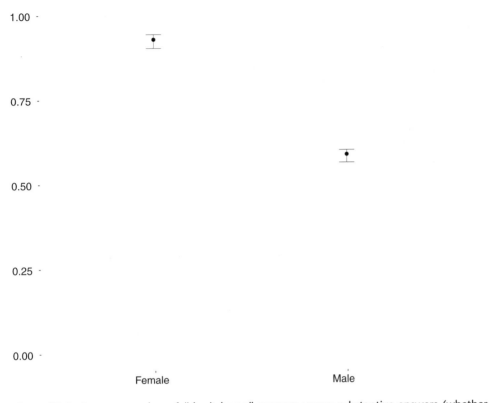

Figure 17.4 Average number of "don't know" answers versus substantive answers (whether correct or incorrect) with 99% t-test confidence intervals
Source: European Parliament Election Study 2014. Four questions about knowledge of the EU and national parliaments. 30,064 respondents in 28 EU countries.

Another branch of research posits that it is also the *types of questions* asked that portray women as less knowledgeable than men. In other words, survey items are gendered in such a way that women are structurally disadvantaged. The bulk of knowledge questions fielded in present-day surveys asks for *factual knowledge*, such as information about politicians in specific positions (e.g. the name of the president of the European Council or the leader of party groups in the European Parliament), political parties (i.e. their ideological position and coalition partners), or technical rules concerning political processes (such as the rules that govern the European elections, or the members of the EU).

By contrast, women's *practical and analytical knowledge* of political processes and institutions is rarely asked in the context of the EU where questions are factual, probing domains where women know least. Due to the prevailing gender role allocation, women are more likely to develop expertise on local politics, public services, and welfare state policies (Rapeli 2014). Being asked, for example, about the head of the local school system (Delli Carpini and Keeter 1996), who is eligible for social benefits or where to place a complaint against discrimination (Stolle and Gidengil 2010), the gender gap closes or even reverses. The same happens if respondents are asked about gender relevant items, such as the degree of women's representation (Dolan 2011) or political offices held by female politicians (Burns et al. 2001; Stolle and Gidengil 2010). Research zooming in on gender differences further indicates that women are more likely to provide correct answers when asked about community-oriented topics such as human and social rights (Ferrín et al. 2018).

The rather distal and complex nature of European multilevel governance suggests that women might be less likely to be interested in and thus less knowledgeable about EU issues. Given that citizens tend to gather additional information on topics about which they are already most informed (Iyengar 1990), these informational differences grow as people become more informed in a domain-specific way.

Taken together, these findings carry three implications. (1) The gender gap in political knowledge about the EU shows no signs of abating, as contradictory forces push in different directions. (2) The current mode, setting, and content of surveys measuring political knowledge give an undue advantage to men's habits of acquiring and accessing knowledge, thus inflating their scores on political knowledge scales. A sizable part of the knowledge gap is likely an artifact of the way we have chosen to measure the concept rather than an accurate reflection of how knowledge is distributed among men and women. (3) Perhaps most importantly, we need to rethink what political knowledge is in the context of the EU. Women might know less about distant political problems but, as things draw closer to daily life, the gender gap closes or even reverses. We have not yet been able to design survey items that can adequately capture this relevant information.

The road ahead: challenges to political knowledge research

We have emphasized that the literature on gender differences in political knowledge casts light on substantive as well as measurement factors affecting women's test performance differently than that of men. First, socialization and its byproducts, such as gendered labor market participation, education, or efficacy lead men to outperform women on traditional political knowledge tests. Second, gender gaps can be artifacts of measurement. Both pathways provide us with valuable insights to deal with levels of political knowledge in the EU. To move forward, some quintessential obstacles need to be overcome.

Regarding measurement, researchers face a series of challenges. Despite its importance, we are still lacking a valid and reliable way to capture the target concept of political knowledge. We know even less about suitable approaches to measurement in the multilevel institutional context of the EU. So far, the bulk of research on the EU has relied on factual knowledge questions, treating knowledge as an absolute property, allocating full points for correct answers and zero points for incorrect answers, without the possibility of partially correct answers. To what extent does knowing whether the EU has 27 or 26 members justify a score of one or zero for a respondent? What are the implications of treating respondents who answered the EU has 25 or 51 members as exactly the same, namely, as having no knowledge? Does knowing if Switzerland is formally a member of the EU provide a substantive measure of the target concept? Or is there more substance the standard items fail to capture?

With regard to these *factual questions*, another pressing challenge is to find items allowing for comparisons across countries and regions. Designing questions that are equally demanding in different contexts is intricate (Turgeon 2008). What people (do not) know in large part hinges on the media environment. Imagine, for instance, a question probing the knowledge about EU migration policies. While Greek or Italian respondents might be well informed about the current debates and decisions since this issue is of high importance to them, as both are frontline states when it comes to intra-EU migration, respondents in other countries, e.g. Estonia or Ireland, might follow less closely as it does not affect their daily lives to the same degree. This salience problem equally affects comparisons over time: information about certain aspects of politics are easily accessible in times of high media coverage but might not be recalled as easily once public

The privilege of (defining) knowledge

attention fades. Most factual knowledge scales produce marked variations in the size of gender gaps across and within countries over time. As a result we do not know the exact magnitude of these gender gaps (Fortin-Rittberger 2020). This challenge opens avenues for research seeking to control for context salience.

The alternative to factual questions is to use ideological *placement measures* (Luskin and Bullock 2011). These, by contrast, do not linger on specific political features, but probe the ability of respondents to position political parties or issues along an ideological continuum (such as the left–right scale). Addressing the central aspect around which political competition is organized in established democracies, placement items might allow for more reliable comparisons overtime (Gordon and Segura 1997; Turgeon 2008). We still know very little about the impact of using placement items on gender gaps. Recent work suggests that these items yield more stable results than factual questions (Fortin-Rittberger 2020) but testing these items in the context of the EU remains uncharted territory. However, placement knowledge brings its own set of challenges. Whether parties can be placed correctly on the left–right continuum in large part hinges on the complexity of the party system. While situating parties in countries with a two-party system is manageable for most respondents, getting the situation right in dispersed and volatile multi-party arrangements is considerably more demanding (Busch 2016). Against the backdrop of increasing instability in European party systems (Dalton and Flanagan 2017), which are mostly multi-party systems, knowledge assessments based on party placement might have to be treated with caution.

More recent research seeks to circumvent these pitfalls by stepping away from factual knowledge. Cramer and Toff (2017) suggest taking into account *experiential knowledge*. Whether factual knowledge fosters norms of good citizenship depends on how it is interpreted and used. Knowing facts about policies, institutions, and processes might be a valuable building block in decision-making processes, but it does not necessarily make for a considerate citizen: it is not primarily facts that inform "good" decisions, it is the capacity to capture interconnectedness, to understand one another.

Future research should investigate substantive factors influencing political knowledge. First, existing research lacks insights into *intersectionality*. We know by now that political sophistication is gendered, but other individual characteristics, such as race, income, and age play a major role in the level of political knowledge, too (Abrajano 2015; Delli Carpini and Keeter 1996). What we still have to investigate is how these dimensions interact. If we consider them as overlapping, some segments of societies, for instance young Romanian women who belong to an ethnic minority and are socioeconomically disadvantaged, would be in a dramatically different position than older, white Swedish males with high incomes.

Second, the *effect of contextual variables* emerges as one of the most promising avenues for new research. The causal linkage between institutional variables (such as electoral system or party system institutionalization) and gendered differences in political knowledge is very distal. A series of intervening mechanisms are implied but remain untested. Disentangling this causal chain will require looking deeper into how some institutional contexts are shaping gender gaps in political knowledge. In turn, the consequences of knowledge differences also open up paths for research on pressing questions concerning the future of the EU: how does political knowledge affect Euroscepticism? Does Euroscepticism affect people's willingness to acquire knowledge or to collect biased and factually incorrect information? Future research might also want to investigate the intricate path between men's higher level of (factual) knowledge and women's lower propensity to support populists at the ballot box and beyond (see also Siim and Fiig in this volume).

217

Moving forward

Citizens delegate power to those who best represent their preferences. This holds for modern democracies as well as for the EU and its directly elected European Parliament. To know who of all candidates and parties does the best job of representing my interests as citizen requires political knowledge. Yet, citizens seem to know little about political institutions, processes, and substantive policies. This is particularly relevant with regard to EU politics and the still existing second order character of European elections whereby citizens are less motivated to acquire knowledge and participate in the political process. Even worse, what citizens know is asymmetrically distributed: certain segments of society are systematically advantaged over others. Across countries and over time, women seem to know less about the political sphere than men: the EU has not evaded this trend.

Assessing how much people know about politics has proven to be elusive with our best estimates remaining uncertain. For the time being, all we know is that there is a gendered political knowledge gap, but we know little about its current magnitude and development over time. Since gendered differences are fragile to measurement issues and dependent on both the context and content of questions, we still have to investigate the degree to which findings are generalizable beyond unique settings. It remains difficult to tell whether the gender gap in EU political knowledge is comparable to those we observe in national politics. In the best-case scenario, the EU-national gender gaps are similar in magnitude (Fraile 2014a); in the worst case, the EU gender gap is larger (Kostelka et al. 2019).

Recent research further challenges the alleged consensus regarding the existence of gender gaps in political knowledge. Asking what the knowledge items administered in surveys actually capture, sheds light on the gendered nature of measurement approaches. What knowledge is, how it is assessed and interpreted is a product of (predominantly male) construction. Shifting the focus away from factual questions about politicians and institutions, women's ways of knowing materialize: as questions draw closer to daily life, pertaining to practical knowledge, or asking for analytical skills, women catch up with men and, at times, overtake them. Yet for the majority of citizens, the EU and its politics seems to be too far away from daily life.

Scale and shape of gendered differences remain contested. We know that socialization and its companion, gendered socioeconomic resources, put women at a structural disadvantage in acquiring *factual* knowledge about politics. Building on the premise that voting preferences are formed in a process of rational reasoning, this gap in political knowledge is worrisome. If we want women's voices to be equally heard in the political process, action to narrow this gap is imperative. Research offers tracks for intervention: if women are given space and security to deliberate about political issues (Fraile 2014b), especially if this takes place in environments of political consensus (Wolak and McDevitt 2011), gender differences diminish.

Factual knowledge is a valuable instrument in the toolbox of good citizenship. Without downplaying its importance, a healthy dose of skepticism is in order because knowledge alone does not make a good citizen. In days of tailored media consumption, filter bubbles, and partisan news, people retain facts selectively, tuning out information contradicting their convictions (Iyengar and Hahn 2009). Research on societal polarization indicates that those best informed also tend to be those most likely to process new information in a biased way (Gaines et al. 2007).

We need to rethink the ways in which different forms of knowledge inform political attitudes and behavior. Whether factual knowledge helps people to be "good citizens," to make decisions benefitting not only them but also society as a whole, depends on how they use it. Cramer and Toff (2017) argue that facts are inevitably embedded in experience. We cannot separate them from daily life and from the circumstances we find ourselves entrapped in. Factual information is always seen through a very personal lens. This is a call not to underestimate the intervening factors between facts and decisions. In a world of abundant information, where every fact seems to have its counter-fact, future research might want to ask: how does knowledge help us to be "good"? What sort of knowledge fosters norms of good citizenship? What makes a good EU citizen? What makes people engage with (multilevel) politics in a pursuit of the common good? For researchers, seeking answers to these questions will require a more precise and substantive grasp of what people know and understand about the EU, so that we can better make sense of the puzzling gendered differences lingering around most of our variables of interest. The few factual questions we have drawn upon to theorize about political knowledge might only have let us glimpse at a fragment of what citizens understand and know. This fragment is not enough.

References

Abrajano M (2015): Reexamining the " racial gap " in political knowledge, *Journal of Politics* **77** (1), 44–54.

Armingeon K, Ceka B (2014): The loss of trust in the European Union during the great recession since 2007. The role of heuristics from the national political system, *European Union Politics* **15** (1), 82–107.

Atkeson L, Rapoport RB (2003): The more things change the more they stay the same: Examining gender differences in political attitude expression, 1952–2000, *The Public Opinion Quarterly* **67** (4), 495–521.

Barber JD (1969): *Citizen Politics*, Chicago, IL: Markham.

Benesch C (2012): An empirical analysis of the gender gap in news consumption, *Journal of Media Economics* **25** (3), 147–167.

Bennett L, Bennett S (1989): Enduring gender differences in political interest: The impact of socialization and political dispositions, *American Politics Quarterly* **17** (1), 105–122.

Braun D, Tausendpfund M (2019): Politisches Wissen und Europawahlen, in: Westle B, Tausendpfund M. (eds.): *Politisches Wissen*, Wiesbaden: Springer, 207–236.

Burns N, Schlozman KL, Verba S (2001): *The Private Roots of Public Action: Gender, Equality, and Political Participation*, Cambridge, MA: Harvard University Press.

Busch KB (2016): Estimating parties' left–right positions: Determinants of voters' perceptions' proximity to party ideology, *Electoral Studies* **41** (1), 159–178.

Converse P (1964): The nature of belief systems in mass publics, *Critical Review* **18** (1–3), 1–74.

Cramer KJ, Toff B (2017): The fact of experience: Rethinking political knowledge and civic competence, *Perspectives on Politics* **15** (3), 754–770.

Dalton RJ, Flanagan SE (2017): *Electoral Change in Advanced Industrial Democracies: Realignment or Dealignment?* Princeton, NJ: Princeton University Press.

Dassonneville R, McAllister I (2018): Gender, political knowledge, and descriptive representation: The impact of long-term socialization, *American Journal of Political Science* **62** (2), 249–265.

Delli Carpini MX, Keeter S (1996): *What Americans Know About Politics and Why It Matters*, New Haven, NJ: Yale University Press.

Dolan K (2011): Do women and men know different things? Measuring gender differences in political knowledge, *Journal of Politics* **73** (1), 97–107.

Dow J (2009): Gender differences in political knowledge: Distinguishing characteristics-based and returns-based differences, *Political Behavior* **31** (1), 117–136.

Eurostat (2018): Educational Attainment Statistics, URL: https://ec.europa.eu/eurostat/statistics-explained/index.php/Educational_attainment_statistics#Level_of_educational_attainment_by_sex (download: February 28, 2019).

Eurostat (2019): Gender Statistics, URL: https://ec.europa.eu/eurostat/statistics-explained/index.php/Gender_statistics#Education (download: July 10, 2019).

Ferrín M, Fraile M, García-Albacete G (2018): Is it simply gender? Content, format, and time in political knowledge measures, *Politics and Gender* **14**(2), 162–185.

Ferrín M, Fraile M, García-Albacete G (2019): Adult roles and the gender gap in political knowledge: A comparative study, *West European Politics* **42** (7), 1368–1389.

Fortin-Rittberger J (2016): Cross-national gender gaps in political knowledge: How much is due to context? *Political Research Quarterly* **69** (3), 391–402.

Fortin-Rittberger J (2020): Political knowledge: assessing the stability of gender gaps cross-nationally, *International Journal of Public Opinion Research* **32** (1), 46–65.

Fraile M (2014a): Do women know less than men? The gender gap in political knowledge, *Social Politics* **21** (2), 261–289.

Fraile M (2014b): Does deliberation contribute to decreasing the gender gap in knowledge?, *European Union Politics* **15** (3), 372–388.

Fraile M, Gomez R (2017): Bridging the enduring gender gap in political interest in Europe: The relevance of promoting gender equality, *European Journal of Political Research* **56** (3), 601–618.

Fraile M, Sánchez-Vítores I (2020): Tracing the gender gap in political interest over the life span: A panel analysis, *Political Psychology* **41** (1), 89–106.

Frazer E, Macdonald K (2003): Sex differences in political knowledge in Britain, *Political Studies* **51** (1), 67–83.

Gaines BJ, Kuklinski JH, Quirk PJ, Peyton B, Verkuilen J (2007): Same facts, different interpretations: partisan motivation and opinion on Iraq, *Journal of Politics* **69** (4), 957–974.

Gidengil E, Giles J, Thomas M (2008): The gender gap in self-perceived understanding of politics in Canada and the United States, *Politics & Gender* **4** (4), 535–561.

Gordon SB, Segura GM (1997): Cross-national variation in the political sophistication of individuals: capability or choice?, *Journal of Politics* **59** (1), 126–147.

Harkness S. (2018): Gender and Economic Inequality, in: Shaver S (ed.): *Handbook on Gender and Social Policy*, Aldershot: Edward Elgar, 113–128.

Hobolt SB, de Vries C (2016): Public support for European integration, *Annual Review of Political Science* **19**, 413–432.

Ihme TA, Tausendpfund M (2018): Gender differences in political knowledge: Bringing situation back, *Journal of Experimental Political Science* **5** (1), 39–55.

Inglehart R, Norris P (2003): *Rising Tide. Gender Equality and Cultural Change Around the World*, Cambridge: Cambridge University Press.

Inter-Parliamentary Union (2019): Women in National Parliaments, URL: http://archive.ipu.org/wmn-e/world.htm (download: July 8, 2019).

Iyengar S (1990): The accessibility bias in politics: Television news and public opinion, *International Journal of Public Opinion Research* **2** (1), 1–15.

Iyengar S, Hahn KS (2009): Red media, blue media: Evidence of ideological selectivity in media use, *Journal of Communication* **59** (1), 19–39.

Jennings K (1996): Political knowledge over time and across generations, *Public Opinion Quarterly* **60** (2), 228–252.

Karp JA, Banducci SA, Bowler S (2003): To know it is to love it? Satisfaction with democracy in the European Union, *Comparative Political Studies* **36** (3), 271–292.

Kittilson MC, Schwindt-Bayer L (2012): *The Gendered Effects of Electoral Institutions: Political Engagement and Participation*, Oxford: Oxford University Press.

Kostelka F, Blais A, Gidengil E (2019): Has the gender gap in voter turnout really disappeared?, *West European Politics* **42** (3), 437–463.

Lizotte MK, Sidman AH (2009): Explaining the gender gap in political knowledge, *Politics and Gender* **5** (2), 127–151.

Lupia A, McCubbins M (1998): *The Democratic Dilemma: Can Citizens Learn What They Need to Know?* Cambridge: Cambridge University Press.

Luskin RC, Bullock JG (2011): "Don't know" means "don't know". DK responses and the public's level of political knowledge, *Journal of Politics* **73** (2), 547–557.

Maier J, Bathelt S (2013): Unbekanntes Europa? Eine vergleichende Analyse zu Verteilung und Determinanten von Kenntnissen über die Europäische Union, in: Keil S, Thaidigsmann I (eds.): *Zivile Bürgergesellschaft und Demokratie. Aktuelle Ergebnisse der empirischen Politikforschung*, Wiesbaden: Springer, 413–432.

McAllister I. (2019): The gender gap in political knowledge revisited. Australia's Julia Gillard as a natural experiment, *European Journal of Politics and Gender* **2** (2), 197–220.

McGlone MS, Aronson J, Kobrynowicz D (2006): Stereotype threat and the gender gap in political knowledge, *Psychology of Women Quarterly* **30** (4), 392–398.

Mondak J, Anderson M (2004): The knowledge gap: A reexamination of gender-based differences in political knowledge, *Journal of Politics* **66** (2), 492–512.

Mondak J, Canache D (2004): Knowledge variables in cross-national social inquiry, *Social Science Quarterly* **85** (3), 539–558.

Niedermayer O, Sinnott R (1995): *Public Opinion and Internationalized Governance*, Oxford: Oxford University Press.

Norris P (2002): The Gender Gap: Theoretical Frameworks and New Approaches, in: Caroll S (eds.): *Women and American Politics: New Questions, New Directions*, New York: Oxford University Press, 146–172.

O'Brien DZ (2015): Rising to the top: Gender, political performance, and party leadership in parliamentary democracies, *American Journal of Political Science* **59** (4), 1022–1039.

OECD (2018): *OECD Labour Force Statistics 2018*, Paris: OECD Publishing.

Pereira MF, Fraile M, Rubal M (2015): Young and gapped? Political knowledge of girls and boys in Europe, *Political Research Quarterly* **68** (1), 63–76.

Quaranta M, Dotti Sani GM (2018): Left behind? Gender gaps in political engagement over the life course in twenty-seven European countries, *Social Politics* **25** (2), 254–286.

Rapeli L (2014): Comparing local, national and EU knowledge: The ignorant public reassessed, *Scandinavian Political Studies* **37** (4), 428–446.

Rodriguez MC (2005): Three options are optimal for multiple-choice items, *Educational Measurement: Issues and Practice* **24** (2), 3–13.

Sanbonmatsu K (2003): Gender-related political knowledge and the descriptive representation of women, *Political Behavior* **25** (4), 367–388.

Simon A (2017): How can we explain the gender gap in children's political knowledge?, *American Behavioral Scientist* **61** (2), 222–237.

Singh S, Roy J (2014): Political knowledge, the decision calculus, and proximity voting, *Electoral Studies* **34**, 89–99.

Stolle D, Gidengil E (2010): What do women really know? A gendered analysis of varieties, *Perspectives on Politics* **8** (1), 93–109.

Tillman ER (2012): Support for the Euro, political knowledge, and voting behavior in the 2001 and 2005 UK general elections, *European Union Politics* **13** (3), 367–389.

Turgeon M (2008): Measuring and Explaining Political Sophistication in a Comparative Context, *Paper presented at the Annual Meeting of the ISPP*, Paris: Sciences Po.

United Nations Girls' Education Initiative (2018): *Global Education Monitoring Report Gender Review 2018: Meeting Our Commitments to Gender Equality in Education*, UNESCO.

van Deth J (2017): Children and politics. An empirical reassessment of Early political socialization, *Political Psychology* **32** (1), 147–173.

Verba S, Burns N, Schlozman KL (1997): Knowing and caring about politics gender and political engagement, *Journal of Politics* **59** (4), 1051–1072.

de Vries C, Giger N (2014): Holding governments accountable? Individual heterogeneity in performance voting, *European Journal of Political Research* **53** (2), 345–362.

Wolak J, McDevitt M (2011): The roots of the gender gap in political knowledge in adolescence, *Political Behavior* **33** (3), 505–533.

Zaller J (1993): Who gets the news? Alternative measures of news. Reception and their implications for research, *Public Opinion Quarterly* **57** (2), 133–164.

18
Civil society

Sabine Lang[1]

The 20th century is called the century of parties; the 21st century, in turn, is believed to become that of civil society. Interest in civil society surged with the end of the Cold War and the east central European transformations. After 1989, strong civil societies were perceived to be prerequisites for democratic political institutions and liberal economies. Thirty years onwards, as more and more traditional political parties are being challenged or replaced by movements or "movement parties," the demarcation between political institutions and civic mobilization is becoming weaker. Concurrently, civil society has fundamentally changed its means and modes of communication. The digital rights and #MeToo movements stand for civic mobilizations moving from offline to online spaces, showcasing that online activism can be just as, or even more, powerful than street and face-to-face-based protest. Online activism, however, also enables the proliferation of hate speech and dissonant publics. Whether or not civil society is the best buffer against autocratic regime change, global neoliberalism, or social injustice is still up for debate (Cohen and Arato 1992; Rosanvallon 2007; Thiel 2017).

As power, visibility, and diversity of civil society have increased across Europe, its very idea and functions remain contested. Broadly speaking, civil society is a space between the state, the economy, and private life in which citizens associate and work towards what they perceive as the common good. Its "betweenness" raises a number of unsettling questions about its autonomy from, or relationship to, government, markets, and private life. Transposing this definition onto the European Union's (EU) geographical, political, and cultural spaces renders additional ambiguities: Since the EU is not a state but a complex governance structure in which civil society organizations (CSO) play a central part, Brussels-based civil society cannot claim to be "separate" from EU-level institutions such as the European Commission or the European Parliament. Associating and working together, likewise, poses organizational challenges for the 513 million EU citizens. As civic engagement is still mostly rooted in local and regional activities, how can it scale up to the transnational level? Finally, the "good" in civil society does not exist outside of the post-Cold War neoliberal order and, therefore, it is not immune against reifying gender, race, and class biases and fueling rightwing reactionary and renationalization movements.

Gender has long been neglected in civil society research. In fact, civil society was, and to some degree still is, treated as a gender-neutral space (Monzon and Chaves 2017). The dynamics replicating issue-specific as well as institutional masculinity in civil society have been largely overlooked (e.g. Kohler-Koch and Quittkat 2012; Ruzza 2004; Steffek et al 2008). Only recently has the field started acknowledging the genderedness of their object (e.g. Bee and Guerrina 2017; Hinterhuber 2014; Kalm and Johannson 2015; Schwabenland et al. 2016). While resonating with the social movement literature, feminist contributions have long existed in a parallel intellectual universe to national and EU level civil society research (e.g. Fuchs and Payer 2012; Halsaa et al. 2012; Sanchez Salgado 2014). Gender research challenged the sectoral schism between movement mobilization and institutionalized civil society, but also between civil society and EU institutions, instead emphasizing the ties in the EU within what Alison Woodward (2004) called the "velvet triangle." This triangle visualized informal interactions between European women's movements, policy-makers and politicians, as well as feminist experts and academics working together to place gender on the policy agenda (Lang 2014; Woodward 2004, 2015). As biographical lines blurred, turning feminist experts into movement actors and/or politicians, feminist research highlighted that women as policy insiders and outsiders formed flexible networks, questioning the post-Cold War "state vs. civil society" categorizations.

In the past decade, gender research has contributed, firstly, to ongoing discussions on where to locate European civil society. At the center of this debate is a rift between supra- or transnationally focused civil society concepts and those who perceive it more as scaled aggregates of member state civil societies. Some see "a new transnational intermediary sphere, a pluralist social space between EU governance and European citizens that is populated by non-state agents claiming to represent, speak for or participate in EU decision making on behalf of the most varied social constituencies" (Liebert and Trenz 2012, 2). Others argue that much of what we perceive as EU-level civil society are in fact scaled-up aggregates of member state activism (Sanchez Salgado and Demidov 2018). Feminist scholarship acknowledges the different power dynamics and effects of bottom-up and top-down mobilizations (Cullen 2015; Knappe and Lang 2014; Pudrovska and Ferree 2004; Rolandsen Agustín 2013) and emphasizes the need to build on local, regional, and national mobilizations in order to form and legitimize larger advocacy networks on the EU level (Ahrens 2018; Lang and Sauer 2016; Zippel 2006).

A second debate arises from the tensions between normative and institutional approaches. Normatively, EU civil society is argued to provide the connective tissue between citizens and the Brussels-based edifice by advancing the basic EU Treaty norms. Since participatory modes for EU citizens – aside from elections to the European Parliament since 1979 – are far and few in between (e.g. public consultations or the European Citizens' Initiative), civil society is seen as the normative "glue" that provides democratic legitimacy. Gender research critically interrogates these normative claims by pointing to the multiple intersections of exclusivity running through European integration and its civic articulations. Institutional approaches to assess EU civil society, by contrast, have been called out for being blind to the genderedness of formal and informal EU institutions and their civic infrastructure. As powerful associations, for instance trade unions or employer organizations, across Europe are still dominated by men, women demand not just access to clubs and lobbies, but also more transparency and public visibility for marginalized voices. Feminist research thus critically engages which normative claims about civil society providing EU legitimacy as well as with the architecture of EU civil society itself (Ahrens 2018; Cullen 2015; Rolandsen Agustín 2008; Wilde 2016; Woodward 2015).

A third contention runs between approaches writing the "civil" in civil society in capital letters, and those considering uncivil society as a legitimate, albeit sometimes ugly, part of it. What is considered "uncivil" is culturally overdetermined and open to contestation. "Uncivil" society manifests itself across Europe in many ways, from verbal and physical attacks on ethnic, religious, and sexual minorities to the rise of anti-genderism tropes that defame and slant feminists (e.g. Koettig et al. 2017; Kuhar and Paternotte 2017; see Siim and Fiig in this volume). Increasingly, nationalist and misogynist articulations of masculinity (see Hearn in this volume) take place in online public fora that become echo chambers for particular groups. What is uncivil, however, is always contested. Accepting "uncivility" as a paradoxical precondition of civil society (Edwards 2014, 81) is intrinsic to feminist civil society discourse and practices (Lang 2013), such as Femen activists using their bodies for protest or Pussy Riot mobilizing in sacred religious spaces. Feminist researchers force debate on this paradox as they point to state protection of masculinist notions of civility while also critically engaging with women's complicity in some of these frames (Farris 2017).

These contestations notwithstanding, civil society is one of the cornerstones of EU democracy and legitimacy. Beyond EU institutions relying on civil society actors as informational resource, experts, and interlocutors for policy change, civil society remains maybe the only, but clearly the best hope for increasing citizen buy-in into EU integration (Ruzza 2004). It has advanced to represent both a normative "imagined European community" of citizens as well as an empirically grounded architecture of scaled civil society organizations and mobilizations from the local to the transnational level. This chapter investigates the EU as a civil society promoter, and then asks how women's movements and gender advocacy fit within the EU's civil society framework. A third section addresses how transnational and national civil society articulations intersect in the EU. The final section identifies gaps and future topics for researching gendered civil society.

The EU as civil society promoter

Since the 1990s, the Commission has paved the way for a participatory turn in European governance. With the 1997 Amsterdam Treaty, CSOs were provided with increasing legitimacy as the EU embarked on a rights-based take-off that extended its portfolio beyond economy and employment. The broader application of the open method of coordination (OMC), as well, incentivized the EU to increase openness and transparency vis-à-vis civil society (Lang 2013). Article 11 of the TEU stipulates: "1. The institutions shall, by appropriate means, give citizens and representative associations the opportunity to make known and publicly exchange their views in all areas of Union action" and "2. The institutions shall maintain an open, transparent and regular dialogue with representative associations and civil society." Formally, the EU has codified this interaction by way of instituting civil dialogue, consultations, and the European Citizens' Initiative (ECI; Regulation (EU) 2019/788; see https://europa.eu/citizens-initiative/home_en). These formats, however, while intended to involve broad European publics, in practice overwhelmingly privilege already established and well-organized interests (García 2015; Lang 2020).

Formally, the European Economic and Social Committee (EESC) functions as a hub and clearinghouse for CSO interactions with EU institutions. From its inception, nourishing civic dialogue with representative civil society organizations (CES/CSS/01/2017/EESC, foreword) was central to the EESC mission, and it conceived of EU-level CSOs as mediators between the institutions and EU citizens (Busschaert 2016, 24). Over the past decades, EU-level institutions have opened up more spaces for civil society in different arenas and by way of diverse modalities: The European Commission invites civil society input during regular meetings with stakeholders as well as via online consultations, and it funds civil society actors to professionally fulfill their remit. The European Parliament utilizes public hearings to incorporate civil society actors and engages with CSOs in their areas of specializations on a regular basis (Ahrens 2018). The EU thus provides a political opportunity structure, the key elements of which are "access to EU officials, policy-setting contexts, and funding opportunities" (Cullen 2015: 413).

The Commission, in particular, has encouraged the formation of EU-level civil society networks since the mid-1990s (Bretherton and Sperling 1996). Its insistence on Union-wide international collaborations, e.g. within the European Structural Funds and the European Regional Development Fund, has provided incentives for national and regional CSOs to collaborate across borders and invest in Brussels-based advocacy. The European Women's Lobby (EWL) was founded in 1990 through the initiative of femocrats from the EU Commission (Strid 2009, 15) in order to facilitate coordination of European women's CSOs. In 1996, ILGA-Europe was founded as a transnational advocate for LGBTI citizens. Whereas ILGA has broad-based membership from local and regional organizations, EWL is primarily based on national organizations' membership and distinct from other, more issue-based EU gender networks such as WAVE (Women Against Violence Europe), WIDE (Women in Development Europe), or ENoMW (European Network of Migrant Women). In 2019, the EWL had 31 national coordination organizations in addition to 18 European-wide member organizations and professional associations such as Soroptimist International Europe and University Women of Europe. In total, EWL represents roughly 2,000 women's CSOs across Europe (EWL: www.womenlobby.org/-Our-membership-?lang=en). Its organizational structure relies on national coordination platforms, in fact privileging vertical lines of association to horizontal networking with issue-specific gender CSOs. In 2016, 76% of the EWL operating budget of 1.2 million Euros came from the Commission, down from 80% in 2015; 13% came from foundation grants, 4% each from memberships fees and governments, 2% from individuals and 1% from corporations (EWL 2015, 2018a).

This EU support, however, is facing increasing scrutiny, as resources for and substantive commitment to advancing women and sexual minorities have been called into question by a reframed equality agenda and shifting priorities during and after the financial crisis. Moreover, transnational CSOs' privileged position as representing gender equality issues is challenged by the EU's diversity agenda, with resource constraints producing competition among diversity claims and actors. This coincides with gender mainstreaming replacing hard gender equality policies and soft law being more commonly applied than directives, resulting in equality claims moving further into the Commission (see Hartlapp et al. in this volume) and established civil society actors such as EWL being potentially sidelined. The policy process of the "Roadmap for Equality Between Women and Men 2006–2010" illustrates this. Here, the Commission "invented something entirely new in EU's gender equality policy and at the EU level overall: a policy program without a clear budget and no defined future plans" in which "connections to civil society were used less" and CSOs were excluded (Ahrens 2018, 244). The Roadmap process also exposes the ambivalent nature of a mainstreamed notion of gender moving into the institutions, professionalizing in-house mainstreaming experts, and in the process closing itself off to civil society input.

Thus, the balance sheet is mixed. Historically, the extensive EU political opportunity structure has promoted organized women's interests while simultaneously curating civil society. The constraints invoked by the professionalization necessary for applying for EU funds, by financial dependencies as well as a particular habitus of representation, have led to a dominantly 'NGOized' civil society on the EU level as well as across member states (e.g. Heideman 2017; Lang 2013; Paternotte 2016).

In the aftermath of the financial crisis, austerity policies impacted smaller and/or local CSOs more than Brussels-based umbrella networks (EESC/COMM/12/2012). During the same period, EU institutions have substantially diversified and mainstreamed gender equality across programs and Directorates-General (DGs). Simultaneously, they have downsized and, to some degree, invisibilized gender equality policy, not least by moving it from DG Employment and Social Affairs to DG Justice in 2010. On the upside, these processes have ignited contestations and in turn led to women's CSOs and their networks seeking alternative ways to generate sustainable income and engagement (EWL 2015).

Gender advocacy and women's movements in the EU

EU-level civil society in the gender arena displays a panoply of diverse issue-driven alliances and networks that range from education and welfare to science and development. Even though the "velvet triangle" might have stretched its triadic shape into multi-stakeholder and complex networks of engagement, European institutions remain central to women's network mobilizations. They have helped to transform what we see as the European women's movement from a stronger grassroots orientation in the 1970s and 1980s into a more networked fabric of issue-specific alliances, often carried by a set of advocacy CSOs. This section interrogates some of the current challenges, in particular professionalization, insider/outsider dynamics and effects on claim-making, as well as the affordances of intersectional mobilizations.

Professionalization

One of the early and direct effects of the Commission's engagement with women's CSOs was their professionalization (Cullen 2015; Lang 2013; Strid 2009). Acting professionally meant building internal capacity and organizational hierarchy, but also showcasing professionalism towards the public by minimizing transgressional forms of activism that could appear as controversial to EU institutions. EWL, in particular, had to walk a fine line between claiming representativeness of a multitude of European women's voices and projecting competency and expertise towards EU institutions (Cullen 2015). Sofia Strid (2009, 259) attested to EWL's corporatist interest group image, but also argued that it is an "incorporated, not co-opted, independent interest organization with the potential to function as a two-way pipeline facilitator of preferences, interests, and demands." Operating as a two-way pipeline, however, proved only possible with the help of strong national member organizations that likewise showcased high degrees of professionalization, sometimes at the expense of movement building. Since EWL's birthplace was the Commission, it focused on institutional routes of advocacy. Public advocacy, mobilizing broader European constituencies and inviting cross-national movement building, tended to take the backseat.

Professionalization of CSOs did not just occur in Brussels, but also from national to local levels (e.g. Bereni 2016). Dependency on organizational reproduction, in turn, increased internal tensions between promoting a feminist agenda and acquiring or maintaining often service-oriented funding. This tension was showcased in EU tenders that incentivized service provision over networking, advocacy, or research. As national and regional women's CSOs are often unable to scale up to acquire professional staff, they lose out not just on onerous EU-level funding opportunities, but also on domestic resources, thus accelerating processes of NGOization (Lang 2013; Paternotte 2016; for CEE countries see Irvine 2021). In recent years, EWL articulated the problems of CSOs as service providers and under current funding regimes, requesting European and national decision-makers to "allocate funding to women's rights NGOs through funding schemes that cover both service provision and advocacy work and ensure that smaller women's rights NGOs have access to funding" (EWL 2018b, 12). EWL (2018b, 13) asks for establishing "new and innovative ways and methods of financial support, other than highly bureaucratic project budget lines to ensure the survival, independent functioning and strengthening of women's NGOs." But as less professionalized women's CSOs tend to be resource-poor and operate project-oriented, competition for funding and a precarious labor force in women's organizations

Civil society

delineates an unstable future of gendered mobilizations. It might also prevent women's movement actors from articulating how a more gender-sensitive vision of European integration has been under siege within the triangle of neoliberalism, nationalism, and conservatism (Elomäki and Kantola 2018). If the public health crisis of 2020 provides openings for civil society mobilizations to counter these trends is questionable in light of the aforementioned trends.

Insider/outsider claim-making

A second challenge for European women's civil society is navigating insider and outsider claims-making (Bereni and Revillard 2018; Ewig and Ferree 2013, 446). Women's movements were among the first to "see the EU as an arena for political claims making in the 1970s" (Thiel and Pruegl 2009, 10). Advancing gender equality demands from an insider position was more advantageous than outsider mobilizations, as the Commission and the Parliament provided numerous and impactful venues for CSO input (Ahrens 2019). In recent years, however, women's CSOs experience a somewhat diminished institutional presence and impact, as hard gender legislation has given way to mere soft regulations and as EU institutions' internally mainstreamed gender expertise has decreased reliance on CSO input (Ahrens 2018; Cullen 2015). This shift in power and influence stands in notable contrast to other policy fields. CSOs in the public consumer sector, for example, made their mark via insider strategies on the drafting of EU financial regulatory reforms after 2008 (Kastner 2019); we see similar advances in development and environmental policy. EU-level gender umbrella organizations, by contrast, increasingly assume an external watchdog function in EU governance. When in 2018 during the planning for the Common Provisions Regulation (CPR) 2021–2027 to EU Funds (COM(2018) 375 final), the Commission deleted the equality principle between men and women from their draft proposal – which in the previous funding period had been a guiding horizontal principle enshrined in Article 7 CPR – an alliance of EU-level umbrella organizations, including EWL and ILGA, protested in a joint statement (EDF 2018). In subsequent Commission versions, the equality principle was reclaimed. Thus, CSO networks in the gender equality arena still assume a central role in keeping institutions committed to gender equality, but their position seems to have somewhat shifted: they act now more often from the margins or from outside these institutions than from a place at the table. One factor in this positional shift might be paradoxically the democratization of EU consultation processes. By way of the "Better Regulations Initiative" (COM(2015) 215) and the ECI, the EU now provides mostly online gateways for stakeholder and public consultations, as well as the option to elevate an issue from regional and national civil society onto the formal EU policy-making stages. In turn, formerly privileged, longstanding personal and informal access routes might not be as open for gender activists as before.

Tensions in insider/outsider claims-making also arise in terms of legitimate representation. As EU institutions actively promoted CSOs' role as aggregates of European citizen interests, EWL became the legitimized voice and center for gender advocacy. At the same time, however, questions regarding EWL's representativeness and inclusivity abounded. Black, ethnic minority, and migrant women were among the first to challenge EWL's governance structure for not allowing equal participation and demanded a stronger focus on racism and immigration (Kantola 2010, 99). ENoMW was one of the responses to this claim. Created at an EWL seminar in 2007, it was officially launched as an independent network in 2010 with a mission to represent the needs and interests of migrant women across Europe (Rolandsen Agustín 2013, 172; Stubbergaard 2015). Even though it cooperated with EWL on several campaigns, it by far lacks the resources needed to make it a powerful advocate for migrant women's interests. Other minority CSO networks such as the Black European Women's Council, launched with the help

227

of the Global Funds for Women in 2007 (Rolandsen Agustín 2013, 172), in 2019 appear to have been dismantled. Outsider advocacy might not pay (off) in terms of sustainably building organizational capacity for marginalized women's voices in Europe.

Intersectional mobilization

Compounding strategic decisions about how to raise issues in civil society are questions of equity and access. With social and economic inequalities across Europe stagnant or on the rise, efforts to highlight the affordances of continued and ingrained intersectional mobilizations have multiplied (Erzeel and Muegge 2016; Evans and Lépinard 2020; Irvine et al. 2019; Siim and Mokre 2013; Verloo 2013). CSOs and social movements, however, struggle with simultaneously rooting their mobilizations in particular grievances and shifting perspective to acknowledge and act upon intersections with gender, race, class, sexual identity, age, and other markers of exclusion. Awareness that "single-axis conceptualizations of power" (Irvine et al. 2019, 4) distort the complexity of social movement experiences and power dynamics is increasing the quest for strategies and tools to intersectionalize women's and LGBTI issues without creating new hierarchies (Ayoub 2019; Doerr 2019). The question of how to avoid reproducing "exclusionary solidarity" (Ferree and Roth 1998, 629; Roth 2007) in movements while maintaining a collective message poses an ongoing challenge.

Equally unsettled is the role of EU funding in enabling or curating intersectional civil society. Studies of campaigns against violence towards women have found that EU funding mechanisms have increased the intersectional capacity of these groups (Popa and Krizsán 2019). Petra Ahrens' research on access of equality CSOs to EU institutions, however, identifies a clear hierarchy that privileges class over gender, and gender over race (Ahrens 2019). Ahrens' analysis dovetails with the EU in the new millennium embracing a multiple discrimination approach (see Solanke in this volume), and in the process inviting stronger competition among equality grounds into its debates and funding logics. As the Covid-19 crisis starkly exposes inequalities along intersectional parameters, it might provide new momentum for intersectional mobilizations across Europe.

Transnational and national civil societies in the EU: upward and downward influences

Early 21st century European civil society studies focused almost exclusively on transnational actors and mobilizations and their top-down effects on – or, in some cases, plain lack of interaction with – national and regional civil society actors (Ruzza 2004; Steffek et al. 2008). In recent years, however, a stronger multi-focal lens is employed: There is evidence of national and regional CSOs being more involved in the Brussels beltway than earlier studies suggested and newer work showcases the interaction of regional, national, and EU-level mobilizations (Sanchez Salgado and Demidov 2018).

Gender research, in particular, has articulated both the influence of national and subnational civil society networks on the EU level as well as the interaction between different levels of mobilizations. Kathrin Zippel (2006), in her study of sexual harassment policies in Germany, the U.S. and the EU, coined the term "ping-pong effect" for the ways in which national and supranational activists engaged with respective institutions and in the process strengthened cooperation among different scales of civil society. In an attempt to circumvent national blockages, German CSOs and politicians used EU-level policy-making to put pressure on national-level change. Thus, even though EU institutions were historically seen as not being "structurally responsive" (Rolandsen Agustín 2013, 175) to the array of member states' CSOs, these actors in fact utilized EU policy-making to advance domestic political agendas. Celeste Montoya (2013), likewise, shows that national and regional women's CSOs utilized EU-level networks and policy support to mobilize nationally and regionally for establishing anti-violence legislation and infrastructure. Nonetheless, a lack of civil society funding to monitor legislative reforms in member states carried more weight than formal legislation (Montoya 2013, 250).

To what degree the future of European civil society lies in independent and direct linkages between large domestic CSOs and EU institutions, in fact bypassing EU-level umbrella organizations, is unclear. To some degree, it will depend on the fit between domestic and transnational organizations, cultures, and generational "chemistry," as Claire Lafon (2018) illustrates in her ethnography of the French and Belgian national platforms' relationship with EWL. There are signals that EWL is responsive to the decade-old criticism that depicted it as too focused on institutional policy work and less attentive to national and regional civil society development. For example, a 2018 EWL Task Force on the state of women's rights in central eastern Europe, the Balkans and the Baltic states leads their recommendation section on women's rights in these regions *not*, as would have been the case in earlier periods, with economic and social rights, but cites as the number one priority the strengthening, support, and resourcing of a strong women's rights movement (EWL 2018b, 6).

As the EU has become more responsive to direct engagement of national, regional, and local advocacy, umbrella organizations seem to fall in line. Facilitated by the OMC which presents itself as a "fully decentralized approach" in which civil society on all levels of the EU is "actively involved" (Bussschaert 2016, 165), national and subnational voices have already increased in Brussels. With the extension of consultation procedures as well as the ECI in 2011, the Commission now reaches out beyond its institutionalized layers of civil society into member states and their CSOs, movements, and policy activists. The degree to which such input is as impactful as having stakeholders at the table is under scrutiny (Lang 2020).

In sum, the multifocal lens of recent gender research on civil society in Europe presents a panoply of networked nodes from local to the transnational levels. Even though EU-level umbrella organizations still provide for most communicative hubs, attention to regional and multimember state networks not necessarily trafficked through Brussels has increased.

Future challenges for gendered European civil society research

An EESC (2017) study identifies five trends affecting CSOs by 2030: changes in demography, economic crisis, digitalization, populism, and shrinking civic spaces (CES/CSS/01/2017/EESC). All have gendered impact, but I consider three research gaps to be paramount. First, there is a lack of attention regarding the fragile *political economy of gendered mobilizations in civil society*. Even though public records such as the "European Transparency Register" allow new insights into civil society's finances, we still know too little about the funding. Professional gender CSOs as well as their Brussels-based umbrella organizations are mostly dependent on public funding and/or membership fees. Austerity politics has not just reduced national and local funding; realignment on the EU level also will change the political economy of civil society. On the right wing of civil society, questions need to be asked as well. Who funds the international alliance of anti-abortion activists with their increasing public footprint? What are the effects of some EU governments stigmatizing "foreign funding" for their CSO sector, particularly at a time when EU-level and other member countries' funding should actually be increased to counter attacks on women's rights?

More specifically, we know too little about the actual funds the EU commits to gender equality CSOs. Agnès Hubert and Maria Stratigaki (2016, 27), in their analysis of the "major 'recast' exercise" of gender equality funds after the millennium, point to the strategy of combining formerly identifiable gender budget lines with other lines under headers that are non-gender specific. As participating in EU-funded projects has become increasingly complex and onerous, a recent EWL report delineates the post-austerity predicament of many CSOs as being in a "starvation cycle," barely able to sustain operations and serve their constituencies. This cycle is initiated by "funders' unrealistic expectations" (EWL 2015, 4) about what a CSO such as EWL needs in order to meet core operational costs and leads to CSOs "skimping on vital systems such as spending on capacity-building of staff, resource mobilization, technology systems, organizational and management capacities and other essential overhead" (EWL 2015, 4). Focusing on the political economy of civil society, evidently, is a problem for the sector at large, and warrants large-scale and comprehensive comparative analysis.

A second gap opens around the fact that EU institutions have moved an increasingly large segment of *civil society engagement online*, utilizing public consultation procedures to gauge CSOs and individual citizens' opinion on a wide array of policy issues, gender equality among them. It is, however, far from clear how exactly the EU engages with online civil society input (Lang 2020). With campaigns such as #MeToo against sexual assault and harassment, moreover, we witness the emergence of a digital sphere of European activism reaching citizens without institutional anchoring. As feminists debate the democratizing effect of online activism, its ambivalent nature becomes increasingly clear (Baer 2016; McRobbie 2009). While it provides a low-threshold, low-cost, and widely available suite of articulation means enabling time- and resource-constrained citizens to engage more in politics and civic affairs, it is debatable if it not also increases public opinion formation and civic engagement in echo chambers (Margetts 2017). The fact that online platforms such as Facebook, Instagram, or Snapchat do not allow data use for scientific purposes, poses severe challenges for researchers' attempts to understand the democratizing potential of online activism. Private ownership of Europe's arguably most vibrant public (online) spaces, moreover, does make anti-discrimination interventions difficult, and gender researchers need to address this void.

Third, *rightwing populist movements* are not just critical towards the European institutional edifice as a whole, but they also draw on constructions of nationalism in order to disavow national as well as supranational civil society. A case in point is the French Front National. Marine Le Pen's 2017 presidential platform, known as the 144 Commitments, that included as Commitment 95 the "struggle against communitarianism," and called for a constitutional provision that would read "The Republic recognizes no community" (Le Pen 2017; cited in Bastow 2018, 22). While using public spaces and their movements for displays of power, rightwing movements thus are averse to civil society's role as community maker, which, in their construction, stands for diversity and multiculturalism. Public spaces across Europe become, whenever these movements coalesce, overwhelmingly male spaces, with anti-gender ideology fueling new nationalisms.

This trend is evidenced in central and eastern European countries, where civil society is under threat by illiberal governments. In 2014, the Hungarian Women's Lobby and three of its member CSOs were listed by the government as problematic, subjecting them to several audits. In the same year, ILGA Europe commissioned a study to map the shrinking civil society spaces for LGBTQI people (ILGA 2014). Engaging with gender in civil society, the state, or universities is increasingly dangerous, as rightwing reactionary governments, parties, and movements denounce gender as a "criminal ideology" (EWL 2018b, 14), threatening family values and the traditional division of labor. In 2017, the Polish government raided the offices of several women's

Civil society

organizations in the area of violence against women in Warsaw, Gdańsk, Łódź and Zielona Góra, after they had participated in anti-government protests (FRA 2017, 48).

Arguably, rightwing reactionary civil society has adapted to the multilayered alliances in civil society better than established parties and longstanding organizations. Their "skillful use" (Hodžić and Bijelić 2014, 2) of new technologies and tools has led to networked organizing that shows "blurred lines between civil initiatives, organizations of civil society and political parties" (Hodžić and Bijelić 2014, 12). Even though rightwing reactionary movements' visibility and impact varies across the EU (Kuhar and Paternotte 2017, 261), their public footprint is increasing, ranging from festive events to violent attacks on what they demarcate as the "other" civil society. It remains to be seen if gender equality CSOs and movements can mobilize to counter these attacks.

Note

1 I would like to thank Gabi Abels, Jill Irvine, Andrea Krizsán, Effie Zheng and Chloe Bosley for excellent comments and editing suggestions.

References

Ahrens P (2018): *Actors, Institutions, and the Making of EU Gender Equality Programs*, London: Palgrave Macmillan.

Ahrens P (2019): A Mountain Skyline? Gender Equality and Intersectionality in Supranational "Equality CSOs", in: Irvine J, Lang S, Montoya C (eds.): *Gendered Mobilizations and Intersectional Challenges. Contemporary Social Movements in Europe and North America*, Lanham, MD, London: Rowman & Littlefield/ECPR Press, 244–262.

Ayoub P (2019): Intersectional and Transnational Alliances during Times of Crisis. The European LGBTI Movement, in: Irvine J, Lang S, Montoya C (eds.): *Gendered Mobilizations and Intersectional Challenges. Contemporary Social Movements in Europe and North America*, Lanham, MD, London: Rowman & Littlefield/ECPR Press, 111–132.

Baer H (2016): Redoing feminism: digital activism, body politics, and neoliberalism, *Feminist Media Studies* **16** (1), 17–34.

Bastow S (2018): The *Front national* under Marine Le Pen: a mainstream political party?, *French Politics* **16**, 19–37.

Bee C, Guerrina R, eds. (2017): *Framing Citizen Engagement, Political Participation and Active Citizenship in Europe*, London: Routledge.

Bereni, L (2016): Women's Movements and Feminism: French Political Sociology Meets a Comparative Feminist Approach, in: Elgie R, Grossman E, Mazur AG (eds.): *The Oxford Handbook on French Politics*, Oxford: Oxford University Press, 461–482.

Bereni L, Revillard A (2018): Movement institutions. The bureaucratic sources of feminist protest, *Politics and Gender* **14** (3), 407–432.

Bretherton C, Sperling L (1996): Women's networks and the European Union: towards an inclusive approach?, *Journal of Common Market Studies* **34** (4), 487–508.

Busschaert G (2016): *Participatory Democracy, Civil Society, and Social Europe. A Legal and Political Perspective*, Cambridge: Intersentia.

Cohen J, Arato A (1992): *Civil Society and Political Theory*, Cambridge, MA: MIT Press.

Cullen P (2015): Feminist NGOs and the European Union: contracting opportunities and strategic response, *Social Movement Studies* **14** (4), 410–426.

Doerr N (2019): Activists as Political Translators? Addressing Inequality and Positional Misunderstandings in Refugee Solidarity Coalitions, in: Irvine J, Lang S, Montoya C (eds.): *Gendered Mobilizations and Intersectional Challenges. Contemporary Social Movements in Europe and North America*, Lanham, MD, London: Rowman & Littlefield/ECPR Press, 189–207.

Edwards M (2014): *Civil Society*, Cambridge: Polity Press.

Elomäki, A, Kantola, J (2018): Theorizing feminist struggles in the triangle of neoliberalism, conservatism, and nationalism, *Social Politics* **25** (4), 337–360.

Erzeel S, Mügge L (2016) Introduction: intersectionality in European political science research, *Politics* **36** (4), 341–345.

European Disability Forum (EDF) (2018): Joint Statement on EU Funds for equality between men and women, accessibility for persons with disabilities and non-discrimination, URL: www.edf-feph.org/newsroom/news/joint-statement-eu-funds-equality-between-men-and-women-accessibility-persons (download: April 25, 2020).

European Economic and Social Forum (EESC) (2017): The Future Evolution of Civil Society in the European Union by 2030. Study, Brussels: EESC.

European Union Agency for Fundamental Rights (FRA) (2017): *Challenges Facing Civil Society Organisations Working on Human Rights in the EU*, URL: https://fra.europa.eu/sites/default/files/fra_uploads/fra-2018-challenges-facing-civil-society_en.pdf (download: April 25, 2020).

European Women's Lobby (EWL) (2015): *Together for a Feminist Europe. Financial Resilience and Sustainability Plan 2016–2020*, URL: www.womenlobby.org/IMG/pdf/2016_financial_resilience_sustainability_plan_ewl_for_web.pdf (download: April 25, 2020).

European Women's Lobby (EWL) (2018a): *Financial Information and Transparency*, URL: www.womenlobby.org/Financial-Information-and-Transparency-7525?lang=en (download: October 3, 2019).

European Women's Lobby (EWL) (2018b): *Time for Women's Rights. Time for a United Feminist Europe. The state of women's rights in Central Eastern Europe, the Balkans and the Baltic States. Under Attack and Under Resourced*, Report, URL: www.womenlobby.org/IMG/pdf/ceebbs_report_ewl_web.pdf (download: October 4, 2019).

Evans E, Lépinard E, eds. (2020): *Intersectionality in Feminist and Queer Movements. Confronting Privileges*, London: Routledge.

Ewig C, Ferree M M (2013): Feminist Organizing: What's Old, what's New? History, Trends and Issues, in: Waylen G, Celis K, Kantola J, Weldon S.L. (eds.) *The Oxford Handbook of Gender and Politics*, Oxford: Oxford University Press, 437–461.

Farris S R (2017): *In the Name of Women's Rights. The Rise of Femonationalism,* Chapel Hill, NC: Duke University Press.

Ferree MM, Roth S (1998): Gender, class, and the interaction between social movements. A strike of West Berlin day care workers, *Gender & Society* **12** (6), 626–648.

Fuchs G, Payer S (2012): Women's NGOs in EU Governance. Problems of Finance and Access, in: Obradovic D. Pleines, H (eds.) *The Capacity of Central and East European Interest Groups to Participate in EU Governance*, Stuttgart: ibidem, 163–182.

García LB (2015): The Effects of the European Citizens' Initiative in the Field of European Civil Society, in: Kalm S, Johannson H (eds.): *EU Civil Society. Patterns of Cooperation, Competition, and Conflict*, Basingstoke: Palgrave Macmillan, 175–192.

Halsaa B, Roseneil S, Sumer S, eds. (2012): *Remaking Citizenship in Multicultural Europe. Women's Movements, Gender and Diversity*, Basingstoke: Palgrave Macmillan.

Heideman L (2017): Cultivating peace: social movement professionalization and NGOization in Croatia, *Mobilization* **22** (3), 345–362.

Hinterhuber E M (2014): *Time to Tango! Bringing civil society and gender together*. Working Paper No. 3, Münster: Zentrum für Europäische Geschlechterstudien (ZEUGS).

Hodžić A, Bijelić N (2014): *Neo-Conservative Threats to Sexual and Reproductive Health & Rights in the European Union*, URL: www.cesi.hr/attach/_n/neo-conservative_threats_to_srhr_in_eu.pdf (download: October 21, 2019).

Hubert A, Stratigaki M (2016); 20 years of gender mainstreaming: rebirth out of the ashes?, *Femina Politica* **25** (2), 21–36.

ILGA Europe (2014): *Civil Society Space*, URL: www.ilga-europe.org/what-we-do/our-advocacy-work/civil-society (download: May 30, 2020).

Irvine J (2021): Contentions of Funding Gender Equality in Eastern Europe, in: Fabian A, Johnson J E, Lazda M (eds.): *Routledge Handbook on Gender in Central Eastern Europe and Eurasia*, Abingdon: Routledge.

Irvine J, Lang S, Montoya C, eds. (2019): *Gendered Mobilizations and Intersectional Challenges. Contemporary Social Movements in Europe and North America*, Lanham, MD, London: Rowman & Littlefield/ECPR Press.

Kalm S, Johansson H (2015): *EU Civil Society: Patterns of Cooperation, Competition, and Conflict*, Basingstoke: Palgrave Macmillan.

Kantola J (2010): *Gender and the European Union*, Basingstoke: Palgrave Macmillan.

Kastner, L (2019): From outsiders to insiders: a civil society perspective on EU financial reforms, *Journal of Common Market Studies* **57** (2), 223–241.

Civil society

Knappe H, Lang S (2014): Between whisper and voice. NGOized women's movement outreach in the UK and Germany, *European Journal of Women's Studies* **21** (4), 361–381.

Koettig M, Bitzan R, Peto A, eds. (2017): *Gender and Far Right Politics in Europe*, Cham: Springer.

Kohler-Koch B, Quittkat C (2012): What Is 'Civil Society' and Who Represents It in the European Union?, in: Liebert U, Trenz HJ (eds.): *The New Politics of European Civil Society*, London, New York: Routledge, 19–39.

Kuhar R, Paternotte D, eds. (2017): *Anti-Gender Campaigns in Europe. Mobilizing against Equality*, Lanham, MD: Rowman & Littlefield.

Lafon C (2018): Europeanization through the European Women's Lobby. A sociological comparison of the French and Belgian national coordinations, *Journal of Contemporary European Research* **14** (2), 154–168.

Lang S (2013): *NGOs, Civil Society, and the Public Sphere*, Cambridge, New York: Cambridge University Press.

Lang S (2014): Women's Advocacy Networks: The European Union and the Velvet Triangle, in: Grewal I, Bernal V (eds.): *Theorizing NGOs, Feminist Struggles, States, and Neoliberalism*, Durham, NC: Duke University Press, 266–284.

Lang, S (2020): Consulting Publics in European Union Gender Policies. Organising Echo Chambers of Facilitation Critical Norm Engagement?, in: Engberg-Pedersen L, Fejerskow A, Cold-Ravnkilde M (eds.): *Rethinking Gender Equality in Global Governance*, Cham: Palgrave Macmillan, 213–236.

Lang S, Sauer B (2016): European Integration and the Politics of Scale: A Gender Perspective, in: Abels G, McRae H (eds.): *Gendering European Integration Theory*, Opladen: Barbara Budrich, 217–236.

Liebert U, Trenz HJ (2012): *The New Politics of European Civil Society*, London, New York: Routledge.

Margetts H (2017): Political behaviour and the acoustics of social media, *Nature Human Behaviour* **17** (1), 1–3.

McRobbie A (2009): *The Aftermath of Feminism. Gender, Culture, and Social Change*, London: Sage.

Montoya C (2013): *From Global to Grassroots. The European Union, Transnational Advocacy, and Combating Violence Against Women*, Oxford, New York: Oxford University Press.

Monzon JL, Chaves R (2017): *Recent Evolutions of the Social Economy in the European Union*, Brussels: European Economic and Social Forum.

Paternotte D (2016): The NGOization of LGBT activism: ILGA-Europe and the Treaty of Amsterdam, *Social Movement Studies* **15** (4), 388–402.

Popa RM, Krizsán A (2019): The Politics of Intersectionality in Activism against Domestic Violence in Hungary and Romania, in: Irvine J, Lang S, Montoya C (eds.): *Gendered Mobilizations and Intersectional Challenges. Contemporary Social Movements in Europe and North America*, Lanham, MD, London: Rowman & Littlefield/ECPR Press, 5–73.

Pudrovska T, Ferree M.M. (2004): Global activism in 'virtual space': the European Women's Lobby in the network of transnational women's NGOs on the web, *Social Politics* **11**(1), 117–143.

Rolandsen Agustín L (2008): Civil society participation in EU gender policy-making. Framing strategies and institutional constraints, *Parliamentary Affairs* **61** (3), 419–425.

Rolandsen Agustin L (2013): Transnational Collective Mobilisation: Challenges for Women's Movements in Europe, in: Siim B, Mokre M (eds.): *Negotiating Gender and Diversity in an Emergent European Public Sphere*, London: Palgrave Macmillan, 161–178.

Rosanvallon P (2007): *The Demands of Liberty. Civil Society in France since the Revolution*, Cambridge, MA: Harvard University Press.

Roth S (2007): Sisterhood and solidarity? Women's organizations in the expanded European Union, *Social Politics* **14** (1), 460–487.

Ruzza C (2004): *Europe and Civil Society. Movement Coalitions and European Governance*, Manchester: Manchester University Press.

Sanchez Salgado R (2014): *Europeanizing Civil Society. How the EU Shapes Civil Society Organizations*, Basingstoke: Palgrave Macmillan.

Sanchez Salgado R, Demidov A (2018): Beyond the Brussels bubble? National civil society organisations in the European Union, *Journal of Contemporary European Research* **14** (2), 56–67.

Schwabenland C, Lange C, Onyx J, Nakagawa S, eds. (2016): *Women's Emancipation and Civil Society Organisations. Challenging or maintaining the status quo?*, Bristol: Policy Press.

Siim B, Mokre M, eds. (2013): *Negotiating Gender and Diversity in an Emergent European Public Sphere*, London: Palgrave Macmillian.

Steffek J, Kissling C, Nanz P, eds. (2008): *Civil Society Participation in European and Global Governance. A Cure for the Democratic Deficit?*, Basingstoke: Palgrave.

Strid S (2009): *Gendered Interests in the European Union. The European Women's Lobby and the Organisation and Representation of Women's Interests*, Örebro: Örebro University Publishers.

Stubbergaard Y (2015): Conflict and Cooperation: Interactions among EU-Level Civil Society Organisations in the Field of Gender Equality, in: Kalm S, Johansson H (eds.): *EU Civil Society: Patterns of Cooperation, Competition, and Conflict*, Basingstoke: Palgrave Macmillan, 119–136.

Thiel M (2017): *European Civil Society and Human Rights Advocacy*, Philadelphia: University of Pennsylvania Press.

Thiel M, Pruegl E (2009): Understanding Diversity in the European Union, in: Pruegl E, Thiel M (eds.): *Diversity in the European Union*, New York: Palgrave Macmillan, 3–19.

Wilde G (2016): Civil Society and European Integration: The Re-Configuration of Gendered Power Relations in the Public Sphere, in: Abels G, MacRae H (eds.): *Gendering European Integration Theory*, Opladen, Farmington Hills: Barbara Budrich, 257–278.

Verloo M (2013): Intersectional and cross-movement politics and policies: reflections on current practices and debates, *Signs* **38** (4), 893–915.

Woodward A (2004): Building Velvet Triangles: Gender and Informal Governance, in: Christiansen T, Piattoni S, (eds.): *Informal Governance in the European Union*, Cheltenham: Edward Elgar, 76–93.

Woodward A (2015): Travels, triangles and transformations. Implications for new agendas in gender equality policy, *Tijeschrift voor Genderstudies* **18** (1), 5–18.

Zippel K (2006): *The Politics of Sexual Harassment. A Comparative Study of the United States, the European Union, and Germany*, Cambridge, New York: Cambridge University Press.

19
Party politics

Petra Ahrens and Lise Rolandsen Agustín*

Researching transnational party politics is a quite recent addition to the scholarly debate on European integration (e.g. Andeweg 1995; Bardi 1994; Hix and Lord 1997). Mainstream research mainly focuses on formal institutions; it can be broadly divided into: (1) the analysis of parties and political groups as elements of a parliamentary party-based European Union (EU) democracy (Westlake 2019); (2) the electoral successes and failures of (Euro)parties and voter-party congruence in the European Parliament (EP) (Mattila and Raunio 2006; Stockemer and Sundström 2019; Schmitt and Thomassen 1999); (3) political group cohesion and measures to ensure it (Hix et al. 2005, 2007; McElroy and Benoit 2007, 2010, 2012; Yordanova 2013); and (4) party positions towards European integration (Brack 2018; Almeida 2012). Gender perspectives have not played a role in mainstream research, except for studies of women's representation in the European Parliament (Fortin-Rittberger and Rittberger 2014; 2015; Stockemer and Sundström 2019).

Illuminating connections between Europarties, national parties, and European Parliament political groups, this chapter focuses on the latter and their performance regarding gender equality and gendered representation in the European Parliament. After describing the composition, powers, and position of political groups in the EU system, it attends to electoral systems, political recruitment, and gendered representation. This includes insights on (gendered) electoral support, electoral campaigns, political recruitment, and the gendered outcome of European Parliament elections and leadership positions. Next, we explore political groups' position on gender equality and anti-discrimination, as well as the resulting parliamentary output, such as legislation and reports. Finally, the chapter examines formal and informal working procedures in the European Parliament, specifically those regarding group-cohesion rates (roll-call votes) and the left–right divide versus consensus-oriented practices of grand coalitions. Particular attention is paid to the three major committees for gender equality policy: the Committee on Women's Rights and Gender Equality (FEMM), the Committee on Employment and Social Affairs (EMPL), and the Committee on Civil Liberties, Justice and Home Affairs (LIBE). The final section highlights research gaps and directions for future research.

---

* Petra Ahrens' work received funding from the European Research Council (ERC) under grant agreement No. 771676 of the European Union's Horizon 2020 research and innovation program.

Petra Ahrens and Lise Rolandsen Agustín

Europarties and European party groups – transnational and powerless?

At the EU level, party politics are connected with two different, yet to a large extent overlapping party organizations for transnational democracy: Europarties and European party groups (EPGs, i.e. the political groups in the European Parliament). The former are transnational, extra-parliamentary parties composed of national parties from European states (sometimes even including non-European parties), while the latter are the political groups in the European Parliament consisting of parties from EU member states and often subject to change after European elections (see Ahrens and Rolandsen Agustín (European Parliament) in this volume). On this supranational level, party politics differs considerably from party systems and the role of parties at national and internal party level. Europarties and EPGs are less unitary in their formal structures, the EU itself has no government; hence, parties influence on policy outcomes is much weaker (Almeida 2012). Yet, EPGs perform a core role in the EU's functioning, as stipulated in Article 10(4) of the TFEU: "political parties at European level contribute to forming European political awareness and to expressing the will of citizens of the Union." Members of the European Parliament (MEPs) generally vote along EPG party lines when it comes to legislation and the budget (Corbett et al. 2016, 85). Simultaneously, national parties direct the recruitment of candidates for the European Parliament, and the composition of both Councils (European Council, Council of the European Union; see Abels in this volume) as well as the European Commission through their governmental activities. Furthermore, EPGs select the Parliament's (vice)president(s), (co)chairs, committee (vice)chairs, rapporteurs, and so on (Corbett et al. 2016, 85; Ladrech 2006). Thus, EPGs have gained power over time and are crucial for democratic representation in the European Parliament (Brack 2018).

Over the decades, several changes shaped how Europarties and EPGs became institutionalized, resulting in the EU's unique supranational party politics. The first key historical change was the *introduction of direct elections to the European Parliament* in 1979. As an early response to these elections and the concomitant need for better coordination, national parties started founding Europarties in the mid-1970s. This resulted in the first three: Confederation of Socialist Parties in the European Community (CSPEC, 1974; since 1992 Party of European Socialists, PES), the European Peoples Party (EPP, 1976), and the Federation of Liberal and Democrat Parties in Europe (1976; renamed European Liberal Democrat and Reform Party, ELDR, in 2004, since 2012 Alliance of Liberals and Democrats for Europe, ALDE) (Ladrech 2006, 493; see Table 19.1). With the growing importance of the European Parliament, the need to formalize the status of and relationship between Europarties and EPGs increased. Following the growth of Green parties and social-justice movements across Western Europe in the early 1980s, the European Free Alliance (EFA, 1982) and European Green Party (EGP, 1983) were established, forming the joint Greens/EFA Group (with some intermissions) in the European Parliament. The collapse of the Soviet Union led to considerable growth of Europarty membership with new central and eastern Europe parties joining. After the 2004 enlargement the composition of EPGs changed accordingly (von dem Berge 2017). The new millennium witnessed new Europarties, such as the Party of the European Left (EL) and the Alliance of European Conservatives and Reformists (ACRE), as well as new EPGs related to them, such as the European United Left-Nordic Green Left (GUE/NGL) and European Conservatives and Reformists (ECR) (see Table 19.1).

Approved at the Nice summit in 2000, the Statute on European Parties (Regulation (EC) No. 2004/2003) entered into force in 2004, formally and spatially separating Europarties and EPGs: Europarties moved out of European Parliament offices; they received no further subsidies from EPGs, but operational grants from the European Commission instead (Ladrech 2006, 497). As of 2018, the distinct European Parliament Budget Line 402 was established; since then, Europarties receive contributions of up to 90% of their reimbursable expenditure, if they fulfill the following conditions: registering with the Authority for European Political Parties and European Political Foundations (APPF), having at least one MEP, external auditing, and registration in a member state. Furthermore, their parties must be represented in at least one quarter of member states and in different assemblies (Article 3, Regulation (EC) No. 2004/2003). Table 19.1 provides an overview of today's spectrum of Europarties, the composition of EPGs in relation to them, and further details.

Simultaneously, EPG formation follows the European Parliament's Rules of Procedure. Since 2009, an EPG must consist of a minimum of 25 MEPs (after Brexit 23 MEPs) originating from at least seven member states. MEPs not attached to EPGs belong to "non-inscrit", receive fewer resources, and usually cannot perform core tasks such as rapporteurship. Since the individual EPG's compositions often change between (and sometimes even during) legislatures, the European Parliament party system is volatile. Whereas EPP, S&D, and Greens/EFA have remained stable EPGs since their early formation, as has ALDE (even though it changed its name to Renew Europe (RE) after the 2019 elections to include the French La Republic en Marche with its large share of seats), other EPGs on the left and right have (dis)appeared or considerably changed over the years, due to lack of MEPs or conflicts about the group's political goals. On the left, GUE/NGL has existed since the 2004 elections, but its composition has changed depending on wins and losses in member states. On the right, EPG formation has been more volatile, not least because more center-conservative parties like UKIP refused alliances with nationalist and radical right-wing parties (RRP) like the French Front National (today Rassemblement National, RN) or the Italian Lega Nord (today Lega). At the same time, these RRP parties either failed to fulfill the EPGs' requirements or proved unable to find common ground. While ECR has been rather stable since 2009 with the British Conservatives and Polish Law and Justice Party (PiS) forming the core, other far right EPGs like Europe of Freedom and Direct Democracy (EFDD) (forming an EPG from 2009 to 2019)[1] and Europe of Nations and Freedom (ENF) (formed in 2015) constantly reorganized. In 2019 RRPs formed the new Identity & Democracy (ID) political group (consisting of RN, Lega, the German AfD and several small parties from seven more member states). Thus, the current 2019 European Parliament hosts a total of seven political groups, the size of which changed after the UK left the EU – and thus British MEPs the European Parliament – at the end of January 2020. Since then the number of seats was slightly redistributed among member states and overall lowered to 705 MEP of which the EPP now holds 187 seats, the S&D 147, RE 98, ID 76, Greens/EFA 67, ECR 61, and GUE/NGL 29 seats, plus 29 non-inscrit MEPs (European Parliamentary Research Service, February 2020).

According to Brack (2018, 56, 83), party competition within the European Parliament is today structured along two dimensions: "the left/right economic cleavage and the GAL/TAN (Green-Alternative-Libertarian versus Traditional-Authoritarian-Nationalist) dimension on noneconomic issues such as the environment, lifestyle and values." It is important to note that the national level is generally a poor predictor for party positions on EU integration; parties exhibit considerable cross-family variation (Almeida 2012). The social–democratic party family was internally divided about the future of the welfare state, for instance, and the liberal family about whether to take up a neoliberal or social liberal position. On the left, the party family is generally heterogeneous due to the varying national contexts (Almeida 2012, 153). The Christian democrat party family hold similar positions on EU integration, but CEE enlargement challenged its self-understanding by including "non-Christian but conservative" parties (Almeida 2012, 153; see also Put et al. 2016, 14). Only the RRP family maintained a homogenous stance while turning away from their original Ethno-Europeanism to solid Euroscepticism (Almeida 2012, 154). Hence, EU party politics exhibits a clear divide between supporters and opponents of the EU as a polity (Wiesner 2019, 193). This has repercussions on party stances on anti-discrimination and gender equality policy (Falkner and Plattner 2018).

Table 19.1 Overview of Europarties and EPGs

Name as of 2019 election	Founding Year	Previous party names	Number of national parties	Country representation	Relationship to EPGs	APPF registered	EU funding 2017 in €
Alliance for Peace and Freedom (APF)	2015	–	13	9 EU	Only non-inscrit	No (removed by APPF)	-
Alliance of European National Movements (AEMN)	2009	–	6	5 EU	No MEPs	No (removed by APPF)	342,788
Alliance of Liberals and Democrats for Europe (ALDE)	1975	Federation of Liberal and Democrat Parties in Europe (1976); European Liberals and Democrats (ELD, 1977); European Liberal Democrats and Reformists (ELDR, 1986); European Liberal Democrat and Reform Party (ELDR, 2004)	52	38 European	Renew Europe (RE)	Yes	2,449,108
European Christian Political Movement (ECPM)	2002	–	19	18 European	2 ECR, 1 EPP	Yes	499,993
European Conservatives and Reformists Party (ECR)	2009	Alliance of European Conservatives and Reformists (AECR) (2009–2016); Alliance of Conservatives and Reformists in Europe (ACRE) (2016–2019)	44 (24 none-European)	39 worldwide	ECR	Yes	1,439,310

European Democratic Party (EDP)	2004	–	20	16 European	Renew Europe, 2 S&D	Yes	532,072
European Free Alliance (EFA)	1981	–	47	21 European	Greens-EFA, 1 GUE/ NGL, 3 ECR	Yes	779,408
European Green Party (EGP)	1984	European Green Coordination (EGC, 1984); European Federation of Green Parties (1993)	41	34 European	Greens/EFA	Yes	1,865,999
European People's Party (EPP)	1976	–	84 (37 non-EU)	43 (16 non-EU)	EPP	Yes	8,018,034
European Pirate Party (PPEU)	2014	–	21	20 European	Greens/EFA	No, in preparation	-
Identity and Democracy Party (ID)	2014	Movement for a Europe of Nations and Freedom (MENF; 2014–2019)	12	11 European	Identity and Democracy (ID)	Yes	-
Initiative of Communist and Workers' Parties (INITIATIVE)	2013	–	30	27 European	Non-inscrits	No	-
Now the people!	2018	–	6	6 European	GUE/NGL	No	-
Party of European Socialists (PES)	1974	Confederation of the Socialist Parties of the European Community (CSPEC, 1974)	33	29 (EU, UK, Norway)	S&D	Yes	6,901,688
Party of the European Left (EL)	2004	–	27	25 European	GUE/NGL	Yes	1,342,594
VOLT Europa	2017	–	Pan-European, no national parties	n.a.	Greens/EFA	No	-

Source: Data compiled by the authors from Europarty websites, European Parliament website (www.europarl.europa.eu/pdf/grants/funding_amounts_parties_01-2019.pdf, accessed November 6, 2019), APPF website (www.appf.europa.eu/appf/en/parties-and-foundations/registered-parties.html, accessed November 6, 2019), and Morijn 2019, 631–633.

The 1993 Maastricht Treaty introduced the second decisive historical change to the EPGs' role: the *co-decision procedure*, which put the European Parliament and the Council on equal footing in legislation. The 2009 Lisbon Treaty turned co-decision into the ordinary legislative procedure (OLP) and expanded its application to almost all policy fields, including those important for gender equality: employment, social policy, and justice and home affairs (Abels 2019). Moreover, given that the Parliament obliged itself to implement gender mainstreaming, this would potentially offer fertile ground for EPGs to promote gender equality in all policy fields. As a legislator, it thus became more important which political group and rapporteur were in charge of a legislative proposal. As most parliamentary work is done in the committees, political groups shape the European Parliament's output by assigning MEPs as (vice)chairs, coordinators, and (shadow) rapporteurs. The EPGs assign these tasks as a measure of recognition to enhance group discipline (Yordanova 2013). In the absence of a European "government," the EPP and S&D often formed a decisive "grand coalition," guiding (legislative) proposals through the European Parliament legislative process (Abels 2019; Corbett et al. 2016). With the 2019 electoral losses for the EPP and S&D, this grand coalition ended, emphasizing the need for more ideology-driven coalition-building (centre/left versus centre/right).

A third key historical development came in 2003 with the adoption of the Nice Treaty, which aimed to bring Europarties and EPGs further in line with *fundamental rights and values enshrined in EU treaty bases*. Already in 2001, the European Commission had proposed a Council regulation on Europarties, with the aim of linking funding for Europarties to Article 2 TEU, which contains the EU's legal and political foundations (Morijn 2019). Requiring unanimity, the Council originally blocked the proposal, adopting it only after amendments in 2014 together with the European Parliament (Regulation (EU, Euratom) No. 1141/2014) and amending it in 2018 (Regulation (EU/Euratom) 2018/673. This "EU-values compliance mechanism" (Morijn 2019, 617) requires Europarties to adhere to fundamental values, among them gender equality, anti-discrimination, and tolerance for minorities. Populist and right-wing parties immediately complained it was targeting them unfairly (Morijn 2019, 619). The EU required Europarties striving for EU funding to register with the newly created authority APPF; the Commission, the Council, the European Parliament, or a member state where the Europarty resides could now ask the APPF to check for the party's value compliance. As of 2018 even citizens can request the European Parliament to act (Morijn 2019, 629). If compliance cannot be verified, the Europarty is deregistered and loses its funding. Apparently, the requirement of a written pledge of allegiance to Article 2 TEU (including gender equality and non-discrimination) was too much to ask of some right-wing and populist Europarties; they decided not to register with APPF (Morijn 2019, 631–633; see Table 19.1).

The 2014 European elections witnessed a fourth landmark development: the first *Spitzenkandidatur process* for the European Commission presidency, invented by Europarties, stipulating that the European Council should be "taking into account the elections to the European Parliament" in the nomination (Article 17(7) TEU). Historically, however, supranational party programs had not been common in the electoral campaigns, and only in 2009 did EPGs start to prepare joint election programs (Wiesner 2019, 190). In the 2014 elections, five Europarties – EPP, PES, ALDE, EGP, and EL – each selected one (or two) lead candidates running for Commission presidency. Eurosceptic parties "saw this development as too 'federalist' and refused to appoint Spitzenkandidaten" (Lefkofridi and Katsanidou 2018, 1469). The selection process differed considerably between Europarties. Among the five, only the EL formally subscribed to gender equality, committing to a 50% share of women (and men) in all intra-party bodies. The EGP was the only party practically committed to equal representation by selecting two lead candidates – one woman and one man; all other EPGs nominated only men (Put et al. 2016, 12–16). In 2019, the same Europarties plus ACRE participated in the *Spitzenkandidatur* process, but this time women were slightly better represented. EPP, PES, and ACRE nominated men, ALDE nominated five women and two men, and EL and EGP nominated duos. Yet, famously in 2019 the lead candidate procedure failed; in the end the European Council nominated a non-*Spitzenkandidat*, the German conservative Ursula von der Leyen, who was then elected by the European Parliament in July 2019 (see also Hartlapp et al. and Abels in this volume).

Gendered representation, gender equality policy, and gendered working procedures

Although research on Europarties and EPGs is still developing, it has received more attention over the past decade; gendered perspectives are no exception. Furthest evolved are comparative studies on gendered representation in parties and among MEPs. There is a growing literature on EPG (and Europarty) positions on gender equality and anti-discrimination, and how this plays out in the European Parliament's everyday work, mostly in the committees. Recently, research attends to the EPGs, covering gender aspects of their policies, their formal and informal procedures (groundbreaking is the EUGenDem project, https://research.uta.fi/eugendem/).

European Parliament elections and gendered representation

As MEPs are still elected from national party lists through different national voting systems (European Parliament Research Service PE 635.515, 6), political recruitment and gender quotas are not homogenous across the board (Praud 2012). Some MEPs are subject to electoral gender quotas, some national parties use voluntary party quotas, and some countries have no gender quotas at all.[2] Moreover, quotas allow no straightforward prediction about gender balance. For example, in the 2014 European Parliament election Finland, operating without any quota, had 76.1% women MEPs, while Portugal, with a 33% legislative quota, had 28.6% women MEPs (European Parliament Research Service PE 635.515, 5). European elections thus display gender gaps that mirror those in national parties. In representative terms, EPGs translate the election outcome also differently into the core functions they assign, like political group leaders, European Parliament (vice-)presidents, committee leadership, group coordinators, and rapporteurs.

The share of women MEPs in EPGs varies, ranging after the 2019 elections from 32.3% in ECR to 52.7% in Greens/EFA (Abels 2020, 415). Figure 19.1 illustrates the differences as well as the steadily increasing numbers for all EPGs. A closer look nevertheless reveals important differences. While many green and left-wing parties work with quotas to reach gender balance, this is uncommon for right-wing populist and radical right parties. Hence, women MEPs are unequally distributed across EPGs (cf. Figure 19.1). Some RRP, however, have considerable numbers of women MEPs because of national quota legislation. For instance, the Italian Lega and French RN delegations belonging to the new ID group are gender-balanced because of national quotas, whereas women are clearly underrepresented in the German AfD party (only 18.2%; cf. Abels 2020, 416). Similarly, the largest national delegation of the EPP, the German CDU, only sends 21.7% women MEPs while the overall share of EPP women is 34.1% (Abels 2020, 416).

Based on the analysis of how gendered EPGs' everyday activities are, Kantola and Miller (2019) conclude that EPGs present a unique and complex transnational setting where negotiations need to attend to political as well as state-specific dividing lines. The latter is articulated through national party delegations, which are characterized as "mediating structures": "informational flows from the bureau … are disseminated down and the NPD [national party delegations] can be a filter. This matters for gender experts and civil society organizations who may seek to lobby political groupings more holistically" (Kantola and Miller 2019, 23). When Kantola and Rolandsen Agustín (2019, 774) investigated EPG practices for advancing the position of women MEPs, they found that "unequal gendered norms and practices continue to exist" and "relate to gendered divisions of labor, interaction, symbols, and subjectivities." If we take a closer look at EPGs' current composition, GUE/NGL and Greens/EFA, followed by S&D and ALDE, were the most gender-equal EPGs. ECR and EPP range at the lower end, even though the latter recently did develop steps towards enhancing women's representation and tackling gender inequality internally.

Recently, the #MeToo campaign also reached the European Parliament, and parliamentary staff set up #MeTooEP (see www.metooep.com). The discursive constructions around sexual harassment in the Parliament further showed the differentiated positions on gender equality issues. While many MEPs advocate legal action or structural reforms, others show resistance either by calling the problem an individual or cultural one, or they defend "the EP as a 'good' institution by emphasizing the need to protect its reputation" (Berthet and Kantola 2020).

The unequal share of women MEPs and the EPGs' diverging positions on whether intra-group gender equality promotion is necessary both affect how the EPGs distribute intra-parliamentary and EPG leadership positions. Manon Aubry (GUE/NGL), Iratxe García Pérez (S&D), and Ska Keller (Greens/EFA) (co-)chair their EPGs, yet theirs are only three out of ten available chair positions (Abels 2020, 417). After the 2019 elections, the 22 committee chairs were for the first time equally distributed from the beginning of the legislature. EPP, RE, and ECR delivered an equal number of women and men, S&D three men out of five chairs, GUE/NGL one male chair, and Greens/EFA two women chairs (Abels 2020, 417–418). Committee coordinators were not equally distributed in the last legislature, though they became more balanced over time: the highest level of women's representation was found for GUE/NGL (58%), S&D (57%), and

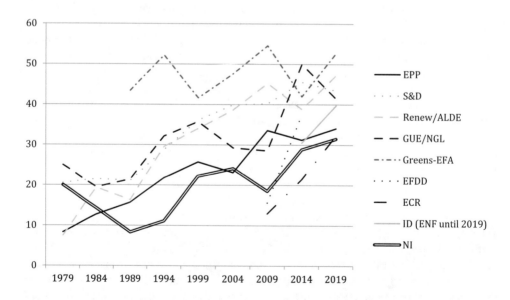

Figure 19.1 Gender composition by European Parliament political group, 1979–2019
Source: Own calculation on the basis of European Parliament data. Please note party name changes: until the 2019 election, RE operated as ALDE and ID operated as ENF.

Greens/EFA (56%), then ALDE (43%) and EFDD (35%), and very low shares for ECR (22%) and EPP (13%) (Kantola and Rolandsen Agustín 2019, 771).

EPG positions on gender equality and anti-discrimination

Research on the EPGs' gender equality and anti-discrimination positions on European Parliament output, such as legislation and reports, sheds light on substantive representation. Party groups are divided on gender equality in relation to substantive representation along the left/right axis. Analyzing the 8th legislature (2014–2019), Kantola and Rolandsen Agustín (2019) find that S&D, ALDE, GUE/NGL, and Greens/EFA all maintain relatively strong pro gender equality policy profiles. The latter two also have a high level of women's descriptive representation among MEPs, both at leadership level and regarding committee coordinators. EFDD, EPP, and ECR show weak gender-equality profiles and a mixed picture of descriptive representation (see above). Analyses of EPGs' internal cultures show that gender stereotypes around the division of labor or policy areas are still existing, and that perceptions about MEPs' interests and competences remain gendered. Stereotypical perceptions – for instance, women MEPs as not interested in or capable of taking key positions in economic policy-making – do still persist, as do expectations around visibility and (lack of) presence, which to some women MEPs translates into perceived irreconcilable spheres of politics and motherhood (Kantola and Rolandsen Agustín 2019).

Though EPGs' policy-making takes place in a broader context of lobbying, the relations between party groups and interest groups in the field of gender equality have remained underexplored. Kluger Dionigi (2017) provides an instructive case of party politics related to negotiations on the maternity-leave directive, which failed in 2015. Though the Parliament's FEMM Committee had the lead on this directive, the European Women's Lobby and trade unions successfully lobbied the S&D rapporteur and other FEMM members to extend the Commission's proposal, thereby increasing controversies among member states in the Council (Kluger Dionigi 2017, 129–130, 135; see also Ahrens and Abels 2017). Meanwhile, employers' associations and member states lobbied MEPs in center-right EPGs, particularly EPP, to vote against the FEMM committee report. EPP hesitated to do so, both because they lacked a majority and because voting against improving women's rights was inopportune (Kluger Dionigi 2017, 132). While the European Parliament in the end adopted its position with a slim majority, several national delegations in EPP and ALDE voted against the proposal, departing from their official group line, which is quite unusual (Kluger Dionigi 2017, 137). Thus, EPG party positions on gender equality depend on the context and political constraints, making them highly issue-specific and marked by divergent opinions. This especially comes to the fore around controversial policy debates, such as abortion and the financial crisis (see also Kantola and Rolandsen Agustín 2016).

Committees are an important arena of party politics. The FEMM, LIBE, and EMPL committees are usually considered progressive regarding gender equality and anti-discrimination policies. The research on other committees' gender equality policy and gender mainstreaming does not attend to differences between EPGs (see Ahrens and Rolandsen Agustín (European Parliament) this volume). Since 2019, the FEMM Committee is led by Evelyn Regner (S&D), EMPL by Lucia Duris Nicholsonová (ECR), and LIBE by Juan Fernando López Aguilar (S&D). This means that one of the most important committees, EMPL, is chaired by an MEP from an EPG which often holds conservative positions on gender equality issues. How this impacts committee work has not yet been investigated, though gender equality and anti-discrimination in all three committees is expected to be contested by right-wing and populist EPGs (Abels 2020; Kantola and Rolandsen Agustín 2016, 2019; Krizsán and Siim 2018). Previously, the three

Eurosceptic political groups – ECR, EFDD, ENF – within the FEMM Committee usually voted against committee compromises, while not taking up any proposals themselves (Ahrens 2018). Furthermore, the intersection of gender equality with migration policies exacerbated tensions within and between EPGs (Nissen and Rolandsen Agustín 2018). In the 7th European Parliament legislature (2009–2014), ALDE, EPP, and S&D shared the conviction that intertwining labor market mobility with gender equality will trigger economic growth; yet, this consensus was founded on silencing other conflicts around the transferability of social rights (Nissen and Rolandsen Agustín 2018).

While EPG cohesion in voting terms is usually high (Hix et al. 2018; see also www.votewatch. eu), this is not the case in the FEMM Committee, which has recently shifted from a consensus orientation (based partially on feminist alliances) to conflictual inter-group relations (Warasin et al. 2019). While in the 7th legislature EPP, S&D, and ALDE aligned, FEMM's agenda was disproportionately influenced by a coalition among S&D, ALDE, Greens/EFA, and GUE/NGL. Furthermore, gender equality policies have become increasingly politicized. This is visible in intra-group cohesion, which is lower than average on gender equality issues compared to other sectors. In the EPP, for instance, internal cleavages are common and some MEPs frequently vote against the party line; this is also the case, to some extent, in ALDE (Warasin et al. 2019). The politicization of equality policies not only occurs in FEMM, but also in the LIBE and EMPL Committees. Engaging with the literature on norm dynamics, Ahrens and van der Vleuten (2019) illustrate how MEPs from ECR, EFDD, ENF, and EPP pulled the "subsidiarity card," i.e. they used the subsidiarity principle to avoid effective actions by the EU against actors attacking gender equality in the member states and to oppose specific policy content, for instance related to sexual education and abortion, in FEMM committee reports (see also Kantola and Rolandsen Agustín 2016). Until recently, the European Parliament hardly ever referred to the subsidiarity principle, because of its overarching institutional interest in expanding its competences. However, MEPs from the right-wing conservative groups begin to strategically use subsidiarity to delegitimize engagement with the EU values enshrined in Article 2 of the TEU: human rights, gender equality, and democracy (Ahrens and van der Vleuten 2019). Analyzing MEPs' voting behavior, Mondo and Close (2018) uncovered that morality issues such as abortion and human embryonic stem-cell research are increasingly politicized. Among the interviewed MEPs, "cohesion was perceived as a strength, excess of party discipline was negatively assessed, revealing some EPGs' incapacity to build a common position, but also impeding MEPs to express their own convictions." However, when religion and personal values are at odds with their EPG position, "most respondents emphasized the great degree of freedom that the European parliamentary arena usually offers" (Mondo and Close 2018, 1014).

MEPs' national origin also affects their engagement in gender equality and anti-discrimination policy-making – regardless of their EPG's position. Cullen (2018, 2019) traced the activities of female Irish MEPs; she observed that the national political context, including party political discipline, limited female political agency. While some Irish female MEPs acted as gender-conscious actors in committees other than FEMM, centrist and right-wing MEPs have been especially constrained; they refused membership in the FEMM Committee due to the issue of abortion (Cullen 2019). Chiva (2019), however, found no fundamental differences in voting patterns along EPG lines among female MEPs from "old" and "new" member states. Overall, female MEPs from central and eastern European (CEE) countries are better represented in the European Parliament than at national level. Since gender equality issues are less contested in the European Parliament, this indeed enhances their possibilities to act in favor of women's interests. Thus, MEPs from CEE are socialized into a gender equality mindset rather than influencing the European Parliament in a conservative direction (Chiva 2019).

The literature on Eurosceptic and populist parties has expanded considerably over the last decade, not least in response to their growing numbers and electoral support in EU member states (see Siim and Fiig in this volume). Falkner and Plattner compared the claim coherence of populist RRPs regarding EU integration in the fields of foreign policy, security and defense, the single market and anti-discrimination (including gender equality). Regarding the latter, they found that only ENF directly positioned itself in this policy field, but there was "no absolute coherence and no goal coherence" (Falkner and Plattner 2018, 18). As for EFDD and ECR, even though the EPGs themselves took no positions, their national parties show clear opposition and the wish to dismantle EU anti-discrimination policies (Falkner and Plattner 2018, 17–18). Looking at same-sex unions as a specifically salient issue, Lefkofridi and Katsanidou (2018, 1173–1174) track down that for the last two legislatures the full spectrum of the left–right divide (pro vs. contra legalizing same-sex unions) was articulated through the EPGs; yet, all differed regarding intra-party coherence. Only the Greens/EFA (pro) and EFDD (contra) were coherent in both elections, while national parties within the other EPGs formed no majority on either the pro or the contra side (Lefkofridi and Katsanidou 2018, 1175–1176).

The arrival of Eurosceptic and far-right conservative nationalists since the late 1990s brought about two fundamental changes in the European Parliament: "outspoken essentializing views on women were voiced" and "subsidiarity, respect for sovereignty, and cultural differences were used as arguments to undermine initiatives for the supranational promotion of gender equality" (van der Vleuten 2019, 45; see also Siim and Fiig in this volume). Zacharenko (2019) calculated anti-gender MEPs numbers as clearly above 170, with additional EPP MEPs from the Hungarian Fidesz and the Polish PiS possibly supporting such positions, too. This "could present a strong front against the alleged threat of 'gender ideology'" (Zacharenko 2019). Yet, Abels (2020, 419) points out that some outspoken feminists also took up important positions in the European Parliament. The literature thus reflects the way in which the Parliament and its political groups constitute sites of gender struggle where divergent norms and values around gender equality and anti-discrimination clash. In recent years this struggle has become accentuated and intertwined with opinions and positions for and against European integration, thus combining nationalist and anti-feminist agendas in the opposition to the EU and its transnational articulation of gender equality policies.

Conclusion

Engaging with European party politics clearly benefits from integrating a gender perspective. We gain better insights about differences between Europarties and EPGs regarding gendered representation and policy positions, about cohesion, consensus and contestation dynamics in the European Parliament and its committees as well as about national peculiarities and traditions in dealing with gender equality. Nevertheless, we observe a range of gaps in the mainstream literature as well as in the gender and anti-discrimination research, revealing underexplored potential for innovative insights on party politics on gender equality and anti-discrimination, and thus on key issues of European integration in general.

The EU and many member states are amidst a crisis of representation, and some parties face a legitimacy crisis as Eurosceptic, populist, and right-wing parties gain support. Although these parties increased their number of seats in the 2019 elections, they do not strictly verify older findings according to which the number of women among their ranks and in their intra-party leadership positions is low, that is their "*Männerparteien*" image (Abels 2020; Ahrens 2018; Meret and Siim 2013; Meret et al. 2017; Mudde and Rovira Kaltwasser 2015). Whether or not this is simply an effect of national quota legislation or a general trend requires more research. Studies also need to address the question of how national electoral systems disrupt the possibilities in reaching parity. Connected to this, it would be worthwhile to investigate EPGs' internal recruitment procedures for positions such as committee coordinators and chairs, and to study in which EPGs women are either sidelined or recognized.

The Eurosceptic, populist, and right-wing EPGs usually have no particular rules on parity or gender equality in place. Some of them are outspoken critics of gender equality, anti-discrimination, and multiculturalism (Krizsán and Siim 2018; van der Vleuten 2019). Yet, mainstream EPGs are also not free from internal struggles around promoting gender equality, showing low levels of intra-group coherence (Warasin et al. 2019). Fascinating examples show, for instance, the utilization of the subsidiarity principle against gender equality within the EPP (Ahrens and van der Vleuten 2019), and reveal opposition by national delegations against the EU's ratification of the Council of Europe's Convention on preventing and combating violence against women and domestic violence (Istanbul Convention; see Roggeband in this volume) in the S&D (Hein 2018). How will EPGs' decision-making processes change when single party delegations speak up against EU equality norms, when they want to limit marriage to heterosexual couples, or even constitutionally ban same-sex marriage (Kuhar and Paternotte 2017; Roggeband and Krizsán 2018; Verloo 2018)?

Future research needs to decipher EPGs' internal struggles and policy position-formation regarding complex gender equality issues. A change in the majority position will probably bring fundamental changes to the overall majority in the European Parliament – regardless of existing anti-gender mobilization in other EPGs. Cullen (2019) and Chiva (2019) demonstrate that national origin and parliamentary culture are important and that we need to better understand how this impacts upon supranational gender equality policy.

Finally, the connection between EPGs and "the people" requires more attention: who can mobilize which parts of the population? Here, EPGs' relationships to civil society and other organized interests are key, such as anti-gender and anti-LGBT movements. Do we see these movements gaining influence via EPGs? More informal modes of exchange between EPGs come into play here: European Parliament intergroups such as "Anti-Racism and Diversity" and "Lesbian, Gay, Bisexual, Transgender and Intersex rights" have received almost no attention in terms of their involvement and impact in this policy field. They cut across EPGs and could be fruitful to further explore coalition formation, be it in favor of gender equality or against, but also broader issues of anti-discrimination and intersectional politics in European politics.

Notes

1   EFDD was closely related to the Europarty Alliance for Direct Democracy in Europe (ADDE, founded 2014), with main member being the UK Independence Party (UKIP). ADDE legally dissolved in 2017 after misusing EU funds.
2   In 2019, legislative electoral quotas are in place in Belgium, Croatia, France, Greece, Ireland, Italy, Luxemburg, Poland, Portugal, Slovenia, Spain. Voluntary party quotas are in place (2019) in Austria, Cyprus, Czech Republic, Germany, Hungary, Lithuania, Malta, Netherlands, Romania, Slovakia, Sweden, United Kingdom. Bulgaria, Denmark, Estonia, Finland, Latvia have no quotas at all.

References

Abels G (2019): The Powers of the European Parliament. Implications for Gender Equality Policy, in Ahrens P, Rolandsen Agustín L (eds.): *Gendering the European Parliament. Structures, Policies and Practices*, London: Rowman & Littlefield, 19–34.

Abels G (2020): Gender and Descriptive Representation in the 2019–2024 European Parliament, in: Kaeding M, Müller M, Schmälter J (eds.): *Die Europawahl 2019*, Wiesbaden: Springer VS, 407–421.

Ahrens P (2018): Anti-feministische Politiker★innen im Frauenrechtsausschuss des Europäischen Parlaments. Wendepunkt oder Resilienz in der EU Gleichstellungspolitik?, *Feministische Studien* **36** (2), 403–416.

Ahrens P, van der Vleuten A (2019): The strategic use of the subsidiarity argument in the European Parliament in debates about gender equality, *Paper for General Conference of the European Consortium on Political Research*, Wroclaw, unpublished.

Ahrens P, Abels G (2017): Die Macht zu gestalten. Die Mutterschutzrichtlinie im legislativen Bermuda-Dreieck der Europäischen Union, *Femina Politca* **26** (1), 39–54.

Almeida D (2012): *The Impact of European Integration on Political Parties. Beyond the Permissive Consensus*, London, New York: Routledge.

Andeweg R (1995): The reshaping of national party systems, *West European Politics* **18** (3), 58–78.

Bardi L (1994): Transnational Party Federations, European Parliamentary Groups and the Building of Europarties, in: Katz RS, Mair P (eds.): *How Parties Organize. Change and adaptation in party organizations in Western Democracies*, London: Sage, 46–76.

Berthet V, Kantola J (2020): Gender, violence and political institutions. Struggles over sexual harassment in the European Parliament, Social Politics: International Studies in Gender, State & Society, https://doi.org/10.1093/sp/jxaa015.

Brack N (2018): *Opposing Europe in the European Parliament. Rebels and Radicals in the Chamber*, Basingstoke: Palgrave Macmillan.

Chiva C (2019): Overcoming Male Dominance? The Representation of Women in the European Parliament Delegations of the Post-Communist EU Member States, in: Ahrens P, Rolandsen Agustín L (eds.): *Gendering the European Parliament. Structures, Policies and Practices*, London: Rowman & Littlefield, 177–197.

Corbett R, Jacobs F, Neville D (2016): *The European Parliament*, London: John Harper.

Cullen P (2018): Irish female members of the European Parliament. Critical actors for women's interests?, *Politics & Gender* **14** (3), 483–511.

Cullen P (2019): The European Parliament and Irish Female MEPs. Female Political Agency for Gender Equality, in: Ahrens P, Rolandsen Agustín L (eds.): *Gendering the European Parliament. Structures, Policies and Practices*, London: Rowman & Littlefield, 159–175.

Falkner G, Plattner G (2018): Populist Radical Right Parties and EU Policies. How coherent are their claims, *Robert Schuman Centre for Advanced Studies Research Paper* No. RSCAS 2018/38.

Fortin-Rittberger J, Rittberger B (2014): Do electoral rules matter? Explaining national differences in women's representation in the European Parliament, *European Union Politics* **15** (4), 496–520.

Fortin-Rittberger J, Rittberger B (2015): Nominating women for Europe: exploring the role of political parties' recruitment procedures for European Parliament elections, *European Journal of Political Research* **54** (4), 767–783.

Hein M (2018): Bulgaria. I·CONnect-Clough Center Global Review of Constitutional Law. URL: www.nhri.no/wp-content/uploads/2019/10/ICON.pdf (download: July 4, 2020).

Hix S, Lord C (1997): *Political Parties in the European Union*, London: Macmillan.

Hix S, Noury A, Roland G (2005): Power to the parties. Cohesion and competition in the European Parliament, 1979–2001, *British Journal of Political Science* **35**, 209–234.

Hix S, Noury A, Roland G (2007): *Democratic Politics in the European Parliament*, Cambridge: Cambridge University Press.

Hix S, Noury A, Roland G (2018): Is there a selection bias in roll call votes? Evidence from the European Parliament, *Public Choice* **176** (1–2), 211–228.

Kantola J, Miller C (2019): Everyday activities of the European Parliament's political groupings: Gendered dynamics and practices, *Paper prepared for European Conference on Politics and Gender (ECPG)*, Amsterdam, unpublished.

Kantola J, Rolandsen Agustín L (2016): Gendering transnational party politics: the case of European Union, *Party Politics* **22** (5), 641–51.

Kantola J, Rolandsen Agustín L (2019): Gendering the representative work of the European Parliament. A political analysis of women MEP's perceptions of gender equality in party groups, *Journal of Common Market Studies* **57** (4), 768–786.

Kluger Dionigi M (2017): *Lobbying in the European Parliament. The Battle for Influence*, Cham: Palgrave Macmillan.

Krizsán A, Siim B (2018): Gender Equality and Family in Populist Radical Right Agendas. Similarities and Differences in European Parliamentary Debates 2014, in: Knijn T, Naldini M (eds.): *Gender and Generational Division in EU Citizenship*, Cheltenham: Edward Elgar, 39–59.

Kuhar R, Paternotte D, eds. (2017): *Anti-Gender Campaigns in Europe. Mobilizing against Equality*, London: Rowman & Littlefield.

Ladrech R (2006): The European Union and Political Parties, in: Katz RS, Crotty W (eds.): *Handbook of Party Politics*, London: Sage, 492–498.

Lefkofridi Z, Katsanidou A (2018): A step closer to a transnational party system? Competition and coherence in the 2009 and 2014 European Parliament, *Journal of Common Market Studies* **56** (6), 1462–1482.

Mattila M, Raunio T (2006): Cautious voters and supportive parties. Opinion congruence between voters and parties on the EU dimension, *European Union Politics* **7** (4), 427–449.

McElroy G, Benoit K (2007): Party groups and policy positions in the European Parliament, *Party Politics* **13** (1), 5–28.

McElroy G, Benoit K (2010): Party policy and group affiliation in the European Parliament, *British Journal of Political Science* **40**, 377–398.

McElroy G, Benoit K (2012): Policy positioning in the European Parliament, *European Union Politics* **13** (1): 150–167.

Meret S, Siim B (2013): Gender, Populism and Politics of Belonging: Discourses of Right-Wing Populist parties in Denmark, Norway and Austria, in: Siim B, Mokre M (eds.): *Negotiating Gender and Diversity in an Emergent European Public Sphere*, Basingstoke: Palgrave Macmillan, 78–96.

Meret S, Siim B, Pingaud E (2017): Men's Parties with Women Leaders. A Comparative Study of Right-Wing Populist Leaders Pia Kjærsgaard, Siv Jensen and Marine Le Pen, in: Lazaridis G, Campani G (eds.): *Understanding the Populist Shift*, London, New York: Routledge, 122–149.

Mondo E, Close C (2018): Morality politics in the European parliament. A qualitative insight into MEPs' voting behaviour on abortion and human embryonic stem cell research, *Journal of European Integration* **40** (7), 1001–1018.

Morijn J (2019): Responding to the "populist" politics at EU level: Regulation 1141/2014 and beyond, *International Journal of Constitutional Law* **17** (2), 617–640.

Mudde C, Rovira Kaltwasser C (2015): Vox populi or vox masculini? Populism and gender in Northern Europe and South America, *Patterns of Prejudice* **49** (1–2), 16–36.

Nissen A, Rolandsen Agustín L (2018): Rights for Women, Migrants, and Minorities. Consensus and Silences in the European Parliament, in: Knijn T, Naldini M (eds.): *Gender and Generational Division in EU Citizenship*, Cheltenham: Edward Elgar, 21–38.

Praud J (2012): Introduction: gender parity and quotas in European Politics, *West European Politics* **35** (2), 286–300.

Put G-J, Van Hecke S, Cunningham C, Wolfs W (2016): The choice of Spitzenkandidaten. A comparative analysis of the Europarties' selection procedures, *Politics and Governance* **4** (1), 9–22.

Roggeband C, Krizsán A (2018): *The Gender Politics of Domestic Violence. Feminists Engaging the State in Central and Eastern Europe*, London, New York: Routledge.

Stockemer D, Sundström A (2019): Do young female candidates face double barriers or an outgroup advantage? The case of the European Parliament, *European Journal of Political Research* **58**, 373–384.

Schmitt H, Thomassen J (1999): *Political Representation and Legitimacy in the European Union*, Oxford: Oxford University Press.

van der Vleuten A (2019): The European Parliament as a Constant Promoter of Gender Equality. Another European Myth?, in: Ahrens P, Rolandsen Agustín L (eds.): *Gendering the European Parliament. Structures, Policies and Practices*, London: Rowman & Littlefield, 35–49.

Verloo M, ed. (2018): *Varieties of Opposition to Gender Equality in Europe*, London, New York: Routledge.

von dem Berge B (2017): Europarty Eastern enlargement. An empirical analysis of Europarty influence on Central and Eastern European parties and party systems, *East European Politics* **33** (4), 472–495.

Warasin M, Kantola J, Rolandsen Agustín L, Coughlan C (2019): Politicisation of Gender Equality in the European Parliament: Cohesion and Inter-Group Coalitions in Plenary and Committees, in: Ahrens P, Rolandsen Agustín L (eds.): *Gendering the European Parliament. Structures, Policies and Practices*, London: Rowman & Littlefield, 141–158.

Westlake M (2019): Possible Future European Union Party-Political Systems, in: Costa O (ed.): *The European Parliament in Times of EU crisis. Dynamics and Transformations*, Cham: Palgrave Macmillan, 321–340.

Wiesner C (2019): *Inventing the EU as a Democratic Polity*, Basingstoke: Palgrave Macmillan.

Yordanova N (2013): *Organising the European Parliament. The Role of Committees and their Legislative Influence*, Colchester: ECPR Press.

Zacharenko E (2019): Political reshuffle of European Parliament. What Consequences for Gender Equality in Europe? URL: www.fes.de/themenportal-gender-jugend-senioren/gender-matters/artikelseite/politische-umstrukturierung-der-europaeischen-kommission-und-des-europaeischen-parlaments (download: June 12, 2020).

Part IV

Gender equality and EU policies

Gendering European studies has always included a strong focus on policies. This goes back to the very beginning with equal pay included as a social policy provision (Article 119 of the Treaty on European Economic Community) in 1957. As the scope of social policy expanded in the 1980s and 1990s, so has gender studies' focus on policy.

Since the adoption of the Treaty of Amsterdam in 1997, the EU is bound by the obligation to eliminate inequalities and promote equality between men and women in all of its activities: this is the famous 'gender-mainstreaming article' (now Article 8 TFEU). Long before 1997, EU policies already aimed at combatting sex-based discrimination, mainly in the labour market, but the adoption of gender mainstreaming was hailed by feminists and 'femocrats' as a window of opportunity to finally address the gendered impacts of all policies – including those that were thus far, viewed as gender-blind.

This part of the Handbook sets out to take the balance of more than 20 years of bringing gender into EU policies. Each chapter discusses a specific policy domain and considers its evolution in general, and the actors who have formal or informal access to policy-making. Next, all chapters offer a gendered perspective on the policies developed, their biases, gaps and impact. They take stock of feminist research regarding the policy domain and offer a future-oriented perspective, specifically highlighting gaps in research.

While some of the policy fields discussed here are more 'the usual suspects' for a gender analysis, other chapters focus on policies which have only been inspected with a gender lens more recently. The overall picture which emerges from these nine chapters is one of scattered patterns of gender mainstreaming as regards EU policies and policymaking, and scattered feminist scholarship. The policy selection here is not comprehensive. However, we can take four key points from their collective analysis.

First, some policy domains are clearly more permeable than others when it comes to taking potentially gendered effects into account. This has to do with their institutional design, which influences access for feminist actors, and the mobilization of women's movements and other civil society actors. It also depends on the positioning of the policy domain as either close to the EU core of market-making and liberalisation (social policies, employment, trade, development, research, climate) or further away (security, migration and violence against women). Those areas

Gender equality and EU policies

close to the core of the EU's policy purview are more likely to have been subject to gender analysis both by the institutions and in academic settings.

Second, it is clear that some policies are not designed with a feminist perspective. Policies reflect gendered thinking (social policy) or gender-blind thinking. Often, gender impact assessments are performed as an add-on, a potential correction to a draft directive or other policy instrument. This is even more obvious when assessing the extent to which policy design reflects not only gender-awareness, but an intersectional awareness.

Third, attention to gender in mainstream EU studies is scarce. The mainstream academic handbooks on EU policymaking only briefly refer to the equal pay article, or contain one chapter on gender equality policies. In these Handbooks all other policy domains are discussed as if gender is irrelevant to them, and without referring to feminist scholarship. In general, mainstream EU scholarship tends to be predominately gender-blind.

Fourth, feminist scholarship has also paid unequal attention to issues across policy domains. While, for instance, social policies have been studied by gender scholars since the 1980s, it is much more difficult to find scholarship taking a gender perspective and addressing gendered impacts as regards climate change or trade, to name but two topics. The selection of policy domains covered by the Handbook reflects the relative attention of feminist scholarship and the uneven attention given to specific domains.

In sum, this Handbook offers an unmatched discussion of gender and intersectionality in no less than nine policy domains. And yet, despite its relatively extensive coverage of policy areas, it does not contain chapters on agriculture and fisheries; competition and internal market; education and culture; foreign policy and neighbourhood policy; health; justice; regional policy; taxation and fraud, transportation, to name but a few domains where the European Union has developed activities and deployed resources. Although there are some analyses that address these policy domains from a gender perspective, feminist scholarship is limited, as is sustained attention to gender equality and intersectionality in policymaking in these areas. In times of crises and contestations, this poses a major challenge to scholars, activist, and policymakers.

20

Social and employment policy

Susan Milner

The European Union's (EU) social and employment policy and gender equality policy intersect in some important respects (Lahuerta and Zbyszewska 2018). Both policy areas fell under the general heading of 'Social Policy' (Title III) in the Treaty establishing the European Economic Community (EEC) in 1958, meaning that gender equality policy was initially a field of European social policy (Abels 2011). Under this heading, Article 117 EEC Treaty provided the overarching basis for actions in the social policy field, stipulating that as well as resulting from the action of establishing the Common Market, policy could be adopted through the 'approximation of legislative and administrative provisions'. Article 118 EEC Treaty stipulates that 'it shall be the aim of the Commission to promote close collaboration between Member States in the social field'. Article 119 EEC Treaty laid down a legal 'principle of equal remuneration for equal work as between men and women workers'. The articles on social policy merely allowed for 'close cooperation' between member states and gave the Commission the authority to gather information 'by means of studies, the issuing of opinions, and the organising of consultations' (Article 118 EEC Treaty) on any actions that might be needed. Article 119 EEC Treaty (today Article 157 TFEU) did not specify action to achieve pay equality but established a non-discrimination principle which could be challenged through the courts. Thus, from the beginning, social policy and gender equality policy derived from the same policy domain but with different logics of policy action.

Both areas of action were initially delimited as sets of actions related to the labour dimension of economic production (Collins 1975; Hoskyns 1991). Member states retained autonomy over areas such as childcare, welfare and taxation, and education, which form the 'policy hinterland' (Mazey 1998) where gender inequalities are produced and reproduced. Gender equality policy was framed narrowly as the principle of equal pay for equal work (Article 119 a, b EEC Treaty), whilst social policy was specifically related to aspects of paid employment: 'employment, labour law and working conditions, occupational and continuation training, social security; protection against occupational accidents and diseases; industrial hygiene; the law as to trade unions, and collective bargaining between employers and workers' (Article 118 EEC Treaty). As policy developed later in both areas, it did so in different but related ways, due to this grounding in aspects of paid employment. Policy was extended into the 'hinterland' but mostly in softer forms of governance which placed only weak adaptational pressures on domestic governments.

The main thrust of policy throughout has been regulatory (Liebert 2003), as there was never political consensus to delegate significant distributive competence to the European level, and therefore no chance of a fully developed European welfare state (Hantrais 2007). Regulatory politics takes second place to market integration (Leibfried 2015). The result is a multi-level system with tensions between the national (and sub-national) and European levels of policy-making, and uneven degrees of integration of discrete sub-fields of policy, in particular gender equality, health and safety at work (and various related areas of working conditions such as working time), and workers' rights to information and consultation, alongside limited policy coordination in social security (Heidenreich and Bischoff 2008).

The main policy actors are the European Commission, the Council of Ministers (since 1993 called Council of the EU; of the ten Council formations especially the Employment, Social Policy, Health and Consumer Affairs Council configuration, in short: EPSCO), and the European Parliament, as well as the Court of Justice of the EU. Social and employment policy has also led to the development of specific mechanisms for deliberative policy-making: the Social Dialogue, whereby trade unions and employers' associations have a role in preparing legislative proposals; and the horizontal forms of policy learning associated with the open method of coordination (OMC), which involves government ministers and reserves an important steering and coordination role for the Commission. Auxiliary redistributive policy through the various structural and investment funds (e.g. European Social Fund/ESF, European Regional Development Fund/ERDF, Cohesion Fund) has constituted a limited but useful resource for feminist activists and scholars, helping to build an evidence base and epistemic networks.

This chapter provides an overview of the development of social and employment policy from a gender equality perspective. In the first section it adopts a broadly chronological order, outlining the shift from a regulatory approach towards softer forms of policy coordination in which gender has purportedly been mainstreamed, and shows that both approaches hold significant weaknesses from a gender perspective. From the beginning, social and employment policy has been subservient to broader economic policy objectives (Daly 2006) and dependent on a favourable ideological environment within the key institutions, particularly the Commission (Hoskyns 1991, 1996; Kantola 2010). From the 1990s, the rights-building approach weakened, and policy became more explicitly instrumentalised in support of market objectives (Daly 2020). After 2004, enlargement and the financial crisis eroded political will to advance and implement social and employment policy other than as a support for macroeconomic objectives (Guerrina 2015a, 2015b; Kantola and Lombardo 2017; Wöhl 2016; Kantola and Lombardo in this volume) and diminished the link between gender equality objectives and social policy (Jacquot 2015).

As discussed in the subsequent section, feminist scholarship contributes significantly to study of EU social and employment policy, particularly from the 1990s when gender mainstreaming approaches overlapped with the dominant policy mode of OMC. Unlike areas of high politics characterised by intergovernmental modes of governance, where gender perspectives have struggled to gain visibility or traction (van der Vleuten 2007), social and employment policy as relatively under-developed policy areas provided a more open and flexible arena enabling feminist agency (van der Vleuten 2016). Indeed, in building this policy area during the early years, the Commission deliberately sought to build expert and activist networks (Hoskyns 1996; Mazey 1998; Wilde 2016). In these respects, the low politics of social and employment policy constitutes an advantage in a multi-scalar polity, allowing innovation and a space for feminist activists to use gaps between domestic and European policy as a lever for change. However, this advantage is fragile and easily contested, and it leaves significant weaknesses, omissions and possibilities for inertia (Abels and MacRae 2016).

Social and employment policy: ambiguous, subordinate and contested

The early years: uneven legislative activism

The early years were characterised by Commission entrepreneurship, backed up later by emerging networks within the European institutions (particularly the European Parliament) or sponsored by them. The principle of non-discrimination to facilitate free movement of labour was subject to Article 49 EEC Treaty, which laid out a precise decision-making route, based on proposals by the Commission and adoption by the Council of Ministers, with consultation of the Economic and Social Committee (ESC). A series of regulations (the hardest form of legislative instrument as regulations are binding in their entirety on member states and immediately applicable, compared to directives, which are binding but are transposed according to national legislative practice) were adopted between 1961 and 1970, establishing the right of European citizens to take up residence, employment and self-employment in other member states, access housing, and bring their family with them (Collins 1975). These initiatives and the wider principles underpinning them formed the basis for the first social action plans proposed by the Commission (Bercusson 2009).

The 1974 Social Action Programme (SAP) laid the basis for around 30 proposals for legislative action over three to four years. Including initiatives to regulate the mutual recognition of vocational training, it focused on the improvement of living and working conditions as a counterpart to plans to establish an economic and monetary union, and sought to strengthen workers' voice in organisational decision-making. Among the most important pieces of legislation from this programme was the 1977 directive on the transfer of public undertakings (TUPE, substantially amended in 2001, 2006 and 2014), which established the principle that not only should workers affected by the transfer of public organisations to the private sector be consulted, but that they should retain employment rights after the transfer. Given that a majority of public sector workers (around two thirds in most member states) are women, the TUPE directive (Directive 77/187/EEC) has been an important piece of protective legislation for women, although it is interpreted in different ways across member states (Grimshaw et al. 2012).

In addition, the 1974 SAP included the concept of reconciliation between work and family, 'albeit in a way that was hardly revolutionary' (Anderson 2015, 129), consisting of measures to support a more equal sharing of parental responsibilities, and the provision of childcare services (Moss 1990, 30). No legislative proposals ensued, because of resistance by many member states, and it was judged that childcare fell under exclusive national competence. However, the Women's Bureau of the Commission set up the Childcare Network which began to produce national reports comparing the situation in different countries and analysing the effect of policies on women's labour market participation (Moss 1988, 1990). The Childcare Network was one of a set of (then nine) influential epistemic communities fostering a favourable environment for work–family policy (Mazey 1998).

The 1987 Single European Act (SEA) extended the use of Qualified Majority Voting (QMV) in the Council to measures supporting the construction of the single market (Article 100 of the SEA), and the definition of health and safety – initially a technical standard – was broadened to encompass wider working and living conditions (Hantrais 2007, 97–98). This change was significant because it allowed an entrepreneurial Commission to put forward legislation that framed social rights as market-supporting measures, without fear of veto by the UK, which under Conservative governments opposed EC competence in the field of social policy.

Amongst the most significant and most controversial initiatives from this period was the working time directive (Council Directive 93/104/EC, amended in 2003: Council Directive 2003/88/EC) which limited the standard working week to 48 hours and gave employees the right to rest breaks and a minimum of four weeks' paid holidays. Given feminist concerns over gender polarisation in working hours, working time limitation is an important instrument for equalisation of working conditions and a more equal sharing of domestic responsibilities (Rubery et al. 2010), but the directive's impact was weakened by growing use of opt-outs for specific groups of employees.

Also amongst legislation from this period was a health and safety directive in 1992 to protect pregnant women and breastfeeding mothers at work (Directive 92/85/EEC; known as the maternity leave directive). This directive responded to European case law, which had upheld individual rights protecting pregnant workers and those on maternity leave (Cichowski 2004).

The European Parliament had, in 1983, called on the Commission to produce an action plan on family policy, based on Article 2 of the EEC Treaty giving the Community the task of raising living standards. The Commission did not act until 1989. Prompted by concerns about demographic trends it produced a report setting out the case for European action in support of the most deprived families, and on the reconciliation of work and family life and the need for parents to share childcare responsibilities. Instead of taking action, however, the Council shifted discussion towards equal opportunities, which had a softer legal approach (Hantrais 2007, 104; Lewis 2006; Stratigaki 2004). Besides resistance from member states, the Commission's hierarchical structure has been seen as responsible for reluctance to act in a more directive fashion to achieve stated policy objectives (Stratigaki 2005).

The 1990s: broadening and softening

Alongside the shift towards QMV in the Council in some areas of social policy, the 1993 Maastricht Treaty on European Union (TEU) fundamentally changed European law by introducing a new mechanism in the form of 'social dialogue', which had been promoted by then Commission president Jacques Delors. Article 118b TEU drew the 'social partners' (the European Trade Union Confederation, the main employers' confederation UNICE, later re-named BusinessEurope, and the public sector employers' confederation CEEP) into the policy process by inviting them to draw up their own agenda and to make policy through framework agreements, which could then form the basis of a Commission proposal for legislation. The first two framework agreements reached in this way were on parental leave (1995) and part-time work (1997), and both led to EU law (Council Directive 1996/34/EC on parental leave and Directive 1997/81/EC on part-time work); both are important parts of the social policy acquis from a gender perspective.

Council Directive 1996/34/EC on parental leave formed the basis for subsequent initiatives around leave and shared parenting, up to the most recent 2019 directive and associated work–life balance package (Directive (EU) 2019/1158). From the beginning, however, it proved highly controversial, and was adopted 13 years after the initial proposal by the Commission (Fusulier 2009). The 1995 agreement between trade unions and employers established parental leave as an individual right for parents (fathers or mothers) of at least three months, to be taken up until the child's eighth birthday (as in Sweden, considered to be have the best example of leave policy). The directive reproducing the content of the social dialogue agreement led to the adoption of leave arrangements in all member states (Haas 2008). However, the absence of explicit instructions concerning the share of leave between parents and especially on payment left considerable leeway to national transposition. Significant variation in leave entitlements and payments continue to exist between member states (Blum et al. 2018).

Directive 1997/81/EC on part-time work proved even more controversial. The employers' association opposed the social justice arguments put forward by the European Trade Union Confederation (ETUC), supported by the Commission (and European Parliament), and insisted on framing the agreement as a move to boost labour market participation. Consequently, the equalisation of working conditions between full-time and part-time employees, which the agreement and directive guaranteed, did not include social security coverage (Bleijenbergh et al. 2004). Member states retained discretion in transposing the directive, resulting in uneven regulation of part-time employment across member states (Hardy and Adnett 2002). The part-time work directive has been substantially strengthened by case law since its adoption, based on the concept of indirect discrimination, since most part-time employees are women, and now equal rights for part-time employees cover social security rights. Implementation has however depended on the capacity of individuals and campaign organisations to pursue litigation, which is easier in northern and western Europe than in other member states (Mulder 2017). The part-time work directive, like the parental leave directive, thus highlights the ambiguities of European social policy legislation. Both directives changed the way in which policy is framed and enacted in many countries, but in an even way which allowed strong implementation in countries where women's and equality groups are strong, and weak implementation elsewhere (Bleijenbergh and Roggeband 2007).

The Social Chapter of the 1997 Treaty of Amsterdam (adopted by the UK, which had previously opted out of the Maastricht Treaty's Social Protocol) arguably marked the high point of developments during this period. Regulation of health and safety of workers and of gender equality, was now extended to cover all aspects of 'labour force' rather than just pay, and subject to QMV (Leibfried 2015). At the same time, the Treaty included (in a new Title VIII) policy coordination on employment and the possibility of complementary action (Article 125 TEU), which was subsequently extended to pensions, social inclusion, health and migration (Zeitlin et al. 2005). Thus, the Amsterdam Treaty ushered in a new phase, extending the scope of social and employment policy and introducing softer, horizontal ways of coordinating policy. This new phase coincided with the adoption of gender mainstreaming by the Treaty.

Childcare exemplifies the weaknesses in the soft policy approach (Plantenga et al. 2008). In 1992 the Council adopted Recommendation 92/241/EEC urging member states to take actions to facilitate women's labour market participation, rather than a directive. Although childcare now became a matter of EU concern, member states faced no adaptational pressure (Bleijenbergh et al. 2004). Only a decade later did the Council finally agree to set targets for the provision of childcare places to at least 33% for under-threes and 90% for pre-school children by 2010. Although by 2019 all member states had met the targets for pre-school provision, only 13 had achieved the target of places for at least 33% of under threes (EIGE 2020), and formal figures often hide very low hours of provision (Ciccia and Bleijenbergh 2014). The lack of binding regulation or strong 'naming and shaming' mechanisms meant that those countries with poor provision failed to invest.

The unrealised potential of gender mainstreaming

Gender mainstreaming came onto the political agenda after the fourth World Conference on Women in Beijing in 1995. In 1996, the Commission formally adopted gender mainstreaming, defined as the need to take account of the respective situation of women and men in the planning, implementation, monitoring and evaluation of policy (COM(1996)67 final). The political opportunity structure for the shift from an equal opportunities approach of minor adjustments to a potentially transformative mainstreaming approach (Rees 1998, 2005) had been prepared by the Maastricht and Amsterdam Treaties, which established employment policy as a new EU objective, and it was expanded by the accession of Nordic member states in 1995 (Mazey 2002; Pollack and Hafner-Burton 2000). An Equality Group of Commissioners was established to oversee mainstreaming across the policy areas for which the Commission was responsible, starting with the structural funds where there was relative consensus in the Council.

Gender mainstreaming was applied to the new European Employment Strategy (EES), replacing the earlier approach of focusing on vulnerable groups, including women. Under the OMC, the Council, acting on a proposal from the Commission and after consulting the Parliament and the ESC, set guidelines for policy, targets and indicators concerning the employment rate, overall, and for women, young people and older people.

Overall, gender mainstreaming in employment policy has been weak due to inadequate and inconsistent use of the tools it provides (statistics, monitoring and impact assessment) and lack of political attention in the hierarchy of EU policy-making (Rees 2005). The result has been an unevenly applied 'constellation' of approaches (Daly 2020, 135) in which the centre of expertise became dispersed. The 2004 'eastern enlargement' increased the degree of variation between member states. Two structural changes further stripped the soft coordination approach of what remained of its transformative potential. First, the hardening of fiscal discipline as a response to financial crisis management after 2008 meant that member states were penalised for not enacting macroeconomic policy changes that had the effect of reducing welfare spending and weakening social rights (Jacquot 2017; see Scheele as well as Kantola and Lombardo in this volume).

Second, social rights that might have been expected to build on earlier initiatives in the sphere of family rights such as parental leave were effectively abandoned. A proposal to strengthen Directive 1996/34/EC on parental leave was finally withdrawn in 2015 on the pretext of 'better regulation', after opposition from the UK and Hungary. Only one labour law directive was adopted between 2005 and 2009 (Directive 2008/104/EC on temporary agency work), compared with the eight new directives passed in the first half of the decade (Smith and Villa 2010, 530). Without producing any new approaches to policy, the period after the ratification of the 2009 Lisbon Treaty saw moves to reactivate social and employment policy, in unfavourable economic and political conditions.

Mainstreaming has also allowed political marginalisation of key gender equality concerns such as actions to tackle gender pay gaps (Meier and Celis 2011; Perruzzi 2015; Smith and Villa 2010; Woodward 2012) whereas in theory statistical tools and evidence-gathering should have led to focused actions. In 2014, under pressure from the European Parliament, a Commission Recommendation (COM(2014) 1405 final, 2014/124/EU) was adopted, urging member states to adopt measures on pay transparency, in order to address gender pay gaps. Ten member states subsequently introduced pay transparency regulations, but all adopting different methods, whilst the majority of states did not act (Veldman 2017). In response to this lack of action, the new Commission president Ursula von der Leyen announced her intention to introduce binding regulation on pay transparency. However, as a study commissioned by the European Parliament illustrates (European Parliament PE 642.379), the lack of member state activism for the introduction of such measures, coupled with business opposition, indicates that any regulation may present the same problems of loose design and weak implementation identified for other social policy initiatives.

Feminist scholarship: identifying and theorising the 'bottlenecks' and gaps

Feminist critique of social and employment policy, analysing the power relations within and between institutions (Kronsell 2005), highlights the relatively low status of this policy area in

Social and employment policy

relation to macroeconomic policy (see also Cavaghan and Elomäki in this volume). Commission initiative has been contingent on the prevailing political ideology as well as the agency of individual Commissioners (Hafner-Burton and Pollack 2009). Since the mid-2000s, the subordination of social policy to market priorities has intensified. Institutionalist analysis highlights the practices and resources of institutions and the individuals within them, whilst social constructivists analyse the way in which dominant ideational frames undermine stated gender equality objectives and reinforce conservative norms of hegemonic masculinity (Locher and Prügl 2009). Both these approaches shed light on the way in which equality concerns take second place to powerful intergovernmental actors and prevailing preferences for weak regulation, market solutions and individual choice. As Jane Jenson (2015) argues, discourse and institutional power relations are mutually reinforcing and their intersection helps to explain the persistence of gender equality in the EU.

Policy development has overlapped significantly with the emerging EU gender regime 'encompassing a variety of soft law instruments in addition to treaty provisions, directives, and court rulings' (Locher and Prügl 2009, 183; see von Wahl in this volume). Significant pieces of legislation have resulted from the interplay of policy actors (Laatikainen 2001), but even these flagship policies (on protection of part-time workers, limitation of working hours, protection of pregnant employees and new mothers, and parental leave) were substantially hollowed out during the adoption process and are subject to domestic transposition, which often weakens their impact and results in considerable variety between member states (Liebert 2003). Social policy and gender equality were not prioritised in accession negotiations or the implementation of the acquis after accession, leading to further variation (see Chiva in this volume). For example, across member states, a significant proportion of men and women (10% of working women and 12% of working men on average) are ineligible for any form of parental leave, with strong differences between states and uneven conditions of eligibility (EIGE 2020, 15).

The pincer effect created by the interplay of case law through Court of Justice rulings (see Solanke and also Guth and Elfving in this volume) and regulatory intervention (by the Commission) led to regulatory innovation (van der Vleuten 2007). However, it also generated a 'boomerang' effect whereby member states became reluctant to accept further regulatory proposals and established strategies to veto them. This led, for example, to the adoption in 2015 of the 'better regulation' approach within the Commission (Kantola and Lombardo 2018, 344) which effectively excluded significant regulatory development in the field of social and employment policy. It also discouraged the Commission from putting effort into compliance enforcement. Anna van der Vleuten (2007) has shown how this process of erosion of supranational regulation took place precisely in those areas where there was early policy activism: equal pay for work of equal value, and social security.

When work–family policy developed later, it was mainly in the form of soft law, which allowed governments to interpret and present domestic policy in ways that formally complied with European objectives but in practice responded to domestic practice and preference. Inconsistencies arose from the 'absence of a cohesive policy and legislative strategy' (Busby and James 2015, 303). Consequently, the motherhood penalty remains strong in the EU, hindering women's economic empowerment (EIGE 2020).

Soft law can promote policy learning through socialisation and dissemination of knowledge, and it can provide a new opportunity structure for domestic actors and especially for transnational epistemic networks (Beveridge and Velluti 2008). However, feminist scholars have shown the weakness of policy coordination, and have highlighted the lack of transformation afforded by the adoption of gender mainstreaming. Sophie Jacquot (2015) has shown how the polysemic nature of gender mainstreaming, like many concepts deployed in EU social and employment policy, allows it to be used even in ways that do not further gender equality but rather serve to window-dress existing national policy preferences. At Commission level, too, by combining gender mainstreaming with more powerful, market-driven ideological frames, choices made in funding projects have effectively downgraded the objective of gender equality in relation to other concerns (Ahrens 2018).

A key contribution of feminist scholarship concerns the nature and impact of equality activism and the resources afforded to it by EU opportunity structures (Locher and Prügl 2009, 185). This observation was made early on in Catherine Hoskyns' pioneering work, which highlighted both the sponsorship of transnational networks by a supportive Commission directorate (Hoskyns 1996). Later this finding was theorised using the concept of 'velvet triangles' or informal advocacy relations between equality activists, feminist Commission officials, politicians, and academics (Woodward 2004). However, this advocacy depends on individual agency of 'femocrats' (i.e. feminist bureaucrats) at EU and national government level; in practice they have often encountered strong resistance from within their own institutions (vertically) as well as horizontally in the interplay of institutions and especially the possibility of veto politics in the Council.

Activism has also been found to depend strongly on existing domestic resources. Weak capacity for transnational networking, or a preference for domestic over transnational action, and weak access to national decision-making institutions constitute domestic bottlenecks preventing activists from exploiting the opportunities provided by EU regulation across countries (Liebert 2003, 16–17). Bottlenecks are more prevalent in southern than northern member states, and more in eastern than western member states. Ulrike Liebert's Europeanisation approach rests on the notion that the EU policy environment provides ideational resources encouraging change over time, allowing domestic equality activists to benefit from a more feminised policy environment at domestic level, and gain stronger leverage over even weak regulatory European instruments as a result.

However, ideational resources for gender equality have diminished in the face of powerful competing frames, in particular the dominance of neoliberal thinking. From the 1990s, European employment policy has instrumentalised labour market participation, framing work–family policy as a market-supporting mechanism and narrowing the discursive space in which feminist agency is able to mobilise. This neoliberalisation of gender expertise has intensified in recent decades (Elomäki 2020), in the context of market-driven reforms imposed by tighter rules for Eurozone macroeconomic governance (Chieregato 2020a). It is accompanied by other discursive trends in which inequalities rooted in structural disadvantage based on gender are downplayed (Daly 2020; Jenson 2015). Thus the potentially transformative emphasis on the adult worker model has not been realised due to the weakness of incentives it offers and the depolitisation of gender relations in policy framing.

With reference to the new parental leave directive adopted in 2019 (Directive 2019/1158/EU), which gives fathers or equivalent second parent the right to two months' non-transferable leave after the birth of a child, the strengthening of fathers' rights represents a move towards more egalitarian forms of parenting but in the form of 'light-touch fatherhood' that does not fundamentally question the domestic division of labour (Daly 2020). Moreover, whilst EU policy framing acknowledges the diversity of family forms and needs, in practice it fails to account for the growing numbers of workers in non-standard employment or in non-traditional family arrangements (Chieregato 2020b). Access to rights is still conditional on domestic legal definitions of parenthood (see also Guerrina 2015a), whilst workplace rights are often ineffective in practice due to the prevalence of non-standard and precarious employment. Feminist scholars argue that an intersectional approach would help policy-makers to understand and assess who has access to rights, since women facing disadvantage on grounds of race and ethnicity, disability, social class, age are over-represented amongst those in precarious employment. Employment rates of women with disabilities and those with low qualifications remain low, and the gender income gap in old age is stubbornly high. Poverty risk is particularly acute for women born outside the EU (EIGE 2020).

Feminist scholars have highlighted the weakness of the EU's gender regime in referring to multiple rather than intersectional discrimination (Kantola 2010; Kantola and Lombardo 2018). In the case of race and ethnicity, social policy remains at the level of a passive anti-discrimination framework, and it derives from citizenship of an EU member state (including Third Country Nationals with residence rights only), which separates social rights from immigration policy (see Siim and Mokre in this volume). This gap is also seen in the most recent framework for social policy initiatives, the Pillar of Social Rights proclaimed by the Parliament, the Council and the Commission in 2017 (Official Journal C 428/2017), which brings together basic social rights with work–family policy, within a framework of non-discrimination and equality of opportunity. The rights enshrined in the pillar derive from EU citizenship and the document does not set out a rationale or plan of action for tackling structural disadvantage.

Conclusion

From the beginning social and employment has been a relatively weak and subordinate policy area. When social objectives are seen as having equal status with economic objectives, significant policy effort has helped enhancing social rights and gender equality rights alike (Hoskyns 1996). The resulting political opportunity structure has enabled women campaigners within the institutions, supported by the informational resources supplied by activist networks, to push for transformative change. In most cases, however, outputs have had ambiguous effects. Hard forms of regulation have largely taken the form of lowest common denominator policy, in the form of directives that depend on national conditions for transposition, yet allowing member states to set higher national standards. Soft forms of regulation have paid formal attention to gender mainstreaming but, in reality, have subordinated social justice claims to the market logic. Overall, efforts to achieve gender equality have been forced to adapt to the constraints of 'neoliberally informed "rules of the game"' (Weiner and MacRae 2017, 87).

Nevertheless, the EU has undoubtedly influenced national policies, partly through landmark legal rulings and directives, partly through a more diffuse form of norm entrepreneurship, particularly in its sponsorship of a gender-egalitarian Scandinavian-style adult worker model (Busby 2018). Although the impact of membership has posed a challenge to equality policy in countries with high existing regulatory standards, notably the Scandinavian welfare states, its impact has been more positive in countries with gaps in provision, such as the UK, where the withdrawal process (Brexit) has highlighted negative consequences of the loss of hard and soft regulation (Fagan and Rubery 2018; see Guerrina and Masselot in this volume). However, the piecemeal way in which policy developed and its dependence on different legal bases has hampered innovation and weakened outputs, reflecting the low status of women's rights in relation to the priorities of EU decision-makers. Activists have been able to keep policy alive, but not to reverse the dominant policy preferences. The weak dynamics of work–family policy persist, despite the 2019 Commission's stated intention to relaunch gender equality policy.

Looking ahead, it is possible to identify a number of agendas for future research and activism. The first concerns the way in which social rights can be defended in the context of uneven

Susan Milner

compliance and backlash in some member states (Holst 2018). Defending the 'gender acquis' and ensuring adequate and consistent implementation form an important first step. The second seeks to integrate gender into ongoing debates about how the Eurozone's economic model can cope with asymmetry long term and how member states under the austerity regimes can find sustainable growth models. The challenges posed by Brexit and a more hostile international environment, as well as domestic divisions and the current Covid-19 pandemic, will make it imperative to find answers to these questions, although it is far from clear that the EU has the capacity or will to do so. Finally, whilst intersectionality provides a strong epistemic and normative basis for action, there is still no legal or political framework for its translation into strong, enforceable rights allowing equality work to progress at EU level.

References

Abels G (2011): Gender Equality Policy, in: Heinelt H, Knodt M (eds.): *Policies Within the EU Multi-Level System. Instruments and Strategies of European Governance*, Baden-Baden: Nomos, 325–348.

Abels G, MacRae H (2016): Why and How to Gender European Integration Theory? in: Abels G, MacRae H (eds.): *Gendering European Integration Theory. Engaging New Dialogues*, Opladen, Toronto: Barbara Budrich Publisher, 9–37.

Ahrens P (2018): *Actors, Institutions, and the Making of EU Gender Equality Programs. Roadmap to Nowhere?*, Basingstoke: Palgrave Macmillan.

Anderson KM (2015): *Social Policy in the European Union*, Basingstoke: Palgrave Macmillan.

Bercusson B (2009): *European Labour Law*, 2nd ed., Cambridge: Cambridge University Press.

Beveridge F, Velluti S, eds. (2008): *Gender and the Open Method of Coordination. Perspectives on Law, Governance and Equality in the EU*, Aldershot: Ashgate.

Bleijenbergh I, de Bruijn I, Bussemaker J (2004): European social citizenship and gender: the part-time work directive, *European Journal of Industrial Relations* **10** (3), 309–328.

Bleijenbergh I, Roggeband C (2007): Equality machineries matter: the impact of women's political pressure on European social-care policies, *Social Politics* **14** (4), 437–459.

Blum S, Kowslowski A, Macht A, Moss P, eds. (2018): *International review of leave policies and research 2018*, URL: www.leavenetwork.org/annual-review-reports/country-reports/ (download: May 9, 2020).

Busby N (2018): The evolution of gender equality and related employment policies: The case of work-family reconciliation, *International Journal of Discrimination and the Law* **18** (2–3), 104–123.

Busby N, James G (2015) Regulating working families in the European Union: a history of disjoined strategies, *Journal of Social Welfare and Family Law* **37** (3): 295–308.

Chieregato E (2020a): Gender equality and the EU's economic governance: women's employment within labor market reforms in Italy, *Social Politics*, https://doi.org/10.1093/sp/jxaa012.

Chieregato E (2020b): A work–life balance for all? Assessing the inclusiveness of EU directive2019/1158. *International Journal of Comparative Labour Law and Industrial Relations* **36** (1), 59–80.

Ciccia R, Bleijenbergh I (2014): After the male breadwinner model? Childcare services and the division of labor in European countries, *Social Politics* **21** (1), 50–79.

Cichowski RA (2004): Women's rights, the European Court, and supranational constitutionalism, *Law & Society Review* **38** (3), 489–512.

Collins D (1975): *The European Communities. The Social Policy of the First Phase. Volume II. The European Economic Communities, 1958–1975*, London: Martin Robertson.

Daly M (2006): EU Social policy after Lisbon, *Journal of Common Market Studies* **44** (3), 461–81.

Daly M (2020): *Gender Inequality and Welfare States in Europe*, Cheltenham: Edward Elgar.

Elomäki A (2020): Economization of expert knowledge about gender equality in the European Union, *Social Politics*, https://doi.org/10.1093/sp/jxaa005.

European Institute for Gender Equality (EIGE) (2020): *Gender Equality Index 2019: Work–Life Balance*, Vilnius: EIGE.

Fagan C, Rubery J (2018): Advancing gender equality through European employment policy. The impact of the UK's EU membership and the risks of Brexit, *Social Politics* **17** (2), 297–317.

Fusulier B (2009): The European Directive: Making Supra-National Leave Policy, in: Kamerman S, Moss P (eds.): *The Politics of Parental Leave Policies. Children, Parenting, Gender and the Labour Market*, Bristol: Policy Press, 243–258.

Grimshaw D, Rubery J, Marino S (2012): *Public sector pay and procurement in Europe during the crisis. The challenges for local government and the prospects for segmentation, inequalities and social dialogue*, Report for European Commission, Manchester: University of Manchester.

Guerrina R (2015a): *Mothering the Union: Gender Politics in the EU*, Manchester: Manchester University Press.

Guerrina R (2015b) Socio-economic challenges to work-life balance at times of crisis, *Journal of Social Welfare and Family Law* **37** (3): 368–377.

Haas L (2008): Parental leave and gender equality: lessons from the European Union, *Review of Policy Research* **20** (1), 89–114.

Hafner-Burton EM, Pollack MA (2009): Mainstreaming gender in the European Union: getting the incentives right, *Comparative European Politics* **17** (1), 114–138.

Hantrais L (2007): *Social Policy in the European Union*, 3rd ed., Basingstoke: Palgrave Macmillan.

Hardy S, Adnett N (2002): The parental leave directive. Towards a "family friendly" social Europe?, *European Journal of Industrial Relations* **8** (2), 157–172.

Heidenreich M, Bischoff G (2008): The open method of co-ordination: a way to the Europeanization of social and employment policies?, *Journal of Common Market Studies* **46** (3), 497–532.

Holst C (2018): *Promoting Global Justice When Backlash Strikes*, Oslo: University of Oslo.

Hoskyns C (1991): Working Women and Women's Rights. The Development and Implications of EC policy, in: Milner S, Hantrais H (eds.): *Workers' rights in Europe. Cross-National Research Papers* **5**, Birmingham: Aston University, 23–32.

Hoskyns C (1996): *Integrating Gender. Women, law and politics in the European Union*, London: Verso.

Jacquot S (2015): *Transformations in EU Gender Equality*, Basingstoke: Palgrave Macmillan.

Jacquot S (2017): A Policy in Crisis. The Dismantling of the EU Gender Equality Policy, in: Kantola J, Lombardo E (eds.): *Gender and the economic crisis in the EU*, Basingstoke: Palgrave Macmillan, 27–48.

Jenson J (2015): The fading goal of gender equality: three policy that underpin the resilience of gendered socio-economic inequalities, *Social Politics* **22** (4), 539–560.

Kantola J (2010): *Gender and the European Union*, Basingstoke: Palgrave Macmillan.

Kantola J, Lombardo E (2017): *Gender and the Crisis in Europe. Politics, Institutions, and Intersectionality*, Basingstoke: Palgrave Macmillan.

Kantola J, Lombardo E (2018): EU Gender Equality Policies, in: Heinelt H, Münch S (eds.): *Handbook of European Policies. Interpretive Approaches to the EU*, Cheltenham: Edward Elgar, 331–349.

Kronsell A (2005): Gender, power and European integration theory, *Journal of European Public Policy* **12** (6), 1022–1040.

Laatikainen KV (2001): Caught Between Access and Activism in the Multilevel European Union Labyrinth, in: Mazur AG (ed.): *State Feminism, Women's Movements and Job Training. Making Democracies Work in a Global Economy*, New York, London: Routledge, 79–109.

Lahuerta SB, Zbyszewska A (2018): Taking stock of twenty years of EU equality law and policy-making and looking ahead, *International Journal of Discrimination and the Law* **18** (2–3), 55–59.

Leibfried S (2015): Social Policy. Left to the Judges and the Markets?, in: Wallace H, Pollack MA, Young AR (eds.): *Policy-Making in the European Union*, 7th ed., Oxford: Oxford University Press, 263–292.

Lewis J (2006): Work/family reconciliation, equal opportunities and social policies. The interpretation of policy trajectories at the EU level and the meaning of gender equality, *Journal of European Public Policy* **13** (3), 420–437.

Liebert U (2003): Gendering Europeanisation: Patterns and Dynamics, in: Liebert U (ed.): *Gendering Europeanisation*, Brussels: Peter Lang, 11–46.

Locher B, Prügl E (2009): Gender and European Integration, in: Wiener A, Diez T (eds.): *European Integration Theory*, 2nd ed., Oxford: Oxford University Press, 181–297.

Mazey S (1998): The European Union and Women's Rights. From the Europeanisation of National Agendas to the Nationalisation of a European Agenda?, in: Hine D, Kassim H (eds.): *Beyond the Market. The EU and National Social Policy*, London, New York: Routledge, 134–155.

Mazey S (2002): Gender mainstreaming in the E.U.: delivering on an agenda? *Feminist Legal Studies* 10 (3–4), 227–240.

Meier P, Celis K (2011): Sowing the seeds of its own failure. Implementing the concept of gender mainstreaming, *Social Politics* **18** (4), 469–489.

Moss P (1988): *Childcare and Equal Opportunity*, Brussels: Commission of the European Communities.

Moss P (1990): Childcare and Equality of Opportunity, in: Hantrais L, Mangan S, O'Brien M (eds.): *Caring and the Welfare State*, Cross-National Research Papers **2**, Birmingham: Aston University, 23–31.

Mulder J (2017): *EU Non-Discrimination Law in the Courts*, London: Hart/Bloomsbury.

Perruzzi M (2015): Contradictions and misalignments in the EU approach towards the gender pay gap, *Cambridge Journal of Economics* **39** (2), 441–465.

Plantenga J, Remery C, Siegel M, Sementini L (2008): Childcare Services in 25 European Union Member States: The Barcelona Targets Revisited, in: Leira A, Saraceno C (eds.): *Childhood: Changing Contexts*, Bingley: Emerald, 27–53.

Pollack MA, Hafner-Burton E (2000): Mainstreaming gender in the European Union, *Journal of European Public Policy* **7** (3), 432–456.

Rees T (1998): *Mainstreaming Equality in the European Union: Education, Training and Labor Market Policies*, New York: Routledge.

Rees T (2005): Reflections on the uneven development of gender mainstreaming in Europe, *International Feminist Journal of Politics* **7** (4), 555–574.

Rubery J, Smith M, Fagan C (2010): National working time regimes and equal opportunities, *Feminist Economics* **4** (1), 71–101.

Smith M, Villa P (2010): The ever declining role of gender equality in the European employment strategy, *Industrial Relations Journal* **41** (6), 526–543.

Stratigaki M (2004): The cooptation of gender concepts in EU policies. The case of 'Reconciliation of work and family', *Social Politics* **11** (1), 30–56.

Stratigaki M (2005): Gender mainstreaming vs positive action: an ongoing conflict in EU gender equality policy, *European Journal of Women's Studies* **12** (2), 165–86.

van der Vleuten A (2007): *The Price of Gender Equality*, Aldershot: Ashgate.

van der Vleuten A (2016): Intergovernmentalism: Gendering a Dinosaur?, in: Abels G, MacRae H (eds): *Gendering European Integration Theory. Engaging New Dialogues*, Opladen, Toronto: Barbara Budrich Publisher, 77–104.

Veldman AG (2017): *Pay Transparency in the EU. A Legal Analysis of the Situation in the EU Member States, Iceland, Liechtenstein and Norway*, Brussels: European Commission.

Weiner E, MacRae H (2017): Opportunity and Setback? Gender Equality, Crisis and Change in the EU, in: Kantola J, Lombardo E (eds): *Gender and the Economic Crisis in the EU*, Basingstoke: Palgrave Macmillan, 73–93.

Wilde G (2016): Civil Society and European integration. The Re-Configuration of Gendered Power Relations in the Public Sphere, in: Abels G, MacRae H (eds.): *Gendering European Integration Theory. Engaging New Dialogues*, Opladen, Toronto: Barbara Budrich Publisher, 257–278.

Wöhl S (2016): Gendering Intergovernmentality and European Integration Theory, in: Abels G, MacRae H (eds.): *Gendering European Integration Theory. Engaging New Dialogues*, Opladen, Toronta: Barbara Budrich Publisher, 237–255.

Woodward AE (2004): Building Velvet Triangles. Gender and Informal Governance, in: Christiansen T, Piattoni S (eds.): *Informal Governance and the European Union*, Cheltenham: Edward Elgar, 76–93.

Woodward AE (2012): From Equal Treatment to Gender Mainstreaming and Diversity Management, in: Abels G. Mushaben JM (eds.): *Gendering the European Union*, Basingstoke: Palgrave Macmillan, 85–103.

Zeitlin J, Pochet P, Magnusson L, eds. (2005): *The Open Method of Coordination in Action: The European Employment and Social Inclusion Strategies*, Brussels: Peter Lang.

21

Economic and monetary union

Alexandra Scheele

From its beginnings, better economic cooperation and coordination between the European states was paramount for the European Union (EU) and its predecessor organizations, i.e. the European Coal and Steel Community (ECSC) founded in 1951 and the European Economic Community (EEC) established in 1957. This was lifted to a new stage with the founding of the Economic and Monetary Union (EMU) in 1992 and accompanying special institutions such as the common currency – the Euro – and the European Central Bank (ECB). The EMU remit also covers joint monetary policy and macro-economic coordination. While initially the Euro was hailed by many as a symbol of and major step towards an 'ever closer Union', with the onset of the economic debt crisis – often called Euro crisis – it became the source of contestation and disintegration in and among the member states (see also Kantola and Lombardo in this volume; Genschel and Jachtenfuchs 2018), particularly as not all EU member states are part of what is called the 'Euro area' (initially 11, today 19 of 27 EU member states).

The institutionalization of EMU has been labelled as a case of 'two-speed Europe'. This means deepening of cooperation in single policy areas without comprising all member states the same way. The Lisbon Treaty as of 2009 grants such 'differentiated integration'. This functional proceeding allows for acknowledging differences between member states and reaching policy consensus; simultaneously, it hinders comprehensive European integration. Both, (potential) conflicts between member states as well as partial membership in EMU result from the combination of regulatory integration and horizontal differentiation characterizing the initial EMU agreement (Genschel and Jachtenfuchs 2018). Regulatory integration means that EMU fiscal policies remained national responsibility but had to be in accordance to common European rules; horizontal differentiation means that not all member states participate at the same time and in the same way in EMU, because they do not want to or they do not fulfil the EMU convergence criteria. Some scholars argue that '(self-) exclusion of unwilling or unable Member States reduced the distributive conflicts involved' (Genschel and Jachtenfuchs 2018, 183), while the focus on formal rules and regulation through institutions, instead of effective policy coordination, lead to a rather fragile construction of EMU.

This chapter provides an overview of EMU and its background, institutions and mechanisms and highlights some crucial points. First, the introduction itself was highly contested, even more so in the aftermath of the financial and economic crisis 2007/2008. EMU policies are largely criticized for fixation on budget stability by all means, thus enforcing social inequalities, social deprivation and budget cuts in social sectors and healthcare. Feminist scholars emphasize the (gender-)democratic deficit of EMU governance and policies. Second, gender analyses examine gendered impacts, and criticize the lack of such impact assessments. EU's commitment to gender equality in regard to economic policies has been and still is inconsistent. In addition, women are largely underrepresented in EMU institutions notwithstanding that the ECB now has its first ever female president, Christine Lagarde, and the key role of the German Chancellor Merkel in the management of the Euro crisis. The underrepresentation of women in decision-making positions of key regulatory institutions and central banks became an issue for researchers as well as for the public and policy actors during the financial and economic crisis since 2008. Yet, this public discourse had no effect and one can still find male dominance in EU institutions. Without a doubt, political and economic decisions have an impact on the private and reproductive sphere. Hence, the structural linkage between production, finance and social reproduction constitutes an important field of analysis. Third, feminist political economists (FPE) denounce mainstream economics as gender-blind; they call for a systematic integration of gender (as an intersectional category) in the design, implementation and evaluation of economic policies at all levels (see Cavaghan and Elomäki in this volume).

In this chapter I first provide an introduction to the idea and history of EMU. Second, I present the institutions and mechanisms for economic coordination. I then illustrate how the economic governance has changed due to the Euro crisis affecting democratic processes at member state level. Next, a gender critique of EMU follows investigating the gender democratic deficits, the lack of gender mainstreaming in the economic governance cycle and, finally, the ignorance towards gendered impacts of economic, fiscal and structural reforms. The chapter concludes with a general analysis of current finance and economics and reconstructs how abstract steering mechanisms and technocratic governance structures hamper a substantial dismantling of existing gender inequalities.

EMU idea and history

EMU means the coordination of economic policy-making between member states, the coordination of fiscal policies, an independent monetary policy orchestrated by the ECB, shared rules and supervision of financial institutions and a single currency in the Euro area. EMU consists of three institutions: ECB, the Euro and the Single Market. Responsibility for economic development is divided between member states and EU institutions.

A vital discussion among policy-makers was whether EMU should be introduced as a trigger towards 'ever closer Union' or if it could only be the final high point of integration. The first interpretation succeeded. First plans for a monetary union and common currency date back to 1970 and the so-called Werner Report (Bulletin of the EC, Supplement 11, 1970), initiated at the Hague Summit in December 1969. This report by the Luxembourgish then prime minister and finance minister Pierre Werner developed a comprehensive plan for the establishment of economic and monetary union in three stages over one decade. It involved significant transfers of responsibility from states to the European Community in the field of monetary policy and aimed at realizing a single currency by the year 1980. The discussion came to a stop because of the international economic and financial turmoil of the 1970s. However, the report is an important milestone and often interpreted as a blueprint for the latter EMU formation nearly 20 years later.

Economic and monetary union

Of particular importance was the adoption of the European Currency Unit (ECU) on 13 March 1979 by the, at this time, 12 European Union member countries. It served as a standard monetary unit used by the European Monetary System (EMS). In June 1988, the European Council confirmed the objective of the successive realization of a multilateral surveillance process of national economic policies. A committee, chaired by Commission President Jacques Delors, developed a report with concrete stages towards joint economic policies. This 'Report on economic and monetary union in the European Community' (Delors Report), presented in April 1989, suggested the gradual coordination of economic and fiscal policies; it aimed at economic and fiscal integration until the end of 1998, when a single currency was to be introduced and a ECB established.

The 1993 Maastricht Treaty laid the foundations, stating that 'Member states shall regard their economic policies as a matter of common concern and shall coordinate them within the Council' (Article 99 TEU); this led to the construction of the Euro area. It started with the introduction of complete freedom for capital transactions on July 1, 1990, increased cooperation between national central banks, the free use of the ECU and the improvement of economic coherence. In a second stage, member states had to meet four 'convergence criteria' to become EMU members in the period between January 1, 1994 and December 31, 1998. These criteria were rather strict: (1) *Price stability*: the inflation rate should not be higher than 1.5% above the rate of the three best-performing member states; (2) *government budget deficit*: government deficit should not be higher than 3% of GDP and government debt not be higher than 60% of GDP; (3) *interest rate*: the long-term interest rate should not be higher than 2% above the rate of the three best-performing member states in terms of price stability; (4) *currency stability*: a country must participate in the European Exchange Rate Mechanism II (ERM II) without severe tensions for at least two years, before it can qualify to adopt the Euro. ERM II fixes the exchange rate of a non-Euro area member state against the Euro and sets limits within the national currency can fluctuate. The ERM II entry is based on an agreement between the ministers and governors of national central banks of the non-Euro zone member state and the Euro-area member states, and the ECB (European Commission n.d.). In May 1998, Austria, Belgium, Finland, France, Germany, Ireland, Italy, Luxembourg, the Netherlands, Portugal and Spain had qualified for EMU, and on January 1, 1999, the third and final stage of the EMU began. On that date, those 11 countries adopted the Euro as their common currency, with monetary and exchange rate policy determined by the ECB. Until the end of 2001, the Euro could only be used in its scriptural form; from January 1, 2002 it became cash money as well. In 2020, the Euro is the official currency for 19 of the 28 resp. 27 EU member countries. For those states, the Euro has at least two advantages: The single currency puts an end to exchange rate fluctuations and provides investors and companies a secure basis for calculating cross-border investments and income. Furthermore, the Euro has created a global currency besides the US Dollar, backed by great economic strength. This economic strength ensured lower interest rates in the Euro area. However, these advantages came with a price tag: the member states subjected themselves to the stability criteria, thus losing their freedom for indebtedness. Hence, budgetary decision-making power moved from national to EU level (Cavaghan 2017, 60).

Institutions and mechanisms for economic coordination

EMU works through several institutions, which have changed over time. The ECB acts as central supervisor of financial institutions in the Euro area and sets monetary policy. It has the task to guarantee price stability. However, ECB's powers are tightly constrained by the EU treaties:

267

in order to prevent any supranational encroachment on national budgets and economic policies: Art. 123 TFEU prohibits the monetary financing of public debts; Art. 125 bans fiscal burden-sharing among Member States or with EU institutions ("no bail out"); Art. 127 essentially restricts the ECB's mandate to the maintenance of price stability.

(Genschel and Jachtenfuchs 2018, 182–183)

The Economic and Financial Affairs Council (ECOFIN; see Abels in this volume) is responsible for economic policy, taxation and the regulation of financial services; it coordinates national economic policies, furthers the convergence of member states' economic performance and monitors their budgetary policies. The Eurogroup is an informal body consisting of the finance ministers of the Euro area member states meeting monthly (at the eve of ECOFIN meetings) to discuss matters related to the Euro. Though the Eurogroup is not mentioned in the Treaty and does not have any formal decision-making competences, it is a widely accepted powerful body scrutinizing the enforcement of restrictive fiscal policy (Cavaghan and O'Dwyer 2018). The position of the European Commission was strengthened through the European Semester (see below), which establishes country-specific recommendations (CSRs) in order to monitor the development of the national budgetary situation and compliance with budgetary discipline. In this process the government budget deficit criteria are taken into account. EMU also empowers the European Parliament, since it has the opportunity to employ control mechanisms around Euro summits, during Economic Dialogues and in the European Parliamentary Week and the interparliamentary conference on Stability, Economic Coordination and Governance (Fromage 2018).

According to the 1999 Stability and Growth Pact (SGP) member states must comply with the budget deficit threshold fixed in the convergence criteria. Under the 2005 reformed SGP, member states must set a budgetary target for the next three years (Medium-Term Objective, MTO) and yearly targets for how to achieve the MTO. Targets are laid out in so-called stability programmes for Euro area member states, and in convergence programmes for non-Euro member states. Within the parameters of the SGP, member states keep their sovereignty on their national policies (Crum 2013) and the state monopoly regarding taxation, welfare entitlements and public service obligations is secured (Genschel and Jachtenfuchs 2018).

As part of the EU's annual economic governance cycle, the Commission assesses the national programmes both before and after implementation. This allows to identify risks of non-compliance before they occur and actual instances of non-compliance that could ultimately warrant sanctions. This guidance and surveillance cycle proceeds as follows: (1) The European Semester, introduced in 2010, aims at enabling coordinate of national economic policies throughout the year in close collaboration with the Commission and the European Council; the focus is on addressing economic challenges. This 'new working method' was implemented 'to ensure that discussion on key issues takes place at EU level, *before* and *not after* national decisions are taken' (European Parliament 2012, PE 462.510, 6; emphasis in original). During this Semester, lasting from January to July, national fiscal and structural reform policies are analysed by the Commission, which then provides policy recommendations and monitors implementation. 'The *second phase* is the National Semester, when the Member States implement the policies they have agreed' (Kerschen and Sweeney 2016, 842).

Within the European Semester member states have to report their economic analyses and priorities for the subsequent year back to the Commission on a regular basis. These reports neither systematically include a gender impact assessment nor require a gender budget analysis. Some authors (e.g. Addabbo et al. 2018) have highlighted that gender equality is hardly mentioned in any of the coordination processes or documents; within the whole economic governance mechanism gender mainstreaming does not play any role. Only with regard to employment, member states are asked to ensure an increase of female employment and to tackle gender inequalities regarding the quantity and quality of employment (part-time, marginal time employment etc.) (Klatzer and Schlager 2016, 41; see also Milner in this volume).

Through the excessive deficit procedure (EDP) the Commission wants to ensure that member states adopt appropriate policy responses to correct excessive deficits (and/or debts). EDP provisions are defined in the 2012 consolidated version of the Treaty on the Functioning of the European Union (TFEU). They comprise schedules and deadlines for the Council, following reports from the Commission and the Economic and Financial Committee, which is an advisory body composed of senior officials from national administrations and central banks, the ECB and the Commission (Article 134 TFEU). Furthermore, opinions on how to judge whether a member state has an excessive deficit are included. The EU calls the EDP the SGP's 'corrective arm'. Since EDP's introduction no member state has been sanctioned, even if the Treaty explicitly links violations to sanctions. Thus, in practice regulations prove to be rather 'soft law' (Kerschen and Sweeney 2016, 836).

Reaction to the crisis since 2008: new economic governance

Rooted in the financial turmoil in 2007/2008, a financial crisis – leading to the Eurozone sovereign debt crisis in 2010 – emerged resulting in a new economic governance framework at the end of 2011. This is considered as 'the most comprehensive reinforcement of economic governance in the European Union and the Euro-area since the launch of the Economic and Monetary Union' (European Commission, MEMO/11/898). This new set of rules for economic and fiscal surveillance is called 'Six Pack' – a package of six new legislative acts adopted by the European Parliament and the Council in December 2011. Bruff and Wöhl (2016) decipher the gendered symbolic meaning, since 'six-pack' does not only refer to a set of six beer cans or bottles but also to a trained man's abdomen. Two years later, on May 30, 2013, an additional 'Two Pack' came into force in the Euro area heading for increased transparency on budgetary decisions. Furthermore, the 2014 budgetary cycle started a stronger coordination in the Euro area 'and the recognition of the special needs of Euro area Member States under severe financial pressure' (European Commission, MEMO/13/457).

With the 2012 Treaty on Stability, Coordination and Governance (TSCG) the member states commit themselves 'to regard their economic policies as a matter of common concern' (TSCG, DOC/12/2). With these reforms the EU aims at improving procedures to reduce public deficits and to address macro-economic imbalances. However, the new economic governance framework does not include any social or gender equality policy dimension (Addabbo et al. 2018).

New tools for budgetary discipline were implemented, yet, regulations do not apply in the same way to all member states. Instruments such as the EFSF/ESM, the Euro Plus Pact (EUPP) or the Fiscal Compact are based on treaties negotiated outside of the EU legal framework (but some later on included in EU primary law) and apply to countries inside the Eurozone only.

> For example, the country specific MTO was introduced as a 'preventive mechanism' permitting ex-ante surveillance on the budgetary policy of the member states. Euro-area countries had to enshrine it into their national law. It was complemented by a common budgetary annual agenda. This correction mechanism played especially a role for the Member States which were not subject to an EDP.
>
> *(Kerschen and Sweeney 2016, 842)*

Member states subjected to a macro-economic adjustment programme (i.e. Greece, Ireland, Portugal and Cyprus) are exempt from the monitoring and assessment of the EU Semester for the duration of the programme. The EU provided financial support in the form of bilateral loans, which were conditional; recipient countries had to guarantee increases in government income, structural budget cuts and the strengthening of tax collection capabilities (Crum 2013). The specific conditions were set up and monitored by a 'troika' consisting of ECB, International Monetary Fund (IMF) and EU Commission delegates.

Throughout the crisis, European executives were further empowered. The European Council became the 'most important forum for decision-making in EMU affairs' and the number of summits increased largely (Auel and Höing 2015, 378). In addition, the Euro summit (see above) became a decisive body for the new economic government (Auel and Höing 2015). These developments follow the form of executive-dominated federalism. Among other aspects, national governments have delegated the mutual supervision of member states' financial and economic policies to technocratic authorities, namely the Commission and the ECB (Crum 2013). This has been accompanied by a loss of political debate in national governments fostering a de-democratization and de-politicization of economic policy (Auel and Höing 2015; Bruff 2014; Cavaghan and Elomäki in this volume).

Benchmarks are in place for national debt and a wide range of economic indicators – from unit labour costs to export market shares and unemployment rates. If a member state deviates from these indicators, the Commission can demand changes in economic policy. If the state in question does not comply with this requirement, the Commission can impose penalties – if agreed by the European Council. Consequently, surveillance takes place through de-politicized procedures and technocratic institutions (Crum 2013, 616). Furthermore, the technocratic procedures adopt a policy style of 'authoritarian neoliberalism' (Bruff 2014), especially since all decisions to tackle the crisis were taken under time pressure and executive dominance (Auel and Höing 2015). Hence, national parliaments – the heart of national democracies – were no longer involved in the process of enforcing austerity mechanisms following the 'debt-brake' rules while the European Commission was entitled 'to install independent bodies at the member state level [i.e. the troika] to monitor the implementation of the rules imposed' (Bruff and Wöhl 2016, 100).

In their review of articles in political sciences journals between 2004 and 2015, Höing and Kunstein (2019, 299) identify five pre-eminent 'narratives' for understanding the EMU – and the roots of the Eurozone crisis in the post-2010 period: (1) fiscal and economic coordination, (2) the construction of EMU, (3) questions of trust, (4) financial regulation, and (5) the democratic legitimacy of the institutional framework. These narratives represent the mainstream debate on the EMU and reflect that the focus is mainly on regulatory aspects and less on democratic implications.

Impacts of the new economic governance at member state level

The economic crisis and the political response is an example for the social and equality impacts of economic decisions – and also for an institutional (re-)configuration of European economic regimes, which are deeply gendered (Kantola and Lombardo 2017; von Wahl in this volume). From the beginning, economic and monetary integration was marked by significant regional inequalities between member states, in which different dynamics of capital accumulation and various forms of its political regulation in the areas of taxes, collective bargaining or welfare policies can be found (Bieling 2015). The creation of centralized fiscal, administrative, and coercive capacities at EU level allowed to foster integration despite differences between member states. However, 'the creation of such a capacity is likely to fuel distributive conflict among the Member States: who pays for, and who benefits from, the joint resources?' (Genschel and Jachtenfuchs 2018, 182).

Economic and monetary union

Many states had to cut spending and raise taxes to reduce their debts risen during the financial crisis. States also lowered their minimum wages, curtailed workers' rights, and the validity of collective bargaining systems to meet the targets set by the new economic governance. Particularly economically weaker states were forced to make cuts. This pressure came not only from EU institutions but also from other member states via fierce debates about welfare and pension systems or public spending in the southern member states, namely Greece.

EMU policies have been and still are criticized by many for their fixation on budget stability by all means and, in doing so, enforcing social inequalities, social deprivation and budget cuts in social sectors and healthcare. National governments can hardly oppose the imposed 'austerity measures', as the Greek example illustrates. Since 2010, the country had to accept two 'Euro rescue packages' to deal with its debt burden; these packages – a 'shock therapy' (Karamessini 2012, 193) – were tied to the implementation of large-scale austerity measures. Greece was put under massive pressure by the Eurogroup and the troika. The latter threatened not to extend the 'aid package' and to cut off the Greek banks' money, if the government were not to follow the imposed austerity plans.

These policies were criticized by many as biased since they were only supporting the financial and industrial sectors. The unequal distribution of the burden and the economic risks between as well as within member states has also led to the formation of Eurosceptical social movements. They express their discontent with the social, economic and political situations as well as the role of political and economic elites; they focus on practical constraints through protests, demonstrations, occupations of public spaces and new forms of political articulation. The 15-M movement in Spain during the regional and local elections in May 2011 is an example as well as the 24-hour general strikes in Greece in 2010. In both protest movements, women and various economically vulnerable groups were active. The protests took on a new character, i.e. mass protests in many Spanish cities, square occupations and tent camps in Athens, but also showed new policy forms. New 'solidarity structures' emerged, which had the character of 'experimental laboratories' (Vogiatzoglou 2014, 366–367). Especially young Spaniards used the civil protest movement to articulate their distrust in the political class – including established interest groups such as trade unions. The objective was to change the functioning of the legislative, governmental and judicial organs (Castellanos, Henar and Gonzales 2011). In accordance with the demand 'Democracia real YA!' (True Democracy NOW!), the movement began to test alternative forms of information, discussion and decision-making, e.g. discussion of central social and political issues at large assemblies, in which a domination-free, equal exchange was attempted (Scheele 2015). The new communities tried 'to reconstruct a space for those who have lost their place in the polity' (Athanasiou 2014, 3).

Such protest also highlighted the (gender) democratic deficit of political and economic decisions and their highly technocratic approach. Feminists participated in these protests to reveal that neoliberalism is a gendered configuration of power, 'both in terms of enhancing gender inequalities in the allocation of livelihood resources and of entrenching neoconservative, sexist, and heteronormative conceptions of the political' (Athanasiou 2014, 4). In sum, the crisis revealed the primacy of financial and economic interests in the EU over social issues and gender equality.

Gendering EMU

The EU's commitment to gender equality in relation to economic policies has been and still is inconsistent. On the one hand, equality at work such as equal pay was included in the 1958

EEC Treaty; subsequent treaties and policy documents codified gender equality particularly in employment as a goal. On the other hand, a gender impact analysis was never and is still not systematically included in EU's policy responses to economic and/or social crises (Cavaghan 2017, 50–51; Hubert and Helfferich 2016, 7) – despite the fact that gender mainstreaming as a tool for securing gender equality in policy, legislation and spending programmes was formally included in the 1997 Amsterdam Treaty (Hubert and Stratigaki 2016, 22). This is also true for the EU's macro-economic policy: 'While the OECD, the World Bank and the World Economic Forum repeatedly and convincingly argue that gender equality generates growth as well as justice, European Union policy-makers do not seem to have integrated this thinking into their macroeconomic policy' (Hubert and Helfferich 2016, 7). This might be due to the reorganization of gender quality policies within the Commission (from GD Employment to the GD Justice; see Hartlapp et al. in this volume); thus, the 'economic and coordination instruments tended to fade into the background while the spotlight remained on legal instruments' (Jacquot 2015, 138). EU priorities shifted from gender mainstreaming to anti-discrimination policies (see also Solanke in this volume) with a tendency to focus on individual cases rather than structural inequalities (Hubert and Stratigaki 2016).

Furthermore, gender analyses of the national reform programmes, which member states have to present regularly, as well as of the Commission's CSRs expose that gender equality measures play only a marginal role and are treated as a mere add-on. A study commissioned by the European Parliament (2012, PE 462.510, 7) points out that 'the gender dimension has a low profile in all the documents developing the Europe 2020 strategy and the European Semester', and that '[n]one of these instruments sets specific targets in gender equality'. The main targets of the Europe 2020 strategy are 'neither disaggregated by sex nor do they contain specific gender targets' (European Parliament 2012, PE 462.510, 7), existing gender inequalities are not recognized, and gender is not considered systematically in the monitoring mechanisms. Finally, 'flagship initiatives' or the 'integrated guidelines' do not explicitly tackle gender equality although the EU economic governance framework strongly affects national policies. Hence '(t)he link between macroeconomics and gender balance should not be overlooked' (European Parliament 2012, PE 462.510, 13).

Feminist researchers have explored the gendered foundation of the separation between production and reproduction in capitalist economies. However, the gendered division of labour in general and the provision of care predominantly by women in particular is not part of established economic models and policies; it remains solely a topic for feminist economic scientists. Feminist research has shown that the salient 'private' sphere of reproduction is, indeed, central for capitalist production. The term 'social reproduction' is to capture the overall meaning of reproducing the species, reproducing labour force and providing care for those in need (Bakker 2007). Therefore, the separation between the spheres of production and social reproduction is only simulated since both spheres are largely interdependent.

Especially social reproduction and its gendered substructure is largely affected by the 'international economic and financial architecture' (Bakker 2002) through liberalization, employment and welfare policies, budget shifts or budget cuts. Thus, it is not surprising that women's organizations in Denmark, opposed the idea of joining EMU – in a referendum held in 2000 – justified by the argument that this would endanger the universalistic welfare system. A similar opposition was active in Sweden. Through the mobilization of women, Sweden highlighted gender equality as a key target for its 2001 Council Presidency. Both countries had to convince female voters that EMU membership would not endanger existing achievements in gender equality (Young 2003, 99f.). Up to today both countries are not Eurozone members.

The global economic crises and the associated 'financialization' processes (i.e. the increase of the financial sector in size and importance) negatively affected the conditions of social reproduction services. For instance, families lost access to social infrastructure or had to fight against forced evictions in European countries as well as in the US (Roberts 2018). Studies (e.g. Bettio et al. 2012) illustrate that, in general, austerity policies hit women harder, since they often have to compensate for welfare cuts and accompanying re-commodification of social services. Marginalized women, e.g. due to their migrant/ethnic background or social status, are even more affected by austerity, while simultaneously lacking recognition when the effects of the crisis are investigated (Emejulu and Bassel 2017).

Numerous analyses (e.g. Annesley and Scheele 2011; Kantola and Lombardo 2017; Walby 2009; Young and Schuberth 2010) have displayed that gender equality was clearly not a consideration of the fiscal and policy responses in the EU. Especially, political decisions on financial subsidies and austerity measures were not subject to gender budgetary analysis so as to ensure that their costs and impacts were evenly distributed. In some countries and in some economic areas gender disparities have narrowed during the crisis and following austerity policies, yet, not resulting from improved living and working conditions of women, but from deteriorating conditions for men (Bettio et al 2012; Karamessini and Rubery 2014). Because of the negative impacts of austerity on women and gender equality – still unacknowledged by policymakers – some feminist researchers view this as a 'U-turn' in EU gender equality policy and 'reversion to an un-apologetically gender-blind EU strategic policy agenda, since the financial crisis' (Cavaghan 2017, 51). Whether the EU Commission under its new president, the German Christian Democrat Ursula von der Leyen, will turn this process around needs to be monitored. Though she is the first female Commission President in EU history and sometimes called a 'feminist' (von Wahl 2019) because of her successful policies regarding family policies and women's representation in corporate boards in Germany, this does not automatically mean that she will be successful in placing gender equality policies on the EMU agenda. However, among the six priorities of the new 2019–2024 Commission is 'An economy that works for the people'; this collects all policy areas dealing with the EMU, its institutions and procedures as well as with investments and labour markets. Whether the term 'the people' reflects gender differences regarding the access to resources or labour market participation remains ambiguous. Yet, the new Commission Gender Equality Strategy (COM(2020) 152 final) addresses some relevant issues.

Economic governance and its bodies are beyond democratic influence or democratic control; and national scope and options of actions are limited through the strict Stability and Convergence Programmes. Klatzer and Schlager (2016, 38–39) characterize the economic steering as follows: (1) the rule-based fiscal policy, with its focus on national deficit reduction, leads to austerity policies and cuts in social policies; (2) the credo of competitiveness created growing wage pressure, the deregulation of labour rights and weakened the power of trade unions; (3) large parts of economic and budget policies were transferred to a rather small group of elites and are characterized by a lack of transparency. They are highly technical policies and their conception as abstract rule-based policies conceals their gendered effects and impede a reflection on including gender equality issues.

This process can be described, as Birgit Sauer (2011) has proposed, as a form of 'depublicizing' (*Entöffentlichung*) of political decision-making arenas, since democratically legitimized bodies such as the European Parliament or national parliaments have no longer (or much less) the 'power of the purse' and competencies for economic decisions. Especially parliaments in member states most severely affected by the financial crisis partly lost their freedom of action and had to meet EU obligations for budget consolidation (Auel and Höing 2015). Since decision-making with 28 resp. now 27 member states has become very difficult, single representatives of governments or 'a

Alexandra Scheele

small group of states that matter most take the decisions that the remaining states have no other choice than to swallow or veto' (Mény 2014, 1340). Mény (2014) calls this an 'UN-ization' of European institutions and a de-politicized integration by stealth. In sum, powers are moved from parliaments to governments at national and supranational level (Bruff and Wöhl 2016).

This democratic deficit affects gender equality. In terms of descriptive representation and compared to other policy arenas, the number of women in fiscal institutions is rather low and the financial sector is disproportionately male (Prügl 2016). While the share of women in other democratic institutions has increased over time (e.g. 40% women in the European Parliament after the 2019 election), there are only two women among the 25 members (8%) in the Governing Council of the ECB and only a few in the ECFIN council. Even with Christine Lagarde becoming ECB President in 2019, the general underrepresentation of women in economic and monetary policies remains a problem since the dominance of men in these institutions is related to particular forms of hegemonic masculinity (see Hearn et al. in this volume) privileging an understanding of economics in which reproductive work, i.e. the 'women's sphere', is externalized or made invisible. However, in 2013 the ECB introduced gender quotas. The target was to fill 35% of management positions and 28% of senior posts with women by 2020. In May 2020, the ECB announced to further improve the gender balance of its staff at all levels until 2026 – the year when the mandate of Christine Lagarde ends.

Moving forward: key issues

Isabella Bakker (1994) once spoke of the 'strategic silence' in relation to gender and economic policy: (1) Though 'every institution, including markets and states construct and reproduce various kinds of femininity and masculinity that constitute an unequal gender order marked by a gender division of labour and structure of power' (Bakker 2002, 17), women are not or only marginally represented in economic institutions; gendered impacts of economic policies are ignored. (2) Simultaneously, feminist discourse and gendered analyses of economic questions have – compared to other areas of feminist scholarship – a marginal position not only within economics, but also within gender studies. Brigitte Young (2013, 37ff.) argued that this follows the assumption that, in contrast to micro-economics, macro-economics are defined as 'gender-neutral'. Since it does not explicitly focus on people, but on monetary aspects, prices and goods – measured with the gross domestic product (GDP), investments, savings, imports and exports, balances of trade (for trade see Garcia in this volume) etc. – it is more demanding to identify their impact on living and working conditions, on intersecting social and gender (in)equalities. Therefore, some feminist economists prefer to analyse the micro and meso level of capitalist economy.

However, feminist political economy scholars questioned the differentiation in micro, meso and macro levels in economics, since it hampers grasping a comprehensive understanding, the whole picture, of structural gender inequalities (Elson 1994). If gender is only considered as an attribute of individuals at micro level, then the impact of the social construction of gender at all levels of the economy is overlooked. Since economic and work organizations are highly gendered (Acker 1991) and since the regulation of labour markets as well as normative ideals of productive and unproductive work, public spending, welfare institutions and macro-economic settings have great impact on gender and gender relations and form particular gender regimes (Pascall and Lewis 2004) it is necessary to conceptualize institutions as materialization of unequal and gendered power relations (Bruff and Wöhl 2016).

In sum, EMU represents a policy sector with quantitative targets laid down at supranational level. This causes manifold contradictions: First, while the EU sets economic key figures to be fulfilled by the member states, it does not develop a framework or a guideline for national policies by which these targets can be met – the social impact has been neglected and relegated to a matter of national responsibility (Hubert and Helfferich 2016, 5). Second, the European mantra of 'growing by numbers' (Hubert and Helfferich 2016, 8), the 3% resp. 60% threshold of budget and public debt levels measured against the GDP stands in opposition to an alternative approach employing qualitative indicators such as environmental issues, gender equality or social aspects as innovative factors for creating wealth and prosperity.

To include gender into the EMU framework seems to be today more difficult than ever before. While in earlier times, gender and gender equality were considered as an important factor, a 'must-have' for social cohesion as well as for economic growth, it is now only considered 'nice to have' and optional. Regarding EMU and its different procedures of monitoring and steering national economic and fiscal developments it is necessary to disaggregate targets by gender, to include appropriate indicators to monitor gender equality, to systematically include gender specific recommendations in the CSRs, and to guarantee that fiscal consolidation priorities match gender equality objectives (see European Parliament 2012, PE 462.510, 12).

The Covid-19 crisis underlines again the need for such a systematic gender impact analysis. In answer to the pandemic and its massive economic and social consequences, the European Commission has proposed a recovery plan for Europe, consisting of a two-fold strategy: The 'Next Generation EU' instrument with which public investment and key structural reforms in the member states are to be fostered and a long-term financial framework. A first gender impact assessment (Klatzer and Rinaldi 2020) of the recovery plan shows that it is gender blind and that the funds do not address the impact of the Covid-19 crisis in the care sector. In addition, it fails to address the specific challenges for women or the increasing inequalities (Klatzer and Rinaldi 2020, 8).

References

Acker J (1991): Hierarchies, Jobs, Bodies: A Theory of Gendered Organizations, in: Lorber J, Farrell S (eds.): *The Social Construction of Gender*, London: Sage, 162–179.

Addabbo T, Klatzer E, Schlager C, Villa P, de Villota P (2018): Challenges of Austerity and Retrenchment of Gender Equality, in: O'Hagan A, Klatzer E (eds.): *Gender Budgeting in Europe. Developments and Challenges*, Basingstoke: Palgrave Macmillan, 57–86.

Annesley C, Scheele A (2011): Gender capitalism and economic crisis. Impact and responses across Europe, *Journal of Contemporary European Studies* **19** (3), 335–347.

Athanasiou A (2014) Precarious intensities. Gendered bodies in the streets and squares of Greece, *Signs* **40** (1), 1–9.

Auel K, Höing O (2015): National parliaments and the Eurozone crisis. Taking ownership in difficult times?, *West European Politics* **38** (2), 375–395.

Bakker I, ed. (1994): *The Strategic Silence. Gender and Economic Policy,* London: Zed Books.

Bakker I (2002): Who built the pyramids? Engendering the new international economic and financial architecture, *Femina Politica* **11** (1), 13–25.

Bakker I (2007): Social reproduction and the constitution of a gendered political economy, *New Political Economy* **12** (4), 541–556.

Bettio F, Corsi M, D'Ippoliti C, Lyberaki A, Samek L, Verashchagina A (2012): The Impact of the Economic Crisis on the Situation of Women and Men and on Gender Equality Policies. Synthesis Report for the European Commission, URL: https://op.europa.eu/en/publication-detail/-/publication/4a10e8f6-d6d6-417e-aef5-4b873d1a4d66/language-en (download: January 15, 2020).

Bieling HJ (2015): Uneven development and 'European crisis constitutionalism', or: the reasons and conditions of a 'passive revolution in trouble', in: Jäger J, Springler E (eds.): *Asymmetric Crisis in Europe and Possible Futures. Critical Political Economy and Post-Keynesian Perspectives*, London, New York: Routledge 98–113.

Bruff I (2014): The rise of authoritarian neoliberalism, *Rethinking Marxism. A Journal of Economics, Culture & Society* **26** (1), 113–129.

Bruff I, Wöhl S (2016): Constitutionalizing Austerity, Disciplining the Household. Masculine Norms of Competitiveness and the Crisis of Social Reproduction in the Eurozone, in: Hozic AA, True J (eds.): *Scandalous Economics. Gender and the Politics of Financial Crises*, Oxford: Oxford University Press, 92–108.

Castellanos C, Henar L, Gonzales E (2011): Protests in Spain. A gender review, *Femina Politica* **20** (2), 109–112.

Cavaghan R (2017): The Gender Politics of EU Economic Policy. Policy Shifts and Contestations Before and After the Crisis, in: Kantola J, Lombardo E (eds.): *Gender and the Economic Crisis in Europe*, Cham: Palgrave Macmillan, 49–71.

Cavaghan R, O'Dwyer M (2018): European economic governance in 2017. A recovery for whom?, *Journal of Common Market Studies* **56** (S1), 96–108.

Crum B (2013): Saving the euro at the cost of democracy?, *Journal of Common Market Studies* **51** (4), 614–630.

Elson D (1994): Micro, Meso, Macro. Gender and Economic Analysis in the Context of Policy Reform, in: Bakker I (ed.): *The Strategic Silence. Gender and Economic Policy*, London: Zed Books, 33–45.

Emejulu A, Bassel L (2017): Whose Crisis Counts? Minority Women, Austerity and Activism in France and Britain, in: Kantola J, Lombardo E (eds.): *Gender and the Economic Crisis in Europe*, Cham: Palgrave Macmillan, 185–208.

European Commission (n.d.): ERM II – the EU's Exchange Rate Mechanism, URL: https://ec.europa.eu/info/business-economy-euro/euro-area/introducing-euro/adoption-fixed-euro-conversion-rate/erm-ii-eus-exchange-rate-mechanism_en (download: April 22, 2020).

Fromage D (2018): The European Parliament in the post-crisis era. An institution empowered on paper only?, *Journal of European Integration* **40** (3), 281–294.

Genschel P, Jachtenfuchs M (2018): From market integration to core state powers. The eurozone crisis, the refugee crisis and integration theory, *Journal of Common Market Studies* **56** (1), 178–196.

Höing O, Kunstein T (2019): Political science and the eurozone crisis. A review of scientific journal articles 2004–15, *Journal of Common Market Studies* **57** (2), 298–316.

Hubert A, Helfferich B (2016): *Integrating Gender into EU Economic Governance. Oxymoron or Opportunity?*, Brussels: Friedrich-Ebert-Stiftung EU Office.

Hubert A, Stratigaki M (2016): Twenty years of EU gender mainstreaming. Rebirth out of the ashes?, *Femina Politica* **25** (2), 21–36.

Jacquot S (2015): *Transformations in EU Gender Equality*, Basingstoke: Palgrave Macmillan.

Kantola J, Lombardo E (2017): *Gender and the Economic Crisis in Europe*, Basingstoke: Palgrave Macmillan.

Karamessini M (2012): Strukturkrise, Schocktherapie und Gender in Griechenland, in: Kurz-Scherf I, Scheele A (eds.): *Macht oder ökonomisches Gesetz? Zum Zusammenhang von Krise und Geschlecht*, Münster: Westfälisches Dampfboot, 187–205.

Karamessini M, Rubery J, eds. (2014): *Women and Austerity. The Economic Crisis and the Future for Gender Equality*, London, New York: Routledge.

Kerschen N, Sweeney M (2016): Chances and Limits of the European Social Integration, in: Schubert K, Villotta P, Kuhlmann J (eds.): *Challenges to European Welfare Systems*, Basel: Springer International, 823–854.

Klatzer E, Schlager C (2016): Gender Mainstreaming oder Mainstream ohne Gender? Wirtschaftspolitische Steuerung in der Europäischen Union. Geschlechterblind und gleichstellungsriskant, *Femina Politica* **25** (2), 37–48.

Klatzer E, Rinaldi A (2020): '#nextGenerationEU' leaves Women behind. Gender Impact Assessmentof the European Commission Proposals for the EU Recovery Plan. Study commissioned by The Greens/EFA Group in the European Parliament, initiated by Alexandra Geese, MEP (Juni 2020).

Mény Y (2014) Managing the EU crises. Another way of integration by stealth?, *West European Politics* **37** (6), 1336–1353.

Pascall G, Lewis J (2004): Emerging gender regimes and policies for gender equality in a wider Europe, *Journal of Social Policy* **3** (33), 373–394.

Prügl E (2016): 'Lehman Brothers and Sisters'. Revisiting Gender and Myth after the Financial Crisis, in: Hozic AA, True J (eds.): *Scandalous Economics. Gender and the Politics of Financial Crises*, Oxford: Oxford University Press, 21–40.

Roberts A (2018): Financialization and the Production of Gender and Class Relations, in: Scheele A, Wöhl S (eds.): *Feminismus und Marxismus*, Weinheim, Basel: Beltz Juventa, 187–201.

Sauer B (2011): Die Allgegenwärtigkeit der "Androkratie". Feministische Anmerkungen zur "Postdemokratie", *Aus Politik und Zeitgeschichte* (1–2), 32–36.

Scheele A (2015): Prekäre Proteste als eine Reformulierung des Politischen? Reflexionen über das Krisenhandeln, in: Amacker M, Völker S (eds.): *Prekarisierungen. Arbeit, Sorge und Politik*, Weinheim: Beltz Juventa, 128–145.

Vogiatzoglou M (2014): Die griechische Gewerkschaftsbewegung. Protest- und Sozialbewegungen im Kontext der Austeritätspolitik, *WSI-Mitteilungen* 67 (5), 361–368.

von Wahl A (2019: The EU elects a feminist leader, *Femina Politica* 28 (2), 154–156.

Walby S (2009): *Gender and the Financial Crisis*, URL: www.lancs.ac.uk/fass/doc_library/sociology/Gender_and_financial_crisis_Sylvia_Walby.pdf (download: July 4, 2020).

Young B, Schuberth H (2010): *The global financial meltdown and the impact of financial governance to gender*, Garnet Policy Brief **10**.

Young B (2003): Economic and Monetary Union, Employment and Gender Politics. A Feminist Constructivist Analysis of Neo-Liberal Labour-Market Restructuring in Europe, in: Overbeek H. (ed.): *The Political Economy of European Employment. European Integration and the Transnationalization of the (Un)Employment Question*, London: Routledge, 99–112.

Young B (2013): Zwei getrennte Welten? Finanzökonomie und Geschlechterforschung, in: Kurz-Scherf I, Scheele A (eds.): *Macht oder ökonomisches Gesetz? Zum Zusammenhang von Krise und Geschlecht*, Münster: Westfälisches Dampfboot, 36–52.

22
Trade policy

Maria García

Since its inception in the 1957 Treaty of Rome, the European Union's (EU) trade policy has aimed to lower barriers to trade beyond the EU's borders, mirroring the liberalising underpinning of the EU's single market project. With the exception of agriculture, the EU has pursued trade liberalisation within the World Trade Organization (WTO) and through its own preferential trade agreements (PTA) and trade policies to support an economic growth agenda. However, trade liberalisation is not uniformly beneficial (Dunkley 2003). The United Nations (UN), developmental non-governmental organisations (NGO) and feminist scholars have highlighted the gendered effects of trade liberalisation (Carr and Williams 2010; Randriamaro 2006). Whilst liberalisation can increase jobs for some women (Nordas 2003), it can also lead to increased jobs in poor conditions (UNCTAD/DITC/2014/3), and lost government income from tariff cuts can result in reduced social spending, which disproportionately affects women (Williams 2007).

In its promotion of trade liberalisation, the EU has gradually turned attention to social and environmental consequences of trade, but explicit consideration of gender has lagged behind. The Treaty of Lisbon (2009) mandates all EU external policies, including trade, to support EU values enshrined in the Treaty (human rights, rule of law, sustainable development, equality). The 2015 'Trade for All' strategy placed values at the heart of trade policy. However, in practice, EU trade policy has been gender-blind and, until recently, has not explicitly been used to foster gender equality (García and Masselot 2015; Vilup 2015). Moreover, it has failed to address inequalities that can arise from trade liberalisation. Explicit consideration of trade and gender began within the European Parliament only in 2016. Soon after, the EU signed up to the 2017 WTO's Declaration on Women and Trade, and moved towards explicit inclusion of gender clauses in its PTAs and policies. This chapter discusses the belated inclusion of concerns about the gendered consequences of trade agreements. It shows how gender considerations are, nonetheless, underpinned by a narrow understanding of women as economic actors. This is a common approach to gender in trade policy criticised by feminist scholars (Hannah et al. 2020; True 2009; van der Vleuten 2017a) for ignoring structural inequalities in terms of education, opportunity and access to power in societies, requiring broader regulation and resources to rebalance.

Against this backdrop, the chapter addresses the following questions: Why has the EU finally started gendering its trade policies? And how has it gendered its approach to preferential trade agreements? To answer these, I first illustrate the background to EU trade policy, which shows the liberalising bias within the policy; this has determined the way gender has been approached. I then summarise the mainstream literature on trade and gender, highlighting the tensions which EU trade policy has failed to fully address. The next section focuses on gender in EU trade policy. It charts the shift from implicit inclusion of gender to incipient explicit gender specificity in EU trade policy and trade agreements, and demonstrates a significant impact of the WTO's recent attention to gender on the EU's approach. This section also discusses the shape, and possible implications, of proposed gender clauses in new EU trade agreements, with special attention to the modernised PTA with Chile since this contains the first Trade and Gender chapter. I conclude that the explicit inclusion of gender in EU PTAs is based on international developments, and that its focus on women as economic actors precludes a fully transformational agenda.

Background and bias of trade policy in the EU

The liberalising ethos in EU trade policy objectives and outcomes has been explained by different factors: (1) particular ideas regarding the purported economic benefits of trade liberalisation, which have been discursively reinforced over time (García 2013; Orbie and De Ville 2011; Siles-Brügge 2011); (2) the institutional arrangements for EU trade policy; and (3) the interplay of economic groups and interests. Institutionally, the Council of the EU negotiates broad guidelines for trade policies and negotiations, which take account of national governments' different material interests. It then delegates to the Commission the task of enacting trade policy and negotiating trade agreements on its behalf. Scholars argue that this division of labour has helped to isolate the Commission from pressures of domestic interest groups, enabling it to focus on a contested liberalising agenda (Meunier 2005; Meunier and Nicolaïdis 1999). The role of the European Parliament in trade policy has been a more recent focus of scholarly attention (Devuyst 2013; Van den Putte et al. 2015; Yan 2019), following the increased oversight and decision-making powers over trade policy granted to the Parliament in the Lisbon Treaty (Rosén 2017). The Parliament has used its new powers to insist on the inclusion of social and environmental chapters in trade negotiations, so as to assuage fears of competition from countries with cheaper costs, and to promote greater consideration of social matters, including gender, in trade policy. It has also echoed civil society concerns around social impacts of trade policy, and civil society positions on unpopular trade negotiations (e.g. Anti-Conterfeiting Treaty, the Transatlantic Trade and Investment Partnership (TTIP)) (Meissner 2016) becoming a forum for politicisation of trade policy (Rosén 2019).

EU institutions do not operate in a vacuum. Interactions with business and interest groups frame the key objectives they wish to attain from trade policies and negotiations, and determine red lines. Focusing on these interactions, scholars have highlighted how the competing interests of business groups, importers and exporters at a given moment in time shape the specific outcomes of EU trade policy (De Bièvre and Eckhardt 2011; Dür 2008; Eckhardt and Poletti 2016). In general, big business has been favourable to trade liberalisation (ALTER-EU 2018), but particular interest group pressures can explain idiosyncrasies in EU trade policy, such as protectionist impulses in the agricultural sector (Daugbjerg and Swinbank 2009).

As international trade negotiations have evolved beyond trade in goods to complex areas like intellectual property rights, public procurement and investment protection, which can impact domestic policy space, trade policy has become more politicised and new actors have become involved. Civil society organisations have increased their presence through the Civil Society Dialogue and public consultations, but have not necessarily managed to translate this into influence (Dür and De Bièvre 2007). Controversial negotiations between the EU and USA for a TTIP

(2013–2016) sparked an unprecedented level of public interest in, and politicisation of, EU trade policy (De Ville and Siles-Brügge 2015; Duina 2019; Eliasson and García Duran-Huet 2018).

Anti-TTIP protests led former Trade Commissioner Cecilia Malmström to introduce the 'Trade for All' strategy (2015), which emphasises European standards shall not be eroded in PTAs, and reiterates that EU treaties require trade policy to promote sustainable development, human rights and good governance. Simultaneously, it maintains the EU's liberalising ethos stressing at the start that trade and investment are powerful engines for growth and job creation. Whilst the normative emphasis is stronger than in previous EU trade policies (e.g. 'Global Europe' 2006), the combination of normative values and utilitarian-motivated liberalisation has been a historical constant in EU trade policy (García 2013; Young 2019). Despite the emphasis on EU values, 'Trade for All' makes no specific mention of gender. This is surprising as the interdependence of sustainable development, labour rights and gender equality is widely acknowledged (Fontana et al. 1998; Frohman 2017; Randriamaro 2006), including in EU development policy (see Debusscher in this volume).

Literature exploring normative impacts of EU trade policy reveals disappointing outcomes. Cancellation of preferential trade privileges due to rights infringements has only been used as a last resort and always in conjunction with international organisations' sanctions (Portela and Orbie 2014). The EU makes trade agreements contingent on parties acquiescing to human rights clauses, and signing up to International Labour Organisation (ILO) Fundamental Conventions and international environmental agreements. This reflects EU's normative aspirations (Manners 2002), its internal legal obligations (García and Masselot 2015), and pressures against trade liberalisation from civil society in Europe. These linkages have been contested by partners, claiming it is an attempt by developed states to thwart developing states' comparative advantages (Bhagwati 1995). Moreover, a growing literature on social clauses in EU trade policy shows their limitations given a lack of resources and willingness to implement commitments (Marx et al. 2016; Orbie et al. 2016; Van Roozendaal 2017). A combination of opposition from trade partners and EU commercial interests in accessing new markets can dilute commitments to values in agreements (García and Masselot 2015; Hoang and Sicurelli 2017; Meissner and McKenzie 2019). Subsequent sections expand on how external challenges and internal interests drive the design of social and prospective gender clauses in PTAs and steer these towards a more limited approach.

Key issues in trade policy and gender

Literature linking EU trade policy and gender is very scarce, reflecting a wider trend in the literature on trade and gender, which has focused instead on the intersection with development (see Debusscher in this volume). Economists, generally, support the idea that trade liberalisation leads to economic growth, which promotes development and poverty alleviation (Krueger 1998; Winters 2004). However, even where on aggregate this is the case, the benefits of growth are not distributed equally amongst populations. Researchers and development advocacy groups highlight how liberalisation impacts women in different ways (Suare and Zoabi 2014; UNCTAD/DITC/2014/3; WIDE Plus and Concord 2018), but there is no agreement on whether liberalisation is overall positive or negative for women (Frohman 2017, 5). Economic analyses show liberalisation can generate increased exports, and with them new jobs and income, facilitating the empowerment of women, thus benefiting some women (Nordas 2003). However, other economists demonstrate that women's ability to benefit from these opportunities is contingent on which sector they work in, socioeconomic and educational levels. Case studies on women in developing states show increased imports can negatively affect certain sectors and female employment, and how additional jobs related to trade openness tend to be in low-paying sectors at times with inadequate working conditions (UNCTAD/DITC/2014/3). Studies of trade impacts in African countries of agreements with the EU show these have not necessarily benefited women. Small-scale female farmers suffer from trade distortions arising from EU agricultural subsidies, and many women are unable to access new export opportunities due to low levels of technical capacity and funds, infrastructure and market standards (Ulmer 2004, 57).

Feminist political economists have highlighted the pitfalls in these analyses, even gender-disaggregated ones, posed by the underlying assumption that the household and domestic arena lie outside the market, therefore ignoring care and unpaid work of women, and focusing exclusively on those women in paid employment (Elson 2000; Folbre 2003; see also Cavaghan and Elomäki in this volume). Instead, they have demonstrated that women are often less able than men to take advantage of new opportunities due to the gender-specific constraints (limited access to and control over resources, limited access to markets, social responsibility for unpaid domestic work, legal discrimination and discriminatory cultural norms) that can be exacerbated by trade liberalisation and trade agreements (Carr and Williams 2010). Moreover, effects of trade liberalisation extend beyond job markets. Services liberalisation can affect access to health services (through privatisation and higher drug prices) for vulnerable groups (Wichterich and Menon-Sen 2009). NGOs also worry that investment arrangements in PTAs, including the potential of services privatisation and the potential for investor–state dispute mechanisms can discourage regulation in the public interest, disproportionally affecting women (WIDE Plus and Concord 2018). However, these broader impacts are obscured by the framing of gender and trade, within the trade community, as a matter of improving access to work opportunities and linking women's enterprises to global markets (Roberts et al. 2019).

Gender in EU trade policy

Social rights and the implicitness of gender in EU trade policy

Successive EU trade policies have failed to specifically address gender issues explicitly (Vilup 2015). Consequently, EU trade agreements have also been silent on gender until negotiations for the first gender chapter in an EU PTA started in 2017 with the modernisation of the EU–Chile agreement. This notwithstanding, two aspects of trade policy and PTAs have implicitly touched upon gender affairs prior to 2017, specifically trade agreements' impact assessments, and the commitment to the ILO and its decent work agenda in trade policy.

In the early 2000s, the Commission developed sustainability impact assessments (SIAs) as a tool to gauge the potential impact of PTAs. These studies, commissioned to independent consultants, forecast outcomes of trade agreement negotiations and highlight potential flanking measures to mitigate sectorial social losses derived from trade liberalisation. The European Commission (2016, 22) Handbook on SIAs incorporates specific instructions for consultants to pay attention to the impacts on human rights, vulnerable groups, and on 'women's rights and the effect that the agreement under negotiation could have on gender equality', expanding the narrow focus on trade and investment impacts of prior SIAs. Recent SIAs include consideration of effects on women; however, the level of detail differs between SIAs.[1] The SIA for the EU–Japan PTA barely mentions women. The one for the modernisation of the agreement with Mexico suggest the agreement will improve wages in Mexico. This SIA places stronger emphasis on the human rights situation in the country, including equality, and goes beyond merely scrutinising labour indicators. It summarises Mexican legislation and compliance with international conventions, but admits that the agreement is unlikely to alter how the government acts towards women's rights making no suggestions on how to address this (SIA EU–Mexico 2019,

102). The SIA for negotiations with Indonesia looks at gendered economic sectors, stressing how increased exports in the garment and textile sector could help women to be more empowered through independent incomes. It admits that rapid growth in the sector, without mitigating policies, could lead to strains in the oversight systems to ensure decent work conditions, but fails to suggest mitigating measures (SIA EU–Indonesia 2019, 107). Given the additional focus on gender placed on the modernisation of the EU–Chile PTA, this SIA is the most detailed in terms of gender. The consultants use UNCTAD's 2017 Trade and Gender Toolbox to undertake a gender disaggregated analysis of the job market, from which it expects the PTA to lead to wage increases in Chile. The SIA also considers women as entrepreneurs, traders and consumers. Its recommendations are to encourage gathering more gender disaggregated data about the economy and developing policies to support women (as traders) taking advantage of the PTA (SIA EU–Chile 2019, 177).

Despite a more considered focus on social issues in SIAs since 2016, the emphasis remains on the collection of quantifiable economic indicators (labour data, wages), a focus on the impacts on employment sectors and opportunities that can obscure wider matters underpinning inequalities (Taylor and von Arnim 2007). Although recent SIAs complement these analyses with overviews of healthcare costs, and adoption of international labour standards and conventions, they fail to make an effective link between the PTA and how to improve human and social rights, including equality, on the ground. Whilst helpful in focusing attention, the methodologies used fail to address the intersection between trade practices and pre-existing social and economic hierarchies, and are often used to legitimate trade policy choices rather than to mitigate the adverse effects of such policies (Hannah et al. 2020, 8).

Gender equality is also implicit in the inclusion in trade policies of respect for the ILO's Fundamental Conventions on decent work. The latter include the elimination of gender discrimination in respect of employment and occupation. The EU has encouraged the promotion of ILO standards, especially by including the Fundamental Conventions in the EU's Generalised System of Preferences (GSP). This system affords unilateral preferential access to the EU market to a series of products from developing states. States can gain even better terms of market access if they accede to the GSP+ system. To do so they ratify and implement ILO Fundamental Conventions.[2] Breaches of these can result in suspension of preferential access to the EU market. However, the application of such sanctions is challenging and a highly politicised process (Portela and Orbie 2014).

Through the inclusion of social and environmental clauses, and referencing of the UN's CEDAW, ILO and human rights conventions in preambles, gender equality has been present in EU PTAs. Economic Partnership Agreements (EPAs), a subset of EU PTAs with developing countries (former European colonies in Africa, Caribbean and Pacific (ACP) countries), address gender impacts. The Caribbean Forum States–European Union Economic Partnership Agreement (EPA), signed in 2008, 'reaffirms the commitment of the parties to promote the development of international trade in a way that is conducive to full and productive employment and decent work for all, including men, women and young people' (Article 191). Older EU PTAs, such as the Global Agreement with Mexico (2000) and the Association Agreement with Chile (2002) included, under sections on development cooperation, the need to promote gender equality. Sections on development cooperation fell under the remit of DG Development, where gender concerns have been incorporated in policy for a longer time, than in DG Trade.

Since 2011, gender non-discrimination at work, is implicit in EU PTAs through the new trade and sustainable development (TSD) chapters, which encourage the parties to accede to the ILO Fundamental Conventions and ensure domestic laws comply with these. TSD chapters fall short of some of these societal demands for two main reasons: first, lack of consensus within

EU member states on the desirability of legally binding social clauses in PTAs, and, second, other states fundamentally disagree with such linkages. Even the inclusion of non-binding TSD chapters is traded against greater access to the EU's market, and complicate negotiations of European commercial interests. Disappointment with the implementation of these chapters (Marx et al. 2016; Orbie et al. 2016), led the Commission to launch a 'non paper' on reform of the TSD chapters. Following extensive consultations amongst EU institutions and with civil society, the European Commission (2018) determined there was insufficient consensus to move to a sanctions-based system. Instead, it proposed reforms for improved implementation and monitoring of the chapters through closer work with social partners, the European Parliament and ILO. These did not explicitly mention gender. This is surprising given that by 2018 gender had firmly arrived as a focus of attention in DG Trade, and more globally in trade negotiations.

Towards explicit inclusion of gender in international trade negotiations

2017 marks the start of explicit references to gender in EU trade policy. In June, the Commission's Chief Economist published a note on women's participation in exports (http://trade.ec.europa.eu/doclib/docs/2017/june/tradoc_155632.pdf). It showed that women's jobs attributable to trade represented only 38% of the total employment in the EU supported by exports to the rest of the world, due to the concentration of female employment in less export-oriented sectors, notably in services. This report was specifically addressing how European women are not benefitting from trade liberalisation. However, it shared the focus on employment and women as economic actors that feminist scholars have critiqued (True 2009).

On June 20, 2017 the European Commission co-hosted with the International Trade Centre (ITC) its first International Forum on Women and Trade for policy-makers, the business community and NGOs. It aimed to galvanise support for inclusive trade policies and the ITC SheTrades initiative, using trade as a lever for women's economic empowerment. The Commission's 'Report on the Implementation of the Trade Policy Strategy Trade for All' (COM(2017) 491) mentioned gender equality in a trade policy document for the first time. It specifies it as essential for EU decision-makers to improve their understanding of the impact of trade instruments on gender equality. The European Parliament welcomed these developments in its 2018 Report on Gender and Trade (A8-0023/2018) and called on the Commission to 'ensure that the gender perspective is included and mainstreamed in the EU's trade and investment policy' (A8-0023/2018, 16). The WTO Trade Review (WT/TPR/G/357, 20) states that the EU 'has an ambitious agenda on gender equality and the economic empowerment of women' to which trade policy contributes through facilitation of SME participation in international trade and digital trade. The EU clearly emphasises the positive aspects of trade and promotes a market-based approach to deal with the unequal distribution of trade opportunities, ignoring other gendered consequences of trade. This mirrors the internal EU approach to gender equality policies which has justified them, as van der Vleuten (2017b, 16) states, 'in terms of the logic of the playing field: non-discrimination in the labour market, preventing unfair competition, strengthening the economic position of the EU ("not waste female talent" as Timmermans aptly called it)'.

The sudden explicit inclusion of gender in DG Trade's agenda dovetails with a focus on gender at the international trade level. As noted previously, the study of the intersection between gender and trade has occurred mostly within the field of development, and it is from the mainstreaming of gender in development and advocacy group's insistence on addressing these matters cross-sectionally that gender has made it onto the international trade agenda. The inclusion of gender in the EU's trade agenda complements its commitments at the international level, and represents their operationalisation.

The UN Sustainable Development Goals (SDG) include an explicit focus on gender inequality; SDG5 calls to 'achieve gender equality and empower all women and girls'. UNCTAD's Nairobi Maafikiano Declaration (UNCTAD TD/519/Add.2, 11) links the SDGs to international trade calling to 'reinforce work on the links between gender equality, women's and girls' empowerment and trade and development'. In response, in 2017 WTO members adopted their first Declaration on Women and Trade (www.wto.org/english/thewto_e/minist_e/mc11_e/genderdeclarationmc11_e.pdf). The brief declaration reiterates how trade can support SDG 5. It frames women as economic actors, especially as entrepreneurs, and focuses efforts on future collaborative activities to identify statistical information needs to comprehend the gendered impact of trade and WTO policies, and to share experiences in programmes to enhance women entrepreneurs' participation in export activities. The approach has been criticised in a letter signed by 160 advocacy groups for failing to take account of the unequal distribution of trade liberalisation gains, and to acknowledge potential negative impacts of liberalisation derived from privatisation or reduced government income (from tariffs) for public service provision, which can disproportionately affect women (WTO Women 2017). Instead, the declaration upholds the WTO's, and its members', including the EU's, belief in the wealth generation effects of trade liberalisation.

Gender chapters in preferential trade agreements

Against this backdrop, in 2017 the negotiations for the modernisation of the EU–Chile Agreement started. The inclusion in the PTA of a gender specific chapter marks the EU's first such chapter and Chile's third. Chile's trade policy took an active stance towards gendering trade negotiations during Michelle Bachelet's second term as President (2014–2018) following her stint as Executive Director of UN Women.[3] Chile incorporated gender chapters in its renewed trade agreements with Uruguay and Canada, and wanted to include a gender chapter in the modernisation of its Association Agreement with the EU. In June 2017, Commissioner Malmström announced she would like to discuss a gender chapter with Chile, to see what they could learn from Chile and develop a model of gender chapters in PTAs (eurefe.es 2017). In 2018, following from the European Parliament's declaratory resolution in favour of some consideration of gender in trade agreements, Social Affairs Commissioner Marianne Thyssen announced on March 12 the inclusion of provisions on gender in the trade agreement with Chile (Guyot 2018). As the EU uses its latest PTA as the starting basis for its future ones, it is expected that future EU PTAs will also include gender-specific chapters.

Despite the novelty of including gender chapters in trade agreements, these build on existing cooperation and inclusion of social clauses in EU trade agreements, displaying little innovation. In line with the design of TSD chapters, the draft text for a chapter on gender equality and trade in the EU–Chile Agreement incorporates a reaffirmation of domestic and international commitments on gender equality and non-discrimination in economic opportunities. It introduces commitments to (1) eliminate discrimination in relation to economic opportunities arising from the trade relationship; (2) progressively close the gender pay gap; (3) facilitate non-discrimination in employment for pregnancy and maternity (EU–Chile 2018, 3). Aims remain firmly grounded in a neoliberal conceptualisation of women as workers. Moreover, like TSD chapters, this chapter is not subject to the PTA's dispute settlement mechanism, meaning financial sanctions or rescinding trade preferences cannot be used to enforce the implementation of the gender chapter. Instead, the chapter revolves around cooperation between the parties, information exchanges, sharing best practices, and cooperation in gathering gender-disaggregated data. Institutionally, it creates a sub-committee on trade and gender that will be tasked with monitoring the implementation of the chapter, suggesting cooperation activities, and consulting with civil society. There is less specification of how this consultation will take place, other than that representatives of civil society must include representation from organisations promoting equality between men and women (EU–Chile 2018, 7). The chapter establishes a mechanism for dispute settlement modelled on the mechanism in TSD chapters. Just like the soft law approach to dispute settlement in TSD chapters has drawn criticism from NGOs, unions and activist groups, so too, has the proposed text for gender chapters. The NGOs WIDE Plus and Concord (2018, 3) in a joint position paper call for gender and other social chapters in EU PTAs to be made binding and 'for a fundamental shift towards an EU trade policy that gives as much importance to human rights and environmental standards as to economic indicators – especially the questionable indicator of GDP growth'. The draft text is based on the EU's approach to TSD chapters, but is also consistent with the Chile's gender chapters. These are exempt from the general dispute resolution mechanism of the PTA, and are resolved through consultation between the parties, and the Trade and Gender Committee is established to decide upon opportune cooperation activities.

Beyond the gender chapter with Chile, the EU is giving more consideration to gender matters in the implementation of other PTAs. However, it is only with other states that, like Chile, are pursuing more gender-sensitive policies that headway is made. At the first meeting of the EU–Japan PTA TSD Committee, inclusion of gender was limited to the EU presenting its work on gender in other PTAs. By contrast, within the Comprehensive Economic and Trade Agreement (CETA) with Canada, in Recommendation 002/2018 the Joint Committee suggests the creation of a specific committee on trade and gender, and reaffirms the parties' commitment to international standards such as SDG 5, CEDAW, ILO, the Beijing Declaration and Platform Action, and the WTO's Declaration on Trade and Women's Economic Empowerment (2017). CETA's trade and gender committee is tasked with sharing best practices on gender equality promotion, engaging in cooperation activities, especially on methods for gender-disaggregated data collection to better understand the impact of trade on equality and facilitate women's participation in international trade. This focus on data and limited approach is unsurprising as these countries are all conducting trade agreement policies inspired by a belief in the desirability of trade liberalisation, and following approaches to trade and gender from emerging practices in multilateral institutions and fora (WTO, ICT, UN SDGs).

A transformative approach would involve changing the focus of trade policy away from economic growth that pays attention to social issues, to trade policy aimed at societal goals instead (Hannah et al. 2020, 9). It would move away from the focus on women as economic actors in paid employment, to broader considerations of women's unpaid work in households and caring, and unequal access to resources and power in societies (Elson 2000; Folbre 2003; True 2009). Although new gender chapters ensure the participation of women's groups in monitoring the impacts of PTAs, a more gender-sensitive approach would actively involve these voices in negotiations for the PTA and drafting of trade policy (Hannah et al. 2020, 11). This would ensure that consideration of gender issues is not limited to the gender chapter and employment opportunities, but instead accounts for broader concerns that arise from other parts of PTAs, for instance regarding rising health costs due to intellectual property rights chapters or access to public services (Wichterich and Menon-Sen 2009).

Conclusion

The explicit incorporation of gender in EU trade policy and trade agreements is a recent phenomenon, greatly influenced by increased attention paid to the gender development–trade nexus at the international level with the UN SDGs and UNCTAD's calls for consideration of these matters by international financial institutions. The WTO's Declaration on Trade and Women marked the official explicit linking of trade and gender. Actions derived from this focus on increasing women's participation in trade and gathering gender-disaggregated data, mostly based on labour markets and economic data. It is evident that in taking this approach, international financial institutions, and the EU, which has followed a similar route in trade policy, have equated gender with women and, more crucially, have tended to focus on working women exclusively and especially female employment in export sectors. This approach is underpinned by the belief that trade liberalisation is beneficial, and assumes that making it easier for women to engage in international trade will prove improve their financial outcomes and eliminate negative externalities of trade liberalisation. This neoliberal understanding of the link between trade and gender, however, fails to take account of the differences that exist amongst groups of women: women in developed and developing countries, women with different educational attainment levels and women of different ethnicities and circumstances, all of whom will be affected differently by trade liberalisation. The focus on quantifiable employment, trade and business owner data ignores caring roles, work in non-traded economic sectors, educational and cultural situations, as well as public service provision, all of which impact women and men, and different groups of women, differently and can be impacted by trade policies and trade agreements.

Consequently, the new focus on trade and women cannot address feminists' calls for trade policies that consider underlying inequalities in societies (Carr and Williams 2010; Hannah et al. 2020; True 2009) and 'the interrelationship between the formal and informal, between productive and reproductive sectors of the economy, and the distributional consequences of liberalisation across these sectors' (van der Vleuten 2017b, 20). It will, therefore, be necessary for researchers to develop more effective tools to measure and evidence the intersectionality of the impacts of trade policies. At the very least the current push for gender-disaggregated data on engagement with trade and employment in exporting sectors should be widened to also account for intersectional issues such as ethnicity, access to education, investment funding, caring facilities. Beyond this positivist approach, a more multidisciplinary research agenda will be needed, including rich ethnographic case studies, to fully appreciate the impact of intersectionality on both (1) abilities to benefit from the new women and trade initiatives, and (2) more generally, on how trade liberalisation affects different groups. In the absence of more fine-grained and nuanced approaches, gender and trade policies will remain very limited in their scope and fall short of transforming women's situations on the ground.

The EU's incorporation of gender in its trade policy has mirrored the WTO's agenda on trade and women. The text of the EU's first proposed gender chapter in a PTA (modernisation agreement with Chile) fails to create enforceable commitments, and is based on data gathering, information sharing and working towards eliminating gender pay gaps and discrimination in the workplace. Work by the Joint Committee on Trade and Gender under CETA has focused on methodologies for gathering gender-disaggregated data. Explicit chapters and joint committees, even if only with like-minded countries, are a starting point only. Future research will have to track the work of these committees and how they monitor impacts of the agreements, and assess the extent to which gender mainstreaming extends beyond specific chapters in PTAs to more holistic approaches, as states improve gender-specific data collection and impact assessments (Fitzgerald 2019).

While the EU is a self-proclaimed leader in the promotion of values (human rights, democracy, sustainable development, equality), it has been a follower in terms of the incorporation of gender into trade policy and PTAs. The EU's approach to gender in PTAs mirrors the processes, procedures, and language adopted at the WTO on the matter. The EU has also eschewed, for now,

Trade policy

'pushing' the issue in recent negotiations and, instead, has taken it on board with the leader on the matter (Chile) and with another convinced state (Canada) within the context of the implementation of CETA. Understanding the specific dynamics determining when the EU furthers engagement on gender and trade, beyond the convergence of interest observed, will require further scrutiny from EU trade and international relations scholars. The dynamics of negotiations, and how these can affect outcomes, both in terms of PTAs and international initiatives, is an area that feminist work on the impacts of trade liberalisation on women (Carr and Williams 2010; Fontana et al.1998; Frohman 2017; Ulmer 2004), and the incipient feminist literature assessing recent international initiatives on trade and gender (She Trades, gender chapters in PTAs, impact assessments) (Hannah et al. 2020; Roberts et al. 2019) have overlooked. Addressing this complex area in the future would allow for a more nuanced understanding of other structural barriers (e.g. decision-making rules in international organisations, how negotiations are conducted) to the holistic incorporation of gender into trade policies that feminist scholars aspire for.

Notes

1   The SIAs that are referenced in the text can be accessed on: https://ec.europa.eu/trade/policy/policy-making/analysis/policy-evaluation/sustainability-impact-assessments/.
2   See www.ilo.org/global/standards/introduction-to-international-labour-standards/conventions-and-recommendations/lang–en/index.htm.
3   From private interview between author and Chilean diplomat (Brussels, March 16, 2017).

References

ALTER-EU (2018): Corporate capture in Europe, URL: www.alter-eu.org/corporate-capture-in-europe-when-big-business-dominates-policy-making-and-threatens-our-right-0 (download: December 20, 2019).
Bhagwati J (1995): Trade liberalisation and 'fair trade' demands. Addressing the environmental and labour standards issues, *World Economy* **18** (6), 745–759.
Carr H, Williams M (2010): *Trading Stories: Experiences with Gender and Trade,* London: Commonwealth Secretariat.
CETA Joint Committee (2018): Declaration on Trade and Gender, September 28, URL: http://trade.ec.europa.eu/doclib/docs/2018/september/tradoc_157419...pdf (download: March 20, 2019).
Daugbjerg C, Swinbank A (2009): *Ideas, Institutions, and Trade: The WTO and the Curious Role of EU Farm Policy in Trade Liberalization,* Oxford: Oxford University Press.
De Bièvre D, Eckhardt J (2011): Interest groups and EU anti-dumping policy, *Journal of European Public Policy* **18** (3), 339–360.
De Ville F, Siles-Brügge G (2015): *TTIP: The Truth about the Transatlantic Trade and Investment Partnership,* London: John Wiley & Sons.
Devuyst Y (2013): The European Parliament and International Trade Agreements. Practice after the Lisbon Treaty, in: Govaere I, Lannon E, van Elsuwege P, Adam S (eds.): *The European Union in the World,* Leiden: Martinus Nijhoff, 171–189.
Duina F (2019): Why the excitement? Values, identities, and the politicization of EU trade policy with North America, *Journal of European Public Policy* **26** (12), 1886–1882.
Dunkley G (2003): *Free Trade: Myth, Reality and Alternatives,* London: Zed.
Dür A (2008): Bringing economic interests back into the study of EU trade policy-making, *British Journal of Politics and International Relations* **10** (1), 27–45.
Dür A, De Bièvre D (2007): Inclusion without Influence? NGOs in European trade policy, *Journal of Public Policy* **27** (1), 79–101.
Eckhardt J, Poletti A (2016). The politics of global value chains. Import-dependent firms and EU–Asia trade agreements, *Journal of European Public Policy* **23** (10), 1543–1562.
Eliasson LJ, García Duran-Huet P (2018): TTIP negotiations: interest groups, anti-TTIP civil society campaigns and public opinion, *Journal of Transatlantic Studies* **16** (2), 101–116.

Elson D (2000): Gender at the Macroeconomic Level, in: Cook J, Roberts J, Waylen G (eds.): *Towards a Gendered Political Economy*, Basingstoke: Palgrave Macmillan, 77–97.

EU-Chile (2018): Draft provisions on Trade and Gender Equality in the context of the Modernisation of the EU-Chile Association Agreement, URL: http://trade.ec.europa.eu/doclib/docs/2018/june/tradoc_156962.pdf (download: July 19, 2020).

eurefe.es (2017): EU wants gender chapter included in Chile trade deal update, EurActiv June 21, URL: www.euractiv.com/section/economy-jobs/news/eu-wants-gender-chapter-included-in-chile-trade-deal-update/ (download: December 20, 2019)

European Commission (2016): *Handbook for Trade Sustainability Impact Assessment*, 2nd ed., Luxembourg: Publications Office of the European Union.

European Commission (2018): Feedback and way forward on improving and enforcing the implementation of trade and sustainability chapters in trade agreements. Non paper of the Commission Services, 26 February, URL: http://trade.ec.europa.eu/doclib/docs/2018/february/tradoc_156618.pdf (download: December 15, 2019).

Fitzgerald O (2019): Why trade negotiators should take a whole agreement approach to gender mainstreaming in trade agreements, CIGI online, URL: www.cigionline.org/articles/why-negotiators-should-take-whole-agreement-approach-mainstreaming-gender-trade-agreements (download: July 19, 2020).

Folbre N (2003): 'Holding Hands at Midnight'. The Paradox of Caring Labor, in: Baker DK, Kuiper E(eds.): *Towards a feminist Philosophy of Economics*, London: Routledge, 213–230.

Fontana M, Joekes S, Masika R (1998): Global trade expansion and liberalisation: Gender issues and impacts, *BRIDGE Development-Gender Report* no. 42.

Frohman A (2017): Gender Equality and Trade Policy, *World Trade Institute Working Paper* 24.

García M (2013): From idealism to realism. EU preferential trade agreement policy, *Journal of Contemporary European Research* **9** (4), 521–541.

García M, Masselot A (2015): The Value of Gender Equality in the EU–Asian Trade Policy, in: Björkdahl A, Chaban N, Leslie J, Masselot A (eds.): *Importing EU Norms. Conceptual Framework and Empirical Findings*, Cham: Springer, 191–209.

Guyot C (2018): EP wants to include gender equality in free-trade agreements, EurActiv March 14, URL: www.euractiv.com/section/politics/news/ep-wants-to-include-gender-equality-in-free-trade-agreements/ (download: July 19, 2020)

Hannah E, Roberts A, Trommer S (2020): Towards a feminist global trade politics. *Globalizations*, DOI: 10.1080/14747731.2020.1779966.

Hoang HH, Sicurelli D (2017): The EU's preferential trade agreements with Singapore and Vietnam. Market vs. normative imperatives, *Contemporary Politics* **23** (4), 369–387.

Krueger AO (1998): Why trade liberalisation is good for growth, *The Economic Journal* **108** (450), 1513–1522.

Manners, I. (2002): Normative power Europe: a contradiction in terms? *Journal of Common Market Studies*, **40** (2), 235–258.

Marx A, Lein B, Brando N (2016): The protection of labour rights in trade agreements. The case of the EU–Colombia agreement, *Journal of World Trade* **50** (4), 587–610.

Meissner K (2016): Democratizing EU external relations. The European Parliament's informal role in SWIFT, ACTA, and TTIP, *European Foreign Affairs Review* **21** (2), 269–288.

Meissner K, McKenzie L (2019): The paradox of human rights conditionality in EU trade policy. When strategic interests drive policy outcomes, *Journal of European Public Policy* **26** (9), 1273–1291.

Meunier, S. (2005): *Trading Voices: The European Union in International Commercial Negotiations.* Princeton, NJ: Princeton University Press.

Meunier S, Nicolaïdis K (1999): 'Who speaks for Europe? The delegation of trade authority in the EU', *Journal of Common Market Studies* **37** (3), 477–501.

Nordas H (2003): The impact of trade liberalisation on women's job opportunities and earnings in developing countries, *World Trade Review* **2** (2), 221–231.

Orbie J, De Ville F (2011): The European Union's trade policy response to the crisis. Paradigm lost or reinforced? *European Integration Online Papers* **15**.

Orbie J, Martens D, Oehri M, Van den Putte L (2016): Promoting sustainable development or legitimising free trade? Civil society mechanisms in EU trade agreements, *Third World Thematics. A TWQ Journal* **1** (4), 526–546.

Portela C, Orbie J (2014): Sanctions under the EU generalised system of preferences and foreign policy. Coherence by accident? *Contemporary Politics* **20** (1), 63–76.

Randriamaro Z (2006): *Gender and Trade. Overview Report*, BRIDGE Development-Gender, URL: www.bridge.ids.ac.uk/reports/CEP-Trade-OR.pdf (download: December 23, 2019).

Roberts A, Trommer S, Hannah E (2019). Gender impacts of trade and investment agreements. Policy, Briefing prepared for the UK Women's Budget Group, URL: https://wbg.org.uk/analysis/uk-policy-briefings/gender-impacts-of-trade-and-investment-agreements/ (download: May 25, 2020).

Rosén G (2017): The impact of norms on political decision-making. How to account for the European Parliament's empowerment in EU external trade policy, *Journal of European Public Policy* **24** (10), 1450–1470.

Rosén G (2019): Proving their worth? The Transatlantic Trade and Investment Partnership and the members of the European parliament, *Politics and Governance* **7** (3), 266–278.

Siles-Brügge G (2011): Resisting protectionism after the crisis. Strategic economic discourse and the EU–Korea free trade agreement, *New Political Economy* **16** (5), 627–653.

Suare P, Zoabi H (2014): International trade, the gender gap and female labor participation, *Journal of Development Economics* **111**, 17–33.

Taylor L, von Arnim R (2007): *Modelling the Impact of Trade Liberalisation. A Critique of Computable General Equilibrium Models,* Oxfam Research Report, Oxford: Oxfam.

True J (2009): Trading-off gender equality for Global Europe: The European Union and free trade agreements, *European Foreign Affairs Review* **14**, Special Issue, 723–742.

Ulmer K (2004): Are trade agreements with the EU beneficial to women in Africa, the Caribbean, and the Pacific? *Gender & Development* **12** (2), 53–57.

Van den Putte L, De Ville F, Orbie J (2015): The European Parliament as an International Actor in Trade: From Power to Impact, in: Stravidis S, Irrera D (eds.): *The European Parliament and its international relations*, London, New York: Routledge, 52–69.

van der Vleuten JM (2017a): The Conflicting Logics of Regionalism and Gender Mainstreaming: EU Trade Agreements with Southern Africa, in: Kruessmann T, Ziegerhofer A (eds.): *Promoting Gender Equality Abroad. An assessment of EU action in the external dimension,* Wien: LIT, 94–116.

van der Vleuten A (2017b): The Merchant and the Message. Hard conditions, soft power and empty vessels as regards gender in EU external relations, ACCESS EUROPA Research Paper no. 03.

Van Roozendaal G (2017): Where symbolism prospers. An analysis of the impact on enabling rights of labour standards provisions in trade agreements with South Korea, *Politics and Governance* **5** (4), 19–29.

Vilup E (2015): *The EU's Trade Policy. From gender-blind to gender-sensitive?* Policy Department, European Parliament.

Williams M (2007): Gender Issues in the Multilateral Trading System, in: van Staveren I, Elson CG, Çağatay N (eds.), *The Feminist Economics of Trade*, London: Routledge, 277–291.

Wichterich C, Menon-Sen K (2009): *Trade liberalisation, gender equality, policy space. The case of the contested EU-India FTA*, URL: https://wideplus.org/wp-content/uploads/2012/10/eu-india-09-wide20095.pdf (download: March 20, 2019)

Wide Plus, Concord (2018): Women's Rights and Trade, URL: https://wideplusnetwork.files.wordpress.com/2018/06/wide-concord-2018-trade-and-gender.pdf (download: March 20, 2019).

Winters LA (2004): Trade liberalisation and economic performance: An overview, *The Economic Journal* **114** (493), F4–F21.

WTO Women (2017): Global call on Governments to Reject the WTO Declaration on 'Women's Economic Empowerment'. Letter signed by 160 organisations, 12 December, URL: https://wideplusnetwork.files.wordpress.com/2017/12/wtowomen2017.pdf (download: March 20, 2019).

Yan S (2019): The European Parliament in EU Trade Relations with China. A Norm and Policy Advocate?, in: Raube K, Müftüler-Baç M, Wouters J (eds.): *Parliamentary Cooperation and Diplomacy in EU External Relations. An Essential Companion,* Aldershot: Edward Elgar, 432–448.

Young AR (2019): Two wrongs make a right? The politicization of trade policy and European trade strategy, *Journal of European Public Policy* **26** (12), 1883–1899.

23
Development policy

Petra Debusscher

Despite its generally critical nature, gender has been largely absent from the mainstream literature on development policy. As the European Union (EU) has long claimed gender equality to be part of its core values and identity in the world, a gender perspective is indispensable to understand the EU's role as a global actor. Scholarship has shown a rhetorical emphasis on gender, but when push comes to shove, the results are uneven: gender is not systematically mainstreamed across the EU's development policy and often instrumentalised to support economic goals. It has shown how seemingly gender-neutral policy is gendered and gendering, both reflecting as well as producing (unequal) gender relations. This scholarship has also investigated gender imbalances and male work cultures in EU development policy-making, demonstrating that 'who decides what matters' is a highly gendered matter, with real life consequences for men and women across the world.

This chapter starts with an overview of EU development policy, introducing its history, main themes, and policy actors as well as some key directions in scholarship. Next, I trace the emergence of gender from the first attempts to integrate women's issues in European development until present day. Then I delve into the respective scholarship and sketch the main routes it has taken so far. Following, I discuss some limitations within this scholarship, including a focus on decision-making and 'policy on paper' rather than on impact on the ground, as well as a compartmentalised and at times rather Eurocentric approach focussed mainly on gender alone and on the European Commission as the key policy actor. Finally, I discuss how the EU is currently at a crossroad in a volatile global context and propose directions for future research.

EU development policy and its scholarship

The EU is a key player in global development, both as a development actor and a system of collective norms and rules (Bodenstein et al. 2017). It is the world's largest aid donor distributing, together with its member states, almost 57% of global aid in 2018 (European Commission, Press Release IP/19/2075). The EU's development action is based on the EU treaties and on the 'European Consensus on Development' (ECD), which commits the Council of the EU, the European Parliament and the European Commission to a common vision on '5 Ps': people, planet, prosperity, peace, partnership. The EU has always claimed to have a strong focus on global poverty reduction as well as on other normative principles such as sustainable development, gender equality, democracy and human rights promotion. The goal of poverty reduction has been present since the establishment of the European Development Fund (EDF) under the 1957 Treaty of Rome establishing the European Economic Community (EEC), covering its former colonies in the African, Caribbean and Pacific (ACP) regions. The then six member states had agreed to set up a European twin package for the ACP region: a free trade area and an aid programme (the EDF) – next to their own bilateral programmes. These provisions were driven by a historical responsibility for Europe's colonial past, but there was also a clear interest in ensuring access to Africa's raw materials as well as opening up the former colonies to further trade and investments from European firms (Carbone 2017). In the early 1960s, these European aid and trade provisions were formalised in the Yaoundé Conventions, which have continued to the present day under different names (Lomé I-IV bis, Cotonou I-III). These agreements encompass two main instruments: (1) preferential trade agreements, supposed to provide development countries easier export access to the EU; (2) financial aid in the form of grants or loans.

Development policy dates back to the 1950s, but the early 2000s signalled a 'new season' aiming at a more harmonised or even 'federated' development policy and a commitment to boost the EU volume of aid and its effectiveness, with poverty reduction as its guiding principle (Carbone 2008). In September 2000, global leaders signed the 'Millennium Declaration' containing eight goals, placing the fight against poverty high on the world's agenda. In accordance with this changing international context and resulting from Commission initiatives endorsed by the member states, EU development policy entered a new phase characterised by a series of new commitments. These range from the ECD, over a 'Code of Conduct on Complementarity and Division of Labour', to specific targets on Official Development Assistance budgets. This led to an increase in volumes of aid as well as a new emphasis on aid effectiveness, particularly donor coordination and recipient country ownership – in the context of various international conferences (Monterrey 2002, Rome 2003, Paris 2005, Accra 2008 and Busan 2011). Consensus exists that the EU has taken a leading role in defining the global development agenda (Carbone 2017). The new phase involved an organisational reform of the Commission, including the creation of a new body, the EuropeAid Co-operation Office (AIDCO) in charge of implementing all external aid across the various regions, next to the existing Directorate-General (DG) Development mainly responsible for policy formulation. The organisational reorganisation also involved the further devolution of activities and responsibilities from the headquarters to the European Commission's external delegations present in recipient countries.

In 2011, the Commission adopted the 'Agenda for Change' (COM(2011) 637) and set out a more targeted approach to reducing poverty, including a more concentrated funding allocation to increase policy impact. The 'Agenda for Change' established the promotion of human rights, democracy, the rule of law and good governance and 'inclusive and sustainable growth' as the two basic pillars of development policy.

The world's leaders adopted the UN Agenda for Sustainable Development (UN A/RES/70/1) in September 2015 setting 17 Sustainable Development Goals (SDGs) focussing on economic, social, environmental and governance objectives to be achieved by 2030. In the aftermath, the EU revised its 2005 ECD as a new common vision for development policy for the EU and its member states. The new 2017 ECD 'Our World, Our Dignity, Our Future' sets out a strategy for reaching the main SDG principles, to guide EU and national development policy over the next 15 years through external and internal policies. Eradicating global poverty remains paramount.

European development policy is formulated by the Commission's DG for International Cooperation and Development (DG DEVCO, previously DG Development and the AIDCO). DG DEVCO also fosters coordination between EU institutions and member states and ensures the EU's external representation abroad. Commission DGs (in)directly responsible for development policy do not always share the same views. Traditionally, DG DEVCO has advanced the interests and needs of the Global South, while DG Trade, DG Agriculture, DG Migration and Home Affairs have primarily pursued the EU's own economic and security interests. This creates problems of policy coherence (Carbone 2017). In the current 2019–2024 European Commission, DG DEVCO is now headed by a Commissioner for International Partnerships (the Finnish Jutta Urpilainen). The renaming of the Commission's development portfolio is setting out a more strategic course with regard to development cooperation and EU–Africa relations in particular, as it restates the EU's commitment to a 'partnership of equals'. Indeed, the von der Leyen Commission has a distinctively more 'geopolitical' agenda in its international relations, and a more strategic relationship with Africa and other developing nations is becoming increasingly important – both as partners in multilateralism and as markets for European investment and trade.

Development policy is implemented on the ground by 141 delegations and offices, representing the EU abroad and managing development and cooperation programmes in recipient countries. While DG DEVCO is responsible for defining policy and the EU delegations for coordinating the implementation of aid on the ground, other EU policies have an impact on development policy as well. To strengthen coherence between EU external relations and development policy, the framework of external action is coordinated by the European External Action Service (EEAS, see Chappell in this volume). The EEAS is led by the High Representative for Foreign Affairs and Security Policy, who is also responsible for coordinating the work of all Commissioners working on EU external relations. While the EEAS has certainly managed a degree of leadership and coherence by setting the EU agenda, a set of institutional challenges is manifest. Problems of coordination and of division of labour continue to arise between the Commission and the EEAS, creating tensions in the formulation and implementation of development initiatives, both at the headquarters and between the headquarters and the EU delegations on the ground (Carbone 2017).

The Council of the EU adopts the framework for development policy and approves the budget together with the European Parliament, which is a co-legislator in development policy and aid expenditure. It approves general policies, budgets, regulations and funding decisions by majority. The Parliament has increasingly influenced this policy area and is often considered a 'friend of the developing world', referring to its close ties with development NGOs and developing countries (e.g. via delegations), as well as to its proactive role on human rights, gender equality, democracy and sustainable development issues (Delputte and Verschaeve 2015, 35).

Member states have their additional policies towards developing countries, often connected to (perceived) historical, cultural, economic and political ties (Delputte and Orbie 2018). Hence, the EU plays two roles simultaneously: as development actor in its own right and as European coordinator. The EU's main purpose, however, is not so much to be 'just another donor' in addition to the member states, but rather to foster a European development policy, aiming to coordinate and harmonise member states' aims, approaches and activities. The absence of a clear delineation of power and the fact that only soft tools for coordination among national policies exist, create a challenge (Delputte and Orbie 2018).

Several authors have traced these evolutions and examined the extent to which harmonisation has taken place (e.g. Lightfoot and Szent-Ivanyi 2014; Orbie and Carbone 2016). The debate about the 'EU factor', examining synergies between the EU and member states, continues to be a key research topic. Another important topic is the role of ethical principles (Bodenstein et al. 2017). A plethora of researchers have examined to what extent the EU is distinctive in its development policy, hypothesising it to be more focussed on ethical norms than other donors, since it has long claimed to be a 'normative power' pursuing ethical principles around the world (Manners 2002; van der Vleuten 2020; Whitman 2011 and van der Vleuten in this volume). Accordingly, the EU can wield power and define the normal in international relations as its norms are attractive to others to the extent that they are emulated by them, or are able to impose norms through conditionality or in exchange for access to the EU market (van der Vleuten 2017, 10). Some authors have shown how the pivotal role of ideas, identities and ideologies is more prominent compared to other international donors, making it normatively distinctive (Orbie et al. 2017). However, others have also criticised the idea of a normative and distinctive EU foreign policy by emphasising inconsistencies (for an overview, see Whitman 2011: 13–16), its interest-based nature and its unreflexivity (e.g. Diez 2005).

Gender in EU development policy

Gender issues were first introduced in EU development policy in the 1980s, focussing mainly on women in education and the health sector. These first attempts were fostered by the UN Decade for Women (1975–1985) and the Third World Conference on Women in Nairobi in 1985. Against this background, the Commission established its 'Women in Development' (WID) policy, including its first specialised units, communiqués and references to women in the Third (1984) and Fourth Lomé conventions (1989). The WID paradigm dominated at the time and addressed the exclusion of women from development by creating specific projects in training, education or health services. Increasingly, however, the WID paradigm was criticised by feminist scholars, activists and practitioners worldwide pointing out that solely focussing on women (and their lack of access to resources) was insufficient. They argued that WID policy was ineffective as it ignored the relational nature of women's subordination as well as underlying structural power issues in women's access to resources (Moser 1993; Razavi and Miller 1995). Although these feminist critiques go back to the late 1970s, it was the Beijing 1995 Fourth World Conference on Women that played a pivotal role in renewing the international community's philosophy about women and development. Consequentially, a shift occurred to the gender and development (GAD) paradigm and the strategy of gender mainstreaming. GAD was considered innovative, as it recognises the need to focus on gender (relations) and men's roles, and brings women's specific projects from the margins to the centre of policy-making. Gender mainstreaming as GAD's implementing strategy would integrate a gender equality perspective across all aspects of development policy. Hence, gender mainstreaming flourished in the EU in the run-up and follow-up to the Beijing Women's Conference. Being among the first EU policies to be gender mainstreamed, development policy is thought to have been particularly 'amenable' (Lister and Carbone 2006, 25); compared to other policy areas it is the most successful. This has prompted scholars to point out the paradox that it seems easier to address gender inequality elsewhere than in one's own context and structures (e.g. Kantola 2010, 130). Some scholars have used the concept of 'enabling and constraining logics' to help understand the different trajectory in different policy fields (van der Vleuten 2017). Accordingly, gender mainstreaming is based upon an 'interventionist logic', i.e. the state is supposed to actively intervene in the market to redress power relations and include gender in all policy processes and outcomes. Thus, DG DEVCO, being relatively interventionist in character, has been more receptive, while market-oriented DGs with a strong neoliberal logic, e.g. DG Trade, have remained insusceptible (van der Vleuten 2017).

Since Beijing, the EU has adopted several high-level policy commitments to mainstream gender in all areas of development and into all programmes and projects at regional and country levels. In 2000, gender mainstreaming was taken up in the EU–African development policy when the Lomé Convention was replaced by a new partnership agreement between ACP states and the EU. In Article 1 of the Cotonou Agreement, gender equality and mainstreaming are explicitly put forward as areas of priority, stating that 'systematic account shall be taken of the situation of women and gender issues in all areas – political, economic and social' (Partnership Agreement 2000/483/EC). A year later, the Commission released the 'Programme of Action for the Mainstreaming of Gender Equality in Community Development Co-operation', which proposes a twin-track strategy according to which the EU includes 'gender equality goals in the mainstream of EC development co-operation policies, programmes and projects', while at the same time taking 'concrete actions targeting women (specific actions)' to reinforce these processes (COM(2001) 295 final, 8–13). In the following years EU institutions took further steps to ameliorate the integration of gender mainstreaming and gender equality into the development agenda. In 2007, the Commission released the 'Communication on Gender Equality and Women's Empowerment in Development Cooperation' (COM(2007) 100 final) with the aim of increasing the efficiency of gender mainstreaming and refocusing specific actions for women's empowerment, providing 41 concrete suggestions in the areas of governance, employment, education, health and domestic violence. In the same year the Commission requested that each delegation appointed a gender focal person (GFP) – defined as a staff 'member who is responsible for facilitating the promotion of women's empowerment and gender equality issues in the activities of the Delegation' (EU Gender Advisory Services 2010, 36). In response, 66 delegations in partner countries nominated a GFP that year (Debusscher 2014). With the (re)establishment of the expertise-sharing network consisting of GFPs of EU delegations as well as representatives from all external DGs, the Commission aimed to kick-start gender mainstreaming in development practice, moving from lip-service to real implementation on the ground. In 2010, the Commission issued its 'EU Plan of Action on Gender Equality and Women's Empowerment in Development 2010–15' (in short: Gender Action Plan, GAP I; SEC(2010) 265 final). GAP moves beyond the twin-track strategy to a 'three-pronged approach' adding a 'political and policy dialogue on gender equality' (SEC(2010) 265 final, 7). In the run-up to GAP I, the Commission again insisted the delegations appoint a GFP and provided guidance, capacity-building and numerous gender trainings. Despite its merits, GAP I suffered from a scant prioritisation in EU external action and a weak institutional leadership and capacity (O'Connell 2015). For instance, despite pressure from the EU headquarters to formalise the GFP's role, often there was little time or budget allocated for this function and tasks had to be carried out on top of existing job responsibilities (Debusscher 2014). The disinterest of some heads of delegation caused a lack of incentives to deliver on gender commitments and implied that the responsibility fell predominantly on the shoulders of the GPFs, who were often junior and placed low on the hierarchy.

In 2015 the EU released its GAP II (SWD(2015)0182): The document 'Gender Equality and Women's Empowerment: Transforming the Lives of Girls and Women through EU External Relations (2016–20)' shows a marked shift. First, it seeks to concentrate the efforts of *all* EU actors – especially its leadership – on changing institutional culture and monitoring, i.e. of the EEAS, delegations, Commission services and member states and services in all partner countries, including fragile and conflict-affected states. Second, it focuses on three thematic areas: girls' and women's physical and psychological integrity, their economic and social rights, and voice and participation. Thus, GAP II actively tries to move away from a compartmentalised approach and links GAD to human rights, security or conflict prevention. An evaluation (Allwood 2018) illustrates GAP's positive impact on promoting gender equality and women's empowerment in the mid to long term, especially in countries where there is already awareness and political commitment.

Nonetheless, GAP II has important lacunas and weaknesses, such as trade policy. Although trade has major links with gender and development policy, DG Trade remains strangely absent from GAP II reporting. The past, however, has shown how EU development finance in support of women can be impeded by trade policy and, thus, jeopardise women's livelihoods (ACDIC et al. 2007). Furthermore, despite a more ambitious agenda, no new money was assigned. This is especially problematic with regards to lack of gender expertise. Serious and long-term investment in human resources as well as investing in high-quality gender expertise are vital to embed a continuous analytical capacity throughout the EU institutions. Finally, without extra funding it is likely that the scale of the specific initiatives in the three thematic areas has been limited (O'Connell 2015).

Scholarship on gender and development

Since the 1990s, an important body of scholarly work on gender and the EU has developed. Initially, scholarship focused on gender policies and mainstreaming *within* the EU but, more recently, the lens was turned to EU external and development policy. Several studies have concentrated on the (lack of) adoption and/or implementation of gender principles and policies in EU external relations, mostly focussing on development policy (e.g. Holvoet and Inberg 2015; Lister and Carbone 2006). This scholarship asks whether the EU practices what it preaches; it examines the extent to which it has indeed gender mainstreamed its external and development policies (van der Vleuten 2017). Results are mixed. While good progress has been made in some areas, gender is not systematically mainstreamed and often understood instrumentally to support economic rather than equality goals (Debusscher 2011). Furthermore, it reveals that the strong rhetoric of gender in external and development policy is often just that: rhetoric (van der Vleuten 2017).

Another strand of research draws on the normative power concept analysing whether the EU indeed 'defines the normal' as regards gender equality in international politics and whether or not it offers an attractive model to others (David and Guerrina 2013; Debusscher 2010a, 2011; Hulse 2017; Petó and Manners 2006; van der Vleuten et al. 2014; van der Vleuten 2017). This research displays that the EU bases its policy on standard-setting by global organisations (such as the United Nations, the ILO, the OECD, and the Council of Europe), hence, the EU is not so much of a norm *setter* – or certainly less so than we could expect from a normative power – but rather '*transfers*' or diffuses the 'normal' as regards gender equality in international politics (van der Vleuten 2017, 12). Other studies contribute a post-colonial lens and argue that the distinctive identity of the EU and its 'partners' is continuously constructed and reproduced through practices of 'Othering' (Kunz and Maisenbacher 2017).

Studies have also raised the question of voice. In other words, are privileged Europeans speaking on behalf of women outside of Europe? (Debusscher and Manners 2020) These questions have come to the fore over the past years (Kunz and Maisenbacher 2017), in particular questions of 'who has a say?' (Debusscher 2011, 45), 'telling silences' (Debusscher and van der Vleuten 2012), and 'including gender advocates' voices' (Debusscher 2020; Debusscher and Hulse 2014). Another strand of literature focusses on how gender equality norms are constructed in EU development policy (Elgström 2000) and diffused between the EU, South America and southern Africa and their regional organisations (Roggeband et al. 2020; van der Vleuten et al. 2014).

Several studies focus on specific geographical regions such as ACP states (Arts 2006; Debusscher and van der Vleuten 2012), Latin America (Angulo and Freres 2006; Debusscher 2012a), the European Neighbourhood (Debusscher 2012b; Giusti 2017; Hulse 2017; Kunz and Maisenbacher 2017; Orbie 2006) and Asia (Debusscher 2010b; Sobritchea 2006). Others apply a more global or comparative approach (Calvo 2013; Debusscher 2011; Roggeband et al. 2020; van der Vleuten et al. 2014).

Methodologically, several studies apply interpretative policy analysis such as Carol Bacchi's 'what's the problem?' approach (Bacci 2009) or Mieke Verloo's (2007) critical frame analysis (e.g. Allwood 2013; Calvo 2013; Debusscher 2011). These studies illustrate how problem definitions (diagnosis) influence solutions that are deemed conceivable (prognosis), how it matters who has voice – or not, who is supposed to act or acted upon. If, for instance, policymakers equate gender inequality in development with 'women (as a single group) as the problem/the victim', without questioning how underlying structures of hegemonic masculinity constrain agency and women's access to resources, then well-intended aid might remain ineffective or even become counter-productive (van der Vleuten 2017).

A gender lens is largely missing from mainstream EU development scholarship; this research demonstrates, at best, limited gender awareness. If included, gender is misunderstood as just another variable or policy goal to examine. The absence in mainstream EU development litera-ture renders the picture of the EU and its identity as a global development power incomplete. For understanding the extent to which the EU is a distinctive normative power, a gender per-spective needs to be explicitly present, as the EU has long claimed gender equality to be part of its core values and identity.

Thus, to understand the EU's global identity it is key to examine how gender equality issues are included in development policy. On a deeper analytical level, it implies analysing how seem-ingly gender-neutral development policy is gendered and gendering, both reflecting as well as (re)producing (unequal) gender relations (Debusscher 2014). A gender lens also takes into account policy-making, its impact on policy content, the gendered power relations involved, and the representation of women. Who decides what matters is indeed a deeply gendered issue, as gender imbalances and male work cultures in the hierarchies of EU headquarters, delegations and partner country governments determine policy contents and have real-life consequences for men and women and gender relations across the world (Debusscher 2020).

Research gaps in gender and EU development studies

Existing scholarship is highly relevant for understanding and assessing the EU's role as a global development actor from a gender perspective. However, research gaps still exist. First, this schol-arship has dealt almost exclusively with studying EU development policy and decision-making, while only very few studies scrutinise actual implementation on the ground and policy impact on the lives of women and men across the world. Such implementation studies are essential. Yet, they are time-consuming and costly: a context-sensitive approach is needed which accounts for the wider social, political and cultural and social environment. Such an approach asks for the inclusion of multiple standpoints: the experiences and views of women's organisations and beneficiaries, as well as those responsible for implementing, are all crucial to take on board in such case studies, to fully understand the actual implementation and real-life impact on people's lives. Exceptions exist such as an evaluation of GAP II in Ghana, Rwanda and Vietnam (Allwood 2019), and case studies in Liberia (Debusscher 2013), Rwanda (Debusscher 2014), South Africa (Debusscher 2016) and Botswana (Debusscher 2020).

Second, much scholarship is based on an analysis of EU policy documents and/or expert interviews with Europeans, leading to a Brussels-centric, institution-centric or even Eurocentric view (Debusscher and Manners 2020). To get a comprehensive perspective, non-European sources need to be consulted and the wider national context in the receiving countries needs to be taken into account. These non-European voices need to be represented in order to fully understand why gender mainstreaming works or does not work in a particular case (see Debusscher 2016; Kunz and Maisenbacher 2017). Depending on the research question, it is

Development policy

therefore crucial to focus on what happens in the EU's partner countries where EU gender policies are implemented and have real-life consequences for non-EU citizens. The fact that scholarship analyses policies destined for a non–European context, renders research questions more complex and often requires an inclusive, participatory dialogue-based approach to fully understand the (un)intended consequences of policies on the lives of others. A methodological approach to be taken in future research is to explicitly include the voices of the women and men affected, for instance by including perspectives of women's organisations or gender advocates from countries receiving EU aid (Debusscher 2016; 2020).

Third, research often suffers from a compartmentalised approach on one (or maximum two) policy sectors. However, gender mainstreaming cannot be seen in isolation. Looking at development policy alone is insufficient to analyse the success or failure of gender policies and mainstreaming (see Allwood 2015). Development is a policy area related to other key policy areas such as climate change (see Allwood 2014, 2019, in this volume), human rights, migration and asylum (see Krause and Schwenken in this volume), security, environment, trade (van der Vleuten et al. 2014; García in this volume), external relations (see Mühlenhoff in this volume) or agriculture. Trade liberalisation promoted by the EU, for example, might have a disproportionate effect on women's livelihoods and economic independence because of unequal divisions of labour, resources and power. In the past for instance, massive exports of frozen chicken parts from the EU have ruined domestic markets in west Africa, thereby destroying women's livelihoods (ACDIC et al. 2007). Despite the many connections between development policy and other policy areas, scholars have not yet systematically analysed gender equality across the whole of EU external actions. Studies analysing intersections of policy areas are still relatively rare. A comparative approach taking into account multiple policy areas as well as policy actors (both European and non-European) is key to generate a deeper understanding (Debusscher and Manners 2020). With this in mind, future research could also involve newer policy areas, such as von Leyen's Green Deal, or the gendered effects of global pandemics such as Covid-19 on EU development policy.

Fourth, research has mostly focussed on gender in isolation. The link to other sources of discrimination has received little academic attention. However, focusing on gender equality alone, creates an incomplete research picture as gender, race, class, sexuality, age, ethnicity and ability cannot be analytically understood in isolation from each other, as they are linked in an 'intersecting constellation of power relationships that produce unequal material realities and distinctive social experiences' for the individuals and groups positioned within them (Hill Collins and Chepp 2013, 58; see also Solanke in this volume). The way in which gender, race and class intersect and, thus, impact the outcome of EU development policies is relevant for answering the question whether the EU is contributing to social and gender justice. For instance, (probably well-intended) EU discourses of 'poor women' in development cooperation with South Africa were criticised by black South African gender activists as being harmful and counterproductive. They criticised the paternalistic and stigmatising language, as it confines black women in presumably permanent stereotypical roles with no upward mobility (Debusscher 2016). Research into intersectionality demonstrates how one identity marker – class, for instance – may alter the meaning of, and is thus interlinked with, other social identity markers such as gender or race. Intersectionality is thus key to understand the impact of EU development policy on actual people's lives. Including the relation between gender and other inequalities also provides deeper insight into the artificial division between high and low politics, e.g. what, who (and why) something matters or why it does not in EU development policy.

Fifth, much scholarship focuses on the Commission. However, the constellation of actors is complex and multiple, operating and influencing each other at different levels – both at EU level as well as at the level of each partner country through permanent diplomatic EU staff. The specific roles of this multitude of policy actors and the interplay between different external relations arenas require more scholarly attention, as each arena has its own constraining or enabling logics, which can help us understand why gender mainstreaming EU development is (in-)effective (van der Vleuten 2017). To grasp why and in which way gender is taken up, we need to spend more time considering the differences and similarities between key EU actors, such as the European Parliament, the EEAS and the different DGs (see also David and Guerrina 2013). In particular, the role of the European Parliament is, so far, not sufficiently addressed. It has long acted as one of the primary advocates of a more forceful EU gender policy and has repeatedly called on the Commission to enhance consistency in external policies including aid, trade, migration and asylum and climate change, since gender often slips off the agenda once other policies intersect with development (Allwood 2013). Existing literature typically tends to focus on the role the Commission and the policy documents produced but remains silent on the Parliament's proactive role.

Conclusion and directions for future research

EU development policy is currently at a crossroads: the EU is negotiating a post-Cotonou agreement with ACP countries. In addition, the EU is operating today in a totally different global context. The global implications of the Covid-19 pandemic are still unclear: it might have devastating effects on the world's economy for years to come, but also on some developing countries given the high vulnerability of their healthcare systems. At the same time, previous allies are no longer reliable and even waging aggressive trade wars against Europe.

In this volatile and often hostile global context, achieving a more 'geopolitical' and assertive Union with a focus on securing economic competitiveness is at the top of Commission President von der Leyen's European agenda. The question arises whether this focus on geopolitical interests affects the EU as a promoter of human and women's rights. Preliminary research shows positive signs with the EU upholding its commitment to a rights-based approach to development in the post-Cotonou negotiations rather than using its development cooperation to advance its geostrategic interests (Saltnes 2020). However, more research is required, especially regarding gender equality and women's rights as these are the core of the EU's identity as a normative power and fundamental to a broader human rights policy.

In addition, Brexit may affect the EU as a global gender actor (Haastrup et al. 2019; see also Guerrina and Masselot in this volume). On the one hand, the EU might take a more socially progressive turn after the UK's withdrawal, as the UK has traditionally been blocking an expansion of European social and women's rights (see Milner in this volume). The EU's ability to proceed more smoothly and swiftly on its social and gender equality policy internally would greatly enhance its ability to 'lead by example' and, thus, directly impact on the role as a global gender actor. On the other hand, Brexit may diminish the EU's soft and normative power and challenge the EU's role as the world's leading donor (European Parliament 2017). The UK has been 'a norm entrepreneur' in preventing sexual violence in conflict as part of its commitment to the global UN 'Women, Peace and Security Agenda'; its policymakers have often claimed leadership in shaping the EU's development policy according to their own principles, including an expertise on gender issues globally and human rights in external policy (European Parliament 2017; Haastrup et al. 2019, 65). Arguably, the EU would then need to compensate for the loss of the UK's contribution to EU aid in qualitative terms, e.g. in gender expertise, knowledge and networks.

The loss is undeniable in quantitative terms as the UK was the third largest contributor to the EU budget (after Germany and France). Thus, Brexit causes a significant shortfall in the EU's development budget (Bond 2017: European Parliament 2017). The EU-27 need to decide whether to increase contributions, cut spending or a combination thereof. Development aid may be cut substantially as part of a broader austerity drive in response to global recession. Cuts in funding may address certain policy areas more than others and have gendered effects. The departure of the UK may also accelerate progress towards financing development outcomes through means other than Official Development Assistance, such as blended financial instruments through public–private partnerships (PPP) (Bond 2017). Shifts in financing and in development instruments will most likely have gendered effects. These are worth analysing; for instance, the PPP focus might strengthen the tendency to include gender in an instrumental and neoliberal manner rather than as a social justice goal. It is necessary to analyse these shifts in the changing global context with a gender+ lens, focussing both on what happens within the responsible EU institutions as well as on what happens in the EU's partner countries, as EU development policies have real-life consequences for women and men across the world.

References

ACDIC, ICCO, Aprodev, EED (2007): No more chicken, please: How a strong grassroots movement in Cameroon is successfully resisting damaging chicken imports from Europe, which are ruining small farmers all over West Africa, Yaounde: ACDIC, URL: https://actalliance.eu/wp-content/uploads/2016/04/071203_chicken_e_final.pdf (download: May 9, 2020).

Allwood G (2013): Gender mainstreaming and policy coherence for development: unintended gender consequences and EU policy, *Women's Studies International Forum* **39**, 42–52.

Allwood G (2014): Gender Mainstreaming and EU Climate Change Policy', in: Weiner, Elaine and Heather MacRae (eds.): 'The persistent invisibility of gender in EU policy' *European Integration online Papers (EIoP)* **18**, http://eiop.or.at/eiop/texte/2014-006a.htm.

Allwood G (2015): Horizontal policy coordination and gender mainstreaming: the case of the EU's global approach to migration and mobility, *Women's Studies International Forum* **48**, 9–17.

Allwood G (2018): *Transforming lives? CONCORD Report EU Gender Action Plan II. From implementation to impact*, Brussels: CONCORD Europe.

Allwood G (2019): Gender Equality in European Union Development Policy in Times of Crisis, *Political Studies Review* 18 (3), 329-345.

Angulo G, Freres C (2006): Gender Equality and EU Development Policy Towards Latin America, in: Lister M, Carbone M (eds.): *New Pathways in International Development. Gender and Civil Society in EU Policy*, Aldershot: Ashgate, 45–57.

Arts K (2006): Gender in ACP–EU Relations: The Cotonou agreement, in: Lister M, Carbone M (eds.): *New Pathways in International Development. Gender and Civil Society in EU Policy*, Aldershot: Ashgate, 31–43.

Bacci C (2009): *Analysing Policy: What's the Problem Represented To Be?*, Frenchs Forest: Pearson Education.

Bodenstein T, Faust J, Furness M (2017): European Union development policy: collective action in times of global transformation and domestic crisis, *Development Policy Review* **35** (4), 441–453.

Bond (2017): The impact of Brexit on UK and EU international development and humanitarian policy, URL: www.bond.org.uk/sites/default/files/resource-documents/the_impact_of_brexit_on_uk_and_eu_international_development_policy_0.pdf (download: May 9, 2020).

Calvo D (2013): *What is the Problem of Gender? Mainstreaming Gender in Migration and Development in the European Union*, Doctoral dissertation, University of Gothenburg.

Carbone M (2008): The new season of EU development policy, *Perspectives on European Politics and Society* **9** (2), 111–113.

Carbone M (2017): The European Union and International Development, in: Hill C, Smith M, Vanhoonacker S (eds.): *International Relations and the European Union,* Oxford: Oxford University Press, 292–315.

David M, Guerrina R (2013): Gender and European external relations: dominant discourses and unintended consequences of gender mainstreaming, *Women's Studies International Forum* **39**, 53–62.

Debusscher P (2010a): *Gender Mainstreaming in European Commission Development Policy*, Doctoral dissertation, Ghent University.

Debusscher P (2010b): Gender mainstreaming in European Commission development policy in Asia: a transformative tool? *Asian Journal of Women's Studies* **16** (3), 80–111.

Debusscher P (2011): Mainstreaming gender in European Commission development policy: conservative Europeanness? *Women's Studies International Forum* **34**, 39–49.

Debusscher P (2012a): Gender mainstreaming in European Union development policy toward Latin America. Transforming gender relations or confirming hierarchies? *Latin American Perspectives* **39** (6), 181–197.

Debusscher P (2012b): Mainstreaming gender in European Commission development policy in the European Neighborhood, *Journal of Women, Politics and Policy*, **33** (4): 322–344.

Debusscher P (2013): Gendered assumptions, institutional disconnections and democratic deficits: the case of European Union development policy towards Liberia, *Women's Studies International Forum* **40**, 212–221.

Debusscher P (2014): Gender mainstreaming on the ground? The case of EU development aid towards Rwanda, *European Integration online Papers* **18**, 1–23.

Debusscher P (2016): Analysing European gender equality policies abroad: a reflection on methodology, *European Journal of Women's Studies* **23** (3), 265–280.

Debusscher P (2020): Budget support through a gender lens. The case of EU development cooperation with Botswana, *The European Journal of Development Research*, **32** (3), 718–737.

Debusscher P, Hulse M (2014): Including women's voices? Gender mainstreaming in EU and SADC development strategies for Southern Africa, *Journal of Southern African Studies* **40** (3), 559–573.

Debusscher P, Manners I (2020): Understanding the European Union as a global gender actor. The holistic intersectional and inclusive study of gender+ in external actions, *Political Studies Review* 18 (3), 410–425.

Debusscher P, van der Vleuten A (2012): Mainstreaming gender in EU development cooperation with sub-Saharan Africa: promising numbers, narrow contents, telling silences, *International Development Planning Review* **34** (3), 319–338.

Delputte S, Orbie J (2018): EU development policy: abduction as a research strategy, in: Heinelt H, Münch S (eds.): *Handbook of European Policies. Interpretive Approaches to the EU*, Cheltenham: Edward Elgar, 288–305.

Delputte S, Verschaeve J (2015): The Role of the European Parliament in EU Development Policy, in: Stavridis S, Irrera D (eds.): *The European Parliament and its International Relations*, Abingdon: Routledge, 35–54.

Diez T (2005): Constructing the self and changing others. Reconsidering 'normative power Europe', *Millennium* **33** (3), 613–636.

Elgström O (2000): Norm negotiations. The construction of new norms regarding gender and development in EU foreign aid policy, *Journal of European Public Policy* **7** (3), 457–476.

EU Gender Advisory Services (2010): What Can GFPs Do to Promote Gender Equality in EU Development Cooperation? Gender Focal Persons Workshop, Report, Brussels, June 16–18, URL: https://europa.eu/capacity4dev/file/7774/download?token=ci8fl6BQ (download May 9, 2020).

European Parliament (2017): Possible impacts of Brexit on EU development and humanitarian policies, Study, Brussels, URL: www.europarl.europa.eu/RegData/etudes/STUD/2017/578042/EXPO_STU%282017%29578042_EN.pdf (download: May 16, 2020).

Giusti S (2017): Gender mainstreaming towards the Mediterranean. The case of the ENP, *Journal of Balkan and Near Eastern Studies* **19** (5), 524–540.

Haastrup T, Wright KA, Guerrina R (2019): Bringing gender in? EU foreign and security policy after Brexit, *Politics and Governance* **7** (3), 62–71.

Hill Collins P, Chepp V (2013): Intersectionality, in: Waylen G, Celis K, Kantola J, Weldon L (eds.): *The Oxford Handbook of Gender and Politics*, Oxford: Oxford University Press, 57–87.

Holvoet N, Inberg L (2015): Gender mainstreaming in sector budget support. The case of the European Commission's sector support to Rwanda's agriculture sector, *Journal of International Women's Studies* **16** (2), 155–169.

Hulse, H (2017): Be free? The European Union's post-Arab Spring women's empowerment as neoliberal governmentality, *Journal of International Relations and Development* **22** (1), 136–158.

Kantola J (2010): *Gender and the European Union*, Basingstoke, New York: Palgrave Macmillan.

Lightfoot S, Szent Iványi B (2014): Reluctant donors? The Europeanization of international development policies in the new member states, *Journal of Common Market Studies* **52** (6), 1257–1272.

Lister M, Carbone M (2006): *New Pathways in International Development. Gender and Civil Society in EU Policy*, Aldershot: Ashgate.

Kunz R, Maisenbacher J (2017): Women in the neighbourhood: reinstating the European Union's civilising mission on the back of gender equality promotion?, *European Journal of International Relations* **23** (1), 122–144.

Manners I (2002): Normative power Europe: a contradiction in terms?, *Journal of Common Market Studies*, **40** (2), 235–258.

Moser C (1993): *Gender Planning and Development: Theory, Practice and Training*, London: Routledge.

O'Connell H (2015): *The European Union's new Gender Action Plan 2016–2020 Gender Equality and Women's Empowerment in External Relations*, London: Overseas Development Institute.

Orbie J (2006): Gender in the Euro-Mediterranean Partnership, in: Lister M, Carbone M (eds.): *New Pathways in International Development. Gender and Civil Society in EU Policy*, Aldershot: Ashgate, 59–73.

Orbie J, Carbone M (2016): The Europeanisation of development policy, *European Politics and Society* **17** (1), 1–11.

Orbie J, Bossuyt F, Debusscher P, Delputte S, Delbiondo K, Reynaert V, Verschaeve J (2017): The normative distinctiveness of the European Union in international development. Stepping out of the shadow of the World Bank?, *Development Policy Review* **35** (4), 493–511.

Pető A, Manners I (2006): The EU and the Value of Gender Equality, in: Lucarelli, Manners I (eds.): *Values and Principles in EU Foreign Policy*, London: Routledge, 97–113.

Razavi S, Miller C (1995): From WID to GAD Conceptual Shifts in the Women and Development Discourse, *UNRISD Occasional Paper* **1**, URL: www.unrisd.org/80256B3C005BCCF9/(httpPublications)/D9C3F CA78D3DB32E80256B67005B6AB5 (accessed May 13, 2020).

Roggeband C, van der Vleuten A, van Eerdewijk A (2020): Feminist Engagement with Gender Equality in Regional Governance, in: Engberg-Pedersen L, Fejerskov A, Cold-Ravnkilde S (eds.): *Rethinking Gender Equality in Global Governance*, Cham: Palgrave Macmillan, 71–95.

Saltnes J (2020): A Break from the Past or Business as Usual? EU-ACP Relations at a Crossroad, *GLOBUS Research Paper no.* 10, ARENA Centre for European Studies.

Sobritchea, C (2006): Gender in European Union Development Cooperation Initiatives in Asia, in: Lister M and Carbone M (eds.): *New Pathways in International Development. Gender and Civil Society in EU Policy*, Aldershot: Ashgate, 75–87.

van der Vleuten A, Van Eerdewijk A and Roggeband C (2014): *Gender Equality Norms in Regional Governance. Transnational Dynamics in Europe, South America and Southern Africa*, Basingstoke: Palgrave Macmillan.

van der Vleuten, A (2017): The Merchant and the Message. Hard Conditions, Soft Power and Empty Vessels as Regards Gender in EU External Relations, *ACCESS EUROPE Research Paper* no. 3, URL: https:// ssrn.com/abstract=3057350 (download May 13, 2020).

Verloo M (2007): *Multiple Meanings of Gender Equality. A Critical Frame Analysis of Gender Policies in Europe*, Budapest: Central European University Press.

Whitman R (2011): *Normative Power Europe. Empirical and Theoretical Perspectives*, Basingstoke: Palgrave Macmillan.

24

Gender and EU climate policy

Gill Allwood

Climate change emerged as a policy issue in the 1980s and gradually gained prominence on the EU's policy agenda. The new Commission president, Ursula von der Leyen, has declared climate policy to be one of her six top priorities. Shortly after taking office in December 2019, she presented her 'European Green Deal' promising that Europe would become the first climate-neutral continent by 2050. This commitment reflects a long-term development, but also the prominence that climate change has gained in the last two years – often called the Greta Thunberg effect – and its impact, for example, on the 2019 European Parliament elections. Alongside the European Green Deal, von der Leyen promised a 'Union of Equality', with the appointment of the first ever Commissioner for Equality, a statement of commitment to diversity and intersectionality, and a revised Gender Equality Strategy, presented within her first 100 days in office.

This chapter focuses on the relation between the EU's climate action and its gender equality agenda. It argues that there is potential for this traditionally gender-blind area of EU policy-making to become more gender-just. Whereas formerly climate change policy was concerned almost exclusively with seeking technological solutions, since 2018 there have been slight but encouraging signs of change. References to 'people' have begun to seep into EU climate policy documents, opening up the possibility for gender equality to be included. A statement of commitment to gender equality is regularly tagged onto Council climate change documents. Although this is not the same as mainstreaming gender throughout all climate policy, neither is it meaningless. However, climate change and gender equality risk remaining separate and parallel, unless there is strong political will to see them mutually integrated. This requires concerted effort throughout all EU institutions and on the part of those responsible for important related policy areas, such as trade, energy and transport.

EU climate policy

Climate change as a policy issue is closely related to energy, which has always been at the heart of the EU's policy remit. Energy use makes a major contribution to greenhouse gas emissions, and strategies for addressing climate change include improving energy efficiency and reducing reliance on fossil fuels. Climate change is also closely related to environmental policy, which arrived on the EU's agenda in the 1960s with the recognition that environmental issues do not respect national borders. EU competence in this policy area has grown with successive treaty changes. The Single European Act (1987) put environmental policy on a legal footing; the Treaty of Amsterdam introduced sustainable development into the Community's objectives; and the Lisbon Treaty included the objective of promoting measures on an international scale to address regional or global environmental problems, in particular the fight against climate change.

EU climate policy has three main components: mitigation, adaptation and climate diplomacy. Mitigation refers to strategies for reducing climate change, largely through the reduction of greenhouse gas emissions. Adaptation refers to strategies for adapting to the effects of climate change, such as increased flooding, droughts and unpredictable weather patterns. Climate diplomacy refers to the EU's role in international climate negotiations and agreements, an area in which it has sought to assert leadership. However, financial, economic and political crises from 2008 slowed internal climate policy, and internal opposition to strong climate action has grown, particularly from central and eastern European member states, including Poland (Dupont and Oberthür 2015, 229). While initially the EU's ambitions exceeded its own internal practice, since the mid-2000s it has tried to 'lead by example'. The EU, along with its member states, is a party to the United Nations Framework Convention on Climate Change (UNFCCC) and plays a key role in trying to reach agreements on global targets. The EU was an influential player in the 2015 Paris Agreement, the first universal, legally binding climate agreement, and continues to try to push global targets upwards.

Key policy frameworks are the Climate and Energy Package for the period 2020–2030 (COM(2014) 15 final), which sets out targets for greenhouse gas emissions reductions, renewable energy and energy efficiency; and the Environmental Action Programme, which provides an overarching framework for all environmental and climate policy and is due to be updated in early 2020. The European Green Deal sets out a strategy for achieving net-zero greenhouse gas emissions by 2050 while sustaining economic growth. The first 'climate laws' will be proposed in early 2020, enshrining in legislation the objective of climate neutrality by 2050.

Since 2013, internal EU climate policy has also included an adaptation strategy, in recognition that climate change is having an impact within the EU, as well as, more obviously, elsewhere. Adaptation to the effects of climate change arrived on the EU internal policy agenda later than concerns with mitigation. While climate change mitigation was more readily framed as an issue to be dealt with at the EU level, adaptation to the effects of climate change appeared, until recently, to require local responses or to be of concern only in countries most severely hit by the impact of climate change, which are concentrated in the Global South. The floods and heatwaves of the early 2000s raised awareness of the impact of climate change within the EU and of its cross-border nature (Rayner and Jordan 2010). As a consequence, the EU's adaptation strategy was adopted in 2013 (COM(2018) 738 final). Member states are encouraged to produce national adaptation strategies, setting out, for example, how they will climate-proof their transport, energy and agriculture sectors, and protect their populations from flooding, droughts and heatwaves. As part of EU external relations, however, adaptation has a longer history. The visible impact of climate change in developing countries, and the use of development aid for adaptation purposes, mean that climate change has been prominent in EU development policy. A Commission Communication in 2003 (COM(2003) 85 final) declared climate change a development, as well as an environmental problem. This has implications for the study of gender and EU climate policy, as will be demonstrated later. The well-established nature of gender and development within the European Commission and the European Parliament (especially its FEMM Committee on Women's Rights and Gender Equality and the Committee on Development; see Ahrens and Rolandsen Agustín (European Parliament) in this volume) means that adaptation has been the core concern of gender and climate change analyses and policy proposals emanating from these institutions.

Mainstream studies of EU climate policy

In common with scholars of other areas of EU policy and policy-making, those who study EU climate policy want to understand what the EU is and how it works. They have considered how climate change arrived on the EU agenda; how climate policy-making has contributed to EU integration; and what role it plays in establishing the EU as a global actor (Jordan and Rayner 2010; Jordan et al. 2010; Keleman 2010; Oberthür and Roche Kelly 2008; Schreurs and Tiberghien 2007; Wettestad et al. 2012). Reflecting the priorities of EU climate policy, the main focus of the studies has been on climate change mitigation, which refers to strategies for reducing climate change, largely through the reduction of greenhouse gas emissions. They include studies of the Emissions Trading System (ETS), the EU's main instrument for reducing greenhouse gas emissions from industry and the promotion of renewable energy (Hildingsson et al. 2010; Torbjørg and Wettestad 2017; van Asselt 2010). Scholars have traced climate policy from its origins in EU environmental policy, noting the landmark Climate and Energy Package of 2009 and the creation of DG Climate Action within the Commission in 2010. They have analysed the decision-makers, the decision-making process, and the content of the resulting policy. Dupont and Oberthür (2015), for example, argue that, despite the EU's relatively ambitious goals, its climate policies have so far remained inadequate to ensure that it achieves its objective of decarbonising by 2050. They, and others, have noted the impact of the economic crisis and growing internal opposition to strong climate action, particularly from central and eastern European member states. Studies have shown that member states are divided over the economic costs of mitigation and adaptation versus the opportunities of green growth, and disagree about whether emissions reduction targets should be increased (Skovgaard 2014). An institutional focus has suggested that the shift of climate decision-making towards the Council (see Abels in this volume) has given more weight to climate laggards, such as Poland, and has reduced the influence of the European Parliament, which has traditionally been the greenest of the EU institutions. Dupont (2019, 2) argues that the European Council has played an unusually active role in climate policy, demonstrating member states' desire to retain control in this area of decision-making.

Drawing on Bretherton and Vogler's (2006) work on EU actorness, mainstream scholars of EU climate policy have sought to explain why the EU globalised its environmental policy and became a global leader in climate policy. They analyse the EU as a global climate power and examine its ability to influence international negotiations through climate diplomacy (Biedenkopf and Dupont 2013; Oberthür and Groen 2018). The study of EU climate policy is situated within a broader study of climate governance, characterised by the move from governments to a heterogenous collection of actors and complex layers of rule-making and implementation. The theorisation of international climate cooperation has become less state-centric and has extended beyond the international climate regime. Different theoretical stances drawn from International Relations lead to different analyses of responses to climate change at a global level, for example, whether competing costs and benefits will prevent effective international cooperation, and whether diplomatic efforts will succeed in achieving a global response (Bäckstrand and Lövbrand 2015, xix). The framing of climate change in the EU's Global Strategy as a threat multiplier and a root cause of conflict marks a shift from an environmental and development issue to a core strategic challenge. Youngs (2014) explores the construction of climate change as a foreign and security issue, and its relation, in this context, with migration policy.

It has long been argued by activists and researchers that environmental policy cannot be effective if it remains isolated from other policy areas. Instead, they argue, it needs to be fully integrated into policies that have an impact on the environment, such as energy, transport and agriculture. The same argument has been applied to climate policy, and a commitment to climate policy integration or climate mainstreaming appears in EU policy documents (Dupont 2016). Scholars have examined the extent to which this integration takes place, both in terms of process and outcome, as well as the factors that affect its success or failure (Adelle and Russel 2013; Dupont and Oberthür 2012). De Roeck, Orbie and Delputte (2018) investigate how climate change is mainstreamed into EU development cooperation and Dupont and Oberthür (2012) explore how climate is mainstreamed into EU energy policy.

Gender and climate change

The effects of climate change are not the same for everyone. Existing inequalities affect the impact of climate change and the ability to respond to it. Measures introduced to reduce climate change or to adapt to it also have different effects on people, according to their gender, class, wealth, ethnicity, physical ability and other structural inequalities. There are gender differences in the production of climate change, in attitudes towards it, and in access to climate decision-making.

A substantial feminist literature demonstrates the ways in which climate change is a feminist issue, and this acts as an important context in which research on gender and EU climate policy has taken place. The gender and climate change literature has its origins in gender, development and environment activism and research, some of which is informed by a rich tradition of feminist theory. Much of this literature is influenced by the work of activists, international organisations and NGOs, and has a policy and practice focus (MacGregor 2010, 126). The close relations between academia and activism in the area of gender and development mean that research from both has had an impact on the field, and on policy-making and policy studies related to EU gender, development and climate change. This literature has concentrated on three main areas: the vulnerability to climate change of rural women in the Global South; women's ability to adapt to the effects of climate change; and the under-representation of women and gender in climate decision-making.

Scholarly research on gender and climate change has highlighted the need to move beyond a focus on the impact of climate change on women and instead to explore gendered power relations in climate change adaptation and mitigation. Rather than focusing on women's innate vulnerability, they have drawn attention to the gendered power relations that produce this vulnerability. For example, Alston argues that

> gender inequalities make change more difficult for women because of uneven power relations, lack of resource control and low levels of institutional support. Women's increased vulnerability to climate events is therefore very much shaped by pre-existing inequitable gender relations and gender blind policies and practices.
>
> *(Alston 2013, 352)*

She states that responses to climate change must recognise pre-existing social structures and inequalities, rather than assuming that they do not exist. Some scholars have focused on masculinity (see Hearn et al. in this volume) and some have taken an intersectional approach (see Solanke in this volume), highlighting the many inequalities that come together to influence vulnerability, responsibility and adaptability to climate change. They challenge the focus on women as a homogenous category and the equation of gender with women.

Equating gender with women risks ignoring women's agency; ignoring differences between women; ignoring change, social struggle and contestation; and diverting attention from gendered power relations. (Kaijser and Kronsell 2014, 421; Kronsell 2015, 75–76; Resurrección 2013, 41). Researchers call for attention to be paid to the gendered construction of the problem of climate change and proposed solutions to it; the gendered nature of institutions that respond to climate change; and the role of dominant group identities and cultures in climate decision-making. For example, Nagel (2012) stresses the importance of understanding the role and attitudes of men in responses to climate change. She states that 'the policies that shape local, national and international responses to climate change reflect the gendered power, privilege and preoccupations of mostly male policy-makers around the world' (Nagel 2012, 470). Including men means asking questions about historically-derived normative structures that privilege masculinities and influence decisions on climate issues. Ignoring men means ignoring, for example, the links between the fossil fuel economy and masculine elites (Kronsell 2015, 80–81).

A handful of scholars have taken an intersectional approach to understanding the impact of climate change and responses to it (Kaijser and Kronsell 2014; MacGregor 2014; Nagel 2012; Sultana 2014; Tschakert and Machado 2012). Intersectionality can help us understand individual and group-based differences in relation to climate change. Rather than designating women as vulnerable victims of climate change, an intersectional approach demonstrates that social structures based on characteristics such as gender, socio-economic status, ethnicity, nationality, health, sexual orientation, age and place influence the responsibility, vulnerability and decision-making power of individuals and groups. The impact of climate change, and responses to it, 'may reinforce or challenge such structures and categorisations' (Kaijser and Kronsell 2014, 420). Focusing on gender is useful, but does not give us a full picture. We need to consider how gender intersects with other axes of power. For example, Kronsell's (2013) study of Sweden shows that there are gendered differences in energy consumption and transportation. She argues, however, that it is important to recognise that gender is not the only relevant factor. She states that class sometimes matters more than gender and that there are considerable differences within the Global North and within the Global South. An intersectional analysis asks which social categories are included in, and excluded from, the cases in question, what assumptions are made about social categories, and what type of knowledge is privileged (Kaijser and Kronsell 2014, 422).

Gender and climate change in EU policy

Feminist EU climate policy literature is influenced by feminist theory; intersectionality; gender, environment and development activism and research; mainstream EU climate policy analysis; and the mainstream climate governance literature. It is open, interdisciplinary and innovative. It is, however, currently very small. This is partly because EU climate policy is relatively new and has had a scientific and technological focus. The only area in which gender has been included in EU climate policy is in relation to international development. Internal climate policy, which largely focuses on mitigation, is gender blind. Feminist policy scholars have not yet paid much attention to the related areas of EU energy or transport policy, although they have highlighted their importance. Key contributions to the feminist EU climate change literature are Magnusdottir and Kronsell (2016) and Allwood (2014). Magnusdottir and Kronsell build on their work on gender and climate change in Scandinavia (Kronsell 2013; Kronsell et al. 2016; Magnusdottir and Kronsell 2015) and on Kronsell's extensive publications on feminist and International Relations theory and on EU policy (Kronsell 2016a, 2016b). Allwood's research forms part of her work on EU external policy, which focuses on the relations between development, migration and climate

Gender and EU climate policy

change (Allwood 2013, 2014, 2015). Magnusdottir and Kronsell (2016) focus on women and men's presence in EU climate policy-making in the Commission; the institutional environment in which EU climate policy is formulated; and its policy outcomes. Allwood (2014, 2020b) focuses on the way in which gender and climate change are mainstreamed (or not) into EU development policy (see Debusscher in this volume), arguing that this takes place in two parallel processes, leaving climate policy gender blind. She finds that the construction of climate change as a problem which can be solved with market, technological and security solutions excludes a people-centred approach, which could favour gender-sensitive policy.

Allwood (2014, 2020b) and Magnusdottir and Kronsell (2016) find that EU climate documents pay little attention to gender, despite the EU's gender mainstreaming obligations and despite the requirement for impact assessments to be conducted and to include an assessment of the gender impact of proposed policies. They have attributed this to the way in which climate change is framed as a technical and security problem, to the deeply engrained masculinity of the policy-making environment, and to the shift of decision-making power from more environmentally aware and gender-sensitive institutions (especially the European Parliament) to the Council, which articulates a gender-sensitive approach to climate change only on the rare occasions when a Danish or Swedish presidency is able to exert influence.

Both articles take a feminist institutionalist approach (see MacRae and Weiner in this volume). Magnusdottir and Kronsell (2016) focus on the European Commission, whereas Allwood also takes into account the European Parliament and the Council. Allwood (2014, 11; 2020b, 6) shows that the European Parliament has been more active in addressing climate change from a gender perspective, but that inter-institutional power relations mean that European Parliament resolutions have had little impact. The European Parliament's FEMM Committee has been a key actor, working with civil society organisations. However, powerful institutional actors are able to ignore the gender agenda and gender mainstreaming obligations. Underlying norms and values which are at the core of the EU, including competitiveness and the free market, take precedence, and gender appears to be a luxury which, at best, is added onto already formulated policies. Adaptation policies have, until recently, been targeted at countries in the Global South, which have been worse affected by the consequences of climate change. Adaptation has therefore featured more prominently in EU development policy than in internal climate policy. However, EU trade, energy and transport interests have been shown to override development objectives in relations with third countries (Allwood 2014, 14).

Magnusdottir and Kronsell (2016, 66) show that focusing on a homogenous category of women in research and policy practice is misguided: 'Well-educated, female climate experts most likely have less in common with low-income working class women across Europe than with their male colleagues at the Commission and this applies to their climate impact as well as climate vulnerability.' They studied the presence of women in the Commission Directorates-General (DGs) responsible for climate change, energy, mobility and transport, and the environment. They also studied the policy documents produced by these departments. They found no difference in the content of policies produced by DG CLIMA (which has a critical female mass) and the others (which do not). They argue that gender is invisible in these areas of the Commission because of decisions which have been made before. The Commission is a masculine institutional environment which constrains the space for gender mainstreaming and the development of gender-sensitive institutional norms and practices (see Hartlapp et al. in this volume). Masculinity is read as normality and gender refers to women. Masculine norms and powers are so deeply engrained in the climate institutions that 'policy-makers, *regardless of their sex*, accept and adapt their views to the masculinised institutional environment in which EU climate policies are formulated' (Magnusdottir and Kronsell 2016, 73).

307

Outside academia, research on gender and EU climate policies has been conducted by think tanks, such as the Heinrich Böll Stiftung (2017), the EU's Institute for Gender Equality (EIGE 2012, 2016; see Jacquot and Krizsán in this volume), and the FEMM Committee (see European Parliament Resolutions (2011/2197(INI) and 2017/2086(INI)).

The first report by EIGE (2012) on gender and climate change was commissioned by the Danish Council presidency in 2012. It had a heavy focus on the number of women in climate decision-making and was designed to develop indicators to monitor progress towards achieving the first of the three objectives under women and the environment in the Beijing Platform for Action, i.e. 'involve women actively in environmental decision-making at all levels'. Scholars and activists have pointed out that women's presence in climate decision-making is poor, and some have called for this to be rectified (Women's Environment and Development Organisation (WEDO) 2018). Some studies have found that women in climate decision-making make a difference. For example, a global quantitative comparative study showed that countries with a higher proportion of women in parliament are more likely to ratify environmental treaties. Another study showed that carbon emissions are lower in countries where women have higher political status (Kronsell 2015, 77). These findings would support the argument that women should be included in climate decision-making because they bring different perspectives, knowledge and experience, which would lead to different policy outputs.

However, not all agree that there is a direct positive correlation between the presence of women in climate decision-making and gender-sensitive policy outputs. Magnusdottir and Kronsell (2016) find that a critical mass of women does not automatically result in gender-sensitive climate policy-making. Their study finds that, even in the most gender-sensitive European countries, gender differences in material conditions and in attitudes towards climate issues were completely invisible and excluded from climate policy texts. Policy-makers were largely unaware of the relevance of gender differences and how to consider them in relation to climate policy-making, despite the gender balance of the institutions where climate policy is made (Kronsell 2015, 77). In an earlier publication, Kronsell (2013, 12) argues that 'gender sensitivity will not come about simply through the inclusion of women in policy-making [...] For equal representation to add substantial input, it requires the input from those actors who are knowledgeable about gender aspects on climate issues'. This is not to say that women and men should not be equally represented in all sites of decision-making, but this would be on grounds of equality and justice, rather than substantive policy change.

The second EIGE report (2016) is very different from the first, taking a broader view of the relation between gender and climate change. It highlights the under-representation of women in climate decision-making and gender differences in adaptation and mitigation. In contrast to EIGE (2012), which was very much about women and climate change, EIGE states:

> This is not just a question of women's vulnerability and the fact that they generally hold less power and are, therefore, less able to mitigate and cope with climate change. It is also a question of understanding how women and men relate to one another and how these relationships influence the ways that households, communities, countries and the global community are affected by, and respond to, climate change.
>
> *(EIGE 2016, 6)*

It states that mitigation strategies need to address women and men's energy needs and uses; and the incorporation of traditional knowledge and practices into mitigation strategies (EIGE 2016, 7).

The European Parliament Resolution (2017/2086(INI)) on women, gender equality and climate justice focuses largely on women and on adaptation to climate change in the Global South. It argues that climate change has a more destructive impact on the countries and communities least responsible for global warming and that those with fewer financial resources will be the hardest hit and the least able to adapt. It emphasises women's vulnerability to climate change and their exclusion from climate decision-making. It calls for their inclusion in order to meet commitments under international conventions and on the grounds that involving women and using their knowledge will make adaptation and mitigation measures more effective. It argues that women are the most severely affected by climate-induced disasters and displacement and that it is important to implement 'a rapid, inclusive and gender-responsive development agenda focused on mitigation and adapting to changing climate conditions' (2017/2086(INI), 7).

In contrast to the 2018 resolution's emphasis on women and adaptation in the Global South, and despite its title, the earlier European Parliament Resolution of 20 April 2012 (2011/2197(INI)) presents a sophisticated gender analysis of the issue, incorporating both adaptation and mitigation. Based on a report by the French Green MEP, Nicole Kiil-Nielsen, this resolution does not equate gender with women, nor does it focus exclusively on adaptation or on the Global South. It takes an intersectional approach, stating that 'sources of discrimination and vulnerability other than gender (such as poverty, geography, traditional and institutional discrimination, race, etc.), all combine to obstruct access to resources and to means to cope with dramatic changes such as climate change' (2011/2197(INI), 4). It argues that climate change will amplify inequalities, including gender inequality and that 'there will not be any climate justice without true gender equality'. Due to gendered roles, women's impact on the environment is not the same as men's, and women's access to resources and their ability to adapt is severely affected by discrimination. As well as addressing adaptation, there is a section on mitigation, which calls for research on the gender dimension of mitigation policies; for the green economy to be opened up to both women and men, and for women as well as men to pursue careers in the environment and energy and technology sectors; for gender impact assessments of projects and programmes and the promotion of gender budgeting in climate-related policies; and for gender analysis of mitigation policies and related research programmes (2011/2197(INI), 15). The resolution does not call simply for the numerical presence of women in climate decision-making, but for the inclusion at all levels of decision-making of 'gender equality and gender justice objectives in policies, action plans and other measures', systematic gender analyses, and the inclusion of gender equality principles at all stages of climate change negotiation. In all of these respects, it stands out from other EU policy documents, including the European Parliament Resolution of 2018 (2017/2086(INI)). This can be attributed to Kiil-Nielsen's report on which it was based and that demonstrates that the relation between gender and climate change extends far beyond the impact of climate change on women and the number of women in climate decision-making.

These reports produced by EIGE and the FEMM Committee appear to be having limited influence on mainstream climate policy. Since 2018, there has been a very gradual appearance of references to 'people' creeping into EU climate policy documents. There is some recognition of young citizens, activists and consumers as climate actors. For example, the Council Conclusions 12795/19 of 4 October 2019 on the 8th Environmental Action Programme stress the need to involve civil society, including young people, the private sector and academia, in active dialogue both before the 8th Environmental Action Programme is adopted and throughout its lifespan. Council Conclusions on external climate action tend to contain a standard statement of commitment to gender equality. For example, the Council Conclusions 6153/19 on Climate Diplomacy of 18 February 2019 state: 'The EU will continue to uphold, promote and protect human rights, gender equality and women's empowerment in the context of climate action.'

The next challenge is seeing this translated into action across all decision-making that intersects with climate change, and this requires strong political will and policy coherence (Allwood 2020a, b).

Conclusion

With a few exceptions, EU climate policy has remained gender blind. The construction of climate change as a problem that can be solved with market, technological and security solutions has, until recently, excluded a people-centred approach, which could favour gender-sensitive policy. There are signs that this is very slowly beginning to change. The good news is:

> EU climate policy is edging away from an exclusive focus on technological solutions towards a recognition that climate change affects people, and that people are part of the solution. However, integrating diversity and intersectionality into the analysis of climate change and proposed responses to it is still a marginal concern.
>
> *(Allwood 2020, 10)*

Efforts to address gender inequality and efforts to address climate change continue to exist in parallel, rather than being fully integrated into each other. Gender equality is not integrated into all aspects of decision-making and at all stages. Instead, it is tagged on or addressed in separate documents and debates.

A 'European Green Deal' and 'A Union of Equality' are headline ambitions set out in von der Leyen's Political Guidelines for the European Commission 2019–2024. The first ever Commissioner for Equality, Helena Dalli, launched a new Gender Equality Strategy 2020–2025 in March 2020. It is based on the dual approach of targeted measures to achieve gender equality, combined with strengthened gender mainstreaming. It emphasises that 'the inclusion of a gender perspective in all EU policies and processes is essential to reach the goal of gender equality'. However, the Strategy mentions climate change only in relation to international partnership, especially with African countries. Achieving a comprehensive approach requires strong political will on the part of all those responsible for climate policy, but also throughout all related policy areas, including trade, transport and energy. The Council Conclusions 6153/19 on Climate Diplomacy describe 2019 as the year of pushing further convergence between the Sustainable Development Goals and climate agendas. A successful integration of these two agendas would make a substantial contribution to a gender- and climate-just future, but again, this requires strong political will and effective policy coherence.

The mainstream literature on EU climate policy has a strong focus on climate change mitigation and climate diplomacy. The gender and climate change literature is strongly influenced by gender, environment and development activism and research, and focuses on women's vulnerability to the impact of climate change; their role in adaptation; and the under-representation of women and gender in climate decision-making. Feminist scholars add a concern with masculinity, gendered power relations and intersectionality. There has been less feminist engagement with EU mitigation strategies, although institutionalist studies of the decision-makers, analyses of problem-framing, and the study of the policy-making process make important contributions. For example, they find that impact assessments are not always done and, when they are, they rarely include gender.

Future research directions in the area of gender and EU climate policy include a much more detailed focus on EU mitigation measures, building on the work that has already been done in

Scandinavian countries (Magnusdottir and Kronsell 2015) and investigating the links between climate policy and energy, transport and other related policy areas, such as trade. Transport, for example, is a major source of greenhouse gas emissions in the EU, and research elsewhere has demonstrated that it is highly gendered. Research could productively explore the links between big business and EU climate and energy policy, and ask whose voices are included and excluded in climate policy-making. Social movement studies of climate activism could also be applied to the EU, exploring the links between civil society and institutional decision-making (see Siim and Mokre in this volume). Bridging the gap between EU internal and external climate policy, the UN Sustainable Development Goals act as a focus for measuring the success of current approaches and designing new ones. With gender and climate change both running throughout all of the Sustainable Development Goals, this is a highly topical area for researchers to explore how such crosscutting issues can be successfully integrated into EU strategies. In terms of EU external action, there is still much to be understood about the relation between the EU's commitment to gender equality and its engagement in international climate diplomacy. Finally, as migration rises yet further up the EU's policy agenda, the relation between gender and the displacement of people as a result of climate change requires critical analysis by feminist scholars.

References

Adelle C, Russel D (2013): Climate policy integration: a case of déjà vu?, *Environmental Policy and Governance* **23** (1), 1–12.

Allwood G (2013): Gender mainstreaming and Policy coherence for development. unintended gender consequences and EU policy, *Women's Studies International Forum* **39**, 42–52.

Allwood G (2014): Gender mainstreaming and EU climate change policy, *European Integration online Papers (EIoP)* **18**, Special issue 1, 1–26, URL: http://eiop.or.at/eiop/texte/2014-006a.htm.

Allwood G (2015): Horizontal policy coordination and gender mainstreaming. The case of the European Union's global approach to migration and mobility, *Women's Studies International Forum* **48**, 9–17.

Allwood G (2020a): Gender equality in European Union development policy in times of crisis, *Political Studies Review* 18 (2), 329–345.

Allwood G (2020b): Mainstreaming gender and climate change to achieve a just transition to a climate-neutral Europe, *Journal of Common Market Studies, Annual Review*, 1–14, DOI: 10.1111/jcms.13082.

Alston M (2013): Women and adaptation, *Wiley Interdisciplinary Reviews. Climate Change* **4** (5), 351–358.

Bäckstrand K, Lövbrand E (2015): Climate Governance after Copenhagen: Research Trends and Policy Practice, in: Bäckstrand K, Lövbrand E (eds.): *Research Handbook on Climate Governance*, Cheltenham: Edward Elgar, xvii–xxx.

Biedenkopf K, Dupont C (2013): A Toolbox Approach to the EU's External Climate Governance, in: Boening A, Kremer J-F, van Loon A (eds.): *Global Power Europe Volume 1*, Berlin: Springer-Verlag, 181–199.

Bretherton C, Vogler J (2006): *The European Union as a Global Actor*, 2nd ed., London, New York: Routledge.

De Roeck F, Orbie J, Delputte S (2018): Mainstreaming climate change adaptation into the European Union's development assistance, *Environmental Science and Policy* **81**, 36–45.

Dupont C (2016): *Climate Policy Integration into EU Energy Policy. Progress and Prospects*, London, New York: Routledge.

Dupont C (2019): The EU's collective securitisation of climate change, *West European Politics* **42** (2), 369–390.

Dupont C, Oberthür S (2012): Insufficient climate policy integration in EU energy policy: the importance of the long-term perspective, *Journal of Contemporary European Research* **8** (2), 228–247.

Dupont C, Oberthür S (2015): The European Union, in: Bäckstrand K and Lövbrand E (eds.): *Research Handbook on Climate Governance*, Cheltenham: Edward Elgar, 224–236.

EIGE (2012): *Review of the Implementation in the EU of Area K of the Beijing Platform for Action. Women and the Environment Gender Equality and Climate Change*, Luxembourg: Publications Office of the European Union.

EIGE (2016): *Gender in Environment and Climate Change*, Luxembourg: Publications Office of the European Union.

Heinrich Böll Stiftung (2017): *The Road from Paris to Sustainable Development. Effectively Integrating Human Rights and Gender Equality into Climate Actions of EU Institutions*, Brussels: Heinrich Böll Stiftung.

Hildingsson R, Stripple J, Jordan A (2010): Renewable Energies: A Continuing Balancing Act?, in: Jordan A, Huitema D, van Asselt H, Rayner T, Berkhout F (eds.): *Climate Change Policy in the European Union*, Cambridge: Cambridge University Press, 103–124.

Jordan A, Rayner T (2010): The Evolution of Climate Policy in the European Union: An Historical Overview, in: Jordan A, Huitema D, van Asselt H, Rayner T, Berkhout F (eds.): *Climate Change Policy in the European Union*, Cambridge: Cambridge University Press, 52–80.

Jordan A, Huitema D, van Asselt H, Rayner T, Berkhout F (2010): *Climate Change Policy in the European Union*, Cambridge: Cambridge University Press.

Kaijser A, Kronsell A (2014): Climate change through the lens of intersectionality, *Environmental Politics* **23** (3), 417–433.

Keleman RD (2010): Globalising European Union environmental policy, *Journal of European Public Policy* **17** (3), 335–349.

Kronsell A (2013): Gender and transition in climate governance, *Environmental Innovation and Societal Transitions* **7**, 1–15.

Kronsell A (2015): Feminism, in: Bäckstrand K and Lövbrand E (eds.): *Research Handbook on Climate Governance*, Cheltenham: Edward Elgar, 73–83.

Kronsell A (2016a): Sexed bodies and military masculinities: gender path dependence in EU's common security and defense policy, *Men and Masculinities* **19** (3), 311–336.

Kronsell A (2016b): The power of EU masculinities: a feminist contribution to European integration theory, *Journal of Common Market Studies* **54** (1), 104–120.

Kronsell A, Rosqvist LS, Hiselius LW (2016): Achieving climate objectives in transport policy by including women and challenging gender norms: the Swedish case, *International Journal of Sustainable Transportation* **10** (8), 703–711.

MacGregor S (2010): A stranger silence still: the need for feminist social research on climate change, *Sociological Review* **57**, 124–140.

MacGregor S (2014): Only resist: feminist ecological citizenship and the post-politics of climate change, *Hypatia* **29** (3), 617–633.

Magnusdottir GL, Kronsell A (2015): The (in)visibility of gender in Scandinavian climate policy-making, *International Feminist Journal of Politics* **17** (2), 308–326.

Magnusdottir GL, Kronsell A (2016): The double democratic deficit in climate policy-making by the EU Commission, *Femina Politica* **25** (2), 64–76.

Nagel J (2012): Intersecting identities and global climate change, *Identities* **19** (4), 467–476.

Oberthür S, Groen L (2018): Explaining goal achievement in international negotiations. The EU and the Paris Agreement on Climate Change, *Journal of European Public Policy* **25** (5), 708–727.

Oberthür S, Roche Kelly C (2008): EU Leadership in international climate policy: acheivements and challenges, *The International Spectator* **43** (3), 35–50.

Rayner T, Jordan A (2010): Adapting to a Changing Climate: An Emerging EU Policy?, in: Jordan A, Huitema D, van Asselt H, Rayner T, Berkhout F (eds.): *Climate Change Policy in the European Union*, Cambridge: Cambridge University Press, 145–166.

Resurrección BP (2013): Persistent women and environment linkages in climate change and sustainable development agendas, *Women's Studies International Forum* **40**, 33–43.

Schreurs MA, Tiberghien Y (2007): Multi-level reinforcement: explaining European Union leadership in climate change mitigation, *Global Environmental Politics* **7** (4), 19–46.

Skovgaard J (2014): EU climate policy after the crisis, *Environmental Politics* **23** (1), 1–17.

Sultana F (2014): Gendering climate change: geographical insights, *The Professional Geographer* **66** (3), 372–381.

Torbjørg J, Wettestad J (2017): EU Emissions Trading: Frontrunner–and 'Black Sheep'?, in: Wettestad J, Gulbrandsen LH (eds.): *The Evolution of Carbon Markets*, London, New York: Routledge, 42–64.

Tschakert P, Machado M (2012): Gender justice and rights in climate change adaptation: opportunities and pitfalls, *Ethics and Social Welfare* **6** (3), 275–289.

van Asselt H (2010): Emissions trading. The enthusiastic adoption of an 'alien' instrument?, in: Jordan A, Huitema D, van Asselt H, Rayner T, Berkhout F (eds.): *Climate Change Policy in the European Union*, Cambridge: Cambridge University Press, 125–44.

Wettestad J, Eikeland PO, Nilsson M (2012): EU climate and energy policy: a hesitant supranational turn? *Global Environmental Politics* **12** (2), 67–86.

Women's Environment and Development Organisation (WEDO) (2018): *Pocket Guide to Gender Equality under the UNFCCC*, Brussels: European Capacity Building Initiative.

Youngs R (2014): *Climate Change and EU Security Policy: An Unmet Challenge*, Brussels: Carnegie Europe.

25

Research policy

Marcela Linková and Lut Mergaert

Research and technological development policy (RTD) has been part of the European Community remit since its foundation in 1957. Whereas the 1986 Single European Act already put more emphasis on research and development (R&D), it was not until the 1997 Amsterdam Treaty that conducting research policy and implementing Framework Programmes (FP)[1] to support European research through funding were explicitly integrated in the EU mandate. Implemented by the European Commission's Directorate-General for Research and Innovation (DG RTD; now renamed Innovation, Research, Culture, Education and Youth), the FPs operationalise this policy, with budget allocations steadily increasing since their launch in 1984. While FP1 (1984–1988) had a budget of 3.8 billion euro, that of the current FP, Horizon 2020, (2014–2020) amounts to 77 billion euro. The proposed budget for the next FP, Horizon Europe, is 94.1 billion euro, though an important #EUInvestInKnowledge call has been published in July 2019 to increase it to at least 120 billion euro. Importantly, DG RTD has not been doing gender budgeting, failing to implement the 2017 recommendations of the European Parliament (IPOL_STU(2019)621801). Furthermore, only a tiny portion of the budget is allocated specifically to projects advancing gender equality in research.

For most of its early history, European research policy was gender blind, with no attention paid to how research affects the lives of women and men or to what extent women contribute to research. Once gender issues garnered political attention worldwide in the 1990s, DG RTD picked up the topic in 1999, with the Communication on 'Women in science: Mobilising women to enrich European research' (COM(1999) 76 final) and the establishment of the Commission's advisory group Helsinki Group on Women and Science (HG, later Gender and Science, 1999–2017).[2] Since then, there has been fluctuation in how gender equality in European research is addressed and in the instruments used to promote it. The policy for gender equality in European research moves unevenly, not along a linear line of increasingly complex and comprehensive solutions based on a growing volume of studies and increasing understanding of what is at stake. Rather, the advancement of gender equality in research and innovation comes with considerable struggles and seems under constant threat of backsliding.

This chapter focuses on EU level policy driven through the political concept of the European Research Area (ERA), launched in 2000 and implemented through FPs and at member state level via the ERA Roadmap National Action Plans and Strategies. While a wide range of actors

314

Research policy

is involved in the policy-making process, the chapter focuses on the Commission's DG RTD and its FPs. The latter act as a crucial structuring and integrating instrument to drive deliberate collaboration among EU member states and their policies and objectives (e.g. large infrastructures; partnerships; and newly for Horizon Europe, the missions, being high-ambition challenges such as climate change or cancer).

This chapter draws on existing scholarship on gender equality in EU RTD, insights gained from the review of grey literature and policy texts as well as the authors' own experience and expertise based on their long-term involvement in policy, expert and advisory roles. It is structured as follows: the next section outlines the history of EU RTD, situating gender equality in it. It charts the fluctuation in support for gender equality and the most recent developments in an evolving gender equality discourse. This is followed by a review of existing research on EU research policy in general and gender equality in EU research policy specifically. It argues that scholarly work on gender in EU RTD is scarce, whereas the bulk of mainstream academic work is gender blind. The last section outlines the topics that emerge as relevant for ensuring a sustainable and effective integration of gender equality in EU RTD and identifies research gaps and suggestions for future research.

Evolution of EU RTD and gender equality in it

This section focuses on the period from FP5 (1998–2002) until the preparations of the next funding programme Horizon Europe (starting 2021), hence covering the 20 years when gender equality has been explicitly addressed in EU research policy. The evolution of policy objectives is discussed with shifts in emphases, which have had clear effects on the instruments supported in individual FPs. A trajectory is followed from 'research by, on and for women' to the 'structural change approach' adopted since 2009. In conclusion, a seemingly disappearing consensus on gender equality at member state level is considered posing challenges to EU policy design and implementation.

From industrial competitiveness to a broader policy framework

Before the institution of FPs in 1984, European RTD tended to be reactive (Andrée 2009, 8) and focused on coordination among member states in a limited number of research areas (coal and steel, agriculture; see HM Government 2014, 13–19; Abels 2012, 188). The peaceful use of nuclear energy had a specific support under the Euratom Treaty of 1957. The Joint Research Centre (JRC), originally established to fund research in this area, expanded its portfolio during the 1970s to renewable energy, informatics, materials and environment (HM Government 2014, 14). Another important area of intervention was space, dating back to the 1970s and part of the FPs since the first one. In 1982, the Council of Ministers (since 1992 Council of the EU) launched ESPRIT as a research and development programme in information and communication technologies, followed by the launch of FP1 in 1984, which focused on agricultural and industrial competitiveness and nuclear energy (HM Government 2014, 14). During the 1980s, EU RTD became more closely aligned with economic development and industrial competitiveness following an economic downturn and the Single Market project (Abels 2012; Sanz Menéndez and Borrás 2000). This focus was reaffirmed in the 1992 Maastricht Treaty on European Union and has remained ever since.

The Amsterdam Treaty, which entered into force in 1999, made policies in the area of research compulsory. The European Commission subsequently launched the ERA in 2000 (COM(2000) 6 final) and reaffirmed it in the 2007 Treaty of Lisbon (in force since 2009) with an objective to

315

Marcela Linková and Lut Mergaert

strengthen Europe's scientific and technological bases where researchers, scientific knowledge and technology circulate freely, with a view to creating a more competitive European industry. Notwithstanding the introduction of Ethical, Legal and Social Aspects (ELSA) in 1994 as part of FP4 (see also Abels 1998, 684), the 2000 ERA Communication was the first major EU research policy initiative where economic objectives were coupled with social ones. The Communication addressed elements such as social issues, citizen involvement and responsibility (Ulnicane 2015). This Communication proclaims a more prominent role for women in research and promotion of social and ethical values in research.

Since then, social aspects have been addressed under the heading of several other policy initiatives. Two important ones have been '3Os – Open Science, Open Innovation and Open to the World' and 'Responsible Research and Innovation' (RRI). First introduced by Commissioner Carlos Moedas in 2015, the 3Os policy was launched to reinforce the existing funding programme Horizon 2020 and reinvigorate the European Research Area policy by bringing the physical and digital together (European Commission 2016). The 3Os policy is gender blind (GENDERACTION 2018). Unlike 3Os, RRI lists gender equality among its six priorities, together with governance, public engagement, open access, ethics and science education (for relations between RRI and Ethical, Legal and Social Aspects (ELSA) in the Human Genome project see Forsberg 2015). RRI is linked to the need to address so-called 'grand challenges' and was a cross-cutting issue in Horizon 2020 (2014–2020). However, the original Commission's vision for RRI did not address gender equality either, although it did mention non-discrimination and social justice among the anchors of EU policy and equality between women and men when addressing the social desirability of product development and design (von Schomberg 2013).

In 2012, under female Commissioner Máire Geoghegan-Quinn, the Commission presented the Communication 'A Reinforced European Research Area Partnership for Excellence and Growth' (COM(2012) 392 final), which defined gender equality and gender mainstreaming in research as one of the ERA priorities and set ambitious goals both for member states and the European Commission. Member states reaffirmed these ERA policy priorities in Council Conclusions (17649/12) of December 11, 2012 on 'A reinforced European research area partnership for excellence and growth' and further in Council Conclusions (14846/15) of December 1, 2015 on 'Advancing Gender Equality in the European Research Area'. These Conclusions set the most ambitious vision for gender equality in European RTD to date. The current approach for ERA is dual: gender equality is an independent, self-standing agenda; concurrently, it is a cross-cutting issue to be mainstreamed in other priorities and policies. The next section charts the evolution towards this comprehensive conceptualisation and considers the most recent developments as the EU negotiates the next framework programme and prepares a substantial revision of the ERA objectives. In autumn 2020 Communication and Council Conclusions on the new ERA were adopted, mentioning gender equality plans as the instrument for advancing gender equality in ERA.

Gender equality in EU research policy: losing the consensus?

Over the past two decades, gender equality and gender mainstreaming in research and innovation have garnered sustained policy attention at EU and member state level (Lipinsky 2014; Marchetti and Raudma 2010; Ruest-Archambault et al. 2008). Gender equality appeared in EU RTD at the end of the 20th century and has been addressed to a greater or lesser extent in each FP since, starting with FP5 in 1998. In 2012, gender equality and gender mainstreaming became one of the ERA priorities. Major steps in the evolution of the gender equality policy are listed in Table 25.1 (see Abels 2012).[3]

Research policy

Table 25.1 Major steps in the evolution of gender equality in RTD, 1993–2020

1993	International workshop 'Women in Science' and proceedings
1998	Commission–Parliament joint conference on 'Women and Science' and proceedings
1999	Commission Communication 'Women and Science. Mobilising Women to Enrich European Research' (COM (1999) 76) published
	Women and Science Sector, later Unit, established in DG RTD
	Council Resolution 'Women and Science' adopted (1999/C 201/01)
	Helsinki Group on Women and Science established
2000	EP resolution on the Communication 'Women and Science' (PE 284.646)
	Commission ETAN report 'Promoting excellence through mainstreaming gender equality'
2001	Commission conference 'Gender and Research'
	Council Conclusions on science and society and on women in science (2001/C 199/01)
	Commission report 'FP5 Gender Impact Assessment Studies'
2002	FP6 establishes link between science policy and gender mainstreaming
	Introduction of Gender Action Plans (GAPs) in FP6 Networks of Excellence and Integrated Projects
	Commission report on 'National Policies on Women and Science in Europe'
2003	Launch of She Figures
	Commission report on 'Women in Industrial Research' (WIR report)
2004	Commission report 'Waste of talents: turning private struggles into a public issue' (Enwise report)
	Commission report 'Gender and excellence in the making'
	Launch of the Gender Monitoring Studies, published later in 2009
2006	European Platform of Women Scientists established
	She Figures 2006
2007	Discontinuation of GAPs in FP7
2008	Commission report 'Benchmarking Policy Measures for Gender Equality in Science'
	European Parliament resolution of May 21, 2008 on women and science (2007/2206(INI))
	Commission report 'Mapping the Maze'
2009	She Figures 2009
	Commission report 'Gender challenge in research funding: Assessing the European national scenes'
	Commission launches structural change projects through gender equality plans
	Commission publication 'Gender in EU-funded Research Toolkit and accompanying training programme'
	Commission report 'FP6 Gender Monitoring Studies'
2012	Commission report 'Structural change in research institutions: Enhancing excellence, gender equality and efficiency in research and innovation'
	Communication from the Commission 'A Reinforced European Research Area Partnership for Excellence and Growth'
	Council Conclusions 'A reinforced European research area partnership for excellence and growth'
2013	Commission report 'Gendered Innovations. How gender analysis contributes to research'
2014	Commission report 'Gender equality policies in public research'
2015	Council Conclusions on 'Advancing Gender Equality in the European Research Area'
	European Parliament resolution 'Women's careers in science and universities, and glass ceiling encountered' (2014/2251(INI)

(continued)

317

Table 25.1 Cont.

2016	European Institute for Gender Equality launches the GEAR tool Member states start adopting national action plans and strategies to implement the ERA Roadmap, including gender equality actions
2017	Discontinuation of the Helsinki Group under the Commission and establishment of the ERAC Standing Working Group on Gender in Research and Innovation (SWG GRI) under the Council
2018	Commission / HG report 'Guidance to facilitate the implementation of targets to promote gender equality in research and innovation' SWG GRI Report on the implementation of Council Conclusions of December 1, 2015 on 'Advancing Gender Equality in the European Research Area' (ST 1213 2018 INIT) SWG GRI policy brief 'Tackling gender bias in research evaluation: Recommendations for action for EU Member States' (ST 1204 2019 INIT)
2019	SWG GRI policy brief on gender and innovation: 'Innovating Innovation' (ST 1210 2019 INIT)
2020	SWG GRI report 'Sexual Harassment in the Research and Higher Education Sector: National Policies and Measures in EU Member States and Associated Countries' (ST 1205 2020 REV 1) and policy brief 'Mobilising to eradicate gender-based violence and sexual harassment: A new impetus for gender equality in the European Research Area' (ST 1206 2020 INIT)

As stated above, the issue of equal opportunities and, with it, the issue of women and science entered the policy space in the EU in the run-up to FP5. While prominence was given to the role of women in research, mainly with the aim to expand the workforce, there was a clear indication that the Commission intended to conceptualise the issue more broadly. In the 1999 Communication on 'Women and Science' (COM (1999) 76) the Commission defined its understanding of promoting equal opportunities as research by, for and on women. Research by women was to address women's workforce participation in research; research for women was to ensure that EU-funded research addresses the needs of both women and men (along the lines of the current attention to the gender dimension in research content) and research on women was to address gender relations specifically, thus bringing into focus the need for specific gender research. Today, 20 years later, EU RTD revolves around three objectives: gender balance in research teams, gender balance in decision-making, and the gender dimension in research. These three objectives are to be achieved through a comprehensive 'structural change approach', which is expected from the Commission, member states, research funding and performing organisations alike. Despite this seeming complexity, the conceptualisation of gender equality has been unwaveringly binary and did not address intersectional inequalities.

The evolution of the RTD policy has not been a steady path of growing evidence-based policy complexity. During the negotiation of FP7 (2007–2013), there was a pushback against gender equality issues. The Commission claimed there was pressure from the research community to eliminate the gender-related requirements as part of 'simplification', although no evidence of this could be found (Mergaert 2012). FP7 thus tended to focus on 'fixing women' with funding allocated to role models through women ambassadors projects or mentoring, especially in its early stages. In the 2010 report 'Stocktaking 10 years of "Women and Science" policy by the European Commission 1999–2009' drafted by Commission staff it is admitted that:

> [S]ome of these actions have been very visible at the political level and can be considered to have had a fair amount of impact. But this does not imply long lasting change. From 2010, the Commission intends to support actions to implement change at a structural level, in the research organisations themselves, rather than among women scientists, meaning that the cultural and structural environment that women scientists face in their everyday work will be modernised and improved.
>
> *(Marchetti and Raudma 2010, 113)*

This fluctuation in support for gender equality actions is related to the presence of 'femocrats' in the Commission and their ability to mobilise internal and external stakeholders (Linková 2011; Linková and Červinková 2011; Mergaert 2012). Commissioners have played a highly important role, with notably two women Commissioners, Edith Cresson and Máire Geoghegan-Quinn, standing out: Cresson introduced the gender equality agenda in FP5, Geoghegan-Quinn reinforced gender equality actions at the end of FP7 and in Horizon 2020.

The structural change approach has been in place since 2009 and has become the dominant approach to advancing gender equality, as evidenced in the already mentioned 2012 and 2015 Council Conclusions and in the support for the implementation of gender equality plans in the work programmes to implement FP7 and Horizon 2020, and as an announced requirement for Horizon Europe applicants. It has contributed to an important shift in the EU's landscape. However, despite the robust policy framework, recent analyses identify a growing gap in the EU, which runs along the EU-13 and EU-15 countries or lower and higher innovators (ST 1213 2018 INIT; Wroblewski 2018). The structural change approach has become a key element in national policy for advancing gender equality in seven EU-15 but only two EU-13 countries, as reported by the ERAC Standing Working Group on Gender in Research and Innovation (ST 1213 2018 INIT, 18). In 2019 and 2020, the structural change approach was reviewed, towards its refashioning in Horizon Europe. Recent policy advice to the Commission and member states calls for taking an intersectional approach when implementing gender equality plans to address other axes of inequality (race and ethnicity, disability, age, LGBT+ etc.), and the involvement of the private business sector as a dominant employer of research staff (see the GENDERACTION 2019 and EU2019.FI 2019).[4]

While the attention for the gender dimension in research has been growing in recent years within the research community and among research funding organisations, it has been present in EU RTD from the very early days, with the two objectives of the initial policy, research for and on women. In its 2001 Staff Working Document, the Commission recognised the importance of the gender dimension in research when it stated: 'Integrating the gender dimension in research requires a deep transformation of research design and also of paradigms and concepts underlying this research design. It touches upon the very nature of science' (SEC(2001) 771, 12). Despite this and despite some Horizon 2020 calls for proposals, which indicate the need to address the gender dimension in research proposals (but, notably, not to include gender experts in the consortium), this requirement continues to be misunderstood by applicants and it is not well evaluated (European Commission 2017, 174). Sanctions are not applied to projects that ignore the requirement, nor do proposing teams have to explain why they do not address the gender dimension in 'flagged up' topics.

Regarding the objective of gender balance, the 40% target was set at the start of the policy. This objective had been almost achieved by the time of the interim evaluation of Horizon 2020, where women make up 53% of members of advisory groups and 36.7% of evaluation panels. Furthermore, women constitute 31% of project coordinators but only 24.5% of European Research Council Principal Investigators. Overall, women's participation has increased since FP7 (European Commission 2017, 173). One major shortcoming in monitoring this objective is that the Commission does not distinguish in Horizon 2020 between scientific and administrative coordinators, increasing the proportion of women as they predominate among the latter. A review is also necessary as to how the legal obligation for gender balance in research teams is implemented by consortia.

A topic that has eluded many of the stakeholders, including the DG RTD, is gender-based violence and harassment. Given the fifth freedom of free movement and stress on academic mobility with the various Marie Curie schemes, there is an urgent need to address this problem in the next FP and at the MS level. The ERAC Standing Working Group on Gender in Research and Innovation published a review of policies in place at national and Research Funding Organisations level, with findings and recommendations delivered in June 2020.

While gender equality will be addressed in Horizon Europe, the preparation and negotiation process underlines the difficulty of maintaining it as a priority as well as ensuring policy learning between cycles. Despite clear recommendations for improvements coming from various stakeholders, including the HG (Helsinki Group on Gender in Research and Innovation 2017) and the Commission's own evaluation (SWD(2017)221/F1), compared to Horizon 2020 the initial proposal for Horizon Europe scaled down gender equality provisions. Major pushback against gender equality was also evident among some member states during Council negotiations. On November 30, 2018, the Council adopted the 'Partial General Approach to Horizon Europe' (15102/18). For the first time in 20 years, this document referred to 'equal opportunities for all' as opposed to gender equality, suggesting that member states no longer align on the concept of gender equality.[5] This is linked to the political developments in several EU countries (including Hungary, Czech Republic, Poland) and the backlash against gender studies and gender research,[6] expressions of which are the ban on gender studies in Hungary and the move of the Central European University from Budapest to Vienna. With the attention given to gender equality by the new Commission President Ursula von der Leyen and the newly appointed female Commissioners (including for the first time a Commissioner with equality as a sole portfolio), the erosion of gender equality seems to have been reversed in the concrete regulations for the implementation of Horizon Europe. Clearly, equality is prominent on the President's as well as the new Commissioner's agenda. In March 2020, the Commission published its new EU Gender Equality Strategy. The most important of the three areas addressing research and innovation is the possibility to require a Gender Equality Plan from Horizon Europe applicants. The other two are an initiative to increase the number of women-led technology start-ups and to make funds available for gender and intersectional research. The concrete implementation of the meanwhile confirmed requirement is under consideration with a view to ensuring that the provision does not exclude research organisations at the start of Horizon Europe while making sure that it does not become a tick-box exercise. The introduction of GEPs as eligibility criterion in Horizon Europe is a key signal of the importance of the agenda for the new Commission and R&I Commissioner.

Critical scholarship about EU research policy

A verification of whether, how and to what extent gender has been addressed in 'mainstream' authors' works leads to the conclusion that EU research policy seems to be a 'masculine' field of interest (predominantly male authors are identified) that focuses on techno-economic topics. The subjects of attention are impact assessment (Luukkonen 1998), EU research as a source of economic growth (Ulnicane 2015), limits of EU R&D funding (Pavitt 1998; Luukkonen 2000), techno-economic impact of EU RTD support at regional level (Clarysse and Muldur 2001), company participation (Luukkonen 2002), approaches to how policy is and can be shaped (Edler

Research policy

and James 2015; Georghiou 2001; Grande and Peschke 1999), network formation (Breschi and Cusmano 2004), evolution of the ERA (Ulnicane 2015) and the future governance of EU research and innovation policy (Kuhlmann 2001), changes in the social contract for European research and legitimisation strategies (Flink and Kaldewey 2018) etc. These topics are addressed in a gender-blind way. There is no reference to gender nor to other social concerns in these works, neither before nor after the European Commission started mainstreaming gender in the FPs. Even a publication that addresses the science and society link mentions the integration of gender studies within the scope of the FPs only in passing (Rodríguez et al. 2013).

It could be argued that much like the mainstream literature and EU research policy fail to address gender concerns, the scholarly work on gender in EU research policy focuses on analysing the specific gender equality provisions but less on the ways in which EU RTD is (or rather is not) gendered. Notably the ERA, the extent to which and how gender equality has been taken up in it, have hardly been addressed, except by Abels (2012).

While in the early days of gender mainstreaming by the European Commission, Pollack and Hafner-Burton (2000) concluded through a comparative analysis of several EU policy domains that the research area was performing quite well, later scholarship has been more critical. Still, only a handful of (female) scholars have studied gender equality in EU research policy (Abels 2012; Cavaghan 2012, 2013, 2017; Linková 2011; Linková and Červinková 2011; Mergaert 2012; Mergaert and Demuynck 2011; Mergaert and Lombardo 2014; Mergaert and Minto 2015). Although they all draw attention to shortcomings in the gender mainstreaming approach, several specific issues are highlighted. Abels (2012) traces the history of gender in EU science and research policy, pointing out the strong emphasis on women's participation in research at the expense of the gender dimension of research content. Looking back at how gender equality was taken up during FP5, considering the comprehensive gender mainstreaming approach under FP6 and pointing out its shrinking in FP7, Mergaert and Demuynck (2011) denounce the variable support for gender equality over time and across framework programmes. Both Linková (2011) and Linková and Červinková (2011) identify a highly non-linear evolution of gender equality policies in research and institutional problems that weaken their implementation. Even within DG RTD, the support for gender equality and gender mainstreaming is not ubiquitous, and the existence of clear resistance has been exposed (Cavaghan 2012, 2013; Linková 2011; Linková and Červinková 2011; Mergaert 2012; Mergaert and Lombardo 2014). Furthermore, several institutional problems have been identified that hinder policy learning over time, thus critically affecting the effectiveness of gender mainstreaming in the research domain, and these can be considered of wider relevance within the European Commission. Among these are the lack of effective connections between the policy cycles, whereby evaluation findings fail to feed the next policy cycle, and gender not being adequately mainstreamed into the 'regular' evaluation processes and procedures (Linková 2011; Mergaert and Minto 2015). This concerns all the expert group reports since FP5 listed above; the gender monitoring studies and their synthesis report about FP6; the evaluation of gender as a cross-cutting issue in Horizon 2020, and more. While the purpose of these exercises has always been to inform policy-making, and despite the fact that such reports often present pertinent recommendations for advancing gender equality, the uptake of these has been very limited (Mergaert and Minto 2015).

Seeking to explain the shortcomings of gender mainstreaming and using the DG RTD as a case study, Mergaert (2012, 235; also see Roggeband and Verloo 2006) has shown that the Commission features as a 'liquid bureaucracy', which she defines as

> an administration that is marked by a very high level of staff mobility, while there are no adequate institutional measures in place to compensate for the disadvantages of this mobility,

> notably in terms of accountability, hand-over of responsibilities, 'ownership' over results, the institutional learning capacity and the institutional memory.

As a result, the conditions for and local attitudes towards gender mainstreaming can change rapidly and windows of opportunity may open and close quickly, which makes it difficult for civil society organisations and lobby groups to understand what happens and where influence is possible or required. The policy-making process is rendered opaque and intangible, and the stability of policy direction even within one policy cycle is undermined. In this context, the role of individuals is of crucial importance. People in positions of power (such as directors-general or heads of unit) can hold back gender mainstreaming, which de facto means they actively counter the EU's democratically adopted and constitutionalised commitment to gender equality and gender mainstreaming (Article 8 TFEU), but individual actors can also push forward gender equality. In this respect, Mergaert (2012) and Linková and Červinková (2011) showed how 'femocrats' have played a key role across the framework programmes. Mergaert furthermore pointed out that a way to 'fix' the policy and to avoid the undoing of gender equality provisions is by enshrining these into firm and formally adopted commitments, such as legal texts. But of course, this comes with the disadvantage that 'shrunk' approaches in a fixed framework are also harder to rectify (Mergaert 2012, 222–227).

Conditions for sustainability of gender equality policy and areas for future research

Several conditions emerge as crucial for ensuring a sustainable and effective integration of gender equality as a policy concern in EU RTD (or, in other words, effective gender mainstreaming), which existing scholarship (see the previous section) identifies as lacking or insufficient.

Stability of gender equality as a strategic priority

As mentioned above, several studies underscore the variability in emphasis on gender equality and gender mainstreaming, resulting in a non-linear evolution and the need for constant vigilance within and outside the Commission. Indeed, the recent developments underscore the continued precariousness of the gender equality agenda in the EU as well as the fact that gender equality can be used as a bargaining chip (e.g. by the parties involved in the trilogue), which may be to the detriment of the robustness of EU gender equality policy.

Policy monitoring and evaluation

There is evidence that ex-post and ex-ante evaluations do not 'feed' each other; that recommendations are not taken up; that gender-specific evaluation-related exercises remain isolated from 'mainstream' policy evaluations; and that gender as a cross-cutting issue is not mainstreamed to other policy priorities. These observations all flag the need for closer follow-up of the policy processes.

Institutional capacity

Additional factors impeding gender equality promotion by DG RTD are related to institutional fluidity (liquid bureaucracy) involving staff rotation rules and changes in the remit under which the gender equality agenda falls. This is further aggravated by the shrinking of resources of the responsible DG RTD unit/sector as well as the potential lack of expertise of responsible staff and the related lack of institutional memory and loss of tacit knowledge. This can severely compromise policy and institutional learning. Analyses also underscore the importance of the individual agency (both for and against gender equality) within the DG RTD, particularly the role of the Commissioners, directors-general and femocrats.

Stakeholder mobilisation

The advancement of gender equality can also suffer due to the multiplicity of actors involved, particularly at times when their values and interests in promoting gender equality in research do not align. Involved in policy implementation are the Commission, Parliament, Council, together with research funding and performing organisations, umbrella organisations including the ERA Stakeholder Platform, the research community and non-governmental organisations (such as the European Women's Lobby, the European Platform of Women Scientists). Misalignments in the gender equality discourse in the EU hamper policy implementation and require vigilance and mobilisation to counter attacks on gender equality objectives.

Cooperation between femocrats at the EU and member state level and external supporters

Committed femocrats in the bureaucracies who safeguard the gender equality agenda are of crucial importance, as was for example clearly evident in the negotiation of the robust framework for FP6 under the steering of the then head of unit, Nicole Dewandre. Equally important is the existence of a policy platform for sharing and coordinating between the EU and member state femocrats and civil servants, as the experience in the HG/SWG GRI underscores the crucial importance of using examples and developments to push agendas. Lastly, it is vital that communication channels exist between femocrats and external actors (gender equality practitioners, scholars, the 'sister projects' as well as NGOs). This makes it possible to coordinate pressure and make the best use of windows of opportunity when they present themselves. Equally, such mobilisations can also help to halt or at least call negative attention to planned developments.

These conditions for sustainable and effective promotion of gender equality have served as a starting point to define areas for future research: (1) policy development and implementation, including policy protection against backlash, with a focus on policy monitoring, evaluation and criteria for good examples of policy design and implementation; (2) the effects of the institutional features of the European Commission and specifically DG RTD on the effectiveness of the policy with a focus on the effects of the 'liquid bureaucracy'; (3) the complex interplay between EU and national policy for gender equality in research and innovation, policy translations, reinforcements and weakenings; (4) intersectionality in EU research and innovation policy, including examination of the shift in some countries towards diversity as opposed to gender equality and its implications for gender equality (Lombardo and Verloo 2009); and (5) the neoliberal framing of research and innovation policy and its impact on the framing of gender equality and gender mainstreaming, expected policy outcomes and impacts, as well as the tools used to achieve those. Another area that will require research attention is gender in the business enterprise sector and innovation with a focus on gendered innovations (European Innovation Council, SME instruments, patenting, entrepreneurship etc.).

Notes

1 Following the adoption of the Maastricht Treaty in 1992, the European Parliament joined the Commission and the Council representing member states in negotiating the FPs, starting with FP4 (Peterson and Sharp 1998, 8).

2 The HG consisted of appointed representatives of member state national authorities. In 2017, in relation to a change in the advisory structure of the ERA, the HG transitioned under the Council of the EU and was constituted as an ERA-related group, the Standing Working Group on Gender in Research and Innovation (SWG GRI). For more information, see https://era.gv.at/directory/85.

3 For the Commission, the list contains major policy documents and work carried out by expert groups but not monitoring and evaluation reports prepared by Commission staff.

4 A study was carried out as part of the Finnish Presidency reviewing the structural change approach, also to inform the future policy.

5 This is also evidenced in the Council Conclusions (14516/18), which call on all parties involved to acknowledge the cross-cutting nature of 'equal opportunities', which replaced the expression gender equality. Only Spain expressed reservations about this.

6 Apart from the growing body of scholarly work (see Siim and Fiig in this volume), see also the European Parliament's 'Resolution on experiencing a backlash in women's rights and gender equality in the EU' (T8-0111/2019).

Acknowledgements

Marcela Linková acknowledges the support for long-term conceptual development of a research organisation RVO:668378025 and grant no. LTI17013.

References

Abels G (1998): The European Community as an Ethical Actor? Policy-Making on the Human Genome and the Role of the European Parliament, in Wheale P, von Schomburg R and Glasner P (eds.): *The Social Management of Genetic Engineering*, Aldershot: Ashgate, 45–62.

Abels G (2012): Research by, for and about Women. Gendering Science and Research Policy, in: Abels G and Mushaben JM (eds.): *Gendering the European Union. New Approaches to Old Democratic Deficits*, Basingstoke: Palgrave Macmillan, 187–207.

Andrée D (2009): *Priority-Setting in the European Research Framework Programmes*, VA 2009–17, VINNOVA. Swedish Governmental Agency for Innovation Systems, URL: www.vinnova.se/upload/EPiStorePDF/va-09-17.pdf (download: March 3, 2020).

Breschi S, Cusmano L (2004): Unveiling the texture of a European Research Area: Emergence of oligarchic networks under EU Framework Programmes, *International Journal of Technology Management* **27** (8), 747–772.

Cavaghan R (2012): *Gender Mainstreaming as a Knowledge Process: Towards an Understanding of Perpetuation and Change in Gender Blindness and Gender Bias*, PhD thesis, The University of Edinburgh.

Cavaghan R (2013): Gender mainstreaming in the DGR as a knowledge process: epistemic barriers to eradicating gender bias, *Critical Policy Studies* **7** (4), 407–421.

Cavaghan R (2017): Bridging rhetoric and practice: new perspectives on barriers to gendered change, *Journal of Women, Politics & Policy* **38** (1), 42–63.

Clarysse B, Muldur U (2001): Regional cohesion in Europe? An analysis of how EU public RTD support influences the techno-economic regional landscape, *Research Policy* **30** (2), 275–296.

Edler J, James AD (2015): Understanding the emergence of new science and technology policies. Policy entrepreneurship, agenda setting and the development of the European Framework Programme, *Research Policy* **44** (6), 1252–1265.

European Commission (2015): *Strategic Engagement for Gender Equality 2015–2019*, Luxembourg: Publications Office of European Union.

European Commission (2016): *Open Innovation, Open Science, Open to the World. A Vision for Europe*, Luxembourg: Publications Office of the European Union.

European Commission (2017): *Gender Equality as a Crosscutting Issue in Horizon 2020.* Interim Evaluation, Luxembourg: Publications Office of the European Union.

Flink T, Kaldewey D (2018): The new production of legitimacy: STI policy discourses beyond the contract metaphor, *Research Policy* **47** (1), 14–22.

Forsberg EM (2015): ELSA and RRI. Editorial, *Life Sciences, Society and Policy* **11** (2), URL: https://doi.org/10.1186/s40504-014-0021-8 (download: March 3, 2020).

GENDERACTION (2018): *Report on Strategic Advice for Enhancing the Gender Dimension of Open Science and Innovation Policy*, URL: http://genderaction.eu/wp-content/uploads/2019/04/GENDERACTION_Report-5.1_D11_OSOI.pdf (download: August 2, 2019).

GENDERACTION (2019): *Taking Structural Change into the Future*, Policy Brief n. 13 of October 1, URL: https://genderaction.eu/wp-content/uploads/2017/07/GENDERACTION_PolicyBriefs_13_web.pdf (download: February 29, 2020).

Georghiou L (2001): Evolving frameworks for European collaboration in research and technology, *Research Policy* **30** (6), 891–903.

Grande E, Peschke A (1999): Transnational cooperation and policy networks in European science policy-making, *Research Policy* **28** (1), 43–61.

EU2019.FI (2019): *Helsinki Call for Action*, URL: www.lyyti.fi/p/NEWPATHWAYS/en/outcomes (download: February 29, 2020).

Helsinki Group on Gender in Research and Innovation (2017): *Position Paper on H2020 Interim Evaluation and Preparation of FP9*, URL: https://s3-eu-west-1.amazonaws.com/data.epws.org/EPWS+NEWSPAGE/2017/HG+position+paper_H2020+interim+evaluation_adopted.pdf (download August 2, 2019).

HM Government (2014): *Review of the Balance of Competences between the United Kingdom and the European Union: Research and Development,* URL: https://gcn.civilservice.gov.uk/ (download: August 2, 2019).

Kuhlmann S (2001): Future governance of innovation policy in Europe: three scenarios, *Research Policy* **30** (6), 953–976.

Linková M (2011): Genderová rovnost v evropské vědní politice: Politická ekonomie strukturální změny, *AULA: Časopis pro vysokoškolskou a vědní politiku* **19** (2), 8–22.

Linková M, Červinková A (2011): What matters to women in science? Gender, power and bureaucracy, *European Journal of Women's Studies* **18** (3), 215–30.

Lipinsky A (2014): *Gender Equality Policies in Public Research*, Luxembourg: Office for Official Publications of the European Communities.

Lombardo E, Verloo M (2009): Institutionalizing intersectionality in the European Union? Policy developments and contestations, *International Feminist Journal of Politics* **11** (4), 478–495.

Luukkonen T (1998): The difficulties in assessing the impact of EU framework programmes, *Research Policy* **27** (6), 599–610.

Luukkonen T (2000): Additionality of EU framework programmes, *Research Policy* **29** (6), 711–724.

Luukkonen T (2002): Technology and market orientation in company participation in the EU framework programme, *Research Policy* **31** (3), 437–455.

Marchetti M, Raudma T, eds. (2010): *Stocktaking 10 Years of "Women in Science" Policy by the European Commission 1999–2009,* Luxembourg: Publications Office of the European Union.

Mergaert L (2012): *The Reality of Gender Mainstreaming Implementation. The Case of the EU Research Policy*, Nijmegen: Radboud Universiteit.

Mergaert L, Demuynck K (2011): The Ups and Downs of Gender Mainstreaming in the EU Research Policy. The Gender Toolkit and Training Activities in FP7, in: Motmans J, Cuypers D, Meier P, Mortelsmans D, Zanoni P (eds.): Equality is not enough: challenging differences and inequalities in contemporary societies: Conference proceedings, 218-234, URL: https://www.researchgate.net/profile/Joz_Motmans/publication/279334714_EINO-2010-web/links/5592489708ae15962d8e5640/EINO-2010-web.pdf#page=218 (download: December 8, 2020).

Mergaert L, Lombardo E (2014): Resistance to Implementing Gender Mainstreaming in EU Research Policy, in: Weiner E, MacRae H (eds.): *The Persistent Invisibility of Gender in EU Policy,* European Integration online Papers (EIoP) **1** (18), 1–21.

Mergaert L, Minto R (2015): Ex ante and ex post evaluations: two sides of the same coin?, *European Journal of Risk Regulation* **6** (1), 47–56.

Pavitt K (1998): The inevitable limits of EU R&D funding, *Research Policy* **27** (6), 559–568.

Peterson J, Sharp M (1998): *Technology Policy in the European Union,* Basingstoke: Macmillan.

Pollack MA, Hafner-Burton E (2000): Mainstreaming gender in the European Union, *Journal of European Public Policy* **7** (3), 432–456.

Rodríguez H, Fisher E, Schuurbiers D (2013): Integrating science and society in European Framework Programmes: trends in project-level solicitations, *Research Policy* **42** (5), 1126–1137.

Roggeband C, Verloo M (2006): Evaluating gender impact assessment in the Netherlands (1994–2004): a political process approach, *Policy & Politics* **34** (4), 615–632.

Sanz Menéndez L, Borrás S (2000): *Explaining Changes and Continuity in EU Technology Policy. The Politics of Ideas*, Working Paper 00-01, Madrid, URL: ftp://ftp.repec.org/opt/ReDIF/RePEc/ipp/wpaper/dt-0001.pdf (download: August 2, 2019).

Ulnicane I (2015): Broadening aims and building support in science, technology and innovation policy: the case of the European Research Area, *Journal of Contemporary European Research* **11** (1): 31–49.

von Ruest-Archambault E, Tunzelmann N, Iammarino S, Jagger N, Miller L, Kutlaca D, Semencenko D, Popvic-Pantic S, Mosurovic M (2008): *Benchmarking Policy Measures for Gender Equality in Science*, Luxembourg: Office for Official Publications of the European Communities.

von Schomberg, R (2013): A Vision of Responsible Research and Innovation, in: Owen R, Bessant J, Heintz M (eds.): *Responsible Innovation. Managing the Responsible Emergence of Science and Innovation in Society*, Chichester: J. Wiley, 51–74.

Wroblewski A (2018): *D 3.1 Report on National Roadmaps and Mechanisms in ERA Priority 4*, URL: https://genderaction.eu/wp-content/uploads/2018/12/741466_GENDERACTION_D05_NAPS_submitted.pdf (download: August 2, 2019).

26
Security and defence policy

Hanna L. Muehlenhoff

All European Union (EU) policies are gendered in terms of their inclusion of women in decision-making processes, their norms and impact. Yet security and defence policy is a particularly strongly gendered field, visible in the dominance of men, the strong association of weapons and war with masculinity, and the disproportionate effects of war on women in terms of physical and structural violence. It is therefore not surprising – yet indispensable – that the EU has only recently considered gender as part of its Common Security and Defence Policy (CSDP)[1] and that research on gender in CSDP is rare. The EU is expected to be a frontrunner in gender equality because it understands itself and it is understood by others (even if debated) as a 'normative power' in the world promoting norms of democracy and human rights, including gender equality (Guerrina and Wright 2016; Manners 2006; see van der Vleuten in this volume). This stems from the EU's equality policies in relation to the Single Market (van der Vleuten 2017; Woodward and van der Vleuten 2014) and is underlined by its commitment in the Amsterdam Treaty 1997 to implement gender mainstreaming in all EU policies (Guerrina and Wright 2016). However, not only in security and defence but in EU external relations more generally there is little evidence of gender-sensitive policies (cf. Special Issue ed. Muehlenhoff, van der Vleuten and Welfens 2020). By now, international organisations, states, practitioners and scholars have recognised that it is crucial to include gender considerations into security policies. The United Nations Security Council Resolution (UNSCR) on Women, Peace and Security (WPS), in short: UNSCR 1325 as of 2000, including its follow-up resolutions, is the most powerful manifestation of this realisation.

Why do gender norms hardly figure in CSDP and its analysis? First, security and defence policy has remained strongly intergovernmental and been less subject to gender-mainstreaming efforts by the Commission and the European Parliament than other sectors. Second and related, EU scholars have focused on discussing the 'capabilities-expectations gap' (Hill 1993) in CSDP (cf. Bickerton et al. 2011). As a consequence, the mainstream literature has 'been either descriptive or prescriptive or both' (Bickerton et al. 2011, 7). This 'prescriptive concern' is characteristic of EU's Studies more generally; it has favoured further integration with little questioning of its politics and the consequences of specific policy choices (cf. Kurowska 2012). Unsurprisingly, an investigation and challenging of gender norms has not been part of this research agenda.

However, the EU Gender Action Plan (GAP I) for External Relations (SEC(2010) 265 final) and the EU Global Strategy (European Union 2016) promise that the EU includes gender considerations in all its external relations, including security and defence. The EU intends to implement the UN WPS agenda (15782/3/08/EC). Some feminist scholars have hence started analysing security and defence, pushing a research agenda on gender norms in CSDP institutions, policies and discourses. This work is especially important at this point in time when the EU and its member states are strengthening cooperation in security and defence as a reaction to what they perceive as an increasingly insecure geopolitical situation. In the following, I will first introduce EU security and defence policy and discuss mainstream approaches to CSDP pointing to their failure to consider gender. Second, I will present existing work on gender and CSDP. Third, I will discuss its gaps and suggest that future research should centre militarism in its analysis of EU institutions, policies and discourses and study security bottom-up.

Mainstream perspectives on the development of EU security and defence policy

The EU is usually *not* described as a security and defence actor, let alone a military power. *The Economist* (February 2, 2019, 21) writes that 'Europeans still seem better at producing bureaucracy than battalions', referring to the attempts of the EU to increase cooperation in defence as a 'paper Euro-army'. Such an understanding of EU security and defence policy as underdeveloped and weak is widespread amongst media, scholars and practitioners alike.

Although from its early beginnings European integration was supposed to provide security and peace for Europe, security and defence initiatives never really took off. In 1954, the European Defence Community (EDC) failed because the French National Assembly declined to ratify the EDC Treaty. Instead, the Western European Union (WEU) was established as an intergovernmental organisation outside the European Community. It mainly served as a discussion forum for European members of the North Atlantic Treaty Organization (NATO), which was already set up in 1949 (Bretherton and Vogler 2005). In fact, some European states long rejected a stronger role for the EU in security and defence because it would question NATO and the involvement of the US in the defence of (Western) Europe. This is the position of the so-called 'Atlanticists' such as the UK, Denmark, the Netherlands and Poland, whereas 'Europeanists' – Germany and France – have traditionally favoured the development of a European security and defence policy (Bretherton and Vogler 2005; Howorth 2014). Some scholars also took the position that the EU should stay a 'civilian power' (Bull 1982; Duchêne 1972) and not develop military capabilities, presenting an alternative to classic military powers such as the US. The 1993 Maastricht Treaty introduced the Common Foreign and Security Policy (CFSP), which remained strictly intergovernmental (Howorth 2014). The treaty mentioned that the WEU would be an integral part of the EU. The same year, the WEU decided on the so-called Petersberg Tasks, including humanitarian and rescue tasks, peacekeeping, crisis management, peace-making, disarmament and military advice (Bretherton and Vogler 2005).

The perceived failure of the EU to act effectively during the war in the Balkans – the first war on the European continent since World War II – in the 1990s changed the discourse. According to Bretherton and Vogler (2005, 191), there was one clear lesson: 'that a more robust approach to conflict management in the early stages would have been preferable to the EU's exclusively civilian efforts'. The Treaty of Amsterdam (1999) incorporated the WEU and the Petersberg Tasks in CFSP, and created the function of a High Representative for CFSP. Next, in 1998, in response to the Kosovo conflict, France and the UK adopted the Saint-Malo declaration calling for a European Security and Defence Policy (ESDP) enabling autonomous European military action. 'Saint-Malo' motivated the European Council in 1999 to adopt the Helsinki Headline Goal, which set out to have 60,000 troops deployable by 2003, and, in 2000, to adopt the Civilian Headline Goals, planning 5,000 police officers, 200 judges and prosecutors and civil protection teams of 2,000 people. In 2003, the EU launched its first military operation and published its first common foreign policy strategy, the European Security Strategy (ESS) (Howorth 2014). However, the EU remained careful to avoid presenting ESDP as a competitor of NATO. The Lisbon Treaty of 2009 introduced a mutual assistance clause, which stipulates that '[c]ommitments and cooperation in this area shall be consistent with commitments under the North Atlantic Treaty Organisation, which, for those States which are members of it, remains the foundation of their collective defence and the forum for its implementation' (Article 42(7) TEU). Together with the EU's solidarity clause (Article 222 TFEU), which clarifies that a member state that is the victim of a terrorist attack will get assistance from the other member states, the EU has established a norm of collective defence while acknowledging NATO's dominant role. The Lisbon Treaty renamed ESDP into the Common Security and Defence Policy (CSDP); it strengthened it institutionally by creating the European External Action Service (EEAS) and introducing a double-hatted High Representative of the Union for Foreign Affairs and Security (HR/VP) who chairs the Foreign Affairs Council and is Vice-President of the Commission (see Chappell in this volume). Although over time former 'Atlanticists', such as the Netherlands and Poland, have 'shifted from an exclusively pro-NATO stance to one in which positive benefits are seen to derive from both NATO and CSDP' (Howorth 2014, 120), CFSP remained a predominately intergovernmental policy in which only the Council decides, mostly by consensus or, if voted on at all, unanimously (Vanhoonacker and Pomorska 2017).

It was only in 2016 that member states agreed to new initiatives for cooperation in security and defence. In a changing international context with the election as President of Donald Trump in the US, an assertive Russia and Brexit on the horizon, EU leaders pushed for more cooperation and spending in CSDP. The reforms are part of the implementation of the Global Strategy, which argues that 'as Europeans we must take greater responsibility for our security', and that 'while NATO exists to defend its members ... from external attacks, Europeans must be better equipped, trained and organised to contribute decisively to such collective efforts, as well as to act autonomously if and when necessary' (European Union 2016, 19). In November 2016, the Council agreed on a 'new level of ambition in security and defence' (EEAS 2018). It established a European Defence Fund (EDF) for research and development in defence equipment and technologies managed by the newly created Directorate-General for Defence Industry and Space (DG DEFIS). On November 13, 2017, ministers from 25 member states – except for the UK, Denmark and Malta – signed a joint notification on permanent structured cooperation (PESCO) and decided to jointly develop capabilities, invest in shared projects and enhance operational readiness and contribution of their armed forces. The EU also introduced the Coordinated Annual Review on Defence (CARD), enabling member states to coordinate their defence spending. A European command centre named Military Planning and Conduct Capability (MPCC) was set up, currently 'only' for military training missions but meant for military operations in the future (Tocci 2018).

Overall, concerns about damaging the transatlantic relationship have lost some significance. While some of these initiatives, such as PESCO, build on past proposals, member states show a growing commitment to implementing them. For example, within two years the Council adopted 47 projects within PESCO, ranging from military training to developing military capabilities (European Union 2020). Similarly, EU defence ministers expressed their (financial) commitment to make use of the EU battlegroups, i.e. two rapid reaction forces of 1,500 personnel on standby, which were established in 2007 but so far never employed (EEAS 2017b).

329

Member states also increased their defence spending by 3.3% in 2018 and 4.6% in 2019 (Council of the EU 2019). In fact, in 2018 and 2019, French President Emmanuel Macron and German Chancellor Angela Merkel called for a European army (*The Economist*, February 2, 2019). The context of perceived crisis has created a sense of urgency to act and 'protect' Europe (Hoijtink and Muehlenhoff 2020).

As indicated above, the mainstream literature has focused on assessing EU (lack of) actorness in security and defence (Hill 1993; Holland 1995), and arguing that the EU should become a more autonomous military actor (Howorth and Keeler 2006). EU normative power scholars have challenged this assessment (Björkdahl 2011; Manners 2006). Manners (2006, 183) argued

> that militarization of the EU need not necessarily lead to the diminution of the EU's normative power, if critical reflection characterised the process. However, I will further argue that militarizing processes beyond the crossroads provided by the European Security Strategy are already weakening the normative claims of the EU in a post-11 September world characterised by the drive towards 'martial potency' and the growth of a Brussels-based 'military-industrial simplex'.

Yet, most mainstream scholars find that even the policies initiated since 2016 do not make the EU a 'serious' actor in security and defence. They welcome the EU Global Strategy with 'one-and-half cheers' (Dijkstra 2016, 371) and argue that the EU has to do more (Biscop 2016). This literature fails to analyse the implications of stepping up security and defence (cf. Kurowska 2012). It pays no attention to how CSDP affects gender relations and people's security in and outside Europe. Moreover, it ignores how security and defence policies re-inscribe or change gender roles in their institutions, discourses and policies. Feminist research has started to address this gap.

Gendered institutions, policies and discourses in CSDP

Although still relatively small, the research field on gender and EU security and defence has grown since 2000. There is now important work on the gendered institutions and policies of CSDP and on the EU's implementation of the WPS agenda. All these contributions start from the assumption that the field of security, defence and military has traditionally been, and largely remains to be, highly masculine, with women's bodies and experiences extremely invisible. This research can be classified as either feminist institutionalist or feminist poststructuralist, both of which I will discuss in the following.

Gendered institutions in CSDP

Feminist institutionalists have studied CSDP looking for so-called 'femocrats' (Guerrina et al. 2018; Guerrina and Wright 2016; Joachim et al. 2017). They assume that feminist actors have to be in strategic positions and form networks in policy-making institutions in order for gender equality to become an accepted norm. Their analysis builds on Woodward's (2004) concept of 'velvet triangles'. Velvet or feminist triangles consist of femocrats (i.e. feminist bureaucrats), organised civil society and epistemic communities that build a strategic alliance and push a feminist agenda in institutions (Guerrina et al. 2018, 1039). Guerrina et al. (2018) consider the lack of gender-sensitive security and defence policy in the EU to be rooted in the nature of CSDP. Firstly, it has been strictly intergovernmental with member states' geopolitical interests dominating. Supranational institutions such as the Commission and the European Parliament, which have typically pushed for gender policies inside the EU (see Hartlapp et al. as well as Ahrens and Rolandsen Agustín in this volume), are rather absent from EU external relations. Secondly, the authors suggest that since its beginning CSDP has mainly been envisioned as a military instead of a civilian policy, dating back to the decisive Saint-Malo summit in 1998. Thus, CSDP has been institutionally dominated by military staff present in the Political and Security Committee, EU Military Committee and EU Military Staff. Because military epistemic communities shape this context, the introduction of gender equality norms has been extremely difficult (Guerrina et al. 2018).

Thirdly and related, feminist triangles hardly exist in security and defence policy. The promising appointment of a Principal Advisor on Gender and WPS in the EEAS has remained rather symbolic because she does not directly report to the HR/VP. The Gender Advisor Mara Marinaki, appointed in 2015, has only two officials in her staff (and eventually an intern). The EEAS Task Force on Women, Peace and Security, established in 2009, is attended by officials from EU institutions, international organisations – including the UN – civil society organisations and the member states (Guerrina and Wright 2016, 299; Joachim et al. 2017). Member states' attendance has increased in the last years (author's interview with EU official, January 2020). Yet, with two members of staff Marinaki's office neither has the institutional standing nor the resources to have a consistent impact on CSDP policies. As feminist institutionalist research on the EU and other international organisations such as the Organisation for Security and Co-operation in Europe (OSCE) (Jenichen et al. 2018) and NATO (Wright et al. 2019) shows, feminist bureaucrats often face considerable resistance to mainstreaming gender within their institutions. While former HR/VP Federica Mogherini did not prioritise the implementation of UNSCR 1325, the new Commission of Ursula von der Leyen might provide a window of opportunity. It published a Gender Equality Strategy in March 2020 (COM (2020)152 final) underlining the EU's commitment to the WPS agenda.[2] HR/VP Josep Borrell (2019, 4) has emphasised the importance of 'mainstreaming a gender perspective in all policies and actions' and assigned gender equality and WPS to the portfolio of one of his cabinet members (European Commission 2020). In an interview (January 2020) with the author, an EU official revealed that since Borrell took office the appointed cabinet member has attended the EAAS weekly gender coordination meetings. It remains to be seen how this translates into policies.

Although the European Parliament only has an advisory role in CFSP, it has supported the WPS agenda, e.g. adopting a resolution on UNSCR 1325 already in 2000 (2000/2025 (INI)) and commissioning several studies (European Parliament 2010, 2017, 2019) on its implementation. The Council published its first document on the implementation of the WPS agenda in the context of ESDP only in 2005 (11932/2/05/EC). This also stands in contrast to the OSCE, which already considered gender in security policies in the early 2000s (Jenichen et al. 2018).

Regarding the role of civil society in the EU's WPS implementation, Guerrina and Wright (2016, 298) argue that 'in this area civil society and epistemic communities have fewer opportunities to access and influence policy process'. Although the European Women's Lobby (EWL; see Lang in this volume) has strongly lobbied for gender mainstreaming in 'internal' EU policies, it has been absent in 'external' policies. Instead, the European Peacebuilding Liaison Office (EPLO), which is a non-feminist umbrella NGO with a working group on gender, peace and security, has been the key civil society actor in this context (Joachim et al. 2017). It has provided 'evidence-based analysis' on the WPS agenda and its implementation in Europe (Guerrina and Wright 2016, 299). Yet, as Haastrup (2018, 226) notes, 'EPLO is not driven by a feminist ethos; any interest in the EU's internalization of the WPS agenda is simply functional'.

With the exception of Sweden (Joachim et al. 2017, 115f.) most member states have not been very active in pushing the WPS agenda in the EU; the UK – with four National Action

Plans for WPS a leader in this field – did 'see its role as a member state of the EU, in promoting the WPS agenda by leveraging its experiences to develop collective European approaches to WPS implementation' (Haastrup et al. 2019, 7). Yet, the UK's approach has been characterised by 'the valorisation of militarism' (Haastrup et al. 2019, 8) – similar to the one of NATO, which adopted UNSCR 1325 in 2007 (Wright 2016). Furthermore, the UK's Withdrawal Agreement hardly mentions gender (Haastrup et al. 2019, 12). Despite the UK's role, Brexit does not seem to diminish the EU's commitment to WPS, as visible in the EU's Strategic Approach from 2018 (15086/18/EC), discussed below.

There is very little research on the impact of the EU's WPS implementation. Haastrup (2018) analysed how the WPS agenda influences EU mediation efforts. Mediation is a rather 'soft' area of security policy where gender considerations should take hold more easily than in 'harder' areas. However, the EU has paid more attention to implementing the WPS agenda in its civilian and military missions than in mediation (Haastrup 2018, 230), where it is basically non-existent. In fact, the EU mediation unit could not point to anyone for Haastrup to interview (Haastrup 2018, 230). For the case of the EU's civilian missions in the security sector reform in Ukraine and Afghanistan, Ansorg and Haastrup as well as Haastrup (2018) show that they mainly consider gender in the form of equality in representation instead of aiming at the transformation of gender relations and gender justice. Olsson et al. (2015) found that the number of women in EU missions varies between 0% and 27% across and within missions (changing over time) with women more often being deployed in less risk locations and serving more in 'softer' fields such as justice or administration. Overall, there is hardly any research on gender considerations in EU military missions, although it is a central component of the EU's implementation of WPS in CSDP. For example, the 2018 Council conclusion on the EU's Strategic Approach to WPS (15086/18/EC) states that the EU needs to 'ensure that all EU-deployed military and civilian personnel are sufficiently trained on gender equality and WPS from induction' and to '[p]romote the meaningful and equitable participation of women security (military/police) personnel in security/military operations'. The 2017 study 'Women in CSDP missions' commissioned by the European Parliament provides limited findings, but suggests that having more women in leading roles in CSDP missions has elevated the importance of gender issues and led to more consensus-driven and safer work environments (European Parliament 2017, 23–24). The EU has established gender advisors in civilian missions, while in military missions these positions have been difficult to fill (15086/18/EC, 61). Yet, for both civilian and – even more so – military missions, feminist research is needed.

Gendered discourses and policies in CSDP

Although the work discussed follows an understanding of gender as socially constructed, it is mainly interested in the role of *institutions* and *actors* in gendering CSDP. Feminist institutionalists focus less on *what kind* of policies feminist triangles promote, despite the fact that the meaning of gender equality is contested among policy-makers and scholars. Moreover, as Kronsell (2016b, 105) argues, a feminist analysis is not simply about studying gender and women's policies, but about analysing 'the power relations around difference and identity'. Poststructuralist feminist work interrogates CSDP as such by making its gendered discourses visible, especially where they are not explicitly about gender. It is less interested in actors and institutions but in discursive representations, such as (official) EU discourse.

Policies define our understanding of masculinities and femininities and their hierarchical order. Their analysis helps understanding the EU's power and identity (Kronsell 2016b). Perhaps unsurprisingly, CSDP (re)produces ideas of masculinity and femininity (Kronsell 2016a, 2016b).

Although Kronsell (2016a) uses a feminist institutionalist perspective, her study centres on the discursive production of femininities and masculinities and the gendered relations of power in CSDP. She shows that institutional path dependency of gender norms in CSDP along with the dominance of masculinity in the military have created lasting ideas of masculinity and femininity in military institutions. Yet, CSDP is not only gendered but also racialised in its discourses. It mainly relies on an image of white heterosexual 'protector masculinity', which legitimises the idea that EU military is employed to protect women abroad (Kronsell 2016a). At the same time, the latest commitments to PESCO and the battlegroups strengthen more traditional 'combat masculinity', valuing strength and aggression. 'Entrepreneurial masculinity' privileging economic rationality is dominant in the EDF (Hoijtink and Muehlenhoff 2020). Thus, CSDP centres masculinities while women hardly appear in the textual and visual material. Women of colour are only visible as victims of (brown) masculine aggression (EEAS 2017a; Hoijtink and Muehlenhoff 2020). Similarly, in 2003, the ESS portrayed Europe as in need of protection from danger located outside Europe: 'Europe is thus painted as a model of masculinity and modern rationality and order, in relation to its chaotic (and implicitly, inferior) Others' (Stern 2011, 38). The EU's security discourses 'Others' those abroad as aggressively masculine or passively feminine and thus deficient. Thereby, it upholds its own identity as being civilised, gender-equal and exhibiting the 'right' types of femininities and masculinities and constitutes its role as 'superior (being the teacher)' (Giusti 2020, 8). As Bilgic (2015, 201) puts it: 'Politics of masculinities is closely related to the process of 'othering' in West/Non-West relations.' This way, CSDP (re)produces hierarchical relations of gender and race legitimising the use of military force and the production of military instruments.

The CSDP's rationale is in stark contrast to the WPS agenda, which is very critical of using military instruments, considering them to contribute to women's insecurity. It aims at overcoming war instead of 'making war safe for women' (Shepherd 2016). This implies centring (in)securities of the most marginalised, including women (Cohn 2004; Tickner 2004). Feminist research shows how the EU's WPS implementation documents focus on the security of the EU and rationalise WPS as contributing to it (Muehlenhoff 2017). For instance, the first EU WPS implementation document assumes that gender equality increases the effectiveness of EU missions:

> Gender mainstreaming in the area of ESDP is not a goal in itself; the ultimate objective is to increase the EU's crisis management capacity by mobilizing additional resources and *exploiting* the full potential of human resources available and to make the mission more effective in establishing peace and security and strengthening democratic values.
>
> *(11923/2/05/EC; emphasis added)*

Tickner (2014, 26) once argued: 'If women become warriors, it reinforces the war system. If women are seen only as peacemakers, it reinforces both militarized masculinity and women's marginality.' The EU is doing both. EU documents define women as neoliberal *and* liberal subjects by emphasising their agency and rights as well as their societal and economic self-responsibility. Victims of gender-based and sexual violence should take 'ownership' and become 'stakeholders' in peace processes (Muehlenhoff 2017). Women are responsible for their own and family's health (15671/1/08/EC). Hence, the EU acknowledges that women are agents in conflicts. In so doing, it reinforces the reductionist understanding of women as mothers, peacemakers and victims (Muehlenhoff 2017, 160f.), combining dominant ideas of femininity as weak and caring with neoliberal rationalities of agency.

Hanna L. Muehlenhoff

The Strategic Approach on WPS presented in 2018 (15086/18/EC) is a step forward in several regards. First, it includes the notion of '[a]voiding instrumentalization by recognising women's rights on their own right, while ensuring that all programming is evaluated against, and shows verifiable contributions to gender equality' (15086/18/EC, 20). Despite this emphasis, the document rationalises gender mainstreaming as contributing to the effectiveness of different security goals, including 'conflict prevention, stabilisation, peacebuilding' (15086/18/EC, 24). Second, the approach refers to 'gender' instead of 'women' and presents women rather as agents than as victims (Haastrup et al. 2019). It aims at '[p]romoting engagement on positive masculinity and supporting activities that challenge gender stereotypes' (15086/18/EC, 19). Yet, it arguably still 'reinforces the notion that the norm is violent masculinity' (Haastrup et al. 2019, 10) and pays little attention to structural barriers to gender equality (Haastrup et al. 2019, 11). The EU Action Plan on WPS for 2019–2024 (1103/19) adopted by the Council in July 2019 sets out actions to be undertaken and ways to monitor the implementation of the Strategic Approach. It centres mainstreaming a gender analysis and achieving gender equality in institutions and operations. Overwhelmingly, the evaluation indicators are quantitative and conceptualised as 'numbers of' documents, staff, projects, girls and women etc. (1103/19, 15–16), which reiterates a neoliberal rationality of effectiveness based on numbers and says little about qualitative change (cf. Muehlenhoff 2019, 61–68).

To sum up, feminist work on CSDP has made the highly gendered nature of this policy field visible by analysing its institutions, policies and discourses. However, it has focused little on (rising) militarism within CSDP and, moreover, it should challenge dominant security understandings more radically. Both determine the EU's impact on gender relations and equality and security.

Research gaps and directions for future research: centring EU militarism and studying security abroad

In the following, I suggest that feminist scholarship on EU security and defence policy should advance its research agenda, first, by centring militarism in CSDP and beyond and, second, by challenging more radically how the EU understands and enacts 'security'. Such a research agenda implies a more systematic analysis of how EU institutions, policies and discourses are gendered and militarised and a move towards studying EU security policies bottom-up.

Feminist research should analyse militarism – defined 'as the preparation for war, its normalization and legitimation' (Stavrianakis and Stern 2018, 4) – in its study of CSDP. As Basham (2018, 33) highlights, most (critical) scholars talk about security but omit militarism. Drawing on Critical Military Studies, feminist scholarship should take the EU's military power seriously (Hoijtink and Muehlenhoff 2020) and study military institutions within CSDP to uncover how ideas of masculinity and femininity define military spheres. Centring militarism means analysing military masculinities and showing how they make possible the 'practices of militarization and war' (Duncanson 2015, 235) and (re)produce our everyday understandings of masculinity (Hutchings 2004). This also implies researching EU military operations, building on existing feminist research on international peacekeeping missions, gender and WPS (Higate 2007; Kronsell and Svedberg 2012; Reeves 2012).

Moreover, scholars should attend to how the boundaries between the military and civilian sphere are blurred (Basham 2018). This leads to an analysis of gender, security and militarism beyond CSDP and towards a study of how other EU policies are increasingly militarised and dominated by different military masculinities (Hoijtink and Muehlenhoff 2020). For example, since 2017 the Instrument contributing to Stability and Peace (IcSP), part of EU development policy (see Debusscher in this volume) and financed through the EU budget, 'may be used to

Security and defence policy

build the capacity of military actors in partner countries, under the exceptional circumstances as set out in paragraph 3, to deliver development activities and security for development activities' (Article 3a of the PE-CONS 54/1/17). Militarism becomes normalised beyond security policies, including development, economic, migration and climate change policies (cf. Allwood 2019). Feminist research has to interrogate the consequences for gender relations and WPS, and how militarism affects the security of women and marginalised people.

This relates to the second focus of a future research agenda, which is a more serious engagement with what 'security' is, how it is understood and enacted in EU security and defence. Here, scholars can engage more with the Feminist Security Studies literature, which has interrogated dominant security understandings and shown how they have co-opted gender for the legitimation of military interventions. For example, concerns for women's rights have served as discursive legitimisation for military interventions, such as in Afghanistan (Shepherd 2006). States and international organisations have implemented the WPS agenda by increasing gender equality in their militaries for the goal of *national* security. (cf. Wright 2016; Wright 2019). Similarly, National Action Plans for USNCR 1325 are often legitimised by reference to state security goals instead of security needs of people affected (Cohn 2004; Pratt and Richter-Devroe 2011). Feminist scholars ask 'whose security' is being produced or protected by policies. One avenue for research is to study how new developments in EU security and defence policy change what is understood and done as 'security'. Until now, what we have seen is that the EU tends to reproduce statist discourses (cf. Borg 2015). The discourses of threat and protection underlying the reforms of CSDP between 2016 and 2020, for example, resonate with long internalised ideas of defending state's borders, territories and populations (Hoijtink and Muehlenhoff 2020).

Linked to that, feminist research should challenge the EU's understanding of security more fundamentally. Can we imagine a different form of security policy that would radically break with traditional security understandings? One way of getting closer to answering this question could be to focus on alternative stories of (in)security moving from the EU level to the abroad and local. 'Telling security narratives from the ground up' (Wibben 2011, 21) implies fieldwork in contexts where the EU intervenes, e.g. with civilian and military missions, and making the experiences and perspectives of women and marginalised people visible.

Research on militarism in EU policies, institutions and discourses and the study of security bottom-up have both to be informed by an intersectional understanding of gender (in)equality, taking other categories of discrimination such as class, race/ethnicity, religion and ability into account. The concept of intersectionality (Crenshaw 1989) underlines that the interaction of different categories, especially race and gender, creates a specific experience of marginalisation (see Solanke in this volume). Some of the above discussed contributions raise questions about race, for example when Kronsell (2016a) describes how CSDP is constituted by ideas of white protector masculinity going out into a dangerous world shaped by the bad masculinity of 'Others' (see Hearn et al. in this volume). While future work should continue paying attention to how militarism is legitimised through the creation of these racialised images, it also needs to investigate whether and how CSDP acknowledges and affects intersectionality. For example, which women benefit from EU policies? The new Gender Equality Strategy (COM(2020)152 final) and GAP II (SEC(2010) 265 final) mention intersectionality. The Strategic Approach often refers to women and girls (and sometimes men and boys) 'from diverse backgrounds' (e.g. 15086/18/EC,7), yet, it fails to seriously consider the implications of an intersectional approach. Otherwise, intersectionality has not been brought up in the WPS context, not even by the European Parliament, which has a good track record on intersectionality EU-internally (cf. Lombardo and Rolandsen Agustín 2016). In addition, despite the Parliament's strong support for WPS, it has not come out as a strong critique of the EU's development of military instruments since 2016, hence failing to consider the implications for the goals of UNSCR 1325 and the effects on the security of people in the Global South. Similarly, policy-makers and scholars should pay attention to whether and how LGBTI+ rights and people are considered and impacted.

To conclude, existing feminist work has analysed CSDP institutions, policies and discourses to show whether and how gender is considered and to deconstruct the gendered and racialised discourses. Future scholarship should analyse militarism in EU institutions, policies and discourses more systematically and demonstrate what militarism does to security and gender. Moreover, feminist research has to challenge dominant security understandings more radically by telling different stories about security and studying bottom-up. This is even more important in times when the EU and its member states are increasing cooperation and spending in security and defence and the EU wants to become a more masculine power in international relations.

Notes

1 This chapter focuses on CSDP and does not discuss other security-related policy fields. For a discussion of gender in migration see Krause and Schwenken in this volume.
2 A third Gender Action Plan (GAP III) for EU external relations was launched in November 2020 (SWD(2020) 284 final).

References

Allwood G (2019): Gender equality in European Union development policy in times of crisis, *Political Studies Review* **18** (3), 329–345.
Ansorg N, Haastrup T (2018): Gender and the EU's support for security sector reform in fragile contexts, *Journal of Common Market Studies* **56** (5), 1127–1143.
Basham VM (2018): Liberal militarism as insecurity, desire and ambivalence: Gender, race and the everyday geopolitics of war, *Security Dialogue* **49** (1–2), 32–43.
Bickerton CJ, Irondelle B, Menon A (2011): Security co-operation beyond the nation-state: the EU's common security and defence policy, *Journal of Common Market Studies* **49** (1), 1–21.
Bilgic A (2015): 'We are not barbarians': gender politics and Turkey's quest for the West', *International Relations* **29** (2): 198–218.
Biscop S (2016): All or nothing? The EU Global Strategy and defence policy after the Brexit, *Contemporary Security Policy* **37** (3), 431–445.
Björkdahl A (2011): Normative and military power in EU peace support operations, in: Whitman RG (ed.): *Normative power Europe: Empirical and theoretical perspectives,* Basingstoke, New York: Palgrave Macmillan, 103–126.
Borg S (2015): *European Integration and the Problem of the State: A Critique of the Bordering of Europe,* Basingstoke, New York: Palgrave Macmillan.
Borrell J (2019): Josep Borrell-Fontelles' answers to the European Parliament questionnaire. URL: https://ec.europa.eu/commission/commissioners/2019–2024/borrell-fontelles_en (download: March 27, 2020).
Bretherton C, Vogler J (2005): *The European Union as a Global Actor,* London, New York: Routledge.
Bull H (1982): Civilian power Europe: a contradiction in terms?, *Journal of Common Market Studies* **21** (2), 149–170.
Cohn C (2004): *Mainstreaming Gender in UN Security Policy: A Path to Political Transformation,* Working Paper No. 204/2004, Boston Consortium on Gender, Security and Human Rights.
Crenshaw K (1989): Demarginalizing the intersection of race and sex: a black feminist critique of antidiscrimination doctrine, feminist theory and antiracist politics, *University of Chicago Legal Forum* (8), 139–167.
Council of the EU (2019): *Defence Cooperation: Council assesses progress made in the framework of PESCO after first year of implementation,* Press Release, 14 May, Brussels.
Dijkstra H (2016): Introduction: one-and-a-half cheers for the EU global strategy, *Contemporary Security Policy* **37** (3), 369–373.
Duchêne F (1972): Europe's Role in World Peace, in: Mayne R (ed.): *Europe Tomorrow: Sixteen Europeans Look Ahead,* London: Fontana, 32–47.

Security and defence policy

Duncanson C (2015): Hegemonic masculinity and the possibility of change in gender relations, *Men and Masculinities* **18** (2), 231–248.

EEAS (2017a): *EU Global Strategy – The story of Sophia*, URL: https://eeas.europa.eu/delegations/united-states-america/22979/eu-global-strategy-story-sophia_ku (download: April 19, 2020).

EEAS (2017b): EU Battlegroups, URL: https://eeas.europa.eu/headquarters/headquarters-homepage/33557/eu-battlegroups_en (download: July 25, 2019).

EEAS (2018): Implementation Plan on Security and Defence – Factsheet, URL: https://eeas.europa.eu/headquarters/headquarters-Homepage/34215/node/34215_en (download: March 25, 2020).

European Commission (2020): Josep Borrell Fontelles' team, URL: https://ec.europa.eu/commission/commissioners/2019–2024/borrell-fontelles/team_en (download April 15, 2020).

European Parliament (2010): *Implementation of EU policies following the UN Security Council Resolution 1325*. Brussels.

European Parliament (2017): *Women in CSDP missions*, Brussels.

European Parliament (2019): *Women's role in peace processes*. Brussels.

European Union (2016): Shared Vision, Common Action: A Stronger Europe: A Global Strategy for the European Union's Foreign and Security Policy, Brussels.

European Union (2020): PESCO: Member States Driven, URL: https://pesco.europa.eu/ (download: April 15, 2020).

Giusti S (2020): The European Union Global Strategy and the EU's Maieutic Role, *Journal of Common Market Studies*, https://doi.org/10.1111/jcms.13047.

Guerrina R, Chappell L, Wright KAM (2018): Transforming CSDP? Feminist triangles and gender regimes, *Journal of Common Market Studies* **56** (5), 1036–1052.

Guerrina R, Wright KAM (2016): Gendering normative power Europe: lessons of the women, peace and security agenda, *International Affairs* **92** (2), 293–312.

Haastrup T (2018:) Creating Cinderella? The unintended consequences of the women peace and security agenda for EU's mediation architecture, *International Negotiation* **23** (2), 218–237.

Haastrup T, Wright K, Guerrina R (2019): Bringing gender in? EU foreign and security policy after Brexit, *Politics and Governance* **7** (3), 62–71.

Higate P (2007): Peacekeepers, masculinities, and sexual exploitation, *Men and Masculinities* **10** (1), 99–119.

Hill C (1993): The capability–expectations gap, or conceptualizing Europe's international role, *Journal of Common Market Studies* **31** (3), 305–328.

Hoijtink M, Muehlenhoff HL (2020): The European Union as a masculine military power: European Union security and defence policy in 'times of crisis', *Political Studies Review* **18** (3), 362–377.

Holland M (1995): Bridging the capability–expectations gap: a case study of the CFSP joint action on South Africa, *Journal of Common Market Studies* **33** (4), 555–572.

Howorth J (2014): *Security and Defence Policy in the European Union*, Basingstoke: Palgrave Macmillan.

Howorth J, Keeler JTS (eds.) (2006): *Defending Europe: NATO and the Quest for European Autonomy*, Basingstoke, New York: Palgrave Macmillan.

Hutchings K (2004): From morality to politics and back again: feminist international ethics and the civil-society argument, *Alternatives: Global, Local, Political* **29** (3), 239–263.

Jenichen A, Joachim J, Schneiker A (2018): "Gendering" European security: policy changes, reform coalitions and opposition in the OSCE, *European Security* **27** (1), 1–19.

Joachim J, Schneiker A, Jenichen A (2017): External networks and institutional idiosyncrasies: the Common Security and Defence Policy and UNSCR 1325 on women, peace and security, *Cambridge Review of International Affairs* **30** (1), 105–124.

Kronsell A (2016a): Sexed bodies and military masculinities, *Men and Masculinities* **19** (3), 311–336.

Kronsell A (2016b): The power of EU masculinities: a feminist contribution to European integration theory, *Journal of Common Market Studies* **54** (1), 104–120.

Kronsell A, Svedberg E (eds) (2012): *Making Gender, Making War: Violence, Military and Peacekeeping Practices*, London: Routledge.

Kurowska X (2012): Introduction: The Role of Theory in Research on Common Security and Defence Polic, in: Kurowska X, Breuer F (eds.): *Explaining the EU's Common Security and Defence Policy: Theory in Action*, Basingstoke, New York: Palgrave Macmillan, 1–15.

Lombardo E, Rolandsen Agustín L (2016): Intersectionality in European Union policymaking: the case of gender-based violence, *Politics* **36** (4), 364–373.

Manners I (2006): Normative power Europe reconsidered: beyond the crossroads, *Journal of European Public Policy* **13** (2), 182–199.

Muehlenhoff HL (2017): Victims, soldiers, peacemakers and caretakers: the neoliberal constitution of women in the EU's security policy, *International Feminist Journal of Politics* **19** (2), 153–167.

Muehlenhoff HL (2019): *EU Democracy Promotion and Governmentality: Turkey and Beyond*, London, New York: Routledge.

Muehlenhoff HL, van der Vleuten A, Welfens N (2020): Slipping off or turning the tide? Gender equality in European Union's external relations in times of crisis, *Political Studies Review* **18** (3), 322–328.

Olsson L, Schjølset A, Möller F (2015): Women's Participation in International Operations and Missions, in: Olsson L, Gizelis TI (eds.): *Gender, Peace and Security: Implementing UN Security Council Resolution 1325,* London, New York: Routledge, 37–61.

Pratt N, Richter-Devroe S (2011): Critically examining UNSCR 1325 on women, peace and security, *International Feminist Journal of Politics* **13** (4), 489–503.

Reeves A (2012): Feminist knowledge and emerging governmentality in UN peacekeeping, *International Feminist Journal of Politics* **14** (3), 348–369.

Shepherd LJ (2006): Veiled references: constructions of gender in the Bush administration discourse on the attacks on Afghanistan post-9/11, *International Feminist Journal of Politics* **8** (1), 19–41.

Shepherd LJ (2016): Making war safe for women? National Action Plans and the militarisation of the women, peace and security agenda, *International Political Science Review* **37** (3), 324–335.

Stavrianakis A, Stern M (2018): Militarism and security: dialogue, possibilities and limits, *Security Dialogue* **49** (1–2), 3–18.

Stern M (2011): Gender and race in the European security strategy: Europe as a 'force for good'?, *Journal of International Relations and Development* **14** (1), 28–59.

The Economist (2019): The paper Euro-army, *The Economist,* February 2, 21–22.

Tickner JA (2004): Feminist responses to international security studies, *Peace Review* **16** (1), 43–48.

Tickner JA (2014): *A Feminist Voyage Through International Relations*, Oxford: Oxford University Press.

Tocci N (2018): Towards a European security and defence union: was 2017 a watershed? *Journal of Common Market Studies* **56**, 131–141.

van der Vleuten A (2017): *The Merchant and the Message: Hard Conditions, Soft Power and Empty Vessels as Regards Gender in EU External Relations, ACCESS EUROPE Research Paper* 3, The Amsterdam Centre for Contemporary European Studies.

Vanhoonacker S, Pomorska K (2017): The Instiutional Framework, in: Hill C, Smith M, Vanhoonacker S (eds.): *International Relations and the European Union,* Oxford: Oxford University Press, 97–122.

Wibben ATR (2011): *Feminist Security Studies: A Narrative Approach*, London: Routledge.

Woodward AE (2004): Building Velvet Triangles: Gender and Informal Governance, in: Christiansen T, Piattoni S, (eds.): *Informal Governance in the European Union*, Cheltenham: Edward Elgar, 76–93.

Woodward AE, van der Vleuten A (2014): EU and the Export of Gender Equality Norms: Myth and Facts, in: van der Vleuten A, van Eerdewijk A, Roggeband C (eds.) *Gender Equality Norms in Regional Governance: Transnational Dynamics in Europe, South America and Southern Africa*, London: Palgrave Macmillan, 67–92.

Wright H (2019): 'Masculinities perspectives': advancing a radical women, peace and security agenda?, *International Feminist Journal of Politics* **18** (1), 1–23.

Wright KAM (2016): NATO'S adoption of UNSCR 1325 on women, peace and security: making the agenda a reality, *International Political Science Review* **37** (3), 350–361.

Wright KAM, Hurley MM, Gil Ruiz J (2019): *NATO, Gender and the Military: Women Organising From Within*, New York: Routledge.

27

Migration and asylum policy

Ulrike Krause and Helen Schwenken

Mobility in a broad sense – including migration and displacement – has been a concern for politicians, civil society organizations, and the public in the European Union (EU) for decades. The influx of numbers of asylum seekers and migrants since 2015 not only led to logistical challenges to receiving refugees and processing asylum cases in a number of EU countries, but also intensified conflicts between and within member states. They reacted with restrictive internal and external policies, and also securitized (forced) migration (see Carrera et al. 2019; Lavenex 2018; Trauner 2016). While one part of civil society organizations and citizens responded with extensive support (della Porta 2018), another part of right-wing parties and movements mobilized against migrants and refugees. The latter problematized the initial gender composition of asylum seekers and migrants – about two-thirds being male – and activated prejudices among the public.

Focusing on migration more generally, differences exist between mobility within the EU and into the EU. Mobility *within* the EU belongs to the Community's founding principles, i.e. it is one of the "four freedoms" in the founding treaties and the 1985 Schengen Agreement, granting the free movement of nationals between signatory states. Migration *into* and asylum *in* the EU are in contrast relatively new policy fields (see Geddes et al. 2020). After the 1993 Maastricht Treaty laid out the first regulations on access for third-country nationals (TCNs), the EU increasingly promoted joint migration and asylum policies. These were not only initially gender-blind but also limited in scope, because the EU considered external border and asylum regulations its main migration-related responsibilities. During enlargement (2004–2013), border security became crucial and itself part of the *acquis communautaire* (i.e. the body of EU law) as external borders moved further to the east and southeast. This was also reflected in the external-ization of EU border policies and migration-related prerequisites in development cooperation (e.g. the readmission of migrants with a deportation order; see also Debusscher in this volume). The Tampere Programme (1999–2004) represented a milestone on the path toward a common migration regime and its four areas are still key today: "partnership with countries of origin," a "common European asylum system," "fair treatment of third-country nationals," and "management of migration flows." The 2009 Lisbon Treaty ultimately formulated a "common" migration and asylum policy (Articles 77–80 TFEU), involving qualified majority voting in the Council, the codecision process (ordinary legislative procedure) between the European Parliament and the Council, and jurisdiction of the European Court of Justice (ECJ). Elements from the Tampere Programme were also further detailed in later documents, including those currently guiding EU policies: the 2011 "Global Approach to Migration and Mobility" (COM(2011) 743 final) and the 2015 "European Agenda on Migration" (COM(2015) 240 final). The goal of these policies is to mainstream migration into the relevant policy fields.

Such developments notwithstanding, there is no unified process of "Europeanization" (see Forest in this volume) for migration as a whole. Instead, EU migration and asylum policies constitute a cross-sectoral policy field generally characterized by horizontal coordination (see Allwood 2015). This field encompasses policies on various types of migration, including intra-EU mobility, labor migration by TCNs (from seasonal work to highly skilled labor), forced migration and asylum, irregular migration, family migration, and EU border externalization, as well as a broad field of socioeconomic integration, political rights, other rights of TCNs and concerning their naturalization. Due to the path dependency of national migration regimes, major differences among the member states prevail in terms of immigration regulations and integration policies. It remains, for example, a national responsibility to determine the number or profile of TCNs given access to national labor markets. In the EU, migration is simultaneously understood "as a solution (to an ageing population, skills shortages), [and] a problem (because of labour market competition or as a threat to national identity)" (Geddes et al. 2020, 2). This ambiguity implies that the prevention of unwanted migration and hence the exclusion of certain groups of migrants – including the usage of gendered discourses – are part of EU migration and asylum policies.

In this chapter, we retrace the patchy coverage of gender in migration and asylum policies and vice versa. Migration and asylum policies address gender in highly varying degrees, from total neglect to continuous coverage (see Mügge and van der Haar 2016; Pruitt et al. 2018; Schrover and Moloney 2013 Welfens 2020). Exclusion tendencies are thus built-in policy features. In turn, gender policies began addressing the situation of migrant, refugee, and minority women relatively early – in the mid-1980s. Yet disagreements surfaced between feminist activists and migration networks over anti-discrimination legislation and intersectionality in the 2000s, which were said to undermine gender equality strategies (see Lombardo et al. 2017; Verloo and Walby 2012).

In what follows, we first illustrate EU citizens' attitudes towards the issue, before focusing on migration and asylum policies. Although such policies are intertwined, we analytically separate them to shed light on a few key developments. We conclude by reconnecting the fields and arguing that they are relatively weakly gendered; migrant and refugee women are often victimized, the need for gendered policies is externalized to territories outside the EU, and intersectional gender equality is, in general, considered an issue of "disadvantaged groups" and is not dealt with as a question of social justice.

Attitudes towards migration and asylum in the EU

In 2018, the Special Eurobarometer 469 presented EU citizens' attitudes toward the integration of immigrants. A majority grossly overestimated the number of undocumented migrants residing in their country: Almost half of the respondents (47%) believed that the number of undocumented migrants is about the same or even higher (29%) than the one of legally staying migrants (Eurobarometer 469, 14). This stands in stark contrast to the actual scope in 2016 with an estimated 984,000 undocumented migrants and 21.6 million with legal residency status (Eurobarometer 469, 5, 10). Such overestimation echoes the strong politicization in the aftermath of 2015. Feminist media studies have stressed the discursive figure of male refugees "being in danger" and "being a danger" for "white" women (Allsopp 2017; Gray and Franck 2019). Such threat-discourses are a characteristic of right-wing parties and movements all over Europe, but mainstream media and parties have also reproduced them (Köttig and Blum 2017). This is reflected in the attitudes towards migration in general: While 38% of surveyed citizens regarded immigration from outside the EU as more problematic, 31% considered it both a problem and opportunity, and 20% saw it as more of an opportunity (by contributing to diversity and economic prosperity); 8% were indifferent (Eurobarometer 469, 7).

The anti-migration discourses are not congruent with the realities in Europe. The majority of EU citizens feel comfortable with having social relations with migrants and have more or less frequent interactions with migrants (about 40% have migrants as friends or family members). Nevertheless, significant differences exist: In Sweden, Spain, and Ireland, more than 80% reported that they felt comfortable with social interactions with migrants, whereas only 17% did so in Hungary and 15% in Bulgaria (Eurobarometer 469, 38). Despite high levels of skepticism, 69% believed that active facilitation of immigrants' integration would benefit their countries in the long term (Eurobarometer 469, 7). Interestingly, only 20% saw the major responsibility for integration as lying with the migrants, while 69% saw it as a two-way process (Eurobarometer 469, 8). This mirrors long-time societal change concerning immigration, departing from assimilationist approaches to understanding migration as a social reality and an issue for everybody in "post-migration societies." However, given the huge differences between and within countries, migration obviously remains a highly divisive subject. While hardly any attitudinal gender differences exist, "gender" – such as discursive repertoires of "dangerous masculinities" – can easily be activated whenever it seems opportune. The concurrence of skepticism and optimism towards migration is exactly the approach we find in current EU policies.

Migration policies and gender

The genderedness of selected migration types and policies

Although migration policies might seem gender-blind at first sight, they are profoundly gendered when we look at the key approaches and controversies of two types of immigration – family migration and labor migration. The first field, *family migration,* receives little academic interest, although about half of all permanent migration to the EU is family reunification and family formation. Policies have prioritized labor migration, which have led to "the separation of the economic – associated with males and the public sphere – from the social, linked with females and the private sphere" (Kofman 2004, 256). Family migration is thus often understood as a "traditional" form of migration, rather than the way the EU envisions flexible (highly-skilled) labor migration. The right to family life is recognized as a human right in international law. Since 2003, Council Directive 2003/86/EC on the right to family reunification has been in place, covering all EU member states except Ireland and Denmark. The authority over admission regulations (e.g. eligibility of adult children or grandparents) rests, however, largely with member states. Key controversies in the negotiations of Directive 2003/86/EC and family migration in general have focused on definitions of eligible family members and the "integration performance" of family migrants. It is disputed whether family reunification facilitates or hinders "successful integration" (Block 2015). This dispute is strongly gendered, because the "facilitation argument" mobilizes stereotypes about women's specific social skills to hold families together and to domesticize their husbands. The counterargument also refers to gendered stereotypes, pointing to high fertility rates in certain immigrant groups. These points homogenize the group of "family migrants," and are often grounded in racist notions of reproduction and behavior. In addition, regulations concerning family migration that define preconditions (i.e. language proficiency) have a class bias, which can also be interpreted as translating racist stereotypes (about "uneducated" groups of migrants) into formal regulations.

In the second field, *labor migration*, a broad utilitarian-based consensus among EU member states exists allowing for – temporary and selective – admission of workers (in particular Directive 2014/36/EU on seasonal workers, the Blue Card Directive 2009/50/EC and Directive 2014/66/EU on intra-corporate transferees). Such directives have served as a compromise between proponents of restrictive entry policies, and supporters of more liberal policies in light of economic and demographic considerations. Such selectivity is not specific to the EU, but reflects a global trend combining restrictive and liberal policies (de Haas et al. 2018). The more open policy orientation reflects the neoliberal, global competition to attract highly skilled workers and, at the same time, to fill positions in sectors that are labor-intensive and have poor working conditions, such as agriculture, logistics, the hospitality sector, or care. Gender becomes relevant here because western European states facilitate or tolerate the entry of migrant women as domestic and care workers – only a few are male – mainly from eastern European countries, both EU member states and beyond. Most of the time, these types of labor migration fall outside the above-mentioned EU Directives, especially when care and domestic workers are self-employed or perform their work informally. Nonetheless, domestic work has frequently been put on the agenda of the FEMM Committee and in the plenary of the European Parliament (e.g. OJ C 75, February 26, 2016, 130–141, 2015/2094(INI)). The European Commission has adopted various support projects (e.g. within DAPHNE-financed projects combatting violence against women; see Schwenken 2006). A great deal of research has been conducted on domestic and care worker migration in the past 20 years (e.g. the pioneering study by Anderson and Phizacklea 1997; see also Lutz 2011; Schwenken 2006; Triandafyllidou 2016). Academic and public attention led to the documentation, analysis, and political recognition (FRA 2011, 2018) of exploitative working conditions, the de-skilling of many domestic workers (who cannot work in their original professions) and the unequal division of household labor between genders and in the international context. Simultaneously, most studies on this particular type of feminized employment reinforce the stereotypical impression that migrant women primarily work as domestic and care workers. The coverage of gender issues is much lower when investigating other types of labor migration. Only few studies have addressed, for example, highly-skilled migration from a gender perspective (such as Kofman 2014), and gender is barely an issue in policy deliberations on labor migration at the EU level. This neglect is problematic, particularly as the share of highly skilled female migrants is increasing (Docquier et al. 2009; Kofman 2014). Turning to migration of highly-skilled workers and the Blue Card (Directive 2009/50/EC), women are a clear minority. Although Eurostat does not publish gender ratios for Blue Card holders, Germany does: while issuing about 87% of all Blue Card visas in the EU, only 23.7% were women in 2015 (BAMF 2016). One reason is the relatively high annual minimum income threshold for Blue Card eligibility (the 2020 salary threshold ranges from €8,168 in Bulgaria to €71,946 in Luxembourg) and the lower average wages of women. Salary in labor migration policies is considered a proxy for skills as well as social and economic desirability. As long as a gender pay gap exists, gender-biased outcomes are predictable. Indeed, all types of labor migration reflect the gendered structure of labor markets and associated gender pay gaps, which have influenced the access to mobility within the EU's legal framework.

When we expand our view to the current core of EU migration policy documents more generally, the mentioning of gender issues is scarce: The 2011 "Global Approach to Migration and Mobility" (COM(2011) 743 final) only mentioned gender in relation to trafficking; the Annex mentioned the "specific needs" of migrant women, but without any further elaboration.

The 2015 "European Agenda on Migration" (COM(2015) 240 final) lacks any reference to gender and women.

In a nutshell, current EU migration governance reflects the fact that migration issues have become more important and are subject to common policies. However, huge differences persist among EU member states. Overall, gender issues do not play a major role in this policy field. Feminist and intersectional researchers, however, have produced significant knowledge on gender and migration in the EU, even leading to over-studying in fields such as domestic work by migrant women.

Gendering migration: key actors and instruments

Attempts to include gender equality and intersectionality into migration issues, and vice versa, can only be understood when looking at the interaction of the actors involved and connected in various positions inside and outside official EU institutions. Since the mid-1980s, a policy advocacy network for migrant women has steadily developed, joined by members from inside EU institutions (Commission, European Parliament, esp. FEMM) and from the outside (women's and migrants' organizations active on European level and academics). This network works similarly to Woodward's (2004) "velvet triangle," describing an informal governance mechanism of gender equality actors with a shared identity, consisting of Commission officials, member state representatives, and NGO activists. Gender equality and migrant women's rights networks overlap significantly. Women migrants rarely represented themselves (and this is still the case); they are mainly represented by feminist, pro-migrant, or antiracist actors. Some national-level women migrants' organizations managed to get access to the EU level in the 1990s. Contact by migrant women to the European Women's Lobby (EWL; see Lang in this volume) also intensified at that time, and the EWL actively lobbied for migrant women's rights. However, minority women's issues and diversity were contested within the EWL, resulting in boundary-drawing between "minority" and "majority" women's issues (Bygnes 2012). EWL members and leaders feared that diversity would dilute political attention to gender and gender equality (Lombardo and Verloo 2009). In the 2000s, the EWL became more active in supporting migrant women's claims, hiring staff, launching campaigns, and ultimately contributing to founding the European Network of Migrant Women (ENoMW) in 2009, which is today a EWL member. The ENoMW describes itself as a "migrant-women-led feminist, secular, non-partisan platform that advocates for the rights, freedoms and dignity of migrant, refugee and ethnic minority women and girls in Europe." Its membership includes migrant women from various world regions and extends to over 40 grassroots and advocacy groups in more than 20 European countries (www.migrantwomennetwork.org/).

Since the mid-1980s, the advocacy network for migrant women has managed to set the issue of migrant women on the EU gender equality policy agenda, in particular resulting in soft law (e.g. action plans, strategies). Gender equality strategies and action plans (AP) are important policy instruments. These documents have shown the role of women migrants changing over time (Schwenken 2006, 111–117). The first action plan, AP 1 (1982–1985), proposed the principle of equal treatment for migrant women. The first studies on the situation of migrant women were commissioned; most of them were employment-related. In 1987, the European Parliament's Women's Rights Committee (later renamed FEMM) issued the Heinrich Report, which highlighted discrimination against women in immigration and alien law. Gradually, a more differentiated picture of migrant women began to develop. In the mid-1980s, member states denied the Commission competence in migration issues and the ECJ reaffirmed this position. Accordingly, migrant and ethnic minority women were not directly mentioned in

AP 2 (1986–1990), AP 3 (1991–1995), and AP 4 (1996–2000). Nevertheless, many EU-funded projects have focused on marginalized and disadvantaged (migrant) women, often as part of the Daphne programs (1997–2013) or the successor program (Rights, Equality and Citizenship, 2014–2020). This period saw the adoption of the Amsterdam Treaty, which in Article 13 TEU extended the concept of discrimination from gender to other forms (e.g. ethnic origin, disability, sexual orientation; see Solanke in this volume). AP 5 (2001–2005) limited the territorial scope of action for women who were "victims of multiple discrimination" to third countries. For the EU itself, the document only called for information campaigns against trafficking. Hence, although migrant women and women from ethnic minorities were again explicitly mentioned, no need for EU-internal measures was identified. This upheld the neocolonial impression that third countries had to catch up on recognizing migrant and minority rights. The 2016–2020 EU Gender Action Plan specific to external relations (GAP II, Council Conclusion 13201/15) refers to migrant women's exploitation (labor exploitation, trafficking) and calls for women's and girls' empowerment. Other gender equality-related policy documents also show a mixed picture range from omission of migrant women to explicitly mentioning the challenges they face, even on the same policy issues. For example, the EU Action Plan entitled "Tackling the gender pay gap" (COM(2017) 678 final) completely ignores migrant women, racism, or intersectionality, although we know that migrant women face a high risk for deskilling and working in precarious (care) jobs (EIGE 2017). Simultaneously, the "Strategic Engagement for Gender Equality (2016–2019)" (SWD(2015) 278 final) details labor market integration of migrant women within the EU as an objective. The "Gender Equality Strategy 2020–2025" (COM(2020) 152 final) emphasizes intersectional patterns of discrimination, referring to the experiences of migrant and Roma women.

During all phases, it was easiest for the (migrant) women's advocacy network to emphasize violence against migrant women, trafficking (see the Anti-Trafficking Directive 2011/36/EU) and exploitation in domestic work. However, a fine line exists between highlighting gendered violence and reifying victimization. The latter has been harshly criticized because it reinforces certain narratives and images, i.e. of female migrants as passive victims (e.g. of "organized crime") (Andrijasevic 2007). Concurrently, countering gender stereotypes has become an EU gender equality issue (COM(2020) 152 final, 5–6).

Asylum policies and gender

International and European entanglements

European and international refugee and asylum policies are deeply entangled (Lavenex 2001). EU policies are rooted in international refugee law and policies, but the latter were and still are also influenced by Western (European) states (Krause forthcoming; Lambert et al. 2013). Based on prior treaties, the Convention Relating to the Status of Refugees was adopted in 1951 and its Protocol in 1967. These represent today's internationally binding legal framework on the rights and duties of refugees and countries of asylum. All EU member states have ratified the Convention and the Protocol, and EU regulations draw on both.

The 1951 Convention constitutes a milestone for articulating refugees' rights globally, but criticism prevails. The early focus on refugees in and from Europe with respective time and geographic constraints in the refugee definition mirrors the Convention's Eurocentric character, which the Protocol sought to overcome (see Krause forthcoming). Furthermore, the Convention lacks any reference to gender, signaling a "gender bias," a "male bias," or a "male paradigm," as feminist scholars have emphasized since the 1980s (Firth and Mauthe 2013, 475, 473; Greatbatch

1989, 518; Indra 1987, 3). This bias stems from the patriarchal values of the Western powers that contributed to the Convention – and, more generally, international law and politics – and established a critical divide between the public and the private.

This divide shaped the refugee figure in the early times as only dangers in (male-associated) public domains were assumed to be relevant for asylum and protection. In the 1950s and 1960s, a refuge was typically seen as a white, young, politically active man fearing and fleeing state persecution. "Voting with *his* feet" (Johnson 2011, 1020) became a common paradigm of Western powers to ideologize flight from the former Soviet Union to the West as a political act for freedom and democracy (Loescher 1996, 21, 59). This highly politicized and gendered approach posed difficulties for women and "the Others" worldwide. Refugees escaping from decolonization struggles, for example, received different, less ideologized ascriptions and were often subsumed as subaltern "Others" – a postcolonial perspective that has continued, and also exists concerning TCNs in the EU (Wikström and Johansson 2013). Until the 1990s, political actors rarely found women and girls to meet the stereotypical features of a refugee, among others because their reasons for flight were also located in the private sphere, e.g. gender-based violence (Greatbatch 1989; Indra 1987). A great deal has indeed changed in how gender-related issues are considered in asylum internationally (see Edwards 2010; Martin 2017), and the EU particularly (see Berkowitz 2006; Freedman 2019), but issues remain.

Varying attention to gender in EU asylum policies

Since the 1980s and especially the 1990s, a number of agreements have paved the way for establishing EU's Common European Asylum System (CEAS), including the 1990 Dublin Convention, the 1993 Maastricht Treaty, the 1999 Amsterdam Treaty, the 1999 Tampere Program, the 2004 Hague Program, the 2009 Lisbon Treaty, and subsequent directives and regulations. The aim of CEAS has been to streamline and harmonize asylum standards and procedures across member states (see Hatton 2015; Ripoll Servent and Zaun 2020). Following the 2015 influx of numbers of asylum seekers and migrants, several major policy initiatives arose. By no means were these limited to targeting harmonized responses to those seeking asylum: a key objective was to reduce and prevent forced migration toward Europe and amplify border control. Hidden under the umbrella of "migration," the 2015 "Ten Point Action Plan on Migration" (IP/15/4813) and the "European Agenda on Migration" (COM(2015) 240 final) represented examples of such initiatives seeking to thwart arrivals to "Fortress Europe." Others included the "EU–Turkey Deal"; strategies for addressing apparent root causes of forced migration through development and self-reliance in third countries (e.g. COM(2016) 234 final); partnership frameworks with third countries for migration control (e.g. COM(2016) 960 final); and extended border control by expanding the role of FRONTEX (the EU's border control agency), partly with the aim of tackling smuggling and human trafficking (COM(2018) 631 final; see Carrera et al. 2019; Joly 2016; Lavenex 2018; Ripoll Servent and Zaun 2020; Trauner 2016).

Perhaps surprisingly in light of the critical biases in international policies and EU migration ones, some EU asylum policies adopted even prior to the founding of the CEAS incorporated gender-related concerns. European Parliament resolutions, for example, called on member states to consider women seeking asylum as a "particular social group" in 1984 (OJ C 127, 14.5.1984, 137). This was reinforced in the context of violence against women in 1986 (OJ C 176, 14.7.1986, 73), and the EP urged member states to more broadly consider persecution due to person's sex or sexual tendencies in 1987 (OJ C 99, 13.4.1987, 167). This was innovative in those days and important for providing protection to women, but scholars began to address the risks of depoliticizing and essentializing "women" with their individual reasons for flight due to this ascribed group membership (e.g. Firth and Mauthe 2013).

Moreover, despite these early developments, asylum policies have never reflected gender-related concerns consistently (Allwood 2015; Freedman 2017; Welfens 2016, 2020). The 2001 Temporary Protection Directive (2001/55/EC) disregards gender and only calls for necessary assistance for victims of sexual and other forms of violence. The Qualification Directive – adopted in 2004 (2004/83/EU) and revised in 2011 (2011/95/EU) – explicitly considers gender-specific acts as particular forms of persecution (2011/95/EU, Articles 9, 10). This corresponds with international guidelines on the interpretation of the definition of "refugee" according to the 1951 Convention on gender-related persecution and membership of a particular social group (Markard 2007). The Asylum Procedure Directive – adopted in 2005 (2005/85/EC), recast in 2013 (2013/32/EU) – stresses the protection of applicants' interests in cases of gender, gender identity, and sexual orientation (2013/32/EU, Article 11), and notes the need for gender-related requirements in asylum application examinations (Article 10) and personal interviews with applicants (Article 11). Moreover, the Reception Conditions Directive – adopted in 2003 (2003/9/EC) and revised in 2013 (2013/33/EU) – requires member states to consider "gender and age-specific concerns and the situation of vulnerable persons" in accommodation centers and to ensure protection against "assault and gender-based violence, including sexual assault and harassment" (Article 18). The Qualification Directive and the Reception Conditions Directive furthermore list "pregnant women" as "vulnerable persons" (2011/95/EU, Article 20; 2013/33/EU, Article 21).

These references to gender and partly to women indicate some progress, but they hardly illustrate structural inclusion and thus gender mainstreaming. Gender is primarily noted in selective areas and to varying degrees, which the following policies further demonstrate. Although central to the CEAS, neither the Eurodac Regulation (603/2013/EU) nor the Dublin III Regulation (604/2013/EU) allude to gender; the latter mentions "pregnant women" once – in the context of health data. Also the "European Agenda on Migration" (COM(2015) 240 final), as noted above, and the "EU Action Plan against migrant smuggling" disregard gender; the latter at least calls for providing assistance to "smuggled migrants, in particular vulnerable groups such as children and women" (COM(2015) 285 final, 7). The Communication entitled "Lives in Dignity: from Aid-dependence to Self-reliance" similarly notes that the "needs of vulnerable people due to gender, age and disability" (COM(2016) 234 final, 10–11) require attention. In contrast, a 2016 Parliamentary Resolution (2015/2325(INI)) on the situation of women refugees and asylum seekers in the EU stresses different forms of the gender-based violence encountered by women in particular, recognizes the risks for children and LGBTI individuals, and calls for increased protection efforts. The 2020–2025 Gender Equality Strategy also addresses gendered vulnerability; its Asylum and Migration Fund calls on member states have been to "support the specific needs of women in the asylum procedure," facilitate their integration, and increase the "protection of vulnerable groups, including women victims of gender-based violence in asylum and migration contexts" (COM(2020) 152 final, 16–17). Moreover, the European Asylum Support Office (EASO), established in 2010 to enhance cooperation among member states and facilitate the implementation of the CEAS, has initiated a training tool for staff who examine asylum applications; according to Welfens (2016) this also encompasses intersectional perspectives.

The erratic gender references in EU asylum policies from complete neglect to (partly) intersectional views reveal the patchy and still marginalized coverage of gender. Freedman argues that the "refugee crisis" has revealed various problems, above all the neglect of gender, regarding the creation of a common system. This echoes the "more long-term and fundamental failure on the part of the EU to mainstream gender in this area of policy making" (Freedman 2017, 146). The patchy way in which gender concerns are addressed is rooted in and shaped by the diverse influences, interests, negotiations, contestations, and power tensions of actors involved in policy-making and implementation. These actors include member states as well as institutions such as the Council, the Justice and Home Affairs Council, the Parliament and the Commission; later, EU agencies such as EASO, FRONTEX, and the Fundamental Rights Agency (FRA) in addition to advocacy groups and NGOs (Lavenex 2001; Trauner 2016) also began to get involved. The composition of actors along with their different interests (which can also change over time) complicates a streamlined and harmonized approach toward mainstreaming gender into all asylum policies.

Member states carry particular weight. They not only influence policymaking (Zaun 2016), but also align norms and handle gender in widely differing ways, including credibility assessments of asylum claims and protection of people based on gender, sexual identity, and sexual orientation (Emmenegger and Stigwall 2019; also European Parliament PE 462.481). This contradicts the supposed pursuit of Europeanization and thus harmonization (Lavenex 2008, 310). It in turn also grants an important role to the ECJ and the Council of Europe's European Court of Human Rights (see also Guth and Elfving in this volume). Both courts have received several cases related to gender equality, gender identity, and sexual orientation, but scholars partly also reflect these judgements and reasoning critically (Güler et al. 2019). Moreover, despite increased protection standards in the EU and its member states, empirical studies reveal that gender-specific risks continue to affect those seeking asylum in member states (see Freedman 2016; Gerard and Pickering 2014).

The insufficient ways gender is included demonstrate how policies continue to draw on a hegemonic understanding of gender, maintain a male paradigm, and reflect men as the standard model of a refugee. The references to gender and (pregnant) women as vulnerable groups exemplify tendencies of perceptions where "gender = women," and of reifying the victimization of women in policies similar to those on migration (see Part 2) and in international policies (Krause 2017). Freedman (2019) likewise records the gendered conceptualization of vulnerability in EU policies, which women appear to fulfill *par excellence* due to the weakness and dependency ascribed to them. Thus, women, men, and all others need to prove that they are vulnerable enough in various different ways to qualify for asylum (Griffiths 2015). This entails risks of essentializing identities and homogenizing groups; Wikström and Johansson (2013) furthermore stress this postcolonial "Othering" by framing women as "victims" and men as "non-victims" or even "perpetrators."

Such gendered stereotyping of asylum seekers and refugees varies across policies and is applied differently in member states' national asylum procedures (e.g. Emmenegger and Stigwall 2019). Moreover, Welfens (2020) shows that internal and external EU asylum policies use differing ascriptions: internal policies tend to employ more comprehensive approaches to gendered vulnerabilities, whereas external policies concentrate on women refugees reduced to the figure of "womenandchildren," and the labels ultimately serve to decrease the number of refugee arrivals on European soil (Welfens 2020, 511). This corresponds to broader political attitudes, which aim to not only reduce the suffering and vulnerabilities of those seeking asylum, but also ensure the internal security of EU member states. In light of the politically produced divide of the safety of forced migrants versus the security of the state, (forced) migration has been securitized (Huysmans 2006) – with gendered effects (Gerard 2014).

Conclusion

Migration and asylum are relatively new EU policy fields, in which the degree of gender mainstreaming varies and lacks systematical integration. As noted above, the diversity of actors and interests influencing policymaking and implementation certainly complicate harmonized processes. However, the main reason for these complications is the field's continued overwhelming domination by member states and the high politicization of this field; some rather progressive policies, such as gender-sensitive Parliament resolutions thus remain paper tigers. Also, "the EU legal framework [has been] merely juxtaposing inequalities rather than intersecting them, and [has not been giving] equal importance to the different inequalities" (Lombardo and Verloo 2009, 478).

Hence, the policy orientation appears contradictory. In the EU, women's political issues nowadays go far beyond the initial employment-related sphere and are informed by perspectives of diversity and intersectionality, while the explicit mention of migrant and refugee women in various strategies is simultaneously decreasing. Allwood (2015, 9) has argued that the "structures and processes for mainstreaming gender and migration are parallel, rather than crosscutting or integrated." That said, the EU has become, and remains, a framework in which the concerns of migrant and refugee women are institutionally heard and material resources are made available. Also, the expansion of the very concepts of discrimination and intersectionality has opened up more discursive and institutional points of entry for gendering migration and asylum policies, which is particularly relevant in those member states with weak gender equality policies. Yet, beyond a focus on "women," additional perspectives are also critical. If gender is understood in its full complexity, by also including LGBTQI★ people and men, broader variation is apparent. Although asylum policies have increasingly addressed gender identity and sexual orientation in recent years, general migration policies have rarely done so. EU asylum and migration policies thus maneuver from gender-blind and gender-biased tendencies to partly intersectional ones.

A core theme that runs through the way gender is taken into account in EU migration and asylum policies is the labeling of women as "victims" of male violence and trafficking. We do not deny that violence in various forms is a serious issue (see Roggeband in this volume), but the discursive effects matter. An anti-trafficking approach prioritizes a "securitized" response, while a rights-based approach would recognize individuals as rights-holders and would address the structural conditions that cause exploitation and trafficking. The focus on protecting EU's external borders against the influx of refugees and unauthorized migrants has resulted in prioritizing securitized and restrictive approaches, including violations of the human and civil rights of those on the move. The character of these EU policies is an enduring issue of controversy among the EU, its member states, and civil society organizations. A feminist research agenda needs to look deeper into EU external and security policies in order to more thoroughly understand the genderedness of securitized (migration) policies.

Another point on the feminist research agenda is to further develop a critical perspective on civil society. Not all civil society groups support the rights-based approach, either on gender or on migration, and more restrictive policies have recently been adopted in many member states. These movements and forces combine anti-migrant and anti-feminist sentiments and demands (see Siim and Fiig in this volume). In recent years, anti-feminist and (Christian) conservative forces including in the European Parliament (and even on the FEMM Committee; see Ahrens and Rolandsen Agustín in this volume) have become stronger, rallying around strong anti-migration rhetoric. How to save existing spaces as well as develop emancipatory policies – that also tackle structural issues and thus go beyond the individualism of anti-discrimination policies – and support structures for all migrant women in light of strengthened anti-immigration and anti-gender-equality forces will be a major issue for the years to come, for feminist activists as well as scholars.

References

Allsopp J (2017): Agent, Victim, Soldier, Son: Intersecting Masculinities in the European "Refugee Crisis", in: Freedman J, Kivilcim Z, Özgür Baklacıoğlu N (eds.): *A Gendered Approach to the Syrian Refugee Crisis*, London, New York: Routledge, 165–184.

Allwood G (2015): Horizontal policy coordination and gender mainstreaming. The case of the European Union's Global Approach to Migration and Mobility, *Women's Studies International Forum* **48**, 9–17.

Anderson B, Phizacklea A (1997): *Migrant Domestic Workers: A European Perspective. Report to DG V of the European Commission*, Brussels: European Commission.

Andrijasevic R (2007): Beautiful dead bodies: gender, migration and representation in anti-trafficking campaigns, *Feminist Review* **86** (1), 24–44.

Bundesamt für Migration und Flüchtlinge (BAMF) (2016): Die Blaue Karte EU in Deutschland. Kontext und Ergebnisse der BAMF-Befragung, *Forschungsbericht* **27**, URL: www.bamf.de/SharedDocs/Anlagen/DE/Forschung/Forschungsberichte/fb27-blaue-karte-eu.pdf (download: June 14, 2020).

Berkowitz NP (2006): Gender and EU Asylum Law, in: Peers S, Moreno-Lax V, Garlick M, Guild E (eds.): *EU Immigration and Asylum Law*, 2nd revised ed., Leiden, Boston: Brill Nijhoff, 539–569.

Block L (2015): Regulating membership: explaining restriction and stratification of family migration in Europe, *Journal of Family Issues* **36** (11), 1433–1452.

Bygnes, S (2012): "We are in complete agreement". The diversity issue, disagreement and change in the European Women's Lobby, *Social Movement Studies* **12** (2), 199–213.

Carrera S, Santos Vara J, Strik T, eds. (2019): *Constitutionalising the External Dimensions of EU Migration Policies in Times of Crisis. Legality, Rule of Law and Fundamental Rights Reconsidered*, Cheltenham: Edward Elgar.

de Haas H, Natter K, Vezzoli S (2018): Growing restrictiveness or changing selection? The nature and evolution of migration policies, *International Migration Review* **52**, 324–367.

della Porta D, ed. (2018): *Solidarity Mobilizations in the "Refugee Crisis"*, Cham: Palgrave Macmillan.

Docquier F, Lowell BL, Marfouk A (2009): A gendered assessment of highly skilled emigration, *Population and Development Review* **35** (2), 297–321.

European Institute for Gender Equality (EIGE) (2017): Gender, skills and precarious work in the EU. *Research note*, URL: https://eige.europa.eu/resources/ti_pubpdf_mh0217250enn_pdfweb_20170503163908.pdf (download: June 14, 2020).

Edwards A (2010): Transitioning gender. Feminist engagement with international refugee law and policy 1950–2010, *Refugee Survey Quarterly* **29** (2), 21–45.

Emmenegger P, Stigwall K (2019): Women-friendliness in European asylum policies. The role of women's political representation and opposition to non-EU immigration, *Comparative Political Studies* **52** (9), 1293–1327.

Firth G, Mauthe B (2013): Refugee law, gender and the concept of personhood, *International Journal of Refugee Law* **25** (3), 470–501.

Fundamental Rights Agency of the European Union (FRA) (2011): Migrants in an Irregular Situation Employed in Domestic Work: Fundamental Rights Challenges for the European Union and Its Member States, URL: https://fra.europa.eu/sites/default/files/migrants_in_an_irregular_situation_employed_in_domestic_work_en.pdf (download: June 14, 2020).

Fundamental Rights Agency of the European Union (FRA) (2018): Out of Sight: Migrant Women Exploited in Domestic Work, URL: http://dx.publications.europa.eu/10.2811/064348 (download: May 24, 2020).

Freedman J (2016): Engendering security at the borders of Europe. Women migrants and the Mediterranean "crisis", *Journal of Refugee Studies* **29** (4), 568–582.

Freedman J (2017): Mainstreaming Gender in EU Immigration and Asylum Policy, in: MacRae H, Weiner E (eds.): *Towards Gendering Institutionalism. Equality in Europe*, London: Rowman & Littlefield, 145–164.

Freedman J (2019): The uses and abuses of "vulnerability" in EU asylum and refugee protection. Protecting women or reducing autonomy?, *Papeles del CEIC, International Journal on Collective Identity Research* 2019 (1), 1–15.

Geddes A, Hadj-Abdou L, Brumat L (2020): *Migration and Mobility in the European Union*, 2nd ed., Basingstoke, New York: Palgrave Macmillan.

Gerard A (2014): *The Securitization of Migration and Refugee Women*, Abingdon: Routledge.

Gerard A, Pickering S (2014): Gender, securitization and transit. Refugee women and the journey to the EU, *Journal of Refugee Studies* **27** (3), 338–359.

Gray H, Franck AK (2019): Refugees as/at risk. The gendered and racialized underpinnings of securitization in British media narratives, *Security Dialogue* **50** (3), 275–291.

Greatbatch J (1989): The gender difference. Feminist critiques of refugee discourse, *International Journal of Refugee Law* **1** (4), 518–527.

Griffiths M (2015): "Here, man is nothing!" Gender and policy in an asylum context, *Men and Masculinities* **18** (4), 468–488.

Güler A, Shevtsova M, Venturi D, eds. (2019): *LGBTI Asylum Seekers and Refugees from a Legal and Political Perspective. Persecution, Asylum and Integration*, Cham: Springer.

Hatton TJ (2015): Asylum policy in the EU: the case for deeper integration, *CESifo Economic Studies* **61** (3–4), 605–637.

Huysmans J (2006): *The Politics of Insecurity: Fear, Migration and Asylum in the EU*, London, New York: Routledge.

Indra DM (1987): Gender. A key dimension of the refugee experience, *Refuge* **6** (3), 3–4.

Johnson HL (2011): Click to donate. Visual images, constructing victims and imagining the female refugee, *Third World Quarterly* **32** (6), 1015–1037.

Joly D (2016): *Haven or Hell? Asylum Policies and Refugees in Europe*, Basingstoke: Palgrave Macmillan.

Kofman E (2004): Family-related migration. A critial review of European studies, *Journal of Ethnic and Migration Studies* **30** (2), 243–262.

Kofman E (2014): Towards a gendered evaluation of (highly) skilled immigration policies in Europe, *International Migration* **52** (3), 116–128.

Köttig M, Blum A (2017): Introduction, in: Köttig M, Bitzan R, Petö A (eds.): *Gender and Far Right Politics in Europe*, Cham: Springer, 1–10.

Krause U (2017): Die Flüchtling – der Flüchtling als Frau. Genderreflexiver Zugang, in: Ghaderi C, Eppenstein T (eds.): *Flüchtlinge: Multiperspektivische Zugänge*, Wiesbaden: Springer, 79–93.

Krause U (forthcoming): Colonial roots of the 1951 Refugee Convention and its effects on the global refugee regime, *Journal of International Relations and Development*.

Lambert H, McAdam J, Fullerton M (2013): *The Global Reach of European Refugee Law*, Cambridge: Cambridge University Press.

Lavenex S (2001): *The Europeanisation of Refugee Policies. Between Human Rights and Internal Security*, Aldershot: Ashgate.

Lavenex S (2008): Asylum Policy, in: Graziano P, Vink MP (eds.): *Europeanization: New Research Agendas*, Basingstoke: Palgrave Macmillan, 309–320.

Lavenex S (2018): "Failing forward" towards which Europe? Organized hypocrisy in the Common European Asylum System, *Journal of Common Market Studies* **56** (5), 1195–1212.

Loescher G (1996): *Beyond Charity. International Cooperation and the Global Refugee Crisis*, Oxford, New York: Oxford University Press.

Lombardo, E, Verloo, M (2009): Institutionalizing intersectionality in the European Union? *International Feminist Journal of Politics* **11** (4), 478–95.

Lombardo E, Meier P, Verloo M (2017), Policymaking from a gender+ equality perspective, *Journal of Women, Politics & Policy* **38** (1), 1–19.

Lutz, H (2011): *The New Maids. Transnational Women and the Care Economy*, London, New York: Zed Books.

Markard N (2007): Fortschritte im Flüchtlingsrecht? Gender Guidelines und geschlechtsspezifische Verfolgung, *Kritische Justiz* **40** (4), 373–390.

Martin SF (2017): UNHCR Policy on Refugee Women. A 25-Year Retrospective, in: Buckley-Zistel S, Krause U (eds.): *Gender, Violence, Refugees*, New York, Oxford: Berghahn, 21–43.

Mügge L, van der Haar M (2016): Who is an Immigrant and Who Requires Integration? Categorizing in European Policies, in: Garcés-Mascareñas B, Penninx R (eds.): *Integration Processes and Policies in Europe*, Cham: Springer, 77–90.

Pruitt L, Berents H, Munroe G (2018): Gender and age in the construction of male youth in the European migration "crisis," *Signs: Journal of Women in Culture and Society* **43** (3), 687–709.

Ripoll Servent A, Zaun N (2020): Asylum Policy and European Union Politics, in: Beach D, Dominguez R, Park SH, Vanhoonacker S, Verdun A (eds.): *Oxford Research Encyclopedia of Politics*, Oxford: Oxford University Press.

Schrover M, Moloney DM, (eds.) (2013): *Gender, Migration and Categorisation. Making Distinctions between Migrants in Western Countries, 1945–2010*, Amsterdam: Amsterdam University Press.

Schwenken H (2006): *Rechtlos, aber nicht ohne Stimme. Politische Mobilisierungen um irreguläre Migration in die Europäische Union*, Bielefeld: transcript.

Trauner F (2016): Asylum policy. The EU's "crises" and the looming policy regime failure, *Journal of European Integration* **38** (3), 311–325.

Triandafyllidou A, ed. (2016): *Irregular Migrant Domestic Workers in Europe. Who Cares?* London: Routledge.

Verloo M, Walby S (2012), Introduction. The implications for theory and practice of comparing the treatment of intersectionality in the equality architecture in Europe, *Social Politics: International Studies in Gender, State & Society* **19** (4), 433–445.

Welfens N (2016): "This Module is not only about Women and Gay People" – Gender Mainstreaming in der europäischen Asylpolitik. Von einem essentialisierenden zu einem intersektionalen Genderverständnis?, *Femina Politica* **25** (2), 77–92.

Welfens N (2020): Protecting refugees inside, protecting borders abroad? Gender in the EU's responses to the "refugee crisis," *Political Studies Review* **18** (3), 510–524.

Wikström H, Johansson T (2013): Credibility assessments as "normative leakage". Asylum applications, gender and class, *Social Inclusion* **1** (2), 92–101.

Woodward A (2004): Building Velvet Triangles: Gender and Informal Governance, in: Christiansen T, Piattoni S (eds.): *Informal Governance in the European Union*, Cheltenham: Edward Elgar, 76–93.

Zaun N (2016): Why EU asylum standards exceed the lowest common denominator. The role of regulatory expertise in EU decision-making, *Journal of European Public Policy* **23** (1), 136–154.

28

Violence against women and gender-based violence

Conny Roggeband

Over the past decades the European Union (EU) developed a patchwork approach towards the problem of violence against women (VAW),[1] both in terms of scope, addressing only some forms of violence, and in terms of strength, developing mainly soft law measures and no comprehensive legal framework. Protection of women from gender-based violence is neither enshrined in the EU treaties nor in the Charter of Fundamental Rights. Feminist activists, scholars and politicians identify VAW as a key manifestation of inequality between women and men and a form of gender discrimination that should be strategically addressed by the EU. According to the EU's Agency for Fundamental Rights survey (FRA 2014) it is a pervasive problem affecting women across Europe: one in every three women has experienced physical and/or sexual violence, whereas one in two experienced sexual harassment. Its high social and economic costs negatively affect the common market (Walby and Olive 2014). The feminist framing of VAW as a human rights issue calls upon the EU and its expressed commitment to protect and promote human rights to address this violation of women's human rights (Benlolo-Carabot et al. 2013; Walby and Olive 2014). In addition to this, advocates have pointed to the large variations in national legislation and resulting different levels of protection for women across member states as a ground for a common EU framework (Benlolo-Carabot et al. 2013; Walby 2013). This reason is also stated in the European Parliament Resolution on combating VAW from February 2014 (Resolution (2013/2004(INL)): 'women in the Union are not equally protected against male violence, due to differing policies and legislation across Member States, as regards among other the definition of offenses and the scope of the legislation, and are therefore vulnerable to such violence'. Yet, despite decades of lobbying from women's organizations and repeated calls from the European Parliament (EP) and its Committee for Women's Rights and Gender Equality (FEMM) to develop a comprehensive legal instrument aimed at combatting all forms of VAW, the European Commission developed only a limited set of directives to directly combat specific aspects of gender-based violence, mainly in areas where the EU has legal competences, like human trafficking (free movement) and sexual harassment in the workplace (internal market). This may change now that the European Commission in its Gender Equality Strategy stated that accession to the Council of Europe Convention is a key priority and that in case this remains blocked 'it will propose measures to achieve the same objectives as the Istanbul Convention' (COM(2020) 152 final, 3). In addition, the Commission intends in particular to present an initiative with a view to extending the areas of crime where harmonization is possible to specific forms of gender-based violence in accordance with Article 83(1) TFEU, the so-called Eurocrimes.

Why was 'gender champion' EU so slow and limited in its response to VAW? One of the most important explanations of the impervious EU activities may be that involvement in gender equality issues has been largely limited to employment policy, making VAW only a relevant issue whenever it affects the employability of women. The lack of a strong treaty hook has prevented a more comprehensive approach (Kantola 2010; Woodward and van der Vleuten 2014). Yet, remarkably in its external action the EU has acted as a strong advocate of women's rights, with a special focus on VAW through a range of concrete actions and policies (Benlolo-Carabot et al. 2013; see Debusscher in this volume). What explains this inconsistency between its internal and external policies to combat VAW? And can we expect a change in this vacillating approach now that the EU signed the 2011 Council of Europe (CoE) Convention on preventing and combating VAW, also known as the Istanbul Convention (CETS No. 210) and the Commission expressed its will to propose measures in line with this Convention? In this chapter I will answer these questions through an analysis of EU's actions on VAW since the 1980s. In the first part, I discuss how and why VAW entered the EU agenda and the policies developed to deal with it. The second part provides an overview of the key feminist research on VAW and the EU. The final part identifies the gaps in the research and discusses ways forward.

EU action on the issue of violence against women

In this section I will discuss how the European Parlimant (EP), in particular the FEMM committee, played a core role in placing VAW on the EU agenda. Yet, in time the Commission and also the Council took a more active role. We also see differences across sub-issues. The Council played a particularly active role in developing legislation on trafficking, whereas the Commission pushed for legislation on sexual harassment.

VAW became one of the core feminist concerns in many European countries in the 1970s and women's movements started to push for the recognition of violence as a public problem requiring state action (Dobash and Dobash 1979). The establishment of broad and inclusive definitions of violence encompassing a wide range of manifestations like sexual assault and rape, domestic abuse, incest, sexual harassment, and female genital mutilation was central to these feminist mobilizations. VAW was understood as a gendered phenomenon disproportionally occurring to women, because they are women. This claim was adopted by the UN General Assembly in December 1993 in the Declaration on the Elimination of Violence against Women (DEVAW; (Resolution 48/104), which defined VAW as 'any act of gender-based violence that results in, or is likely to result in, physical, sexual or psychological harm or suffering to women, including threats of such acts, coercion, or arbitrary deprivation of liberty, whether occurring in public or private life' (Article 1 DEVAW).

Feminists argue that violence is intimately linked to existing gendered inequalities that make women more vulnerable to power abuse and make it more difficult for them to escape abusive relationships (Montoya 2013; Weldon 2002). EU member states were slow and often reluctant to respond to the feminist claim that women as citizens should be protected against violence. After a decade of mobilization, some countries eventually started to develop different forms of intervention in the 1980s, ranging from social programs and shelters, to awareness-raising campaigns and legislative reform. Increased transnational networking on the issue also targeted international and regional organizations (Montoya 2013; Zippel 2004). The formation of an ad-hoc committee on Women's Rights within the first directly elected EP in 1979 (see Ahrens and Rolandsen

Agustín (European Parliament) in this volume) provided a first important opportunity to call for EU action. This committee was chaired by socialist MEP and French feminist Yvette Roudy. It worked for 14 months preparing a major debate leading to the adoption of a 'Resolution on the position of women in the European Community' in February 1981 (*Official Journal* C 50, March 9, 1981, 35). The resolution included an exhaustive list of specific problems experienced by women, among them violence, in particular domestic violence (then called ill-treatment in the family), rape and sexual assault. When the Committee on Women's Rights (later re-named FEMM) was set up permanently in 1984, VAW became one of its focal points (*Official Journal* C 46, February 20, 1984, 42). In 1986, MEP Hedy d'Ancona presented a first report particularly focused on VAW, which led to the European Parliament Resolution (A2-44/86) of June 11, 1986. This resolution presents VAW as a gender equality problem, linking it to structural inequalities between men and women. It takes a comprehensive approach addressing rape and sexual assault – calling to review the legal distinction between rape and indecent assault, and demanding more adequate responses from police and judiciary –, violence in the private sphere – including the legal recognition of rape within marriage–, and sexual abuse of children. It also takes into account the different positioning of women in relation to ethnicity, sexual preferences, age and religion. Yet, the labour market focus of the EU proved to be an important limitation for the diligent efforts of women's movements and feminist politicians to lobby for a EU-wide integral policy to tackle VAW (Kantola 2010; Locher 2007). What developed instead over time is a patchy approach, in which some specific sub-issues closer to core EU competences, such as trafficking and sexual harassment, were more developed than others. The development of EU policies combatting VAW can be distinguished in four main policy dimensions: (1) sexual harassment; (2) trafficking in women, (3) VAW and domestic violence; and (4) VAW in EU relations with third countries.

Sexual harassment

Sexual harassment in the workplace is the sub issue where the EU has demonstrated a significant degree of activism (Zippel 2006). EU measures were responsive to feminist demands by defining sexual harassment from a victim's perspective as 'unwanted behavior' and sex discrimination (Zippel 2006, 83). Also, EU policies often preceded and served as a catalyst for national legislation (Zippel 2006). In response to the EP's call to harmonize national legislation on sexual harassment, the Council of Ministers (today called Council of the EU) tasked the Commission to undertake a study on 'The dignity of women at work' (Rubenstein 1988). The study revealed that workplace harassment affected a large share of the European workforce, both women and men, and that legislation was absent in most member states. The Rubenstein report defined sexual harassment as 'the violation of dignity' and linked it to the existing legitimate field of intervention on equal treatment of women and men in the workplaces as defined by the Council Equal Treatment Directive (76/207/EEC) of 1976. In its conclusion, the report argued in favour of a specific directive to offer adequate protection against sexual harassment, but Manuel Marín, then Commissioner for Social Affairs, Education and Employment, feared that no consensus on hard law could be reached among member states (van der Vleuten 2007, 165). His successor Vasso Papandreou did take the initiative to draft a resolution that framed sexual harassment as an obstacle to the full participation of women in the labour market and protection against harassment as a precondition for equal treatment (van der Vleuten 2007, 165). This mainly symbolic resolution was adopted in 1990 and was followed by the legally non-binding Council Resolution 92/C 27/01 in 1992. The Commission formulated a 'Recommendation on the protection of the dignity of women and men at work' (92/131/EEC) and 'Code of Practice on Measures to Combat Sexual Harassment' (*Official Journal* L 49, February, 24, 1992, 4) in 1991; both focused on the importance of national legislative reform to ensure the rights of employees and called upon governments, employers and unions to include specific regulations and procedures in collective labour agreements. Recommendation 92/131/EEC had important limitations. Sexual harassment was not recognized as a form of sex discrimination, the list of offensive types of behaviours was eliminated from the recommendation, and the recommendation was not binding, yet: it placed the issue on the agenda of member states and even led to the adoption of some national legislation (van der Vleuten 2007, 164).

Hard law to deal with sexual harassment started to develop after the turn of the millennium, when Anna Diamantopolou, Commissioner for Employment, Social Affairs and Equal Opportunities, defined sexual harassment as one of her priorities (for a discussion of directives in social and employment policy see Milner in this volume). Following the Rubenstein report, she pushed to include a definition of harassment as the 'violation of dignity', in the revision of the 1976 Equal Treatment Directive which dealt with equal opportunities and equal access for women and men in the labour market. Her efforts were supported by EP and non-governmental actors like the European Trade Union Confederation (ETUC) and the European Women's Lobby (EWL) (Zippel 2006). The revised Equal Treatment Directive (2002/73/EC) defined harassment as 'where an unwanted conduct related to the sex of a person occurs with the purpose or effect of violating the dignity of a person, and of creating an intimidating, hostile, degrading, humiliating or offensive environment' (Article 2 (2) Directive 2002/73/EC). Article 3 then defined harassment and sexual harassment as 'discrimination on the grounds of sex and therefore prohibited'. The scope of the Directive was limited to working conditions. Directive 2004/113/EC acknowledged that 'discrimination based on sex, including harassment and sexual harassment, also takes place in areas outside of the labour market' (Recital 9) and extended the scope to include the access to and supply of goods and services. In 2006, the Recast Directive 2006/54/EC that merged previous directives on the equal treatment of women and men in employment characterizes sexual harassment as both a form of sex discrimination and a violation of the dignity in the workplace. Through these directives the EU crafted a particular approach in which harassment is understood as a violation of the dignity of workers and a form of sex discrimination (Zippel 2006). Yet, a report of the European Network of Legal Experts in the Field of Gender Equality (in 2014 merged with the network on non-discrimination) noted that not all member states transposed the directives into national law and that many countries did not adopt specific regulations to deal with sexual harassment in the workplace (Numhauser-Henning and Laulom 2012).

Trafficking in women

A second field where the EU developed binding instruments is trafficking of women. In the early 2000s, the EU adopted two binding legal instruments dealing with trafficking (see also Krause and Schwenken in this volume) in which exploitation and abusive power relations often play a major role. In 2002, the Council Framework Decision 2002/629/JHA on combating trafficking in human beings was adopted, followed by the 2004 Council Directive 2004/81/EC on the short-term residence permit for victims of trafficking. The topic of trafficking had a long history as international policy issue and EU action in this field strongly relied on pre-existing UN frameworks (Kantola 2010). The 1997 Amsterdam Treaty provided a new legal basis for joint action. Article 29 TEU calling for an Area of Freedom, Security and Justice mentioned the fight against trafficking as one of its objectives (Kantola 2010, 148). The new EU competence, however, only partly covers the issue, since prostitution policies and criminal justice policies remain under member state jurisdiction (Kantola 2010, 151). Directive 2004/81/EC turned trafficking in women into part of EU primary law. The situation of victims was addressed by granting them temporary permits in the destination country, but subordinate to member state legislation, which is allowed to define the length and availability of legal and psychological assistance (Kantola 2010, 152). The 2005 EU Action Plan (COM(2005) 514 final) to enhance EU-wide police cooperation against trafficking called for fighting some of the root causes of trafficking such as gender inequality. Yet, critics argued trafficking in women is primarily approached as an issue of illegal migration or transnational organized crime instead of VAW (Goodey 2003, cited in Kantola 2010, 152). In 2011, the EP and the Council adopted Directive 2011/36/EU on preventing and combating trafficking in human beings and protecting its victims, which is broader and more ambitious in scope (Benlolo-Carabot et al. 2013). Deriving its legal authority from Articles 82(2) and 83(1) TFEU, the Directive 'adopts an integrated, holistic, and human rights approach to the fight against trafficking in human beings' (Recital 7, Directive 2011/36/EU). It recognizes the gender-specific nature of trafficking and that women and men are often trafficked for different purposes (Recital 3, Directive 2011/36/EU). The situation of victims is improved through a set of

> minimum rules concerning the definition of criminal offences and sanctions in the area of trafficking in human beings. It also introduces common provisions, taking into account the gender perspective, to strengthen the prevention of this crime and the protection of the victims thereof.
>
> *(Article 1, Directive 2011/36/EU)*

A report of the FEMM committee showed that despite transposition the implementation the Directive's requirements is uneven across member states, in particular in relation to its gender dimension; it prevents victims of trafficking from receiving adequate support and assistance (EPRS Study (2017) 598614).

Violence against women and domestic violence

As argued before, the EU has not developed a legal framework to address the wider issue of VAW, yet, the issue has slowly become recognized as a major problem in Europe. The development of international norms and rules, in particular the UN DEVAW Declaration and the Platform for Action, adopted at the UN Fourth World Conference on Women held in Beijing in 1995, gave some impetus to processes within the EU (Kantola 2010; Montoya 2013). Based on the Beijing Platform, the 1995 Spanish Council presidency held a public debate and issued a statement according to which 'the member states of the European Union, are resolved to condemn and eradicate any form of violence against women, which must be regarded as a violation of their basic rights and freedoms, both domestic violence and violence in other areas of society' (European Council 1995) This supportive statement did lead to some policy action, mainly in the form of soft law measures like awareness-raising campaigns, declarations, and publications. Anita Gradin, Commissioner of Justice, Home Affairs and Fundamental Rights seized the momentum of international shock around the Belgian Dutroux affair in 1996[2] to push for two new Commission programmes addressing violence: STOP and Daphne (Montoya 2013). The first programme 'Sexual Trafficking of Persons' (STOP) was launched in November 1996. The programme's objective was to stimulate cooperation between law-enforcement agencies, policymakers and NGOs engaged in the fight against human trafficking and child sexual exploitation. The positive response to this programme inspired the launch of the follow-up Daphne initiative in 1997, a three-year pilot programme aimed at violence against children, but also women, recognizing the link between the two (Montoya 2013). It provided a specific budget line to finance projects to combat VAW and children, stimulate transnational cooperation and exchange, and build capacity at the local level through NGOs and local institutions. Daphne ran in four phases and started with a modest funding of 13 million Euro for the Daphne Initiative (1997–1099), expanding to 20 million Euro for the Daphne Programme (2000–2003), 50 million Euro for Daphne II (2004–07) and, finally, 116 million Euro for Daphne III (2008–2013). Yet, turning the initiative into a more permanent programme raised the question of what provision could be used as the legal basis for the programme. The FEMM Committee proposed to use Article 235 EC Treaty (now Article 352 TFEU), a general provision that enables the Commission to draft a proposal for actions lacking a treaty base but deemed necessary 'to attain one of the objectives set out in the Treaties', whereas the Council pushed for a narrower basis. A long battle followed, resulted in a reframing of Daphne to fit under the EU provision on public health (Article 129 EC Treaty, now Article 168 TFEU) (Locher 2007, 278; Rolandsen Agustín 2013). The public health frame proved instrumental for the approval of the Daphne programme in 1999 and gave the EP more competences in the area because Article 129 EC Treaty (now Article 168 TFEU) was covered by the co-decision procedure that required the Council to act in tandem with the Parliament. Gender scholars consider the Daphne programmes important for capacity-building and networking, the dissemination and exchange of information, and raising awareness on VAW across Europe (Benlolo-Carabot et al. 2013; Montoya 2013). Simultaneously, the programme was criticized for not acknowledging gender inequality as underlying structural problem (Krizsán et al. 2007; Rolandsen Agustín 2013), the short-term funding of projects leaving the burden of action mainly with NGOs instead of member states (Askola 2007), and the fact that it did not provide new rights for women enforceable before national or European courts or tribunals (Benlolo-Carabot et al. 2013; Woodward and van der Vleuten 2014).

Since 2010, VAW has become more prominent on the EU agenda and a number of additional directives focusing on victims of different forms of violence were issued. The 2010 Women's Charter positions gender-based violence as one of the priorities for EU action. In this document, the Commission promised to 'put in place a comprehensive and effective policy framework to combat gender-based violence' and urged to strengthen EU action 'to eradicate female genital mutilation and other acts of violence, including by means of criminal law within the limits of our [the Commission's] powers' (COM(2010) 78 final, 4). This statement was followed by two important directives issued by the EP and the Council: Directive 2011/99/EU and Directive 2012/29/EU. The first Directive on European Protection Orders (EPOs) is relevant for victims of violence, in particular instances of intimate partner violence (Walby and Olive 2014), because it seeks to regulate cross-border protection measures enabling victims to avoid contact with offenders. Yet, the Directive does not explicitly refer or deal with VAW. The Directive is based on Article 83(1) TFEU, which allows the EP and the Council to adopt measures 'to lay down rules and procedures for ensuring recognition throughout the Union of all forms of judgments and judicial decisions', which means it is solely related to criminal law. Much room is given to member states to adopt and enforce protection measures in line with national legislation (Benlolo-Carabot et al. 2013). A recent assessment of the EP makes clear that the instrument remains under-used. (EPRS 2017). The second directive strengthens rights of victims of crime to 'appropriate information, support and protection' (Article 1, Directive 2012/29/EU). The instrument seeks to reinforce existing relevant national measures by guaranteeing a minimum level of rights for crime victims across the EU, irrespective of their nationality or country of residence. It defines gender-based violence as 'violence that is directed against a person because of that person's gender, gender identity or gender expression or that affects persons of a particular gender disproportionately' (Recital 17). Gender-based violence is understood to be a form of discrimination and a violation of the fundamental freedoms of the victim and includes violence in close relationships, sexual violence (including rape, sexual assault and harassment), trafficking in human beings, slavery, and different forms of harmful practices, such as forced marriages, female genital mutilation and so-called 'honour crimes' (Recital 17). This can be considered a significant step because this definition is now part of a binding provision and brings EU legislation more in line with existing UN and CoE frameworks.

A recent important step towards a more extensive EU policy approach is the decision to ratify the CoE 'Convention on preventing and combating violence against women and domestic violence' adopted in Istanbul in 2011 (CETS No. 210). This Convention provides a binding legal framework to protect women and girls from gender-based violence and is open to international organizations, such as the EU, in addition to member states and non-member states of the CoE. In October 2015, the European Commission published a 'Roadmap' (2015/JUST/010) on the (possible) EU accession to the Istanbul Convention (De Vido 2016). In March 2016, the Commission presented the proposal for a Council Decision on the signing of the Convention (COM(2016) 109 final). Following debate in the Council, it was decided to split the signing of the Convention in two separate decisions: one covering judicial cooperation in criminal matters, the other asylum and non-refoulement, both adopted in May 2017, followed by the signing of the Convention on June 13, 2017. The EP responded with Resolution (P8_TA(2017)0329) of September 12, 2017, calling for a broad EU accession to the Istanbul Convention without any limitations. It noted that VAW is an obstacle to equality between women and men, which is one of the EU's founding values and aims, as laid down in Articles 2 and 3 TEU, and that the EU has overall competence to protect fundamental rights. The EP – supported by the Commission – asked the opinion of the Court of Justice of the EU (CJEU) regarding the compatibility of the proposals for EU accession with the Treaties, as well as regarding the accession procedure in April 2019. This means that at the time of writing (May 2020) further steps in the ratification process depend on the CJEU's response.

Combatting violence against women in EU external actions

Critics have pointed to the sharp contrast between the priority given to violence in the EU's internal policies and its external action (Benlolo-Carabot et al. 2013; Woodward and van der Vleuten 2014). VAW is an important issue in the economic, development and humanitarian policies of the EU, of what is required from candidates for EU membership, and of EU foreign policy within broader organizations and universal initiatives. The Union addresses VAW in its specific dialogues on human rights and supports projects to combat such violence by means of the programme European Instrument for Democracy and Human Rights (EIDHR).

In the field of EU external action, the Council of the EU adopted the 'Guidelines on violence against women and girls' (Council Decision 16173/08) in 2008. They affirm the EU's commitment to promote and protect the rights of women in third countries. Their value is mainly political as the guidelines are legally non-binding. Article 3.1.1 states that

> the strategies of the Member States and of the EU in its external action must in particular focus on legislation and public policies which discriminate against women and girls, and the lack of diligence in combatting discrimination practiced in the private sphere and gender-stereotyping.

> *(Article 3, Council Decision 16173/08)*

In 2015, the European Commission and the European External Action Service (EEAS; see Chappell in this volume) adopted a Gender Action Plan for external relations for 2016–2020 (GAP II, SWD (2015) 182 final), which prioritizes VAW and girls (see also Debusscher in this volume). In 2017, the EU and the UN launched the Spotlight Initiative, with an initial investment of around 500 million Euro, to support measures to eliminate VAW and girls, in line with the 2030 Agenda for Sustainable Development. This is taken forward in the GES 2020 plan. These policies indicate that VAW is an important hallmark of the EU's external gender equality policies.

Gender research and feminist engagement with the topic

Feminist research on VAW and the EU reflects the limited and slow development of EU policies. Mainstream EU studies have altogether ignored the topic. Feminist scholarship can be divided in three line of research: (1) studies explaining the development of specific policies; (2) feminist proposals to develop EU regulation on VAW; and (3) research into the incidence and consequences of VAW in Europe.

The first line has traced the development of (specific) policies in the field of violence like trafficking (Askola 2007; Kantola 2010; Locher 2007), sexual harassment (Roggeband 2002; Roggeband and Verloo 1999; Zippel 2004, 2006), VAW and domestic violence (Elman 1996; Krizsán et al. 2007; Montoya 2013; Rolandsen Agustín 2013), VAW policies in external action (Woodward and van der Vleuten 2014), and the Istanbul Convention (De Vido 2016; Jones 2018; Nousiainen and Chinkin 2016). These studies examine the role of (feminist) actors, EU institutions and agencies, strategies and framing. Feminist advocacy is generally identified as a key factor in the emergence of the issue on the EU agenda and the advances made since the 1980s. Feminist activists located outside and within the EU have used transnational networking to promote the issue on the national and regional level. The EWL, the umbrella organizations focused on EU advocacy created in 1990 (see Lang in this volume), included 'the elimination of all forms of violence against women' in its core mission. To this end it established the Policy Action Centre on Violence against Women and the European Observatory on Violence against Women in 1997 (Montoya 2013, 70). Grassroots activists have been critical of EWL's work on the issue, often also sceptical of the (potential) role of the EU in fighting VAW (Joachim 2007, 170). A more bottom-up, autonomous and sectoral European network of women's NGOs organizing is Women Against Violence Europe (WAVE), established in 1994 during a preparatory meeting for the 1995 Beijing conference. It received funding through the Daphne Initiative in 1997 and thereby rapidly expanded the network and increased activity. Its relative autonomy vis-à-vis the EU allowed it to be a more critical voice compared to EWL (Kantola 2006). WAVE has become a crucial source of information and expertise through conferences, research and monitoring, but also played an important role in setting up services across Europe. WAVE actively represents women's organizations in a number of international fora, like the UN or CoE. Beyond these main players, issue-specific women's organizations like AVFT (Association des victimes de harcèlement moral, psychologique, sexuel, dans le cadre du travail), WasH (Women against sexual harassment), or Hands Off in the field of sexual harassment, or the Rape Crisis Network Europe and general women's NGOs like the European Feminist Forum, the International Lesbian, Gay, Bisexual, Trans and Intersex Association (ILGA), and Women in Development Europe (WIDE) are identified as advocates on the issue (Kantola 2010; Montoya 2013; Strid 2009).

Particular emphasis is also given to the role of academics and practitioners who are often called upon to serve as experts. This crucial role is highlighted in Zippel's study of the development of the Directives 2002/73/EC on sexual harassment where 'professional, scientific language' became 'the currency' in transnational communication among feminists, policy-makers, and politicians, and helped to advance feminist claims (Zippel 2006, 91). The Commission made use of individual experts – like in the case of the Rubinstein report– but also expert groups such as the European Equality Law Network and Expert Group on Trafficking in Human Beings for external consultation on VAW (Kantola 2010; Montoya 2013).

The EU actors identified as most active on VAW are the EP, in particular the FEMM Committee, and some entrepreneurial Commissioners. Also the establishment of the Fundamental Rights Agency (FRA) and the European Institute for Gender Equality (EIGE; see Jacquot and Krizsán in this volume) are mentioned as important. FRA conducted one of the most prominent pieces of EU-level gender research in the last decades: the European comparative gender-based violence survey (FRA 2014). EIGE, established in 2007, has gender-based violence as one of its priorities and runs the European Union Observatory on Violence against Women to research gender-based violence and monitor mechanisms for the EU to evaluate member state policies. It has developed a gender equality index, which includes violence as one out of seven dimensions.

The active lobbying of women's organizations and feminist experts has resulted in a relatively strong feminist framing of violence as a gender equality issue and violation of women's human rights within EU documents (Kantola 2010; Krizsán et al. 2007; Locher 2007; Montoya 2013; Zippel 2006). Yet, scholars also argue that this framing is largely inconsistent and can be predominantly found in EP documents, although the Council and Commission also increasingly adopted feminist frames (Krizsán et al. 2007). An intersectional approach to violence is, however, still lacking (Krizsán et al. 2007; Lombardo and Rolandsen Agustín 2016). Lombardo and Rolandsen Agustín (2016) also point to a tendency to 'culturalize' violence, in particular in debates in the EP, but also Commission documents, where VAW is connected mainly to migrants or Muslims, and ample attention has gone 'harmful customary or traditional practices' (COM(2010) 78 final, 4), in particular female genital mutilation (FGM).[3]

Gender scholars have criticized ways in which gender equality issues were incorporated into the EU accession process of candidate countries. VAW was very inconsistently addressed: it was neither part of the major accession documents, nor part of the acquis-related negotiations. Some of the progress reports paid attention to how countries were acting on these issues, but not in any systematic way (Fábián 2010; Krizsán and Roggeband 2018; Montoya 2013).

A second research strands concerns feminist proposals to improve EU policies and extend legislative frameworks. Scholars have explored the legal grounds for a more comprehensive EU approach based on existing treaties and frameworks (Benlolo-Carabot et al 2013; Nousiainen and Chinkin 2016; Walby 2013). Benlolo-Carabot et al. (2013) argue that Article 83(1) TFEU, which stipulates that 'the Council may adopt a decision identifying other areas of crime that meet the criteria specified in this paragraph' provides legal competence to combat VAW. If the Council decided to extend the list of offences contained in this provision, as is now proposed in the GES 2020, then EU institutions could propose minimum standards of definition and sanctions in order to combat VAW at a larger scale (Benlolo-Carabot et al. 2013, 59). Nousiainen and Chinkin (2016) also argue that the EU should use its competence in the area of criminal law. They refer to Article 67(3) TFEU, according to which the EU must ensure a high level of security by taking measures to prevent and combat crime, racism and xenophobia by measures for coordination and cooperation between authorities, mutual recognition of judgments in criminal matters and, if necessary, by approximation of criminal legislation. Article 84 TFEU also offers opportunities to develop rules of prevention as it allows for the adoption of rules that 'promote and support the action of Member States in the field of crime prevention, excluding any harmonization of the laws and regulations of the Member States'. According to Benlolo-Carabot et al. (2013) this provides a 'useful legal basis for a directive that would not seek to harmonize national legislations, but to efficiently supplement existing EU law on victims' (I-60). Walby (2013) argues that a VAW directive could draw on either Article 157 or Article 19 TFEU. In her view, the legal competence to combat VAW as a form of discrimination is firmly, but narrowly based on Article 157 TFEU, within the field of employment. Article 19 TFEU extends this competence to combat sex discrimination – including harassment and VAW – to a wider range of fields (Walby 2013).

A final strand of research are feminist efforts to investigate the incidence of different forms of violence across Europe, but also its implications for health and its economic costs. In particular, the FRA European-wide survey stands out. It has been critical in raising awareness at EU level of the significance of the problem, and to advance claims for EU policy and research development. While the survey was undertaken by FRA staff, feminist experts played an important role in developing its methodology. An important limitation is that the survey only includes women; comparisons between violence against women and against men cannot be made. Walby and Towers (2017, 21) point to several problems with the sample of 42,000 respondents as it is too small to robustly compare member states, too small to compare by severity of violence within member states, and too small to analyse less frequent forms of violence, such as rape, even at EU level. The economic impact of VAW has been the topic of a report commissioned by EIGE (Walby and Olive 2014).

Moving forward: key issues

Despite promising initiatives, persistent lobbying and strong proposals to extend EU regulation to combat VAW, the EU has been a laggard and poor performer. It remains to be seen if the EU will extend its competences in the near future, but the new von der Leyen Commission in its Gender Equality Strategy 2020–2025 certainly formulated an ambitious agenda to combat VAW. A key priority remains the EU ratification of the Istanbul Convention on violence against women. In addition, the Commission intends to extend the areas of crime where harmonization is possible, adding VAW to the list of EU crimes defined in the Treaty (so-called 'Eurocrimes'). The Commission will also propose additional measures to prevent and combat specific forms of gender-based violence, including sexual harassment, abuse of women and FGM (Article 83 TFUE). The EWL has expressed its concern that the ambition to extend areas of crime is only limited to those areas where harmonization is possible and to those forms of violence 'already apprehended by the existing Eurocrimes'. The Gender Equality Strategy also squarely advocates a more intersectional approach to gender equality. In relation to VAW, the specific vulnerabilities of women with disabilities and migrant women are mentioned and the need for intersectional data on VAW, paying attention to the role of age, disability status, migrant status and rural–urban residence is emphasized. To realize these ambitions, it is important to link the Gender Equality Strategy to other EU instruments like the Action Plan on Integration and Inclusion and the EU strategic frameworks on Disability, LGBTI+, Roma Inclusion and Children's Rights to ensure they are integrated into a comprehensive European framework addressing all forms of intersecting discriminations.

In addition to taking stock of the partial response of the EU to combat VAW, the chapter makes clear that research on EU initiatives is somewhat limited, largely following the pattern of EU policy development. This research provides an in-depth analysis of the development of the sexual harassment and trafficking directives and the Daphne programmes, but not much beyond it. This is perhaps indicative of a certain scepticism among feminist scholars about the potential of the EU to become a more proactive and significant policy actor in the field of VAW.

Notes

1 In this chapter I use both the terms of violence against women (VAW) and gender-based violence as both concepts also appear in EU documents. The concept of gender-based violence is generally seen as a more encompassing concept referring to violence directed against a person because of that person's gender or violence that affects persons of a particular gender disproportionately. The concept of VAW in international law is understood as a violation of human rights and a form of discrimination against women.

2 In Belgium two young girls abducted and raped by Marc Dutroux were discovered in his house. Four other young girls had been murdered by him.

3 See, for instance, the European Parliament resolutions (2012/2684(RSP); 2014/2511(RSP)); Commission Communication (COM(2013) 833 final); and Council Conclusion (9543/14).

References

Askola H (2007): *Legal Responses to Trafficking in Women for Sexual Exploitation in the European Union*, Oxford, Portland: Hart.

Benlolo-Carabot M, Bories C, Hennette-Vauchez S, Möschel M (2013): *European Added Value of a Directive on Combatting Violence Against Women. ANNEX I Assessing the Necessity and Effects of Intervention at EU Level*, Brussels: European Union, DOI: 10.2861/20396.

De Vido S (2016): The ratification of the Council of Europe Istanbul Convention by the EU. A step forward in the protection of women from violence in the European legal system, *European Journal Legal Studies* **9**, 69–102.

Dobash RE, Dobash R (1979): *Violence Against Wives: A Case Against the Patriarchy*, New York: Free Press.

Elman RA, ed. (1996): *Sexual Politics and the European Union: The New Feminist Challenge*, Oxford, New York: Berghahn Books.

EPRS (2017) European Protection Order Directive 2011/99/EU European Implementation Assessment. PE 603.272 – September 2017, URL: www.europarl.europa.eu/RegData/etudes/STUD/2017/603272/EPRS_STU(2017)603272_EN.pdf (download: May 26, 2020).

European Council (1995): *Fourth World Conference on Women. Information from the Presidency and Public Debate*, URL: www.consilium.europa.eu/uedocs/cms_data/docs/pressdata/en/lsa/017a0003.htm (download: May 17, 2020).

European Union Agency for Fundamental Rights (FRA) (2014): *Violence Against Women: An EU-Wide Survey, Main Results*, Luxembourg: Publications Office of the European Union.

Fábián K (2010): Mores and gains: the EU's influence on domestic violence policies among its new post-communist member states, *Women's Studies International Forum* **33** (1), 54–67.

Joachim JM (2007): *Agenda Setting, the UN, and NGOs: Gender Violence and Reproductive Rights*, Washington DC: Georgetown University Press.

Jones J (2018): The European Convention on Human Rights (ECHR) and the Council of Europe Convention on Violence Against Women and Domestic Violence (Istanbul Convention), in: Manjoo R, Jones J (eds.): *The Legal Protection of Women From Violence: Normative Gaps in International Law*, Milton Park, New York: Routledge, 147–173.

Kantola J (2006): *Feminists Theorize the State*, Basingstoke: Palgrave MacMillan.

Kantola J (2010): *Gender and the European Union*, Basingstoke: Palgrave MacMillan.

Krizsán A, Bustelo M, Hadjiyanni A, Kamoutis F (2007): Domestic Violence: A Public Matter, in: Verloo M (ed.): *Multiple Meanings of Gender Equality. A Critical Frame Analysis of Gender Policies in Europe*, Budapest: Central European University Press, 141–184.

Krizsán A, Roggeband C (2018): Towards a conceptual framework for struggles over democracy in back-sliding states. Gender equality policy in central eastern Europe, *Politics and Governance* **6** (3), DOI: http://dx.doi.org/10.17645/pag.v6i3.1414.

Locher B (2007): *Trafficking in Women in the European Union: Norms, Advocacy-Networks and Policy-Change*, Wiesbaden: Springer VS.

Lombardo E, Rolandsen Agustín L (2016): Intersectionality in European Union policymaking. The case of gender-based violence, *Politics* **36** (4), 364–373.

Montoya C (2013): *From Global to Grassroots: The European Union, Transnational Advocacy, and Combating Violence Against Women*, Oxford: Oxford University Press.

Nousiainen K, Chinkin C (2016): *Legal Implications of EU Accession to the Istanbul Convention*, Luxembourg: Publications Office of the European Union.

Numhauser-Henning A, Laulom S (2012): *Harassment Related to Sex and Sexual Harassment Law in 33 European Countries: Discrimination versus Dignity*, Brussels: European Union.

Roggeband C (2002): *Over de grenzen van de politiek. Een vergelijkende studie naar de opkomst en ontwikkeling van de vrouwenbeweging tegen seksueel geweld in Nederland en Spanje*, Assen: Uitgeverij Van Gorcum.

Roggeband C, Verloo M (1999): Global Sisterhood and Political Change: The unhappy 'Marriage' of Women's Movements and Nation States, in: van Kersbergen K and Lieshout R, Lock G (eds.): *Expansion and Fragmentation. Internationalization, Political Change and the Transformation of the Nation State*, Amsterdam: Amsterdam University Press, 177–194.

Rolandsen Agustín L (2013): *Gender Equality, Intersectionality, and Diversity in Europe*, Basingstoke: Palgrave Macmillan.

Rubenstein M (1988): *The Dignity of Women at Work. A Report on the Problem of Sexual Harassment in the Member States of the European Communities. Parts I-II,* Luxembourg: Office for Official Publications of the European Communities.

Strid S (2009): *Gendered Interests in the European Union. The European Women's Lobby and the Organisation and Representation of Women's Interests*, Doctoral dissertation, Örebro universitet.

van der Vleuten A (2007): *The Price of Gender Equality. Member States and Governance in the European Union*, New York: Routledge.

Walby S (2013): Legal perspectives for action at EU level. Research paper. Annex II of the European Added Value of a Directive on combatting violence against women (Research paper), DOI: 10.2861/20760.

Walby, S., Olive, P. (2014) 'Estimating the costs of gender-based violence in the European Union', URL: https://eige.europa.eu/gender-based-violence/estimating-costs-in-european-union [accessed May 22, 2020].

Walby S, Towers J (2017): Measuring violence to end violence: Mainstreaming gender, *Journal of Gender-Based Violence* **1** (1), 11–31.

Weldon SL (2002): *Protest, Policy, and the Problem of Violence Against Women: A Cross-National Comparison*, Pittsburgh, PA: University of Pittsburgh Press.

Woodward A, van der Vleuten A (2014): EU and the Export of Gender Equality Norms: Myth and Facts, in: van der Vleuten A, van Eerdewijk A, Roggeband C (eds): *Gender Equality Norms in Regional Governance*, Basingstoke: Palgrave Macmillan, 67–92.

Zippel K (2004): Transnational advocacy networks and policy cycles in the European Union: The case of sexual harassment, *Social Politics: International Studies in Gender, State & Society* **11** (1), 57–85.

Zippel K (2006): *The Politics of Sexual Harassment. A Comparative Study of the United States, the European Union, and Germany*, Cambridge: Cambridge University Press.

Part V
A gender lens on key issues and debates

Since its founding, the European Union (EU) has developed and evolved in a number of different ways. One of the major drivers for changes and reforms, according to much of the literature, has been the challenges and periods of crises that have historically provided both opportunities for reform as well as for retrenchment. This is particularly true of the last decade, which has been marked by a series of crises, which combine to what Jean-Claude Juncker referred to as a 'poly-crisis'. These interconnected issues and crises additionally form an overarching crisis of legitimacy which impacts on every aspect of EU governance, institutions, policies and politics. Neither the crises, nor their responses are gender neutral. In fact, gender research has demonstrated that they are gendered in numerous ways.

This part of the Handbook considers three of the key challenges that the EU, and its constituencies have navigated over the last 12 years, specifically considering the gendered nature of these challenges and the ways in which their resolution may advance or detract from gender equality as European integration moves forward. The chapters in this section show all three challenges: the economic and financial crisis; the rise of populism; and Brexit. They demonstrate remarkably gendered political and policy processes which have unequal consequences for EU integration and EU citizens. We also see the absence of gender mainstreaming, and even gender exclusionary logics, in how the EU responds to these outstanding challenges. These chapters demonstrate the sidelining, or even exclusion of women in policy. Without gender awareness, there are extreme consequences, including increased gender violence and lack of recognition and neglect of its ramifications, and often an EU that backs out from important previous commitments to gender equality, or remains incapable of enforcing these.

The economic crisis brings backsliding in various gender equality fields in many member states, and along with national processes of dismantling, we can see a deterioration of the EU gender equality governance model. Whereas the EU itself was once a leader in gender equality policy, in the wake of the crisis, we witness EU patterns that mirror national patterns supporting rather than challenging the dismantling of social and equality policies. A variety of strands of gender research contribute prominently to identifying gendered aspects of the economic crises for EU and member state policies and governance as well as their impact on women and gender

365

A gender lens on key issues and debates

equality in European societies. But gender research also contributes with forward-looking thinking in terms of the future of Europe and a better integrated and more gender equal EU.

Partly as a result of the economic crisis and the austerity it imposed, numerous member states saw a rise in right-wing radicalism and populism lately. While mainstream research on populism, including research on the nature and origins of populism in the EU, has flourished in the last decade, this research remains remarkably ignorant of the highly gendered nature of populism itself, and the gendered consequences that it can have on politics and society. Gendered aspects remain almost exclusively a topic for gender research, even though many of the populist battlefields are prominent gender equality fields. Gender research shows how the intersectional and masculinity research lens can contribute to more gender-sensitive populism research, which can help us to understand populist successes and limitations, within the EU system. It can also further highlight the need for more conceptual work on notions of gender democracy and gender justice, to augment mainstream conceptualizations of democracy.

Brexit has highlighted similar issues. It highlights both the gender exclusive nature of the process and its exclusionary consequences as well as its racialised pattern. Importantly, it also draws attention to the absence of a gender lens on both sides of the Brexit process. The exclusion of women and gender/intersectional concerns speak volumes about the position that gender concerns have in times of crisis.

All of these chapters point to the ways in which gender is not fundamentally entrenched into the EU processes. But, these challenges can also offer key opportunities to make the necessary changes. Even as they all underscore political polarization, they also show examples of pushback and of revitalizing gender politics and reconfiguring political arenas, which in the longer run could have beneficial consequences for the EU. Whether the challenges discussed in this part of the Handbook further deepen the legitimacy crisis that the EU faces or bring input and inspiration towards further integration; whether they cause disintegration or integration, is too early to say. Especially the manifold implications of the still ongoing Covid-19 pandemic on gender relations in Europe need to be addressed in future research. In the following chapters, the authors consider how these processes are gendered, what is there to be gained or lost in terms of gender rights, and how gender research can contribute to the mainstream analysis of these processes.

29

The populist challenge to gender equality

Birte Siim and Christina Fiig

There is an increasing scholarly interest in populism in contemporary Europe. The rise of right-wing populism (RWP) parties in several European nation states and within the European Parliament is usually interpreted as a challenge to liberal values, such as democracy, freedom and equality, that hints at fundamental problems for European societies and the European Union (Loch and Norocel 2015; Müller 2016; Verloo 2018a). This chapter discusses the relations between populism and gender in EU member states and EU institutions. While mainstream literature on populism, with few exceptions, has neglected gender issues, there is a new body of work on gender and right-wing populism and neo-nationalism. Gender scholars usually agree that nationalist (and populist) discourses have a gender bias, which constructs men and women differently in their public and private lives. Yet, no agreement exists on the implications of populism for gender equality and feminist politics in contemporary Europe (cf. Knijn and Naldini 2018)

The chapter first presents the concept of populism and key issues in scholarly debates on populism in mainstream and gender research. What populism means for democracy, gender equality and the future of the EU is a contested issue. We discuss Cas Mudde's influential approach to populism as a 'thin ideology' combining authoritarianism and nativism (cf. Mudde 2007; Mudde and Kaltwasser 2015) and show that there is a 'gender gap' in the literature on populism, since it lacks systematic studies of gender and populism. Next, we provide an overview of research reframing populism, gender equality and feminist politics in contemporary Europe. Comparative studies of European RWP parties have identified a shift in their discourses on gender and family away from the patriarchal, conservative family model (Farris 2017; Krizsán and Siim 2018; Norocel 2017). As a result, most RWP parties have adopted a version of gender equality and sexual rights, abandoning the male-breadwinner model of the family (Farris 2017; Krizsán and Siim 2018). At the same time, a number of such parties call for a dismantling of anti-discrimination legislation in the EU (Falkner and Plattner 2019). These studies emphasize that European populism is contextual and may express a variety of positions opposing gender equality (Verloo 2018a). Finally, we review the scholarly debates featuring the challenges that recent right-wing populism pose to liberal democracy, EU gender equality norms and feminist politics and point to future challenges in both national and transnational arenas. One urgent

367

Birte Siim and Christina Fiig

issue is how to address the growing opposition to gender equality and anti-discrimination policies from RWP parties in the EU member states and within the European Parliament. In the conclusions we point to empirical and theoretical gaps in the literature and propose two areas for future gender research: first, the implications of populist opposition to gender equality and anti-discrimination with a focus on the interactions of the national and transnational EU-arena; second, the effects of national dynamics of populist anti-gender civil society mobilizations for feminist politics as well as for the future of the EU.

Reframing populism in mainstream and gender literature

Populism is a contested concept with contextual variations. Scholars often disagree about its definition, the relations between right-wing and left-wing populism as well as its relation to democracy and liberal values. Cas Mudde's approach to populism as nativist, anti-elitist and anti-establishment refers to populism as a 'thin ideology' associated with diverse political content (Mudde 2007); this can be attached to different ideologies and thus manifests itself in different forms (Spierings et al. 2015, 8). Another example is Benjamin Moffit's study of the global rise of populism, emphasizing its political style 'performed, embodied and enacted in a variety of political and cultural contexts' (Moffit 2016, 12). Jan-Werner Müller (2016, 2017) provides a somewhat different definition of populism. He claims that populism is a dangerous anti-pluralist and anti-democratic ideology, which aims to make opposition to populism illegitimate in contemporary Europe. This understanding makes a crucial distinction between the discourse of populism in opposition and populists' politics in power, which aims to remake political institutions to reflect their image of the real, authentic people (Müller 2017, 602–603).

The recent rise of left-wing populism in Europe has provoked scholarly debates about the similarities and differences between right-wing and left-wing parties and movements (Mudde and Kaltwasser 2011; Moffit 2016; Müller 2016). The notion of left-wing populism fits well with theoretical approaches,[1] such as Mudde and Kaltwasser's categorizing, but is more difficult to reconcile with Müller's claims that populism is always anti-pluralist (Müller 2016, 128–138).

These different approaches have implications for the relation between populism and gender. Some scholars tend to emphasize the similarities, rather than the variations, regarding gender politics in diverse cultural and historical contexts, such as Latin America and Europe (Mudde and Kaltwasser 2011), or across Europe (Mudde and Kaltwasser 2015). Populism has generally been associated with charismatic leadership, and Mudde's term 'Männerpartien' (*men's parties*; Mudde 2007) fits well with male leaders of the majority of RWP parties but less with female leadership of these parties (Meret et al. 2017). Interestingly, Mudde and Kaltwasser (2015, 17) have recently argued that conceptually populism has no specific relationship to gender. According to Müller, however, populism is not necessarily associated with charismatic (male) leaders. Instead, he refers to the importance of contextual factors, such as the gender gap in voting for European populist parties, with more men than women as voters and supporters, different from Latin America (Müller 2016, 35). Müller (2016, 24–28) does not address the conceptual relation between populism and gender, but according to his understanding populism makes diversity – including diversity among women – illegitimate.

To summarize, mainstream literature demonstrates a variety of ways to understanding populist challenges to democratic legitimacy, liberal values and equality, but has not conceptualized gender as a defining characteristic of populist parties (cf. Dietze and Roth 2020). We argue that a focus on gender can reveal how notions of 'the people' embody highly gendered expectations of the roles of both women and men, as part of the ideology of populism and as a performative style (Geva 2018, 16–17; Kantola and Lombardo 2019, 1).

Reframing populism through the gender lens

Feminist scholarship has begun to explore relations of gender equality, sexuality and the family to populism. It claims that gender perspectives have an unacknowledged significance to populism, nationalism/nativism and authoritarianism and that research needs to explore to what extent and in what form gender is a defining characteristic of nationalism and radical-right politics (RRP) (Spierings et al. 2015, 1–15; Spierings 2020). To capture the gender aspects of populism, we propose to combine insights from different approaches, specifically studies of nationalism/nativism, intersectionality and critical masculinity studies.

Gender scholars have not explicitly conceptualized the relationship between gender and populism, but many have analysed the links between gender and the nation, nationalism /nativism and autochthonic politics (i.e. to be of the soil). They claim that nationalist projects often construct women and mothers as the embodiment of imaginary homelands (Yuval-Davis 1997, 2011, 94–96) and as 'biological reproducers of the nation' (Farris 2017, 72). One example is Nira Yuval-Davis's influential approach to national belongings inspired by Benedict Anderson's work on imagined communities (Yuval-Davis 1997, 2011). Another is Sara Farris' (2017) more recent notion of femo-nationalism. Both approaches emphasize how nationalist projects identify women as 'bearers of the collective' and as 'biological reproducers of the nation' rather than as individuals (Farris 2017, 72). However, this literature rarely appears in mainstream discussions on populism.

In Yuval-Davis' work on gendering nationalism, the intersectional approach is crucial for analysing belonging/s and political projects of belonging. Here different groups of women are located as members of different collectivities with different identifications and normative value systems (Yuval-Davis 2011, 25). This work identifies the move towards 'cultural racism', which does not rest on notions of 'race' or 'ethnic origin' but on culture, religion and tradition perceived to threaten the nation. Yuval-Davis (2011, 99–102) argues that the notion of 'autochthonic politics of belonging' is crucial for right-wing politics in contemporary Europe and elsewhere since it defines who belongs to the nation.

Feminist scholars propose that European RWP parties use anti-gender equality positions to exclude minority groups such as Muslims, Roma, 'persons of colour', migrants and refugees (Meret and Siim 2013, 90–92; Verloo 2018a, 50). Farris (2017, 57–67) links the concept of populism closely to theories of nationalism and emphasizes the racialist underpinnings of the populist radical approach to nationalism. Her coinage of 'femo-nationalism', short for 'feminist and femocratic nationalism' (Farris 2017, 4, 6), points to the ways gender equality is used to define or draw borders between Muslim women and native-born women, the ways feminist themes are exploited by nationalism and neoliberalism in anti-Islam and anti-immigration campaigns and used for the stigmatization of Muslim men. Farris' studies document how the far right in Italy, France and the Netherlands advance their anti-Islam agenda in the name of women's rights.

Comparative studies of European RWP parties with women leaders propose to revise Mudde's definition of these parties as 'Männerparteien', which is premised on charismatic leadership and on women's reproductive and symbolic role as 'mothers' of the nation (Erzeel and Rashkova 2017; Geva 2018; Meret et al. 2017). These studies point to female leadership of some of these parties and show that most of them accept some version of gender equality. In the same vein, research on populist parties has emphasized the nativist/neo-nationalist character of European populism (Krizsán and Siim 2018). These studies demonstrate how national histories, political institutions and culture influence RWP parties' leadership style and ideologies. They point to the influence of the heritage of the Nordic welfare states, post-communist states and countries with a heritage of Nazism and fascism (cf. Krizsán and Siim 2018; Sauer et al. 2017).

Some studies propose to gender populism (and nationalism) by employing an intersectional analysis as a tool to understand the multiple ways gender intersects with other categories of difference and axes of inequality (Siim and Mokre 2013). An intersectional analysis of the populist right can show that support for these parties is not only tied to gender – meaning that men rather than women support these parties – but also to race (white) and class (lower) (Spierings et al. 2015, 11). The intersectionality approach has evolved through comparative studies of the rise of RWP parties in contemporary Europe, for example, analysis looking at the interface between immigration, race/ethnicity, gender and sexuality (Krizsán and Siim 2018; Meret and Siim 2013; Mulinari and Neergaard 2014; Sauer and Ajanovic 2016; Sauer et al. 2017). The RWP parties often combine exclusionary neo-nationalist positions with nativist discourses and liberal values such as gender equality and women's rights (de Lange and Mügge 2015; Meret and Siim 2013, 93; Siim and Meret 2016). Based on studies of actors' identity constructions in the European public sphere, scholars propose to distinguish between two contradictory developments towards either 'exclusionary' or 'inclusionary' framings of the interaction of gender equality and ethnic diversity (Siim and Mokre 2013, 34–35). 'Exclusionary' intersectionality refers to the belief by the populist right in irreconcilable conflicts between the value of gender equality and diversity and in minority groups' inability to accept gender equality. This contrasts with 'inclusionary' intersectionality that refers to a non-hierarchical understanding of equality and ethnic diversity as positive values to be reconciled by common struggles against all forms of discrimination and for justice.

Critical masculinity studies (see also Hearn et al. in this volume) have contributed to a reframing of populism with insights into party leaders' and members' identities and performative practices (Christensen and Qvotrup Jensen 2014; Geva 2018), adding affects and emotions (Dietze and Roth 2020, 11). One example is Norocel's study of the Sweden Democrats, which demonstrates the gradual normalization of populist radical discourses in Swedish politics (Norocel 2017). He identifies the discursive link between controlling migration and ensuring (Swedish) women's safety in public space. The analysis specifies gender as an important social position in the dichotomous relationship between Swedish native majority and the migrant (Muslim) others and the majority's opposition to the presence of the migrants in the Swedish *Folkheim*'s homeland (Norocel 2017, 101–102). Another example is Kantola and Lombardo's comparison of left-wing populism (in Spain) and right-wing populism (in Finland). The authors point to the 'ethos of hegemonic masculinity' as a common characteristic of two populist political parties and propose that both are dominated by hegemonic masculinity (Kantola and Lombardo 2019). However, we still need more systematic knowledge of the relationship of left-wing populism to gender equality discourses, policies and political styles, which compares right-wing and left-wing populism in diverse national contexts.

In sum, gender scholars have made important contributions to reframing our thinking of populism, but we still lack systematic knowledge about the relationship between gender and the populist right and the populist left. It is an emergent research field and many research gaps still exist, especially knowledge about the explanatory potential of the category gender (cf. Dietze and Roth 2020). Systematic, context-sensitive intersectional analyses of the relation of gender with other forms of inequality is a way to expand our knowledge of diverse and complex neo-nationalist and right-wing – or radical-right – populist projects across Europe.

Overview of research on gender and populism in the EU and its member states

This section addresses the conflicts about gender equality, welfare and migration within the EU, the European Parliament and within some of the member states. It aims to contextualize

The populist challenge to gender equality

opposition to gender equality in Europe by paying attention to national historical legacies and to diversity in the political and cultural developments in different regions of the EU. Next, it aims to analyse opposition to gender equality by neo-nationalist and anti-migration discourses and policies within the EU and in the European Parliament.

Since the early 2000s, Europe has witnessed a strengthening of neo-nationalist and anti-migration discourses and policies. Feminist scholars have started to study the varieties of opposition to gender equality. These studies identify the multiple actors that take part in the anti-movements, such as the Manif Pour Tous against French laws legalizing same-sex marriage; Catholic groups against legislation concerning violence against women as well as opposition from inside political and legal institutions (cf.Verloo 2018b).

Research has emphasized that contextual varieties in the relationship between RWP ideologies and gender equality are crucial for understanding the opposition to EU gender equality norms (Verloo 2018a). Comparative studies have identified tensions in discourses and policies about gender, family, migration and mobility premised on exclusive intersectionality (Krizsán and Siim 2018; Sauer et. al. 2017). A study of seven RWP parties concludes that these parties adopt different discursive strategies concerning gender and homosexuality, influenced by their countries' welfare, gender and migration regimes. Some employ bio-political, ethno-nationalist or racist arguments; others use a pragmatic appeal to liberal values and good morals; only a few support the mainstream European discourse gender equality and LGBTQ rights[2] (cf. Sauer et al. 2017, 110–118).

Studies of RWP parties in the EU resp. European Parliament have confirmed that important differences exist in their constructions of welfare, gender and family issues (Knijn and Naldini 2018). A study of RWP parties at the European Parliamentary elections in 2014 illustrates that these parties, selected from different European regions, disagreed on gender, sexual and family policies.The RWP parties promoted both neoliberal and social welfare policies, instrumentalizing gender equality, sexuality and family issues to serve their versions of exclusive welfare nationalisms (cf. Farris 2017; Krizsán and Siim 2018; see also Ahrens and Rolandsen Agustín (Party politics) in this volume).With the exceptions of Alternative für Deutschland (AfD), the analysed parties expressed a pragmatic acceptance of the principle of gender equality and support for women's wage work and childcare, justified with reference to nativist or reproductive claims (Krizsán and Siim 2018, 39–59). Interestingly, this study has also found that RWP parties promoted different family models. The major difference emerged between the two Northern parties (the Danish Peoples' Party, DF, and the Dutch Freedom Party, PVV) and the rest of the parties, which supported the traditional family (model) and advocated for state intervention due to low fertility and deteriorating morals. The German AfD was an outlier in rejecting any state or EU intervention, which could promote 'gender ideology' (Krizsán and Siim 2018, 55).The study concluded that immigration generally trumps gender and family issues. It found that RWP parties within the European Parliament share exclusionary versions of nationalism favouring native-born citizens. They justify these with reference to norms in their own national gender and welfare regimes. However, research shows that after the 2014 European election the RWP parties decided to join parliamentary political groups with different political profiles guided by domestic benefits (cf. McDonnell and Werner 2018).

Literature points to a triumvirate of actors that plays a role in articulating the relationship between gender and the ideology of populism: its political leaders, party members and voters/supporter (Abi-Hassan 2017; Spierings and Zaslove 2015). Research has identified a gender gap in radical-right votes: greater reluctance of women to vote for these parties in Europe (Barisione and Mayer 2015). The large quantitative study of voter choice for RWPs in Austria, Belgium, Denmark, France, the Netherlands and Sweden based on the 2014 European Election Studies

371

confirmed the slight gender gap (roughly 4–5 percentage points) in the electoral support for RWP parties (Barisione and Mayer 2015, 18). More important, the gap does not depend exclusively on educational or religious gender differences, but on mediators such as left–right self-placement and attitudes towards immigrants and sexual minorities. The study points towards intra-gender heterogeneity, with women appearing particularly split along societal and ideological lines. It concludes that the gender gap in radical-right voting appears closely linked to two patterns: the 'traditional support' (i.e. that women are less often on the right of the ideological spectrum and tend to be more tolerant than men vis-à-vis social outgroups), and the 'modern rejection'. The latter refers to an ideal-type of younger highly educated left-wing women with modern political attitudes, who are very far from the profile of the women on which the traditional RR gender gap rests – i.e. older, less educated, more religious and politically conservative (Barisione and Mayer 2015, 19–20).

Studies on the influence of female leadership on populism as a political style and ideology in RWP parties are still scarce. RWP parties with male (or female) leaders may publicly support gender equality and women's rights, while they direct their discourses and policies mainly against the supposedly patriarchal migrant (Muslim) 'Other' (Farris 2017; Meret et al. 2017). One case study of Marine le Pen's leadership of the French Rassemblement National argues that structures and performance of hegemonic masculinity and hegemonic femininity provide the content for the performative repertoire linking populism with the radical right (Abi-Hassan 2017, 436–437; Geva 2018, 16–18).

From the EU perspective the context of multiple crises, i.e. the sovereign debt crises, the migration/Schengen crisis, Brexit and most recently the Covid-19 crisis, have led to an increase in right-wing populism and its influence on gender equality policies (Fiig 2020).

Research on the varieties of opposition to gender equality in Europe has focused on opposition to feminist politics, labelled gender+ equality, that refers to 'the importance of paying attention to the intersectional inequalities that are interwoven with gender equality' (Verloo 2018b, 7). This research confirms that opposition to gender+ equality has become unacceptable, a 'taboo', on the supranational EU level, leading to a low prevalence of 'politically incorrect' direct opposition and to more indirect forms of opposition (Ahrens 2018, 77). This absence of direct opposition results from the self-image of the EU as the defender of equality between women and men (Ahrens 2018, 82). Ahrens' study, based on expert interviews with gender+ policy stakeholders in key institutions, finds that direct opposition to gender+ policies mostly comes from the European Parliament and from actors external to the network of EU gender+ equality actors (Ahrens 2018) – for example with reference to Malta, Poland and Ireland, often labelled as a 'backlash triangle' due to their opposition to abortion and reproductive rights (Ahrens 2018, 81). Ahrens (2018) identifies a typology of indirect opposition to gender+ equality that effectively hampers further improvements. Its techniques include inertia (inactivity), evasion (avoiding participating in exchanges about gender+ equality) and degradation (actors isolate and devalue gender+ equality policies).

Over the past six decades, the European Parliament has promoted gender equality in terms of agenda setting and adoption of resolutions on new issues at times when no clear treaty base existed. Recent research has pointed to changes in the Parliament's ability to promote gender equality (van der Vleuten 2019). It shows that electoral gains of RWP parties, following the elections of 2014 and 2019, have created political groupings able to challenge the Parliament as an engine for gender equality (Ahrens and Rolandsen Agustín 2019; see also Rolandsen Agustín and Ahrens in this volume). RWP party groups have sharpened the rhetoric about women's and gender issues, essentializing views of women and strengthening opposition to the supranational promotion of gender equality. The result has been a shift from gender at the EU level to a stronger focus on national politics. Given increased contestation of gender 'ideology' and LGBTI+ rights, the domain of gender equality is no longer a simple legitimacy booster (van der Vleuten 2019, 48). A recent study addresses what the impact of the changed composition of the European Parliament in 2014 and 2019 means for its openness to transnational 'equality civil society organizations' that promote gender equality and anti-discrimination (Ahrens and Woodward 2020). The study finds that these CSOs despite the changing environment in the European Parliament have maintained an effective presence on the political stage albeit moving their activities from formal to more 'informal venues' in order to avoid polarization and conflict (Ahrens and Woodward 2020, 12).

One area where knowledge remains limited is the impact of discourses on the threat of gender ideology on left wing parties/movements in Europe. Feminist research has been more attentive to the effects of right-wing than left-wing populism (cf. Kantola and Lombardo 2019). One exception is the study of the Spanish Podemos party pointing towards an ambiguity between the feminization of the political discourses and the party's lack of gender equality and feminist policies (Lombardo and Verge 2017).

Given the increasing power of the European Parliament and its participation in European legislative procedures, the question of what the potential impact of right-wing political groups on gender equality will be is an important one (Ahrens and Rolandsen Agustín 2019, 2, and in this volume). We need knowledge about the implications of recent political transformations for gender equality, knowledge that explores the complex links between the national and transnational levels of the EU.

Moving forward: future challenges for gender research and politics

This section offers reflections on the future challenges for research on gender equality politics and policies in the context of populism, growing resistance to feminist norms in the European Parliament and across member states (Köttig et al. 2017; Pajnik and Sauer 2017; Verloo 2018a). The focus is on two issues: the growing opposition to gender equality in the Parliament and the normalization of right-wing populism in EU member states, followed by an increase of anti-gender movements.

First, scholars have emphasized that despite its history as a promoter of gender equality and women's rights, the European Parliament no longer acts as a unified and agenda-setting actor for gender equality. They point to the importance of considering national party frames, which have become predictors of voting positions within the European Parliament regarding anti-discrimination (Falkner and Plattner 2019) and emphasize that gender equality is increasingly politicized within the Parliament (Meier et al. 2019; Warasin et al. 2019). In principle, populist radical-right parties may influence policy outcomes both directly (via increased presence and via their voice in EU decision-making) and indirectly (via 'nudging' other parties to take on board their preferred topics or even viewpoints) (Falkner and Plattner 2019).

Secondly, research pays increasing attention to the implications for gender equality of the gradual 'normalization' of RWP parties in EU member states. The mainstreaming of anti-migration and exclusive nationalism by a number of socially conservative, liberal and in some cases social-democratic parties, taking over the claims of RWP parties' discourse and policies, is famously labelled 'the politics of fear' (Wodak 2015, 2019). The recent political transformations have led to growing opposition to the EU's fundamental values of (gender) equality, human rights and the rule of law, social justice and (ethnic and family) diversity, and increased the populist (right-wing) parties' ability to influence public debate and the future of EU gender policies. This includes the impact of the political transformations following the entry of RWP

Birte Siim and Christina Fiig

parties in governments in countries such as Austria, Finland, Norway, Hungary, Poland and Italy. It also includes the growing political influence of RWP parties as coalition parties in minority governments, as in the Danish case, or with growing parliamentary support, as for the Sweden Democrats (Norocel 2017).

Comparative studies on populism and anti-democratic tendencies emphasize that political actors in a number of countries actively oppose the values of gender equality with the label 'gender ideology'. They show that these movements have successfully mobilized against human rights and equality, for instance to limit women's reproductive rights, curtail LGBTI+ rights etc. (Grzebalska et al. 2017, 3; Verloo 2018a) or even the fight against domestic and gender-based violence as in the case of opposition against ratification of the Istanbul Convention (see Roggeband in this volume). One observed strategy is to use political arguments to create moral panics in opposition to promoters of gender-progressive politics (Svatonova *forthcoming*).

Cases where RWP parties are in power are particularly acute. For example, Hungary is characterized by a transition to illiberalism, a system that rests on the rejection of civic liberalism (i.e. checks and balances, civil liberties) and that undermines democracy in the process (Grzebalska at al. 2017, 2). In this case, Prime Minister Victor Orbán is effectively challenging EU values of liberal democracy, human rights and gender equality, and currently instrumentalizes the Covid-19 pandemic for moving forward on his autocratic path. Another worrying case is Poland, where the government combines anti-liberal, anti-abortion, anti-pluralist and anti-feminist rhetoric and policies (Grzebalska 2015; Grzebalska at al. 2017).

Feminist scholars have begun to identify the different dimensions of anti-gender-equality policies. These include increasingly hostile policy processes, dismantling of existing policies or amending policies so that their priorities or objectives change, undermining implementation and institutional design and erosion of inclusion and accountability mechanisms, for example by dismantling formal consultation structures (Krizsán and Roggeband 2018). However, only a few gender studies focus on the implications of these anti-democratic, anti-pluralist and anti-liberal national policies for the transnational EU arena.

In all, there is growing concern that negative attitudes to key aspects of gender equality and anti-discrimination at the national level may spill over to affect gender equality policies in the European Parliament, a consequence of the growth of RWP parties across the EU (Krizsán and Siim 2018). The threats to liberal democracy and legal rights in a number of member states have added to the impression that the EU is not able to deal with populist politics. Democratic backsliding (Sedelmeier 2014) and de-democratization processes have serious consequences, and often include opposition to (gender) equality. Research convincingly documents the need for more systematic analyses of the opposition to gender equality and feminist norms at the regional, national and transnational levels (Ahrens and Rolandsen Agustín 2019; Verloo 2018a).

Concluding reflections

Scholars are concerned that the political transformations in contemporary Europe have serious implications for democracy, equality and social justice. Gender scholars add that new forms of populism and neo-nationalism present particular challenges for gender equality policies and feminist politics (Ahrens and Rolandsen Agustín 2019; Verloo 2018a). The chapter concludes that we need to overcome the gender gap in mainstream literature about populism and proposes to reframe gender and populism inspired by different bodies of literature bridging studies of populism in political science and political sociology with gender research. Furthermore, future studies of populism and gender need to be more concerned with the complex interactions of national and transnational arenas, political institutions and activism in civil society. In addition,

374

we need comparative studies of similarities and differences between right and left populism in various cultural and political contexts, as well as between gender and populism in Europe and other parts of the world.

One theoretical challenge is placing populist opposition to gender equality and the feminist project in relation to larger macro-level forces, such as neo-nationalist, neoliberal and anti-democratic projects (Verloo and Paternotte 2018). Gender scholars have proposed different concepts and research strategies, which tend to focus either predominantly on populism's relation to nationalism/nativism, to racism/ethnicity, or to capitalism/neoliberalism. The concept of femo-nationalism presents an exception, since it rests upon the theoretical and empirical hypothesis of 'a convergence between feminism, neo-nationalism and neo-liberalism' (Farris 2017, 144), but further research must either confirm or reject this premise. Arguably, it is both possible and desirable for future research on gender, populism and neo-nationalism to combine insights from diverse approaches, such as intersectionality, critical masculinity studies and nationalism/femo-nationalism. We have proposed that the intersectionality approach (see also Solanke in this volume) is a fruitful theoretical and methodological research strategy for analysing gender aspects of populism. It can combine diverse approaches and has the potential as an analytical tool to explore the complex intersections of gender and other inequalities in relation to social locations, political values and identities in the European context.

Empirically, the existing literature argues convincingly that the rise of populist parties in European nation states, the EU and the European Parliament presents a potential threat to liberal values, such as anti-discrimination, gender equality and reproductive rights. Research also demonstrates that populism in contemporary Europe takes different forms, influenced by political and cultural contexts, and that some RWP parties currently support liberal values in relation to family and gender issues. At the same time, recent studies have identified a growing opposition in some member states to liberal values, such as gender equality, minority and sexual rights, including by RWP parties in government (Ahrens and Rolandsen Agustín 2019, 2).

It is still debatable what the recent political mainstreaming of populism and normalization of anti-migration policies in many member states might imply for the future development of liberal democracy and gender equality policies in the EU. In the short-term perspective, one key issue is whether populist parties will be able to unite on an anti-EU, anti-migration and anti-gender agenda within the present EP legislature, or remain divided on key issues, as was the case after the previous European Parliament legislature of 2014–2019. It is a crucial political as well as a research challenge to study whether and how the EU will be able to defend liberal democracy, human rights and gender equality in member states, such as Hungary and Poland. Another major challenge is whether political parties, civil society groups and movements advocating for democracy, gender equality and social justice will be able to mobilize and build alliances across political differences and social categories on common (trans) national platforms in defence of (gender) equality and social justice. Recent developments in EU member states as well as in the European Parliament demonstrate that future research needs to combine studies of the implications of political transitions for gender equality at EU level with sensitivity to national contexts.

Finally, we propose that future studies need to address the normative challenges presented by populism's opposition to the Union's values such as democracy, human rights and (gender) equality laid down in the treaties and the Copenhagen Criteria for enlargement (1993; see Chiva in this volume). One crucial research area could be the politics and acts of solidarity against growing inequality, discrimination and racism in social movements and civil society organizations across Europe (Agustín and Bak Jørgensen 2016; Della Porta 2018). Studies (cf. Sauer 2018; Siim et al. 2018; Verloo 2018b) of the responses by civil society and feminist actors

Birte Siim and Christina Fiig

are powerful means to make visible the local/regional, national/transnational level mobilization for gender equality and anti-discrimination.

Notes

1 Scholars employing Mudde's minimal definition often differentiate between exclusionary populism in Europe and inclusionary populism in Latin America (cf. Mudde and Kaltwasser 2011), while Müller's approach to populism as an anti-pluralist discourse provides a more critical understanding of left-wing populism (cf. Müller 2016, 123–128).
2 The first strategy was adopted by the Greek Golden Dawn and the Bulgarian National Union, the second by the Austrian Freedom Party and the Italian Forza Nuova, and the third by the Danish Peoples' Party and the Finns (cf. Sauer et al. 2017, 110–118).

References

Abi-Hassan S (2017): Populism and Gender, in: Kaltwasser C R, Taggart P, Ochoa Espejo P, Ostiguy P (eds.): *The Oxford Handbook of Populism,* Oxford: Oxford University Press, 426–444.

Agustin O G, Bak Jørgensen M (2016): *Solidarity without Borders. Gramscian Perspectives on migration and civil society alliances,* London: Pluto Press.

Ahrens P (2018): Indirect Opposition: Diffuse Barriers to Gender Equality in the European Union, in: Verloo M. (ed.): *Varieties of Opposition to Gender Equality in Europe,* New York: Routledge, 77–97.

Ahrens P, Rolandsen Agustín L (2019): Gendering the European Parliament. Introducing Structures, Policies and Practices, in: Ahrens P, Rolandsen Agustín L (eds.): *Gendering the European Parliament. Structures, Policies and Practices,* London: Rowman & Littlefield, 1–16.

Ahrens P, Woodward A (2020): Adjusting venues and voices: populist and right-wing parties, the European Parliament and civil society organizations 2014–2019, *European Politics and Society,* 1–18, DOI: 10.1080/23745118.2020.1801181.

Barisione M, Mayer N (2015): The Transformation of the Radical Right Gender Gap. The case of the 2014 EP Election, paper presented at the 4th European Conference on Politics and Gender, Uppsala, June 11–13.

Christensen AD, Qvotrup Jensen S (2014): Combining hegemonic masculinity and intersectionality, *NORMA: International Journal of Masculinity Studies* **9** (1), 60–75.

de Lange S, Mügge L (2015): Gender and right wing populism in the Low Countries. Ideological variations across parties and time, *Patterns of Prejudice* **49** (1–2), 61–80.

Della Porta D, ed. (2018): *Solidarity Mobilizations in the 'Refugee Crisis',* Cham: Palgrave Macmillan.

Dietze G, Roth J, eds. (2020): *Right-Wing Populism and Gender. European Perspectives and Beyond,* Bielefeld: transcript.

Erzeel S, Rashkova E (2017): Still men's parties: gender and the radical right in comparative perspective, *West European Politics* **40**, 812–820.

Falkner G, Plattner G (2019): EU policies and populist radical right parties' programmatic claims. Foreign policy, anti-discrimination and the Single Market, *Journal of Common Market Studies* **58** (3), 723–739.

Farris SR (2017): *In the Name of Women's Rights. The Rise of Femo-nationalism,* Durham, NC, London: Duke University Press.

Fiig C (2020). Gender Equality Policies and European Union Politics, in: Laursen F (ed.): *Encyclopedia of European Union Politics,* Oxford: Oxford University Press, 1–27.

Geva D (2018): Daugther, mother, captain: Marine le Pen, gender, and populism in the French National Front, *Social Politics* **27** (1), 1–26.

Grzebalska W (2015): Poland, in: Kováts E, Põim M (eds.): *Gender as Symbolic Glue– The Position and Role of Conservative and Far Right Parties in the Anti-Gender Mobilizations in Europe,* Budapest: Foundation for European Progressive Studies in cooperation with the Friedrich Ebert Stiftung, 83–102.

Grzebalska W, Kováts E, Petö A (2017). *Gender as the sympolic glue: How 'gender' became an umbrella term for the rejection of the (neo)liberal order,* URL: http://politicalcritique.org/long-read/2017/gender-as-symbolic-glue-how-gender-became-an-umbrella-term-for-the-rejection-of-the-neoliberal-order (download: May 13, 2020).

Kantola J, Lombardo E (2019): Populism and feminist politics: the cases of Finland and Spain, *European Journal of Political Research* **58** (4), 1108–1128.

Kantola, J, Lombardo E (2020): Populism and Feminist Politics, *International Political Science Review*, Special Issue: Populism Symposium, 1–4, https://doi.org/10.1177/0192512120972609

Knijn T, Naldini M, eds (2018): *Gender and Generational Division in EU Citizenship,* Cheltenham: Edward Elgar.

Köttig M, Bitzan R, Peto A, eds. (2017): *Gender and Far Right Politics in Europe*. Basingstoke: Palgrave Macmillan.

Krizsán A, Roggeband C (2018): Towards a conceptual framework for struggles over democracy in backsliding states. Gender equality Policy in central eastern Europe, *Politics and Governance* **6** (3), 90–100.

Krizsán A, Siim B (2018): Gender Equality and Family in European Populist Radical-Right Agendas: European Parliamentary Debates 2014, in: Knijn T, Naldino M (eds.): *Gender and Generational Division in EU Citizenship*, Cheltenham: Edward Elgar, 39–59.

Loch D, Norocel OC (2015): The Populist Radical Right in Europe. A Xenophobic Voice in the Global Economic Crisis, in: Guiraudon V, Ruzza C, Trenz HJ (eds.): *Europa's Prolonged Crisis. The Making of the Unmaking of a Political Union*, Basingstoke: Palgrave Macmillan, 251–269.

Lombardo E, Verge T (2017): Cuotas de género en política y economía Regulación y configuración institucional en Espana, *Politica y Gobierno* **24** (2), 301–331.

McDonnell D, Werner A (2018): Respectable radicals: why some radical right parties in the European Parliament forsake political congruence, *Journal of European Public Policy* **25** (5), 747–763.

Meier P, Ahrens P, Rolandsen Augustin L (2019). ★Gender★ Power★? On the Multiple Relations between Gender and Power in the European Parliament, in: Ahrens P, Rolandsen Agustín L (eds.): *Gendering the European Parliament. Structures, Policies and Practices*, London: Rowman & Littlefield, 199–212.

Meret S, Siim B (2013): Gender, Populism and Politics of Belonging. Discourses of Right-Wing Populist Parties in Denmark, Norway and Austria, in: Siim B, Mokre M (eds.): *Negotiating Gender and Diversity in an Emergent European Public Sphere*, Basingstoke: Palgrave Macmillan, 78–96.

Meret S, Siim B, Pingaud E (2017): Men's parties with women leaders. A comparative study of right-wing populist leaders Pia Kjærsgaard, Siv Jensen and Marine Le Pen, in: Lazaridis G, Campani G (eds.): *Understanding the Populist Shift*, London, New York: Routledge, 122–149.

Moffit B (2016): *The Global Rise of Populism. Performance, Political Style, and Representation*, Stanford, CA: Stanford University Press.

Mudde C (2007): *Populist Radical Right Parties in Europe*, Cambridge: Cambridge University Press.

Mudde C, Kaltwasser C (2011): Voices of the Peoples. Populism in Europe and Latin America compared, Helen Kellogg Institute for International Studies, *Working Paper* **378**.

Mudde C, Kaltwasser C (2015): Vox populi or vox masculini? Populism and gender in Northern Europe and South America, *Patterns of Prejudice* **49** (1–2), 16–36.

Mulinari D, Neergaard A (2014): We are Sweden Democrats because we care for others. Exploring racisms in the Swedish extreme right, *European Journal of Women's Studies* **21** (1), 43–56.

Müller JW (2016): *Hvad er populisme*, [What is populism], Viborg: Informations Forlag.

Müller JW (2017): Populism and Constitutionalism, in: Kaltwasser CR, Taggart P, Ochoa Espejo P, Ostiguy P (eds.): *The Oxford Handbook of Populism,* Oxford: Oxford University Press, 590–606.

Norocel C (2017): Åkesson and Almedalen. Intersectional tensions and normalization of populist right discourse in Sweden, *Nora: Nordic Journal of Feminist and Gender Research* **25** (2), 91–106.

Pajnik M, Sauer S, eds. (2017): *Populism and the Web: Communicative Practices of Parties and Movements in Europe*, London, New York: Routledge.

Sauer B, Ajanovic E (2016): Hegemonic Discourses of Difference and Inequality: Right-Wing Organisations in Austria, in: Lazaridis G, Campani G, Benveniste A (eds.): *The Rise of the Far Right in Europe. Populist Shifts and 'Othering'*, Basingstoke: Palgrave Macmillan, 81–108.

Sauer B, Kuhar R, Ajanovic E, Saarinen S (2017): Exclusive Intersections: Constructions of Gender and Sexuality, in: Lazaridis G, Campone G (eds.): *Understanding the Populist Shift. Othering in a Europe in Crisis,* London, New York: Routledge, 104–121.

Sauer B (2018): The (Im)possibility of Creating Counter-Hegemony against the Radical Right. The Case of Austria, in: Siim B, Krasteva A, Saarinen A (eds.): *Citizens' Activism and Solidarity Movements in contemporary Europe. Contending with Populism*, Cham: Palgrave Macmillan, 111–136.

Sedelmeier U (2014): Anchoring democracy from above? The European Union and democratic backsliding in Hungary and Romania after accession, *Journal of Common Market Studies* **52** (1), 105–121.

Siim B, Mokre M, eds. (2013): *Negotiating Gender and Diversity in an Emergent European Public Sphere,* Basingstoke: Palgrave Macmillan.

Siim B, Meret S (2016): Right wing populism in Denmark. People, nation and welfare in the construction of the 'Other', in: Lazaridis G, Campani G, Benveniste A (eds.): *The Rise of the Far-Right in Europe. Populist Shifts and Othering*, Basingstoke: Palgrave Macmillan, 109–136.

Siim B, Krasteva A, Saarinen S (2018): *Citizens' Activism and Solidarity Movements in contemporary Europe. Contending with Populism*, Cham: Palgrave Macmillan.

Spierings N (2020): Why Gender and Sexuality are both Trivial and Pivotal in Populist Radical Right Politics, in: Dietze G, Roth J (eds.): *Right-Wing Populism and Gender. European Perspectives and Beyond*, Bielefeld: transcript, 41–58.

Spierings N, Zaslove A (2015): Conclusion: dividing the populist radical right between 'liberal nativism' and traditional conceptions of gender, *Patterns of Prejudice* **49** (1–2), 163–173.

Spierings N, Zaslove A, Mügge LM, de Lange SL (2015): Gender and populist radical-right politics: an introduction, *Patterns of Prejudice* **49** (1–2), 3–15.

Svatonova E (forthcoming): 'Gender Activists Will Kidnap Your Kids'. The Construction of Feminist and LGBT+ Rights Activists as the Modern Folk Devils in Czech Anti-gender Campaigns, in: Harboe I, Demant Frederiksen M (eds.): *Modern Folk Devils: The Construction of Evil in the Contemporary World*, Helsinki: Helsinki University Press.

Verloo M, Paternotte D (2018): The feminist project under threat in Europe, *Politics and Governance* **6** (3), 1–5.

Verloo M (2018a): How to Study Varieties of Opposition to Gender+ Equality in Europe? Lessons from This Book, Conceptual Building Blocks, and Puzzles to Address, in: Verloo M (ed.): *Varieties of Opposition to Gender Equality in Europe*, New York: Routledge, 38–54.

Verloo M (2018b): Introduction: Dynamics of Opposition to Gender+ Equality in Europe, in Verloo M (ed.): *Varieties of Opposition to Gender Equality in Europe*, New York: Routledge, 3–18.

van der Vleuten A (2019): The European Parliament as a Constant Promoter of Gender Equality. Another European Myth?, in: Ahrens P, Rolandsen Agustín L (eds.): *Gendering the European Parliament. Introducing structures, Policies and Practices*, London: Roman & Littlefield, 35–50.

Warasin, M, Kantola J, Rolandsen Agustin L, Coughlan C (2019): Politicisation of Gender Equality in the European Parliament: Cohesion and Inter-Group Coalitions in Plenary and Committees in: Ahrens P, Rolandsen Agustín L (eds.): *Gendering the European Parliament. Introducing Structures, Policies and Practices*, London: Roman & Littlefield, 141–158.

Wodak R (2015): *The Politics of Fear. What Right-Wing Populist Discourses Mean*, Newbury Park, CA: Sage.

Wodak R (2019): Entering the 'post-shame era'. The rise of illiberal democracy, populism and neo-authoritarianism in Europe, *Global Discourse* 9 (1), 195–2013.

Yuval-Davis N (1997): *Gender and Nation*, London: Sage.

Yuval-Davis N (2011): *The Politics of Belonging: Intersectional Contestations*, London: Sage.

30
Economic crisis and the politics of austerity

Johanna Kantola and Emanuela Lombardo

The last decade of gender and EU politics has been strongly marked by the economic crisis that began in 2008 and the austerity politics that followed. The national economies of European countries such as Iceland, Ireland, Greece, Spain, Portugal and Italy were brought down and others were significantly affected. The Euro faced an existential crisis with the crisis in Greece spiralling. No sphere of society – including gender relations and politics – was completely out of the reach of the economic crisis.

Feminist researchers from different disciplines provide perspectives to these multifaceted gendered effects of the crisis. Economists have shown how – as a result of the cuts to the public sector services, benefits and jobs – women's unemployment, poverty and discrimination increased with minority women from different racial and ethnic backgrounds or with disabilities being disproportionately affected (Karamessini 2014a; Pearson and Elson 2015). Political scientists and sociologists documented how the harder economic climate was combined with a turn to conservatism. The rise of the populist right parties, anti-Islamic and anti-Semitic sentiments as well as racism and resentment towards migrants have included attacks on migrant women and veiled women (Athanasiou 2014; Emejulu and Bassell 2017). At the same time progressive gender and wider anti-discrimination policies, policy instruments and institutions that might counter these trends have suffered from significant cuts to their resources (Elomäki 2019; Jacquot 2017). Feminist cultural studies analyse the 'commodification of domestic femininities': the idealisation and promotion of female resourcefulness at times of recession and cuts in family income in various television programmes and series (Negra and Tasker 2014, 7).

EU's political engagements with gender and its gender policy during that decade and after cannot be understood without understanding the economic as well as the political effects of the crisis. Thus, it is necessary to write about *crises* in the plural (Hozic and True 2016, 12; Walby 2015). The long-standing EU legitimacy crisis reached new heights with the crumbling of social rights of European citizens for example in Greece, with the 'troika' of the European Central Bank (ECB), the European Commission and the International Monetary Fund (IMF) dictating austerity politics on member states. The Commission has since attempted to amend some of these injustices through the adoption of the so-called European Pillar of Social Rights (EPSR)

(Elomäki and Kantola 2020; Plomien 2018) combining both hard and soft law and representing an attempt to address the cuts to social rights caused by EU's austerity politics.

In this chapter, we first discuss mainstream approaches to economic crisis and austerity. Second, we focus upon different feminist approaches, which expose the costs of any gender-blind approaches (Kantola and Lombardo 2017a, 2017b). We conclude with some future directions.

Mainstream approaches to the economic crisis and austerity

Whilst the economic crisis presented the EU an opportunity for adopting either stimulus or austerity politics, the Commission opted for austerity (O'Dwyer 2018). Austerity then is 'a form of voluntary deflation in which the economy adjusts through the reduction of wages, prices and public spending to restore competitiveness, which is (supposedly) best achieved by cutting the state's budgets, debts and deficits' (Blyth 2013, 2). Austerity policies can be defined as a 'set of measures and regulatory strategies in economic policies aimed to produce a structural adjustment by reducing wages, prices and public spending' (Addabbo et al. 2013, 5). This agenda signified strengthening the deregulatory impetus within a new economic governance regime. Gender equality and wider social equalities were marginalised within the Commission's 'Europe 2020' economic strategy (COM(2010) 2020 final). This entailed institutional changes in the EU and in member states particularly. For feminist scholars it gives rise to questions such as: how are the shifts in the EU economic governance regime in crisis times and in the EU institutional balance affecting gender equality policy agendas and struggles for wider equalities?

In her award-winning article Myriann O'Dwyer (2018) argues that austerity is economically not sensible. A number of commentators have indeed argued that austerity solutions are based on the transformation of a financial crisis – the result of an over-financialisation of the economy and the prioritisation of the requirements of financial capital at the expense of paid and domestic economies (Walby 2015) – into a public debt crisis (Bettio et al. 2012; Busch et al. 2013; Rubery 2014). This conversion pushed European states to buy out the unsustainable levels of banks and household debts built up within the financial sector – bailing out failing banks – in an effort to re-stabilise the markets, which in turn then began questioning the ability of states to finance them (Rubery 2014), thus rendering borrowing on newly established sovereign debt increasingly expensive and unsustainable (Busch et al. 2013; Karamessini 2014a). This has had implications for the repertoire of policy responses, which policymakers could conceive of and their impact. In line with neoliberal economic analyses, Busch et al. (2013, 4) argue that the EU 'has interpreted the main cause of the crisis as debt and, based on this reversal of cause and effect' it has implemented severe austerity rather than growth measures, especially in the Eurozone countries, with negative social and equality impacts for the already indebted southern European states.

The EU's neoliberal regime and its emerging institutional configuration have heavily influenced the policies in the aftermath of the crisis; the new economic governance regime has reorganised the coordination of economic policy along the lines of 'disciplinary neoliberalism' (Cavaghan and O'Dwyer 2018; Kantola and Lombardo 2017a). The latter 'involves both a discourse of political economy and a relatively punitive programme of social reform' (Gill and Roberts 2011, 162). Strict rules of fiscal and monetary policies are imposed on member states that have bailed out failing banks. The main institutional actors shaping this new regime are the European Council, the ECB, ECOFIN (i.e. Economic and Financial Affairs Council), the Eurogroup, the European Commission, and political leaders of the member state governments, enjoying Germany the greater relative power in this process (Klatzer and Schlager 2014). The

Economic crisis and austerity

European Parliament has limited voice; for instance, it does neither control the European Stability Mechanism nor the European Semester.

EU crisis responses have primarily comprised efforts to encourage and coordinate states' reduction of sovereign debt through various instruments and discourses designed to enforce states' reductions in public spending. The austerity agenda includes measures that promote deregulation and liberalisation of the market, including the labour market, through the reduction of labour rules, the decentralization of collective bargaining from state to enterprises, and cuts in wages (Busch et al. 2013; Klatzer and Schlager 2014).

The new regime comprises institutions, rules and procedures to coordinate member states' macroeconomic policy. The Commission's 'Europe 2020' strategy sets the framework for the surveillance of member states' economic policies through new governance mechanisms. These are the 'Euro Plus Pact', the 'Stability and Growth Pact', the 'Fiscal Compact' and a 'Six-pack' of EU regulations that tie member states into a commitment to keep their annual budgetary deficit below 3% and their debt below 60% of GDP, targets established with the adoption of the EMU (Klatzer and Schlager 2014; Maier 2011; see also Scheele in this volume). The new economic governance tools challenge representative democracies by moving powers from parliamentary to executive branches of polities both at the national and supranational levels (Bruff and Wöhl 2016, 98; Kantola and Lombardo 2017a).

In particular, the 'Stability and Growth Pact' included expenditure and debt rules and severely increased sanctions for Eurozone countries. The 'macroeconomic imbalance procedure' gave the European Commission and ECOFIN the power to guide member states' economic policy and sanction non-compliance. The 'Fiscal Compact', an international treaty, severely constrains member states' (except UK and Czech Republic) fiscal policy and imposes debt reduction. The 'Euro Plus Pact', adopted in 2011 by initiative of German Chancellor Angela Merkel and then French President Nicolas Sarkozy, put pressure on member states to adopt reforms in the labour market, health and pension policies aiming at greater market liberalisation. It set the basis for the EU intervention in wage policy, since it considers wage policy a key factor for promoting competitiveness (Busch et al. 2013; Klatzer and Schlager 2014). A so-called 'Six-pack' of EU regulations entered into force in 2011 to implement the 'Euro Plus Pact' with the objective of 'enforcing measures to correct excessive macroeconomic imbalances in the euro area' (Bruff and Wöhl 2016, 98–99). The 'European Semester' reinforced the EU surveillance of member states' economic and budget policy procedures and decisions, establishing an annual cycle of pre-set economic targets member states have to achieve (Europe 2020), translation of these targets into country objectives through national reform programmes combined with stability programmes (where each member state plans the country's budget for the coming three or four years), EU recommendations to member states, and European Council and Commission monitoring of implementation and imposing of financial sanctions to member states in case of non-compliance (Elomäki and Kantola 2020). The 'European Stability Mechanism', through an intergovernmental treaty adopted in 2012, establishes the rules for providing EU financial support to member states in economic difficulty; loans are subject to strict conditionality and structural economic reforms through a process controlled by the EC, in cooperation with ECB and IMF (Kantola and Lombardo 2017a).

These macroeconomic policies aim to stabilise the European economy, stimulate growth and achieve price stability; concurrently, they narrow the definition of the role of government in the macroeconomic arena, thus reducing the ability of the state to act as the financier and employer of last resort (Maier 2011; Rubery 2014). These policies are thus politically contested due, among other things, to the high social costs in terms of increasing inequality (Klatzer and Schlager 2014; Rubery 2014).

381

Indeed, gender analyses criticise that gender has not been mainstreamed neither in policy design nor implementation of 'crisis measures' (Bettio et al. 2012; Karamessini and Rubery 2014; Klatzer and Schlager 2014; Villa and Smith 2014, 2011; Weiner and MacRae 2017). Only in 9.8% of the cases was some assessment of national measures from a gender perspective conducted (Bettio et al. 2012;Villa and Smith 2011).The European Employment Strategy, which had formerly integrated gender, has progressively made gender invisible, so that it would have disappeared completely from EU2020, if it had not been reinserted last minute after amendments from specific member states (Villa and Smith 2014; see Milner in this volume). Even the 'European Economic Recovery Plan' makes no mention of 'gender', 'women', or 'equality', a fact that was criticised by the Commission's Advisory Committee on Equal Opportunities for Women and Men. As gender experts denounce, 'the "urgency" of a response to the crisis seems to have pushed gender mainstreaming further down the priority list' (Bettio et al. 2012, 97–98), including the basic presentation of gender-disaggregated statistical data. There was some consensus in the European Parliament's Committee for Women's Rights and Gender Equality (FEMM) about the importance of tackling the gendered aspects of the crisis. However, political disagreements about austerity broke this consensus between the political groups (Kantola and Rolandsen Agustín 2016).

Sophie Jacquot (2017) has analysed the fate of the EU gender policy in the midst of the economic crisis. She concludes that the economic crisis has exacerbated the already ongoing stagnation in EU gender policy. Parallel to changes made in the aftermath of the 2008 crisis, EU gender equality policies experienced a number of institutional and policy shifts that locate the EU as 'the most striking example of a U-turn in the importance attached to gender equality as a social goal' (Karamessini and Rubery 2014, 333). Although before the crisis gender was not effectively mainstreamed into the EU macroeconomic policies (Villa and Smith 2014), it was in employment policies through the European Employment Strategies (O'Dwyer 2018). However, the EU has shifted its priorities and gender equality is not treated as a social goal and it is not integrated in employment policies any longer. The shift in context helps to understand this gender invisibility in the EU employment agenda (Villa and Smith 2014). In the 1990s, the rise in women's employment improved labour market performance in the member states and was thus considered important for the EU economy, the neoliberal model was accompanied by developments in the social democratic model, and the entry of gender equality supporters such as Sweden and Finland all favoured the integration of gender into the EU employment policies. The economic crisis context is less favourable to gender equality due to a stronger neoliberal ideology in member governments; in addition, 'the key actors in favour of gender equality had been side-lined both internally in the Commission and externally among member states' (Villa and Smith 2014, 288).

A significant shift occurred in the second Barroso Commission in January 2011, when responsibility for gender equality moved within the European Commission from the Directorate-General Employment, Social Affairs and Equal Opportunities (DG EMPL) to the Directorate-General Justice, Fundamental Rights and Citizenship (DG Justice); two dedicated units on gender equality policies and on legal matters in equal treatment were also transferred (e.g. Ahrens 2018). The responsibility for gender equality in the workplace is still in DG EMPL, but no dedicated unit on gender equality is left in the DG. This administrative shift unrooted the portfolio for equal opportunity and non-discrimination from their traditional base (DG EMPL), provoking deep political and strategic consequences on EU gender equality policies (Ahrens 2018; Jacquot 2015; see Hartlapp et al. in this volume). It might be detrimental to gendering European integration in a moment in which a new EU economic governance regime is being built in response to the 2008 financial crisis to strengthen the coordination of national economic, labour market, and social policies (Klatzer and Schlager 2014). It came precisely at the time in which the Council and the Commission, through mechanisms such as the European Semester and the 'Six-pack legislation', tightened control over member states' economic and employment policies, with the consequence that the institutional shift of gender equality from DG EMPL to DG Justice 'distanced gender equality from employment policy and spread gender equality input thinly across the Commission' (Villa and Smith 2014, 288). This could weaken the EU Equal Opportunities unit's capacity of mainstreaming gender into economic and social initiatives.

While the institutional shift boosted new developments in 'justice', evident in the legally binding directives (Directive 2011/99/EU, Directive 2012/29/EU) against some forms of gender-based violence, Jacquot (2015, 2017) argues that it contributed to locate gender equality even more within a legal perspective of rights, and it changed the interconnectedness of the administrative, political, academic and activist actors. The increased weight of member states in times of economic and institutional crisis, with a greater role for the Council of Ministers (see Abels in this volume), blocked developments in EU gender equality policies, as exemplified in the withdrawal of the revision of the maternity leave directive proposal and the blockage of the women on corporate boards directive proposal (Jacquot 2017). Eventually a work–life balance directive was approved in 2019 through the EPSR signalling some positive shifts. The enlargement to central and eastern European (CEE) countries further favoured the spread of neoliberal ideologies and, in some cases, more traditional notions of gender equality (Villa and Smith 2014, 288; Zbyszewska 2017; see Chiva in this volume). This shifting context, radicalised by the urgency to respond to the Eurozone crisis, tilted the balance between economic and egalitarian goals towards a promotion of neoliberal economic goals. In the crisis context the EU shifted its priorities and seemed to forget its commitments to gender equality goals (Karamessini and Rubery 2014).

Gender approaches and their contributions

Five different approaches to the gendered politics of the economic crises and austerity and each analytical perspective sheds different light on various questions: (1) women and the crisis, (2) gender and the crisis, (3) deconstruction of gender and the crisis, (4) intersectionality and the crisis, and (5) post-deconstruction of gender and the crisis (Kantola and Lombardo 2017a, 2017b). Depending on the approach, crisis definitions and concepts to make sense of it vary. The distinctions between these approaches are analytical as most research combines them in a quest to answer empirical real-world puzzles. We suggest that analytically frameworks such as these help to discuss the underpinnings of the approaches and their compatibility.

First, a number of feminist economists map the effects of the crisis on women by using a *women and the crisis approach*. They analyse the different waves of the crisis where men's employment in the private sector, for example in construction businesses, was worst hit at first, and how in the second wave the public sector cuts started to erase women's jobs, as well as the public sector services and benefits that women relied on (Bettio et al. 2012; Karamessini and Rubery 2014). In the field of politics, this has signified studying the numbers of women and men in economic decision-making and banking. Walby's (2015, 57) question 'Would the financial crisis have been different if it had been Lehman Sisters rather than Lehman Brothers?' makes us ask whether a more diverse composition of corporate boards would have moved financial leaders to take less risky decisions (for a critical discussion see Prügl 2016; True 2016). Feminist scholars have argued that it has been a men's crisis in the sense that men have been the dominant actors in the institutions that have inflicted the crisis and attempted to solve it (Pearson and Elson 2015, 14). Whilst taking 'women' and 'men' as relatively unproblematic and unitary categories, the approach has the strength of providing factual evidence for policymakers about statistical patterns of the crisis as well as arguments for activists about who is represented in the institutions involved in solving the crisis and whose voice is heard in policy-making.

Second, the *gender and the crisis approach* investigates the gendered impacts on the crisis. Focussing on gender as opposed to women calls for an understanding of the wider societal structures that reproduce continuing patterns of domination and inequality. Gender norms underpin finance, production and reproduction, resulting in women's overconcentration in the reproductive sphere (O'Dwyer 2018; Pearson and Elson 2015, 10). Neoliberal policy solutions, which require cutting down the public sector, rely on and reproduce traditional gender roles that delegate major care responsibility to women. This changes national and European gender regimes (Walby 2011, 2015); the EU austerity policies represent a 'critical juncture' that could revert long-term progress achieved in gender equality (Rubery 2014). Gender equality policies and institutions – including gender mainstreaming – have been downscaled in numerous countries when they would be needed the most to counter gendered crisis effects (Klatzer and Schlager 2014). Patterns of the feminisation of poverty and increases in gender violence point to the ways in which the economic, political and social consequences of the crisis are gendered in complex ways. At the same time there is increasing space to understand how gender intersects with categories such as race and ethnicity, disability and class, resulting in differentiated crisis impacts (Kantola and Lombardo 2017a, 2017b).

The impact of EU policy responses on member states' gender equality varies depending on factors ranging from the characteristics of *gender regimes* (see also von Wahl in this volume), especially in relation to women's integration in waged labour and extent to which employment and social policies are able to free women from unpaid care work (Karamessini and Rubery 2014; Walby 2009; Wöhl 2014). despite women's increased integration in the labour market, their higher presence in public sector occupations (education and health) and their greater involvement in part-time and temporary jobs, make women more vulnerable to recession and austerity (Rubery 2014). Intersectional differences relate to class, migration (e.g. migrant women encounter more disadvantages in the labour market than native women), nationality, geographical location (e.g. regional disparities in women's employment rates) and age (e.g. young women's difficult integration in the labour market and old women facing higher retirement ages due to pension reforms) (Karamessini 2014b; Karamessini and Rubery 2014).

Gender equality in southern European countries was strongly affected (Lombardo and Bustelo 2012). In Greece, for example, we see the 'deterioration of employment and social conditions of both women and men' (Karamessini 2014b, 183); while fiscal and structural adjustments are spreading part-time among male workers, the 'crisis has interrupted women's progress towards gender equality in paid work through their better integration in employment', thus the restructuring of the welfare state will negatively affect women. Changes in the wage determination system, employment and welfare state have impoverished vulnerable and middle-class women and men, increasing the proportion of jobless households. In Spain, from 2010 onwards, gender equality institutions have been downgraded or eliminated at the central and regional levels, and care and gender equality policies dismantled and reoriented towards more traditional goals (Lahey and de Villota 2013; Lombardo 2017). This could reverse significant progress achieved in the last 20 years (González and Segales 2014). In Italy, most policy reforms reinforce existing gender imbalances, in a context of a high gender pay gap and gender segregation in employment; budget cuts will reinforce traditional gender roles in the family division of paid and unpaid work because '[b]y cutting childcare and elderly care, funds for disabled and immigrants the entire burden of missing welfare is shifted to women' (Verashchagina and Capparucci 2014, 266).

Other EU member states are affected, too. In the UK, EU austerity policies have increased labour market problems. As Rubery (2014, 139) states:

> Women's prospects of both secure employment and reasonable pay and conditions are being eroded by the shrinkage and downgrading of public sector employment while labour market opportunities for lower skilled men are also converging towards those found in the female-dominated private services, with lower pay and more non-standard employment often taken up on an involuntary basis.

The biggest austerity-triggered falls in disposable income have been experienced by the most vulnerable women – lone mothers, single women pensioners and single women without children – while working-age couples without children have been least affected (Pearson and Elson 2015). Despite state cuts in care policies, women are not voluntarily exiting the labour market; thus dual earner households are currently resisting, though in conditions of increased labour exploitation for both women and men, and care exploitation for women (Walby 2015). In Poland, despite a comparatively good economic performance at the outset of the crisis, the government imposed strict austerity policies, unpopular to citizens and labour unions and detrimental to women due to the increased privatisation of care provoked by public cuts. Polish politicians' willingness to belong to the 'EU neoliberal vanguard' revealed that the crisis was functional to the consolidation of the country's ongoing neoliberal reform project (Zbyszewska 2017). Even in the Nordic countries, e.g. Finland, neoliberal austerity policies have arrived later than in other European states, but in 2015 have hit the women-friendly welfare state with cuts in the public budget that will shift the burden of care from the state to families, that is to women (Elomäki and Kantola 2017). There too the 'political usage of the EU' is discernible, namely justifying domestic austerity politics informed by political ideologies of governing parties with reference to the EU requirements (Kantola 2018).

Third, the *deconstruction of gender and the crisis approach* discerns the ways in which the crisis is discursively constructed and how these constructions are gendered and gendering. It allows to understand how some solutions are favoured over others and how gender is silenced, sidelined or employed in particular ways (Kantola and Lombardo 2017a, 2017b). In other words, discursive constructions of gender offer particular subject positions and close off others. These constructions have effects, they can politicise or depoliticise the crisis in particular ways and they impact on perceived solutions. Using this approach, scholars inquire who defines and narrates the crisis, and how is the crisis constitutive of new and old political identities, institutions and practices (Hozic and True 2016, 14). How is knowledge about the crises conditioned and informed by patterns of power (Griffin 2016, 180)? Penny Griffin (2015, 55) suggests that there is a prevalence of governance responses that 'centralise women's "essential" domesticity or fiscal prudence, prevailing representations of men as public figures of authority and responsibility, and techniques of governance that exploit these'. Such techniques include gender quota systems based on the assumption that the presence of women's bodies balances out hypermasculine behaviour, or austerity measures that are instituted on the foundational assumption of women's reproductive work as inferred but unpaid.

Feminist scholarship has studied how neoliberalism has fundamentally shaped the context where feminisms operate and explored *governance feminism* and *market feminism* to grasp their changing forms and practices (Kantola and Squires 2012; Prügl 2011). Griffin (2015, 51) speaks of 'crisis governance feminism' as a 'form of feminist strategy friendly to existing neo-liberal governance and supportive of the resuscitation of neo-liberal global finance'. The concepts illustrate how feminisms may have adapted to the neoliberal context by adopting a role of providing gender expertise into existing policies rather than engaging in more radical political critique (Elomäki et al. 2019). This is not simply a crisis of neoliberalism (Crouch 2011). Instead neo-liberal economic policies have become entrenched in relation to the EU. On the one hand, this could have the potential to transform resistance: new forms of feminist autonomous movements appear (Elomäki and Kantola 2017, 2018), and the strengthening of national and international feminist alliances (Lombardo 2017). On the other hand, the crisis may generate new challenges for feminist and intersectional struggles for equality in the harder political climate (Emejulu and Bassel 2017; Jacquot 2017).

Austerity politics has been accompanied by de-democratisation. The new forms of economic governance are closed off from democratic debate, participation, and civil society lobbying. It has indeed become harder for many feminist organisations to lobby governments and the EU. As economic austerity discourses are dominant equality needs to give way to the perceived economic necessities. There is a powerful discursive construction of exceptional times when equality cannot be afforded and is for the good times. Moreover, changes in the new economic governance regime of the EU and new undemocratic regulations in the member states, such as the constitutional securing of the annual budget deficit below 3% and the 2015 'Law of Citizens' Safety' in Spain – strongly opposed by civil society renaming it 'gag law' due to the restriction of freedom of expression and other human rights it contains – have made political institutions especially impenetrable for citizens and activists.

Fourth, *intersectionality approaches* explore the inequalities, marginalisations and dominations that the interactions of gender, race, class and other systems of inequality produce in times of crisis, such as the differentiated impact of austerity policies on migrant minoritised women or men (Bettio et al. 2012), female refugees in countries like Greece (Athanasiou 2014), younger unemployed women and older women who see their pensions reduced or cut (Bettio et al. 2012; Karamessini and Rubery 2014) and women with disabilities. Heteronormativity is deeply implicated in the dominant narratives about the economic, social and political crises although their implications are detrimental to LGBTQ communities (Smith 2016, 231–232). In the UK, for example, there has been a silence about the impact of government's austerity policies on sexual injustices with the issue of same-sex marriage dominating the agenda (Smith 2016, 232). Intersectionality shows how different organisations and movements representing different groups can be pitted against one another in a seeming competition for scarcer resources or, alternatively, it can point to new alliances and solidarity at times of crisis (Bassel and Emejulu 2014). Populist right parties seeking to protect 'our people' can resort to racist or even fascist discourses that challenge the human rights of racialised others in European countries (Norocel 2013). European media and politicians demonised Greeks as 'whites but not quite', drawing on racialised constructions of otherness, underpinned by presumed 'laziness' and 'criminality' (Agathangelou 2016, 208).

The EU member states dynamics in times of crisis has also implied a turn to conservatism and de-democratisation, which have gendered and racialised consequences (Verloo 2018). National governments worked to formulate austerity politics out of the reach of public democratic debate and civil society contestations. From Finland to Spain, national governments adopted new laws to transpose EU requirements about limits to budget deficit into national law, with negative consequences for women, who are especially affected by public cuts, and for social and gender equality policies (Kantola and Lombardo 2017a). In Spain, the undemocratic reaction of the conservative government to citizens' anti-austerity struggles has been a restriction of freedom of expression and other human rights through the 2014 'Law of citizens' safety', which civil society has strongly opposed, renaming it the 'gag law' (Lombardo 2017).

Economic crisis and austerity

In the UK and France, minority women's daily experiences of economic, social, gender and race inequality before *and* after the 2008 crisis move Emejulu and Bassell (2017) to speak of 'routinised crises'. As the authors write: minority women's

> persistently high unemployment and poverty rates are not 'exceptional' and not necessarily problems to be addressed through policy action since they are indicators of capitalism, patriarchy and white supremacy operating as intended. Once we understand minority women's precarity as the banality of everyday life we can begin to understand the fallacy of the construction of the 2008 economic 'crisis'.

The crucial question that intersectional analyses of the crisis such as Emejulu and Bassell raise is: a crisis for whom? (Cavaghan and O'Dwyer 2018).

A number of countries have witnessed dramatic changes in civil society activism and political party systems as a result of the crisis. New forms of resistance include, for example, new political parties, such as the rise of left populist parties like Podemos in Spain and Syriza in Greece, or strengthening of radical right populist politics in other parts of northern and eastern Europe, France, Germany or the UK (Kantola and Lombardo 2019). At the same time as some groups and peoples have been empowered, others have been further marginalised reflecting, for instance, the existing gendered and racialised inequalities.

The hard climate of neoliberalism and austerity has been combined with overt racism in European societies, brought to the surface with the so-called refugee crisis since 2015 and for example the UK's Brexit vote in 2016, and gender conservatism pushing women away from the labour market. Whilst institutional racism has underpinned European societies before the crisis, few would dispute that racist incidents have surfaced across Europe and been legitimised by the radical right politics of political leaders.

Finally, the *post-deconstruction and the crisis approach* has yet to enter gender and politics research (Kantola and Lombardo 2017a). Post-deconstruction signals a diverse set of debates on feminist new materialism and affect theory that comes analytically (not chronologically, Lykke 2010, 106) 'after' reflections on the deconstruction of gender (Ahmed 2004; Hemmings 2005). These approaches are interested in understanding what effects, emotions and bodily material *do* in gender and politics, beyond discourses (Kantola and Lombardo 2017c). The economic crisis makes the analysis of issues such as the material underpinning of the current political economy, its entrenched relations to neoliberalism, states' biopolitics and emotions and affects and their bodily impacts particularly important (Coole and Frost 2010). Emotions and affects, such as anger, shame, guilt and empathy circulate in the economic crisis. For instance, Cossarini argues that in the recent social movements against capitalism and austerity politics from the Wall Street to Indignados in Spain emotions play a key role in the constructions of the 'political subject – *the people* – as well as in today's struggle for democratic legitimacy and the resistance to the emptying of democracy by global-market forces' (Cossarini 2014, 291). Post-deconstruction analyses suggest that these emotions are social and involve power relations (Ahmed 2004). For instance, the 'austerity' agenda has been accompanied by a moralising discourse 'that passes on the responsibility to citizens together with a feeling of guilt, making easier for governments to impose public expenditure cuts and to increase social control of the population' (Addabbo et al. 2013, 5). Another example is that of Northern women politician's expressing empathy towards 'the other women' in the South, that can read as an affective expression of power that fixes the Southern countries economic and gender policies as failed (Kantola 2018; Pedwell 2014). Feminist analyses using these approaches show that neoliberalism and violence constitute the vulnerabilities of the bodies affected by the crisis and protesting against it (Athanasiou 2014).

Conclusion

The economic crisis and the austerity that followed in Europe and the EU need to be understood from a variety of feminist analytical perspectives. We have discussed both the austerity politics adopted by the EU actors, its gendered consequences, and the feminist analytical perspectives that can be used to analyse these dimensions. The economic crisis resulted in a primacy of the economy, arguments based on economic growth, sidelining of gender mainstreaming and gender equality as a value in itself. Feminist analyses show the severe costs involved in such short-sighted and partial, gender blind, approaches and make a strong case for understanding the economic crisis and austerity from feminist perspectives. The consequences of the economic crisis are not just about policies and the inclusion of a gender perspective in policy fields. Both the economic crisis and austerity have also had profound effects on the EU polity: its democratic legitimacy and functioning.

In future, research about gender inequalities in political representation, political, social and economic rights, which are at the heart of the solutions to the problems caused by the economic crisis and austerity, will be much needed. Future research will also be able to account to the shifts in gender equality policies the economic crisis resulted in. Feminist research into the economic crisis and austerity has also illustrated the dire need for more feminist research in the field of economics and political economy (see also Cavaghan and Elomäki in this volume). This would enable a deeper understanding of the hegemonic position of the austerity solutions adopted to the crisis and challenging them.

Acknowledgement

Johanna Kantola's research has received funding from the European Research Council (ERC) under the European Union's Horizon 2020 research and innovation program grant number 771676.

References

Addabbo T, Rodríguez-Modroño P, Gálvez-Muñoz L (2013): Gender and the Great Recession: Changes in Labour Supply in Spain, *DEMB Working Paper Series* 10, URL: https://ideas.repec.org/p/mod/dembwp/0010.html (download: June 12, 2020)

Agathangelou AM (2016): Global Raciality of Capitalism and "Primitive" Accumulation. (Un)making the Death Limit? in: Hozic AA, True J (eds.): *Scandalous Economics: Gender and the Politics of Financial Crises*, Oxford: Oxford University Press, 205–230.

Ahmed S (2004): *The Cultural Politics of Emotions*, Edinburgh: Edinburgh University Press.

Ahrens P (2018): *Actors, institutions, and the making of EU gender equality programs*, Basingstoke: Palgrave Macmillan.

Athanasiou A (2014) Precarious intensities: gendered bodies in the streets and squares of Greece, *Signs* **40** (1), 1–9.

Bassel L, Emejulu A (2014): Solidarity under austerity: intersectionality in France and the United Kingdom, *Politics & Gender* **10** (1), 130–136.

Bettio F, Corsi M, D'Ippoliti C, Lyberaki A, Samek Lodovici M, Verashchagina A (2012): *The Impact of the Economic Crisis on the Situation of Women and Men and on Gender Equality Policies*, Brussels: European Commission.

Blyth M (2013): *Austerity. The History of a Dangerous Idea*, Oxford, New York: Oxford University Press.

Bruff I, Wöhl S (2016): Constitutionalizing Austerity, Disciplining the Household. Masculine Norms of Competitiveness and the Crisis of Social Reproduction in the Eurozone, in: Hozic AA, True J (eds.): *Scandalous Economics. Gender and the Politics of Financial Crises*, Oxford: Oxford University Press, 92–108.

Busch K, Hermann C, Hinrichs K, Schulten T (2013): *Euro Crisis, Austerity Policy and the European Social Model. How Crisis Policies in Southern Europe Threaten the EU's Social Dimension*, Friedrich Ebert Stiftung, URL: http://library.fes.de/pdf-files/id/ipa/09656.pdf (download: December 10, 2019).

Cavaghan R, O'Dwyer M. (2018): European economic governance in 2017: a recovery for whom? *Journal of Common Market Studies* **56** (Annual Review), 96–108.

Coole D, Frost S (2010): Introducing the New Materialisms, in: Coole D, Frost S (eds.): *New Materialisms: Ontology, Agency and Politics*, Durham, NC: Duke University Press, 1–46.

Cossarini P (2014): Protests, emotions and democracy. Theoretical insights from the *Indignados* movement, *Global Discourse* **4** (2–3), 291–304.

Crouch C (2011): *The Strange Non-Death of Neoliberalism*, Cambridge: Polity Press.

Elomäki A (2019): Governing austerity. Governance reforms as facilitators of gendered austerity in Finland, *Australian Feminist Studies* **34** (100), 182–197.

Elomäki A, Kantola J (2017): Austerity Politics and Feminist Resistance in Finland. From Established Women's Organizations to New Feminist Initiatives, in: Kantola J, Lombardo E (eds.): *Gender and the Economic Crisis in Europe. Politics, Institutions and Intersectionality*, Basingstoke: Palgrave Macmillan, 231–256.

Elomäki A, Kantola J (2018): Theorizing feminist struggles in the triangle of neoliberalism, conservatism, and nationalism, *Social Politics* **25** (3), 337–360.

Elomäki A, Kantola J (2020): European social partners as gender equality actors in EU social and economic governance, *Journal of Common Market Studies* **58** (4), 999–1015.

Elomäki A, Kantola J, Koivunen A, Ylöstalo H (2019): Affective virtuosity: challenges for governance feminism in the context of the economic crisis. *Gender, Work & Organization* **26** (6), 822–839.

Emejulu A, Bassel L (2017): Whose Crisis Counts? Minority Women, Austerity and Activism in France and Britain, in: Kantola J, Lombardo E (eds.): *Gender and the Economic Crisis in Europe. Politics, Institutions and Intersectionality*, Basingstoke: Palgrave Macmillan, 185–208.

Gill S, Roberts A (2011): Macroeconomic Governance, Gendered Inequality, and Global Crises, in: Young B, Bakker I, Elson D (eds.): *Questioning Financial Governance from a Feminist Perspective*, London: Routledge, 155–172.

González E, Segales M (2014): Women, Gender Equality and the Economic Crisis in Spain, in: Karamessini M, Rubery J (eds.): *Women and Austerity. The Economic Crisis and the Future for Gender Equality*, London: Routlegde, 229–247.

Griffin P (2015): Crisis, austerity and gendered governance: A feminist perspective, *Feminist Review* **109** (1), 49–72.

Griffin P (2016): Gender, Finance and the Embodiment of the Crisis, in: Hozic AA, True J (eds.): *Scandalous Economics. Gender and the Politics of Financial Crises*, Oxford: Oxford University Press, 179–203.

Hemmings C (2005): Invoking affect. Cultural theory and the ontological turn, *Cultural Studies* **19** (5), 548–567.

Hozic AA, True J (2016): Making Feminist Sense of the Global Financial Crisis, in: Hozic AA, True J (eds.): *Scandalous Economics. Gender and the Politics of Financial Crises*, Oxford: Oxford University Press, 3–20.

Jacquot S. (2015): *Transformations in EU Gender Equality*, Basingstoke: Palgrave Macmillan.

Jacquot S. (2017): A Policy in Crisis. The Dismantling of the EU Gender Equality Policy, in: Kantola J, Lombardo E (eds.): *Gender and the Crisis in Europe: Politics, Institutions, and Intersectionality*, Basingstoke: Palgrave Macmillan, 27–48.

Kantola J (2018): Gender and the economic crisis. Political parties as sites of feminist struggles, *Social Politics: International Studies in Gender, State & Society* **25** (3), 361–382.

Kantola J, Lombardo E (2017a): Gender and the Politics of the Economic Crisis in Europe, in: Kantola J, Lombardo E (eds.): *Gender and the Economic Crisis in Europe: Politics, Institutions and Intersectionality*, Basingstoke: Palgrave Macmillan, 1–26.

Kantola J, Lombardo E. (2017b): Gender and political analysis: exploring hegemonies, silences, and novelties, *Feminist Theory* **18** (3), 323–341.

Kantola J, Lombardo E (2017c): *Gender and Political Analysis*, Basingstoke: Palgrave Macmillan.

Kantola J, Lombardo E (2019): European integration and disintegration: feminist perspectives to inequalities and social justice, *Journal of Common Market Studies* **57** (S1), 62–76.

Kantola J, Rolandsen Agustín L (2016): Gendering transnational party politics: the case of European Union, *Party Politics* **22** (5), 641–651.

Kantola J, Squires J (2012): From state feminism to market feminism?, *International Political Science Review* **33** (4), 382–400.

Karamessini M (2014a): Introduction – Women's Vulnerability to Recession and Austerity. A Different Context, a Different Crisis, in: Karamessini M, Rubery J (eds.): *Women and Austerity: The Economic Crisis and the Future for Gender Equality*, London: Routledge, 3–16.

Karamessini M (2014b): Structural Crisis and Adjustment in Greece. Social Regression and the Challenge to Gender Equality, in: Karamessini M, Rubery J (eds.): *Women and Austerity: The Economic Crisis and the Future for Gender Equality*, London: Routledge, 165–185.

Karamessini M, Rubery J, eds. (2014): *Women and Austerity. The Economic Crisis and the Future for Gender Equality*, London, New York: Routledge.

Klatzer E, Schlager C (2014): Feminist Perspectives on Macroeconomics. Reconfiguration of Power Structures and Erosion of Gender Equality Through the New Economic Governance Regime in the European Union, in: Evans M, Hemmings C, Henry M, Madhok S, Waring S (eds.): *Feminist Theory Handbook*, London: SAGE, 483–499.

Lahey K, de Villota P (2013): Economic crisis, gender equality, and policy responses in Spain and Canada, *Feminist Economics* **19** (3), 82–107.

Lombardo E (2017): Austerity Politics and Feminists Struggles in Spain: Reconfiguring the Gender Regime? in: Kantola J, Lombardo E (eds.): *Gender and the Economic Crisis in Europe: Politics, Institutions and Intersectionality*, Basingstoke: Palgrave Macmillan, 20–230.

Lombardo E, Bustelo M (2012): Political approaches to inequalities in Southern Europe. A comparative analysis of Italy, Portugal, and Spain, *Social Politics* **19** (4), 572–595.

Lykke N (2010): *Feminist Studies. A Guide to Intersectional Theory, Methodology and Writing*, London: Routledge.

Maier, F (2011): Macroeconomic Regimes in OECD Countries and the Interrelations with Gender Orders, in: Young B, Bakker I, Elson D (eds.): *Questioning Financial Governance from a Feminist Perspective*, London: Routledge, 11–37.

Negra D, Tasker Y (2014) Introduction: Gender and Recessionary Culture, in: Negra D, Tasker Y (eds.): *Gendering the Recession. Media and Culture in an Age of Austerity*, Durham, NC: Duke University Press, 1–30.

Norocel C (2013): 'Give us back Sweden!' A feminist reading of the (re)interpretations of the *Folkhem* conceptual metaphor in Swedish radical right populist discourse, *NORA: Nordic Journal of Feminist and Gender Research* **21** (1), 4–20.

O'Dwyer M (2018): Making sense of austerity. The gendered ideas of European economic policy, *Comparative European Politics* **16** (5), 745–761.

Pearson R, Elson D (2015): Transcending the impact of the financial crisis in the United Kingdom. Towards plan F—a feminist economic strategy, *Feminist Review* **109** (1), 8–30.

Pedwell C (2014): *Affective Relations: The Transnational Politics of Empathy*, Basingstoke: Palgrave Macmillan.

Plomien A (2018): EU social and gender policy beyond Brexit: towards the European Pillar of Social Rights, *Social Policy and Society* **17** (2), 281–296.

Prügl E (2016): 'Lehman Brothers and Sisters'. Revisiting Gender and Myth after the Financial Crisis, in: Hozic AA, True J (eds.): *Scandalous Economics. Gender and the Politics of Financial Crises*, Oxford: Oxford University Press, 21–40.

Prügl E (2011): Diversity management and gender mainstreaming as technologies of government, *Politics and Gender* **7** (1), 71–89.

Rubery J (2014): From Women and Recession to Women and Austerity: A Framework for Analysis, in: Karamessini M, Rubery J (eds.): *Women and Austerity: The Economic Crisis and the Future for Gender Equality*, London: Routledge, 17–36.

Smith N (2016): Toward a Queer Political Economy of the Crisis, in: Hozic AA, True J (eds.) *Scandalous Economics. Gender and the Politics of Financial Crises*, Oxford: Oxford University Press, 231–247.

True J (2016): The Global Financial Crisis's Silver Bullet. Women Leaders and 'Leaning In', in: Hozic AA, True J (eds.): *Scandalous Economics. Gender and the Politics of Financial Crises*, Oxford: Oxford University Press, 41–56.

Verashchagina A, Capparucci M (2014): Living Through the Crisis in Italy: The Labour Market Experiences of Women and Men, in: Karamessini M, Rubery J (eds.): *Women and Austerity: The Economic Crisis and the Future for Gender Equality*, London: Routledge, 248–270.

Verloo M, ed. (2018): *Varieties of Opposition to Gender Equality in Europe*, London: Routledge.

Villa P, Smith M (2014): Policy in the Time of Crisis. Employment Policy and Gender Equality in Europe, in: Karamessini M, Rubery J (eds.): *Women and Austerity: The Economic Crisis and the Future for Gender Equality*, London: Routledge, 273–294.

Villa, P, Smith M (2011): *National Reform Programmes 2011: A Gender Perspective*, External report commissioned by and presented to the European Commission Directorate-General for Justice, Unit D1 'Equality between men and women'.

Walby, S (2009): *Globalization and Inequalities. Complexity and Contested Modernities*, London: Sage.

Walby, S (2011): *The Future of Feminism*, Cambridge: Polity Press.

Walby, S (2015): *Crisis*, Cambridge: Polity Press.

Weiner E, MacRae H (2017): Opportunity and Setback? Gender Equality, Crisis and Change in the EU, in: Kantola J, Lombardo E (eds.): *Gender and the Economic Crisis in Europe: Politics, Institutions and Intersectionality*, Basingstoke: Palgrave Macmillan, 73–93.

Wöhl S (2014): The state and gender relations in international political economy. A state-theoretical approach to varieties of capitalism in crisis, *Capital & Class* **38** (1), 83–95.

Zbyszewska A (2017): Gendering Poland's Crisis Reforms. A Europeanization Perspective, in: Kantola J, Lombardo E (eds.): *Gender and the Economic Crisis in Europe: Politics, Institutions and Intersectionality*, Basingstoke: Palgrave Macmillan, 117–137.

31

The gender story of Brexit

From under-representation of women to marginalisation of equality

Roberta Guerrina and Annick Masselot

The 2016 EU referendum in the United Kingdom (UK) represents a milestone in the history of the European Union (EU). When the British people were asked whether the UK should remain or leave the EU, they embarked on an unprecedented political process that has ramifications for the whole of Europe. The binary nature of the question posed in the referendum helped to oversimplify a complex relationship and opened new socio-political cleavages in the country. Technically the referendum was advisory and thus, not legally binding. The results pointed to a country divided: 51.9% of the votes were cast in favour of leaving the EU against 48.1%. But with a turnout of 72.2% the result provided strong political mandate to the government. Voting preferences highlighted significant cleavages based on class, educational background and age, with 71% of people aged between 18 and 24 voting to remain in the EU, compared with just 36% of people aged over 65. Differences also appeared in regional preferences: Northern Ireland (55.78%) and Scotland (62%) voted in favour of remaining in the EU. Although the data points towards a small gender gap, the nature and quality of public debates, both during the campaign and since the vote, have revealed an overarching blindness, and casual disregard, for gender and intersectional issues.

More than that, it has exposed gendered and racialised patterns underpinning citizens' participation and engagement in the public sphere. Gender hierarchies permeated every aspect of this crisis, 'manufactured not only by a generic male-dominated British political elite but in this case quite literally by men who happen to have gone to the same elite schools and have been competing with each other since adolescence' (Hozic and True 2016, 276). This is not disconnected from the UK government's position on international and external politics since the referendum. The 'war cry' used by Brexiters since the vote – 'achieving the will of the people' – helps to legitimise the downgrading of the concerns about the impact of Brexit on women and other traditionally marginal groups.

The socio-economic and political structures that are becoming established as a result of Brexit will affect EU politics and the relationship between European institutions and the member states for years to come. What is striking about Brexit, and the political economy that has emerged around it, is that it is largely one-dimensional. The reification of binaries at the heart of the debate, e.g. the left behinds vs the rights of migrants, has almost entirely omitted women's interests from the discussion. This chapter explores the story of Brexit through a feminist lens.

392

It seeks to highlight how women's interests, whether as a homogeneous or diverse group, have been sidelined and instrumentalised in the pursuit of a project that is imbued with masculine and nationalist undertones.

Gendering Brexit opens a space for an intersectional feminist agenda to expose silences and structures of power at the heart of both national and European institutions, as well as the very discipline that seeks to study those institutions (Guerrina et al. 2018). More broadly, this new body of work contributes to the feminist approaches about de-democratisation and disintegration as outlined by Lombardo and Kantola (2019). This chapter provides a synthesis of current debates and research on the UK's withdrawal from the EU. Highlighting the omission of gender perspectives from the wider body of research and political economy that has emerged as a result of the 2016 EU referendum provides an entry point for the analysis of the process of evolution of the UK gender regime. This analytical frame helps to understand the links between austerity, Brexit and the growing anti-equality narratives so deeply entrenched in populist discourse.

As a way of context, gender equality is one of the oldest and most sophisticated fields of EU law and policy (Bell 2011; Guerrina and Murphy 2016; Prechal 2004). The EU has undeniably contributed dynamically to the advancement of gender equality in the member states. It is often highlighted as a successful and vigorous field of EU law and policy (Caracciolo di Torella and Masselot 2013), even if indicators – such as the EIGE Gender Equality Index (see Jacquot and Kriszan in this volume) – show that gender equality rights have not yet achieved their full potential (https://eige.europa.eu/gender-equality-index). The footprint of EU law on the UK legal system is no exception as the impact of European law on the development of the national equality policies has clearly been traced by scholars (Annesley and Gains 2013). However, this relationship is not unidirectional. The UK has also helped to shape the development of EU gender equality provisions (Hantrais 2018) and the shape the European gender regime (Fagan et al. 2006; see also von Wahl in this volume). In particular, the UK's bias in favour of deregulation has permeated into the negotiations, limiting the scope of key policy initiatives such as the 1992 Pregnant Workers Directive (Foubert and Imamović 2015; Elomäki 2015; McGlynn 1996, 2000; see also Milner in this volume).

This emphasis is relevant as it relates to the EU's focus on preventing social dumping and maintaining a level playing field. Indeed, Article 8 of the Treaty on the Functioning of the EU (TFEU) requires that '[i]n all its activities, the Union shall aim to eliminate inequalities, and to promote equality, between men and women' (see Guerrina 2005; Mergaert and Lombardo 2014; Pollack and Hafner-Burton 2000). Moreover, under Article 157(4) TFEU, the EU has a positive duty to achieve gender equality (Fredman 2005; McCrudden 2019). The EU's negotiating team thus has a duty to ensure the process and outcomes do not disproportionally disadvantage women and safeguard the gender equality *acquis*. However, Brexit has not happened in a vacuum, but it unfolded in the aftermath of the 2008 financial crisis which had already relegated social cohesion and equality to second order issues (see Kantola and Lombardo in this volume). The key question in the context of the post-Brexit settlement is how much will key foundational principles come to bear on the outcome of the negotiations and, in so doing, shape the future of the equality agenda in the UK and Europe alike.

Referendum: representing women's interests?

In 2013, David Cameron made an electoral pledge to hold a referendum on EU membership. The background to this decision resides, in part, in the internal politics of the Conservative Party. The European question was becoming more pressing for the Conservative Prime Minister who was facing increasing challenge from the right of his party as well as Eurosceptic parties such as

UKIP. In part, 'Cameron's decision to hold an in-out referendum reflected a hubristic attitude … firmly ingrained in his privileged background' (Achilleos-Sarll and Martill 2019, 25). This is important because it sets the scene for the 2016 campaign.

The six weeks of the (official) EU referendum campaign were defined by highly charged and divisive language aimed at arousing deep emotions. Anger and fear were the driving emotions registered by voters during and after the campaign (Manners 2018). The very nature of the political communication strategies was intended to evoke this kind of response. Leave campaigns in particular sought to establish a new form of nationalism rooted in sovereignty, the idea of 'taking back control' and a return to a 'glorious' past. The campaign was marred with language associated with deal-making, militarism and conflictual relations (Achilleos-Sarll and Martill 2019).

What was also notable about the campaign was the absence of women's voices and interests in public debates and media coverage (Achilleos-Sarll and Martill 2019; Deacon et al. 2016). Women featured only in 25% of the Brexit media coverage. This means that in this debate women were marginalised as citizens, political leaders as well as experts (Galpin 2016). It was only at the end of the official campaign (two weeks before the referendum) that both campaigns started targeting women as voters as they realised that they were the largest 'undecided' group. As the official polls started to show an increasingly narrow margin between leave and remain, women political leaders took centre stage, as in the case of the final TV referendum debate.

The official campaigns were likewise high charged and deeply gendered. Issues relating to social policy and social justice were hardly discussed by either campaign, and gender equality featured almost solely in reference to International Women's Day (MacLeavy 2018). The way such arguments were deployed, however, also betrays a functionalist and utilitarian logic that exploits, rather than advances, the principle of equality. For example, Women for Britain, a spin-off of the Vote Leave Campaign, produced a video on that occasion drawing on the history of suffragettes but deforming their spirit[1] with a clear view to tap into a new form of nationalism rooted in the UK's past. The focus here is therefore on the construction of an identity in which feminist language is co-opted to pursue an alternative political agenda. The fact that equality was not discussed in a nuanced way and that no gender impact assessment was conducted at any point is telling of the implicit bias of the campaign and the way Brexit, and EU politics, are discussed.

What captured the voters' imagination, and therefore shaped their motivations for voting either leave or remain, reflected the focus of the campaigns. The EU referendum was therefore decided on issues traditionally defined as 'high politics' (Haastrup et al. 2016), such as the economy, security and migration. Social policies and gender equality were not considered as pertinent to the decision-making process and, as a result, were siloed and largely ignored in the debate (Guerrina and Masselot 2018). The restriction on civil society and charities to partake in political campaigning and therefore the obligation to remain neutral during the campaign period restricted their room for action. Although, this obligation applies to all charities, it has a particular detrimental impact on the ability of women's rights advocacy group to ensure that an impact assessment is included in the process (see Ritch 2019 on the comparative engagement of women's organisations in the 2015 Scottish referendum and 2016 EU referendum in Scotland).

Interregnum – May's leadership years

The conduct of the campaigns, the kind of interests and voices dominating the debate have had a direct impact on the way the post-referendum period has unfolded (MacLeavy 2018). Whilst Cameron resigned as prime minister and the Leave camp's tenors walked away (literally) from responsibilities, it was Theresa May who was elected leader of the Conservative Party and therefore became prime minister. Hozic and True (2016) describe this transition of power as the paradox of Brexit, whereby women who were largely excluded during the campaign came to power to 'clean up' the mess produced by a specific set of interests within the ruling party.

The way May came to power, the challenges she faced throughout her time as premier, and ultimately her fall from the leadership of the Conservative Party is an example of the glass cliff phenomenon (Cook and Glass 2014, 95). It is at times of crisis that women tend to rise to leadership positions. (Gendered) assumptions about women's leadership style, e.g. aversion to risk taking and collaborative management style, make them a better fit to navigate difficult political environments requiring accommodation of divergent interests. Conversely, under the same circumstances, men tend to shy away from leadership positions, as seen as carrying too much personal risk. For Hozic and True (2016), May emerged during the 2016 Conservative leadership contest as a 'safe pair of hands' to see the country through the Brexit crisis.

Theresa May's leadership was forecast to be short, difficult and marred by failure. The gendered resistance she faced as a prime minister is evident in the tabloid press and was never better illustrated than by Sarah Vine's 2017 article on a meeting between May and Nicola Sturgeon, the First Minister of Scotland, which fronted the *Daily Mail* with the headline: 'Never mind Brexit, Who won legsit?' This kind of media framing not only disrespects the political leadership of two leading women, it reduces their position to a hypersexualised commentary on their physical appearance (Guerrina 2017). It also fuelled the internal struggle for power and authority within her party and government.

Two decisions came to define May's tenure as prime minister. First, her cabinet appointments were supposed to unify the party. Leave and Remainers were appointed to senior positions in the cabinet to provide balance. Second, she positioned a group of lead Brexiters to key cabinet positions to signal her intention to deliver 'Brexit'. Looking to bring the Eurosceptic wing of the party into the fold, she appointed leading figures of the Leave campaign to key departments responsible for delivering Brexit, e.g. Boris Johnson as Foreign Secretary, David Davis as Minister for Brexit and Liam Fox to International Trade. Seen as a politically shrewd move, it also provided a platform for the 'Brexit mavericks' to shape the process. The tensions in the cabinet and the challenge to delivering a Brexit 'deal' provided a space for more 'radical' views in the Conservative Party to take centre stage, sidelining May's softer vision for Brexit (for a composition of her cabinet see Mason et al. 2016).

The appointment of those Brexiters had the impact of normalising extreme language associated with high salience policy areas, such as migration. Theresa May's 2017 Florence speech was supposed set the agenda for the government's priorities. It was her high nationalist moment and a rallying cry to appease the Brexit mavericks in her cabinet. Far from supporting May's leadership, these cabinet members ultimately worked against their own policies, including voting against May's Withdrawal Agreement, which ultimately led to her political demise in May 2019.

The growing influence of the European Research Group (ERG) within the Conservative Party is something worth examining in some detail as it represented a form of internal opposition and contestation within the party and made it impossible for May to be effective as prime minister. The ERG consists of leading Eurosceptic members of the Conservative Party and is composed by a majority of men. Since 2018, Jacob Rees-Mogg has been its chair and it has had a number of prominent Vote Leave campaigners associated with it. The ERG has often been defined as a 'party within the party' and as such it lobbies the government and has increasingly achieved positions within the government itself, as in the case of its former chair, Steve Baker, who was appointed as Brexit minister in 2017 (Cusick et al. 2019). The impact of the increasing ERG intra-party influence has crystallised a long-standing cleavage in the party and is evidenced in the resignation of a number of centrist/moderate Conservatives, such as Anna Soubry, Sarah Wollaston and Heidi Allen (BBC 2019), who are also often female politicians.

Internal divisions in the Conservative Party and a shallow majority based on the support of the Northern Irish Democratic Unionist Party[2] proved too much of an insurmountable hurdle for May's version of the Withdrawal Agreement. Although virtually similar to that of May's, Johnson's 2019 Agreement received a different reception by those who staunchly opposed May, indicating that May's leadership was defined by internal obstacles and a deeply gendered narrative within the party of government itself (Haastrup et al. 2019; Holder 2019).

This process facilitated the rise of the ERG and a hard turn to the right for the Conservative Party that would be crystallised under the Johnson's early tenure as prime minister. The shift in political discourse within the party from the centrist 'one nation' ideology to a more socially conservative party is also linked to a deep nostalgia for the UK's past 'greatness' (Bhambra 2017). The impact on the legislative and policy process is clear, however; it is also permeating everyday interactions in deeply gendered and racialised ways that 'have made it so much easier to link eastern European immigration, anti-Muslin sentiments and refugees into the quest for control over sovereign borders' (Hozic and True 2016, 274; see also Gill and Ahmed 2019).

Negotiations

The backdrop to the evolving national political picture were the 2017–2018 negotiations between the UK and the EU on a Withdrawal Agreement. While a comprehensive assessment of the negotiations has not yet been completed, a number of issues are worth noting here. In terms of raw numbers, it is widely accepted that women were largely under-represented, with only one woman included in the team of nine senior civil servants deployed to Brussels. In July 2017, 56 Labour MPs called on the government to carry out a review of the gender balance of the UK team. Government's representatives responded that 'the prime minister is the person ultimately in charge of the Brexit negotiations and is a woman' (Asthana 2017). This simplistic interpretation of representation is intended to obfuscate the conduct of the negotiations, to concentrate power in the hands of the executive and to further sideline 'equality and diversity' in the context of Brexit. Rather, three issues became central to the negotiations: trade, citizens' rights and migration, and the question of Northern Ireland. Although feminist research points to the gendered nature and impact of these policy domains, the process succeeded in de-gendering the issue, treating them as though they were gender neutral. This position would in particular have a significant impact on the rights of female EU national residents in the UK (Brenigan 2017).

In the early days of the UK–EU negotiations, the focus was on arriving at a settlement for trade between the two parties. The focus was on duties, access and third-party agreements. No evidence can be found that gender or equality impact assessments were carried out at any point. Rather both the EU and the UK treated trade as something that is free from gender considerations, disregarding the fact that women and minority groups are unequally positioned in the market due, in particular, to their care responsibilities (Stephenson and Fontana 2019).

The way the negotiations were framed, the focus on 'high politics', the highly technical nature of the issues under discussion made the process itself opaque. At a time when emotions are on the rise as a driver for politics, whereas trust and efficacy are declining, detachment from everyday politics helps to consolidate the EU as 'other' in the eyes of Leave voters. This process was ultimately legitimised through the use of deeply gendered language around 'divorce' settlement and divorce bills. In this context, the citizens are infantilised and stripped of agency, as the 'grown-ups' discuss the future arrangements that will shape their future lives (Millar 2018).

To extend this metaphor, the focus of the negotiations focused on the 'assets', i.e. access to markets and trade in goods and services. Considerations of the social arrangements, such as citizens' rights, were folded into wider discussions about freedom of movement and immigration policy. As such, they became a point for leverage as part of the negotiation process. The residence status of EU nationals resident in the UK and UK nationals resident in the EU was put in question as the negotiating teams struggled to find a way to affirm the rights of citizens, whilst retaining the integrity of the freedom of movement principle. Like trade, the residency question has been considered to be gender neutral even if overwhelming research shows that migration and gender are intertwined (Duda-Mikulin 2018; Kilkey 2017; Shutes and Walker 2018). One notable omission from these discussions was the gendered impact of withdrawing from the labour market to fulfil the function of care (Caracciolo di Torella 2019; O'Brien 2013, 2018; Shutes and Walker 2018). Specifically, as the negotiating teams started from the assumption that the issues at stake were gender neutral, they failed to consider the way each and every one of those policy domains is shaped by the UK's gender regime.

These thorny issues were brought to light during the operationalisation of the 'Settlement Scheme'. Soon after the EU referendum large numbers of EU nationals resident in the UK started to apply for permanent residence in the first instance and from 2018 for Settled Status, the new government scheme introduced to facilitate EU nationals to register their residence status in the UK. At the time of writing, the Conservative Government warned that the Settled Scheme would be open until the end of 2020. At that point, those who had yet to register will become undocumented migrants. The stakes, therefore, could not be higher. Understanding the impact of this process on different groups should have been a priority for the Home Office so that it would not lead to unintended gender outcomes. It is clear that women are more likely to be denied residency rights, if they had withdrawn from the labour market for any period of time to care for children and/or other dependents. Also more vulnerable to not have their status recognised are women who are self-employed in family-run businesses or farms (Dustin et al. 2019; Women's Budget Group 2018).

The situation of third-country national (TNC) women with EU national children resident in the UK is even more precarious. Applying an intersectional feminist lens, Solanke (2019) draws attention to the UK and the EU multi-level abandonment of black British children whose primary carers are TCNs in the UK. This highlights how the process of exiting the EU has become an opportunity to redraw the lines of inclusion and exclusion along racialised and gendered lines aimed at re-asserting the idea of nationhood and Britannia (Bhambra 2017).

The 2018 Withdrawal Agreement concluded two years of negotiations based on two competing mandates. The negotiating teams were clear that the Agreement was the best possible outcome based on the 'red lines' set out by each party. The main focus was to set out regulatory alignment and divergence between the UK and the EU. Divided into six parts, it deals with: 1. Common Provisions; 2. Citizens' Rights; 3. Separation Provisions; 4. Transition; 5. Financial Provisions; 6. Institutional and 7. Final Provisions. In addition, the Agreement includes a number of separate protocols and annexes. Since its publication on 13 November 2018, the focus of political debate has been on citizens' rights, the transition and the Protocol on Northern Ireland, which includes the infamous 'backstop'. It was indeed the inclusion of the backstop, i.e. the provision that there should not be a hard border on the island of Ireland, that would be the downfall of the Withdrawal Agreement in the House of Commons and ultimately Theresa May's leadership in 2019.

A simple content analysis of this Agreement highlights significant gender silences, or blind spots. Where the principle of equality appears, it focuses on preventing discrimination based on nationality. The only explicit mention of socio-economic rights enshrined in EU law occurs in the Protocol on Northern Ireland and its related annexes (European Council, EUCO XT 20015/18). A Scottish Parliament report on the Withdrawal Agreement distils the way in which the principle of equal treatment was handled in the document as follows: 'The Withdrawal Agreement lays down that EU citizens and UK nationals, as well as their respective family members, have the right to not be discriminated against due to nationality, and have the right to equal treatment with host state nationals' (McIver et al. 2018, 27). The lack of foresight and absence of impact assessments will remain one of the most enduring features of this process. Whereas the footprint of EU law is clear in national equality provisions, their absence from the overall withdrawal framework highlights the vulnerability of social rights in the absence of European regulation.

Through the looking glass

It is difficult to map all the way different trends coming together in the process. Brexit has become a bell-weather for wider political trends shaping this decade in European politics, from the rise in populism to culture wars. Nevertheless, public performance of toxic masculinity in the public sphere represents a unifying trend. In many ways, the 2016 EU referendum campaigns and the process of Brexit have normalised such performance in what has become the theatre of politics. Reflecting back on the EU Referendum campaign, one of the key funders of the Leave. EU campaign, Aaron Banks, sees this as the victory of the 'Bad Boys of Brexit' (Caesar 2019). Layering this narrative on to the gender ideology of the members of the ERG, Brexit tells a tale of how toxic masculinity is shaping political and economic institutions.

Ian Manners (2018) highlights the existing linkages between far-right movements concerned with immigration and security; the neo-liberal preoccupation with privatisation of public services through the dismantlement of social welfare; and the ultra-conservatives who long for the return of a melancholic British imperial era (Bhambra 2017). A common feature of these new movements lies in re-asserting 'traditional' gender norms and values. They highlight the rise of a range of ideological traditions with the common goal of retrenching or reversing the social transformations of the last 40 years (see Siim and Fiig in this volume).

The masculine, militaristic, racialised and heteronormative nature of the Brexit debate (Achilleos-Sarll and Martill 2019) has gone a long way into providing legitimation for the opposition to the feminist project as well as generating a range of gendered violence. Women of colour and of ethnic minority backgrounds are possibly the most impacted but also the least visible victims of this violent development. The 'politics of difference' (Rajan-Rankin 2017) conducted during the Brexit process has had a particularly dire impact on the lives of black and minority ethnic (BME) women in the UK. Immediately after the referendum, a spike of racist and islamophobe verbal and physical violence was reported, 'legitimised by the leave result' (Gill and Ahmed 2019). This combination of misogyny and xenophobia crystallised in the Brexit process results in the rejection of the British shared value of diversity and the advent of the rejection of the other. This goes further than the legal and financial consequences, which intersectional lenses tell us always disproportionately impact women of colour and ethnic minority background. In the post-referendum era, the entire identity of the UK has been shaken and much uncertainty lies in relation to gender, race, religious and class relations.

The normalisation of violent rhetoric has further identified women political leaders as targets. No one has paid a higher price than Jo Cox, the MP who was murdered during the referendum campaign, whilst she was out campaigning in her constituency. A member of the Remain campaign and vocal advocate on refugees and migrants' rights, she was shot and stabbed by a supporter of the far-right shouting 'death to the traitor'. This event marked the beginning of an ever-increasing insecurity for female and minority ethnic politicians. Most female members of the British Parliament today feel that their life is at risk and have had to hire security guards. Many of these women have had to move out of their home and have changed their pattern of living – it is likely many will have to keep this life. Although violence against female MPs is found in all European countries (IPU-PACE 2018; Raibaigi 2019), in the UK, the increased violence against women MPs since the referendum is unprecedented and directly linked to Brexit (House of Commons Joint Committee on Human Rights 2019; Sabbagh 2019; Women and Equalities Committee 2019). In fact, a survey from Cardiff University and the University of Edinburgh has revealed that a majority of voters in England, Wales and Scotland believe that some level of violence against MPs is a 'price worth paying' in order to get their way on Brexit (Cardiff University News 2019). According to Metropolitan Police data, MPs reported 151 alleged crimes to the police in 2017, rising to 342 in 2018: a 126% increase (House of Commons Joint Committee on Human Rights 2019). What is more, police data shows that female MPs and MPs from ethnic minorities are disproportionately targeted, and about ten MPs accounted for 29% of reports.

There is a direct link between gender equal society and level of democracy (Inglehart et al. 2002), hence attacks against women and other minorities represent symptoms of democratic deficit and decay (Childs and Campbell 2019). Such violence not only has clear gender implications for women's participation in politics, but it further points towards a decline in the British democracy and has detrimental effects for the polity at large.

The violence, indeed, has not exclusively been directed at women but also against democratic institutions. In reproducing and amplifying political toxic masculinity, the media frames has been setting the scene for a more violent and conflictual discourse in society. This is best illustrated by the *Daily Mail*'s headlines on 4 November 2016: 'Enemies of the People' with an article and the pictures of the three High Court judges[3] who held in the *Miller* case[4] that the government would need to obtain Parliament's consent before it could trigger Article 50 TEU and exit the EU. Similar attacks were reproduced in other newspapers such as 'The judges vs. the people' on the front headline of the *Daily Telegraph*, which accused the three High Court judges of frustrating the will of the people. *The Sun*'s title 'Who do you think you are? Loaded foreign elites defy the will of British voters' added a layer of xenophobia to the charge against the judiciary. Indeed, the case had been initiated by Gina Miller, a Guyanese-British governance and transparency activist of Indian descent (Loveland 2018). As such, she embodied everything that Brexiters loath: an educated, black, independent woman and, in consequence, she quickly became the target of media and social media attacks. Other instances where the media has displayed violence in the course of the Brexit process includes the *Daily Mail*'s headline: 'Crush the Saboteurs' on 19 April 2017, following the prime minister's decision to call a snap election. Here the attack was not focussed on the judiciary, but rather on the 'unelected' House of Lords and the minority of people who voted for Britain to remain in the EU were labelled as 'remoaners'. The violence has also been extended to a range of critical voices in the Brexit process and especially against female experts (Galpin 2018), in an effort to silence women's voice as experts (Haastrup et al. 2016).

Conclusions

Brexit has revealed that EU politics and policies have not succeeded in embedding gender norms in everyday politics. What is remarkable about this process is that women remain excluded and marginalised within the context of major events. Not only women are not part of the debate, they are effectively excluded from the process. It is not that women do not want to be part of the debate, but they are consistently marginalised through discursive frames and the performance of gendered violence in public spaces, whether physical or digital.

There is evidence of an emerging counter discourse that calls on the government to make an open commitment to gender equality policies so that a post–Brexit regime does not lead to lowest common denominator politics that are harmful to women and other under-represented groups. The Face Her Future Campaign (www.faceherfuture.co.uk/) is probably the most wide-reaching campaign to date. It brings together leading women's rights organisations in the UK that have been warning about the gendered impact of Brexit. As part of this campaign, the Fawcett Society and the Women's Budget Group produced a joint report drawing on economic data and highlighting specifically four key areas of concern: workers' rights, access to public services, cost to women as consumers, and finally impact on the national GDP (WGB 2018).

The election of Johnson as leader of the Conservative Party marked the beginning of the end game in the first stage of Brexit. Positioning himself as the one to 'get Brexit done' come what may, his government thus set out to force their way through, doubling down on an open confrontation with Parliament, civil society and the Supreme Court. This points to a way of doing politics that favours open conflict and confrontation over cooperation and mediation. This is also fuelling the highly antagonistic and divisive environment that has become established since the EU referendum campaign in 2016. The result of the 2019 general election[5] gives this government a large enough majority in the House of Commons to push through legislation that consolidates power in the hands of the executive, sidelining open deliberation and citizens' rights. The gendered and racialised nature of this new form of nationalism is ultimately intended to disrupt progress towards equality and social justice and is linked to a deeper challenge to the very foundations inclusive governance (Briant 2018). Going forward, it is therefore important to examine the compounded impact of the 2008 financial crisis, with associated austerity, Brexit, and the Covid-19 pandemic. The failure of policy-makers and political leaders to carry out impact assessments and therefore the racialised and gendered impact of these processes will likely have long term unintended consequences on British and European gender regimes.

Notes

1   The video highlighted that the suffragettes died for independence, which membership of the EU violated.
2   The Democratic Unionist Party (DUP) is a unionist political party in Northern Ireland committed to maintain links to London and British identity. It is a right-wing party, which has been linked to various loyalist paramilitary groups and is socially conservative (opposed to abortion, same-sex marriage). The party is Eurosceptic and supported the Leave campaign.
3   The newspaper article written by James Slack, who was later appointed as Theresa May's official spokesman, was initially complemented by homophobic commentaries on the *Daily Mail*'s website describing Lord Etherton as an 'openly-gay ex-Olympic fencer'.
4   *Miller & Anor, R (On the Application Of) v The Secretary of State for Exiting the European Union (Rev 1)* [2016] EWHC 2768 (Admin) (3 November 2016). The Supreme Court dismissed the Government's appeal against the High Court's decision and confirmed that the government cannot trigger Article 50 without an Act of Parliament. *Miller & Anor, R (on the application of) v Secretary of State for Exiting the European Union (Rev 3)* [2017] UKSC 5 (24 January 2017).
5   This majority results from the electoral system; in terms of the popular vote 53% of votes went to Remain parties.

References

Achilleos-Sarll C, Martill B (2019): Toxic Masculinity: Militarism, Deal-Making and the Performance of Brexit, in: Dustin M, Ferreira N, Millns S (eds.): *Gender and Queer Perspectives on Brexit*: Cham: Palgrave Macmillan, 15–44.

Annesley C, Gains F (2013): Investigating the economic determinants of the UK gender equality policy agenda, *The British Journal of Politics and International Relations* **15** (3), 125–146.

Asthana A (2017): Female MPs urge May to Review Brexit Team's Gender Balance, *The Guardian*, 18 July, URL: www.theguardian.com/politics/2017/jul/18/female-mps-urge-may-to-review-brexit-teams-gender-balance (download: 28 February 2020).

BBC (2019): Tory MP's resignation letter, *BBC*, 20 February, URL: www.bbc.co.uk/news/uk-politics-47304424 (download: 28 February 2020).

Bell M (2011): The Principle of Equal Treatment: Widening and Deepening, in: Craig P, De Búrca G (eds.): *The Evolution of EU Law*, Oxford: Oxford University Press, 611–639.

Bhambra G (2017): Brexit, Trump, and 'methodological whiteness'. On the misrecognition of race and class, *British Journal of Sociology* **68** (S1), 214–232.

Brenigan T (2017): All white and just one woman. Why is our Brexit team like this?, *The Guardian*, 22 June.

Briant E (2018): Our governments share responsibility for the Cambridge Analytica crisis … and here's how they should fix it, *openDemocracy*, 8 October, URL: www.opendemocracy.net/en/dark-money-investigations/our-governments-share-responsibility-for-cambridge-analytica-crisis-and-her/ (download: 28 February 2020).

Caesar E (2019): The Chaotic Triumph of Arron Banks, the "Bad Boy of Brexit", The New Yorker. 25 March 2019, URL: www.newyorker.com/magazine/2019/03/25/the-chaotic-triumph-of-arron-banks-the-bad-boy-of-brexit (download: 14 November 2020).

Caracciolo di Torella E (2019): The Unintended Consequences of Brexit: The Case of Work–Life Balance, in: Dustin M, Ferreira N, Millns S (eds.): *Gender and Queer Perspectives on Brexit*, Cham: Palgrave Macmillan, 61–92.

Caracciolo di Torella E, Masselot A (2013): Work and family life balance in the EU law and policy 40 years on: still balancing, still struggling, *European Gender Equality Law Review* **2**, 6–14.

Cardiff University News (2019): Future of England Survey reveals public attitudes towards Brexit and the union, 24 October, URL: www.cardiff.ac.uk/news/view/1709008-future-of-england-survey-reveals-public-attitudes-towards-brexit-and-the-union (download: 28 February 2020).

Childs S, Campbell R (2019): It's not all humbug. The Toxification of British Politics, *The Global Institute for Women's Leadership*, URL: www.kcl.ac.uk/news/its-not-all-humbug-the-toxification-of-british-politics (download: 3 June 2020).

Cook A, Glass C (2014): Women and top leadership positions. Towards an institutional analysis, *Gender, Work & Organization* **21** (1), 91–103.

Cusick J, Corderoy J, Geoghegan P (2019): The files that expose the ERG as a party within a party, *openDemocracy*, 22 July 2019, URL: www.opendemocracy.net/en/dark-money-investigations/revealed-the-files-that-expose-erg-as-a-militant-party-within-a-party/ (download: 25 June 2020)

Deacon D, Harmer E, Downey J, Stanyer J, Wring D (2016): UK news coverage of the 2016 EU Referendum. Report 3 (6 May–8 June 2016), Loughborough: Loughborough University.

Duda-Mikulin E (2018): Gendered migrations and precarity in the post-Brexit-vote UK. The case of Polish women as workers and carers, *Migration and Development* **9** (1), 92–110.

Dustin M, Ferreira N, Millns S (2019): Brexit: Using Gender and Queer Lenses, in: Dustin M, Ferreira N, Millns S (eds.): *Gender and Queer Perspectives on Brexit*, Cham: Palgrave Macmillan, 3–14.

Fagan C, Grimshaw D, Rubery J (2006): The subordination of the gender equality objective. The National Reform Programmes and 'making work pay' policies, *Industrial Relations Journal* **37** (6), 571–592.

Foubert P, Imamović Š (2015): The Pregnant Workers Directive: must do better – lessons to be learned from Strasbourg?, *Journal of Social Welfare & Family Law* **37** (3), 309–320.

Fredman S (2005): Changing the norm. Positive duties in equal treatment legislation, *Maastricht Journal of European and Comparative Law* **12** (4), 369–397.

Elomäki A (2015): The economic case for gender equality in the European Union. Selling gender equality to decision-makers and neoliberalism to women's organizations, *European Journal of Women's Studies* **22** (3), 288–302.

Galpin C (2018): 'Video must not kill the female stars of academic debate', *Times Higher Education*, 8 November, URL: www.timeshighereducation.com/opinion/video-must-not-kill-female-stars-academic-debate (download: 28 February 2020).

Galpin C (2016): Project Fear: how the negativity of the referendum campaign undermines democracy, *LSE Brexit*, 13 June, URL: https://blogs.lse.ac.uk/brexit/2016/06/13/project-fear-how-the-negativity-of-the-referendum-campaign-undermines-democracy/ (download: 28 February 2020).

Gill A, Ahmed N (2019): A New World Order? in: Dustin M, Ferreira N, Millns S (eds.): *Gender and Queer Perspectives on Brexit*, Cham: Palgrave Macmillan, 45–58.

Guerrina R (2005): Mothering the Union: gender politics in the EU, Manchester: Manchester University Press.

Guerrina R (2017): 'Legsit' is not joke. It's symptomatic of a reactionary political culture, *LSE Brexit Blog*, 28 April, URL: https://blogs.lse.ac.uk/brexit/2017/04/28/legsit-is-no-joke-its-symptomatic-of-a-reactionary-brexit-political-culture/#comments (download: 26 June 2020).

Guerrina R, Haastrup T, Wright K, Masselot A, Macrae H, Cavaghan R (2018): Does EU studies have a gender problem? Experiences from researching Brexit, *International Feminist Journal of Politics* **20** (2), 252–257.

Guerrina R, Masselot A (2018): Walking into the footprint of EU Law: unpacking the gendered consequences of Brexit, *Social Policy & Society* **17** (2), 319–330.

Guerrina R, Murphy H (2016): Strategic silences in the Brexit debate: gender, marginality and governance, *Journal of Contemporary European Research* **12** (4), 872–880.

Haastrup T, Wright K, Guerrina R (2016): Women in the Brexit debate. Still largely confined to 'low' politics, *LSE Brexit*, URL: https://blogs.lse.ac.uk/brexit/2016/06/17/women-in-the-brexit-debate-still-largely-confined-to-low-politics/ (download: 5 May 2020).

Haastrup T, Wright KAM, Guerrina R (2019): Brexit: gendered implications for equality in the UK, *European Journal of Politics and Gender* **2** (2), 311–312.

Hantrais L (2018): Review article: assessing the past and future development of EU and UK social policy, *Social Policy & Society* **17** (2), 265–279.

Holder J (2019): How much of Johnson's great new deal is actually new?, *The Guardian*, 18 October 2019.

House of Commons Joint Committee on Human Rights (2019): Democracy, Freedom of Expression and Freedom of Association: Threats to MPs: First Report of Session 2019-20, HC 37 HL Paper 5, 18 October 2019, URL: https://publications.parliament.uk/pa/jt201919/jtselect/jtrights/37/37.pdf (download: 14 November 2020).

Hozic A, True J (2016): Making Feminist Sense of the Global Financial Crisis, in: Hozic A, True J (eds.): *Scandalous Economics: Gender and the Politics of Financial Crises*, Oxford, New York: Oxford University Press, 3–20.

Inglehart R, Norris P, Welzel C (2002): Gender equality and democracy, *Comparative Sociology* **1** (3–4), 235–264.

Inter-Parliamentary Union and Parliamentary Assembly of the Council of Europe (IPU-PACE) (2018): Sexism, harassment and violence against women in parliaments in Europe, *Issue Briefs*, October, Geneva: IPU.

Loveland I (2018) *Constitutional Law, Administrative Law and Human Rights. A Critical Introduction*, Oxford: Oxford University Press.

Mason R, Walker P, Elgot J (2016): Who's who in Theresa May's new cabinet, *The Guardian*, 14 July, URL: www.theguardian.com/politics/2016/jul/13/who-theresa-may-cabinet-boris-hammond-rudd (download: 25 January 2020).

Kilkey M (2017): Conditioning family-life at the intersection of migration and welfare. The implications for 'Brexit families', *Journal of Social Policy* **46** (4), 797–814.

Lombardo E, Kantola J (2019): European integration and disintegration. Feminist perspectives on inequalities and social justice, *Journal of Common Market Studies* **57**, 62–76.

MacLeavy J (2018): Women, equality and the UK's EU referendum. Locating the gender politics of Brexit in relation to the neoliberalising state, *Space and Polity* **22** (2), 205–223.

Manners I (2018): Political psychology of European integration. The (re) production of identity and difference in the Brexit debate, *Political Psychology* **39** (6), 1213–1232.

McCrudden C (2019): *Gender-Based Positive Action in Employment in Europe*, Luxembourg: Publications Office of the European Union.

McGlynn C (1996): Pregnancy dismissals and the Webb litigation, *Feminist Legal Studies* **4** (2), 229–242.

McGlynn C (2000): Ideologies of motherhood in European Community sex discrimination, *European Law Journal* **6** (1), 29–44.

McIver I, Thom I, Evans A, Kenyon W, McCallum F and McGrath F (2018): The UK's departure from the European Union – An overview of the Withdrawal Agreement, *SPICe Briefing*, URL: https://digitalpublications.parliament.scot/ResearchBriefings/Report/2018/11/26/The-UK-s-Departure-from-the-European-Union–An-overview-of-the-Withdrawal-Agreement (download: 25 June 2020).

Mergaert L, Lombardo E (2014): Resistance to Implementing Gender Mainstreaming in EU Research Policy, in: Weiner E, MacRae H (eds.): *The Persistent Invisibility of Gender in EU Policy,* European Integration online Papers (EIoP), Special Issue **1** (18).

Millar J (2018): The Brexiteers represent the four faces of toxic masculinity, New Statesman, 5 July, URL: www.newstatesman.com/politics/staggers/2018/07/brexiteers-represent-four-faces-toxic-masculinity (download 11 November 2020).

O'Brien C (2013): I trade, therefore I am: legal personhood in the European Union, *Common Market Law Review* **50** (6), 1643–1684.

O'Brien C (2018): The rights of EU nationals in the UK post-Brexit. Five pessimistic predictions, *Free movement,* 19 February, URL: www.freemovement.org.uk/rights-eu-nationals-uk-post-brexit-five-pessimistic-predictions/ (download: 5 May 2020).

Pollack M, Hafner-Burton E (2000): Mainstreaming gender in the European Union, *Journal of European Public Policy* **7** (3), 432–456.

Prechal S (2004): Equality of treatment, non-discrimination and social policy: achievements in three themes, *Common Market Law Review* **41** (2), 533–551.

Raibaigi K (2019): In parliaments across Europe women face alarming levels of sexism, harassment and violence, *EDJNet – The European Data Journalism Network,* URL: www.europeandatajournalism.eu/eng/News/Data-news/In-parliaments-across-Europe-women-face-alarming-levels-of-sexism-harassment-and-violence (download: 5 May 2020).

Rajan-Rankin S (2017): Brexit logics: myth and fact – a black feminist analysis, *feminists@law* **7** (2), 1–2.

Ritch E (2019): Foreboding Newness. Brexit and Feminist Civil Society in Scotland, in: Dustin M, Ferreira N, Millns S (eds.): *Gender and Queer Perspectives on Brexit,* Cham: Palgrave Macmillan, 333–362.

Sabbagh D (2019): Violent threats against MPs 'commonplace', report warns, *The Guardian,* 18 October, URL: www.theguardian.com/politics/2019/oct/18/violent-threats-against-mps-commonplace-report-warns (download: 5 May 2020).

Solanke I (2019): Who Speaks for the Zambrano Families? Multi-level Abandonment in the UK and EU, in: Dustin M, Ferreira N, Millns S (eds.): *Gender and Queer Perspectives on Brexit,* Cham: Palgrave Macmillan, 151–183.

Stephenson MA, Fontana M (2019): The Likely Economic Impact of Brexit on Women. Lessons from Gender and Trade Research, in: Dustin M, Ferreira N, Millns S (eds.): *Gender and Queer Perspectives on Brexit,* Cham: Palgrave Macmillan, 415–438.

Shutes I, Walker S (2018): Gender and free movement: EU migrant women's access to residence and social rights in the UK, *Journal of Ethnic and Migration Studies* **44** (1), 137–153.

Women's Budget Group (2018): *Exploring the economic impact of Brexit on women.* March 2018, URL: www.fawcettsociety.org.uk/Handlers/Download.ashx?IDMF=049e3458-12b0-4d0f-b0a6-b086e860b210 (download 25 June 2020).

Women and Equalities Committee (2019): Two thirds of women MPs say that progress on tackling violence against women in politics impacts their willingness to stand for re-election, URL: www.parliament.uk/business/committees/committees-a-z/commons-select/women-and-equalities-committee/news-parliament-2017/women-mps-tackling-violance-letters-2019/ (download: 3 June 2020).

Index

Abels, Gabriele 37, 111, 113, 245, 321
abortion, anti-abortion 25, 195, 202, 229, 243, 244, 372, 374
accession *see* enlargement
acquis communautaire see law
Action Programme (AP) 127, 137–9, 243–4; environmental 303, 309; first (1988–1990) 140, 243–4; fourth (2004–2008) 140, 243–4; second (1992–1996) 140, 243–4; social 255; third (1997–2000) 140, 243–4
Advisory Committee on Equal Opportunities for Women and Men 125, 382
advocacy, transnational 34, 50, 225
African, Caribbean and Pacific (ACP) countries 282, 291, 293–5, 298; *see also* trade
Agenda for Change 291
agenda-setting 11, 108, 113– 16, 126, 128, 133, 372, 373; *see also* policy analysis
Agreement: Comprehensive Economic Trade Agreement (CETA) 285–7; Cotonou 291, 294, 298; Economic Partnership (EPA) 282, 293–4; EU-Chile Association 281, 282, **284–5**, 286–7; Paris 303; Schengen 198, 339; Withdrawal 395–8, 332
agriculture 68, 278, 279, 281, 297, 303, 305, 315, 342
Ahrens, Petra 64, 113, 139, 171, 228, 244, 372
Allen, Heidi 395–6
Alliance of Liberals and Democrats for Europe (ALDE) *see* political party
Allwood, Gill 153, 306–7, 348
Alter, Karen 172
Ansorg, Nadine 332
anti-discrimination *see* discrimination
anti-gender politics/movements *see* backlash
anti-LGBT movement *see* backlash
anti-pluralism *see* illiberalism
approach: rights-based 224, 298, 348; social investment 19; structural change 315, **317**, 318, **319**
Arendt, Hannah 197, 204
Article: Article 2 TEU 185, 240, 244; Article 8 TFEU 138, 251, 322, 393; Article 13 TEU 122,

344; Article 17.7 TEU 240; Article 19 TFEU 93–4, 101, 361; Article 50 TEU 399; Article 119 EEC 7, 12, 18, 82, 93, 137, 185, 251, **253**; *see also* EU law
Ashton, Catherine 9, 123, 147, 150, 152–3
Association against Violence toward Women at Work (AVFT) 359
asylum *see* policy
Atlanticists 328, 329
Aubry, Manon 242
austerity *see* policy
Austria 18, 86, 110, 124, 128, 210–12, 267, 371, 374
Authority for European Political Parties and European Political Foundations (APPF) **237–41**, 240
Ayoub, Phillip 191

Bachelet, Michelle 284
backlash 12, 19, 23–5, 37–8, 50, 113, 166, 182, 223, 230, 245, 246, 261–2, 320, 323, 368, 369, 372, **373–4**, 375
Baker, Steve 395
Bakker, Isabella 274
Balkans 35, 84, 193, 229, 328
Baltics, Baltic states 84, 187, 229
Banks, Arron 398
Barroso Commission 134–6, 142, 382
Beijing Fourth World Conference on Women 1995 21, 127, 257, **293**, 356, 359
Beijing Platform for Action 158, 285, 308, 356
Belgium 4, 109, 210–12, 128, 229, 267, 371
Benlolo Carabot, Myriam 360–1
Black European Women's Council 227–8
Black feminism 46, 68, 94–5
border(s) 6, 25, 72, 84–5, 198, 201, 202, 335, 339–40, 345, 348, 396, 397
Borrell, Josep 123, 331
Börzel, Tanja 33, 189
Brack, Nathalie 237
Bretherton, Charlotte 304, 328
Brexit 4, 12–13, 19, 23, 35, 49, 122, 261–2, 298–9, 332, 366, **392–5**, 396, **398–9**, 400

404

Bruff, Ian 269
Brundtland, Gro Harlem 8
budget deficit 72, 267, **268**, 270–3, 380, 381, 384, 386
Buenos Aires Declaration on Women and Trade *see* declaration
Bulgaria 6, 85–6, 97, 124, 129, 183, 186–7, 211, 341, 342
bureaucracy 70, 141, 321, 323, 328
BusinessEurope 256
Buttiglione, Rocco 108

Cameron, David 393–4
Camps, Miriam 2
capitalism 19, 68, 69, 71, 73, 75, 196, 272, 375, 387
care 45, 48, 164, 196, 200, 272, 275, 281, 384–5; concept of 84, 87; childcare 19, 71, 138, 253, **255**, 256, 257, 371, 384, 397; work 17, 20, 23, 71–3, **86–7**, 201, 342, 344, 384
Cavaghan, Rosalind 47–9
CEDAW *see* discrimination
CEE countries 18–19, 21, 23, 24, 30, 37, 88–9, 111, 165, 182, 183, 186–8, 190–2, 200, 230, 236, 237, 244, 303, 304, 383
Chappell, Laura 61
Charlemagne Prize 8
Charter of Fundamental Rights *see* rights
Chiva, Cristina 110–11, 191, 244, 246
Cichowski, Rachel 172
Citizenship: European 122, 174, 181, 195, **197–9**, 200, 202–3, 255, 261, 379; feminist approach to 181, 195, 196, 203–4; intersectional approach to 195; national 24, 195–7, 199, 200; post-national/pluri-national 201, 203; supranational 199, 203, 204; transnational 84, 203, 204; women's citizenship rights 196, 197, 200–1, **203**
civil society 10, 60, 116, 129, 151, 182, 191, **222–4**, 225, 227–31, 279, 285, 309, 330, 331, 339, 348, 375–6, 386; digital civil society/online civil society 230
civilian mission 332
class *see* difference
climate: change 36, 37, 153, 298, **302–9**, 310–11, 315; diplomacy 303, 304, 309–11; policy 37, 76, **302–4**, 305–11, 335; and energy package 303, 304
Close, Caroline 244
coalition, coalition formation 50, 124, 125, 142, 143, 235, 240, 244, 246, 374
co-decision procedure 107, 114, 240, 340, 357; *see also* European Parliament
Codruţa Kövesi, Laura 9
co-legislator 107, 292; *see also* European Parliament
Combahee River Collective (CRC) 94–5
Comitology 123
Commission *see* European Commission

committee (European Parliament): chair 113, 114, 236, 240–3, 246, 267, 354; rapporteur 2, 112, 113, 236, 237, 240, 241, 243; of Women's Rights and Gender Equality (FEMM) 24, 59, 63, 112, **113–1**, 116, 142, 161, 165, 202, 235, 243–4, 303, 307–9, 342, 343, 352–4, 357, 360, 382; on Civil Liberties, Justice and Home Affairs (LIBE) 113, 235, 243–4; on Constitutional Affairs (AFCO) 113; on Employment and Social Affairs (EMPL) 113, 235, 243–4; on Security and Defence (SEDE) 113; on Transport and Tourism (TRAN) 113
Common European Asylum System (CEAS) 339, 345, 346
Common Foreign and Security Policy (CFSP) *see* policy
common market 26, 82, 93, 253, 352; *see also* single market
Common Security and Defence Policy (CSDP) *see* policy
compliance 32, 33, 165, **186–90**, 191, 240, 259, 268, 270, 381
Comprehensive Economic Trade Agreement (CETA) *see* agreement
conditionality: administrative 186; economic 186; political 184, 185, **186–7**, 258
Conference on the Future of Europe (CoFoE) **10–11**
Connell, Raewyn W./Robert 20, 22, 81
convergence 22, 25, 30, 32–4, **36**, 37, 57, 189, 190, 265, 267, 268, 273
Coordinated Annual Review on Defence (CARD) 329
Copenhagen criteria 32, 186, 375; *see also* enlargement
COREPER 106, **122–3**, 125, 126; *see also* Council
Corradi, Sofia 9
Council: Agriculture and Fisheries (AGRIFISH) 121; Competitiveness (COMPET) 121; of Europe 6, 97, 121, 295, 358, 359; of Ministers 9, 121, 127, 254, 255, 315, 354; of the EU 10, 86, 107, 120, **121**, 122–4, 135, 236, 254, 279, 290, 292, 315, 354, 358; presidency **121**, 123; Economic and Financial Affairs (ECOFIN) 121, 124, 268, 380, 381; Education, Youth, Culture and Sport (EYCS) 121, 124; Employment, Social Policy, Health and Consumer Affairs (EPSCO) 121, 142, 254; Environment (ENVI) 121; European (EUCO) 35, 108, 120, **122–3**, 124–5, 127, 129, 135, 185, 236, 240–1, 267, 268, 270, 304, 329, 380, 381; European Council presidency **122**, 127–9; Foreign Affairs (FAC) 121, 124, 329; General Affairs (GAC) 121, 124; General Secretariat of the (GSC) **122**, 125; Justice and Home Affairs (JHA) 121, 347; Transport, Telecommunications and Energy (TTE) 121

Index

Court of Justice of the EU (CJEU) 12, 33, 65, 94, 98–9, 100, 141, **170–7**, 184, 198, 254, 340, 343, 347, 358

court cases: *Achbita* (C-157/15) **98**, 176; *Bougnaoui* (C-188/15) 98, **99**, 176; *BS v Spain* (no 47159/08; ECtHR) **99**; *Chez Razpredelenie Bulgaria AD,* C 83/14 100; *Defrenne* cases 7, 8, 141; *DeGraffenreid v General Motors Assembly Division* **95–6**, 98–9; *Jefferies v Harris Cty. Community Action Association* 102

Covid-19 pandemic 6, 11, 12, 19, 35, 38, 71, 76, 101, 228, 262, 275, 298, 372, 374

Cox, Jo 398

Cresson, Edith 319

Crisis: of democracy 89; economic 8, 12, 23, 24, 35, 38, 43, 47, 48, **49**, 51, 75, 159, 165, 166, 182, 192, 202, 229, 266, 270, 273, 304, 365–6, 379–80, 382, **384–7**, 388; Euro/Eurozone 2, 17–18, **19**, 23, 68, 69, 124, 265–6, **269–70**, 379, 383; financial 19, 23, 68, **69–70**, 121, 126, 166, 182, 202, 225, 243, 254, 258, 266, 269–71, **273**, 365, 380, 382–3, 393, 400; legitimacy 23, 36, **159–60**, 166, 181, 182, 208, 245, 365–6; poly-crisis 3, **4**, 17–18, 26, 35, 76, 365, 372; refugee/migration 35, 39, 122, 204, 346, 372, 386; rule of law 35–6, 39

Critical Political Economy *see* integration theory

critical race feminism 94, 95, 97; *see also* Black feminism

critical research on men (CROME) 85–6, 87–9; *see also* masculinity/masculinities

Croatia 35, 38, 97, 183, 211

Cullen, Pauline 244, 246

Cyprus 110, 210, 211, 270

Czechia, Czech Republic 84, 85, 89, 129, 183, 187, 189, 191–2, 210–12, 320, 381

D'Ancona, Hedy 354

Dalli, Helena 142, 310

DAPHNE program *see* violence

Davis, David 395

Debusscher, Petra 62

Declaration: on the Elimination of Violence against Women (DEVAW) 353, 356, 359; on Women and Trade 278, 284; Nairobi Maafikiano 284; Universal Declaration of Human Rights (UDHR) 197

decolonization 345

decommodification 20; *see also* welfare state regime

deconstruction 43, **45–7**, 50–1, 81, 336, 383, 385

de-democratization 23, 25, 50, 51, 70, 165, 270, 374, 386, 393; *see also* illiberalism

de-europeanization 31, **35–6**

defence *see* policy

Delors Commission 134–6

Delors, Jacques 127, 256, 267

democracy: democratic backsliding **23**, 50, 192, 374; democratic deficit 107, 129, 181, **200**, 203, 266, 271, 274, 399; democratic legitimacy 19, 116, 200, 223–4, 270, 387, 388; liberal 19; illiberal 35, 89, 367, 374, 375; *see also* de-democratization, illiberalism

Denmark 18, 85, 124, 128, 142, 210, 211, 272, 307, 308, 328, 329, 341, 371, 374

Deshormes La Valle, Fausta 8

development: development aid 299, 303; cooperation 121, 153, 282, 292, 294, 297, 298, 305, 339; Gender and (GAD) 68, **293–8**, 303, 305, 293; Official Development Assistance 291, 299; sustainable 278, 280, 282, 286, 291, 292, 303; Women in Development Europe (WIDE) 225, 285, **293**, 359

Dewandre, Nicole 323

Di Nonno, Maria Pia 2–3, 7

Diamantopolou, Anna 355

Difference: class 11, 24, 46–7, 49, 51, 58, 64, 65, 68–70, 88, 154, 181, 197, 202, 222, 228, 261, 297, 305, 306, 335, 342, 370, 384, 386, 392, 398; gender 12, 26, 46, 64, 72, 94, 102, 154, 181, 197, 202, **210–11**, 213, 215, 216, 218, 222, 228, 273, 297, 305, 306, 308, 333, 335, 341, 370, 372, 384, 386, 398; nationality 24, 93, 181, 197, 202, 203, 205, 306, 384, 397–8; race 11, 24, 46–7, 49, 58, 64, 65, 100, 154, 176, 202, 203, 222, 228, 261, 297, 335, 370, 379, 384, 386, 398

digitalization 229, 230, 316

Dinan, Desmond 2–3

diplomatic corps 125

directives: access to and supply of goods and services (2004/113/EC) 138, 355; European protection order (2011/99/EU) 357, 383; amending Council Directive 76/207/EEC on the implementation of the principle of equal treatment for men and women (2002/73/EC) 355, 359; Asylum Procedure (2005/85/EC), (2013/32/EU) 176, 346, 347; conditions of entry and residence of TNCs (2009/50/EC) (Blue Card Directive) 342; Employment Equality Framework (2000/78/EC) 83, 93–4, 98, 99, 138, 187; Equal Pay (75/117/EEC) 137; Equal Treatment (76/207/EEC), (2002/73/EC) 93, 97, 99, 137, **354–5**; Equal Treatment for the Self-Employed (86/613/EEC) 137, 139; implementation of the principle of equal treatment for men and women a (76/207/EEC) 93, 97, 99, 137, 354, 355; Maternity leave (Pregnant Workers Directive) (92/85/EEC) 35, 114, 137, 243, 256, 383, 393; minimum standards on the rights, support and protection of victims of crime (2012/29/EU) 357, 383; Occupational Pensions Schemes (86/378/EEC) 137; Parental leave (1996/34/EC) 137, 138, 256–8, 260; Part-time work (1997/81/EC)

137, 138, 256, 257; Pregnant Workers (92/85/EEC) *see* Maternity leave Directive; preventing and combating trafficking in human beings and protecting its victims (2011/36/EU) 344, **356**, 361; Race Directive (2000/43/EC) 93, 97, 99, 165, 187, 202; Recast Directive (2006/54/EC) 139, 165, 355; residence permit for victims of human trafficking (2004/81/EC) 355–6; Social Security (79/7/EEC) 137, 257; standards for the qualification of TNCs (Qualification Directive) (2004/83/EU), (2011/95/EU) 346; temporary agency work (2008/104/EC) 258; work–life balance (2019/1158/EU) 35, 139, 256, 260, 383; Temporary Protection (2001/55/EC) 346; Working time (93/104/EC), (2003/88/EC) 256

Director(s) General 134, **135–6**, 141–3, 322–3

Directorate-General (DG) 134–6, 140, 141, 225, 292, 293, 294, 298, 307; *see also* European Commission; Climate Action (CLIMA) 304, 307; Defence, Industry and Space (DG DEFIS) 329; Economic and Financial Affairs (ECFIN) 74, 136, 274; Education, Youth Sport and Culture (EAC) 136, 314; Employment, Social Affairs and Inclusion (EMPL) 140–2, 160, 225, 382–3; European Neighbourhood and Enlargement Negotiations (NEAR) 136, 186; Health and Food Safety (SANTE) 136; International Cooperation and Development (DEVCO) 282, 291–3; Justice, Fundamental Rights and Citizenship (DG Justice) 136, 142, 160, 161, 225, 382–3; Migration and Home Affairs (HOME) 292; RELEX (External Relations) 146; *see also* European External Action Service; DG Research and Innovation (DG RTD) 34, **314–15**, **317**, 320–3

discrimination: age 18, 83, 93, 94, 99, 100, 163, 187, 202, 228, 261, 319, 384; anti-discrimination 16, 18, 21, 22, 34, 37, 39, 83, 94–7, **100**, 102, 126, 128, 138, **139**, 142, 159, **163–4**, 201, 204, 230, 235, 237, 240, 241, **243–5**, 246, 261, 272, 340, 348, 367–8, 373–6, 379; Convention on the Elimination of All Forms of Discrimination against Women (CEDAW) 86, 187, 282, 285; gender 6, 18, 23, 24, 83, 93–4, 96, **100–1**, 102, 128, 141, 163, 174, 202, 282, 286, 344, 352, 357–8; indirect 83, 94, 98, 137, 257; multiple 39, 94, **96–7**, 99, 100, **101–2**, 174, 228, 344; non-discrimination 33, **93**, 97, 141, 183–5, 187, 189, 240, 253, 255, 261, 282–4, 316, 355, 382; intersectional **94–7**, 98–100, **101–2**, 192, 261, 348, 361; sex 7–9, 18, 83, 93–7, 133, 137, 138, 143, 161, 165, 173, 251, 343, 345, **354–5**, 358, 361; race 18, 47, 83, 93–5, **96**, 97, 100, 101, 163, 174, 187, 202, 309, 335; *see also* race; difference

disintegration 25, 26, 36, 46, 48, 76, 265, 366, 393

displacement 59, 309, 311, 339

diversity 17, 22, 47, 59, 65, 105, 140, 141, 147, 154, 163, 165, 167, 182, 195, 196, 201, 225, 230, 302, 310, 323, 341, 343, 347–8, 368, 370, 373, 396, 398; *see also* intersectionality

Diversity and Inclusion Charter (2017) 141; *see also* rights

divorce 6, 396

domestic impact 31–2, 260

Dublin Convention 176, 345, 346

Economic and Monetary Union (EMU) 4, 69, 70, 127, 255, **265–7**, 268–75, 381

ECOFIN (Economic and Financial Affairs Council) *see* council

Economic Partnership Agreement (EPA) *see* agreement

education 19, 71, 72, 83, 84, 86–7, 94, 97, 111, 115, 128, 136, 175, 187, 201, 210, **213**, 216, 226, 244, 253, 278, 280, 286, 293, 294, 316, **318**, 342, 372, 384, 392

EEAS *see* European External Action Service

effect: boomerang 259; pincer 259; ping-pong 228

election: electoral rules 110, 213; electoral turnout **109**, 200, 214, 392; European Election Studies 209, 371–2; European Electoral Act 107, 110; European Parliament 8, 82, **107–11**, 112, 129, 135, 142, 198, 200, 213–14, 223, 236–41, **24–2**, 245, 274, 302, 371, 372; second-order 109, 111, 214, 218

Elson, Diane 274, 281, 285

Emejulu, Akwugo 74, 387

Emissions Trading System (ETS) 304

empowerment 7, 10, 39, 50, 63, 134, **136**, 143, 154, 196, 259, 280, 282–4, **294**, 309, 344, 387

enlargement 4, 12, 18–19, **30–1**, **32–5**, 37, 114, 126, 141–2, 165, 181–4, **184–93**, 200, 254, 258–9, 339, 360, 383; *see also* Copenhagen criteria

enslaved women 94, 95

environment 4, 76, 89, 159, 227, 237, 275, 278–80, 282, 285, 291, 297, **302–3**, 304–5, 306–10, 315

epistemology 44, 57, 60, 70, 73–6, 80, 128

Equal Opportunities Strategy (2010–14) 140

Equal Opportunities Unit 140; *see also* Commission

equal rights *see* rights

equality: bodies 116, **165–6**, 187, 188; Commissioner for Equality *see* European Commission; equal pay *see* directives; equal treatment *see* directives; European Equality Law Network 158, 360; European Institute for Gender Equality (EIGE) *see* EU agency; European Network of Legal Experts in the Field of Gender Equality 355; European Pact for Gender Equality 127; institutions 23, 49, 105, 166, 202, 334, 384; law 7, 95, 170, 172, 173;

Index

race 25, 163, 165; *see also* race; discrimination; Strategic Engagement for Gender Equality (2016–19) **139**, 320, 344; Strategy for Equality between Women and Men (2010–15) 139; Union of Equality 302, 310; *see also* discrimination; gender equality; rights

Erasmus programme 9

Esping-Andersen, Gøsta 20, 22

Estonia 84, 85, 183, **210**, **211**, **212**, 216

Ethical, Legal and Social Aspects of emerging science (ELSA) 316

ethnicity 17, 18, 24, 26, 46, 49, 51, 58, 64, 65, 88, 102, 163–5, 181, 202, 203, 205, 261, 286, 297, 305, 306, 319, 335, 354, 370, 375, 384; *see also* race; minority

EU agency: European Agency for Safety and Health at Work (EU-OSHA) 164; European Asylum Support Office (EASO) 164, 346–7; European Foundation for the Improvement of Living and Working Conditions (EUROFOUND) 164; European Institute for Gender Equality (EIGE) 18, 59, 87, 97, 108, 116, 125, 159, **160–3**, 164–7, 308, 309, 360, 361; European Training Foundation (ETF) 164; FRONTEX (European Border and Coast Guard Agency) 345–6; Fundamental Rights Agency (FRA) 97, 159, 160, 161, **163–4**, 165–7, 347, 352, 360, 361; independent agency 159–61, 163, 166; regulatory agency 166

EU Delegations 10, 147, 149, 150, 155, 291, 292, 294, 296

EU Group of Experts on Trafficking in Human Beings 360

Euratom *see* European Atomic Energy Community

Euro 4, 24, 265, **266–7**, 268, 379; *see also* crisis

Eurobarometer *see* statistics

EURODAC Regulation (603/2013/EU) 346

Eurogroup 74, 121, 122, 268, 271, 380

Europarties 110, **236–41**, 245; *see also* political party

Europe 2020 Strategy 127, 171, 272, 381

EuropeAid Co-operation Office (AIDCO) 291; *see also* Directorate-General (DG)

European Agenda on Migration 340, 343, 345, 346; *see also* policy

European Asylum Support Office (EASO) *see* EU agency

European Atomic Energy Community (Euratom) 4, 107, 158; *see also* treaty

European Central Bank (ECB) 5, 62, 74, 106, 123, 129, 265, 266, **267–8**, 269, 270, 274, 379–81

European Centre of Employers and Enterprises (CEEP) 256

European Citizens' Initiative (ECI) 223, 224, 227, 229

European Coal and Steel Community (ECSC) 2, 4, 82, 107, 198, 265; *see also* treaty

European Commission; *see also* Directorate-General (DG): administration 133, **135–6**, 140, 142, 143, 321; administrative role 134–6; appointment process for Commissioners 134–6; College of Commissioners 108, 134, 135, 141; president 3, 9, **108**, 122, 123, 133–5, 142, 144, 240; Commissioner for Employment 134, 354, 355; Commissioner for Equality 26, 142, 163, 284, 302, 310; *see also* equality; Commissioner for International Partnerships 292; Commissioners 10, 47, 129, 133–6, 142–3, 259, 292, 319, 323, 360; Group of Commissioners on Equal Opportunities 142, 258; Political Guidelines of the (2019–24) 10, 310

European Consensus on Development (ECD) 290, 291

European Convention on Human Rights (ECHR) *see* rights

European Council *see* Council

European Council presidency *see* Council

European Court of Human Rights (ECtHR) *see* rights

European Court of Justice *see* Court of Justice of the EU (CJEU); *see also* court cases

European Defence Community 4, 328

European Defence Fund (EDF) 329, 333

European Economic and Social Committee (EESC) 121, 224, 229, 255, 258

European Economic Community (EEC) 4, 93, 107, 185, 198, 265

European Economic Recovery Plan 275, 382

European Employment Strategies 33, 258, 382; *see also* policy

European Exchange Rate Mechanism (ERM) 267

European External Action Service (EEAS) 5, 9, 12, 106, 136, **146–54**, 155, 292, 294, 297, 330, 329, 359; Gender Advisor(s) 147, 151–3, 331, 332; Task Force on Women, Peace and Security 147, 152, 331

European Feminist Forum 359

European Green Deal 297, 302, 303, 310; *see also* policy

European Institute for Gender Equality (EIGE) *see* EU agency

European Instrument for Democracy and Human Rights (EIDHR) 358

European Neighbourhood Policy (ENP) *see* policy

European Network of Migrant Women (ENoMW) 225, 227, **343**

European Ombudsman 165, 198

European Parliament; *see also* committee; political party: Equality and Diversity Unit 113; European Parliamentary Research Service (EPRS) 114; political groups 108, **111–12**, 113–16, **235–6**, 237, 240, 241, **242**, 245, 371, 372, 373

European Parliamentary Assembly 107, 185

408

European Party Groups (EPGs) *see* political party
European Peacebuilding Liaison Office
  (EPLO) 331
European Pillar of Social Rights (EPSR) *see* rights
European Platform of Women Scientists (EPWS)
  317, 323
European Profeminist Men's Network 85, 87
European Research Area (ERA) 314, **315–16**,
  317–18, 321, 323
European Research Council (ERC) 319
European Security and Defence Policy (ESDP)
  see policy
European Security Strategy (ESS) 329, 330, 333
European Semester 70, **268**, 270, 272, 381, 383;
  see also Euro; governance
European Social Dialogue 138, 253, 256
European Social Survey (ESS) **212**
European Trade Union Confederation (ETUC)
  256–7, 355
European Women's Lobby (EWL) 21, 34, 142, 158,
  161, **225–7**, 229–30, 243, 323, 331, 343, 355,
  359, 361
Europeanisation/Europeanization 21–3, **30**, **31–6**,
  37–40, 44, 115, 116, 126, 159, **165–6**, 184, 186,
  188–90, 191, 192, 202–4, 260, 340, 347
Europeanists 56, 57, 328
Euroscepticism 23, 38, 112, 191, 201, **202**, 217,
  237, 240, 243–6, 271, 393, 395
EU-Turkey Deal 345; *see also* migration
evaluation panels 319
Excessive Deficit Procedure (EDP) 269–70;
  see also Euro; governance
exclusion, social 10, 49, 65, 82, 85, **87–8**, 95, 100,
  181, 182, 228, 340, 369, 397
expertise 21, 49, 73, 74, 149, 160, **162–3**, 167, 226,
  227, 260, 295, 298, 386

Face Her Future Campaign 400
Falkner, Gerda 32, 189, 245
Family: care obligations 86–7, 199, 200, 333;
  members 199, 204, 341, 398; migration 340,
  341–2, 371; model/traditional 24, 37, 87, 125,
  230, 367, **371**; reconciliation of work and 81,
  128, 255, 256, 259–61; reunification 175, **341**
Farris, Sara 369
Fawcett Society 400
female genital mutilation (FGM) 353, 357, 358,
  360, 361; *see also* violence
femininities 12, 16, 20, 57–8, 61, **65**, 80, 82, 151,
  274, **332–3**, 334, 372, 379
feminism: anti-feminist forces 12, 38, 81, 245,
  348, 374; feminist actors 50, 62, 74, 251, 330,
  354, 359, 375; *see also* femocrats; feminist
  movement(s), women's movement(s) 3, 18, 19,
  21, 23, 25, 48, 50, 95, 133, 141–3, 166, **191**, 223,
  224, **226–7**, 228–9, 251, 353, 254, 386; feminist
  politics 367–8, 372, 374; state 158, 191

Feminist Political Economy (FPE) 12, **68–9**, **71–6**,
  266, 274, 281
feminization 49, 111, 373, 384
FEMM *see* committee
femocrats 21, 60, 115, 141, 151, 225, 251, 260, 319,
  322, **323**, 330, 369
Finland 38, 48, 85, 86, 110, 125–8, 151, **210–12**,
  241, 267, 370, 374, 382, 385, 386
Fiscal Compact *see* treaty
Fischer Boel, Mariann 2
Fontaine, Nicole 114
founding fathers/mothers 1, 3, 5–7, 9, 82, 127
Fox, Liam 395
fragmentation 22, 26, 124
Framework Programmes (FP) 37, 85, **314**, 316,
  319–21, 323
frames/framing 22, 30, 33, 34, 37, 45, 47, 49, 86, 88,
  114, 125, 127, 128, 148, 166, 190, 192, 223, 257,
  259, 260, 279, 281, 284, 304, 310, 323, 347, 359,
  360, 370, 373, 395, 399; Critical Frame Analysis
  47, 296; policy 23, 34, 47, **260**, 357
France 3, 4, 8, 9, 38, 48, 97, 110, 124, 134, **210–12**,
  229, 267, 299, 328, 369, 371, 387
freedom: of expression 386; of movement 35, 93,
  198–200, 204, 320, 339, 397; of the press 36
Front National *see* political party
FRONTEX *see* EU agency

Galligan, Yvonne 128
García Pérez, Iratxe 242
García, Maria 76
gayropa 39
Gender Action Plan (GAP) **294–5**, 296, **317**, 309,
  328, 335, **343–4**, 359
gender; *see also* difference, gender mainstreaming:
  advisors 147, **151–2**, 153, 294, 331, 332;
  approaches 12, 19–21, 38, 43–4, **45–7**, 51, 66,
  70, 138, 254, 273, 321, 334, **383–7**; balance
  on company boards 24, 128, 142, 273, 383;
  budgeting 59, **75**, 115, 128, 230, 268, 309, 314;
  composition 110, 111, 120, 124, 125, 136, 140,
  172, **242**, 339, 383; gap **109**, 110, 111, 154,
  209–13, 214–17, **218**, 241, 367, 368, 371–2,
  392; Gender Focal Person (GFP) **294**; gender+
  equality **372**; gender-blind 46, 61, 72, 114, 176,
  251–2, 266, 273, 275, 278, 302, 306, 307, 310,
  314–16, 321, 339, 341, 380, 388, 397; gendered
  innovations 316, **317**, 323; ideology 113, 115,
  125, 129, 166, 230, 245, 371, 373, 374, 398;
  impact assessment (GIA) 252, 258, 266, 268, 275,
  286, 287, 307, 309, 310, **317**, 320, 394, 396, 400;
  opposition to gender equality 23, 38, 127, 142,
  192, 201, 202, 244, 245, 367–8, **371–2**, 373–5,
  398; order 20, 22, 80, 84, 274; pay gap 2, 7,
  17, 18, 21, 82, 93, **137**, 139, 185, 200, 251, 253,
  258, 259, 261, 284, 286, 342, 344, 384; pension
  gap 384, 386; policy 17, 21–3, 34, 49, 62, 128,

137, 139, 142, 143, 159, 241, 274, 297–8, 331, 332, 340, 371–3, 379, 382, 387; politics 167, 366, 368, 373, 387; quota 21, 24, 59, 110, 124, **241**, 245, 274, 385; regime 5, 7, 12, 18, **19–21**, 25–6, 30, 33, 46, **48**, 59, 72, 74, 76, 125, 126, 148, 151, 154, 261, 274, 371, 384, 393, 397, 400; representation 10, 59, 105, 108–11, 125, 129, 140, 141, 332; theory 15–16, 39, 45, 80, 128; stereotyping 34, 127, 154, 214, 243, 334, 341, 344, 347, 358

gender equality; *see also* equality: bodies 23, 49, 158–9, **164–6**; *see also* European Institute for Gender Equality (EIGE); Council 10, 121, 125, 127, 128; Index 125, **162**, 360, 393; norms 8, 111, 146, 151, 165, **188–9**, 203, 246, 295, 331, 367–8, 370, 374; plans **317**, 319, 320, 343; Strategy 11, 26, 37, 39, 102, 127, 128, 134, 163, 171, 175, 273, 302, 310, 320, 331, 335, 340, 343, 344, 346, 352, **361**, 361; regime 16, 17, 19, **21–5**

gender mainstreaming 10–12, 18, 21, 22, 30, **33–4**, 37, 49, 58–9, 61, 63, 74, 75, 82, 113, 115, 126–9, 137, **138**, 140, 142, 143, 146–7, 151–4, 159, 191, 225, 240, 251, 254, **257–8**, 259–60, 266, 272, 286, 293–5, 297–8, 307, 310, 316, **317**, 321–2, 327, 331, 333–4, 347–8, 382

General Secretariat of the Council (GSC) *see* council

Generalised System of Preferences (GSP) 282; *see also* trade

Geoghegan-Quinn, Máire 316, 319

Germany 3, 4, 8, 9, 20, 84, 85, 86, 97, 110, 124–5, 200, **210–12**, 228, 267, 273, 299, 328, 342, 380, 387

glass cliff phenomenon 395

global actor 290, 304, 298

Global Approach to Migration and Mobility 340, 342

Global Europe 280

Global South 292, 303, 305–7, **309**, 336

Global Strategy 153, 304, 328, 329, 330

goodness of fit 32; *see also* integration theory

governance: global 22; feminism 385; economic 48, 68, **69–70**, **73–5**, 266, 268, 269, 272, 273, 380, 382; good 280, 291; macroeconomic 260; multi-level (MLG) 31, 216; new modes of 138–40, 143, 160, 162, 167, 381; new economic 69, **269**, 270–1, 380–1, 386

Gradin, Anita 356

Greece 49, 110, 125, 184, **210**, **211**, 270, **271**, 379, 384, 386, 387

Griffin, Penny 385–6

Gross Domestic Product (GDP) 267, 274–5, 285, 381, 400

Group of Commissioners on Equal Opportunities *see* European Commission

Group of Equality and Diversity Coordinators 113

Grybauskaitė, Dalia 8

Guerrina, Roberta 48, 49, 61, 63, 151, 155, 331

Guigou, Élisabeth 9

Haastrup, Toni 150, 151, 331–2

harassment; *see also* violence: #MeToo 222, 230; #MeTooEP 116, 242; anti-harassment 18, 354; in the workplace 94, 352, **354–5**; racial 99; sexual 21, 162, 228, 230, 242, **318**, 320, 346, 352, 353, **354–5**, 358, 359, 361

harmonisation 6, 93, 122, 165, 181, 291, 292, 345, 347, 348, 353, 354, 360–1

Hayes-Renshaw, Fiona 123

health 6, 71, 85–7, **88**, 97, 112, 114, 159, 176, 227, 252, 254–7, 266, 271, 281, 282, 293, 294, 298, 306, 333, 357, 361, 381, 384

Helsinki Group (HG) 314, **317–18**, 320, 323

heteronormativity 38, 47, 49, 51, 86, 271, 386, 398

High Level Group on Gender Equality and Diversity 113; *see also* European Commission

High Representative of the Union for Foreign Affairs and Security Policy (HR/VP) 9, 121–2, 123, **147–8**, 150–3, 292, 328, 329, 331; *see also* EEAS

hijab 98–9

Hirschmann, Ursula 6

Hoffmann, Stanley 5, 123, 127

Horizon 2020, Horizon Europe 314–16, **319–20**, 321

Hoskyns, Catherine 7, **60**, 105, 172, 260

Hubert, Agnès 230

human rights *see* rights

Hungary 6, 24, 35, 37, 39, 89, 125, 128, 183, 187–9, 191, **210–12**, 258, 320, 341, 374, 375

ILGA Europe 34, 225, 227, 230, 359

illiberalism 166, 230, 368, **374**; *see also* populism

inequality, structural 46–7, 49, 51, 64, 74, 95, 106, 154, 260, 272, 274, 278, **305**, 354, 386

insecurity *see* security

institutional learning 32, 44, 322–3

institutionalism; *see also* integration theory: discursive 33, **34**, 39, 56–7, 190; feminist (FI) 11–12, 34, 37, 39, 46, **56–8**, 58–60, 64, 116, 155, 307, 330–3; historical (HI) 56–8, 66; new/neo (NI) 15, 30, 31, **33–4**, 37, 46, **56–61**, **62–6**, 128; old vs new 33, 57; rational choice 32, 33, 57, 66; sociological 32, 44, **56–7**, 59, 190

Instrument contributing to Stability and Peace (IcSP) 334

integration theory 11, 15, 31, **43–9**, 50, 124, 128; Critical Political Economy (CPE) 68, **69–71**, 74; intergovernmentalism 5, 15, 30, 31, 105, 114, **123–4**, 126, 127, **128**, 139; *see also* intergovernmentalism; multi-level governance (MLG) *see* governance; neo-functionalism 15, 30, 31, 60, 105; neo-institutionalism *see* institutionalism; post-functionalism 128; social constructivism 11, 15, **43–51**, 128, 259, 274

interest rate 267

interest(s): group(s) 173, 226, 243, 271, **279**; political 136, 143, **212**, 214, 298, 330

intergovernmentalism; *see also* integration theory: classical 127; liberal 30, 31, 123–4, 126; new 124, 139

intergroup (European Parliament) 114; on Anti-Racism and Diversity 114, 246; LGBT 114, 246

International Labour Organisation (ILO) 280, 281, **282–3**, 285, 295

International Trade Centre (ITC) 283, 285

International Women's Day 394

intersectionality, intersectional 11–12, 15–16, 24–6, 34, 39–40, 43, 45, **46–50**, 51, **64–5**, 66, 74, 75, 87, **94**, 102, 106, 116, 151, 163, 167, 174–7, 187, 190, 192, 195, 202, 217, **228**, 252, 286, 297, 306, 335, 340, 343, 344, 346, 348, 361, 366, **369–70**, 375, 386; *see also* discrimination

intra-group cohesion 112, 244, 246

Ireland 18, 38, 85, 97, 128, 142, 189, **210–12**, 216, 267, 270, 341, 372, 379, 397

Isin, Engin F. 197, 203

Istanbul Convention *see* violence

Italy 4, 6, 85, 128, 189, **210–12**, 216, 267, 369, 373, 379, 384

Jacquot, Sophie 24, 139, 259, 382, 383

Jenson, Jane 2, 259

Johnson, Boris 395, 396, 400

Joint Research Centre (JRC) 315

Jourová, Věra 142

judicial politics **171**, 172–4, 177; *see also* court cases

Juncker Commission 134–6, 139, 141, 142

Juncker, Jean-Claude 153, 365

Justice and Home Affairs (JHA) 4, 121, 122, 240

Kantola, Johanna 22, 34, 45, 64, 241, 243, 370, 393

Katsanidou, Alexia 245

Keller, Ska 242

Kenney, Sally 172

Kiil-Nielsen, Nicole 309

Klaus, Vaclav 192

Klompé, Marga 2

Kluger Dionigi, Maja 243

Kohl, Helmut 127

Krizsán, Andrea 23, 190–2

Kronsell, Annica 22, 58, 61, 65, 150, **306–7**, 308, 332–3, 335

Lagarde, Christine 62, 129, 266, 274

Latvia 84, 85, 110, 129, 183, 191, **210**, **211**

law; *see also* directives; article: *acquis communautaire* 163, 165, 166, 181–5, **186–7**, 189, 190, 256, 259, 339, 393; European 7, 12, 22, 26, 31, 36, 93, 94,

97–8, **170–1**, 172–4, **175**, 183, 189, 199, 256, 361, 393, 397–8; international refugee 344–5; soft 22, 225, **259**, 269, 285, 343, 352, 356, 380

leadership: charismatic 368, 369; female 5, 113, 127, 136, 143–4, 243, 368, 369, 372, 395; masculine 6, 89, 155, 213, 395; styles 9, 59, 127, 369, 395

Ledru, Madame 2

Lefkofridi, Zoe 245

left-right divide 111, 112, 217, 235, 237, 243, 245, 372

legitimacy 24, 81, 107, 115, 149, 150, 159, 161–3, 172, 191, 223–4, 373; *see also* democracy; crisis

Le Pen, Marine 230, 372

LGBTQI/LGBTIQA+ 21, 25, 34, 80, 83, 129, 141, 154, 164, 190, 191, 202, 225, 228, 230, 319, 346, 348, 361, 386; *see also* equality; rights

Liebert, Ulrike 22, 34, 38, 260

Lisbon Treaty *see* treaty

Lithuania 128–9, 183, 191, **210–12**

Lombardo, Emanuela 11, 34, 37, 45, 190, 370, 393

Lomé Convention 291, 293

López Aguilar, Juan Fernando 243

MacRae, Heather 24, 60, 65

macroeconomic coordination *see* governance

Macron, Emmanuel 124, 330

Männerparteien 245, 369

Magnusdottir, Gunnhildur 65, **306–7**, 308

male-as-norm 82, 96

malestream 73

Malmström, Cecilia 280, 284

Malta 110, 128, **210**, **211**, 329, 372

Manifesto of Ventotene 6; *see also* founding fathers/mothers; Spinelli

Manners, Ian 398

marginalisation 10, 11, 46, 48–9, 70, 73, 87, 96, 101, 105, 151, 174, 196, 223, 228, 273, 333, 335, 344, 386, 387, 394, 399

Marín, Manuel 354

Marinaki, Mara 147, 151, 331

market citizenship *see* citizenship

market feminism *see* feminism

Marshall, Thomas H. 196

masculinity/masculinities: caring 86–7; complicit 81, 151, 224; critical masculinity studies 80–1, **84–5**, 89, 369, 370, 375; Critical Studies on Men and Masculinities (CSMM) 80–1, 85; men's domination/dominance/hegemonic 1, 2, 16, 48, **61**, 81, 83, 87, 105, 155, 259, 274, 296, 333, 370, 372; military/protector 58, 65, 148, 150–2, 155, 327, **333**, 334, 335; toxic 398, 399

Masselot, Annick 76

May, Theresa **394–6**, 397

Mazey, Sonia 137

media 38, 85, 89, 162, 212, 216, 218, 328, 340–1, 386, 394, 395, **399**

411

Index

Merkel, Angela 2, 8, 124, 125, 127, 266, 330, 381
migration: anti-migration 24, 341, 348, 371, 373, 375; family *see* family; highly skilled 101, 340, 341, **342**; labour 340, **341–2**
militarism 89, 328, 332, **334–6**, 394
military 61, 65, 83, 148, 150–1, 153–5, **328–5**
Military Planning and Conduct Capability (MPCC) 329
Miller, Cherry 241
Miller, Gina 399
minority: and sexual rights *see* rights; black 74, **94–6**, 97, 99, 100, 101, 227, 297, 369, 397–9; ethnic 47–9, 65, 74, 174, 186, 187, 189–90, 202, 208, 217, 227, 343, 344, 369, 398–9; Roma **187**, 188, 190, 192, 202, 344, 361, 369; women 47–9, 74, 94–7, 99–101, 176, 187, 188, 190, 192, 202, 297, 340, 342, **343**, 344, 379, 386–7, 398–9
misogyny 224, 398
Moedas, Carlos 316
Moffit, Benjamin 368
Mogherini, Federica 9, 123, 150, 153, 331
Mondo, Emilie 244
monitoring (evaluation) 21, 83, 115, 127, 133, 138, 140, 141, 159, 165, **183–4**, 186, **187–8**, 189, 229, 257–8, 266, 268, 270, 272, 275, 283, 285, 286, 294, 296, 308, **317–8**, 319–21, **322**, 323, 334, 359, 360, 381
Montoya, Celeste 229
Moravcsik, Andrew 123–4
motherhood penalty 259
Mudde, Cas 367, **368**, 369
Muehlenhoff, Hanna L. 151
Müller, Jan-Werner 368
multi-level governance (MLG) *see* integration theory
Mushaben, Joyce M. 37, 114, 127, 201
Muslim 47, 98–9, 176, 360, **369**, 370, 372

nation(-state) 17, 23, 72, 195, 197, 199, 203–5, 367, **369**, 375, 396
National Reform Programmes 272, 381
nationalism: ethno-nationalism 202, 371; exclusive 371, 373; femo-nationalism 18, 369, **375**; gendering 369; nativism 202, 367, 368, **369**, 370, 371, 375; *see also* racism; neo-nationalism 18, 24, 367, **369–70**, 371, 374–5; transnationalism 17
nationality *see* difference
naturalization 150, 199, 201, 203, 340
neo-functionalism *see* integration theory
neo-institutionalism *see* integration theory; institutionalism
neoliberalism/neoliberal 19, 22–6, 45, **48**, 49, 68, **69–70**, 73, 74, 76, 87, 115, 126, 148, 154, 155, 202, 222, 227, 237, 260, 261, 271, 284, 286, 293, 299, 323, 333–4, 342, 369, 371, **375**, **380**, 382–4,

385–6, 387, 398; authoritarian 70, 74, 270; *see also* illiberalism
Netherlands 4, 38, 97, 110, 124, **210–12**, 267, 328, 329, 369, 371
new member states 18, 34, 111, 142, 165, 183, 185, 186, 192, 199, 200, 244; *see also* enlargement
NGO-ization 34, 225, 226
Nicholsonová, Lucia Ďuriš 243
Nonon, Jacqueline 8, 141
Nordic countries 20, 83–5, 258, 369, 385
norm(s): adaptation 30, 32, 36, 188; compliance 33, 165, 189–90, 281; *see also* compliance; formal 62, 63, 120; informal 62, 63, 120, 126, 192–3
North Atlantic Treaty Organization (NATO) 328–9, 331, 332
Northern Ireland 392, 396–8
Norway 85–6, **212**, 374

Official Development Assistance (ODA) *see* development
Olsson, Louise 332
ontology 46, 80
Open Method of Coordination (OMC) 224, 229, 254, 258; *see also* governance
Open Science, Open Innovation and Open to the World **316**
Orbie, Jan 305
Ordinary Legislative Procedure (OLP) 93, 107, 123, 127, 240, 340; *see also* trilogue
Organisation for Security and Co-operation in Europe (OSCE) 331
othering 19, 295, 333, 347

Papandreou, Vasso 9, 134, 354
parachutage 135
parliamentarisation 107, 111
participation: labour force/labour market 19, 21, 139, 210, 216, 255, 257, 260, 273, 318, 354; political 196, 200, 208, 399
Pateman, Carol 196
path dependency 57, **58**, 61, 64, 150, 333, 340
patriarchy **81**, 84, 87, 88, 95, 345, 367, 372, 387
pay: equal pay (gap) *see* gender; transparency 258
Permanent Structured Cooperation (PESCO) 329, 333
Petersberg Tasks 328
Plattner, Georg 245
Poland 35, 37–9, 84, 85, 89, 125, 183, 187, 191, **210–12**, 230–1, 303, 304, 320, 328, 329, 372, 374, 375, 385
Poland and Hungary Assistance for the Restructuring of the Economy (PHARE) Programme 188
policy: asylum 297, 298, **339–40**, **344–7**, 348; *see also* migration policy; austerity 12, 19, 23, 48, 49, **69–70**, 71, 72, 74, 225, 229, **273**, 379, **380**,

381, **384–6**, 387, 388; climate change 37, 68, 76, 153, 297, **302–8**, 309, **310–11**, 335; coherence 148, 155, 292, 310; Common Foreign and Security (CFSP) 4, 146–9, 155, 328–9, 331; Common Security and Defence (CSDP) 61, 121, 146–7, 149, 150–3, 327–9, **330–4**, 335–6; dismantling 24, 139, 163, 166, 245, 365, 374; economic 68–70, **71–4**, 121, 243, 259, **266–8**, 269, 270, 272, 274, 380–2, 386; employment 12, 18, 21, 60, 75, **253–5**, 257, **258**, 259, 260, 353, 382–3; European Neighbourhood (ENP) 30, 31, 35, 36, 39, 148; European Security and Defence (ESDP) 328–9, 331, 333; external 61, 153, 278, 298, 306, 331, 339, 347, 353; macro-economic 49, 68–70, 72–4, **75**, 254, 258, 259, 272, 381, 382; migration 201, 216, 244, 261, 298, 304, **339–42**, 347–8, 375, 397; monetary 5, 24, 69, 76, **265**, 266–8, 274, 380; social 2, 7, 12, 18, 19, 22, 34, 61, 70, 115, 121, 126, 127, 137, 139, 189, 202, 240, 251–2, **253–4**, 255–9, 261, 273, 355, 383, 384, 394; soft policy instruments 31, 33, **37**, 39, 257, 292, 332; *see also* Open Method of Coordination (OMC)

policy analysis: Critical Frame Analysis *see* frames/framing; interpretative 47–8, 50, 296; policy frames *see* frames/framing

political group(s) *see* European Parliament

political party: Alliance for Peace and Freedom (APF) **238**; Alliance of European Conservatives and Reformists (ACRE) 236, **238**, 240–1; Alliance of European National Movements (AEMN) **238**; Alliance of Liberals and Democrats for Europe (ALDE) 111, 112, 236, 237, **238**, 240–1, **242–4**; Alternative für Deutschland (AfD) (Germany) 237, 241, 371; Conservative Party (UK) 393, **394–6**, 400; European Conservatives and Reformists (ECR) 111–12, 236, 237, **238**, **239**, 241, **242–4**, 245; European Party Groups (EPGs) 215, **235–46**; European People's Party (EPP) 108, **111–12**, 236, 237, **238**, **239**, 240, **241–4**, 245; European United Left/Nordic Green Left (GUE/NGL) 111–2, 236, 237, **239**, **242**, 243, 244; Fidesz (Hungary) 245; Front National *see* Rassemblement National; Greens/European Free Alliance (Greens/EFA) **111–12**, 236, 237, **238**, **239**, **241–3**, 244, 245; Identity and Democracy (ID) 111–12, 237, **239**, 241, **242**; Law and Justice Party (PiS) (Poland) 237, 245; Northern Irish Democratic Unionist Party (Northern Ireland) 395; party system 33, 124, **214**, **217**, 236–7, 387; Podemos (Spain) 373, 387; populist parties 12, 17, 24, 38, 126, 166, 240, 245, 246, 368, 369, 370, 375, 379, 387; *see also* populism; populist radical right parties (RWP) 38, 113, 241, **367–8**, 369–70, **371–2**, 373–5, 386; Progressive Alliance of Socialists

and Democrats (S&D) 108, **111–12**, 237, **239**, 240, **242–4**, 246; Rassemblement National (RN) 230, 237, 241, 372; Renew Europe (RE) 108, 111, 237, **238**, **239**, **242**

politics of belonging 203, 369

politics of fear 373, 394

politicisation, de-politicisation 6, 23, 31, 38–9, 70, 112, 129, 143, **162–3**, 167, 244, 270, 274, 279–80, 282, 340, 345–6, 348, 373, 385

populism 12, 19, 23–6, 38, 39, 50, 51, 81, 89, 116, 125, 128, 182, 192, 202, 204, 229, 230, 243, 365, 366, **367–70**, 371–2, **373**, 374, **375**, 387, 393, 398; *see also* illiberalism

Portugal 84, 184, **210–12**, 241, 267, 270, 379

positivism, critique of positivism 73, 286

postcolonialism 39, 46, 80, 81, 84, 295, 345, 347

post-deconstruction 51, 383, **387**

post-migration societies 341

poststructuralism 80, 330, 332; *see also* integration theory

poverty 23, 24, 49, 208, 213, 261, 280, **291**, 297, 309, 379, 384, 387

power: civilian 61, 328; delegation of 159–60, 166, 218; genderedness, gendered nature of **45**, 47, 51, **57**, 60–4, **65–6**, 81, 128, 153, 154, 201, 271, 274, 305–6, 310, 333; normative power Europe 22, 292, **295–6**, 296, 298, 327, 329; resource 21, 30, 278, 285, 293, 296, 297, 305

preliminary reference procedure, preliminary rulings 171; *see also* court cases; CJEU

price stability 267–8, 381

Principal Advisor on Gender and Women, Peace and Security 147, 151, 331

Prodi Commission 134, 135, 142

Prodi-Kinnock reforms 140; *see also* Commission

productive economy 71, 72, 75

Protocol on Northern Ireland 397–8; *see also* Brexit

public: consultations 223, 224, 227, 230, 255, 279, 283, 285; sphere 84, **196**, 213, 341, 370, 392, 398; public-private divide 196, 341, 345

qualified majority voting (QMV) **121–2**, 125, 255, 256, 257, 339–40

Queen Beatrix 8

Quintin, Odile 142

quota *see* gender

race 26, 70, 72, 95, 99, **101–2**, 164, 173, 217, 319, 333, 369, 387; *see also* difference; discrimination

racialisation, de-racialisattion 11, 48, 49, 69, 71, 72, 75, 76, 97, 101, 333, 335–6, 366, **386–7**, 392, 396, 397, 398, 400

racism 72, **83**, 87–9, 96, 99, 101, 202, 227, 341–2, 344, 360, 369, 371, 375, 379, 386, 387, 398

Radaelli, Claudio 32

Rape Crisis Network Europe 359

Index

rapporteur(ship) *see* committee; shadow rapporteur 113, 240

rational economic man 71–2

Reding, Viviane 142

Rees-Mogg, Jacob 395

referendum 23, 37, 49, 89, 272, **392–4**, 397–400; *see also* Brexit

refugees 18, 19, 24, 25, 35, 49, 50, 80, 88, 89, 201, 204, 339, 340, 343, **344–5**, 346–8, 369, 386, 396, 398; *see also* asylum

Regner, Evelyn 243

remoaners 399; *see also* Brexit

Renew Europe (RE) *see* political party

Report: Birkelbach 185; Delors 267; Maij-Weggen 8; Rubenstein 354, 355; Werner 266

representation: descriptive 109, **110**, 112, 114, 115, 210, 243, 274; female 4, 63, 108, 109, **111–12**, 113, 114, 124, 133–6, 141, 143, 148, 150, 181, 201, 209, 213, 235, 240, 242, 273, 296; gendered 235, **241–4**, 245; substantive 11, 108, 111, 112, 114, 115, 125, 243; underrepresentation 10, 109, 113, 128, 140, 150, 174, 177, 200, 212, 241, 266, 274, 305, 308, 310, 396, 400

reproductive economy 49, 68, 72, 75, 286; *see also* care

research and development (R&D) 314, 315, 320

research and technology development (RTD) 314, **315–19**, 320–2

research funding organisations 315, 318–20, 323

resistance 6, 25, 37, 61, **62**, 74, 101, 125–7, 134, 142, 143, 159, 192, 202, 255, 256, 260, 321, 331, 373, 386, **387**, 395

Responsible Research and Innovation (RRI) 316

rights; *see also* equality; discrimination; Charter of Fundamental Rights (2010/C 83/02) 9, 94, 98, 160, 163–4, 176, 198, 352; children's 361; civil 35, 94, 203, 348; equal 18, 195–6, 257; ethnic minority 50, 187, **189–90**, 202; European Convention on Human Rights (ECHR) 94, **97–8**, 99, 173; European Court of Human Rights 94, 97–9, 100, 170, 173, 174, **175–7**, 347; *see also* court cases; European Pillar of Social Rights (EPSR) 35, 261, 379–80; minority and sexual 50, 112, 344, 367, 371, 375; policyhuman 25, 72, 98, 99, 127, 142, 152, 154, 165, 170, 183, 185, 186, **197**, 202, 203, **204**, 216, 244, 278, 280–2, 285, 291, 292, 294, 298, 309, 327, 341, 348, 352, 356, 358, 360, 373–5; 386; LGBTQI 21, 34, 39, 50, 114, 202, 190, 191, 204, 336, 371–2, 374; political 19, 196, **197**, 203–5, 340; reproductive 50, 112, 166, 202, 372, 374, 375; Rights, Equality and Citizenship Programme 344; rights-based approach *see* approach; social 19, 25, 47, 195, 200–4, 216, 229, 244, 255, 258, 261, **281–2**, 294, 379–80, 398; Universal Declaration of Human Rights (UDHR) *see* declaration; Women's Charter, A

142, 139, 357; women's citizenship 196, 203; *see also* citizenship

Risse, Thomas 33, 189

Roadmap: for Equality (2006–2010) 139, 225; European Research Area (ERA) 314, **318**

Rolandsen Agustín, Lise 47, 64, 241–2, 360

Rossi, Ada 6

Roudy, Yvette 354

Russian Federation, Russia 35, 36, 39, 85, 329

Sánchez, Pedro 124

Santer Commission 135, 142

Santer, Jacques 134

Sauer, Birgit 273

Schimmelfennig, Frank 188, 189

Schmidt, Vivien A. 33, 45, 57

Schuman Plan 4; *see also* founding fathers/mothers

Scotland 392, 394, 395, 398, 399

Scrivener, Christiane 134

security 58, 64, 121, **146–7**, 148, 150–1, 153–5, 245, 251, 292, 294, 297, 304, 307, **327–36**, 339, 347, 348, 360, 394, 398

securitization 339, 347, 348

settled status 397; *see also* asylum

Settlement Scheme 397; *see also* asylum

sexual orientation 11, 17, 18, 24, 26, 46, 47, 51, 64, **83**, 84, 88, 93–5, 116, 163, 166, 187, 202, 228, 297, 306, 345–8, 354, 369–71; *see also* LGBTQI/LGBTIQA+

Shaw, Jo 46, 172

simplification 122, 162, 171, 318, 392

Single European Act (SEA) *see* treaty

single market 93, 159, 245, 255, 266, 278, 315, 327

Six-Pack legislation 70, 269, 381, 383; *see also* Two-Pack legislation

slavery **95**, 97, 196, 358; *see also* enslaved women

Slovenia 38, 84, 110, 183, 189, **210–12**

Slovakia 35, 38, 109, 110, 183, **186**, 189, **210**, **211**

social: constructivism *see* integration theory; impact(s) 72, 189, 270, 275, 279, 297, 394, 400; justice 101, 222, 236, 257, 261, 297, 299, 316, 340, 373–5, 379, 394, 400; policy *see* policy; reproduction 72, 74–6, 266, **272**; *see also* care; Action Programme (SAP) 255; Chapter 7, 257, 279, 285; Summit 35

socialization 32, 44, 47, 62, 70–1, 111, 126, 128, 149, 189–90, 209, **211**, 213, 216, 218, 244, 259

solidarity 35, 49, 114–15, 185, 204, 228, 271, 329, 375, 386

Soubry, Anna 396

sovereignty 5–6, 31, 196–7, 201, 245, 268, 394, 396

Spain 38, 48, 99, 124, 184–5, 188, **210–12**, 267, 384, 386

Spitzenkandidatur/Spitzenkandidaten 108, 135, **240–1**

Spinelli, Altiero 3, 6

Stability and Convergence Programme 273

Stability and Growth Pact (SGP) 70, 268–9, 381
stakeholders/stakeholder involvement 10, 87, 116, 129, 141, 224, 226–7, 229, 319–20, **323**, 333, 372; *see also* interest(s)
state feminism *see* feminism
statistics 85, 130, 164, 171, **210–1**, 258, 284, 382, 384; Eurobarometer 25, 128, 340–1; Gender Equality index *see* gender equality; sex-disaggregated 164, 272
stereotyping 100, 129, 214, 297, 342, 345; *see also* gender
stigma, stigmatised 47, 96, **100**, 229, 297, 369; anti-stigma principle 100, 102
Stratigaki, Maria 230
strategic silence 49, 72, 274
structural and investment funds (ESF, ERDF, Cohesion) 254
Sturgeon, Nicola 395
Šuica, Dubravka 10
Sullerot, Evelyne 9
supply-side explanation 110
sustainability 89, 278, 280, 282, 286, 291, 303, 322, 380; Impact Assessment (SIA) **281–2**; Development Goals (SDG) 284–6, 291, 310, 311
Sweden 18, 20, 85, 110, 124–6, 128, 151, 161, 184, **210–12**, 272, 331, 382
synergy 94, **95–6**, 100–2

target (40% target) 139–40, **141**, 143, 257, 272, 274, **318–19**
Tampere Programme 339–40, 345
Thatcher, Margaret 2
third country national (TCN) 195, 198–9, **201–2**, 203–4, 261, 339–40, 345, 397
Thyssen, Marianne 284
trade 68–9, 76, 121, 123, 251–2, 274, **278–87**, 291, 307, 396–7; liberalisation effects 69, 251, **278**, **280–1**, 284, 286–7, 297; Trade for All 278, **280**, 283; unions 9, 253
trafficking 83, 88, 187, 229, 342, 344, 345, 348, 352, 353, 354, **355–6**, 358, 359; *see also* migration; violence
Transatlantic Trade and Investment Partnership (TTIP) 279–80
Transnationalism *see* nationalism
transparency register 229; *see also* interest(s); stakeholder
transport 89, 113, 121, 252, 302–3, 305–7, 310, 311
transposition 34, 50, 183, 185–7, **189–90**, 255–7, 259, 261, 355–6, 386
Treaty: of Amsterdam 18, 26, 33, 82, 83, 93, 107, 126, 138, 163, 185, 199, 201–2, 224, 251, 257, 258, 272, 303, 314, 315, 327, 328, 344, 345, 355; Establishing the European Economic Community 21, 251, 253, 291, 185, 198;

Euratom 315; Fiscal Compact 70, 122, 269, **381**; Lisbon 107, 116, 121–2, 146, 147, 153, 184, 198, 240, 258, 265, 278, 279, 303, 315, 329, 339, 345; of Maastricht 4–5, 9, 18, 122–4, 138, 197–9, 240, 256–8, 267, 315, 328, 339, 345; of Nice 240; of Paris 4, 121; of Rome 2, 4, 18, 93, 183, 184, 278, 291; on Stability, Coordination and Governance (TSCG) 269; Single European Act (SEA) 121, 122, 255, 303, 314
trilogue 113–14, 123, 127; *see also* Council; European Parliament
trio presidency 121; *see also* Council
Troika 270–1, 379
True, Jacqui 76, 395
Two-Pack legislation 70, 269; *see also* Six-Pack legislation

United Kingdom (UK) 4, 12, 18, 20, 48, 76, 89, 142, 172, **210–1**, 237, **239**, 255, 257–8, 261, 298–9, 328–9, 331–2, 381, 385, 387, 392–3, 396–7
United Nations (UN): Agenda for Sustainable Development 291, 359; Conference on Trade and Development (UNCTAD) 282, 284, 286; Framework Convention on Climate Change (UNFCCC) 303; General Assembly 353; Security Council Resolution (UNSCR) 1325 147, 151, 152, 327, 331–2, 335–6
Urpilainen, Jutta 292

V4 (Visegrad) countries 89
van der Vleuten, Anna 2, 7–8, 62, 64, 115, 124, 127, 192, 244, 259, 283
Veil, Simone 3, **8**, 114
velvet triangle 21, 50, 60, 115, 161, 167, **223**, 226, 260, 330, 343
Verloo, Mieke 47, 50, 296
victimization 88, 344, 347
Vine, Sarah 395
violence: against women (VAW) 45, 83, 86, 114, 125–9, 162, 173, 228, 231, 246, 327, 342, 344, 345, 348, **352–4**, **356–61**, 371, 399; Council of Europe Convention on Preventing and Combating Violence against Women and Domestic Violence (Istanbul Convention) 6, 38, 86, 125, 129, 173, 175, 246, 352, 353, 358, 361, 374; DAPHNE programme 342, 344, **356–7**, 359, 361; Declaration on the Elimination of Violence against Women (DEVAW) *see* declaration; domestic 6, 25, 114, 129, 173, 175, 190, 191, 294, 353, 354, **356–7**, 359, 374; European Observatory on Violence against Women 359, 360; European Parliament Resolution (2013/2004(INL) on combating Violence against Women 352; gender-based 37, 47–9, 86, 87, 102, 115, 139, 164, **318**, 320, 333, 345–6, 352–3, **357–8**, **360**, 361, 365, 374, 383,

Index

384; sexual 1, 83, 87–8, 298, 333, 346, 352–4, 358, 361; violence against women survey 164, 360, 261, 399

Vogel-Polsky, Éliane 7, 8, 141

Vogler, John 304, 328

von der Leyen, Ursula 5, 9, 10, 26, 62, 108, 129, 134–6, 139, 142, 163, 241, 258, 273, 292, 298, 302, 310, 331, 361

von Wahl, Angelika 22

Vote Leave campaign 394–5; *see also* Brexit

vulnerability 61, 305–6, 308, 347, 361, 387 398; vulnerable persons 99, 346, 397; vulnerable groups 139, 176, 258, 271, 281, 346–7

Walby, Sylvia 22, 84, 361, 383

Wallace, Helen 123

war 61, 82, 151, 327–8, 333, **334**, **398**; Cold War 222; World War II 4–6, 82; Turf 148; Trade 298

Weiss, Louise 3

welfare state regimes 17, 19, **20**, 125, 371; *see also* gender equality

Welfens, Natalie 346, 347

Wenmakers, Ursula 9

Western European Union (WEU) 328

Wiener, Antje 33

Withdrawal Agreement 332, 396–7; *see also* Brexit

Wöhl, Stefanie 269

Wollaston, Sarah 396

Wollstonecraft, Mary 196

women with disabilities 24, 261, 361, 386

Women against sexual Harassment (WasH) 359

Women Against Violence Europe (WAVE) 225, 359

Women for Britain 394; *see also* Brexit

Women in Development Europe (WIDE) *see* development

Women, Peace and Security (WPS) 147, 151–2, 298, 327–8, **330–2**, 333–5

Women's Budget Group 400

Women's European Council (WEUCO) 129

women's movement *see* feminism

Woodward, Alison 21, **60**, **39**, 223, 330, 343

work: care *see* care; domestic 71, 281, **342–3**, 344; seasonal 342; life balance 18, 19, 21, 35, 141

World Trade Organisation (WTO) 278, 283, 284, 286

Wright, Katharine 61, 151, 155

xenophobia 24, 174, 360, 398, 399; *see also* racism

Young, Brigitte 76, 274

Yuval-Davis, Nira 203, 369

Zippel, Kathrin 228, 359